BERLITZ®

spanish-english
english-spanish
dictionary

diccionario
español-inglés
inglés-español

By the Staff of Editions Berlitz

Revised edition 1979
Library of Congress Catalog Card Number: 78-78079

5th printing 1984
Printed in Switzerland

Contents

Indice

Preface

In selecting the 12.500 word-concepts in each language for this dictionary, the editors have had the traveller's needs foremost in mind. This book will prove invaluable to all the millions of travellers, tourists and business people who appreciate the reassurance a small and practical dictionary can provide. It offers them—as it does beginners and students—all the basic vocabulary they are going to encounter and to have to use, giving the key words and expressions to allow them to cope in everyday situations.

Like our successful phrase books and travel guides, these dictionaries—created with the help of a computer data bank—are designed to slip into pocket or purse, and thus have a role as handy companions at all times.

Besides just about everything you normally find in dictionaries, there are these Berlitz bonuses:

- imitated pronunciation next to each foreign-word entry, making it easy to read and enunciate words whose spelling may look forbidding

- a unique, practical glossary to simplify reading a foreign restaurant menu and to take the mystery out of complicated dishes and indecipherable names on bills of fare

- useful information on how to tell the time and how to count, on conjugating irregular verbs, commonly seen abbreviations and converting to the metric system, in addition to basic phrases.

While no dictionary of this size can pretend to completeness, we expect the user of this book will feel well armed to affront foreign travel with confidence. We should, however, be very pleased to receive comments, criticism and suggestions that you think may be of help in preparing future editions.

Prefacio

Al seleccionar las 12 500 palabras-conceptos en cada una de las lenguas de este diccionario, los redactores han tenido muy en cuenta las necesidades del viajero. Esta obra es indispensable para millones de viajeros, turistas y hombres de negocios, quienes apreciarán la seguridad que aporta un diccionario pequeño y práctico. Tanto a ellos como a los principiantes y estudiantes les ofrece todo el vocabulario básico que encontrarán o deberán emplear en el lenguaje de todos los días; les proporciona las palabras clave y las expresiones que les permitirán enfrentarse a las situaciones de la vida diaria.

Al igual que nuestros conocidos manuales de conversación y guías turísticas, estos diccionarios – realizados en computadora con la ayuda de un banco de datos – han sido ideados para llevarse en el bolsillo o en un bolso de mano, asumiendo de este modo su papel de compañeros disponibles en todo momento.

Además de las nociones que de ordinario ofrece un diccionario, encontrará:

- una transcripción fonética tan sencilla que facilita la lectura, aun cuando la palabra extranjera parezca impronunciable

- un léxico gastronómico inédito que le hará «descifrar» los menús en un restaurante extranjero, revelándole el secreto de los platos complicados y los misterios de la cuenta

- informaciones prácticas que le ayudarán a comunicar la hora y a contar, así como a utilizar los verbos irregulares, las abreviaturas más comunes y algunas expresiones útiles.

Ningún diccionario de este formato puede tener la pretensión de ser completo, pero el fin de este libro es permitir que quien lo emplee posea un arma para enfrentarse con confianza al viaje en el extranjero. Sin embargo, recibiremos con gusto los comentarios, críticas y sugestiones que con toda seguridad nos permitirán preparar las futuras ediciones.

spanish-english

español-inglés

Introduction

This dictionary has been designed to take account of your practical needs. Unnecessary linguistic information has been avoided. The entries are listed in alphabetical order regardless of whether the entry word is printed in a single word or in two or more separate words. As the only exception to this rule, a few idiomatic expressions are listed as main entries alphabetically according to the most significant word of the expression. When an entry is followed by sub-entries, such as expressions and locutions, these, too, have been listed in alphabetical order.[1]

Each main-entry word is followed by a phonetic transcription (see guide to pronunciation). Following the transcription is the part of speech of the entry word whenever applicable. When an entry word may be used as more than one part of speech, the translations are grouped together after the respective part of speech.

Whenever an entry word is repeated in sub-entries a tilde (~) is used to represent the full entry word.

An asterisk (*) in front of a verb indicates that the verb is irregular. For details you may refer to the lists of irregular verbs.

The dictionary is based on Castilian Spanish. All words and meanings of words that are exclusively Mexican have been marked as such (see list of abbreviations used in the text).

Abbreviations

adj	adjective	n	noun
adv	adverb	nAm	noun (American)
Am	American	num	numeral
art	article	p	past tense
conj	conjunction	pl	plural
f	feminine	plAm	plural (American)
fMe	feminine (Mexican)	pp	past participle
fpl	feminine plural	pr	present tense
fplMe	feminine plural (Mexican)	pref	prefix
m	masculine	prep	preposition
Me	Mexican	pron	pronoun
mMe	masculine (Mexican)	v	verb
mpl	masculine plural	vAm	verb (American)
mplMe	masculine plural (Mexican)	vMe	verb (Mexican)

[1] Note that the alphabetical order in Spanish differs from our own in three cases: ch, ll and ñ are considered independent letters and come after c, l and n, respectively.

Guide to Pronunciation

Each main entry in this part of the dictionary is followed by a phonetic transcription which shows you how to pronounce the words. This transcription should be read as if it were English. It is based on Standard British pronunciation, though we have tried to take account of General American pronunciation also. Below, only those letters and symbols are explained which we consider likely to be ambiguous or not immediately understood.

The syllables are separated by hyphens, and stressed syllables are printed in *italics*.

Of course, the sounds of any two languages are never exactly the same, but if you follow carefully our indications, you should be able to pronounce the foreign words in such a way that you'll be understood. To make your task easier, our transcriptions occasionally simplify slightly the sound system of the language while still reflecting the essential sound differences.

Consonants

bh	a rather indecisive **b**, i.e. one verging on **v**
dh	like **th** in **th**is, often rather indecisive, possibly quite like **d**
g	always hard, as in **g**o
ǥ	a **g**-sound where the tongue doesn't quite close the air passage between itself and the roof of the mouth, so that the escaping air produces audible friction; it is also on occasions pronounced as an indecisive **g**
kh	like **ǥ**, but based on a **k**-sound; therefore hard and voiceless, like **ch** in Scottish lo**ch**
lʸ	like **lli** in mi**lli**on
ñ	as in the Spanish se**ñ**or, or like **ni** in o**ni**on
r	slightly rolled in the front of the mouth
rr	strongly rolled **r**
s	always hard, as in **s**o

Vowels and Diphthongs

ah	a short version of the **a** in car, i.e. a sound between **a** in c**a**t and **u** in c**u**t
igh	as in s**igh**
ou	as in l**ou**d

1) Raised letters (e.g. **ay^{oo}**, **^{y}ah**) should be pronounced only fleetingly.

2) Spanish vowels (i.e. not diphthongs) are pure and fairly short. Therefore, you should try to read a transcription like **oa** without moving tongue or lips while pronouncing the sound.

Latin-American Pronunciation

Our transcriptions reflect the pronunciation of Castilian, the official language of Spain. In Latin America, two of the Castilian sounds are practically unknown:

1) **ll** as in the word **calle** (which we represent by **l^y**) is usually pronounced like Spanish **y** (as in English yet); in the Río de la Plata region, though, both **ll** and **y** are pronounced like **s** in pleasure.

2) The letters **c** (before **e** and **i**) and **z** are pronounced like **s** in so instead of **th** as in thin.

A

a (ah) *prep* to, on; at; **a las ...** at ... o'clock

abacería (ah-bhah-thay-*ree*-ah) *f* grocer's

abacero (ah-bhah-*thay*-roa) *m* grocer

abadía (ah-bhah-*dhee*-ah) *f* abbey

abajo (ah-*bhah*-khoa) *adv* downstairs; down; **hacia ~** downwards

abandonar (ah-bhahn-doa-*nahr*) *v* abandon

abanico (ah-bhah *nee*-koa) *m* fan

abarrotería (ah-bhah-rroa-tay-*ree*-ah) *fMe* grocer's

abarrotero (ah-bhah-rroa-*tay*-roa) *mMe* grocer

abastecimiento (ah-bhahss-tay-thee-*mªayn*-toa) *m* supply

abatido (ah-bhah-*tee*-dhoa) *adj* down

abecedario (ah-bhay-thay-*dah*-rªoa) *m* alphabet

abedul (ah-bhay-*dhool*) *m* birch

abeja (ah-*bhay*-khah) *f* bee

abertura (ah-bhayr-*too*-rah) *f* opening

abierto (ah-*bhªayr*-toa) *adj* open

abismo (ah-*bhee*-zmoa) *m* abyss

ablandador (ah-bhlahn-dah-*dhoar*) *m* water-softener

ablandar (ah-bhlahn-*dahr*) *v* soften

abogado (ah-bhoa-*gah*-dhoa) *m* barrister, lawyer, attorney; solicitor; advocate

abolir (ah-bhoa-*leer*) *v* abolish

abolladura (ah-bhoa-lªah-*dhoo*-rah) *f* dent

abonado (ah-bhoa-*nah*-dhoa) *m* subscriber

abono (ah-*bhoa*-noa) *m* manure, dung

aborto (ah-*bhoar*-toa) *m* miscarriage; abortion

abrazar (ah-bhrah-*thahr*) *v* embrace; hug

abrazo (ah-*bhrah*-thoa) *m* hug; embrace

abrecartas (ah-bhray-*kahr*-tahss) *m* paper-knife

abrelatas (ah-bhray-*lah*-tahss) *m* can opener, tin-opener

abreviatura (ah-bhray-bhªah-*too*-rah) *f* abbreviation

abrigar (ah-bhree-*gahr*) *v* shelter

abrigo (ah-bhree-goa) *m* coat, overcoat; **~ de pieles** fur coat

abril (ah-*bhreel*) April

abrir (ah-*bhreer*) *v* open; unlock; turn on

abrochar (ah-bhroa-*chahr*) *v* button

abrupto (ah-*bhroop*-toa) *adj* steep

absceso (ahbhs-*thay*-soa) *m* abscess

absolución (ahbh-soa-loo-*thªoan*) *f* acquittal

absolutamente (ahbh-soa-loo-tah-*mayn*-tay) *adv* absolutely

absoluto (ahbh-soa-*loo*-toa) *adj* sheer; total

abstemio (ahbhs-*tay*-mʸoa) *m* teetotaller

*****abstenerse de** (ahbhs-tay-*nayr*-say) abstain from

abstracto (ahbhs-*trahk*-toa) *adj* abstract

absurdo (ahbh-*soor*-dhoa) *adj* absurd; foolish

abuela (ah-*bhway*-lah) *f* grandmother

abuelo (ah-*bhway*-loa) *m* grandfather, granddad; **abuelos** *mpl* grandparents *pl*

abundancia (ah-bhoon-*dahn*-thʸah) *f* abundance, plenty

abundante (ah-bhoon-*dahn*-tay) *adj* abundant, plentiful

abundar (ah-bhoon-*dahr*) *v* abound

aburrido (ah-bhoo-*rree*-dhoa) *adj* boring, dull

aburrimiento (ah-bhoo-rree-*mʸayn*-toa) *m* annoyance

aburrir (ah-bhoo-*rreer*) *v* bore, annoy

abusar de (ah-bhoo-*sahr*) exploit

abuso (ah-*bhoo*-soa) *m* misuse, abuse

acá (ah-*kah*) *adv* here

acabar (ah-kah-*bhahr*) *v* end; **acabado** finished; over

academia (ah-kah-*dhay*-mʸah) *f* academy; ~ **de bellas artes** art school

acallar (ah-kah-*lʸahr*) *v* silence

acampador (ah-kahm-pah-*dhoar*) *m* camper

acampar (ah-kahm-*pahr*) *v* camp

acantilado (ah-kahn-tee-*lah*-dhoa) *m* cliff

acariciar (ah-kah-ree-*thʸahr*) *v* cuddle

acaso (ah-*kah*-soa) *adv* perhaps

accesible (ahk-thay-*see*-bhlay) *adj* accessible

acceso (ahk-*thay*-soa) *m* entrance, access; approach

accesorio (ahk-thay-*soa*-rʸoa) *adj* ad-

ditional; **accesorios** *mpl* accessories *pl*

accidental (ahk-thee-dhayn-*tahl*) *adj* accidental

accidente (ahk-thee-*dhayn*-tay) *m* accident; ~ **aéreo** plane crash

acción (ahk-*thʸoan*) *f* share; action; deed; **acciones** *fpl* stocks and shares

acechar (ah-thay-*chahr*) *v* watch for

aceite (ah-*thay*-tay) *m* oil; ~ **bronceador** suntan oil; ~ **de mesa** salad-oil; ~ **de oliva** olive oil; ~ **lubricante** lubrication oil; ~ **para el pelo** hair-oil

aceitoso (ah-thay-*toa*-soa) *adj* oily

aceituna (ah-thay-*too*-nah) *f* olive

acelerador (ah-thay-lay-rah-*dhoar*) *m* accelerator

acelerar (ah-thay-lay-*rahr*) *v* accelerate

acento (ah-*thayn*-toa) *m* accent

acentuar (ah-thayn-*twahr*) *v* emphasize, stress

aceptar (ah-thayp-*tahr*) *v* accept

acera (ah-*thay*-rah) *f* pavement; sidewalk *nAm*

acerca de (ah-*thayr*-kah day) about

acercarse (ah-thayr-*kahr*-say) *v* approach

acero (ah-*thay*-roa) *m* steel; ~ **inoxidable** stainless steel

*****acertar** (ah-thayr-*tahr*) *v* *hit; guess right

acidez (ah-thee-*dhayth*) *f* heartburn

ácido (*ah*-thee-dhoa) *m* acid

aclamar (ah-klah-*mahr*) *v* cheer

aclaración (ah-klah-rah-*thʸoan*) *f* explanation

aclarar (ah-klah-*rahr*) *v* clarify

acné (ahk-*nay*) *m* acne

acogida (ah-koa-*khee*-dhah) *f* reception

acomodación (ah-koa-moa-dhah-*thʸoan*) *f* accommodation

acomodado (ah-koa-moa-*dhah*-dhoa) *adj* well-to-do

acomodador (ah-koa-moa-dhah-*dhoar*) *m* usher

acomodadora (ah-koa-moa-dhah-*dhoa*-rah) *f* usherette

acomodar (ah-koa-moa-*dhahr*) *v* accommodate

acompañar (ah-koam-pah-*ñahr*) *v* accompany; conduct

aconsejar (ah-koan-say-*khahr*) *v* recommend, advise

*__acontecer__ (ah-koan-tay-*thayr*) *v* occur

acontecimiento (ah-koan-tay-thee-*mᵞayn*-toa) *m* event; happening, occurrence

*__acordar__ (ah-koar-*dhahr*) *v* agree; *__acordarse__ *v* remember, recollect, recall

acortar (ah-koar-*tahr*) *v* shorten

*__acostar__ (ah-koass-*tahr*) *v* *lay down; *__acostarse__ *v* *go to bed

acostumbrado (ah-koass-toom-*brah*-dhoa) *adj* accustomed; customary; *__estar ~ a__ *be used to

acostumbrar (ah-koass-toom-*brahr*) *v* accustom

*__acrecentarse__ (ah-kray-thayn-*tahr*-say) *v* increase

acreditar (ah-kray-dhee-*tahr*) *v* credit

acreedor (ah-kray-ay-*dhoar*) *m* creditor

acta (*ahk*-tah) *f* certificate; **actas** minutes

actitud (ahk-tee-*toodh*) *f* attitude; position

actividad (ahk-tee-bhee-*dhahdh*) *f* activity

activo (ahk-*tee*-bhoa) *adj* active

acto (*ahk*-toa) *m* act, deed

actor (ahk-*toar*) *m* actor

actriz (ahk-*treeth*) *f* actress

actual (ahk-*twahl*) *adj* present; topical

actualmente (ahk-twahl-*mayn*-tay) *adv* now

actuar (ahk-*twahr*) *v* act

acuarela (ah-kwah-*ray*-lah) *f* watercolour

acuerdo (ah-*kwayr*-dhoa) *m* approval; agreement, settlement; **¡de acuerdo!** all right!, okay!; *__estar de ~ con__ approve of

acumulador (ah-koo-moo-lah-*dhoar*) *m* battery

acusación (ah-koo-sah-*thᵞoan*) *f* charge

acusado (ah-koo-*sah*-dhoa) *m* accused

acusar (ah-koo-*sahr*) *v* accuse; charge

adaptar (ah-dhahp-*tahr*) *v* adapt; suit

adecuado (ah-dhay-*kwah*-dhoa) *adj* adequate; convenient, appropriate

adelantar (ah-dhay-lahn-*tahr*) *v* *get on; **por adelantado** in advance; **prohibido ~** no overtaking

adelante (ah-dhay-*lahn*-tay) *adv* ahead, onwards, forward

adelanto (ah-dhay-*lahn*-toa) *m* advance

adelgazar (ah-dhayl-gah-*thahr*) *v* slim

además (ah-dhay-*mahss*) *adv* moreover, furthermore, besides; **~ de** beyond, besides

adentro (ah-*dhayn*-troa) *adv* inside, in; **hacia ~** inwards

adeudado (ah-dhayᵒᵒ-*dhah*-dhoa) *adj* due

adición (ah-dhee-*thᵞoan*) *f* addition

adicional (ah-dhee-th ᵞoa-*nahl*) *adj* additional

adicionar (ah-dhee-thᵞoa-*nahr*) *v* add; count

¡adiós! (ah-*dhᵞoass*) good-bye!

adivinanza (ah-dhee-bhee-*nahn*-thah) *f* riddle

adivinar (ah-dhee-bhee-*nahr*) *v* guess

adjetivo (ahdh-khay-*tee*-bhoa) *m* adjective

administración (ahdh-mee-neess-trah-

th^yoan) *f* administration; direction
administrar (ahdh-mee-neess-*trahr*) *v*
manage; direct; administer
administrativo (ahdh-mee-neess-trah-
tee-bhoa) *adj* administrative
admirable (ahdh-mee-*rah*-bhlay) *adj*
admirable
admiración (ahdh-mee-rah-*th^yoan*) *f*
admiration
admirador (ahdh-mee-rah-*dhoar*) *m*
fan
admirar (ahdh-mee-*rahr*) *v* admire
admisión (ahdh-mee-*s^yoan*) *f* admission; admittance
admitir (ahdh-mee-*teer*) *v* admit; acknowledge
adonde (ah-*dhoan*-day) *adv* where
adoptar (ah-dhoap-*tahr*) *v* adopt
adorable (ah-dhoa-*rah*-bhlay) *adj* adorable
adorar (ah-dhoa-*rahr*) *v* worship
adormidera (ah-dhoar-mee-*dhay*-rah) *f*
poppy
adorno (ah-*dhoar*-noa) *m* ornament
adquirible (ahdh-kee-*ree*-bhlay) *adj* obtainable, available
*****adquirir** (ahdh-kee-*reer*) *v* acquire;
*buy
adquisición (ahdh-kee-see-*th^yoan*) *f*
acquisition
aduana (ah-*dwah*-nah) *f* Customs *pl*
adulto (ah-*dhool*-toa) *adj* grown-up,
adult; *m* grown-up, adult
adverbio (ahdh-*bhayr*-bh^oa) *m* adverb
advertencia (ahdh-bhayr-*tayn*-th^yah) *f*
warning
*****advertir** (ahdh-bhayr-*teer*) *v* caution,
warn; notice
aerolínea (ah-ay-roa-*lee*-nay-ah) *f* airline
aeropuerto (ah-ay-roa-*pwayr*-toa) *m*
airport
aerosol (ah-ay-roa-*soal*) *m* atomizer
afamado (ah-fah-*mah*-dhoa) *adj* noted

afección (ah-fayk-*th^yoan*) *f* affection
afectado (ah-fayk-tah-dhoa) *adj* affected
afectar (ah-fayk-*tahr*) *v* affect; feign
afeitadora eléctrica (ah-fay-tah-*dhoa*-
rah ay-*layk*-tree-kah) electric razor
afeitarse (ah-fay-*tahr*-say) *v* shave;
máquina de afeitar safety-razor;
shaver
afición (ah-fee-*th^yoan*) *f* hobby
aficionado (ah-fee-th^yoa-*nah*-dhoa) *m*
supporter
afilar (ah-fee-*lahr*) *v* sharpen; **afilado**
sharp
afiliación (ah-fee-l^yah-*th^yoan*) *f* membership
afiliado (ah-fee-*l^yah*-dhoa) *adj* affiliated
afirmación (ah-feer-mah-*th^yoan*) *f*
statement
afirmar (ah-feer-*mahr*) *v* claim
afirmativo (ah-feer-mah-*tee*-bhoa) *adj*
affirmative
aflicción (ah-fleek-*th^yoan*) *f* grief
afligido (ah-flee-*khee*-dhoa) *adj* sad;
***estar** ~ grieve
afluente (ah-*flwayn*-tay) *m* tributary
afortunado (ah-foar-too-*nah*-dhoa) *adj*
fortunate, lucky
África (*ah*-free-kah) *f* Africa
África del Sur (*ah*-free-kah dayl soor)
South Africa
africano (ah-free-*kah*-noa) *adj* African; *m* African
afuera (ah-*fway*-rah) *adv* outside, outdoors; **hacia** ~ outwards
afueras (ah-*fway*-rahss) *fpl* outskirts
pl
agarradero (ah-gah-rrah-*dhay*-roa) *m*
grip
agarrar (ah-gah-*rrahr*) *v* grasp, seize;
agarrarse *v* *hold on
agarre (ah-*gah*-rray) *m* grip, grasp
agencia (ah-*khayn*-th^yah) *f* agency; ~

de viajes travel agency
agenda (ah-*khayn*-dah) *f* diary
agente (ah-*khayn*-tay) *m* agent; ~ de
policía policeman; ~ de viajes
travel agent
ágil (*ah*-kheel) *adj* supple
agitación (ah-khee-tah-*th^yoan*) *f* excitement; bustle
agitar (ah-khee-*tahr*) *v* stir up
agosto (ah-*goass*-toa) August
agotado (ah-goa-*tah*-dhoa) *adj* sold
out
agotar (ah-goa-*tahr*) *v* use up
agradable (ah-grah-*dhah*-bhlay) *adj*
agreeable; enjoyable, pleasing,
pleasant; nice
***agradecer** (ah-grah-dhay-*thayr*) *v*
thank
agradecido (ah-grah-dhay-*thee*-dhoa)
adj grateful, thankful
agrario (ah-*grah*-r^yoa) *adj* agrarian
agraviar (ah-grah-*bh^yahr*) *v* wrong
agregar (ah-gray-*gahr*) *v* add
agresivo (ah-gray-*see*-bhoa) *adj* aggressive
agrícola (ah-*gree*-koa-lah) *adj* agrarian
agricultura (ah-gree-kool-*too*-rah) *f*
agriculture
agrio (*ah*-gr^yoa) *adj* sour
agua (*ah*-gwah) *f* water; ~ corriente
running water; ~ de mar sea-
water; ~ de soda soda-water; ~
dulce fresh water; ~ helada iced
water; ~ mineral mineral water; ~
potable drinking-water
aguacero (ah-gwah-*thay*-roa) *m* shower; downpour
aguafuerte (ah-gwah-*fwayr*-tay) *f* etching
aguanieve (ah-gwah-*n^yay*-bhay) *f*
slush
aguantar (ah-gwahn-*tahr*) *v* *bear
aguardado (ah-gwahr-*dhah*-dhoa) due
aguardar (ah-gwahr-*dahr*) *v* expect

agudo (ah-*goo*-dhoa) *adj* keen; acute
águila (*ah*-gee-lah) *m* eagle
aguja (ah-*goo*-khah) *f* needle; spire;
labor de ~ needlework
agujero (ah-goo-*khay*-roa) *m* hole
ahí (ah-*ee*) *adv* there
ahogar (ah-oa-*gahr*) *v* drown; ahogarse *v* *be drowned
ahora (ah-*oa*-rah) *adv* now; de ~ en
adelante henceforth; hasta ~ so
far
ahorrar (ah-oa-*rrahr*) *v* save
ahorros (ah-*oa*-rroass) *mpl* savings *pl*;
caja de ~ savings bank
ahuyentar (ou-^yayn-*tahr*) *v* chase
aire (*igh*-ray) *m* air; sky; breath; ~
acondicionado air-conditioning;
cámara de ~ inner tube; *tener aires de look
airear (igh-ray-*ahr*) *v* air, ventilate
aireo (igh-*ray*-oa) *m* ventilation
airoso (igh-*roa*-soa) *adj* airy
aislado (ighz-lah-dhoa) *adj* isolated
aislador (ighz-lah-*dhoar*) *m* insulator
aislamiento (ighz-lah-*m^yayn*-toa) *m*
isolation; insulation
aislar (ighz-*lahr*) *v* isolate; insulate
ajedrez (ah-khay-*dhrayth*) *m* chess
ajeno (ah-*khay*-noa) *adj* foreign
ajetrearse (ah-khay-tray-*ahr*-say) *v* labour
ajo (*ah*-khoa) *m* garlic
ajustar (ah-khooss-*tahr*) *v* adjust
ala (*ah*-lah) *f* wing
alabar (ah-lah-*bhahr*) *v* praise
alambre (ah-*lahm*-bray) *m* wire
alargar (ah-lahr-*gahr*) *v* lengthen; renew; hand
alarma (ah-*lahr*-mah) *f* alarm; ~ de
incendio fire-alarm
alarmante (ah-lahr-*mahn*-tay) *adj*
scary
alarmar (ah-lahr-*mahr*) *v* alarm
alba (*ahl*-bhah) *f* dawn

albañil (ahl-bhah-*ñeel*) *m* bricklayer

albaricoque (ahl-bhah-ree-*koa*-kay) *m* apricot

albergue para jóvenes (ahl-*bhayr*-gay pah-rah *khoa*-bhay-nayss) youth hostel

alborotador (ahl-bhoa-roa-tah-*dhoar*) *adj* rowdy

alboroto (ahl-bhoa-*roa*-toa) *m* noise, racket

álbum (*ahl*-bhoom) *m* album

alcachofa (ahl-kah-*choa*-fah) *f* artichoke

alcalde (ahl-*kahl*-dhay) *m* mayor

alcance (ahl-*kahn*-thay) *m* reach, range

alcanzable (ahl-kahn-*thah*-bhlay) *adj* attainable

alcanzar (ahl-kahn-*thahr*) *v* achieve, reach

alce (*ahl*-thay) *m* moose

alcohol (ahl-*koal*) *m* alcohol; ~ **de quemar** methylated spirits

alcohólico (ahl-*koa*-lee-koa) *adj* alcoholic

aldea (ahl-*day*-ah) *f* hamlet

alegrar (ah-lay-*grahr*) *v* cheer up

alegre (ah-*lay*-gray) *adj* cheerful, merry, joyful; glad, gay

alegría (ah-lay-*gree*-ah) *f* gaiety; gladness

alejar (ah-lay-*khahr*) *v* move away

alemán (ah-lay-*mahn*) *adj* German; *m* German

Alemania (ah-lay-*mah*-nʸah) *f* Germany

*alentar (ah-layn-*tahr*) *v* encourage

alergia (ah-*layr*-khʸah) *f* allergy

alfiler (ahl-fee-*layr*) *m* pin

alfombra (ahl-*foam*-brah) *f* carpet

alfombrilla (ahl-foam-*bree*-lʸah) *f* rug

álgebra (*ahl*-gay-bhrah) *f* algebra

algo (*ahl*-goa) *pron* something; *adv* somewhat

algodón (ahl-goa-*dhoan*) *m* cotton;

cotton-wool; **de** ~ cotton

alguien (*ahl*-gʸayn) *pron* someone, somebody

alguno (ahl-*goo*-noa) *adj* any; **algunos** *adj* some; *pron* some

alhaja (ah-*lah*-khah) *f* gem

alharaca (ah-lah-*rah*-kah) *f* fuss

aliado (ah-lʸah-dhoa) *m* associate; **Aliados** *mpl* Allies *pl*

alianza (ah-lʸahn-thah) *f* alliance

alicates (ah-lee-*kah*-tayss) *mpl* pliers *pl*

alienado (ah-lʸay-*nah*-dhoa) *m* lunatic

aliento (ah-lʸayn-toa) *m* breath

alimentar (ah-lee-mayn-*tahr*) *v* *feed

alimento (ah-lee-*mayn*-toa) *m* fare; food

alivio (ah-*lee*-bhʸoa) *m* relief

alma (*ahl*-mah) *f* soul

almacén (ahl-mah-*thayn*) *m* depot, warehouse, depository, store-house; store; ~ **de licores** off-licence; **grandes almacenes** department store

almacenaje (ahl-mah-thay-*nah*-khay) *m* storage

almacenar (ahl-mah-thay-*nahr*) *v* store

almanaque (ahl-mah-*nah*-kay) *m* almanac

almendra (ahl-*mayn*-drah) *f* almond

almidón (ahl-mee-*dhoan*) *m* starch

almidonar (ahl-mee-dhoa-*nahr*) *v* starch

almirante (ahl-mee-*rahn*-tay) *m* admiral

almohada (ahl-moa-*ah*-dhah) *f* pillow; ~ **eléctrica** heating pad

almohadilla (ahl-moa-ah-*dhee*-lʸah) *f* pad

almohadón (ahl-moa-ah-*dhoan*) *m* cushion; pillow

almuerzo (ahl-*mwayr*-thoa) *m* lunch, luncheon

alojamiento (ah-loa-khah-*mʸayn*-toa)

m accommodation, lodgings *pl*

alojar (ah-loa-*khahr*) *v* lodge

alondra (ah-*loan*-drah) *f* lark

alquilar (ahl-kee-*lahr*) *v* hire; rent, lease, *let

alquiler (ahl-kee-*layr*) *m* rent; ~ **de coches** car hire; **de** ~ for hire

alrededor de (ahl-ray-dhay-*dhoar* day) around, round; about

alrededores (ahl-ray-dhay-*dhoa*-rayss) *mpl* environment, surroundings *pl*

altar (ahl *tahr*) *m* altar

altavoz (ahl-tah-*bhoath*) *m* loudspeaker

alteración (ahl-tay-rah-th*Y*oan) *f* alteration

alterar (ahl-tay-*rahr*) *v* alter

alternar con (ahl-tayr-*nahr*) mix with

alternativa (ahl-tayr-nah-*tee*-bhah) *f* alternative

alternativo (ahl-tayr-nah-*tee*-bhoa) *adj* alternate

altiplano (ahl-tee-*plah*-noa) *m* uplands *pl*

altitud (ahl-tee-*toodh*) *f* altitude

altivo (ahl-*tee*-bhoa) *adj* haughty

alto (*ahl*-toa) *adj* high, tall; **en** ~ overhead

¡alto! (*ahl*-toa) stop!

altura (ahl-*too*-rah) *f* height

aludir a (ah-loo-*dheer*) allude to

alumbrado (ah-loom-*brah*-dhoa) *m* lighting

alumna (ah-*loom*-nah) *f* schoolgirl

alumno (ah-*loom*-noa) *m* scholar, pupil; schoolboy

alzar (ahl-*thahr*) *v* raise

allá (ah-*l*Yah) *adv* over there; **más** ~ beyond; **más** ~ **de** past, beyond

allí (ah-*l*Yee) *adv* there

amable (ah-*mah*-bhlay) *adj* kind, friendly

amado (ah-*mah*-dhoa) *adj* dear

amaestrar (ah-mah-ayss-*trahr*) *v* train

amamantar (ah-mah-mahn-*tahr*) *v* nurse

amanecer (ah-mah-nay-*thayr*) *m* sunrise, daybreak

amante (ah-*mahn*-tay) *m* lover

amapola (ah-mah-*poa*-lah) *f* poppy

amar (ah-*mahr*) *v* love

amargo (ah-*mahr*-goa) *adj* bitter

amarillo (ah-mah-*ree*-l*Y*oa) *adj* yellow

amatista (ah-mah-*teess*-tah) *f* amethyst

ámbar (*ahm*-bahr) *m* amber

ambicioso (ahm-bee-th*Y*oa-soa) *adj* ambitious

ambiente (ahm-b*Y*ayn-tay) *m* atmosphere

ambiguo (ahm-*bee*-gwoa) *adj* ambiguous

ambos (*ahm*-boass) *adj* both; either

ambulancia (ahm-boo-*lahn*-th*Y*ah) *f* ambulance

ambulante (ahm-boo-*lahn*-tay) *adj* itinerant

amenaza (ah-may-*nah*-thah) *f* threat

amenazador (ah-may-nah-thah-*dhoar*) *adj* threatening

amenazar (ah-may-nah-*thahr*) *v* threaten

ameno (ah-*may*-noa) *adj* nice

América (ah-*may*-ree-kah) *f* America; ~ **Latina** Latin America

americana (ah-may-ree-*kah*-nah) *f* jacket

americano (ah-may-ree-*kah*-noa) *adj* American; *m* American

amiga (ah-*mee* gah) *f* friend

amígdalas (ah-*meeg*-dhah-lahss) *fpl* tonsils *pl*

amigdalitis (ah-meeg-dhah-*lee*-teess) *f* tonsilitis

amigo (ah-*mee*-goa) *m* friend

amistad (ah-meess-*tahdh*) *f* friendship

amistoso (ah-meess-*toa*-soa) *adj* friendly

amnistía (ahm-neess-*tee*-ah) *f* amnesty

amo (*ah*-moa) *m* master

amoníaco (ah-moa-*nee*-ah-koa) *m* ammonia

amontonar (ah-moan-toa-*nahr*) *v* pile

amor (ah-*moar*) *m* love; darling, sweetheart

amorío (ah-moa-*ree*-oa) *m* affair, romance

amortiguador (ah-moar-tee-gwah-*dhoar*) *m* shock absorber

amortizar (ah-moar-tee-*thahr*) *v* *pay off

amotinamiento (ah-moa-tee-nah-m^yayn-toa) *m* mutiny

ampliación (ahm-pl^yah-*th^yoan*) *f* enlargement; extension

ampliar (ahm-*pl^yahr*) *v* enlarge; extend

amplio (*ahm*-pl^yoa) *adj* broad

ampolla (ahm-*poa*-l^yah) *f* blister

amueblar (ah-mway-*bhlahr*) *v* furnish

amuleto (ah-moo-*lay*-toa) *m* charm

analfabeto (ah-nahl-fah-*bhay*-toa) *m* illiterate

análisis (ah-*nah*-lee-seess) *f* analysis

analista (ah-nah-*leess*-tah) *m* analyst

analizar (ah-nah-lee-*thahr*) *v* analyse; *break down

análogo (ah-*nah*-loa-goa) *adj* similar

anarquía (ah-nahr-*kee*-ah) *f* anarchy

anatomía (ah-nah-toa-*mee*-ah) *f* anatomy

anciano (ahn-*th^yah*-noa) *adj* aged; elderly

ancla (*ahng*-klah) *f* anchor

ancho (*ahn*-choa) *adj* broad; wide; breadth

anchoa (ahn-*choa*-ah) *f* anchovy

anchura (ahn-*choo*-rah) *f* width

andadura (ahn-dah-*dhoo*-rah) *f* walk

andamio (ahn-*dah*-m^yoa) *m* scaffolding

***andar** (ahn-*dahr*) *v* walk

andares (ahn-*dah*-rayss) *mpl* pace

andén (ahn-*dayn*) *m* platform

anemia (ah-*nay*-m^yah) *f* anaemia

anestesia (ah-nayss-*tay*-s^yah) *f* anaesthesia

anestésico (ahn-ayss-*tay*-see-koa) *m* anaesthetic

anexar (ah-nayk-*sahr*) *v* annex

anexo (ah-*nayk*-soa) *m* annex, enclosure

anfitrión (ahn-fee-*tr^yoan*) *m* host

ángel (*ahng*-khayl) *m* angel

angosto (ahng-*goass*-toa) *adj* narrow, tight

anguila (ahng-*gee*-lah) *f* eel

ángulo (*ahng*-goo-loa) *m* angle

angustioso (ahng-gooss-*t^yoa*-soa) *adj* afraid

anhelar (ah-nay-*lahr*) *v* desire, long for

anhelo (ah-*nay*-loa) *m* longing

anillo (ah-*nee*-l^yoa) *m* ring; ~ **de boda** wedding-ring; ~ **de esponsales** engagement ring

animado (ah-nee-*mah*-dhoa) *adj* crowded

animal (ah-nee-*mahl*) *m* beast, animal; ~ **de presa** beast of prey; ~ **doméstico** pet

animar (ah-nee-*mahr*) *v* encourage, inspire; animate

ánimo (*ah*-nee-moa) *m* mind; courage

aniversario (ah-nee-bhayr-*sah*-r^yoa) *m* anniversary; jubilee

anoche (ah-*noa*-chay) *adv* last night

anomalía (ah-noa-mah-*lee*-ah) *f* aberration

anónimo (ah-*noa*-nee-moa) *adj* anonymous

anormal (ah-noar-*mahl*) *adj* abnormal

anotación (ah-noa-tah-*th^yoan*) *f* entry

anotar (ah-noa-*tahr*) *v* *write down

ansia (*ahn*-s^yah) *f* anxiety

ansioso (ahn-*s^yoa*-soa) *adj* anxious, eager

ante (*ahn*-tay) *prep* in front of

anteayer (ahn-tay-ah-*Yayr*) *adv* the day before yesterday

antecedentes (ahn-tay-thay-*dhayn*-tayss) *mpl* background

antena (ahn-*tay*-nah) *f* aerial

anteojos (ahn-tay-*oa*-khoass) *mpl* spectacles, glasses

antepasado (ahn-tay-pah-*sah*-dhoa) *m* ancestor

antepecho (ahn-tay-*pay*-choa) *m* window-sill

anterior (ahn-tay-*rYoar*) *adj* former, prior, previous

antes (*ahn*-tayss) *adv* before; formerly; at first; ~ **de** before; ~ **de que** before

antibiótico (ahn-tee-*bhYoa*-tee-koa) *m* antibiotic

anticipar (ahn-tee-thee-*pahr*) *v* advance

anticipo (ahn-tee-*thee*-poa) *m* advance

anticonceptivo (ahn-tee-koan-thayp-*tee*-bhoa) *m* contraceptive

anticongelante (ahn-tee-koang-khay-*lahn*-tay) *m* antifreeze

anticuado (ahn-tee-*kwah*-dhoa) *adj* old-fashioned; ancient, out of date, quaint

anticuario (ahn-tee-*kwah*-rYoa) *m* antique dealer

antigualla (ahn-tee-*gwah*-lYah) *f* antique

Antigüedad (ahn-tee-gway-*dhahdh*) *f* antiquity

antigüedades (ahn-tee-gway-*dhah*-dhayss) *fpl* antiquities *pl*

antiguo (ahn-*tee*-gwoa) *adj* ancient, antique; former

antipatía (ahn-tee-pah-*tee*-ah) *f* antipathy, dislike

antipático (ahn-tee-*pah*-tee-koa) *adj* nasty, unpleasant

antiséptico (ahn-tee-*sayp*-tee-koa) *m* antiseptic

antojarse (ahn-toa-*khahr*-say) *v* fancy, *feel like

antojo (ahn-*toa*-khoa) *m* fad, whim

antología (ahn-toa-loa-*khee*-ah) *f* anthology

antorcha (ahn-*toar*-chah) *f* torch

anual (ah-*nwahl*) *adj* annual, yearly

anuario (ah-*nwah*-ree-oa) *m* annual

anudar (ah-noo-*dhahr*) *v* tie; knot

anular (ah-noo-*lahr*) *v* cancel

anunciar (ah-noon-*thYahr*) *v* announce

anuncio (ah-*noon*-th Yoa) *m* announcement; advertisement

anzuelo (ahn-*thway*-loa) *m* fishing hook

añadir (ah-ñah-*dheer*) *v* add

año (*ah*-ñoa) *m* year; **al** ~ per annum; ~ **bisiesto** leap-year; ~ **nuevo** New Year

apagado (ah-pah-*gah*-dhoa) *adj* mat

apagar (ah-pah-*gahr*) *v* extinguish; *put out, switch off

aparato (ah-pah-*rah*-toa) *m* appliance, apparatus; machine

aparcamiento (ah-pahr-kah-*mYayn*-toa) *m* parking; **zona de** ~ parking zone

*** aparecer** (ah-pah-ray-*thayr*) *v* appear

aparejo (ah-pah-*ray*-khoa) *m* gear; ~ **de pesca** fishing tackle

aparente (ah-pah-*rayn*-tay) *adj* apparent

aparición (ah-pah-ree-*thYoan*) *f* apparition

apariencia (ah-pah-*rYayn*-thYah) *f* appearance, semblance

apartado (ah-pahr-*tah*-dhoa) *adj* out of the way

apartamento (ah-pahr-tah-*mayn*-toa) *m* suite; apartment *nAm*

apartar (ah-pahr-*tahr*) *v* separate

aparte (ah-*pahr*-tay) *adv* aside; *adj* individual

apasionado (ah-pah-sYoa-*nah*-dhoa)

adj passionate

apearse (ah-pay-*ahr*-say) *v* *get off

apelación (ah-pay-lah-*th^yoan*) *f* appeal

apelmazado (ah-payl-mah-*thah*-dhoa) *adj* lumpy

apellido (ah-pay-*l^yee*-dhoa) *m* family name, surname; ~ **de soltera** maiden name

apenado (ah-pay-*nah*-dhoa) *adj* sorry

apenas (ah-*pay*-nahss) *adv* hardly, barely, scarcely ; just

apéndice (ah-*payn*-dee-thay) *m* appendix

apendicitis (ah-payn-dee-*thee*-teess) *f* appendicitis

aperitivo (ah-pay-ree-*tee*-bhoa) *m* aperitif, drink

apertura (ah-payr-*too*-rah) *f* opening

apestar (ah-payss-*tahr*) *v* *stink

apetito (ah-pay-*tee*-toa) *m* appetite

apetitoso (ah-pay-tee-*toa*-soa) *adj* appetizing

apio (*ah*-p^yoa) *m* celery

aplaudir (ah-plou-*dheer*) *v* clap

aplauso (ah-*plou*-soa) *m* applause

aplazar (ah-plah-*thahr*) *v* postpone, adjourn, *put off

aplicación (ah-plee-kah-*s^yoan*) *f* application

aplicar (ah-plee-*kahr*) *v* apply ; **aplicarse a** apply, *be valid for

apogeo (ah-poa-*khayoa*) *m* height; zenith; ~ **de la temporada** peak season

*apostar (ah-poass-*tahr*) *v* *bet

apoyar (ah-poa-*^yahr*) *v* support; **apoyarse** *v* *lean

apoyo (ah-*poa*-^yoa) *m* support; assistance

apreciar (ah-pray-*th^yahr*) *v* appreciate

aprecio (ah-*pray*-th^yoa) *m* appreciation

aprender (ah-prayn-*dayr*) *v* *learn; **aprenderse de memoria** memorize

apresar (ah-pray-*sahr*) *v* hijack

apresurado (ah-pray-soo-*rah*-dhoa) *adj* hasty

apresurarse (ah-pray-soo-*rahr*-say) *v* hasten, hurry

apretado (ah-pray-*tah*-dhoa) *adj* tight

*apretar (ah-pray-*tahr*) *v* press; tighten

apretón (ah-pray-*toan*) *m* clutch; ~ **de manos** handshake

aprobación (ah-proa-bhah-*th^yoan*) *f* approval

*aprobar (ah-proa-*bhahr*) *v* approve; pass

apropiado (ah-proa-*p^yah*-dhoa) *adj* appropriate, suitable, proper; fit

aprovechar (ah-proa-bhay-*chahr*) *v* profit, benefit

aproximadamente (ah-proak-see-mah-dhah-*mayn*-tay) *adv* about, approximately

aproximado (ah-proak-see-*mah*-dhoa) *adj* approximate

aptitud (ahp-tee-*toodh*) *f* qualification; faculty

apto (*ahp*-toa) *adj* suitable; * **ser ~ para** qualify

apuesta (ah-*pwayss*-tah) *f* bet

apuntar (ah-poon-*tahr*) *v* aim at; point out

apunte (ah-*poon*-tay) *m* note; memo; **libreta de apuntes** notebook

aquel (ah-*kayl*) *adj* that; **aquellos** *adj* those

aquél (ah-*kayl*) *pron* that; **aquéllos** *pron* those

aquí (ah-*kee*) *adv* here

árabe (*ah*-rah-bhay) *adj* Arab; *m* Arab

Arabia Saudí (ah-*rah*-bh^yah sou-*dhee*) Saudi Arabia

arado (ah-*rah*-dhoa) *m* plough

arancel (ah-rahn-*thayl*) *m* tariff; duty

araña (ah-*rah*-ñah) *f* spider; **tela de ~**

cobweb
arar (ah-*rahr*) v plough
arbitrario (ahr-bhee-*trah*-rʸoa) adj arbitrary
árbitro (*ahr*-bhee-troa) m umpire
arbol (*ahr*-bhoal) m tree; ~ **de levas** camshaft
arbolado (ahr-bhoa-*lah*-dhoa) m woodland
arbusto (ahr-*bhooss*-toa) m shrub
arca (*ahr*-kah) f chest
arcada (ahr-*kah*-dhah) f arcade
arce (*ahr*-thay) m maple
arcilla (ahr-*thee*-lʸah) f clay
arco (*ahr*-koa) m arch, bow; ~ **iris** rainbow
archivo (ahr-*chee*-bhoa) m archives pl
arder (ahr-*dhayr*) v *burn
ardilla (ahr-*dhee*-lʸah) f squirrel
área (ah-ray-ah) f area; are
arena (ah-*ray*-nah) f sand
arenoso (ah-ray-*noa*-soa) adj sandy
arenque (ah-*rayng*-kay) m herring
Argelia (ahr-*khay*-lʸah) f Algeria
argelino (ahr-khay-*lee*-noa) adj Algerian; m Algerian
Argentina (ahr-khayn-*tee*-nah) f Argentina
argentino (ahr-khayn-*tee*-noa) adj Argentinian; m Argentinian
argumentar (ahr-goo-mayn *tahr*) v argue
argumento (ahr-goo-*mayn*-toa) m argument
árido (*ah*-ree-dhoa) adj arid
arisco (ah-*reess*-koa) adj unkind
aritmética (ah-reet-*may*-too-kah) f arithmetic
arma (*ahr*-mah) f weapon, arm
armador (ahr-mah-*dhoar*) m shipowner
armadura (ahr-mah-*dhoo*-rah) f frame; armour
armar (ahr-*mahr*) v arm

armario (ahr-*mah*-rʸoa) m cupboard; closet
armonía (ahr-moa-*nee*-ah) f harmony
aroma (ah-*roa*-mah) m aroma
arpa (*ahr*-pah) f harp
arqueado (ahr-kay-*ah*-dhoa) adj arched
arqueología (ahr-kay-oa-loa-*khee*-ah) f archaeology
arqueólogo (ahr-kay-*oa*-loa-goa) m archaeologist
arquitecto (ahr-kee-*tayk* toa) m architect
arquitectura (ahr-kee-tayk-*too*-rah) f architecture
arraigarse (ah-rrigh-*gahr*-say) v settle down
arrancar (ah-rrahng-*kahr*) v uproot, pull out; start off
arranque (ah-*rrahng*-kay) m starter motor
arrastrar (ah-rrahss-*trahr*) v haul, drag; *draw; **arrastrarse** v crawl
arrecife (ah-rray-*thee*-fay) m reef
arreglar (ah-rray-*glahr*) v settle; tidy up; repair, fix; **arreglarse con** *make do with
arreglo (ah-*rray*-gloa) m arrangement; settlement; **con ~ a** in accordance with
arrendamiento (ah-rrayn-dah-*mʸayn*-toa) m lease; **contrato de ~** lease
*** arrendar** (ah-rrayn-*dahr*) v lease
arrepentimiento (ah-rray-payn-tee-*mʸayn*-toa) m regret, repentance
arrestar (ah-rrayss-*tahr*) v arrest
arresto (ah-*rrayss*-toa) m arrest
arriar (ah-*rʸahr*) v *strike, lower
arriate (ah-*rʸah*-tay) m flowerbed
arriba (ah-*rree*-bhah) adv upstairs; up
arriesgado (ah-rryayz-*gah*-dhoa) adj risky
arriesgar (ah-rrʸayz-*gahr*) v venture, risk

arrodillarse (ah-rroa-dhee-*l^yahr*-say) *v* *kneel

arrogante (ah-rroa-*gahn*-tay) *adj* snooty

arrojar (ah-rroa-*khahr*) *v* *throw

arroyo (ah-*rroa*-^yoa) *m* stream, brook

arroz (ah-*rroath*) *m* rice

arruga (ah-*rroo*-gah) *f* wrinkle

arrugar (ah-rroo-*gahr*) *v* wrinkle

arruinar (ah-rrwee-*nahr*) *v* ruin; **arruinado** broke

arte (*ahr*-tay) *m/f* art; **artes industriales** arts and crafts; **bellas artes** fine arts

arteria (ahr-*tay*-r^yah) *f* artery; ~ **principal** thoroughfare

artesanía (ahr-tay-sah-*nee*-ah) *f* handicraft

articulación (ahr-tee-koo-lah-*th^yoan*) *f* joint

artículo (ahr-*tee*-koo-loa) *m* article

artificial (ahr-tee-fee-*th^yahl*) *adj* artificial

artificio (ahr-tee-*fee*-th^yoa) *m* artifice

artista (ahr-*teess*-tah) *m/f* artist

artístico (ahr-*teess*-tee-koa) *adj* artistic

arzobispo (ahr-thoa-*bheess*-poa) *m* archbishop

asamblea (ah-sahm-*blay*-ah) *f* assembly, meeting

asar (ah-*sahr*) *v* roast; ~ **en parrilla** roast

asbesto (ahdh-*bhayss*-toa) *m* asbestos

ascensor (ah-thayn-*soar*) *m* lift; elevator *nAm*

aseado (ah-say-*ah*-dhoa) *adj* tidy

asegurar (ah-say-goo-*rahr*) *v* assure, insure; **asegurarse de** ascertain

asemejarse (ah-say-may-*khahr*-say) *v* resemble

asesinar (ah-say-see-*nahr*) *v* murder

asesinato (ah-say-see-*nah*-toa) *m* murder, assassination

asesino (ah-say-*see*-noa) *m* murderer

asfalto (ahss-*fahl*-toa) *m* asphalt

así (ah-*see*) *adv* thus, so; ~ **que** so that

Asia (*ah*-s^yah) *f* Asia

asiático (ah-s^yah-tee-koa) *adj* Asian; *m* Asian

asiento (ah-s^yayn-toa) *m* seat

asignación (ah-seeg-nah-*th^yoan*) *f* allowance

asignar (ah-seeg-*nahr*) *v* allot; ~ **a** assign to

asilo (ah-*see*-loa) *m* asylum

asimismo (ah-see-*meez*-moa) *adv* also, likewise

*asir (ah-*seer*) *v* grip

asistencia (ah-seess-*tayn*-th^yah) *f* attendance; assistance

asistente (ah-seess-*tayn*-tay) *m* assistant

asistir (ah-seess-*teer*) *v* assist, aid; ~ **a** assist at, attend

asma (*ahz*-mah) *f* asthma

asociación (ah-soa-th^yah-*th^yoan*) *f* association; club, society

asociado (ah-soa-*th^yah*-dhoa) *m* associate

asociar (ah-soa-*th^yahr*) *v* associate; **asociarse a** join

asombrar (ah-soam-*brahr*) *v* amaze, astonish

asombro (ah-*soam*-broa) *m* amazement; wonder

asombroso (ah-soam-*broa*-soa) *adj* astonishing

aspecto (ahss-*payk*-toa) *m* aspect; appearance, look; sight

áspero (*ahss*-pay-roa) *adj* harsh; rough

aspiración (ahss-pee-rah-*th^yoan*) *f* inhalation; aspiration

aspirador (ahss-pee-rah-*dhoar*) *m* vacuum cleaner; **pasar el** ~ hoover

aspirar (ahss-pee-*rahr*) *v* aspire; ~ **a** aim at

aspirina (ahss-pee-*ree*-nah) *f* aspirin

asqueroso (ahss-kay-*roa*-soa) *adj* disgusting

astilla (ahss-*tee*-lYah) *f* splinter; chip

astillar (ahss-tee-*lYahr*) *v* chip

astillero (ahss-tee-*lYay*-roa) *m* shipyard

astronomía (ahss-troa-noa-*mee*-ah) *f* astronomy

astucia (ahss-*too*-thYah) *f* ruse

astuto (ahss-*too*-toa) *adj* cunning; clever, sly

asunto (ah-*soon*-toa) *m* affair, matter; concern, business; topic

asustado (ah-sooss-*tah*-dhoa) *adj* afraid

asustar (ah-sooss-*tahr*) *v* scare; **asustarse** *v* *be frightened

atacar (ah-tah-*kahr*) *v* attack, assault; *strike

atadura (ah-tah-*dhoo*-rah) *f* binding

atañer (ah tah ñayr) *v* concern

ataque (ah-*tah*-kay) *m* attack, fit; stroke; ~ **cardíaco** heart attack

atar (ah-*tahr*) *v* tie, *bind; fasten; bundle

atareado (ah tah ray *ah*-dhoa) *adj* busy

atención (ah-tayn-*thYoan*) *f* attention; consideration, notice; **prestar** ~ *pay attention, look out

atender a (ah-tayn-*dayr*) attend to, see to; nurse

atento (ah-*tayn*-toa) *adj* attentive; thoughtful

ateo (ah-*tay*-oa) *m* atheist

aterido (ah-tay-*ree*-dhoa) *adj* numb

aterrador (ah-tay-rrah-*dhoar*) *adj* terrifying

aterrizar (ah-tay-rree-*thahr*) *v* land

aterrorizar (ah-tay-rroa-ree-*thahr*) *v* terrify

Atlántico (aht-*lahn*-tee-koa) *m* Atlantic

atleta (aht-*lay*-tah) *m* athlete

atletismo (aht-lay-*teez*-moa) *m* athletics *pl*

atmósfera (aht-*moass*-fay-rah) *f* atmosphere

atómico (ah-*toa*-mee-koa) *adj* atomic

átomo (*ah*-toa-moa) *m* atom

atónito (ah-*toa*-nee-toa) *adj* speechless

atontado (ah-toan-*tah*-dhoa) *adj* dumb

atormentar (ah-toar-mayn-*tahr*) *v* torment

atornillar (ah-toar-nee-*lYahr*) *v* screw

atracar (ah-trah-*kahr*) *v* dock

atracción (ah-trahk-*thYoan*) *f* attraction

atraco (ah-*trah*-koa) *m* hold-up

atractivo (ah trahk *tee*-bhoa) *adj* attractive

atraer (ah-trah-*ayr*) *v* attract

atrapar (ah-trah-*pahr*) *v* contract

atrás (ah-*trahss*) *adv* back

atrasado (ah-trah-*sah*-dhoa) *adj* overdue

atravesar (ah-trah-bhay-*sahr*) *v* cross, pass through

atreverse (ah-tray-*bhayr*-say) *v* dare

atrevido (ah-tray-*bhee*-dhoa) *adj* daring

atribuir a (ah-tree-*bhweer*) assign to

atroz (ah-*troath*) *adj* horrible

atún (ah-*toon*) *m* tuna

audacia (ou-*dhah*-thYah) *f* nerve

audaz (ou-*dhahth*) *adj* bold

audible (ou-*dhee*-bhlay) *adj* audible

auditorio (ou-dhee-*toa*-rYoa) *m* audience

aula (*ou* lah) *f* auditorium

aumentar (ou-mayn-*tahr*) *v* increase, raise

aumento (ou-*mayn*-toa) *m* increase; rise; raise *nAm*

aun (ah-*oon*) *adv* (aún) yet; even

aunque (*oung*-kay) *conj* although, though

aurora (ou-*roa*-rah) *f* dawn
ausencia (ou-*sayn*-th^yah) *f* absence
ausente (ou-*sayn*-tay) *adj* absent
Australia (ouss-*trah*-l^yah) *f* Australia
australiano (ouss-trah-*l^yah*-noa) *adj* Australian ; *m* Australian
Austria (*ouss*-tr^yah) *f* Austria
austríaco (ouss-*tree*-ah-koa) *adj* Austrian ; *m* Austrian
auténtico (ou-*tayn*-tee-koa) *adj* authentic ; true, original
auto (*ou*-toa) *m* car
autobús (ou-toa-*bhooss*) *m* coach, bus
autoestopista (ou-toa-ayss-toa-*peess*-tah) *m* hitchhiker
automático (ou-toa-*mah*-tee-koa) *adj* automatic
automatización (ou-toa-mah-tee-thah-*th^yoan*) *f* automation
automóvil (ou-toa-*moa*-bheel) *m* motor-car, automobile ; ~ **club** automobile club
automovilismo (ou-toa-moa-bhee-*leez*-moa) *m* motoring
automovilista (ou-toa-moa-bhee-*leess*-tah) *m* motorist
autonomía (ou-toa-noa-*mee*-ah) *f* self-government
autónomo (ou-*toa*-noa-moa) *adj* independent, autonomous
autopista (ou-toa-*peess*-tah) *f* motorway ; highway *nAm* ; ~ **de peaje** turnpike *nAm*
autopsia (ou-*toap*-s^yah) *f* autopsy
autor (ou-*toar*) *m* author
autoridad (ou-toa-ree-*dhahdh*) *f* authority
autoritario (ou-toa-ree-*tah*-r^yoa) *adj* authoritarian
autorización (ou-toa-ree-thah-*th^yoan*) *f* authorization ; permission
autorizar (ou-toa-ree-*thahr*) *v* allow ; license
autoservicio (ou-toa-sayr-*bhee*-th^yoa)

m self-service
*****hacer autostop** (ah-*thayr* ou-toa-*stoap*) hitchhike
auxilio (ouk-*see*-l^yoa) *m* assistance ; **primeros auxilios** first-aid
avalancha (ah-bhah-*lahn*-chah) *f* avalanche
avanzar (ah-bhahn-*thahr*) *v* advance
avaro (ah-*bhah*-roa) *adj* avaricious
avefría (ah-bhay-*free*-ah) *f* pewit
avellana (ah-bhay-*l^yah*-nah) *f* hazelnut
avena (ah-*bhay*-nah) *f* oats *pl*
avenida (ah-bhay-*nee*-dhah) *f* avenue
aventura (ah-bhayn-*too*-rah) *f* adventure
*****avergonzarse** (ah-bhayr-goan-*thahr*-say) *v* *be ashamed
avería (ah-bhay-*ree*-ah) *f* breakdown
averiarse (ah-bhay-r^y*ahr*-say) *v* *break down ; **averiado** *adj* out of order
aversión (ah-bhayr-*s^yoan*) *f* aversion, dislike
avestruz (ah-bhayss-*trooth*) *m* ostrich
avión (ah-*bh^yoan*) *m* aeroplane ; aircraft, plane ; airplane *nAm* ; ~ **a reacción** jet ; ~ **turborreactor** turbojet
avíos (ah-*bhee*-oass) *mpl* kit ; ~ **de pesca** fishing gear
avisar (ah-bhee-*sahr*) *v* inform
aviso (ah-*bhee*-soa) *m* notice
avispa (ah-*bheess*-pah) *f* wasp
aya (*ah*-^yah) *f* governess
ayer (ah-^y*ayr*) *adv* yesterday
ayuda (ah-^y*oo*-dhah) *f* help ; relief ; ~ **de cámara** valet
ayudante (ah-^yoo-*dhahn*-tay) *m* helper
ayudar (ah-^yoo-*dhahr*) *v* aid, help
ayuntamiento (ah-^yoon-tah-*m^yayn*-toa) *m* town hall
azada (ah-*thah*-dhah) *f* spade
azafata (ah-thah-*fah*-tah) *f* hostess ; stewardess
azar (ah-*thahr*) *m* chance, luck

azor (ah-*thoar*) *m* hawk
azote (ah-*thoa*-tay) *m* whip
azúcar (ah-*thoo*-kahr) *m/f* sugar; **te-rrón de** ~ lump of sugar
azucena (ah-thoo-*thay*-nah) *f* lily
azul (ah-*thool*) *adj* blue
azulejo (ah-thoo-*lay*-khoa) *m* tile

B

babor (bah-*bhoar*) *m* port
bacalao (bah-kah-*lah*-oa) *m* cod; had-dock
bacteria (bahk-*tay*-rʸah) *f* bacterium
bache (*bah*-chay) *m* hole
bahía (bah-*ee*-ah) *f* bay
bailar (bigh-*lahr*) *v* dance
baile (*bigh*-lay) *m* ball; dance
baja (*bah*-khah) *f* slump
bajada (bah-*khah*-dhah) *f* descent
bajamar (bah-khah-*mahr*) *f* low tide
bajar (bah-*khahr*) *v* lower; **bajarse** *v* *bend down
bajo (*bah*-khoa) *adj* low; short; *prep* under, below; *m* bass
bala (*bah*-lah) *f* bullet
baladí (bah-lah-*dhee*) *adj* insignificant
balance (bah-*lahn*-thay) *m* balance
balanza (bah-*lahn*-thah) *f* scales *pl*
balbucear (bahl-bhoo-thay-*ahr*) *v* falter
balcón (bahl-*koan*) *m* balcony; circle
balde (*bahl*-day) *m* pail, bucket
baldío (bahl-*dee*-oa) *adj* waste
balneario (bahl-nay-ah-rʸoa) *m* spa
ballena (bah-*lʸay*-nah) *f* whale
ballet (bah-*lay*) *m* ballet
bambú (bahm-*boo*) *m* bamboo
banco (*bahng*-koa) *m* bank; bench
banda (*bahn*-dah) *f* band; gang
bandeja (bahn-*day*-khah) *f* tray
bandera (bahn-*day*-rah) *f* flag; banner
bandido (bahn-*dee*-dhoa) *m* bandit

banquete (bahng-*kay*-tay) *m* banquet
bañador (bah-ñah-*dhoar*) *m* bathing-trunks
bañarse (bah-*ñahr*-say) *v* bathe
baño (*bah*-ñoa) *m* bath; *mMe* bath-room; ~ **turco** Turkish bath; **cal-zón de** ~ swimming-trunks; **traje de** ~ swim-suit
bar (bahr) *m* bar; saloon, café
barajar (bah-rah-*khahr*) *v* shuffle
baranda (bah-*rahn*-dah) *f* banisters *pl*
barandilla (bah-rahn-*dee*-lʸah) *f* rail; railing
barato (bah-*rah*-toa) *adj* inexpensive, cheap
barba (*bahr*-bhah) *f* beard
barbero (bahr-*bhay*-roa) *m* barber
barbilla (bahr-*bhee*-lʸah) *f* chin
barca (*bahr*-kah) *f* boat
barco (*bahr*-koa) *m* boat
barítono (bah-*ree*-toa-noa) *m* baritone
barman (*bahr*-mahn) *m* bartender, barman
barniz (bahr-*neeth*) *m* varnish; ~ **para las uñas** nail-polish
barnizar (bahr-nee-*thahr*) *v* varnish
barómetro (bah-*roa*-may-troa) *m* ba-rometer
barquillo (bahr-*kee*-lʸoa) *m* waffle
barra (*bah*-rrah) *f* bar, rod; counter
barrer (bah-*rrayr*) *v* *sweep
barrera (bah-*rray*-rah) *f* barrier, rail; ~ **de protección** crash barrier
barril (bah-*rreel*) *m* barrel, cask
barrilete (bah-rree-*lay*-tay) *m* keg
barrio (*bah*-rrʸoa) *m* quarter, district; ~ **bajo** slum
barroco (bah-*rroa*-koa) *adj* baroque
barrote (bah-*rroa*-tay) *m* bar
basar (bah-*sahr*) *v* base
báscula (*bahss*-koo-lah) *f* weighing-machine
base (*bah*-say) *f* basis, base
basílica (bah-*see*-lee-kah) *f* basilica

bastante (bahss-*tahn*-tay) *adv* enough, sufficient; fairly, pretty, rather, quite

bastar (bahss-*tahr*) *v* suffice

bastardo (bahss-*tahr*-dhoa) *m* bastard

bastón (bahss-*toan*) *m* cane; walking-stick; **bastones de esquí** ski sticks

basura (bah-*soo*-rah) *f* trash, rubbish, garbage; **cubo de la** ~ rubbish-bin

bata (*bah*-tah) *f* dressing-gown; ~ **de baño** bathrobe; ~ **suelta** negligee

batalla (bah-*tah*-lʸah) *f* battle

batería (bah-tay-*ree*-ah) *f* battery

batidora (bah-tee-*dhoa*-rah) *f* mixer

batir (bah-*teer*) *v* *beat, whip

baúl (bah-*ool*) *m* trunk

bautismo (bou-*teez*-moa) *m* baptism

bautizar (bou-tee-*thahr*) *v* christen, baptize

bautizo (bou-tee-thoa) *m* christening, baptism

baya (*bah*-ʸah) *f* berry

bebé (bay-*bhay*) *m* baby

beber (bay-*bhayr*) *v* *drink

bebida (bay-*bhee*-dhah) *f* drink, beverage; ~ **no alcohólica** soft drink; **bebidas espirituosas** spirits

beca (*bay*-kah) *f* grant, scholarship

becerro (bay-*thay*-rroa) *m* calf skin

beige (*bay*-khay) *adj* beige

béisbol (*bayz*-bhoal) *m* baseball

belga (*bayl*-gah) *adj* Belgian; *m* Belgian

Bélgica (*bayl*-khee-kah) *f* Belgium

belleza (bay-*lʸay*-thah) *f* beauty; **salón de** ~ beauty salon

bello (*bay*-lʸoa) *adj* fine

bellota (bay-*lʸoa*-tah) *f* acorn

***bendecir** (bayn-day-*theer*) *v* bless

bendición (bayn-dee-*thʸoan*) *f* blessing

beneficio (bay-nay-*fee*-thʸoa) *m* profit, benefit

berenjena (bay-rayng-*khay*-nah) *f* eggplant

berro (*bay*-rroa) *m* watercress

besar (bay-*sahr*) *v* kiss

beso (*bay*-soa) *m* kiss

betún (bay-*toon*) *m* shoe polish

biblia (*bee*-bhlʸah) *f* bible

biblioteca (bee-bhlʸoa-*tay*-kah) *f* library

bicicleta (bee-thee-*klay*-tah) *f* cycle, bicycle

biciclo (bee-*thee*-kloa) *m* cycle, bicycle

bicimotor (bee-thee-moa-*toar*) *m* moped

biela (*bʸay*-lah) *f* piston-rod

bien (bʸayn) *adv* well; **¡bien!** all right!; **bien ... bien** either ... or

bienes (*bʸay*-nayss) *mpl* goods *pl*; possessions

bienestar (bʸay-nayss-*tahr*) *m* ease; welfare

bienvenida (bʸayn-bhay-*nee*-dhah) *f* welcome; *dar la** ~ welcome

bienvenido (bʸayn-bhay-*nee*-dhoa) *adj* welcome

biftec (beef-*tayk*) *m* steak

bifurcación (bee-foor-kah-*thʸoan*) *f* road fork, fork

bifurcarse (bee-foor-*kahr*-say) *v* fork

bigote (bee-*goatay*) *m* moustache

bilingüe (bee-*leeng*-gway) *adj* bilingual

bilis (*bee*-leess) *f* gall, bile

billar (bee-*lʸahr*) *m* billiards *pl*

billete (bee-*lʸay*-tay) *m* ticket; ~ **de andén** platform ticket; ~ **de banco** banknote; ~ **gratuito** free ticket

biología (bʸoa-loa-*khee*-ah) *f* biology

biológico (bʸoa-*loa*-khee-koa) *adj* biological

bisagra (bee-*sah*-grah) *f* hinge

bizco (*beeth*-koa) *adj* cross-eyed

bizcocho (beeth-*koa*-choa) *m* cookie *nAm*

blanco¹ (*blahng*-koa) *adj* white; blank

blanco² (*blahng*-koa) *m* mark, target

blando (*blahn*-doa) *adj* soft
blanquear (blahng-kay-*ahr*) *v* bleach
bloc (bloak) *mMe* writing-pad
bloque (*bloa*-kay) *m* block; writing-pad
bloquear (bloa-kay-*ahr*) *v* block
blusa (*bloo*-sah) *f* blouse
bobina (boa-*bhee*-nah) *f* spool; ~ **del encendido** ignition coil
bobo (*boa*-bhoa) *adj* silly
boca (*boa*-kah) *f* mouth
bocadillo (boa-kah-*dhee*-lʸoa) *m* sandwich
bocado (boa-*kah*-dhoa) *m* bite
bocina (boa-*thee*-nah) *f* horn, hooter; **tocar la** ~ hoot
boda (*boa*-dhah) *f* wedding
bodega (boa-*dhay*-gah) *f* hold
bofetada (boa-fay-*tah*-dhah) *f* smack, slap
boina (*boi*-nah) *f* beret
bolera (boa-*lay*-rah) *f* bowling alley
boletín meteorológico (boa-lay-*teen* may-tay-oa-roa-*loa*-khee-koa) weather forecast
boleto (boa-*lay*-toa) *mMe* ticket
bolígrafo (boa-*lee*-grah-foa) *m* ballpoint-pen, Biro
Bolivia (boa-*lee*-bhʸah) *f* Bolivia
boliviano (boa-lee-*bhʸah*-noa) *adj* Bolivian; *m* Bolivian
bolsa (*boal*-sah) *f* bag; stock market, stock exchange; pocket-book, purse; ~ **de hielo** ice-bag; ~ **de papel** paper bag
bolsillo (boal-*see*-lʸoa) *m* pocket
bolso (*boal*-soa) *m* handbag; bag
bollo (*boa*-lʸoa) *m* bun
bomba (*boam*-bah) *f* pump; bomb; ~ **de agua** water pump; ~ **de gasolina** petrol pump; fuel pump *Am*
bombardear (boam-bahr-dhay-*ahr*) *v* bomb
bombear (boam-bay-*ahr*) *v* pump

bomberos (boam-*bay*-roass) *mpl* fire-brigade
bombilla (boam-*bee*-lʸah) *f* light bulb; ~ **de flash** flash-bulb
bombón (boam-*boan*) *m* chocolate; candy *nAm*
bondad (boan-*dahdh*) *f* goodness
bondadoso (boan-dah-*dhoa*-soa) *adj* good-natured, kind
bonito (boa-*nee*-toa) *adj* pretty; fair, nice, lovely
boquerón (boa-kay-*roan*) *m* whitebait
boquilla (boa-*kee*-lʸah) *f* cigarette-holder
bordado (boar-*dhah*-dhoa) *m* embroidery
bordar (boar-*dhahr*) *v* embroider
borde (*boar*-dhay) *m* edge, border; verge, rim, brim; ~ **del camino** wayside
bordillo (boar-*dhee*-lʸoa) *m* curb
a bordo (ah *boar*-doa) aboard
borracho (boa-*rrah*-choa) *adj* drunk
borrar (boa-*rrahr*) *v* erase
borrascoso (boa-rrahss-*koa*-soa) *adj* gusty
borrón (boa-*rroan*) *m* blot
bosque (*boass*-kay) *m* wood, forest
bosquejar (boass-kay-*khahr*) *v* sketch
bosquejo (boass-*kay*-khoa) *m* sketch
bostezar (boass-tay-*thahr*) *v* yawn
bota (*boa*-tah) *f* boot; **botas de esquí** ski boots
botadura (boa-tah-*dhoo*-rah) *f* launching
botánica (boa-*tah*-nee-kah) *f* botany
bote (*boa*-tay) *m* rowing-boat; ~ **a motor** motor-boat
botella (boa-*tay*-lʸah) *f* bottle
botón (boa-*toan*) *m* button; knob, push-button; ~ **del cuello** collar stud
botones (boa-*toa*-nayss) *mpl* bellboy
bóveda (*boa*-bhay-dhah) *f* vault, arch

boxear (boak-say-*ahr*) v box
boya (*boa*-Yah) f buoy
braga (*brah*-gah) f briefs pl; panties pl
bragueta (brah-*gay*-tah) f fly
branquia (*brahng*-kYah) f gill
Brasil (brah-*seel*) m Brazil
brasileño (brah-see-*lay*-ña) adj Brazilian; m Brazilian
braza (*brah*-thah) f breaststroke; ~ **de mariposa** butterfly stroke
brazo (*brah*-thoa) m arm; **del** ~ arm-in-arm
brea (*bray*-ah) f tar
brecha (*bray*-chah) f breach
bregar (bray-*gahr*) v labour
brema (*bray*-mah) f bream
breve (*bray*-bhay) adj brief; **en** ~ soon
brezal (bray-*thahl*) m moor
brezo (*bray*-thoa) m heather
brillante (bree-lYahn-tay) adj brilliant
brillantina (bree-lYahn-*tee*-nah) f hair cream
brillar (bree-*lYahr*) v glow, *shine
brillo (*bree*-lYoa) m glow, gloss
brincar (breeng-*kahr*) v hop; skip
brindis (*breen*-deess) m toast
brisa (*bree*-sah) f breeze
británico (bree-*tah*-nee-koa) adj British; m Briton
brocha (*broa*-chah) f brush; ~ **de afeitar** shaving-brush
broche (*broa*-chay) m brooch
broma (*broa*-mah) f joke
bronca (*broang*-kah) f row
bronce (*broan*-thay) m bronze; **de** ~ bronze
bronquitis (broang-*kee*-teess) f bronchitis
brotar (broa-*tahr*) v bud
bruja (*broo*-khah) f witch
brújula (*broo*-khoo-lah) f compass
brumoso (broo-*moa*-soa) adj foggy;

hazy
brutal (broo-*tahl*) adj brutal
bruto (*broo*-toa) adj gross
bucear (boo-thay-*ahr*) v dive
bueno (*bway*-noa) adj good; kind; sound; ¡bueno! well!
buey (bway) m ox
bufanda (boo-*fahn*-dah) f scarf
buffet (boof-*fayt*) m buffet
buhardilla (bwahr-*dee*-lYah) f attic
buho (*boo*-oa) m owl
buitre (*bwee*-tray) m vulture
bujía (boo-*khee*-ah) f sparking-plug
bulbo (*bool*-bhoa) m bulb; light bulb
Bulgaria (bool-*gah*-rYah) f Bulgaria
búlgaro (*bool*-gah-roa) adj Bulgarian; m Bulgarian
bulto (*bool*-toa) m bulk
bulla (*boo*-lYah) f fuss
buque (*boo*-kay) m ship; vessel; ~ **a motor** launch; ~ **cisterna** tanker; ~ **de guerra** man-of-war; ~ **velero** sailing-boat
burbuja (boor-*boo*-khah) f bubble
burdel (boor-*dhayl*) m brothel
burdo (*boor*-dhoa) adj coarse
burgués (boor-*gayss*) adj middle-class, bourgeois
burla (*boor*-lah) f mockery
burlarse de (boor-*lahr*-say) mock
burocracia (boo-roa-*krah*-thYah) f bureaucracy
burro (*boo*-rroa) m ass, donkey
buscar (booss-*kahr*) v look for; look up, *seek, search; hunt for; *ir a ~ *get, pick up, fetch
búsqueda (*booss*-kay-dhah) f search
busto (*booss*-toa) m bust
butaca (boo-*tah*-kah) f armchair, easy chair; stall; orchestra seat Am
buzón (boo-*thoan*) m pillar-box, letter-box; mailbox nAm

C

caballero (kah-bhah-*lᵞay*-roa) *m* gentleman; knight

caballitos (kah-bhah-*lᵞee*-toass) *mpl* merry-go-round

caballo (kah-*bhah*-lᵞoa) *m* horse; ~ **de carrera** race-horse; ~ **de vapor** horsepower

cabaña (kah-*bhah*-nah) *f* cabin, hut

cabaret (kah-bhah-*rayt*) *m* cabaret; nightclub

cabecear (kah-bhay-thay-*ahr*) *v* nod

cabeceo (kah-bhay-*thay*-oa) *m* nod

cabello (koh-*bhay*-lᵞoa) *m* hair

cabelludo (kah-bhay-*lᵞoo*-dhoa) *adj* hairy

cabeza (kah-*bhay*-thah) *f* head; ~ **de turco** scapegoat; **dolor de** ~ headache

cabezudo (kah-bhay-*thoo*-dhoa) *adj* head-strong

cabina (kah-*bhee*-nah) *f* cabin; booth; ~ **telefónica** telephone booth

cable (*kah*-bhlay) *m* cable

cablegrafiar (kah-bhlay-grah-*fᵞahr*) *v* cable

cablegrama (kah-bhlay-*grah*-mah) *m* cable

cabo (*kah*-bhoa) *m* cape

cabra (*kah*-bhrah) *f* goat

cabritilla (kah-bhree-*tee*-lᵞah) *f* kid

cabrón (kah-*bhroan*) *m* goat

cacanuate (kah-kah-*wah*-tay) *mMe* peanut

cacahuete (kah-kah-*way*-tay) *m* peanut

cacerola (kah-thay-*roa*-lah) *f* saucepan

cachear (kah-chay-*ahr*) *v* search

cachivache (kah-chee-*bhah*-chay) *m* junk

cada (*kah*-dhah) *adj* every, each; ~ **uno** everyone

cadáver (kah-*dhah*-bhayr) *m* corpse

cadena (kah-*dhay*-nah) *f* chain

cadera (kah-*dhay*-rah) *f* hip

caducado (kah-dhoo-*kah*-dhoa) *adj* expired

*****caer** (kah-*ayr*) *v* *fall; **dejar** ~ drop

café (kah-*fay*) *m* coffee; public house

cafeína (kah-fay-ee-nah) *f* caffeine

cafetera filtradora (kah-fay-*tay*-rah feel-trah-*dhoa*-rah) percolator

cafetería (kah-fay-tay-*ree*-ah) *f* snack-bar, cafeteria

caída (kah-*ee*-dhah) *f* fall

caja (*kah*-khah) *f* box; crate; pay-desk; ~ **de cartón** carton; ~ **de caudales** safe, vault; ~ **de cerillas** match-box; ~ **de colores** paint-box; ~ **de velocidades** gear-box; ~ **fuerte** safe; ~ **metálica** canister

cajera (kah-*khay*-rah) *f* cashier

cajero (kah-*khay*-roa) *m* cashier

cajón (kah-*khoan*) *m* drawer

cal (kahl) *f* lime

calambre (kah-*lahm*-bray) *m* cramp

calamidad (kah-lah-mee-*dhahdh*) *f* disaster

calcetín (kahl-thay-*teen*) *m* sock

calcio (*kahl*-thᵞoa) *m* calcium

calculadora (kahl-koo-lah-*dhoa*-rah) *f* adding-machine

calcular (kahl-koo-*lahr*) *v* reckon, calculate

cálculo (*kahl*-koo-loa) *m* calculation; ~ **biliar** gallstone

calderilla (kahl-day-*ree*-lᵞah) *f* petty cash

calefacción (kah-lay-fahk-*thᵞoan*) *f* heating

calefactor (kah-lay-fahk-*toar*) *m* heater

calendario (kah-layn-*dah*-rᵞoa) *m* calendar

*****calentar** (kah-layn-*tahr*) *v* warm, heat

calidad (kah-lee-*dhahdh*) *f* quality; **de**

primera ~ first-class
caliente (kah-*l*ʸayn-tay) *adj* warm, hot
calificado (kah-lee-fee-*kah*-dhoa) *adj* qualified
calina (kah-*lee*-nah) *f* haze
calinoso (kah-lee-*noa*-soa) *adj* hazy
calma (*kahl*-mah) *f* calm
calmante (kahl-*mahn*-tay) *m* tranquillizer, sedative
calmar (kahl-*mahr*) *v* calm down; **calmarse** *v* calm down
calor (kah-*loar*) *m* warmth, heat
caloría (kah-loa-*ree*-ah) *f* calorie
calorífero (kah-loa-*ree*-fay-roa) *m* hot-water bottle
calumnia (kah-*loom*-nʸah) *f* slander
calvinismo (kahl-bhee-*neez*-moa) *m* Calvinism
calvo (*kahl*-bhoa) *adj* bald
calzada (kahl-*thah*-dhah) *f* carriageway, causeway; drive
calzado (kahl-*thah*-dhoa) *m* footwear
calzoncillos (kahl-thoan-*thee*-lʸoass) *mpl* pants *pl*, briefs *pl*, drawers; shorts *plAm*
callado (kah-*lʸah*-dhoa) *adj* silent
callarse (kah-*lʸahr*-say) *v* *be silent
calle (*kah*-lʸay) *f* street; road; ~ **lateral** side-street; ~ **mayor** main street
callejón (kah-lʸay-*khoan*) *m* alley, lane; ~ **sin salida** cul-de-sac
callo (*kah*-lʸoa) *m* callus; corn
cama (*kah*-mah) *f* bed; ~ **de tijera** camp-bed; cot *nAm*; **camas gemelas** twin beds; ~ **y desayuno** bed and breakfast
camafeo (kah-mah-*fay*-oa) *m* cameo
cámara (*kah*-mah-rah) *f* camera; ~ **fotográfica** camera
camarada (kah-mah-*rah*-dhah) *m* comrade
camarera (kah-mah-*ray*-rah) *f* waitress
camarero (kah-mah-*ray*-roa) *m* waiter; steward; **jefe de camareros** head-waiter
camarón (kah-mah-*roan*) *m* shrimp
camastro (kah-*mahss*-troa) *m* bunk
cambiar (kahm-*b*ʸahr) *v* alter, change; vary; exchange, switch; ~ **de marcha** change gear
cambio (*kahm*-bʸoa) *m* alteration, change, variation; turn; exchange; exchange rate; **oficina de** ~ money exchange
camello (kah-*may*-lʸoa) *m* camel
caminar (kah-mee-*nahr*) *v* *go; hike
caminata (kah-mee-*nah*-tah) *f* walk
camino (kah-*mee*-noa) *m* way; road; **a mitad de** ~ halfway; **borde del** ~ roadside; ~ **de** bound for; ~ **en obras** road up; ~ **principal** main road
camión (kah-*m*ʸoan) *m* lorry; truck *nAm*
camioneta (kah-mʸoa-*nay*-tah) *f* van
camisa (kah-*mee*-sah) *f* shirt
camiseta (kah-mee-*say*-tah) *f* undershirt; vest
camisón (kah-mee-*soan*) *m* nightdress
campamento (kahm-pah-*mayn*-toa) *m* camp
campana (kahm-*pah*-nah) *f* bell
campanario (kahm-pah-*nah*-rʸoa) *m* steeple
campaña (kahm-*pah*-ñah) *f* campaign; **catre de** ~ camp-bed
campeón (kahm-pay-*oan*) *m* champion
campesino (kahm-pay-*see*-noa) *m* peasant
camping (*kahm*-peeng) *m* camping site, camping
campo (*kahm*-poa) *m* countryside, country; field; ~ **de aviación** airfield; ~ **de golf** golf-course; ~ **de tenis** tennis-court; **día de** ~ picnic
Canadá (kah-nah-*dhah*) *m* Canada
canadiense (kah-nah-*dh*ʸayn-say) *adj*

Canadian; *m* Canadian

canal (kah-*nahl*) *m* canal; channel;
Canal de la Mancha English Channel

canario (kah-*nah*-rʸoa) *m* canary

cancelación (kahn-thay-lah-*thʸoan*) *f*
cancellation

cancelar (kahn-thay-*lahr*) *v* cancel

cáncer (*kahn*-thayr) *m* cancer

canción (kahn-*thʸoan*) *f* song

cancha (*kahn*-chah) *f* tennis-court

candado (kahn-*dah*-dhoa) *m* padlock

candela (kahn-*day*-lah) *f* candle

candelabro (kahn-day-*lah*-bhroa) *m*
candelabrum

candidato (kahn-dee-*dhah*-toa) *m* candidate

canela (kah-*nay*-lah) *f* cinnamon

cangrejo (kahng-*gray*-khoa) *m* crab

canguro (kahng-*goo*-roa) *m* kangaroo

canica (kah-*nee*-kah) *f* marble

canoa (kah-*noa*-ah) *f* canoe

cansancio (kahn-sahn-thʸoa) *m* fatigue

cansar (kahn-*sahr*) *v* tire; **cansado**
tired, weary

cantadora (kahn-tah-*dhoa*-rah) *f* singer

cantante (kahn-*tahn*-tay) *m* singer

cantar (kahn-*tahr*) *v* *sing

cántaro (*kahn*-tah-roa) *m* pitcher; jug

cantera (kahn-*tay*-rah) *f* quarry

cantidad (kahn-tee-*dhahdh*) *f* amount,
quantity; number; lot

cantina (kahn-*tee*-nah) *f* canteen; *fMe*
saloon

canto (*kahn*-toa) *m* singing; edge

caña (*kah*-ñah) *f* cane; ~ **de pescar**
fishing rod

cañada (kah-*ñah*-dhah) *f* glen

cáñamo (*kah*-ñah-moa) *m* hemp

cañón (kah-*ñoan*) *m* gun; gorge

caos (*kah*-oass) *m* chaos

caótico (kah-*oa*-tee-koa) *adj* chaotic

capa (*kah*-pah) *f* cloak, cape; layer,
deposit

capacidad (kah-pah-thee-*dhahdh*) *f* capacity

capataz (kah-pah-*tahth*) *m* foreman

capaz (kah-*pahth*) *adj* able; capable;
*ser ~ de *be able to; qualify

capellán (kah-pay-*lʸahn*) *m* chaplain

capilla (kah-*pee*-lʸah) *f* chapel

capital (kah-pee-*tahl*) *m* capital; *adj*
capital

capitalismo (kah-pee-tah-*leez*-moa) *m*
capitalism

capitán (kah-pee-*tahn*) *m* captain

capitulación (kah-pee-too-lah-*thʸoan*) *f*
capitulation

capítulo (kah-*pee*-too-loa) *m* chapter

capó (kah-*poa*) *m* bonnet; hood *nAm*

capricho (kah-*pree*-choa) *m* fancy,
whim

cápsula (*kahp*-soo-lah) *f* capsule

captura (kahp-*too*-rah) *f* capture

capturar (kahp-too-*rahr*) *v* capture

capucha (kah-*poo*-chah) *f* hood

capullo (kah-poo-lʸoa) *m* bud

caqui (*kah*-kee) *m* khaki

cara (*kah*-rah) *f* face

caracol (kah-rah-*koal*) *m* snail; ~ **marino** winkle

carácter (kah-*rahk*-tayr) *m* character

característica (kah-rahk-tay-*reess*-teekah) *f* characteristic, feature; quality

característico (kah-rahk-tay-*reess*-teekoa) *adj* typical, characteristic

caracterizar (kah-rahk-tay-ree-*thahr*) *v*
characterize, mark

caramelo (kah-rah-*may*-loa) *m* caramel, toffee, sweet

caravana (kah-rah-*bhah*-nah) *f* caravan; trailer *nAm*

carbón (kahr-*bhoan*) *m* coal; ~ **de leña** charcoal

carburador (kahr-bhoo-rah-*dhoar*) *m*
carburettor

cárcel (*kahr*-thayl) *f* jail, gaol

carcelero (kahr-thay-*lay*-roa) *m* jailer

cardenal (kahr-dhay-*nahl*) *m* cardinal

cardinal (kahr-dhee-*nahl*) *adj* cardinal

cardo (*kahr*-dhoa) *m* thistle

* **carecer** (kah-ray-*thayr*) *v* lack

carencia (kah-*rayn*-th^yah) *f* want, shortage

carga (*kahr*-gah) *f* charge; cargo, freight, load; batch

cargar (kahr-*gahr*) *v* charge; load

cargo (*kahr*-goa) *m* office; freight

cari (*kah*-ree) *m* curry

caridad (kah-ree-*dhahdh*) *f* charity

carillón (kah-ree-l^yoan) *m* chimes *pl*

cariño (kah-*ree*-ñoa) *m* affection; pet

cariñoso (kah-ree-*ñoa*-soa) *adj* affectionate

carmesí (kahr-may-*see*) *adj* crimson

carnaval (kahr-nah-*bhahl*) *m* carnival

carne (*kahr*-nay) *f* meat; flesh; ~ de cerdo pork; ~ de gallina gooseflesh; ~ de ternera veal; ~ de vaca beef

carnero (kahr-*nay*-roa) *m* mutton

carnicero (kahr-nee-*thay*-roa) *m* butcher

caro (*kah*-roa) *adj* expensive, dear

carpa (*kahr*-pah) *f* carp

carpintero (kahr-peen-*tay*-roa) *m* carpenter

carrera (kah-*rray*-rah) *f* career; race; ~ de caballos horserace; pista para carreras race-track

carretera (kah-rray-*tay*-rah) *f* highway

carretilla (kah-rray-*tee*-l^yah) *f* wheelbarrow

carro (*kah*-rroa) *m* cart; *mMe* car; ~ de gitanos caravan

carrocería (kah-rroa-thay-*ree*-ah) *f* coachwork

carroza (kah-*rroa*-thah) *f* coach

carta (*kahr*-tah) *f* map; letter; ~ certificada registered letter; ~ de crédito letter of credit; ~ de recomen-

dación letter of recommendation; ~ de vinos wine-list; ~ marina chart

cartel (kahr-*tayl*) *m* poster, placard

cárter (*kahr*-tayr) *m* crankcase

cartera (kahr-*tay*-rah) *f* bag; satchel; wallet

cartero (kahr-*tay*-roa) *m* postman

cartílago (kahr-*tee*-lah-goa) *m* cartilage

cartón (kahr-*toan*) *m* cardboard; carton; de ~ cardboard

cartucho (kahr-*too*-choa) *m* cartridge

casa (*kah*-sah) *f* house; home; a ~ home; ama de ~ housewife; ~ de campo cottage; ~ de correos post-office; ~ del párroco vicarage; ~ de pisos block of flats; apartment house *Am*; ~ de reposo rest-home; ~ flotante houseboat; ~ señorial manor-house; en ~ at home; indoors, indoor, home; gobierno de la ~ housekeeping

casarse (kah-*sahr*-say) *v* marry

cascada (kahss-*kah*-dhah) *f* waterfall

cascanueces (kahss-kah-*nway*-thayss) *m* nutcrackers *pl*

cáscara (*kahss*-kah-rah) *f* shell; skin; ~ de nuez nutshell

casco (*kahss*-koa) *m* helmet; hoof

casero (kah-*say*-roa) *adj* home-made

casi (*kah*-see) *adv* almost, nearly

casimir (kah-see-*meer*) *m* cashmere

casino (kah-*see*-noa) *m* casino

caso (*kah*-soa) *m* event; case; instance; ~ de urgencia emergency; en ~ de in case of; en ningún ~ by no means; en tal ~ then; en todo ~ at any rate, anyway

caspa (*kahss*-pah) *f* dandruff

casquillo (kahss-*kee*-l^yoa) *m* socket

castaña (kahss-*tah*-ñah) *f* chestnut

castellano (kahss-tay-l^y*ah*-noa) *adj* Castilian; *m* Castilian

castigar (kahss-tee-*gahr*) *v* punish

castigo (kahss-*tee*-goa) *m* penalty, punishment

castillo (kahss-*tee*-l^yoa) *m* castle

casto (*kahss*-toa) *adj* chaste; pure

castor (kahss-*toar*) *m* beaver

por casualidad (poar kah-swah-lee-*dhahdh*) by chance

catacumba (kah-tah-*koom*-bah) *f* catacomb

catálogo (kah-*tah*-loa-goa) *m* catalogue

catarro (kah-*tah*-rroa) *m* catarrh

catástrofe (kah-*tahss*-troa-fay) *f* disaster, catastrophe, calamity

catedral (kah-tay-*dhrahl*) *f* cathedral

catedrático (kah-tay-*dhrah*-tee-koa) *m* professor

categoría (kah-tay-goa-*ree*-ah) *f* category

católico (kah-*toa*-lee-koa) *adj* catholic, Roman Catholic

catorce (kah-*toar*-thay) *num* fourteen

catorceno (kah-toar-*thay*-noa) *num* fourteenth

caucho (*kou*-choa) *m* rubber

causa (*kou*-sah) *f* cause, reason; case; lawsuit; **a ~ de** because of, on account of, for, owing to

causar (kou-*sahr*) *v* cause

cautela (kou-*tay*-lah) *f* caution

cautivar (kou-tee-*bhahr*) *v* fascinate

cavar (kah-*bhahr*) *v* *dig

caviar (kah-*bh^yahr*) *m* caviar

cavidad (kah-bhee-*dhahdh*) *f* cavity

caza (*kah*-thah) *f* chase, hunt; game; **apeadero de ~** lodge

cazador (kah-thah-*dhoar*) *m* hunter

cazar (kah-*thahr*) *v* hunt; chase; **~ en vedado** poach

cebada (thay-*bhah*-dhah) *f* barley

cebo (*thay*-bhoa) *m* bait

cebolla (thay-*bhoa*-l^yah) *f* onion

cebollino (thay-bhoa-l^y*ee*-noa) *m* chives *pl*

cebra (*thay*-bhrah) *f* zebra

ceder (thay-*dhayr*) *v* indulge, *give in

***cegar** (thay-*gahr*) *v* blind

ceja (*thay*-khah) *f* eyebrow

celda (*thayl*-dah) *f* cell

celebración (thay-lay-bhrah-th^y*oan*) *f* celebration

celebrar (thay-lay-*bhrahr*) *v* celebrate

célebre (*thay*-lay-bhray) *adj* famous

celebridad (thay-lay-bhree-*dhahdh*) *f* celebrity

celeste (thay-*layss*-tay) *adj* heavenly

celibato (thay-lee-*bhah*-toa) *m* celibacy

celo (*thay*-loa) *m* zeal, diligence; **celos** jealousy

celofán (thay-loa-*fahn*) *m* cellophane

celoso (thay-*loa*-soa) *adj* zealous, diligent; envious, jealous

célula (*thay*-loo-lah) *f* cell

cementerio (thay-mayn-*tay*-r^yoa) *m* churchyard, graveyard, cemetery

cemento (thay-*mayn*-toa) *m* cement

cena (*thay*-nah) *f* dinner, supper

cenar (thay-*nahr*) *v* dine, *eat

cenicero (thay-nee-*thay*-roa) *m* ashtray

cenit (thay-*neet*) *m* zenith

ceniza (thay-*nee*-thah) *f* ash

censura (thayn-*soo*-rah) *f* censorship

centelleante (thayn-tay-l^yay-*ahn*-tay) *adj* sparkling

centígrado (thayn-*tee*-grah-dhoa) *adj* centigrade

centímetro (thayn-*tee*-may-troa) *m* centimetre; tape-measure

central (thayn-*trahl*) *adj* central; **central eléctrica** power-station; **central telefónica** telephone exchange

centralizar (thayn-trah-lee-*thahr*) *v* centralize

centro (*thayn*-troa) *m* centre; **~ comercial** shopping centre; **~ de la ciudad** town centre; **~ de recreo** recreation centre

cepillar (thay-pee-l^yahr) v brush

cepillo (thay-pee-l^yoa) m brush; ~ **de dientes** toothbrush; ~ **de la ropa** clothes-brush; ~ **para el cabello** hairbrush; ~ **para las uñas** nail-brush

cera (thay-rah) f wax

cerámica (thay-rah-mee-kah) f ceramics pl; crockery, pottery

cerca (thayr-kah) f fence

cerca de (thayr-kah day) near, by; almost

cercano (thayr-kah-noa) adj close, nearby, near

cercar (thayr-kahr) v encircle, surround

cerdo (thayr-dhoa) m pig

cereales (thay-ray-ah-layss) mpl corn

cerebro (thay-ray-bhroa) m brain; **conmoción cerebral** concussion

ceremonia (thay-ray-moa-n^yah) f ceremony

cereza (thay-ray-thah) f cherry

cerilla (thay-ree-l^yah) f match

cerillo (thay-ree-l^yoa) mMe match

cero (thay-roa) m zero, nought

cerradura (thay-rrah-dhoo-rah) f lock; **ojo de la** ~ keyhole

*****cerrar** (thay-rrahr) v close, *shut; fasten; turn off; ~ **con llave** lock

cerrojo (thay-rroa-khoa) m bolt

certificación (thayr-tee-fee-kah-th^yoan) f certificate

certificado (thayr-tee-fee-kah-dhoa) m certificate; ~ **de salud** health certificate

certificar (thayr-tee-fee-kahr) v register

cervato (thayr-bhah-toa) m fawn

cervecería (thayr-bhay-thay-ree-ah) f brewery

cerveza (thayr-bhay-thah) f beer; ale

cesar (thay-sahr) v cease, quit, stop, discontinue

césped (thayss-paydh) m lawn; grass

cesta (thayss-tah) f basket

cesto (thayss-toa) m hamper; ~ **para papeles** wastepaper-basket

cicatriz (thee-kah-treeth) f scar

ciclista (thee-kleess-tah) m cyclist

ciclo (thee-kloa) m cycle

ciego (th^yay-goa) adj blind

cielo (th^yay-loa) m heaven; sky; ~ **raso** ceiling

ciencia (th^yayn-th^yah) f science

científico (th^yayn-tee-fee-koa) adj scientific; m scientist

ciento (th^yayn-toa) num hundred; **por** ~ percent

cierre (th^yay-rray) m fastener; ~ **relámpago** zipper

cierto (th^yayr-toa) adj certain; **por** ~ indeed

ciervo (th^yayr-bhoa) m deer

cifra (thee-frah) f number, figure

cigarrillo (thee-gah-rree-l^yoa) m cigarette

cigüeña (thee-gway-ñah) f stork

cigüeñal (thee-gway-ñahl) m crankshaft

cilindro (thee-leen-droa) m cylinder; **culata del** ~ cylinder head

cima (thee-mah) f top, summit; hilltop

cinc (theengk) m zinc

cincel (theen-thayl) m chisel

cinco (theeng-koa) num five

cincuenta (theeng-kwayn-tah) num fifty

cine (thee-nay) m pictures

cinematógrafo (thee-nay-mah-toa-grah-foa) m cinema

cinta (theen-tah) f ribbon, tape; ~ **adhesiva** scotch tape, adhesive tape; ~ **de goma** elastic band; ~ **métrica** tape-measure

cintura (theen-too-rah) f waist

cinturón (theen-too-roan) m belt; bypass; ~ **de seguridad** seat-belt

cipo (*thee*-poa) *m* milepost

circo (*theer*-koa) *m* circus

*****circuir** (theer-*kweer*) *v* encircle

circulación (theer-koo-lah-*thᵞoan*) *f* circulation

circular (theer-koo-*lahr*) *v* circulate

círculo (*theer*-koo-loa) *m* circle, ring; club

circundante (theer-koon-*dahn*-tay) *adj* surrounding

circundar (theer-koon-*dahr*) *v* circle

circunstancia (theer-koons-*tahn*-thᵞah) *f* circumstance, condition

ciruela (thee-*rway*-lah) *f* plum; ~ **pasa** prune

cirujano (thee-roo-*khah*-noa) *m* surgeon

cisne (*theez*-nay) *m* swan

cistitis (theess-*tee*-teess) *f* cystitis

cita (*thee*-tah) *f* date, appointment; quotation

citación (thee-tah-*thᵞoan*) *f* summons

citar (thee-*tahr*) *v* quote

ciudad (thᵞoo-*dhahdh*) *f* city, town

ciudadanía (thᵞoo-dhah-dhah-*nee*-ah) *f* citizenship

ciudadano (thᵞoo-dhah-*dhah*-noa) *m* citizen

cívico (*thee*-bhee-koa) *adj* civic

civil (thee-*bheel*) *adj* civilian, civil

civilización (thee-bhee-lee-thah-*thᵞoan*) *f* civilization

civilizado (thee-bhee-lee-*thah*-dhoa) *adj* civilized

claridad (klah-ree-*dhahdh*) *f* clarity

clarificar (klah-ree-tee-*kahr*) *v* clarify

claro (*klah*-roa) *adj* clear; plain, distinct; serene, bright; *m* clearing

clase (*klah*-say) *f* class; sort; form; classroom; ~ **media** middle class; ~ **turista** tourist class; **de primera** ~ first-rate; **toda** ~ **de** all sorts of

clásico (*klah*-see-koa) *adj* classical

clasificar (klah-see-fee-*kahr*) *v* classify, assort, sort, arrange

cláusula (*klou*-soo-lah) *f* clause

clavar (klah-*bhahr*) *v* pin

clavicémbalo (klah-bhee-*thaym*-bah-loa) *m* harpsichord

clavícula (klah-*bhee*-koo-lah) *f* collarbone

clavo (*klah*-bhoa) *m* nail

clemencia (klay-*mayn*-thᵞah) *f* mercy

clérigo (*klay*-ree-goa) *m* clergyman, minister

cliente (klᵞ*ayn*-tay) *m* client, customer

clima (*klee*-mah) *m* climate

climatizado (klee-mah-tee-*thah*-dhoa) *adj* air-conditioned

clínica (*klee*-nee-kah) *f* clinic

cloro (*kloa*-roa) *m* chlorine

club de yates yacht-club

coagularse (koa-ah-goo-*lahr*-say) *v* coagulate

cobarde (koa-*bhahr*-dhay) *adj* cowardly; *m* coward

cobertizo (koa-bhayr-*tee*-thoa) *m* shed

cobrador (koa-bhrah-*dhoar*) *m* conductor

cobrar (koa-*bhrahr*) *v* cash

cobre (*koa*-bhray) *m* copper, brass; **cobres** *mpl* brassware

cocaína (koa-kah-*ee*-nah) *f* cocaine

cocina (koa-*thee*-nah) *f* kitchen; cooker, stove; ~ **de gas** gas cooker

cocinar (koa-thee-*nahr*) *v* cook

cocinero (koa-thee-*nay*-roa) *m* cook

coco (*koa*-koa) *m* coconut

cocodrilo (koa-koa-*dhree*-lᵞoa) *m* crocodile

cóctel (*koak*-tayl) *m* cocktail

coche (*koa*-chay) *m* car; carriage; ~ **cama** sleeping-car; ~ **comedor** dining-car; ~ **de carreras** sportscar; ~ **Pullman** Pullman

cochecillo (koa-chay-*thee*-lᵞoa) *m* pram; baby carriage *Am*

cochinillo (koa-chee-*nee*-lᵞoa) *m* piglet

codicia (koa-*dhee*-th^yah) *f* greed
codicioso (koa-dhee-*th^yoa*-soa) *adj* greedy
código (*koa*-dhee-goa) *m* code; ~ **postal** zip code *Am*
codo (*koa*-dhoa) *m* elbow
codorniz (koa-dhoar-*neeth*) *f* quail
coger (koa-*khayr*) *v* *catch; *take; **llegar a ~** *catch
coherencia (koa-ay-*rayn*-th^yah) *f* coherence
cohete (koa-*ay*-tay) *m* rocket
coincidencia (koa-een-thee-*dhayn*-th^yah) *f* concurrence
coincidir (koa-een-thee-*dheer*) *v* coincide
cojear (koa-khay-*ahr*) *v* limp
cojo (*koa*-khoa) *adj* lame
col (koal) *m* cabbage; **~ de Bruselas** sprouts *pl*
cola (*koa*-lah) *f* queue, file, line; tail; gum, glue; ***hacer ~** queue
colaboración (koa-lah-bhoa-rah-*th^yoan*) *f* co-operation
colcha (*koal*-chah) *f* counterpane, quilt
colchón (koal-*choan*) *m* mattress
colección (koa-layk-*th^yoan*) *f* collection; **~ de arte** art collection
coleccionar (koa-layk-th^yoa-*nahr*) *v* gather
coleccionista (koa-layk-th^yoa-*neess*-tah) *m* collector
colectivo (koa-layk-*tee*-bhoa) *adj* collective
colector (koa-layk-*toar*) *m* collector
colega (koa-*lay*-gah) *m* colleague
colegio (koa-*lay*-kh^yoa) *m* college
cólera (*koa*-lay-rah) *f* anger, passion, temper
colérico (koa-*lay*-ree-koa) *adj* hot-tempered
***colgar** (koal-*gahr*) *v* *hang
coliflor (koa-lee-*floar*) *f* cauliflower

colina (koa-*lee*-nah) *f* hill
colisión (koa-lee-s^yoan) *f* collision
colmena (koal-*may*-nah) *f* beehive
colmo (*koal*-moa) *m* height
colocar (koa-loa-*kahr*) *v* *lay, place, *put
Colombia (koa-*loam*-b^yah) *f* Colombia
colombiano (koa-loam-*b^yah*-noa) *adj* Colombian; *m* Colombian
colonia (koa-*loa*-n^yah) *f* colony; **~ veraniega** holiday camp
color (koa-*loar*) *m* colour; **~ de aguada** water-colour; **de ~** coloured
colorado (koa-loa-*rah*-dhoa) *adj* colourful
colorante (koa-loa-*rahn*-tay) *m* colourant
colorete (koa-loa-*ray*-tay) *m* rouge
columna (koa-*loom*-nah) *f* column, pillar; **~ del volante** steering-column
columpiarse (koa-loom-*p^yahr*-say) *v* *swing
columpio (koa-*loom*-p^yoa) *m* swing; seesaw
collar (koa-*l^yahr*) *m* beads *pl*, necklace; collar
coma (*koa*-mah) *f* comma; *m* coma
comadrona (koa-mah-*dhroa*-nah) *f* midwife
comandante (koa-mahn-*dahn*-tay) *m* commander; captain
comarca (koa-*mahr*-kah) *f* district
comba (*koam*-bah) *f* bend
combate (koam-*bah*-tay) *m* combat, battle, struggle, fight; **~ de boxeo** boxing match
combatir (koam-bah-*teer*) *v* combat, battle, *fight
combinación (koam-bee-nah-*th^yoan*) *f* combination; slip
combinar (koam-bee-*nahr*) *v* combine
combustible (koam-booss-*tee*-bhlay) *m* fuel; **~ líquido** fuel oil
comedia (koa-*may*-dh^yah) *f* comedy;

~ **musical** musical
comediante (koa-may-*dh*ʸ*ahn*-tay) *m* comedian
comedor (koa-may-*dhoar*) *m* dining-room; ~ **de gala** banqueting-hall
comentar (koa-mayn-*tahr*) *v* comment
comentario (koa-mayn-tah-rʸoa) *m* comment
***comenzar** (koa-mayn-*thahr*) *v* commence, *begin
comer (koa-*mayr*) *v* *eat
comercial (koa-mayr-*th*ʸ*ahl*) *adj* commercial
comerciante (koa-mayr-*th*ʸ*ahn*-tay) *m* merchant; trader, dealer; ~ **al por menor** retailer
comerciar (koa-mayr-*th*ʸ*ahr*) *v* trade
comercio (koa-*mayr*-thʸoa) *m* commerce, trade, business; ~ **al por menor** retail trade
comestible (koa-mayss-tee-bhlay) *adj* edible
comestibles (koa-mayss-*tee*-bhlayss) *mpl* groceries *pl*; **tienda de** ~ **finos** delicatessen
cometer (koa-may-*tayr*) *v* commit
cómico (*koa*-mee-koa) *adj* comic, funny; *m* comedian; entertainer
comida (koa-*mee*-dhah) *f* food; meal; ~ **principal** dinner
comidilla (koa-mee-*dhee*-lʸah) *f* hobby-horse
comienzo (koa-*m*ʸ*ayn*-thoa) *m* beginning, start
comillas (koa-*mee*-lʸahss) *fpl* quotation marks
comisaría (koa-mee-sah-*ree*-ah) *f* police-station
comisión (koa-mee-*s*ʸ*oan*) *f* committee, commission
comité (koa-mee-*tay*) *m* committee
comitiva (koa-mee-*tee*-bhah) *f* procession
como (*koa*-moa) *adv* as, like, like; **así**

~ as well as; ~ **máximo** at most; ~ **si** as if
cómo (*koa*-moa) *adv* how
cómoda (*koa*-moa-dhah) *f* chest of drawers; bureau *nAm*
comodidad (koa-moa-dhee-*dhahdh*) *f* comfort, leisure
cómodo (*koa*-moa-dhoa) *adj* convenient, easy
compacto (koam-*pahk*-toa) *adj* compact
compadecerse de (koam-pah-dhay-*thayr*-say) pity
compañero (koam-pah-*ñay*-roa) *m* companion; associate; ~ **de clase** class-mate
compañía (koam-pah-*ñee*-ah) *f* company; society
comparación (koam-pah-rah-*th*ʸ*oan*) *f* comparison
comparar (koam-pah-*rahr*) *v* compare
compartimento (koam-pahr-tee-*mayn*-toa) *m* compartment; ~ **para fumadores** smoking-compartment
compartir (koam-pahr-*teer*) *v* share
compasión (koam-pah-*s*ʸ*oan*) *f* sympathy
compasivo (koam-pah-*see*-bhoa) *adj* sympathetic
compatriota (koam-pah-*tr*ʸ*oa*-tah) *m* countryman
compeler (koam-pay-*layr*) *v* compel
compensación (koam-payn-sah-*th*ʸ*oan*) *f* compensation
compensar (koam-payn-*sahr*) *v* compensate; *make good
competencia (koam-pay-*tayn*-thʸah) *f* competition, rivalry; capacity
competente (koam-pay-*tayn*-tay) *adj* expert, qualified
competidor (koam-pay-tee-*dhoar*) *m* competitor, rival
***competir** (koam-pay-*teer*) *v* compete
compilar (koam-pee-*lahr*) *v* compile

*complacer (koam-plah-*thayr*) v please; *give satisfaction

complejo (koam-*play*-khoa) adj complex; m complex

completamente (koam-play-tah-*mayn*-tay) adv completely, quite

completar (koam-play-*tahr*) v complete; fill in; fill out Am

completo (koam-*play*-toa) adj complete; whole, total, utter; full up

complicado (koam-plee-*kah*-dhoa) adj complicated

cómplice (*koam*-plee-thay) m accessary

complot (koam-*ploat*) m plot

*componer (koam-poa-*nayr*) v compose

comportarse (koam-poar-*tahr*-say) v behave, act

composición (koam-poa-see-*th^yoan*) f composition; essay

compositor (koam-poa-see-*toar*) m composer

compra (*koam*-prah) f purchase; *ir de compras shop

comprador (koam-prah-*dhoar*) m purchaser, buyer

comprar (koam-*prahr*) v purchase, *buy

comprender (koam-prayn-*dayr*) v *understand; *see, *take; comprise, contain

comprensión (koam-prayn-*s^yoan*) m understanding

comprobante (koam-proa-*bhahn*-tay) m voucher

*comprobar (koam-proa-*bhahr*) v ascertain, diagnose, establish, note; prove

comprometerse (koam-proa-may-*tayr*-say) v engage

compromiso (koam-proa-*mee*-soa) m compromise; engagement

compuerta (koam-*pwayr*-tah) f sluice

común (koa-*moon*) adj common; ordinary; en ~ joint

comuna (koa-*moo*-nah) f commune

comunicación (koa-moo-nee-kah-*th^yoan*) f communication

comunicado (koa-moo-nee-*kah*-dhoa) m communiqué, information

comunicar (koa-moo-nee-*kahr*) v communicate, inform

comunidad (koa-moo-nee-*dhahdh*) f congregation

comunismo (koa-moo-*neez*-moa) m communism

comunista (koa-moo-*neess*-tah) m communist

con (koan) prep with; by

*concebir (koan-thay-*bheer*) v conceive

conceder (koan-thay-*dhayr*) v extend, grant; award

concentración (koan-thayn-trah-*th^yoan*) f concentration

concentrarse (koan-thayn-*trahr*-say) v concentrate

concepción (koan-thayp-*th^yoan*) f conception

concepto (koan-*thayp*-toa) m idea

*concernir (koan-thayr-*neer*) v touch, concern; concerniente a concerning

concesión (koan-thay-*s^yoan*) f concession

conciencia (koan-*th^yayn*-th^yah) f conscience; consciousness

concierto (koan-*th^yayr*-toa) m concert

conciso (koan-*thee*-soa) adj concise

*concluir (koang-*klweer*) v conclude

conclusión (koang-kloo-*s^yoan*) f conclusion; issue, ending

*concordar (koang-koar-*dhahr*) v agree

concreto (koang-*kray*-toa) adj concrete

concupiscencia (koang-koo-pee-*thayn*-th^yah) f lust

concurrido (koang-koo-*rree*-dhoa) adj

busy
concurrir (koang-koo-*rreer*) *v* coincide; concur
concurso (koang-*koor*-soa) *m* competition, contest; quiz
concha (*koan*-chah) *f* shell; sea-shell
condado (koan-*dah*-dhoa) *m* county
conde (*koan*-day) *m* count, earl
condena (koan-*day*-nah) *f* conviction
condenado (koan-day-*nah*-dhoa) *m* convict
condesa (koan-*day*-sah) *f* countess
condición (koan-dee-*th*^{Y}*oan*) *f* condition, term
condicional (koan-dee-th^{Y}oa-*nahl*) *adj* conditional
condimentado (koan-dee-mayn-*tah*-dhoa) *adj* spiced
* **conducir** (koan-doo-*theer*) *v* *lead, carry, conduct; *drive
conducta (koan-*dook*-tah) *f* behaviour, conduct
conducto (koan-*dook*-toa) *m* pipe
conductor (koan-dook-*toar*) *m* driver; *mMe* conductor
conectar (koa-nayk-*tahr*) *v* connect
conejo (koa-*nay*-khoa) *m* rabbit; **conejillo de Indias** guinea-pig
conexión (koa-nayk-*s*^{Y}*oan*) *f* connection
confeccionado (koan-fayk-th^{Y}oa-*nah*-dhoa) *adj* ready-made
confederación (koan-fay-day-rah-*th*^{Y}*oan*) *f* union
conferencia (koan-fay-*rayn*-th^{Y}ah) *f* conference; lecture; ~ **interurbana** trunk-call
* **confesarse** (koan-fay-*sahr*-say) *v* confess
confesión (koan-fay-*s*^{Y}*oan*) *f* confession
confiable (koan-*f*^{Y}*ah*-bhlay) *adj* trustworthy
confianza (koan-*f*^{Y}*ahn*-thah) *f* faith,

trust, confidence; **indigno de** ~ untrustworthy
confiar (koan-*f*^{Y}*ahr*) *v* commit; ~ **en** trust
confidencial (koan-fee-dhayn-*th*^{Y}*ahl*) *adj* confidential
confirmación (koan-feer-mah-*th*^{Y}*oan*) *f* confirmation
confirmar (koan-feer-*mahr*) *v* confirm, acknowledge
confiscar (koan-feess-*kahr*) *v* confiscate, impound
confitería (koan-fee-tay-*ree*-ah) *f* sweetshop
confitero (koan-fee-*tay*-roa) *m* confectioner
confitura (koan-fee-*too*-rah) *f* marmalade
conflicto (koan-*fleek*-toa) *m* conflict
conforme (koan-*foar*-may) *adj* alike; in agreement; ~ **a** according to, in agreement with
conformidad (koan-foar-mee-*dhahdh*) *f* agreement
confort (koan-*foart*) *m* comfort
confortable (koan-foar-*tah*-bhlay) *adj* comfortable; cosy
confundir (koan-foon-*deer*) *v* *mistake, confuse
confusión (koan-foo-*s*^{Y}*oan*) *f* confusion; disturbance
confuso (koan-*foo*-soa) *adj* confused
congelado (koang-khay-*lah*-dhoa) *adj* frozen; **alimento** ~ frozen food
congelador (koang-khay-lah-*dhoar*) *m* deep-freeze
congelar (koang-khay-*lahr*) *v* *freeze
congestión (koang-khayss-*t*^{Y}*oan*) *f* jam
congregación (koang-gray-gah-*th*^{Y}*oan*) *f* congregation
congreso (koang-*gray*-soa) *m* congress
conjetura (koang-khay-*too*-rah) *f* guess
conjeturar (koang-khay-too-*rahr*) *v* guess

conjuración (koang-khoo-rah-*th*ʸ*oan*) *f* plot

conmemoración (koan-may-moa-rah-*th*ʸ*oan*) *f* commemoration

conmovedor (koan-moa-bhay-*dhoar*) *adj* touching

* **conmover** (koan-moa-*bhayr*) *v* move

connotación (koan-noa-tah-*th*ʸ*oan*) *f* connotation

* **conocer** (koa-noa-*thayr*) *v* *know

conocido (koa-noa-*thee*-dhoa) *m* acquaintance

conocimiento (koa-noa-thee-*m*ʸ*ayn*-toa) *m* knowledge

conquista (koang-*keess*-tah) *f* conquest, capture

conquistador (koang-keess-tah-*dhoar*) *m* conqueror

conquistar (koang-keess-*tahr*) *v* conquer, capture

consciente (koan-*th*ʸ*ayn*-tay) *adj* conscious, aware

consecuencia (koan-say-*kwayn*-th*ʸ*ah) *f* consequence, result; issue

* **conseguir** (koan-say-*geer*) *v* *get; *make, obtain

consejero (koan-say-*khay*-roa) *m* counsellor; councillor

consejo (koan-*say*-khoa) *m* advice, counsel; council, board

consentimiento (koan-sayn-tee-*m*ʸ*ayn*-toa) *m* consent; approval

* **consentir** (koan-sayn-*teer*) *v* agree, consent

conserje (koan-*sayr*-khay) *m* concierge, janitor

conservación (koan-sayr-bhah-*th*ʸ*oan*) *f* preservation

conservador (koan-sayr-bhah-*dhoar*) *adj* conservative

conservar (koan-sayr-*bhahr*) *v* preserve

conservas (koan-*sayr*-bhahss) *fpl* tinned food

conservatorio (koan-sayr-bhah-*toa*-rʸoa) *m* music academy

considerable (koan-see-dhay-*rah*-bhlay) *adj* considerable

consideración (koan-see-dhay-rah-*th*ʸ*oan*) *f* consideration

considerado (koan-see-dhay-*rah*-dhoa) *adj* considerate

considerando (koan-see-dhay-*rahn*-doa) *prep* considering

considerar (koan-see-dhay-*rahr*) *v* regard, consider; *think over; count, reckon

consigna (koan-*seeg*-nah) *f* left luggage office

por consiguiente (poar koan-see-*g*ʸ*ayn*-tay) consequently

consistir en (koan-seess-*teer*) consist of

* **consolar** (koan-soa-*lahr*) *v* comfort

consorcio (koan-*soar*-th*ʸ*oa) *m* concern

conspirar (koans-pee-*rahr*) *v* conspire

constante (koans-*tahn*-tay) *adj* even, constant; steadfast

constar de (koans-*tahr*) consist of

constitución (koans-tee-too-*th*ʸ*oan*) *f* constitution

* **constituir** (koans-tee-*tweer*) *v* constitute; represent

construcción (koans-trook-*th*ʸ*oan*) *f* construction

* **construir** (koans-*trweer*) *v* construct, *build

consuelo (koan-*sway*-loa) *m* comfort

cónsul (*koan*-sool) *m* consul

consulado (koan-soo-*lah*-dhoa) *m* consulate

consulta (koan-*sool*-tah) *f* consultation

consultar (koan-sool-*tahr*) *v* consult

consultorio (koan-sool-*toa*-rʸoa) *m* surgery

consumidor (koan-soo-mee-*dhoar*) *m* consumer

consumir (koan-soo-*meer*) *v* use up

contacto (koan-*tahk*-toa) *m* contact; touch

contador (koan-tah-*dhoar*) *m* meter

contagioso (koan-tah-*khᵞoa*-soa) *adj* infectious, contagious

contaminación (koan-tah-mee-nah-*thᵞoan*) *f* pollution

*****contar** (koan-*tahr*) *v* count; relate, *tell; ~ con rely on

contemplar (koan-taym-*plahr*) *v* contemplate

contemporáneo (koan-taym-poa-*rah*-nay-oa) *adj* contemporary; *m* contemporary

contenedor (koan-tay-nay-*dhoar*) *m* container

*****contener** (koan-tay-*nayr*) *v* contain; restrain

contenido (koan-tay-*nee*-dhoa) *m* contents *pl*

contentar (koan-tayn-*tahr*) *v* satisfy

contento (koan-*tayn*-toa) *adj* happy, glad, content, joyful; pleased

contestar (koan-tayss-*tahr*) *v* answer

contienda (koan-*tᵞayn*-dah) *f* dispute

contiguo (koan-*tee*-gwoa) *adj* neighbouring

continental (koan-tee-nayn-*tahl*) *adj* continental

continente (koan-tee-*nayn*-tay) *m* continent

continuación (koan-tee-nwah-*thᵞoan*) *f* sequel

continuamente (koan-tee-nwah-mayn-tay) *adv* all the time, continually

continuar (koan-tee-*nwahr*) *v* *go on, *go ahead; carry on, continue, *keep on; *keep

continuo (koan-*tee*-nwoa) *adj* continuous, continual

contorno (koan-*toar*-noa) *m* outline, contour

contra (*koan*-trah) *prep* against, versus

contrabandear (koan-trah-bhahn-day-ahr) *v* smuggle

*****contradecir** (koan-trah-dhay-*theer*) *v* contradict

contradictorio (koan-trah-dheek-*toa*-rᵞoa) *adj* contradictory

contrahecho (koan-trah-*ay*-choa) *adj* deformed

contralto (koan-*trahl*-toa) *m* alto

contrario (koan-*trah*-rᵞoa) *adj* opposite, contrary; *m* contrary, reverse; **al ~** on the contrary

contraste (koan-*trahss*-tay) *m* contrast

contratiempo (koan-trah-*tᵞaym*-poa) *m* misfortune

contratista (koan-trah-*teess*-tah) *m* contractor

contrato (koan-*trah*-toa) *m* agreement, contract

contribución (koan-tree-bhoo-*thᵞoan*) *f* contribution

*****contribuir** (koan-tree-*bhweer*) *v* contribute

contrincante (koan-treeng-*kahn*-tay) *m* opponent

control (koan-*troal*) *m* inspection, control

controlar (koan-troa-*lahr*) *v* check, control

controvertible (koan-troa-bhayr-*tee*-bhlay) *adj* controversial

controvertido (koan-troa-bhayr-*too*-dhoa) *adj* controversial

convencer (koam-bayn-*thayr*) *v* convince, persuade; convict

convencimiento (koam-bayn-thee-*mᵞayn*-toa) *m* conviction

conveniente (koam-bay-*nᵞayn*-tay) *adj* adequate, proper; convenient

convenio (koam-*bay*-nᵞoa) *m* settlement

*****convenir** (koam-bay-*neer*) *v* agree; fit, suit

convento (koam-*bayn*-toa) *m* cloister,

convent; nunnery

conversación (koam-bayr-sah-*th^yoan*) *f* conversation, talk, discussion

* **convertir** (koam-bayr-*teer*) *v* convert; *convertirse en turn into

convicción (koam-beek-*th^yoan*) *f* persuasion

convidar (koam-bee-*dhahr*) *v* invite

convulsión (koam-bool-*s^yoan*) *f* convulsion

cónyuges (*koan*-^yoo-khayss) *mpl* married couple

coñac (koa-*ñahk*) *m* cognac

cooperación (koa-oa-pay-rah-*th^yoan*) *f* co-operation

cooperador (koa-oa-pay-rah-*dhoar*) *adj* co-operative

cooperativa (koa-oa-pay-rah-*tee*-bhah) *f* co-operative

cooperativo (koa-oa-pay-rah-*tee*-bhoa) *adj* co-operative

coordinación (koa-oar-dhee-nah-*th^yoan*) *f* co-ordination

coordinar (koa-oar-dhee-*nahr*) *v* co-ordinate

copa (*koa*-pah) *f* cup

copia (*koa*-p^yah) *f* copy, carbon copy

copiar (koa-*p^yahr*) *v* copy

coraje (koa-*rah*-khay) *m* guts

coral (koa-*rahl*) *m* coral

corazón (koa-rah-*thoan*) *m* heart; core

corbata (koar-*bhah*-tah) *f* tie, necktie; ~ **de lazo** bow tie

corbatín (koar-bhah-*teen*) *m* bow tie

corcino (koar-*thee*-noa) *m* fawn

corcho (*koar*-choa) *m* cork

cordel (koar-*dhayl*) *m* string

cordero (koar-*dhay*-roa) *m* lamb

cordial (koar-*dh^yahl*) *adj* cordial, hearty, sympathetic

cordillera (koar-dhee-*l^yay*-rah) *f* mountain range

cordón (koar-*dhoan*) *m* cord, line; lace, shoe-lace; ~ **de extensión** ex-

tension cord; ~ **flexible** flex

cornamenta (koar-nah-*mayn*-tah) *f* antlers *pl*

corneja (koar-*nay*-khah) *f* crow

coro (*koa*-roa) *m* choir

corona (koa-*roa*-nah) *f* crown

coronar (koa-roa-*nahr*) *v* crown

coronel (koa-roa-*nayl*) *m* colonel

corpulento (koar-poo-*layn*-toa) *adj* corpulent, stout

corral (koa-*rrahl*) *m* yard; **aves de** ~ poultry

correa (koa-*rray*-ah) *f* leash, strap; ~ **del ventilador** fan belt; ~ **de reloj** watch-strap

corrección (koa-rrayk-*th^yoan*) *f* correction

correcto (koa-*rrayk*-toa) *adj* correct; right

corredor (koa-rray-*dhoar*) *m* broker; bookmaker; ~ **de casas** house agent

* **corregir** (koa-rray-*kheer*) *v* correct

correo (koa-*rray*-oa) *m* post, mail; ~ **aéreo** airmail; **enviar por** ~ mail; **sello de correos** postage stamp

correr (koa-*rrayr*) *v* *run; dash; flow

correspondencia (koa-rrayss-poan-*dayn*-th^yah) *f* correspondence

corresponder (koa-rrayss-poan-*dayr*) *v* correspond; **corresponderse** *v* correspond

corresponsal (koa-rrayss-poan-*sahl*) *m* correspondent

corrida de toros (koa-*rree*-dhah day *toa*-roass) bullfight

corriente (koa-*rr^yayn*-tay) *adj* current; regular, customary, plain; *f* current; stream; ~ **alterna** alternating current; ~ **continua** direct current; ~ **de aire** draught

corromper (koa-rroam-*payr*) *v* corrupt

corrupción (koa-rroop-*th^yoan*) *f* corruption

corrupto (koa-*rroop*-toa) *adj* corrupt

corsé (koar-*say*) *m* corset

cortadura (koar-tah-*dhoo*-rah) *f* cut

cortaplumas (koar-tah-*ploo*-mahss) *m* penknife

cortar (koar-*tahr*) *v* *cut; chip, *cut off

corte (*koar*-tay) *f* court

cortés (koar-*tayss*) *adj* civil, courteous, polite

corteza (koar-*tay*-thah) *f* bark; crust

cortijo (koar-*tee*-khoa) *m* farmhouse

cortina (koar-*tee*-nah) *f* curtain

corto (*koar*-toa) *adj* short

cortocircuito (koar-toa-theer-*kwee*-toa) *m* short circuit

cosa (*koa*-sah) *f* thing; **entre otras cosas** among other things

cosecha (koa-*say*-chah) *f* harvest, crop

coser (koa-*sayr*) *v* sew

cosméticos (koaz-*may*-tee-koass) *mpl* cosmetics *pl*

cosquillear (koass-kee-*lʸahr*) *v* tickle

costa (*koass*-tah) *f* coast

costar (koass-*tahr*) *v* *cost

coste (*koass*-tay) *m* cost

costilla (koass-*tee*-lʸah) *f* rib

costoso (koass-*toa*-soa) *adj* expensive

costumbre (koass-*toom*-bray) *f* custom; **costumbres** morals

costura (koass-*too*-rah) *f* seam; **sin ~** seamless

cotidiano (koa-tee-*dhʸah*-noa) *adj* everyday

cotorra (koa-*toa*-rrah) *f* parakeet

cráneo (*krah*-nay-oa) *m* skull

cráter (*krah*-tayr) *m* crater

creación (kray-ah-*thʸoan*) *f* creation

crear (kray-*ahr*) *v* create

crecer (kray-*thayr*) *v* *grow

crecimiento (kray-thee-*mʸayn*-toa) *m* growth

crédito (*kray*-dhee-toa) *m* credit

crédulo (*kray*-dhoo-loa) *adj* credulous

creencia (kray-*ayn*-thʸah) *f* belief

creer (kray-*ayr*) *v* believe; guess, reckon

crema (*kray*-mah) *f* cream; **~ de afeitar** shaving-cream; **~ de base** foundation cream; **~ de noche** night-cream; **~ facial** face-cream; **~ hidratante** moisturizing cream; **~ para la piel** skin cream; **~ para las manos** hand cream

cremallera (kray-mah-*lʸay*-rah) *f* zip

cremoso (kray-*moa*-soa) *adj* creamy

crepúsculo (kray-*pooss*-koo-loa) *m* twilight, dusk

crespo (*krayss*-poa) *adj* curly

cresta (*krayss*-tah) *f* ridge

creta (*kray*-tah) *f* chalk

criada (krʸah-dhah) *f* housemaid

criado (krʸah-dhoa) *m* servant

criar (krʸahr) *v* rear; raise

criatura (krʸah-*too*-rah) *f* creature; infant

crimen (*kree*-mayn) *m* crime

criminal (kree-mee-*nahl*) *adj* criminal; *m* criminal

criminalidad (kree-mee-nah-lee-*dhahdh*) *f* criminality

crisis (*kree*-seess) *f* crisis

cristal (kreess-*tahl*) *m* crystal; pane; **de ~** crystal

cristiano (kreess-*tʸah*-noa) *adj* Christian; *m* Christian

Cristo (*kreess*-toa) Christ

criterio (kree-*tay*-rʸoa) *m* criterion

crítica (*kree*-tee-kah) *f* criticism

criticar (kree-tee-*kahr*) *v* criticize

crítico (*kree*-tee-koa) *adj* critical; *m* critic

cromo (*kroa*-moa) *m* chromium

crónica (*kroa*-nee-kah) *f* chronicle

crónico (*kroa*-nee-koa) *adj* chronic

cronológico (kroa-noa-*loa*-khee-koa) *adj* chronological

cruce (*kroo*-thay) *m* crossroads; **~ pa-**

ra peatones pedestrian crossing;
crosswalk *nAm*
crucero (kroo-*thay*-roa) *m* cruise
crucificar (kroo-thee-fee-*kahr*) *v* crucify
crucifijo (kroo-thee-*fee*-khoa) *m* crucifix
crucifixión (kroo-thee-feek-s*y*oan) *f*
crucifixion
crudo (*kroo*-dhoa) *adj* raw
cruel (krwayl) *adj* harsh, cruel
crujido (kroo-*khee*-dhoa) *m* crack
crujiente (kroo-*kh*y*ayn*-tay) *adj* crisp
crujir (kroo-*kheer*) *v* creak, crack
cruz (krooth) *f* cross
cruzada (kroo-*thah*-dhah) *f* crusade
cruzar (kroo-*thahr*) *v* cross
cuadrado (kwah-*dhrah*-dhoa) *adj*
square; *m* square
cuadriculado (kwah-dhree-koo-*lah*-
dhoa) *adj* chequered
cuadro (*kwah*-dhroa) *m* cadre; picture; **a cuadros** chequered; ~ **de
distribución** switchboard
cuál (kwahl) *pron* which
cualidad (kwah-lee-*dhahdh*) *f* property
cualquiera (kwahl-*k*y*ay*-rah) *pron* anyone, anybody; whichever; **cual-
quier cosa** anything
cuando (*kwahn*-doa) *conj* when; ~
quiera que whenever
cuándo (*kwahn*-doa) *adv* when
cuánto (*kwahn*-toa) *adv* how much;
how many; **cuanto más . . . más**
the … the; **en cuanto a** as regards
cuarenta (kwah-*rayn*-tah) *num* forty
cuarentena (kwah-rayn-*tay*-nah) *f*
quarantine
cuartel (kwahr-*tayl*) *m* barracks *pl*; ~
general headquarters *pl*
cuarterón (kwahr-tay-*roan*) *m* panel
cuarto[1] (*kwahr*-toa) *num* fourth; *m*
quarter; ~ **de hora** quarter of an
hour

cuarto[2] (*kwahr*-toa) *m* chamber; ~ **de
aseo** lavatory; washroom *nAm*; ~
de baño bathroom; ~ **de niños**
nursery; ~ **para huéspedes** spare
room
cuatro (*kwah*-troa) *num* four
Cuba (*koo*-bhah) *f* Cuba
cubano (koo-*bhah*-noa) *adj* Cuban; *m*
Cuban
cubierta (koo-*bh*y*ayr*-tah) *f* cover;
deck
cubierto (koo-*bh*y*ayr*-toa) *adj* cloudy
cubiertos (koo-*bh*y*ayr*-toass) *mpl* cutlery
cubo (*koo*-bhoa) *m* cube; ~ **de la basura** dustbin
cubrir (koo-*bhreer*) *v* cover
cuclillo (koo-klee-*l*y*oa) *m* cuckoo
cuchara (koo-*chah*-rah) *f* spoon; soup-
spoon, tablespoon
cucharada (koo-chah-*rah*-dhah) *f*
spoonful
cucharadita (koo-chah-rah-*dhee*-tah) *f*
teaspoonful
cucharilla (koo-chah-*ree*-l*y*ah) *f* teaspoon
cuchillo (koo-*chee*-l*y*oa) *m* knife
cuello (*kway*-l*y*oa) *m* neck; collar; ~
de botella bottleneck
cuenta (*kwayn*-tah) *f* account; bill;
check *nAm*; bead; ~ **de banco**
bank account; *darse ~ *see
cuento (*kwayn*-toa) *m* story, tale
cuerda (*kwayr*-dhah) *f* cord; string;
*dar ~ *wind
cuerno (*kwayr*-noa) *m* horn
cuero (*kway*-roa) *m* leather; ~ **vacuno** cow-hide
cuerpo (*kwayr*-poa) *m* body
cuervo (*kwayr*-bhoa) *m* raven
cuestión (kwayss-*t*y*oan) *f* matter, issue, question
cueva (*kway*-bhah) *f* cavern, cave;
wine-cellar

cuidado (kwee-*dhah*-dhoa) *m* care; *tener ~ watch out, look out

cuidadoso (kwee-dhah-*dhoa*-soa) *adj* careful; diligent

cuidar de (kwee-*dhahr*) attend to, look after, tend, *take care of

culebra (koo-*lay*-bhrah) *f* snake

culpa (*kool*-pah) *f* guilt, fault, blame

culpable (kool-*pah*-bhlay) *adj* guilty

culpar (kool-*pahr*) *v* blame

cultivar (kool-tee-*bhahr*) *v* cultivate; *grow, raise

cultivo (kool-*tee*-bhoa) *m* cultivation

culto (*kool*-toa) *adj* cultured; *m* worship

cultura (kool-*too*-rah) *f* culture

cultural (kool-too-*rahl*) *adj* cultural

cumbre (*koom*-bray) *f* peak

cumpleaños (koom-play-ah-ñoass) *m* birthday

cumplimentar (koom-plee-mayn-*tahr*) *v* compliment

cumplimiento (koom-plee-*m*ʸ*ayn*-toa) *m* compliment

cumplir (koom-*pleer*) *v* accomplish

cuna (*koo*-nah) *f* cradle; ~ de viaje carry-cot

cuneta (koo-*nay*-tah) *f* ditch; gutter

cuña (*koo*-ñah) *f* wedge

cuñada (koo-*ñah*-dhah) *f* sister-in-law

cuñado (koo-*ñah*-dhoa) *m* brother-in-law

cuota (*kwoa*-tah) *f* quota

cupón (koo-*poan*) *m* coupon

cúpula (*koo*-poo-lah) *f* dome

cura (*koo*-rah) *m* priest; *f* cure

curación (koo-rah-*th*ʸ*oan*) *f* cure, recovery

curandero (koo-rahn-*day*-roa) *m* quack

curar (koo-*rahr*) *v* cure, heal; curarse *v* recover

curato (koo-*rah*-toa) *m* parsonage

curiosidad (koo-rʸoa-see-*dhahdh*) *f* curiosity; sight; curio

curioso (koo-rʸoa-soa) *adj* curious; inquisitive; quaint

cursiva (koor-see-bhah) *f* italics *pl*

curso (*koor*-soa) *m* course; lecture; ~ intensivo intensive course

curva (koor-bhah) *f* turn, curve, bend

curvado (koor-*bhah*-dhoa) *adj* curved

curvo (*koor*-bhoa) *adj* crooked, bent

custodia (kooss-*toa*-dhʸah) *f* custody

cuyo (*koo*-ʸoa) *pron* whose; of which

CH

chabacano (chah-bhah-*kah*-noa) *mMe* apricot

chal (chahl) *m* shawl

chaleco (chah-*lay*-koa) *m* waistcoat; vest *nAm*; ~ salvavidas lifebelt

chalet (chah-*layt*) *m* chalet

champán (chahm-*pahn*) *m* champagne

champú (chahm-*poo*) *m* shampoo

chantaje (chahn-*tah*-khay) *m* blackmail; *hacer ~ blackmail

chapa (*chah*-pah) *f* plate, sheet

chaparrón (chah-pah-*rroan*) *m* cloudburst

chapucero (chah-poo-*thay*-roa) *adj* sloppy

chaqueta (chah-*kay*-tah) *f* jacket; cardigan, ~ ligera blazer

charanga (chah-*rahng*-gah) *f* brass band

charco (*chahr*-koa) *m* puddle

charla (*chahr*-lah) *f* chat

charlar (chahr-*lahr*) *v* chat

charlatán (chahr-lah-*tahn*) *m* chatterbox; quack

charola (chah-*roa*-lah) *fMe* tray

chasis (chah-*seess*) *m* chassis

chatarra (chah-*tah*-rrah) *f* scrap-iron

checo (*chay*-koa) *adj* Czech; *m* Czech

Checoslovaquia (chay-koaz-loa-*bhah*-

kʸah) f Czechoslovakia

cheque (*chay*-kay) *m* cheque; check *nAm*; ~ **de viajero** traveller's cheque

chicle (*chee*-klay) *m* chewing-gum

chico (*chee*-koa) *m* boy; kid

chichón (chee-*choan*) *m* lump

Chile (*chee*-lay) *m* Chile

chileno (chee-*lay*-noa) *adj* Chilean; *m* Chilean

chillar (chee-*lʸahr*) *v* scream, shriek

chillido (chee-*lʸee*-dhoa) *m* scream, shriek

chimenea (chee-may-*nay*-ah) *f* chimney; fireplace

China (*chee*-nah) *f* China

chinche (*cheen*-chay) *f* bug; drawing-pin; thumbtack *nAm*

chinchorro (cheen-*choa*-rroa) *m* dinghy

chino (*chee*-noa) *adj* Chinese; *m* Chinese; *adjMe* curly

chisguete (cheez-*gay*-tay) *m* squirt

chisme (*cheez*-may) *m* gossip; *contar chismes* gossip

chispa (*cheess*-pah) *f* spark

chistoso (cheess-*toa*-soa) *adj* witty, humorous

chocante (choa-*kahn*-tay) *adj* revolting, shocking

chocar (choa-*kahr*) *v* collide, crash, bump; shock; ~ **contra** knock against

chocolate (choa-koa-*lah*-tay) *m* chocolate

chófer (*choa*-fayr) *m* chauffeur

choque (*choa*-kay) *m* crash; shock

chorro (*choa*-rroa) *m* spout, jet

chuleta (choo-*lay*-tah) *f* chop, cutlet

chupar (choo-*pahr*) *v* suck

D

dactilógrafa (dahk-tee-*loa*-grah-fah) *f* typist

dadivoso (dah-dhee-*bhoa*-soa) *adj* liberal

daltoniano (dahl-toa-*nʸah*-noa) *adj* colour-blind

dama (*dah*-mah) *f* lady

danés (dah-*nayss*) *adj* Danish; *m* Dane

dañar (dah-*ñahr*) *v* damage; *hurt

daño (*dah*-ñoa) *m* mischief; harm; *hacer ~ *hurt

dañoso (dah-*ñoa*-soa) *adj* harmful

***dar** (dahr) *v* *give; **dado que** supposing that

dátil (*dah*-teel) *m* date

dato (*dah*-toa) *m* data *pl*

de (day) *prep* of; out of, from, off; with

debajo (day-*bhah*-khoa) *adv* underneath, beneath, below; ~ **de** under, beneath, below

debate (day-*bhah*-tay) *m* debate, discussion

debatir (day-bhah-*teer*) *v* discuss

debe (*day*-bhay) *m* debit

deber (day-*bhayr*) *m* duty; *v* *have to, need to, need; owe; ~ **de** *be bound to

debido (day-*bhee*-dhoa) *adj* due; proper; ~ **a** owing to

débil (*day*-bheel) *adj* faint, weak, feeble

debilidad (day-bhee-lee-*dhahdh*) *f* weakness

decencia (day-*thayn*-thʸah) *f* decency

decente (day-*thayn*-tay) *adj* decent

decepcionar (day-thayp-thʸoa-*nahr*) *v* *let down, disappoint

decidir (day-thee-*dheer*) *v* decide; **de-**

cidido resolute

décimo (*day*-thee-moa) *num* tenth

decimoctavo (day-thee-moak-*tah*-bhoa) *num* eighteenth

decimonono (day-thee-moa-*noa*-noa) *num* nineteenth

decimoséptimo (day-thee-moa-*sayp*-tee-moa) *num* seventeenth

decimosexto (day-thee-moa-*sayks*-toa) *num* sixteenth

*decir (day-*theer*) *v* *say, *tell; ***querer ~** *mean

decisión (day-thee-s^yoan) *f* decision

decisivo (day-thee-*see*-bhoa) *adj* decisive

declaración (day-klah-rah-*th^yoan*) *f* statement, declaration

declarar (day-klah-*rahr*) *v* state, declare

decoración (day-koa-rah-*th^yoan*) *f* decoration

decorativo (day-koa-rah-*tee*-bhoa) *adj* decorative

decreto (day-*kray*-toa) *m* decree

dedal (day-*dhahl*) *m* thimble

dédalo (*day*-dhah-loa) *m* muddle

dedicar (day-dhee-*kahr*) *v* devote, dedicate

dedo (*day*-dhoa) *m* finger; **~ auricular** little finger; **~ del pie** toe

*deducir (day-dhoo-*theer*) *v* infer, deduce; deduct

defecto (day-*fayk*-toa) *m* fault

defectuoso (day-fayk-*twoa*-soa) *adj* defective, faulty

*defender (day-fayn-*dayr*) *v* defend

defensa (day-*fayn*-sah) *f* defence; plea; *fMe* fender

defensor (day-fayn-*soar*) *m* champion

deficiencia (day-fee-*th^yayn*-th^yah) *f* deficiency, shortcoming

déficit (*day*-fee-theet) *m* deficit

definición (day-fee-nee-*th^yoan*) *f* definition

definir (day-fee-*neer*) *v* define; **definido** definite

definitivo (day-fee-nee-*tee*-bhoa) *adj* definitive

deforme (day-*foar*-may) *adj* deformed

dejar (day-*khahr*) *v* *let, *leave; *leave behind, desert; **~ de** stop

delantal (day-lahn-*tahl*) *m* apron

delante de (day-*lahn*-tay day) before, in front of, ahead of

delegación (day-lay-gah-*th^yoan*) *f* delegation

delegado (day-lay-*gah*-dhoa) *m* delegate

deleitable (day-lay-*tah*-bhlay) *adj* enjoyable

deleite (day-*lay*-tay) *m* delight

deleitoso (day-lay-*toa*-soa) *adj* delightful

deletrear (day-lay-tray-*ahr*) *v* *spell

deletreo (day-lay-*tray*-oa) *m* spelling

delgado (dayl-*gah*-dhoa) *adj* thin

deliberación (day-lee-bhay-rah-*th^yoan*) *f* deliberation

deliberar (day-lee-bhay-*rahr*) *v* deliberate; **deliberado** *adj* deliberate

delicado (day-lee-*kah*-dhoa) *adj* delicate, tender

delicia (day-*lee*-th^yah) *f* joy, delight

delicioso (day-lee-*th^yoa*-soa) *adj* wonderful, delightful, delicious, lovely

delincuente (day loong *kwayn* tay) *m* criminal

delito (day-*lee*-toa) *m* crime

demanda (day-*mahn*-dah) *f* request; application; demand

demás (day-*mahss*) *adj* remaining

demasiado (day-mah-s^yah-dhoa) *adv* too

democracia (day-moa-*krah*-th^yah) *f* democracy

democrático (day-moa-*krah*-tee-koa) *adj* democratic

*demoler (day-moa-*layr*) *v* demolish

demolición (day-moa-lee-*th^yoan*) *f* demolition

demonio (day-*moa*-n^yoa) *m* devil

demostración (day-moass-trah-*th^yoan*) *f* demonstration

*demostrar (day-moass-*trahr*) *v* demonstrate, *show, prove

*denegar (day-nay-*gahr*) *v* deny

denominación (day-noa-mee-nah-*th^yoan*) *f* denomination

denso (*dayn*-soa) *adj* thick, dense

dentadura postiza (dayn-tah-*dhoo*-rah poass-*tee*-thah) *f* false teeth, denture

dentista (dayn-*teess*-tah) *m* dentist

dentro (*dayn*-troa) *adv* inside; **de ~** within; **~ de** inside, within; into; in

departamento (day-pahr-tah-*mayn*-toa) *m* department; section, division

depender de (day-payn-*dayr*) depend on

dependiente (day-payn-*d^yayn*-tay) *adj* dependant; *m* shop assistant

deporte (day-*poar*-tay) *m* sport; **conjunto de ~** sportswear; **chaqueta de ~** sports-jacket

deportista (day-poar-*teess*-tah) *m* sportsman

depositar (day-poa-see-*tahr*) *v* bank

depósito (day-*poa*-see-toa) *m* deposit; **~ de gasolina** petrol tank

depresión (day-pray-s^yoan) *f* depression

deprimente (day-pree-*mayn*-tay) *adj* depressing

deprimir (day-pree-*meer*) *v* depress; **deprimido** blue, depressed, low

derecho (day-*ray*-choa) *m* right; law, right, justice, straight; *adj* upright; right-hand; **~ administrativo** administrative law; **~ civil** civil law; **~ comercial** commercial law; **~ electoral** franchise, suffrage; **~ penal** criminal law

derivar de (day-ree-*bhahr*) *be derived from

derramar (day-rrah-*mahr*) *v* *shed

derribar (day-rree-*bhahr*) *v* knock down

derrochador (day-rroa-chah-*dhoar*) *adj* wasteful

derrota (day-*rroa*-tah) *f* defeat

derrotar (day-rroa-*tahr*) *v* defeat

derrumbarse (day-rroom-*bahr*-say) *v* collapse

desabotonar (day-sah-bhoa-toa-*nahr*) *v* unbutton

desacelerar (day-sah-thay-lay-*rahr*) *v* slow down

desacostumbrado (day-sah-koass-toom-*brah*-dhoa) *adj* unaccustomed

desacostumbrar (day-sah-koass-toom-*brahr*) *v* unlearn

desafiar (day-sah-f^y*ahr*) *v* dare; challenge

desafilado (day-sah-fee-*lah*-dhoa) *adj* blunt

desafortunado (day-sah-foar-too-*nah*-dhoa) *adj* unlucky, unfortunate

desagradable (day-sah-grah-*dhah*-bhlay) *adj* nasty, disagreeable, unpleasant; unkind

desagradar (day-sah-grah-*dhahr*) *v* displease

desagüe (day-*sah*-gway) *m* sewer, drain

desaliñado (day-sah-lee-*ñah*-doa) *adj* untidy

desamueblado (day-sah-mway-*bhlah*-dhoa) *adj* unfurnished

desánimo (day-*sah*-nee-moa) *m* depression

*desaparecer (day-sah-pah-ray-*thayr*) *v* disappear; vanish

desaparecido (day-sah-pah-ray-*thee*-dhoa) *adj* lost; *m* missing person

desapasionado (day-sah-pah-s^yoa-*nah*-dhoa) *adj* matter-of-fact

*desaprobar (day-sah-proa-*bhahr*) *v*

disapprove

desarrollar (day-sah-rroa-*lYahr*) v develop

desarrollo (day-sah-*rroa*-lYoa) m development

desasosiego (day-sah-soa-sYay-goa) m unrest

desastre (day-*sahss*-tray) m disaster, calamity

desastroso (day-sahss-*troa*-soa) adj disastrous

desatar (day-sah-*tahr*) v *undo, untie, unfasten

desautorizado (day-sou-toa-ree-*thah*-dhoa) adj unauthorized

desayuno (day-sah-Yoo-noa) m breakfast

descafeinado (dayss-kah-fay-*nah*-dhoa) adj decaffeinated

descansar (dayss-kahn-*sahr*) v rest; relax

descanso (dayss-*kahn*-soa) m rest; break; half-time

descarado (dayss-kah-*rah*-dhoa) adj bold, impertinent

descargar (dayss-kahr-*gahr*) v discharge, unload

descendencia (day-thayn-*dayn*-thYah) f origin

*descender (day-thayn-*dhayr*) v *fall

descendiente (day-thayn-dYayn-tay) m descendant

descolorido (dayss-koa-loa-*ree*-dhoa) adj discoloured

descompostura (dayss-koam-poss-*too*-rah) fMe breakdown

*desconcertar (dayss-koan-thayr-*tahr*) v overwhelm, embarrass

desconectar (dayss-koa-nayk-*tahr*) v disconnect

desconfiado (dayss-koan-*fYah*-dhoa) adj suspicious

desconfianza (dayss-koan-fYahn-thah) f suspicion

desconfiar de (dayss-koan-*fYahr*) v mistrust

descongelarse (dayss-koang-khay-*lahr*-say) v thaw

*desconocer (dayss-koa-noa-*thayr*) v not to *know, fail to recognize

desconocido (dayss-koa-noa-*thee*-dhoa) adj unknown; unfamiliar

descontento (dayss-koan-*tayn*-toa) adj discontented

descorchar (dayss-koar-*chahr*) v uncork

descortés (dayss-koar-*tayss*) adj impolite

describir (dayss-kree-*bheer*) v describe

descripción (dayss-kreep-thYoan) f description

descubrimiento (dayss-koo-bhree-mYayn-toa) m discovery

descubrir (dayss-koo-*bhreer*) v discover, detect

descuento (dayss-*kwayn*-toa) m discount; ~ **bancario** bank-rate

descuidar (dayss-kwee-*dhahr*) v neglect; **descuidado** slovenly

descuido (dayss-*kwee*-dhoa) m oversight

desde (*dayz*-dhay) prep from; since; ~ **entonces** since; ~ **que** since

desdén (dayz-*dhayn*) m disdain

desdichado (dayz-dhee-*chah*-dhoa) adj unhappy

deseable (day-say-*ah*-bhlay) adj desirable

desear (day-say-*ahr*) v desire; wish, want

desecar (day-say-*kahr*) v drain

desechable (day-say-*chah*-bhlay) adj disposable

desechar (day-say-*chahr*) v discard

desecho (day-*say*-choa) m refuse

desembarcar (day-saym-bahr-*kahr*) v disembark; land

desembocadura (day-saym-boa-kah-

dhoo-rah) *f* mouth

desempaquetar (day-saym-pah-kay-*tahr*) *v* unpack

desempeñar (day-saym-pay-*ñahr*) *v* perform

desempleo (day-saym-*play*-oa) *m* unemployment

desengaño (day-sayng-*gah*-ñoa) *m* disappointment

desenvoltura (day-saym-boal-*too*-rah) *f* ease

*****desenvolver** (day-saym-boal-*bhayr*) *v* unwrap

deseo (day-*say*-oa) *m* wish, desire

desertar (day-sayr-*tahr*) *v* desert

desesperación (day-sayss-pay-rah-th^y*oan*) *f* despair

desesperado (day-sayss-pay-*rah*-dhoa) *adj* hopeless, desperate; *****estar ~** despair

desfavorable (dayss-fah-bhoa-*rah*-bhlay) *adj* unfavourable

desfile (dayss-*fee*-lay) *m* parade

desgarrar (dayz-gah-*rrahr*) *v* *tear

desgracia (dayz-*grah*-th^yah) *f* misfortune

desgraciadamente (dayz-grah-th^yah-dhah-*mayn*-tay) *adv* unfortunately

*****deshacer** (day-sah-*thayr*) *v* *undo

deshielo (day-s^yay-loa) *m* thaw

deshilacharse (day-see-lah-*chahr*-say) *v* fray

deshonesto (day-soa-*nayss*-toa) *adj* crooked

deshonor (day-soa-*noar*) *m* disgrace

deshonra (day-*soan*-rah) *f* shame

deshuesar (day-sway-*sahr*) *v* bone

desierto (day-s^y*ayr*-toa) *adj* desert; *m* desert

designar (day-seeg-*nahr*) *v* designate; appoint

desigual (day-see-*gwahl*) *adj* unequal, uneven

desinclinado (day-seeng-klee-*nah*-

dhoa) *adj* unwilling

desinfectante (day-seen-fayk-*tahn*-tay) *m* disinfectant

desinfectar (day-seen-fayk-*tahr*) *v* disinfect

desinteresado (day-seen-tay-ray-*sah*-dhoa) *adj* unselfish

desliz (dayz-*leeth*) *m* slide; slip

deslizarse (dayz-lee-*thahr*-say) *v* *slide; slip

deslucido (dayz-loo-*thee*-dhoa) *adj* dim

deslumbrador (dayz-loom-brah-*dhoar*) *adj* glaring

desmayarse (dayz-mah-^y*ahr*-say) *v* faint

desnudarse (dayz-noo-*dhahr*-say) *v* undress

desnudo (dayz-*noo*-dhoa) *adj* naked, nude, bare; *m* nude

desnutrición (dayz-noo-tree-th^y*oan*) *f* malnutrition

desocupado (day-soa-koo-*pah*-dhoa) *adj* unoccupied; unemployed

desodorante (day-soa-dhoa-*rahn*-tay) *m* deodorant

desorden (day-*soar*-dayn) *m* disorder; mess

despachar (dayss-pah-*chahr*) *v* dispatch, despatch, *send off

despacho (dayss-*pah*-choa) *m* study

despedida (dayss-pay-*dhee*-dhah) *f* parting; departure

*****despedir** (dayss-pay-*dheer*) *v* dismiss; fire; *****despedirse** *v* check out

despegar (dayss-pay-*gahr*) *v* *take off

despegue (dayss-*pay*-gay) *m* take-off

despensa (dayss-*payn*-sah) *f* larder

desperdicio (dayss-payr-*dhee*-th^yoa) *m* litter; waste

despertador (dayss-payr-tah-*dhoar*) *m* alarm-clock

*****despertar** (dayss-payr-*tahr*) *v* *wake, *awake; *****despertarse** *v* wake up

despierto (dayss-p^y*ayr*-toa) *adj*

awake; vigilant

* desplegar (dayss-play-*gahr*) *v* unfold; expand

desplomarse (dayss-ploa-*mahr*-say) *v* collapse

despreciar (dayss-pray-th*Y*ahr) *v* scorn, despise

desprecio (dayss-*pray*-th*Y*oa) *m* scorn, contempt

despreocupado (dayss-pray-oa-koo-*pah*-dhoa) *adj* carefree

después (dayss-*pwayss*) *adv* afterwards; then; ~ **de** after; ~ **de que** after

destacado (dayss tah *kah* dhoa) *adj* outstanding

destacarse (dayss-tah-*kahr*-say) *v* *stand out

destapar (dayss-tah-*pahr*) *v* uncover

destartalado (dayss-tahr-tah-*lah*-dhoa) *adj* ramshackle

destello (dayss-*tay*-l*Y*oa) *m* glare

* desteñirse (dayss-tay-*ñer*-say) *v* fade, discolour; **no destiñe** fast-dyed

destinar (dayss-tee-*nahr*) *v* destine; address

destinatario (dayss-tee-nah-*tah*-r*Y*oa) *m* addressee

destino (dayss-*tee*-noa) *m* fate, destiny, lot; destination

destornillador (dayss-toar-nee-l*Y*ah-*dhoa*) *m* screw-driver

destornillar (dayss-toar-nee-*l*Y*ahr*) *v* unscrew

destrucción (dayss-trook-th*Y*oan) *f* destruction

* destruir (dayss-*trweer*) *v* destroy; wreck

desvalorización (dayz-bhah-loa-ree-thah-th*Y*oan) *f* devaluation

desvalorizar (dayz-bhah-loa-ree-*thahr*) *v* devalue

desvelado (dayz-bhay-*lah*-dhoa) *adj* sleepless

desventaja (dayz-bhayn-*tah*-khah) *f* disadvantage

desviar (dayz-*bh*Y*ahr*) *v* avert; **desviarse** *v* deviate

desvío (dayz-*bhee*-oa) *m* detour; diversion

detallado (day-tah-*l*Y*ah*-dhoa) *adj* detailed

detalle (day-*tah*-l*Y*ay) *m* detail; **vender al** ~ retail

detective (day-tayk-*tee*-bhay) *m* detective

detención (day-tayn-th*Y*oan) *f* custody

* detener (day-tay *nayr*) *v* detain

detergente (day-tayr-*khayn*-tay) *m* detergent

determinar (day-tayr-mee-*nahr*) *v* define, determine; **determinado** definite

detestar (day-tayss-*tahr*) *v* hate, dislike

detrás (day-*trahss*) *adv* behind; ~ **de** behind, after

deuda (*day*⁰⁰-dhah) *f* debt

* devolver (day-bhoal-*bhayr*) *v* *bring back; *send back

día (*dee*-ah) *m* day; **¡buenos días!** hello!; **de** ~ by day; ~ **de trabajo** working day; ~ **laborable** weekday; **el otro** ~ recently

diabetes (d*Y*ah-*bhay*-tayss) *f* diabetes

diabético (d*Y*ah-*bhay*-tee-koa) *m* diabetic

diablo (d*Y*ah-*bhloa*) *m* devil

diabluras (d*Y*ah-*bhloo*-rahss) *fpl* mischief

diagnosis (d*Y*ahg-*noa*-seess) *m* diagnosis

diagnosticar (d*Y*ahg-noass-tee-*kahr*) *v* diagnose

diagonal (d*Y*ah-goa-*nahl*) *adj* diagonal; *f* diagonal

dialecto (d*Y*ah-*layk*-toa) *m* dialect

diamante (dᵛah-*mahn*-tay) *m* diamond

diapositiva (dᵛah-poa-see-*tee*-bhah) *f* slide

diario (*dᵛah*-rᵛoa) *adj* daily; *m* daily, newspaper; diary; **a ~** per day; **~ matutino** morning paper

diarrea (dᵛah-*rray*-ah) *f* diarrhoea

dibujar (dee-bhoo-*khahr*) *v* sketch, *draw

dibujo (dee-*bhoo*-khoa) *m* sketch, drawing; **dibujos animados** cartoon

diccionario (deek-th ᵛoa-*nah*-rᵛoa) *m* dictionary

diciembre (dee-th ᵛ*aym*-bray) December

dictado (deek-*tah*-dhoa) *m* dictation

dictador (deek-tah-*dhoar*) *m* dictator

dictadura (deek-tah-*dhoo*-rah) *f* dictatorship

dictáfono (deek-*tah*-foa-noa) *m* dictaphone

dictar (deek-*tahr*) *v* dictate

dichoso (dee-*choa*-soa) *adj* happy

diecinueve (dᵛay-thee-*nway*-bhay) *num* nineteen

dieciocho (dᵛay-th ᵛoa-choa) *num* eighteen

dieciséis (dᵛay-thee-*sayss*) *num* sixteen

diecisiete (dᵛay-thee-sᵛay-tay) *num* seventeen

diente (dᵛ*ayn*-tay) *m* tooth; **~ de león** dandelion

diesel (*dee*-sayl) *m* diesel

diestro (dᵛ*ayss*-troa) *adj* skilful

diez (dᵛayth) *num* ten

diferencia (dee-fay-*rayn*-th ᵛah) *f* difference; contrast, distinction

diferente (dee-fay-*rayn*-tay) *adj* different; unlike

*** diferir** (dee-fay-*reer*) *v* vary, differ; delay

difícil (dee-*fee*-theel) *adj* hard, difficult

dificultad (dee-fee-kool-*tahdh*) *f* difficulty

difteria (deef-*tay*-rᵛah) *f* diphtheria

difunto (dee-*foon*-toa) *adj* dead

difuso (dee-*foo*-soa) *adj* dim

digerible (dee-khayss-*tee*-bhlay) *adj* digestible

*** digerir** (dee-khay-*reer*) *v* digest

digestión (dee-khayss-t ᵛ*oan*) *f* digestion

dignidad (deeg-nee-*dhahdh*) *f* dignity

digno de (*dee*-ñoa day) worthy of

dilación (dee-lah-th ᵛ*oan*) *f* delay, respite

diligencia (dee-lee-*khayn*-th ᵛah) *f* diligence

diligente (dee-lee-*khayn*-tay) *adj* industrious

*** diluir** (dee-*lweer*) *v* dilute

dimensión (dee-mayn-sᵛ*oan*) *f* extent, size

Dinamarca (dee-nah-*mahr*-kah) *f* Denmark

dínamo (*dee*-nah-moa) *f* dynamo

dinero (dee-*nay*-roa) *m* money; **~ contante** cash

dios (dᵛoass) *m* god

diosa (dᵛ*oa*-sah) *f* goddess

diploma (dee-*ploa*-mah) *m* diploma, certificate

diplomático (dee-ploa-*mah*-tee-koa) *m* diplomat

diputado (dee-poo-*tah*-dhoa) *m* deputy; Member of Parliament

dique (*dee*-kay) *m* dike, dam

dirección (dee-rayk-th ᵛ*oan*) *f* direction; way; address; leadership, lead; **~ de escena** direction; **~ única** one-way traffic

directamente (dee-rayk-tah-*mayn*-tay) *adv* straight; straight away

directo (dee-*rayk*-toa) *adj* direct

director (dee-rayk-*toar*) *m* director,

manager; conductor; ~ **de escuela** head teacher, headmaster; principal

directorio telefónico (dee-rayk-*toa*-rʸoa tay-lay-*foa*-nee-koa) *Me* telephone directory

directriz (dee-rayk-*treeth*) *f* directive

dirigir (dee-ree-*kheer*) *v* head; direct; **dirigirse a** address

disciplina (dee-thee-*plee*-nah) *f* discipline

discípulo (deess-*thee*-poo-loa) *m* pupil

disco (*deess*-koa) *m* disc; record

discreto (deess-*kray*-toa) *adj* inconspicuous

disculpa (deess-*kool*-pah) *f* apology

disculpar (dee-ree-kool-*pahr*) *v* excuse; **disculparse** *v* apologize; ¡**disculpe!** sorry!

discurso (deess-*koor*-soa) *m* speech

discusión (deess-koo-sʸoan) *f* discussion, argument

discutir (deess-koo-*teer*) *v* discuss, deliberate, argue

disentería (dee-sayn-tay-*ree*-ah) *f* dysentery

***disentir** (dee-sayn-*teer*) *v* disagree

diseñar (dee-say-*ñahr*) *v* design

diseño (dee-*say*-ñoa) *m* design; pattern; **cuaderno de** ~ sketch-book

disfraz (deess-*frahth*) *m* disguise

disfrazarse (deess-frah-*thahr*-say) *v* disguise

disfrutar (deess-froo-*tahr*) *v* enjoy

disgustar (deez-gooss-*tahr*) *v* displease

disimular (dee-see-moo-*lahr*) *v* conceal

dislocado (deez-loa-*kah*-dhoa) *adj* dislocated

dislocar (deez-loa-*kahr*) *v* wrench

disminución (deez-mee-noo-*thʸoan*) *f* decrease

***disminuir** (deez-mee-*nweer*) *v* reduce, lessen, decrease

***disolver** (dee-soal-*bhayr*) *v* dissolve

disparar (deess-pah-*rahr*) *v* fire

disparo (deess-*pah*-roa) *m* shot

dispensar (deess-payn-*sahr*) *v* exempt; ~ **de** discharge of; ¡**dispense usted!** sorry!

dispensario (deess-payn-*sah*-rʸoa) *m* health centre

***disponer** (deess-poa-*nayr*) *v* sort; ~ **de** dispose of

disponible (deess-poa-*nee*-bhlay) *adj* available; spare

disposición (deess-poa-see-*thʸoan*) *f* disposal

dispuesto (deess-*pwayss*-toa) *adj* inclined, willing

disputa (deess-*poo*-tah) *f* dispute, argument, quarrel

disputar (deess-poo-*tahr*) *v* argue, quarrel; dispute

distancia (deess-*tahn*-thʸah) *f* distance; space, way

distinción (deess-teen-*thʸoan*) *f* distinction, difference

distinguido (deess-teeng-*gee*-dhoa) *adj* distinguished, dignified

distinguir (deess-teeng-*geer*) *v* distinguish; **distinguirse** *v* excel

distinto (deess-*teen*-toa) *adj* distinct

distracción (deess-trahk-*thʸoan*) *f* amusement

***distraer** (deess-trah-*ayr*) *v* distract

distribuidor (deess-tree-bhwee-*dhoar*) *m* distributor

***distribuir** (deess-tree-*bhweer*) *v* distribute; issue

distrito (deess-*tree*-toa) *m* district, ~ **electoral** constituency

disturbio (deess-*toor*-bhʸoa) *m* disturbance

disuadir (dee-swah-*dheer*) *v* dissuade from

diván (dee-*bhahn*) *m* couch

diversión (dee-bhayr-*sʸoan*) *f* pleasure, fun; diversion, entertainment

diverso (dee-*bhayr*-soa) *adj* diverse

divertido (dee-bhayr-*tee*-dhoa) *adj* amusing, entertaining

*__divertir__ (dee-bhayr-*teer*) *v* amuse, entertain

dividir (dee-bhee-*dheer*) *v* divide

divino (dee-*bhee*-noa) *adj* divine

división (dee-bhee-s*y*oan) *f* division; section

divorciar (dee-bhoar-th*y*ahr) *v* divorce

divorcio (dee-*bhoar*-th*y*oa) *m* divorce

dobladillo (doa-bhlah-*dhee*-l*y*oa) *m* hem

doblar (doa-*bhlahr*) *v* *bend; fold

doble (*doa*-bhlay) *adj* double

doce (*doa*-thay) *num* twelve

docena (doa-*thay*-nah) *f* dozen

doctor (doak-*toar*) *m* doctor

doctrina (doak-*tree*-nah) *f* doctrine

documento (doa-koo-*mayn*-toa) *m* document

*__doler__ (doa-*layr*) *v* ache

dolor (doa-*loar*) *m* ache, pain; grief; **dolores** *mpl* labour; **sin** ~ painless

dolorido (doa-loa-*ree*-dhoa) *adj* painful

doloroso (doa-loa-*roa*-soa) *adj* sore

domesticado (doa-mayss-tee-*kah*-dhoa) *adj* tame

domesticar (doa-mayss-tee-*kahr*) *v* tame

doméstico (doa-*mayss*-tee-koa) *adj* domestic; **faenas domésticas** housework

domicilio (doa-mee-*thee*-l*y*oa) *m* domicile

dominación (doa-mee-nah-th*y*oan) *f* domination

dominante (doa-mee-*nahn*-tay) *adj* leading

dominar (doa-mee-*nahr*) *v* master

domingo (doa-*meeng*-goa) *m* Sunday

dominio (doa-*mee*-n*y*oa) *m* dominion, rule

don (doan) *m* faculty

donación (doa-nah-th*y*oan) *f* donation

donante (doa-*nahn*-tay) *m* donor

donar (doa-*nahr*) *v* donate

doncella (doan-*thay*-l*y*ah) *f* chambermaid

donde (*doan*-day) *conj* where; **en ~ sea** anywhere

dónde (*doan*-day) *adv* where

dondequiera (doan-day-*k*y*ay*-rah) *adv* anywhere; ~ **que** wherever

dorado (doa-*rah*-dhoa) *adj* gilt; golden

dormido (doar-*mee*-dhoa) *adj* asleep; **quedarse ~** *oversleep

*__dormir__ (doar-*meer*) *v* *sleep

dormitorio (doar-mee-*toa*-r*y*oa) *m* bedroom; dormitory

dos (doass) *num* two; ~ **veces** twice

dosis (*doa*-seess) *f* dose

dotado (doa-*tah*-dhoa) *adj* talented

dragón (drah-*goan*) *m* dragon

drama (*drah*-mah) *m* drama

dramático (drah-*mah*-tee-koa) *adj* dramatic

dramaturgo (drah-mah-*toor*-goa) *m* playwright, dramatist

drenar (dray-*nahr*) *v* drain

droguería (droa-gay-*ree*-ah) *f* chemist's, pharmacy; drugstore *nAm*

ducha (*doo*-chah) *f* shower

duda (*doo*-dhah) *f* doubt; *poner en ~ query; sin ~ undoubtedly, without doubt

dudar (doo-*dhahr*) *v* doubt

dudoso (doo-*dhoa*-soa) *adj* doubtful

duelo (*dway*-loa) *m* duel; grief

duende (*dwayn*-dhay) *m* elf

dueña (*dway*-ñah) *f* mistress

dueño (*dway*-ñoa) *m* landlord

dulce (*dool*-thay) *adj* sweet; smooth; *m* sweet; **dulces** cake; sweets; candy *nAm*

duna (*doo*-nah) *f* dune

duodécimo (dwoa-*day*-thee-moa) *num* twelfth

duque (*doo*-kay) *m* duke

duquesa (doo-*kay*-sah) *f* duchess
duración (doo-rah-*th*ⁿoan) *f* duration
duradero (doo-rah-*dhay*-roa) *adj* permanent, lasting
durante (doo-*rahn*-tay) *prep* for, during
durar (doo-*rahr*) *v* last; continue
duro (*doo*-roa) *adj* hard; tough

E

ébano (*ay*-bhah-noa) *m* ebony
eclipse (ay-*kleep*-say) *m* eclipse
eco (*ay*-koa) *m* echo
economía (ay-koa-noa-*mee*-ah) *f* economy
económico (ay-koa-*noa*-mee-koa) *adj* economic; thrifty, economical; cheap
economista (ay-koa-noa-*meess*-tah) *m* economist
economizar (ay-koa-noa-mee-*thahr*) *v* economize
Ecuador (ay-kwah-*dhoar*) *m* Ecuador
ecuador (ay-kwah-*dhoar*) *m* equator
ecuatoriano (ay-kwah-toa-*r*ⁿah-noa) *m* Ecuadorian
eczema (ayk-*thay*-mah) *m* eczema
echada (ay-*chah*-dhah) *f* cast
echar (ay-*chahr*) *v* toss; ~ **al correo** post; ~ **a perder** *spoil; ~ **la culpa** blame
edad (ay-*dhahdh*) *f* age; **mayor de** ~ of age; **menor de** ~ under age
Edad Media (ay-*dhahdh* may-dh*ⁿah*) Middle Ages
edición (ay-dhee-*th*ⁿoan) *f* issue, edition; ~ **de mañana** morning edition
edificar (ay-dhee-fee-*kahr*) *v* construct
edificio (ay-dhee-*fee*-th*ⁿoa*) *m* construction, building

editor (ay-dhee-*toar*) *m* publisher
edredón (ay-dhray-*dhoan*) *m* eiderdown
educación (ay-dhoo-kah-*th*ⁿoan) *f* education
educar (ay-dhoo-*kahr*) *v* educate, *bring up, raise
efectivamente (ay-fayk-tee-bhah-*mayn*-tay) *adv* as a matter of fact, in fact
efectivo (ay-fayk-*tee*-bhoa) *m* cash; * **hacer** ~ cash
efecto (ay-*fayk*-toa) *m* effect
efectuar (ay-fayk-*twahr*) *v* effect; implement
efervescencia (ay-fayr-bhay-*thayn*-th*ⁿah*) *f* fizz
eficacia (ay-fee-*kah*-th*ⁿah*) *f* efficacy
eficaz (ay-fee-*kahth*) *adj* effective
eficiente (ay-fee-*th*ⁿ*ayn*-tay) *adj* efficient
egipcio (ay-*kheep*-th*ⁿoa*) *adj* Egyptian; *m* Egyptian
Egipto (ay-*kheep*-toa) *m* Egypt
egocéntrico (ay-goa-*thayn*-tree-koa) *adj* self-centred
egoísmo (ay-goa-*eez*-moa) *m* selfishness
egoísta (ay-goa-*eess*-tah) *adj* egoistic, selfish
eje (*ay*-khay) *m* axle
ejecución (ay-khay-koo-*th*ⁿoan) *f* execution
ejecutar (ay-khay-koo-*tahr*) *v* perform, execute
ejecutivo (ay-khay-koo-*tee*-bhoa) *adj* executive; *m* executive
ejemplar (ay-khaym-*plahr*) *m* copy
ejemplo (ay-*khaym*-ploa) *m* instance, example; **por** ~ for instance, for example
ejercer (ay-khayr-*thayr*) *v* exercise
ejercicio (ay-khayr-*thee*-th*ⁿoa*) *m* exercise
ejercitar (ay-khayr-thee-*tahr*) *v* exercise

ejército (ay-*khayr*-thee-toa) *m* army

ejote (ay-*khoa*-tay) *mMe* bean

el (ayl) *art* (f la; pl los, las) the *art*

él (ayl) *pron* he

elaborar (ay-lah-boa-*rahr*) *v* elaborate

elasticidad (ay-lahss-tee-thee-*dhahdh*) *f* elasticity

elástico (ay-*lahss*-tee-koa) *adj* elastic; *m* rubber band

elección (ay-layk-*th^yoan*) *f* choice, pick, selection; election

electricidad (ay-layk-tree-thee-*dhahdh*) *f* electricity

electricista (ay-layk-tree-*theess*-tah) *m* electrician

eléctrico (ay-*layk*-tree-koa) *adj* electric

electrónico (ay-layk-*troa*-nee-koa) *adj* electronic

elefante (ay-lay-*fahn*-tay) *m* elephant

elegancia (ay-lay-*gahn*-th^yah) *f* elegance

elegante (ay-lay-*gahn*-tay) *adj* smart, elegant

***elegir** (ay-lay-*kheer*) *v* elect, select

elemental (ay-lay-mayn-*tahl*) *adj* primary

elemento (ay-lay-*mayn*-toa) *m* element

elevador (ay-lay-bhah-*dhoar*) *mMe* lift; elevator *nAm*

elevar (ay-lay-*bhahr*) *v* elevate

eliminar (ay-lee-mee-*nahr*) *v* eliminate

elogio (ay-*loa*-kh^yoa) *m* praise, glory

elucidar (ay-loo-thee-*dhahr*) *v* elucidate

ella (*ay*-l^yah) *pron* she

ello (*ay*-l^yoa) *pron* it

ellos (*ay*-l^yoass) *pron* they

emancipación (ay-mahn-thee-pah-*th^yoan*) *f* emancipation

embajada (aym-bah-*khah*-dhah) *f* embassy

embajador (aym-bah-khah-*dhoar*) *m* ambassador

embalaje (aym-bah-*lah*-khay) *m* packing

embalar (aym-bah-*lahr*) *v* pack

embalse (aym-*bahl*-say) *m* reservoir

embarazada (aym-bah-rah-*thah*-dhah) *adj* pregnant

embarazoso (aym-bah-rah-*thoa*-soa) *adj* embarrassing, awkward; puzzling

embarcación (aym-bahr-kah-*th^yoan*) *f* vessel; embarkation

embarcar (aym-bahr-*kahr*) *v* embark

embargar (aym-bahr-*gahr*) *v* confiscate

embargo (aym-*bahr*-goa) *m* embargo; sin ~ yet, however, though, still

emblema (aym-*blay*-mah) *m* emblem

emboscada (aym-boass-*kah*-dhah) *f* ambush

embotado (aym-boa-*tah*-dhoa) *adj* dull

embotellamiento (aym-boa-tay-l^yah-m^yayn-toa) *m* traffic jam

embrague (aym-*brah*-gay) *m* clutch

embriagado (aym-br^yah-*gah*-dhoa) *adj* intoxicated

embrollar (aym-broa-l^yahr) *v* muddle

embrollo (aym-*broa*-l^yoa) *m* muddle

embromar (aym-broa-*mahr*) *v* kid

embudo (aym-*boo*-dhoa) *m* funnel

emergencia (ay-mayr-*khayn*-th^yah) *f* emergency

emigración (ay-mee-*grah*-th^yoan) *f* emigration

emigrante (ay-mee-*grahn*-tay) *m* emigrant

emigrar (ay-mee-*grahr*) *v* emigrate

eminente (ay-mee-*nayn*-tay) *adj* outstanding

emisión (ay-mee-*s^yoan*) *f* issue

emisor (ay-mee-*soar*) *m* transmitter

emitir (ay-mee-*teer*) *v* *broadcast; utter

emoción (ay-moa-*th^yoan*) *f* emotion

empalme (aym-*pahl*-may) *m* junction

empapar (aym-pah-*pahr*) *v* soak

empaquetar (aym-pah-kay-*tahr*) *v* pack up

emparedado (aym-pah-ray-*dhah*-dhoa) *m* sandwich

emparentado (aym-pah-rayn-*tah*-dhoa) *adj* related

empaste (aym-*pahss*-tay) *m* filling

empeñar (aym-pay-*ñahr*) *v* pawn

empeño (aym-*pay*-ñoa) *m* pawn; determination

emperador (aym-pay-rah-*dhoar*) *m* emperor

emperatriz (aym-pay-rah-*treeth*) *f* empress

****empezar** (aym-pay-*thahr*) *v* *begin, start

empleado (aym-play-*ah*-dhoa) *m* employee; ~ **de oficina** clerk

emplear (aym-play-*ahr*) *v* employ; engage

empleo (aym-*play*-oa) *m* job, employment

emprender (aym-prayn-*dayr*) *v* *undertake

empresa (aym-*pray*-sah) *f* undertaking, enterprise; concern, business

empujar (aym-poo-*khahr*) *v* push; press

empujón (aym-poo-*khoan*) *m* push

en (ayn) *prep* at, in; inside, to

enamorado (ay-nah-moa-*rah*-dhoa) *adj* in love

enamorarse (aynah-moa-*rahr*-say) *v* *fall in love

enano (ay-*nah*-noa) *m* dwarf

encantado (ayng-kahn-*tah*-dhoa) *adj* delighted

encantador (ayng-kahn-tah-*dhoar*) *adj* glamorous; charming, enchanting

encantar (ayng-kahn-*tahr*) *v* delight; bewitch

encanto (ayng-*kahn*-toa) *m* glamour, charm; spell

encarcelamiento (ayng-kahr-thay-lah-*mᵞayn*-toa) *m* imprisonment

encarcelar (ayng-kahr-thay-*lahr*) *v* imprison

encargarse de (ayng-kahr-*gahr*-say) *take over, *take charge of

encargo (ayng-*kahr*-goa) *m* assignment

encariñado con (ayng-kah-ree-*ñah*-dhoa koan) attached to

encendedor (ayn-thayn-day-*dhoar*) *m* cigarette-lighter

****encender** (ayn-thayn-*dayr*) *v* *light; turn on, switch on

encendido (ayn-thayn-*dee*-dhoa) *m* ignition

****encerrar** (ayn-thay-*rrahr*) *v* *shut in; encircle

encía (ayn-*thee*-ah) *f* gum

enciclopedia (ayn-thee-kloa-*pay*-dhᵞah) *f* encyclopaedia

encima (ayn-*thee*-mah) *adv* above; over; ~ **de** over, above, on top of

encinta (ayn-*theen*-tah) *adj* pregnant

encogerse (ayng-koa-*khayr*-say) *v* *shrink; **no encoge** shrinkproof

****encontrar** (ayng-koan-*trahr*) *v* *come across, *find; ****encontrarse con** *meet, encounter, run into

encorvado (ayng-koar-*bhah*-dhoa) *adj* curved

encrucijada (ayng-kroo-thee-*khah*-dhah) *f* crossing, junction

encuentro (ayng-*kwayn*-troa) *m* meeting, encounter

encuesta (ayng-*kwayss*-tah) *f* inquiry; enquiry

encurtidos (ayng-koor-*tee*-dhoass) *mpl* pickles *pl*

enchufar (ayn-choo-*fahr*) *v* plug in

enchufe (ayn-*choo*-fay) *m* plug

endosar (ayn-doa-*sahr*) *v* endorse

endulzar (ayn-dool-*thahr*) *v* sweeten

enemigo (ay-nay-*mee*-goa) *m* enemy

energía (ay-nayr-*khee*-ah) *f* energy;

power; zest; ~ **nuclear** nuclear energy

enérgico (ay-*nayr*-khee-koa) *adj* energetic

enero (ay-*nay*-roa) January

enfadado (ayn-fah-*dhah*-dhoa) *adj* angry, cross

énfasis (*ayn*-fah-seess) *m* stress

enfatizar (ayn-fah-tee-*thahr*) *v* emphasize

enfermedad (ayn-fayr-may-*dhahdh*) *f* disease; ailment, sickness, illness; ~ **venérea** venereal disease

enfermera (ayn-fayr-*may*-rah) *f* nurse

enfermería (ayn-fayr-may-*ree*-ah) *f* infirmary

enfermizo (ayn-fayr-*mee*-thoa) *adj* unsound

enfermo (ayn-*fayr*-moa) *adj* sick, ill

enfoque (ayn-*foa*-kay) *m* approach

enfrentarse con (ayn-frayn-*tahr*-say) face

enfrente de (ayn-*frayn*-tay day) facing, opposite

engañar (ayng-gah-*ñahr*) *v* cheat, deceive; fool

engaño (ayng-*gah*-ñoa) *m* deceit

engrasar (ayng-grah-*sahr*) *v* grease

enhebrar (ay-nay-*bhrahr*) *v* thread

enigma (ay-*neeg*-mah) *m* mystery, enigma, puzzle

enjuagar (ayng-khwah-*gahr*) *v* rinse

enjuague (ayng-*khwah*-gay) *m* rinse; ~ **bucal** mouthwash

enjugar (ayng-khoo-*gahr*) *v* wipe

enlace (ayn-*lah*-thay) *m* connection, link

enlazar (ayn-lah-*thahr*) *v* link

enmaderado (ayn-mah-dhay-*rah*-dhoa) *m* panelling

enmohecido (ayn-moa-ay-*thee*-dhoa) *adj* mouldy

enojado (ay-noa-*khah*-doa) *adj* angry, cross

enojo (ay-*noa*-khoa) *m* anger

enorme (ay-*noar*-may) *adj* huge, enormous, immense

enrollar (ayn-roa-*lʸahr*) *v* *wind

ensalada (ayn-sah-*lah*-dhah) *f* salad

ensamblar (ayn-sahm-*blahr*) *v* join

ensanchar (ayn-sahn-*chahr*) *v* widen

ensayar (ayn-sah-*ʸahr*) *v* test; rehearse; **ensayarse** *v* practise

ensayo (ayn-*sah*-ʸoa) *m* test; rehearsal; essay

ensenada (ayn-say-*nah*-dhah) *f* inlet, creek

enseñanza (ayn-say-*ñahn*-thah) *f* tuition; teachings *pl*

enseñar (ayn-say-*ñahr*) *v* *teach; *show

ensueño (ayn-*sway*-ñoa) *m* day-dream

entallar (ayn-tah-*lʸahr*) *v* carve

***entender** (ayn-tayn-*dayr*) *v* conceive; *take

entendimiento (ayn-tayn-dee-*mʸayn*-toa) *m* insight; conception

enteramente (ayn-tay-rah-*mayn*-tay) *adv* completely, entirely, quite

enterar (ayn-tay-*rahr*) *v* inform

entero (ayn-*tay*-roa) *adj* whole, entire

***enterrar** (ayn-tay-*rrahr*) *v* bury

entierro (ayn-*tʸay*-rroa) *m* burial

entonces (ayn-*toan*-thayss) *adv* then; **de** ~ contemporary

entrada (ayn-*trah*-dhah) *f* entry, entrance, way in; admission; appearance; entrance-fee; **prohibida la** ~ no admittance

entrañas (ayn-*trah*-ñahss) *fpl* insides

entrar (ayn-*trahr*) *v* *go in, enter

entre (*ayn*-tray) *prep* among, amid; between

entreacto (ayn-tray-*ahk*-toa) *m* intermission

entrega (ayn-*tray*-gah) *f* delivery

entregar (ayn-tray-*gahr*) *v* *give; deliver; commit; extradite

entremeses (ayn-tray-*may*-sayss) *mpl* hors-d'œuvre

entrenador (ayn-tray-nah-*dhoar*) *m* coach

entrenamiento (ayn tray nah *m*^y*ayn* toa) *m* training

entrenar (ayn-tray-*nahr*) *v* train, drill

entresuelo (ayn-tray-*sway*-loa) *m* mezzanine

entretanto (ayn-tray-*tahn*-toa) *adv* meanwhile, in the meantime

* **entretener** (ayn-tray-tay-*nayr*) *v* amuse, entertain

entretenido (ayn-tray-tay-*nee*-dhoa) *adj* entertaining

entretenimiento (ayn-tray-tay-nee-*m*^y*ayn*-toa) *m* amusement, entertainment

entrevista (ayn-tray-*bheess*-tah) *f* interview

entumecido (ayn-too-may-*thee*-dhoa) *adj* numb

entusiasmo (ayn-too-s^y*ahz*-moa) *m* enthusiasm

entusiasta (ayn-too-s^y*ahss*-tah) *adj* enthusiastic, keen

envenenar (aym-bay-nay-*nahr*) *v* poison

enviado (aym-b^y*ah*-dhoa) *m* envoy

enviar (aym-b^y*ahr*) *v* dispatch, *send

envidia (aym-bee-dh^yah) *f* envy

envidiar (aym-bee-*dh*^y*ahr*) *v* grudge, envy

envidioso (aym-bee-*dh*^y*oa*-soa) *adj* envious

envío (aym-*bee*-oa) *m* expedition, consignment

* **envolver** (aym-boal-*bhayr*) *v* wrap; involve

épico (*ay*-pee-koa) *adj* epic

epidemia (ay-pee-*dhay*-m^yah) *f* epidemic

epilepsia (ay-pee-*layp*-s^yah) *f* epilepsy

epílogo (ay-*pee*-loa-goa) *m* epilogue

episodio (ay-pee-*soa*-dheeoa) *m* episode ·

época (*ay*-poa-kah) *f* period

equilibrio (ay-kee-*lee*-bhr^yoa) *m* balance

equipaje (ay-kee-*pah*-khay) *m* baggage, luggage; ~ **de mano** hand luggage; hand baggage *Am*; **furgón de equipajes** luggage van

equipar (ay-kee-*pahr*) *v* equip

equipo (ay-*kee*-poa) *m* outfit, equipment; gang, team; crew; soccer team

equitación (ay-kee-tah-*th*^y*oan*) *f* riding

equivalente (ay-kee-bhah-*layn*-tay) *adj* equivalent

equivocación (ay-kee-bhoa-kah-*th*^y*oan*) *f* misunderstanding, mistake

equivocado (ay-kee-bhoa-*kah*-dhoa) *adj* mistaken

equivocarse (ay-kee-bhoa-*kahr*-say) *v* *be mistaken

equívoco (ay-*kee*-bhoa-koa) *adj* ambiguous

era (*ay*-rah) *f* era

erguido (ayr-*gee*-dhoa) *adj* erect

erigir (ay-ree-*kheer*) *v* erect

erizo (ay-*ree*-thoa) *m* hedgehog; ~ **de mar** sea-urchin

* **errar** (ay-*rrahr*) *v* err; wander

erróneo (ay-*rroa*-nay-oa) *adj* wrong

error (ay-*rroar*) *m* mistake, error

erudito (ay-roo-*dhee*-toa) *m* scholar

esbelto (ayz-*bhayl*-toa) *adj* slim, slender

escala (ayss-*kah*-lah) *f* scale; ~ **de incendios** fire-escape; ~ **musical** scale

escalar (ayss-kah-*lahr*) *v* ascend

escalera (ayss-kah-*lay*-rah) *f* stairs *pl*, staircase; ~ **de mano** ladder; ~ **móvil** escalator

escalofrío (ayss-kah-loa-*free*-oa) *m* chill, shiver

escama (ayss-*kah*-mah) *f* scale

escándalo (ayss-*kahn*-dah-loa) *m* scandal; offence

Escandinavia (ayss-kahn-dee-*nah*-bh^yah) *f* Scandinavia

escandinavo (ayss-kahn-dee-*nah*-bhoa) *adj* Scandinavian; *m* Scandinavian

escapar (ayss-kah-*pahr*) *v* escape

escaparate (ayss-kah-pah-*rah*-tay) *m* shop-window

escape (ayss-*kah*-pay) *m* exhaust; **gases de ~** exhaust gases

escaque (ayss-*kah*-kay) *m* check

escarabajo (ayss-kah-rah-*bhah*-khoa) *m* beetle, bug

escarcha (ayss-*kahr*-chah) *f* frost

escarcho (ayss-*kahr*-choa) *m* roach

escarlata (ayss-kahr-*lah*-tah) *adj* scarlet

escarnio (ayss-*kahr*-n^yoa) *m* scorn

escasez (ayss-kah-*sayth*) *f* scarcity, shortage

escaso (ayss-*kah*-soa) *adj* scarce; minor

escena (ay-*thay*-nah) *f* scene; setting

escenario (ayss-thay-*nah*-r^yoa) *m* stage

esclavo (ayss-*klah*-bhoa) *m* slave

esclusa (ayss-*kloo*-sah) *f* lock

escoba (ayss-*koa*-bhah) *f* broom

escocés (ayss-koa-*thayss*) *adj* Scottish, Scotch; *m* Scot

Escocia (ayss-*koa*-th^yah) *f* Scotland

escoger (ayss-koa-*khayr*) *v* *choose, pick

escolta (ayss-*koal*-tah) *f* escort

escoltar (ayss-koal-*tahr*) *v* escort

escombro (ayss-*koam*-broa) *m* mackerel

esconder (ayss-koan-*dayr*) *v* *hide

escribano (ayss-kree-*bhah*-noa) *m* clerk

escribir (ayss-kree-*bheer*) *v* *write; **~ a máquina** type; **papel de ~** notepaper; **por escrito** written, in writing

escrito (ayss-*kree*-toa) *m* writing

escritor (ayss-kree-*toar*) *m* writer

escritorio (ayss-kree-*toa*-r^yoa) *m* desk, bureau

escritura (ayss-kree-*too*-rah) *f* handwriting

escrupuloso (ayss-kroo-poo-*loa*-soa) *adj* careful

escuadrilla (ayss-kwah-*dhree*-l^yah) *f* squadron

escuchar (ayss-koo-*chahr*) *v* listen; eavesdrop

escuela (ayss-*kway*-lah) *f* school; **director de ~** head teacher, headmaster; **~ secundaria** secondary school

escultor (ayss-kool-*toar*) *m* sculptor

escultura (ayss-kool-*too*-rah) *f* sculpture

escupir (ayss-koo-*peer*) *v* *spit

escurridor (ayss-koo-rree-*dhoar*) *m* strainer

ese (*ay*-say) *adj* that; **ése** *pron* that

esencia (ay-*sayn*-th^yah) *f* essence

esencial (ay-sayn-*th^yahl*) *adj* essential; vital

esfera (ayss-*fay*-rah) *f* sphere; atmosphere

*esforzarse (ayss-foar-*thahr*-say) *v* try, bother

esfuerzo (ayss-*fwayr*-thoa) *m* effort; strain; stress

esgrimir (ayz-gree-*meer*) *v* fence

eslabón (ayz-lah-*bhoan*) *m* link

esmaltado (ayz-mahl-*tah*-dhoa) *adj* enamelled

esmaltar (ayz-mahl-*tahr*) *v* glaze

esmalte (ayz-*mahl*-tay) *m* enamel

esmeralda (ayz-may-*rahl*-dah) *f* emerald

esnórquel (ayz-*noar*-kayl) *m* snorkel

eso (*ay*-soa) *pron* that

espaciar (ayss-pah-*th^yahr*) *v* space

espacio (ayss-*pah*-th^yoa) *m* room;

space

espacioso (ayss-pah-*th^yoa*-soa) *adj*
spacious, roomy, large

espada (ayss-*pah*-dhah) *f* sword

espalda (ayss-*pahl*-dah) *f* back; **dolor de ~** backache

espantado (ayss-pahn-*tah*-dhoa) *adj*
frightened

espantar (ayss-pahn-*tahr*) *v* frighten

espanto (ayss-*pahn*-toa) *m* fright; horror

espantoso (ayss-pahn-*toa*-soa) *adj*
dreadful

España (ayss-*pah*-ñah) *f* Spain

español (ayss-pah-*ñoal*) *adj* Spanish;
m Spaniard

esparadrapo (ayss-pah-rah-*dhrah*-poa)
m adhesive tape, plaster

esparcir (ayss-pahr-*theer*) *v* scatter,
*shed

espárrago (ayss-*pah*-rrah-goa) *m* asparagus

especia (ayss-*pay*-th^yah) *f* spice

especial (ayss-pay-*th^yahl*) *adj* special;
peculiar, particular

especialidad (ayss-pay-th^yah-lee-*dhahdh*) *f* speciality

especialista (ayss-pay-th^yah-*leess*-tah)
m specialist

especializarse (ayss-pay-th^yah-lee-*thahr*-say) *v* specialize; **especializado** skilled

especialmente (ayss-pay-th^yahl-*mayn*-tay) *adv* especially

especie (ayss-*payth^yay*) *f* species,
breed

específico (ayss-pay-*thee*-fee-koa) *adj*
specific

espécimen (ayss-*pay*-thee-mayn) *m*
specimen

espectáculo (ayss-payk-*tah*-koo-loa) *m*
spectacle, show; **~ de variedades**
floor show

espectador (ayss-payk-tah-*dhoar*) *m*

spectator

espectro (ayss-*payk*-troa) *m* ghost;
spectrum

especular (ayss-pay-koo-*lahr*) *v* speculate

espejo (ayss-*pay*-khoa) *m* mirror, looking-glass

espeluznante (ayss-pay-looth-*nahn*-tay)
adj creepy

espera (ayss-*pay*-rah) *f* waiting

esperanza (ayss-pay-*rahn*-thah) *f*
hope; expectation

esperanzado (ayss-pay-rahn-*thah*-dhoa)
adj hopeful

esperar (ayss-pay-*rahr*) *v* hope; wait;
expect, await

espesar (ayss-pay-*sahr*) *v* thicken

espeso (ayss-*pay*-soa) *adj* thick

espesor (ayss-pay-*soar*) *m* thickness

espetón (ayss-pay-*toan*) *m* spit

espía (ayss-*pee*-ah) *m* spy

espiar (ayss-*p^yahr*) *v* peep

espina (ayss-*pee*-nah) *f* thorn; fishbone; **~ dorsal** backbone

espinacas (ayss-pee-*nah*-kahss) *fpl*
spinach

espinazo (ayss-pee-*nah*-thoa) *m* spine

espirar (ayss-pee-*rahr*) *v* expire

espíritu (ayss-*pee*-ree-too) *m* spirit;
ghost

espiritual (ayss-pee-ree-*twahl*) *adj*
spiritual

espléndido (ayss-*playn*-dee-dhoa) *adj*
splendid; glorious, enchanting,
magnificent

esplendor (ayss-playn-*doar*) *m* splendour

esponja (ayss-*poang*-khah) *f* sponge

esposa (ayss-*poa*-sah) *f* wife; **esposas**
fpl handcuffs *pl*

esposo (ayss-*poa*-soa) *m* husband

espuma (ayss-*poo*-mah) *f* froth, foam,
lather

espumante (ayss-poo-*mahn*-tay) *adj*

sparkling

espumar (ayss-poo-*mahr*) v foam

esputo (ayss-*poo*-toa) m spit

esquela (ayss-*kay*-lah) f note

esqueleto (ayss-kay-*lay*-toa) m skeleton

esquema (ayss-*kay*-mah) m diagram; scheme

esquí (ayss-*kee*) m ski; skiing; ~ **acuático** water ski; **salto de** ~ ski-jump

esquiador (ayss-kʸah-*dhoar*) m skier

esquiar (ayss-kʸ*ahr*) v ski

esquina (ayss-*kee*-nah) f corner

esquivo (ayss-*kee*-bhoa) adj shy

estable (ayss-*tah*-bhlay) adj permanent, stable

***establecer** (ayss-tah-bhlay-*thayr*) v establish

establo (ayss-*tah*-bhloa) m stable

estación (ayss-tah-*thʸoan*) f season; station; depot nAm; ~ **central** central station; ~ **de servicio** filling station; ~ **terminal** terminal

estacionamiento (ayss-tah-thʸoa-nah-mʸayn-toa) m parking lot Am; **derechos de** ~ parking fee

estacionar (ayss-tah-thʸoa-*nahr*) v park; **prohibido estacionarse** no parking

estacionario (ayss-tah-thʸoa-*nah*-rʸoa) adj stationary

estadio (ayss-*tah*-dhʸoa) m stadium

estadista (ayss-tah-*dheess*-tah) m statesman

estadística (ayss-tah-*dheess*-tee-kah) f statistics pl

Estado (ayss-*tah*-doa) m state

estado (ayss-*tah*-dhoa) m state, condition

Estados Unidos (ayss-*tah*-dhoass oo-*nee*-dhoass) the States, United States

estafa (ayss-*tah*-fah) f swindle

estafador (ayss-tah-fah-*dhoar*) m swindler

estafar (ayss-tah-*fahr*) v cheat, swindle

estallar (ayss-tah-*lʸahr*) v explode

estambre (ayss-*tahm*-bray) m/f worsted

estampa (ayss-*tahm*-pah) f engraving

estampilla (ayss-tahm-*pee*-lʸah) fMe stamp

estancia (ayss-*tahn*-thʸah) f stay

estanco (ayss-*tahng*-koa) m cigar shop, tobacconist's

estanque (ayss-*tahng*-kay) m pond

estanquero (ayss-tahng-*kay*-roa) m tobacconist

estante (ayss-*tahn*-tay) m shelf

estaño (ayss-*tah*-ñoa) m tin; pewter

***estar** (ayss-*tahr*) v *be

estatua (ayss-*tah*-twah) f statue

estatura (ayss-tah-*too*-rah) f figure

este¹ (*ayss*-tay) m east

este² (*ayss*-tay) adj this; **éste** pron this

estera (ayss-*tay*-rah) f mat

estercolero (ayss-tayr-koa-*lay*-roa) m dunghill

estéril (ayss-*tay*-reel) adj sterile

esterilizar (ayss-tay-ree-lee-*thahr*) v sterilize

estético (ayss-*tay*-tee-koa) adj aesthetic

estilo (ayss-*tee*-loa) m style

estilográfica (ayss-tee-loa-*grah*-fee-kah) f fountain-pen

estima (ayss-*tee*-mah) f esteem

estimación (ayss-tee-mah-*thʸoan*) f respect; estimate

estimar (ayss-tee-*mahr*) v esteem; estimate

estimulante (ayss-tee-moo-*lahn*-tay) m stimulant

estimular (ayss-tee-moo-*lahr*) v stimulate; urge

estímulo (ayss-*tee*-moo-loa) m impulse

estipulación (ayss-tee-poo-lah-*thʸoan*)

f stipulation

estipular (ayss-tee-poo-*lahr*) v stipulate

estirar (ayss-tee-*rahr*) v stretch

estirón (ayss-tee-*roan*) m tug

esto (*ayss*-toa) adj this

estola (ayss-*toa*-lah) f stole

estómago (ayss-*toa*-mah-goa) m stomach; **dolor de ~** stomach-ache

estorbar (ayss-toar-*bhahr*) v disturb, embarrass

estornino (ayss-toar-*nee*-noa) m starling

estornudar (ayss-toar-noo-*dhahr*) v sneeze

estrangular (ayss-trahng-goo-*lahr*) v choke, strangle

estrato (ayss-*trah*-toa) m layer

estrechar (ayss-tray-*chahr*) v tighten

estrecho (ayss-*tray*-choa) adj narrow; tight

estrella (ayss-*tray*-lyah) f star

estremecido (ayss-tray-may-*thee*-dhoa) adj shivery

estremecimiento (ayss-tray-may-thee-*myayn*-toa) m shudder

estreñido (ayss-tray-*ñee*-dhoa) adj constipated

estreñimiento (ayss-tray-ñee-*myayn*-toa) m constipation

estribo (ayss-*tree*-bhoa) m stirrup

estribor (ayss-tree-*bhoar*) m starboard

estricto (ayss-*treek*-toa) adj strict

estrofa (ayss-*troa*-fah) f stanza

estropeado (ayss-troa-pay-ah-*dhoa*) adj broken; crippled

estropear (ayss-troa-pay-*ahr*) v mess up

estructura (ayss-trook-*too*-rah) f structure; fabric

estuario (ayss-*twah*-ryoa) m estuary

estuco (ayss-*too*-koa) m plaster

estuche (ayss-*too*-chay) m case

estudiante (ayss-too-*dhyahn*-tay) m

student

estudiar (ayss-too-*dhyahr*) v study

estudio (ayss-*too*-dhyoa) m study

estufa (ayss-*too*-fah) f stove; **~ de gas** gas stove

estupefaciente (ayss-too-pay-fah-*thyayn*-tay) m drug

estupendo (ayss-too-*payn*-doa) adj wonderful

estúpido (ayss-*too*-pee-dhoa) adj stupid; dumb

etapa (ay-*tah*-pah) f stage

etcétera (ayt-*thay*-tay-rah) and so on, etcetera

éter (*ay*-tayr) m ether

eternidad (ay-tayr-nee-*dhahdh*) f eternity

eterno (ay-*tayr*-noa) adj eternal

etíope (ay-*tee*-oa-pay) adj Ethiopian; m Ethiopian

Etiopía (ay-*tyoa*-pyah) f Ethiopia

etiqueta (ay-tee-*kay*-tah) f tag

Europa (ayoo-*roa*-pah) f Europe

europeo (ayoo-roa-*pay*-oa) adj European; m European

evacuar (ay-bhah-*kwahr*) v evacuate

evaluar (ay-bhah-*lwahr*) v evaluate, estimate

evangelio (ay-bhahng-*khay*-lyoa) m gospel

evaporar (ay-bhah-poa-*rahr*) v evaporate

evasión (ay-bhah-*syoan*) f escape

eventual (ay-bhayn-*twahl*) adj eventual; possible

evidente (ay-bhee-*dhayn*-tay) adj evident; self-evident

evidentemente (ay-bhee-dhayn-tay-*mayn*-tay) adv apparently

evitar (ay-bhee-*tahr*) v avoid

evolución (ay-bhoa-loo-*thyoan*) f evolution

exactamente (ayk-sahk-tah-*mayn*-tay) adv exactly

exactitud (ayk-sahk-tee-*toodh*) f correctness

exacto (ayk-*sahk*-toa) adj precise, exact, accurate

exagerar (ayk-sah-khay-*rahr*) v exaggerate

examen (ayk-*sah*-mayn) m examination

examinar (ayk-sah-mee-*nahr*) v examine

excavación (ayks-kah-bhah-*th*ᵧ*oan*) f excavation

exceder (ayk-thay-*dhayr*) v exceed

excelencia (ayk-thay-*layn*-th*ᵧ*ah) f excellence

excelente (ayk-thay-*layn*-tay) adj excellent, fine

excéntrico (ayk-*thayn*-tree-koa) adj eccentric

excepción (ayk-thayp-*th*ᵧ*oan*) f exception

excepcional (ayk-thayp-th*ᵧ*oa-*nahl*) adj exceptional

excepto (ayk-*thayp*-toa) prep except

excesivo (ayk-thay-*see*-bhoa) adj excessive

exceso (ayk-*thay*-soa) m excess; ~ **de velocidad** speeding

excitación (ayk-thee-tah-*th*ᵧ*oan*) f excitement

excitante (ayk-thee-*tahn*-tay) adj exciting

excitar (ayk-thee-*tahr*) v excite

exclamación (ayks-klah-mah-*th*ᵧ*oan*) f exclamation

exclamar (ayks-klah-*mahr*) v exclaim

*excluir (ayks-*klweer*) v exclude

exclusivamente (ayks-kloo-see-bhah-*mayn*-tay) adv exclusively, solely

exclusivo (ayks-kloo-*see*-bhoa) adj exclusive

excursión (ayks-koor-*s*ᵧ*oan*) f trip, excursion

excusa (ayks-*koo*-sah) f apology, excuse

excusar (ayks-koo-*sahr*) v excuse

exención (ayk-sayn-*th*ᵧ*oan*) f exemption

exento (ayk-*sayn*-toa) adj exempt; ~ **de impuestos** duty-free

exhalar (ayk-sah-*lahr*) v exhale

exhausto (ayk-*souss*-toa) adj overtired

exhibir (ayk-see-*bheer*) v exhibit, display

exigencia (ayk-see-*khayn*-th*ᵧ*ah) f demand

exigente (ayk-see-*khayn*-tay) adj particular

exigir (ayk-see-*kheer*) v demand

exiliado (ayk-see-*l*ᵧ*ah*-dhoa) m exile

exilio (ayk-*see*-l*ᵧ*oa) m exile

eximir (ayk-see-*meer*) v exempt

existencia (ayk-seess-*tayn*-th*ᵧ*ah) f existence; **existencias** fpl supply, stock; ***tener en ~** stock

existir (ayk-seess-*teer*) v exist

éxito (*ayk*-see-toa) m success, luck; hit; **de ~** successful; ***tener ~** manage, succeed

exorbitante (ayk-soar-bhee-*tahn*-tay) adj prohibitive

exótico (ayk-*soa*-tee-koa) adj exotic

expansión (ayks-pahn-*s*ᵧ*oan*) f expansion

expedición (ayks-pay-dhee-*th*ᵧ*oan*) f expedition

expediente (ayks-pay-*dh*ᵧ*ayn*-tay) m file

experiencia (ayks-pay-r*ᵧ*ayn-th*ᵧ*ah) f experience

experimentar (ayks-pay-ree-mayn-*tahr*) v experiment; experience; **experimentado** experienced

experimento (ayks-pay-ree-*mayn*-toa) m experiment

experto (ayks-*payr*-toa) m expert

expirar (ayks-pee-*rahr*) v expire

explanada (ayks-plah-*nah*-dhah) *f* esplanade

explicable (ayks-plee-*kah*-bhlay) *adj* accountable

explicación (ayks-plee-kah-*thᵞoan*) *f* explanation

explicar (ayks-plee-*kahr*) *v* explain; account for

explícito (ayks-*plee*-thee-toa) *adj* express, explicit

explorador (ayks-ploa-rah-*dhoar*) *m* scout, boy scout

exploradora (ayks-ploa-rah-*dhoa*-rah) *f* girl guide

explorar (ayks-ploa-*rahr*) *v* explore

explosión (ayks-ploa-*sᵞoan*) *f* explosion, blast; outbreak

explosivo (ayks-ploa-*see*-bhoa) *adj* explosive; *m* explosive

explotar (ayks-ploa-*tahr*) *v* exploit

*** exponer** (ayks-poa-*nayr*) *v* exhibit

exportación (ayks-poar-tah-*thᵞoan*) *f* exportation, export

exportar (ayks-poar-*tahr*) *v* export

exposición (ayks-poa-see-*thᵞoan*) *f* exposition, exhibition, display, show; exposure; ~ **de arte** art exhibition

exposímetro (ayks-poa-*see*-may-troa) *m* exposure meter

expresar (ayks-pray-*sahr*) *v* express

expresión (ayks-pray-*sᵞoan*) *f* expression

expresivo (ayks-pray-*see*-bhoa) *adj* expressive

expreso (ayks-*pray*-soa) *adj* explicit; express; **por** ~ special delivery

expulsar (ayks-pool-*sahr*) *v* chase; expel

exquisito (ayks-kee-*see*-toa) *adj* exquisite; delicious

éxtasis (*ayks*-tah-seess) *m* ecstasy

*** extender** (ayks-tayn-*dayr*) *v* *spread, expand

extenso (ayks-*tayn*-soa) *adj* comprehensive, extensive

extenuar (ayks-tay-*nwahr*) *v* exhaust

exterior (ayks-tay-rᵞ*oar*) *adj* external, exterior; *m* exterior, outside

externo (ayks-*tayr*-noa) *adj* outward

extinguir (ayks-teeng-*geer*) *v* extinguish

extintor (ayks-teen-*toar*) *m* fire-extinguisher

extorsión (ayks-toar-*sᵞoan*) *f* extortion

extorsionar (ayks-toar-sᵞoa-*nahr*) *v* extort

extra (*ayks*-trah) *adj* extra

extracto (ayks-*trahk*-toa) *m* excerpt

*** extraer** (ayks-trah-*ayr*) *v* extract

extranjero (ayks-trahng-*khay*-roa) *adj* alien, foreign; *m* alien, foreigner; stranger; **en el** ~ abroad

extrañar (ayks-trah-*ñahr*) *v* amaze, surprise; banish

extraño (ayks-*trah*-ñoa) *adj* foreign, strange; peculiar, queer, funny

extraoficial (ayks-trah-oa-fee-*thᵞahl*) *adj* unofficial

extraordinario (ayks-trah-oar-dhee-*nah*-rᵞoa) *adj* extraordinary, exceptional

extravagante (ayks-trah-bhah-*gahn*-tay) *adj* extravagant

extraviar (ayks-trah-*bhᵞahr*) *v* *mislay

extremo (ayks-*tray*-moa) *adj* extreme; very, utmost; *m* extreme; end

exuberante (ayk-soo-bhay-*rahn*-tay) *adj* exuberant

F

fábrica (*fah*-bhree-kah) *f* factory; works *pl*, mill; ~ **de gas** gasworks

fabricante (fah-bhree-*kahn*-tay) *m* manufacturer

fabricar (fah-bhree-*kahr*) *v* manufacture

fábula (*fah*-bhoo-lah) *f* fable

fácil (*fah*-theel) *adj* easy

facilidad (fah-thee-lee-*dhahdh*) *f* ease; facility

facilitar (fah-thee-lee-*tahr*) *v* facilitate

factible (fahk-*tee*-bhlay) *adj* attainable

factor (fahk-*toar*) *m* factor

factura (fahk-*too*-rah) *f* invoice

facturar (fahk-too-*rahr*) *v* bill

facultad (fah-kool-*tahdh*) *f* faculty

fachada (fah-*chah*-dhah) *f* façade

faisán (figh-*sahn*) *m* pheasant

faja (*fah*-khah) *f* strip; girdle

falda (*fahl*-dah) *f* skirt

faldón (fahl-*doan*) *m* gable

falsificación (fahl-see-fee-kah-th^yoan) *f* fake

falsificar (fahl-see-fee-*kahr*) *v* forge, counterfeit

falso (*fahl*-soa) *adj* false; untrue

falta (*fahl*-tah) *f* error; want, lack; offence; **sin ~** without fail

faltar (fahl-*tahr*) *v* fail

fallar (fah-l^yahr) *v* fail

*****fallecer** (fah-l^yay-*thayr*) *v* depart

fama (*fah*-mah) *f* fame; **de ~ mundial** world-famous; **de mala ~** notorious

familia (fah-*mee*-l^yah) *f* family

familiar (fah-mee-l^y*ahr*) *adj* familiar

famoso (fah-*moa*-soa) *adj* famous

fanal (fah-*nahl*) *m* headlamp

fanático (fah-*nah*-tee-koa) *adj* fanatical

fantasía (fahn-tah-*see*-ah) *f* fantasy

fantasma (fahn-*tahz*-mah) *m* spook, phantom, ghost

fantástico (fahn-*tahss*-tee-koa) *adj* fantastic

farallón (fah-rah-l^y*oan*) *m* cliff

fardo (*fahr*-dhoa) *m* load

farmacéutico (fahr-mah-*thay^{oo}*-tee-koa) *m* chemist

farmacia (fahr-*mah*-th^yah) *f* chemist's,

pharmacy; drugstore *nAm*

farmacología (fahr-mah-koa-loa-*khee*-ah) *f* pharmacology

faro (*fah*-roa) *m* headlight; lighthouse

farol trasero (fah-*roal* trah-*say*-roa) taillight

farsa (*fahr*-sah) *f* farce

fascismo (fah-*theez*-moa) *m* fascism

fascista (fah-*theess*-tah) *adj* fascist; *m* fascist

fase (*fah*-say) *f* stage, phase

fastidiar (fahss-tee-dh^y*ahr*) *v* annoy, bother

fastidioso (fahss-tee-dh^y*oa*-soa) *adj* difficult

fatal (fah-*tahl*) *adj* fatal; mortal

favor (fah-*bhoar*) *m* favour; **a ~ de** on behalf of; **por ~** please

favorable (fah-bhoa-*rah*-bhlay) *adj* favourable

*****favorecer** (fah-bhoa-ray-*thayr*) *v* favour

favorecido (fah-bhoa-ray-*thee*-dhoa) *m* payee

favorito (fah-bhoa-*ree*-toa) *adj* pet; *m* favourite

fe (fay) *f* faith

febrero (fay-*bhray*-roa) February

febril (fay-*bhreel*) *adj* feverish

fecundo (fay-*koon*-doa) *adj* fertile

fecha (*fay*-chah) *f* date

federación (fay-dhay-rah-th^yoan) *f* federation

federal (fay-dhay-*rahl*) *adj* federal

felicidad (fay-lee-thee-*dhahdh*) *f* happiness

felicitación (fay-lee-thee-tah-th^yoan) *f* congratulation

felicitar (fay-lee-thee-*tahr*) *v* congratulate

feliz (fay-*leeth*) *adj* happy

femenino (fay-may-*nee*-noa) *adj* feminine; female

fenómeno (fay-*noa*-may-noa) *m* phenomenon

feo (*fay*-oa) *adj* ugly

feria (*fay*-r^yah) *f* fair

fermentar (fayr-mayn-*tahr*) *v* ferment

feroz (fay-*roath*) *adj* wild

ferretería (fay-rray-tay-*ree*-ah) *f* hardware store

ferrocarril (fay-rroa-kah-*rreel*) *m* railway; railroad *nAm*

fértil (*fayr*-teel) *adj* fertile

fertilidad (fayr-tee-lee-*dhahdh*) *f* fertility

festival (fayss-tee-*bhahl*) *m* festival

festivo (fayss-*tee*-bhoa) *adj* festive

feudal (fay⁰⁰-*dhahl*) *adj* feudal

fiable (f^yah-bhlay) *adj* reliable

fianza (f^yahn-thah) *f* security; bail; deposit

fiasco (f^yahss-koa) *m* failure

fibra (*fee*-bhrah) *f* fibre

ficción (feek-th^yoan) *f* fiction

ficha (*fee*-chah) *f* chip, token

fiebre (f^yay-bhray) *f* fever; ~ del heno hay fever

fiel (f^yayl) *adj* faithful, true

fieltro (f^yayl-troa) *m* felt

fiero (f^yay-roa) *adj* fierce

fiesta (f^yayss-tah) *f* feast; party; holiday

figura (fee-*goo*-rah) *f* figure

figurarse (fee-goo-*rahr*-say) *v* imagine

fijador (foo khah *dhoar*) *m* setting lotion

fijar (fee-*khahr*) *v* attach; **fijarse en** mind

fijo (*fee*-khoa) *adj* fixed; permanent

fila (*fee*-lah) *f* row, rank

Filipinas (fee-lee-*pee*-nahss) *fpl* Philippines *pl*

filipino (fee-lee-*pee*-noa) *adj* Philippine; *m* Filipino

filmar (feel-*mahr*) *v* film

filme (*feel*-may) *m* movie

filosofía (fee-loa-soa-*fee*-ah) *f* philos-

ophy

filosófico (fee-loa-*soa*-fee-koa) *adj* philosophical

filósofo (fee-*loa*-soa-foa) *m* philosopher

filtrar (feel-*trahr*) *v* strain

filtro (*feel*-troa) *m* filter; ~ **de aire** air-filter; ~ **del aceite** oil filter

fin (feen) *m* end; aim, purpose; **a** ~ **de** so that; **al** ~ at last

final (fee-*nahl*) *adj* eventual, final; *m* end; **al** ~ at last

financiar (fee-nahn-th^yahr) *v* finance

financiero (fee-nahn-th^yay-roa) *adj* financial

finanzas (fee-*nahn*-thahss) *fpl* finances *pl*

finca (*feeng*-kah) *f* premises *pl*

fingir (feeng-*kheer*) *v* pretend

finlandés (feen-lahn-*dayss*) *adj* Finnish; *m* Finn

Finlandia (teen-*lahn*-d^yah) *f* Finland

fino (*fee*-noa) *adj* delicate, fine; sheer

firma (*feer*-mah) *f* signature; firm

firmar (feer-*mahr*) *v* sign

firme (*feer*-may) *adj* steady, firm; secure

física (*fee*-see-kah) *f* physics

físico (*fee*-see-koa) *adj* physical; *m* physicist

fisiología (fee-s^yoa-loa-*khee*-ah) *f* physiology

flaco (*flah*-koa) *adj* thin

flamenco (flah-*mayng*-koa) *m* flamingo

flauta (*flou*-tah) *f* flute

flecha (*flay*-chah) *t* arrow

flexible (flayk-*see*-bhlay) *adj* flexible; supple, elastic

flojel (floa-*khayl*) *m* down

flojo (*floa*-khoa) *adj* weak

flor (floar) *f* flower

florista (floa-*reess*-tah) *m* florist

floristería (floa-reess-tay-*ree*-ah) *f*

flower-shop

flota (*floa*-tah) *f* fleet

flotador (floa-tah-*dhoar*) *m* float

flotar (floa-*tahr*) *v* float

fluido (*floo*-ee-dhoa) *adj* fluid; *m* fluid

*****fluir** (flweer) *v* flow, stream

foca (*foa*-kah) *f* seal

foco (*foa*-koa) *m* focus; *mMe* light bulb

folklore (foal-*kloa*-ray) *m* folklore

folleto (foa-*lʸay*-toa) *m* brochure

fondo (*foan*-doa) *m* background; ground, bottom; *mMe* slip; **fondos** *mpl* fund

fonético (foa-*nay*-tee-koa) *adj* phonetic

foque (*foa*-kay) *m* foresail

forastero (foa-rahss-*tay*-roa) *m* foreigner; stranger

forma (*foar*-mah) *f* form, shape

formación (foar-mah-*thʸoan*) *f* formation

formal (foar-*mahl*) *adj* formal

formalidad (foar-mah-lee-*dhahdh*) *f* formality

formar (foar-*mahr*) *v* form, shape; educate

formato (foar-*mah*-toa) *m* size

formidable (foar-mee-*dhah*-bhlay) *adj* huge

fórmula (*foar*-moo-lah) *f* formula

formulario (foar-moo-*lah*-rʸoa) *m* form; ~ **de matriculación** registration form

forro (*foa*-rroa) *m* lining

fortaleza (foar-tah-*lay*-thah) *f* fortress, fort

fortuna (foar-*too*-nah) *f* fortune

forúnculo (foa-*roong*-koo-loa) *m* boil

*****forzar** (foar-*thahr*) *v* force; strain

forzosamente (foar-thoa-sah-*mayn*-tay) *adv* by force

foso (*foa*-soa) *m* moat

foto (*foa*-toa) *f* photo

fotocopia (foa-toa-*koa*-pʸah) *f* photostat

fotografía (foa-toa-grah-*fee*-ah) *f* photograph; photography; ~ **de pasaporte** passport photograph

fotografiar (foa-toa-grah-*fʸahr*) *v* photograph

fotógrafo (foa-*toa*-grah-foa) *m* photographer

fracasado (frah-kah-*sah*-dhoa) *adj* unsuccessful

fracaso (frah-*kah*-soa) *m* failure

fracción (frahk-*thʸoan*) *f* fraction

fractura (frahk-*too*-rah) *f* fracture, break

fracturar (frahk-too-*rahr*) *v* fracture

frágil (*frah*-kheel) *adj* fragile

fragmento (frahg-*mayn*-toa) *m* fragment, piece; extract

frambuesa (frahm-*bway*-sah) *f* raspberry

francés (frahn-*thayss*) *adj* French; *m* Frenchman

Francia (*frahn*-thʸah) *f* France

franco (*frahng*-koa) *adj* postage paid, post-paid

francotirador (frahng-koa-tee-rah-*dhoar*) *m* sniper

franela (frah-*nay*-lah) *f* flannel

franja (*frahng*-khah) *f* fringe

franqueo (frahng-*kay*-oa) *m* postage

frasco (*frahss*-koa) *m* flask

frase (*frah*-say) *f* sentence; phrase

fraternidad (frah-tayr-nee-*dhahdh*) *f* fraternity

fraude (*frou*-dhay) *m* fraud

frecuencia (fray-*kwayn*-thʸah) *f* frequency

frecuentar (fray-kwayn-*tahr*) *v* associate with

frecuente (fray-*kwayn*-tay) *adj* frequent

frecuentemente (fray-kwayn-tay-*mayn*-tay) *adv* frequently, often

*fregar (fray-*gahr*) *v* wash up; scrub

*freír (fray-*eer*) *v* fry

frenar (fray-*nahr*) *v* slow down

freno (*fray*-noa) *m* brake; ~ **de mano** hand-brake; ~ **de pie** foot-brake

frente (*frayn*-tay) *f* forehead; *m* front

fresa (*fray*-sah) *f* strawberry

fresco (*frayss*-koa) *adj* fresh; chilly, cool

fricción (freek-*th*ᵛ*oan*) *f* friction

frigorífico (free-goa-*ree*-fee-koa) *m* fridge

frío (*free*-oa) *adj* cold; *m* cold

frontera (froan-*tay*-rah) *f* frontier, border; boundary, bound

frotar (froa-*tahr*) *v* rub

fruta (*froo*-tah) *f* fruit

fruto (*froo*-toa) *m* fruit

fuego (*fway*-goa) *m* fire

fuente (*fwayn*-tay) *f* source, fountain; dish

fuera (*fway*-rah) *adv* out; off, away; ~ **de** outside, out of; ~ **de lugar** misplaced; ~ **de temporada** off season

fuerte (*fwayr*-tay) *adj* powerful, strong; mighty; loud

fuerza (*fwayr*-thah) *f* force; power, might, energy; strength; ~ **de voluntad** will-power; ~ **motriz** driving force; **fuerzas armadas** military force, armed forces

fugitivo (foo-khee-*tee*-bhoa) *m* runaway

fumador (foo-mah-*dhoar*) *m* smoker; **compartimento para fumadores** smoker

fumar (foo-*mahr*) *v* smoke; **prohibido** ~ no smoking

función (foon-*th*ᵛ*oan*) *f* function

funcionamiento (foon-th*ᵛ*oa-nah-m*ᵛ*ayn-toa) *m* working, operation

funcionar (foon-th*ᵛ*oa-*nahr*) *v* work, operate

funcionario (foon-th*ᵛ*oa-nah-r*ᵛ*oa) *m* civil servant

funda (*foon*-dah) *f* sleeve; ~ **de almohada** pillow-case

fundación (foon-dah-*th*ᵛ*oan*) *f* foundation

fundamentado (foon-dah-mayn-*tah*-dhoa) *adj* well-founded

fundamental (foon-dah-mayn-*tahl*) *adj* fundamental, basic

fundamento (foon-dah-*mayn*-toa) *m* basis, base

fundar (foon-*dahr*) *v* found

fundir (foon-*deer*) *v* melt

funerales (foo-nay-*rah*-layss) *mpl* funeral

furgoneta (foor-goa-*nay*-tah) *f* delivery van

furioso (foo-r*ᵛ*oa-soa) *adj* furious

furor (foo-*roar*) *m* anger, rage

fusible (foo-*see*-bhlay) *m* fuse

fusil (foo-*seel*) *m* gun

fusión (foo-s*ᵛ*oan) *f* merger

fútbol (*foot*-bhoal) *m* soccer; football

fútil (*foo*-teel) *adj* petty

futuro (foo-*too*-roa) *adj* future

G

gabinete (gah-bhee-*nay*-tay) *m* cabinet

gafas (*gah*-fahss) *fpl* goggles *pl*; ~ **de sol** sun-glasses *pl*

gaitero (gigh-*tay*-roa) *adj* gay

galería (gah-lay-*ree*-ah) *f* gallery; ~ **de arte** art gallery

galgo (*gahl*-goa) *m* greyhound

galope (gah-*loa*-pay) *m* gallop

galleta (gah-*l*ᵛ*ay*-tah) *f* biscuit

gallina (gah-*l*ᵛ*ee*-nah) *f* hen

gallo (*gah*-l*ᵛ*oa) *m* cock; ~ **de bosque** grouse

gamba (*gahm*-bah) *f* prawn

gamuza (gah-*moo*-thah) f suede
gana (*gah*-nah) f fancy; appetite
ganado (gah-*nah*-dhoa) m cattle pl
ganador (gah-nah-*dhoar*) adj winning
ganancia (gah-*nahn*-thʸah) f gain, profit
ganar (gah-*nahr*) v gain; *make, earn
ganas (*gah*-nahss) fpl desire
gancho (*gahn*-choa) m hook
ganga (*gahng*-gah) f bargain
garaje (gah-*rah*-khay) m garage; **dejar en ~** garage
garante (gah-*rahn*-tay) m guarantor
garantía (gah-rahn-*tee*-ah) f guarantee
garantizar (gah-rahn-tee-*thahr*) v guarantee
garganta (gahr-*gahn*-tah) f throat; **dolor de ~** sore throat
garra (*gah*-rrah) f claw
garrafa (gah-*rrah*-fah) f carafe
garrote (gah-*rroa*-tay) m club, cudgel
garza (*gahr*-thah) f heron
gas (gahss) m gas; **cocina de ~** gas cooker
gasa (*gah*-sah) f gauze
gasolina (gah-soa-*lee*-nah) f petrol; gasoline nAm, gas nAm; **puesto de ~** petrol station
gastado (gahss-*tah*-dhoa) adj worn-out, worn, threadbare
gastar (gahss-*tahr*) v *spend; wear out
gasto (*gahss*-toa) m expense, expenditure; **gastos de viaje** fare, travelling expenses
gástrico (*gahss*-tree-koa) adj gastric
gastrónomo (gahss-*troa*-noa-moa) m gourmet
gatear (gah-tay-*ahr*) v *creep
gatillo (gah-*tee*-lʸoa) m trigger
gato (*gah*-toa) m cat; jack
gaviota (gah-*bhʸoa*-tah) f gull, seagull
gema (*khay*-mah) f gem
gemelos (khay-*may*-loass) mpl twins

pl; binoculars pl; cuff-links pl; **~ de campaña** field glasses
***gemir** (khay-*meer*) v groan, moan
generación (khay-nay-rah-*thʸoan*) f generation
generador (khay-nay-rah-*dhoar*) m generator
general (khay-nay-*rahl*) adj general; universal, public, broad; m general; **en ~** in general
generalmente (khay-nay-rahl-*mayn*-tay) adv mostly, as a rule
generar (khay-nay-*rahr*) v generate
género (*khay*-nay-roa) m gender; kind
generosidad (khay-nay-roa-see-*dhahdh*) f generosity
generoso (khay-nay-*roa*-soa) adj generous, liberal
genial (khay-*nʸahl*) adj genial
genio (*khay*-nʸoa) m genius
genital (khay-nee-*tahl*) adj genital
gente (*khayn*-tay) f folk; people pl
gentil (khayn-*teel*) adj gentle
genuino (khay-*nwee*-noa) adj genuine
geografía (khay-oa-grah-*fee*-ah) f geography
geográfico (khay-oa-*grah*-fee-koa) adj geographical
geología (khay-oa-loa-*khee*-ah) f geology
geometría (khay-oa-may-*tree*-ah) f geometry
gerencial (khay-rayn-*thʸahl*) adj administrative
germen (*khayr*-mayn) m germ
gesticular (khayss-tee-koo-*lahr*) v gesticulate
gestión (khayss-*tʸoan*) f administration, management
gesto (*khayss*-toa) m sign
gigante (khee-*gahn*-tay) m giant
gigantesco (khee-gahn-*tayss*-koa) adj enormous, gigantic
gimnasia (kheem-*nah*-sʸah) f gymnas-

tics *pl*

gimnasio (kheem-*nah*-sᵛoa) *m* gymnasium

gimnasta (kheem-*nahss*-tah) *m* gymnast

ginecólogo (khee-nay-*koa*-loa-goa) *m* gynaecologist

girar (khee-*rahr*) *v* turn

giro (*khee*-roa) *m* draft; ~ **postal** postal order

gitano (khee-*tah*-noa) *m* gipsy

glaciar (glah-*thᵛahr*) *m* glacier

glándula (*glahn*-doo-lah) *f* gland

globo (*gloa*-bhoa) *m* globe; balloon

gloria (*gloa*-rᵛah) *f* glory

glorieta (gloa-rᵛay-tah) *f* roundabout

glosario (gloa-*sah*-rᵛoa) *m* vocabulary

glotón (gloa-*toan*) *adj* greedy

gobernador (goa-bhayr-nah-*dhoar*) *m* governor

gobernante (goa-bhayr-*nahn*-tay) *m* ruler

***gobernar** (goa-bhayr-*nahr*) *v* reign, rule

gobierno (goa-*bhᵛayr*-noa) *m* government, rule; ~ **de la casa** housekeeping

goce (*goa*-thay) *m* enjoyment

gol (goal) *m* goal

golf (goalf) *m* golf; **campo de ~** golf-links

golfo (*goal*-foa) *m* gulf

golondrina (goa-loan-*dree*-nah) *f* swallow

golosina (goa-loa-*see*-nah) *f* delicacy; **golosinas** sweets; candy *nAm*

golpe (*goal*-pay) *m* blow; knock, bump; ***dar golpes** bump

golpear (goal-pay-*ahr*) *v* *beat, knock, *strike; thump, tap

golpecito (goal-pay-*thee*-toa) *m* tap

gollerías (goa-lᵛay-*ree*-ahss) *fpl* delicatessen

goma (*goa*-mah) *f* gum; ~ **de borrar**

eraser, rubber; ~ **de mascar** chewing-gum; ~ **espumada** foam-rubber

góndola (*goan*-doa-lah) *f* gondola

gordo (*goar*-dhoa) *adj* big; fat, stout

gorra (*goa*-rrah) *f* cap

gorrión (goa-rrᵛoan) *m* sparrow

gorro (*goa*-rroa) *m* cap; ~ **de baño** bathing-cap

gota (*goa*-tah) *f* drop; gout

gotear (goa-tay-*ahr*) *v* leak

goteo (goa-*tay*-oa) *m* leak

gozar (goa-*thahr*) *v* enjoy

grabación (grah-bhah-*thᵛoan*) *f* recording

grabado (grah-*bhah*-dhoa) *m* engraving; picture, print

grabador (grah-bhah-*dhoar*) *m* engraver

grabar (grah-*bhahr*) *v* engrave

gracia (*grah*-thᵛah) *f* grace

gracias (*grah*-thᵛahss) thank you

gracioso (grah-*thᵛoa*-soa) *adj* funny, humorous; graceful

grado (*grah*-dhoa) *m* degree; grade; **a tal ~** so

gradual (grah-*dhwahl*) *adj* gradual

graduar (grah-*dhwahr*) *v* grade; **graduarse** *v* graduate

gráfico (*grah*-fee-koa) *adj* graphic; *m* graph, chart, diagram

gramática (grah-*mah*-tee-kah) *f* grammar

gramatical (grah-mah-tee-*kahl*) *adj* grammatical

gramo (*grah*-moa) *m* gram

gramófono (grah-*moa*-foa-noa) *m* gramophone

Gran Bretaña (grahn bray-*tah*-ñah) Great Britain

grande (*grahn*-day) *adj* big; great, large, major

grandeza (grahn-*day*-thah) *f* greatness; grandness

grandioso (grahn-*d^yoa*-soa) *adj* superb, magnificent

granero (grah-*nay*-roa) *m* barn

granito (grah-*nee*-toa) *m* granite

granizo (grah-*nee*-thoa) *m* hail

granja (*grahng*-khah) *f* farm

granjera (grahng-*khay*-rah) *f* farmer's wife

granjero (grahng-*khay*-roa) *m* farmer

grano (*grah*-noa) *m* grain; corn; pimple

grapa (*grah*-pah) *f* clamp; staple

grasa (*grah*-sah) *f* fat, grease; *fMe* shoe polish

grasiento (grah-*s^yayn*-toa) *adj* fatty, greasy

graso (*grah*-soa) *adj* fat

grasoso (grah-*soa*-soa) *adj* greasy

gratis (*grah*-teess) *adv* free of charge

gratitud (grah-tee-*toodh*) *f* gratitude

grato (*grah*-toa) *adj* enjoyable

gratuito (grah-*twee*-toa) *adj* gratis, free of charge, free

grava (*grah*-bhah) *f* gravel

grave (*grah*-bhay) *adj* grave; bad

gravedad (grah-bhay-*dhahdh*) *f* gravity

Grecia (*gray*-th^yah) *f* Greece

griego (gr^yay-goa) *adj* Greek; *m* Greek

grieta (gr^yay-tah) *f* cleft, chasm; cave

grifo (*gree*-foa) *m* tap; faucet *nAm*

grillo (*gree*-l^yoa) *m* cricket

gripe (*gree*-pay) *f* influenza, flu

gris (greess) *adj* grey

gritar (gree-*tahr*) *v* cry; yell, scream, shout

grito (*gree*-toa) *m* cry; yell, scream, shout

grosella (groa-*say*-l^yah) *f* currant; ~ **espinosa** gooseberry; ~ **negra** black-currant

grosero (groa-*say*-roa) *adj* gross; coarse, rude, impertinent

grotesco (groa-*tayss*-koa) *adj* ludicrous

grúa (*groo*-ah) *f* crane

gruesa (*grway*-sah) *f* gross

grueso (*grway*-soa) *adj* corpulent

grumo (*groo*-moa) *m* lump

*****gruñir** (groo-*ñeer*) *v* growl

grupo (*groo*-poa) *m* group; party, set, bunch

gruta (*groo*-tah) *f* grotto

guante (*gwahn*-tay) *m* glove

guapo (*gwah*-poa) *adj* handsome

guarda (*gwahr*-dhah) *m* custodian

guardabarros (gwahr-dhah-*bhah*-rroass) *m* mud-guard

guardabosques (gwahr-dhah-*bhoass*-kayss) *m* forester

guardar (gwahr-*dhahr*) *v* *keep, *put away; guard; ~ **con llave** lock up; **guardarse** *v* beware

guardarropa (gwahr-dhah-*rroa*-pah) *m* wardrobe; cloakroom; checkroom *nAm*

guardería (gwahr-dhay-*ree*-ah) *f* nursery

guardia (*gwahr*-dh^yah) *f* guard; *m* policeman; ~ **personal** bodyguard

guardián (gwahr-*dh^yahn*) *m* attendant, warden; caretaker

guateque (gwah-*tay*-kay) *m* party

guerra (*gay*-rrah) *f* war; ~ **mundial** world war

guía (*gee*-ah) *m* guide; *f* guidebook; ~ **telefónica** telephone directory; telephone book *Am*

guiar (g^yahr) *v* guide

guijarro (gee-*khah*-rroa) *m* pebble

guión (g^yoan) *m* dash; hyphen

guisante (gee-*sahn*-tay) *m* pea

guisar (gee-*sahr*) *v* cook

guiso (*gee*-soa) *m* dish

guitarra (gee-*tah*-rrah) *f* guitar

gusano (goo-*sah*-noa) *m* worm

gustar (gooss-*tahr*) *v* care for, like; fancy

gusto (*gooss*-toa) *m* taste; **con mucho ~** gladly

gustosamente (gooss toa sah *mayn* tay) *adv* willingly, gladly

H

*haber (ah-*bhayr*) *v* *have

hábil (*ah*-bheel) *adj* able, skilful, skilled

habilidad (ah-bhee-lee-*dhahdh*) *f* ability; skill, art

habitable (ah-bhee-*tah*-bhlay) *adj* inhabitable, habitable

habitación (ah-bhee-tah-*th*ʸ*oan*) *f* room; **~ para huéspedes** guestroom

habitante (ah-bhee-*tahn*-tay) *m* inhabitant

habitar (ah-bhee-*tahr*) *v* inhabit

hábito (*ah*-bhee-toa) *m* habit

habitual (ah-bhee-*twahl*) *adj* habitual

habitualmente (ah-bhee-twahl-*mayn*-tay) *adv* usually

habla (*ah*-bhlah) *f* speech

habladuría (ah-bhlah-dhoo-*ree*-ah) *f* rubbish

hablar (ah-*bhlahr*) *v* *speak, talk

*hacer (ah-*thayr*) *v* act; *do; *have, cause to, *make; **hace** ago; ***hacerse** *v* *become; *grow, *go, *get

hacia (*ah*-thʸah) *prep* at, towards, to; about; **~ abajo** down; **~ adelante** forward; **~ arriba** upwards, up; **~ atrás** backwards

hacienda (ah-*th*ʸ*ayn*-dah) *f* estate

hacha (*ah*-chah) *f* axe

hada (*ah*-dhah) *f* fairy; **cuento de hadas** fairytale

halcón (ahl-*koan*) *m* hawk

halibut (ah-lee-*bhoot*) *m* halibut

hallar (ah-*lʸahr*) *v* *come across

hallazgo (ah-*lʸahdh*-goa) *m* finding

hamaca (ah-*mah*-kah) *f* hammock

hambre (*ahm* bray) *f* hunger

hambriento (ahm-*br*ʸ*ayn*-toa) *adj* hungry

harina (ah-*ree*-nah) *f* flour

harto de (*ahr*-toa day) fed up with, tired of

hasta (*ahss*-tah) *prep* to, till, until; **~ ahora** so far; **~ que** till

haya (*ah*-ʸah) *f* beech

hebilla (ay-*bhee*-lʸah) *f* buckle

hebreo (ay-*bhray*-oa) *m* Hebrew

hechizar (ay-chee-*thahr*) *v* bewitch

hecho (*ay*-choa) *m* fact

*heder (ay-*dhayr*) *v* *smell

hediondo (ay-*dh*ʸ*oan*-doa) *adj* smelly

helado (ay-*lah*-dhoa) *adj* freezing; *m* ice-cream

*helar (ay-*lahr*) *v* *freeze

hélice (*ay*-lee-thay) *f* propeller

hemorragia (ay-moa-*rrah*-khʸah) *f* haemorrhage; **~ nasal** nosebleed

hemorroides (ay-moa-*rroi*-dhayss) *fpl* haemorrhoids *pl*, piles *pl*

*hender (ayn-*dayr*) *v* *split

hendidura (ayn-dee-*dhoo*-rah) *f* chink, crack

heno (*ay*-noa) *m* hay

heredar (ay-ray-*dhahr*) *v* inherit

hereditario (ay-ray-dhee-*tah*-rʸoa) *adj* hereditary

herencia (ay-*rayn*-thʸah) *f* inheritance, legacy

herida (ay-*ree*-dhah) *f* injury, wound

*herir (ay-*reer*) *v* injure, wound

hermana (ayr-*mah*-nah) *f* sister

hermano (ayr-*mah*-noa) *m* brother

hermético (ayr-*may*-tee-koa) *adj* airtight

hermoso (ayr-*moa*-soa) *adj* beautiful

hernia (*ayr*-nʸah) *f* hernia; **~ intervertebral** slipped disc

héroe (*ay*-roa-ay) *m* hero

heroico (ay-*roi*-koa) *adj* heroic

heroísmo (ay-roa-*eez*-moa) *m* heroism

herradura (ay-rrah-*dhoo*-rah) *f* horse-shoe

herramienta (ay-rrah-*mᵞayn*-tah) *f* tool, utensil, implement; **bolsa de herramientas** tool kit

herrería (ay-rray-*ree*-ah) *f* ironworks

herrero (ay-*rray*-roa) *m* smith, blacksmith

herrumbre (ay-*rroom*-bray) *f* rust

*__*hervir** (ayr-*bheer*) *v* boil

heterosexual (ay-tay-roa-sayk-*swahl*) *adj* heterosexual

hidalgo (ee-*dhahl*-goa) *m* nobleman

hidrógeno (ee-*dhroa*-khay-noa) *m* hydrogen

hiedra (*ᵞay*-dhrah) *f* ivy

hielo (*ᵞay*-loa) *m* ice

hierba (*ᵞayr*-bhah) *f* herb; **brizna de ~** blade of grass; **mala ~** weed

hierro (*ᵞay*-rroa) *m* iron; **de ~** iron; **~ fundido** cast iron

hígado (*ee*-gah-dhoa) *m* liver

higiene (ee-*khᵞay*-nay) *f* hygiene

higiénico (ee-*khᵞay*-nee-koa) *adj* hygienic; **papel ~** toilet-paper

higo (*ee*-goa) *m* fig

hija (*ee*-khah) *f* daughter

hijastro (ee-*khahss*-troa) *m* stepchild

hijo (*ee*-khoa) *m* son

hilar (ee-*lahr*) *v* *spin

hilo (*ee*-loa) *m* yarn, thread; **~ de zurcir** darning wool

himno (*eem*-noa) *m* hymn; **~ nacional** national anthem

hinchar (een-*chahr*) *v* inflate; **hincharse** *v* *swell

hinchazón (een-chah-*thoan*) *f* swelling

hipo (*ee*-poa) *m* hiccup

hipocresía (ee-poa-kray-*see*-ah) *f* hypocrisy

hipócrita (ee-*poa*-kree-tah) *adj* hypocritical; *m* hypocrite

hipódromo (ee-*poa*-dhroa-moa) *m* race-course

hipoteca (ee-poa-*tay*-kah) *f* mortgage

hispanoamericano (eess-pah-noa-ah-may-ree-*kah*-noa) *adj* Spanish-American

histérico (eess-*tay*-ree-koa) *adj* hysterical

historia (eess-*toa*-rᵞah) *f* history; **~ de amor** love-story; **~ del arte** art history

historiador (eess-toa-rᵞah-*dhoar*) *m* historian

histórico (eess-*toa*-ree-koa) *adj* historical, historic

hocico (oa-*thee*-koa) *m* mouth, snout

hogar (oa-*gahr*) *m* hearth

hoja (*oa*-khah) *f* leaf; sheet; blade; **~ de afeitar** razor-blade; **~ de pedido** order-form; **hojas de oro** gold leaf

¡hola! (*oa*-lah) hello!

Holanda (oa-*lahn*-dah) *f* Holland

holandés (oa-lahn-*dayss*) *adj* Dutch; *m* Dutchman

hombre (*oam*-bray) *m* man

hombro (*oam*-broa) *m* shoulder

homenaje (oa-may-*nah*-khay) *m* tribute, homage

homosexual (oa-moa-sayk-*swahl*) *adj* homosexual

hondo (*oan*-doa) *adj* deep

honesto (oa-*nayss*-toa) *adj* honest; honourable, straight

hongo (*oang*-goa) *m* mushroom; toadstool

honor (oa-*noar*) *m* honour; glory

honorable (oa-noa-*rah*-bhlay) *adj* honourable

honorarios (oa-noa-*rah*-rᵞoass) *mpl* fee

honra (*oan*-rrah) *f* honour

honradez (oan-rah-*dhayth*) *f* honesty

honrado (oan-*rrah*-dhoa) *adj* honest

honrar (oan-*rahr*) *v* honour

hora (*oa*-rah) f hour; ~ **de afluencia** rush-hour; ~ **de llegada** time of arrival; ~ **de salida** time of departure; ~ **punta** peak hour; **horas de consulta** consultation hours; **horas de oficina** office hours, business hours; **horas de visita** visiting hours; **horas hábiles** business hours

horario (oa-*rah*-r^yoa) m schedule; timetable; ~ **de verano** summer time

horca (*oar*-kah) f gallows pl

horizontal (oa-ree-thoan-*tahl*) adj horizontal

horizonte (oa-ree-*thoan*-tay) m horizon

hormiga (oar-*mee*-gah) f ant

hormigón (oar-mee-*goan*) m concrete

hornear (oar-nay-*ahr*) v bake

horno (*oar*-noa) m oven; furnace

horquilla (oar-*kee*-l^yah) f hairpin, hair-grip; bobby pin Am

horrible (oa-*rree*-bhlay) adj horrible; hideous

horror (oa-*rroar*) m horror

horticultura (oar-tee-kool-*too*-rah) f horticulture

hospedar (oass-pay-*dhahr*) v entertain; **hospedarse** v stay

hospedería (oass-pay-dhay-*ree*-ah) f hostel

hospicio (oass-*pee*-th^yoa) m home

hospital (oass-pee-*tahl*) m hospital

hospitalario (oass-pee-tah-*lah*-r^yoa) adj hospitable

hospitalidad (oass-pee-tah-lee-*dhahdh*) f hospitality

hostil (oass-*teel*) adj hostile

hotel (oa-*tayl*) m hotel

hoy (oi) adv today; ~ **en día** nowadays

hoyo (*oa*-^yoa) m pit

hueco (*way*-koa) adj hollow; m gap

huelga (*wayl*-gah) f strike; *estar en ~ *strike

huella (*way*-l^yah) f trace

huérfano (*wayr*-fah-noa) m orphan

huerto (*wayr*-toa) m kitchen garden

hueso (*way*-soa) m bone; stone

huésped (*wayss*-paydh) m guest; lodger, boarder

hueva (*way*-bhah) f roe

huevera (way-*bhay*-rah) f egg-cup

huevo (*way*-bhoa) m egg; **yema de ~** egg-yolk

*huir (weer) v escape

hule (*oo*-lay) mMe rubber

humanidad (oo-mah-nee-*dhahdh*) f humanity, mankind

humano (oo-*mah*-noa) adj human

humedad (oo-may-*dhahdh*) f moisture, humidity, damp

*humedecer (oo-may-dhay-*thayr*) v moisten, damp

húmedo (*oo*-may-dhoa) adj moist, humid, damp; wet

humilde (oo-*meel*-day) adj humble

humo (*oo*-moa) m smoke

humor (oo-*moar*) m spirit, mood; humour; **de buen ~** good-tempered, good-humoured

humorístico (oo-moa-*reess*-tee-koa) adj humorous

hundimiento (oon-dee-m^yayn-toa) m ruination

hundirse (oon-*deer* say) v *sink

húngaro (*oong*-gah-roa) adj Hungarian; m Hungarian

Hungría (oong-*gree*-ah) m Hungary

huracán (oo-rah-*kahn*) m hurricane

hurtar (oor-*tahr*) v *steal

hurto (*oor*-toa) m theft

husmear (oos-may-*ahr*) v scent, *get wind of

I

ibérico (ee-*bhay*-ree-koa) *adj* Iberian
icono (ee-*koa*-noa) *m* icon
ictericia (eek-tay-*ree*-thʸah) *f* jaundice
idea (ee-*dhay*-ah) *f* idea
ideal (ee-dhay-*ahl*) *adj* ideal; *m* ideal
idear (ee-dhay-*ahr*) *v* devise
idéntico (ee-*dhayn*-tee-koa) *adj* identical
identidad (ee-dhayn-tee-*dhahdh*) *f* identity; **carnet de ~** identity card
identificación (ee-dhayn-tee-fee-kah-*thʸoan*) *f* identification
identificar (ee-dhayn-tee-fee-*kahr*) *v* identify
idioma (ee-*dhʸoa*-mah) *m* language
idiomático (ee-dhʸoa-*mah*-tee-koa) *adj* idiomatic
idiota (ee-*dhʸoa*-tah) *adj* idiotic; *m* idiot, fool
ídolo (*ee*-dhoa-loa) *m* idol
iglesia (ee-*glay*-sʸah) *f* chapel, church
ignorancia (eeg-noa-*rahn*-thʸah) *f* ignorance
ignorante (eeg-noa-*rahn*-tay) *adj* ignorant
ignorar (eeg-noa-*rahr*) *v* ignore
igual (ee-*gwahl*) *adj* equal, alike; level, even; **sin ~** unsurpassed
igualar (ee-gwah-*lahr*) *v* level, equalize; equal
igualdad (ee-gwahl-*dahdh*) *f* equality
igualmente (ee-gwahl-*mayn*-tay) *adv* alike; equally
ilegal (ee-lay-*gahl*) *adj* illegal, unlawful
ilegible (ee-lay-*khee*-bhlay) *adj* illegible
ileso (ee-*lay*-soa) *adj* unhurt
ilimitado (ee-lee-mee-*tah*-dhoa) *adj* unlimited

iluminación (ee-loo-mee-nah-*thʸoan*) *f* illumination
iluminar (ee-loo-mee-*nahr*) *v* illuminate
ilusión (ee-loo-*sʸoan*) *f* illusion
ilustración (ee-looss-trah-*thʸoan*) *f* illustration; picture
ilustrar (ee-looss-*trahr*) *v* illustrate
ilustre (ee-*looss*-tray) *adj* illustrious
imagen (ee-*mah*-khayn) *f* image, picture; **~ reflejada** reflection
imaginación (ee-mah-khee-nah-*thʸoan*) *f* fancy, imagination
imaginar (ee-mah-khee-*nahr*) *v* conceive; **imaginarse** *v* fancy, imagine
imaginario (ee-mah-khee-*nah*-rʸoa) *adj* imaginary
imitación (ee-mee-tah-*thʸoan*) *f* imitation
imitar (ee-mee-*tahr*) *v* imitate, copy
impaciente (eem-pah-*thʸayn*-tay) *adj* eager, impatient
impar (eem-*pahr*) *adj* odd
imparcial (eem-pahr-*thʸahl*) *adj* impartial
impecable (eem-pay-*kah*-bhlay) *adj* faultless
impedimento (eem-pay-dhee-*mayn*-toa) *m* impediment
*****impedir** (eem-pay-*dheer*) *v* hinder, impede; restrain, prevent
impeler (eem-pay-*layr*) *v* propel
imperdible (eem-payr-*dhee*-bhlay) *m* safety-pin
imperfección (eem-payr-fayk-*thʸoan*) *f* fault
imperfecto (eem-payr-*fayk*-toa) *adj* imperfect
imperial (eem-pay-*rʸahl*) *adj* imperial
imperio (eem-*pay*-rʸoa) *m* empire
impermeable (eem-payr-may-*ah*-bhlay) *adj* waterproof, rainproof; *m* raincoat, mackintosh
impersonal (eem-payr-soa-*nahl*) *adj*

impersonal

impertinencia (eem-payr-tee-*nayn*-thᵞah) *f* impertinence

impertinente (eem-payr-tee-*nayn*-tay) *adj* bold, impertinent

impetuoso (eem-pay-*twoa*-soa) *adj* violent

implicar (eem-plee-*kahr*) *v* imply; **implicado** involved

imponente (eem-poa-*nayn*-tay) *adj* grand, imposing

imponible (eem-poa-*nee*-bhlay) *adj* dutiable

impopular (eem-poa-poo-*lahr*) *adj* unpopular

importación (eem-poar-tah-*thᵞoan*) *f* import

importador (eem-poar-tah-*dhoar*) *m* importer

importancia (eem-poar-*tahn*-thᵞah) *f* importance; *tener ~ matter

importante (eem-poar-*tahn*-tay) *adj* important; considerable, capital, big

importar (eem-poar-*tahr*) *v* import

importuno (eem-poar-*too*-noa) *adj* annoying

imposible (eem-poa-*see*-bhlay) *adj* impossible

impotencia (eem-poa-*tayn*-thᵞah) *f* impotence

impotente (eem-poa-*tayn*-tay) *adj* powerless; impotent

impresión (eem-pray-*sᵞoan*) *f* impression; ~ **digital** fingerprint

impresionante (eem-pray-sᵞoa-*nahn*-tay) *adj* impressive, striking

impresionar (eem-pray-sᵞoa-*nahr*) *v* *strike, impress

impreso (eem-*pray*-soa) *m* printed matter

imprevisto (eem-pray-*bheess*-toa) *adj* unexpected, incidental

***imprimir** (eem-pree-*meer*) *v* print

improbable (eem-proa-*bhah*-bhlay) *adj* unlikely, improbable

ímprobo (*eem*-proa-bhoa) *adj* unfair, dishonest

impropio (eem-*proa*-pᵞoa) *adj* improper; wrong

improvisar (eem-proa-bhee-*sahr*) *v* improvise

imprudente (eem-proo-*dhayn*-tay) *adj* unwise

impudente (eem-poo-*dhayn*-tay) *adj* impudent

impuesto (eem-*pwayss*-toa) *m* taxation, tax; Customs duty; ~ **de aduana** Customs duty; **impuestos de importación** import duty; **libre de impuestos** tax-free

impulsivo (eem-pool-*see*-bhoa) *adj* impulsive

impulso (eem-*pool*-soa) *m* urge, impulse

inaccesible (ee-nahk-thay-*see*-bhlay) *adj* inaccessible

inaceptable (ee-nah-thayp-*tah*-bhlay) *adj* unacceptable

inadecuado (ee-nah-dhay-*kwah*-dhoa) *adj* inadequate; unfit, unsuitable

inapreciable (ee-nah-pray-*thᵞah*-bhlay) *adj* priceless

incapaz (eeng-kah-*pahth*) *adj* unable, incapable

incendio (een-*thayn* dᵞoa) *m* fire

incidente (een-thee-*dhayn*-tay) *m* incident

incienso (een-*thᵞayn*-soa) *m* incense

incierto (een-*thᵞayr*-toa) *adj* uncertain

incineración (een-thee-nay-rah-*thᵞoan*) *f* cremation

incinerar (een-thee-nay-*rahr*) *v* cremate

incisión (een-thee-*sᵞoan*) *f* cut

incitar (een-thee-*tahr*) *v* incite

inclinación (eeng-klee-nah-*thᵞoan*) *f* tendency, inclination; incline

inclinar (eeng-klee-*nahr*) v bow; **inclinado** inclined; sloping, slanting; **inclinarse** v *be inclined to; slope, slant

***incluir** (eeng-*klweer*) v include; enclose; count; **todo incluido** all in

incluso (eeng-*kloo*-soa) adj inclusive, included

incombustible (eeng-koam-booss-*tee*-bhlay) adj fireproof

incomible (eeng-koa-*mee*-bhlay) adj inedible

incomodidad (eeng-koa-moa-dhee-*dhahdh*) f inconvenience

incómodo (eeng-*koa*-moa-dhoa) adj uncomfortable

incompetente (eeng-koam-pay-*tayn*-tay) adj incompetent; unqualified

incompleto (eeng-koam-*play*-toa) adj incomplete

inconcebible (eeng-koan-thay-*bhee*-bhlay) adj inconceivable

incondicional (eeng-koan-dee-th^{y}oa-nahl) adj unconditional

inconsciente (eeng-koan-th^{y}ayn-tay) adj unaware; unconscious

inconveniencia (eeng-koam-bay-n^{y}ayn-th^{y}ah) f inconvenience

incorrecto (eeng-koa-*rrayk*-toa) adj incorrect

increíble (eeng-kray-*ee*-bhlay) adj incredible

incrementar (eeng-kray-mayn-*tahr*) v increase

inculto (eeng-*kool*-toa) adj uncultivated; uneducated

incurable (eeng-koo-*rah*-bhlay) adj incurable

indagación (eeng-dah-gah-th^{y}oan) f inquiry

indagar (een-dah-*gahr*) v query

indecente (een-day-*thayn*-tay) adj indecent

indefenso (een-day-*fayn*-soa) adj unprotected

indefinido (een-day-fee-*nee*-dhoa) adj indefinite

indemnización (een-daym-nee-thah-th^{y}oan) f compensation, indemnity

independencia (een-day-payn-*dayn*-th^{y}ah) f independence

independiente (een-day-payn-d^{y}ayn-tay) adj self-employed, independent

indeseable (een-day-say-*ah*-bhlay) adj undesirable

India (*een*-d^{y}ah) f India

indicación (een-dee-kah-*th^{y}oan*) f indication

indicador (een-dee-kah-*dhoar*) m trafficator, indicator

indicar (een-dee-*kahr*) v indicate; declare

indicativo (een-dee-kah-*tee*-bhoa) m area code

índice (*een*-dee-thay) m index, table of contents; index finger

indiferencia (een-dee-fay-*rayn*-th^{y}ah) f indifference

indiferente (een-dee-fay-*rayn*-tay) adj indifferent; careless

indígena (een-*dee*-khay-nah) m native

indigestión (een-dee-khayss-t^{y}oan) f indigestion

indignación (een-deeg-nah-*th^{y}oan*) f indignation

indio (*een*-d^{y}oa) adj Indian; m Indian

indirecto (een-dee-*rayk*-toa) adj indirect

indispensable (een-deess-payn-*sah*-bhlay) adj essential

indispuesto (een-deess-*pwayss*-toa) adj unwell

individual (een-dee-bhee-*dhwahl*) adj individual

individuo (een-dee-*bhee*-dhwoa) m individual

Indonesia (een-doa-*nay*-s^{y}ah) f Indo-

nesia
indonesio (een-doa-*nay*-s^yoa) *adj* Indonesian ; *m* Indonesian
indudable (een-doo-*dhah*-bhlay) *adj*
undoubted
indulto (een-*dool*-toa) *m* pardon
industria (een-*dooss*-tr^yah) *f* industry ;
ingenuity
ineficiente (ee-nay-fee-*th^yayn*-tay) *adj*
inefficient
inerte (ee-*nayr*-tay) *adj* limp
inesperado (ee-nayss-pay-*rah*-dhoa)
adj unexpected
inestable (ee-nayss-*tah*-bhlay) *adj* unsteady, unstable
inevitable (ee-nay-bhee-*tah*-bhlay) *adj*
unavoidable, inevitable
inexacto (ee-nayk-*sahk*-toa) *adj* incorrect, inaccurate ; false
inexperto (ee-nayks-*payr*-toa) *adj* inexperienced
inexplicable (ee-nayks-plee-*kah*-bhlay)
adj unaccountable
infancia (een-*tahn*-th^yah) *f* infancy
infantería (een-fahn-tay-*ree*-ah) *f* infantry
infantil (een-fahn-*teel*) *adj* childlike
infección (een-fayk-*th^yoan*) *f* infection
infectar (een-fayk-*tahr*) *v* infect ; **infectarse** *v* *become septic
inferior (een-fay-r^yoar) *adj* inferior ;
bottom
infiel (een-f^yayl) *adj* unfaithful
infierno (een-f^yayr-noa) *m* hell
infinidad (een-fee-nee-*dhahdh*) *f* infini-
ty
infinitivo (een-tee-nee-*tee*-bhoa) *m* infinitive
infinito (een-fee-*nee*-toa) *adj* endless,
infinite
inflable (een-*flah*-bhlay) *adj* inflatable
inflación (een-flah-*th^yoan*) *f* inflation
inflamable (een-flah-*mah*-bhlay) *adj*
inflammable

inflamación (een-flah-mah-*th^yoan*) *f*
inflammation
influencia (een-*flwayn*-th^yah) *f* influence
*influir** (een-*flwoer*) *v* influence
influjo (een-*floo*-khoa) *m* influence
influyente (een-floo-*y*ayn-tay) *adj* influential
información (een-foar-mah-*th^yoan*) *f*
enquiry, information ; **oficina de informaciones** inquiry office
informal (een-foar-*mahl*) *adj* informal ;
casual
informar (een-foar-*mahr*) *v* report, inform ; plead ; **informarse** *v* inquire
informe (een-*foar*-may) *m* report ; **informes** *mpl* information ; *pedir
informes** inquire
infortunio (een-foar-*too*-n^yoa) *m* misfortune
infrarrojo (een-frah-*rroa*-khoa) *adj* infra-red
infrecuente (een-fray-*kwayn*-tay) *adj*
infrequent
infringir (een-freeng-*kheer*) *v* trespass
ingeniero (eeng-khay-n^yay-roa) *m* engineer
ingenioso (eeng-khay-n^yoa-soa) *adj* in-
genious
ingenuo (eeng-*khay*-nwoa) *adj* naïve ;
simple
Inglaterra (eeng-glah-*tay*-rrah) *f* England ; Britain
ingle (*eeng*-glay) *f* groin
inglés (eeng-*glayss*) *adj* English ; *m*
Englishman ; Briton
ingrato (eeng-*grah*-toa) *adj* ungrateful
ingrediente (eeng-gray-*dh^yayn*-tay) *m*
ingredient
ingresar (eeng-gray-*sahr*) *v* deposit
ingreso (eenggray-soa) *m* entry
ingresos (eeng-*gray*-soass) *mpl* revenue, earnings *pl*, income ; **impuesto sobre los ~** income-tax

inhabitable (ee-nah-bhee-*tah*-bhlay) *adj* uninhabitable

inhabitado (ee-nah-bhee-*tah*-dhoa) *adj* uninhabited

inhalar (ee-nah-*lahr*) *v* inhale

inicial (ee-nee-*th*ʸ*ahl*) *adj* initial; *f* initial

iniciar (ee-nee-*th*ʸ*ahr*) *v* initiate

iniciativa (ee-nee-th*ʸ*ah-*tee*-bhah) *f* initiative

ininterrumpido (ee-neen-tay-rroom-*pee*-dhoa) *adj* continuous

injusticia (eeng-khooss-*tee*-th*ʸ*ah) *f* injustice

injusto (eeng-*khooss*-toa) *adj* unfair, unjust

inmaculado (een-mah-koo-*lah*-dhoa) *adj* stainless, spotless

inmediatamente (een-may-dh*ʸ*ah-tah-*mayn*-tay) *adv* instantly, immediately

inmediato (een-may-*dh*ʸ*ah*-toa) *adj* immediate, prompt; **de** ~ immediately

inmenso (een-*mayn*-soa) *adj* immense

inmerecido (een-may-ray-*thee*-dhoa) *adj* unearned

inmigración (een-mee-grah-*th*ʸ*oan*) *f* immigration

inmigrante (een-mee-*grahn*-tay) *m* immigrant

inmigrar (een-mee-*grahr*) *v* immigrate

inmodesto (een-moa-*dhayss*-toa) *adj* immodest

inmueble (een-*mway*-bhlay) *m* house

inmundo (een-*moon*-doa) *adj* filthy

inmunidad (een-moo-nee-*dhahdh*) *f* immunity

inmunizar (een-moo-nee-*thahr*) *v* immunize

innato (een-*nah*-toa) *adj* natural

innecesario (een-nay-thay-*sah*-r*ʸ*oa) *adj* unnecessary

innumerable (een-noo-may-*rah*-bhlay) *adj* innumerable

inocencia (ee-noa-*thayn*-th*ʸ*ah) *f* innocence

inocente (ee-noa-*thayn*-tay) *adj* innocent

inoculación (ee-noa-koo-lah-*th*ʸ*oan*) *f* inoculation

inocuo (ee-*noa*-kwoa) *adj* harmless

inoportuno (ee-noa-poar-*too*-noa) *adj* inconvenient; misplaced

inquietarse (eeng-k*ʸ*ay-*tahr*-say) *v* worry

inquieto (een-*k*ʸ*ay*-toa) *adj* restless; uneasy, worried

inquietud (eeng-k*ʸ*ay-*toodh*) *f* unrest; worry

inquilino (eeng-kee-*lee*-noa) *m* tenant

insalubre (een-sah-*loo*-bhray) *adj* unhealthy

insatisfecho (een-sah-teess-*fay*-choa) *adj* dissatisfied

inscribir (eens-kree-*bheer*) *v* enter, book, list; **inscribirse** *v* register, check in

inscripción (eens-kreep-*th*ʸ*oan*) *f* inscription; registration

insecticida (een-sayk-tee-*thee*-dhah) *m* insecticide

insectífugo (een-sayk-*tee*-foo-goa) *m* insect repellent

insecto (een-*sayk*-toa) *m* insect; bug *nAm*

inseguro (een-say-*goo*-roa) *adj* unsafe; doubtful

insensato (een-sayn-*sah*-toa) *adj* senseless

insensible (een-sayn-*see*-bhlay) *adj* insensitive; heartless

insertar (een-sayr-*tahr*) *v* insert

insignificante (een-seeg-nee-fee-*kahn*-tay) *adj* unimportant, petty, insignificant

insípido (een-*see*-pee-dhoa) *adj* tasteless

insistir (een-seess-*teer*) v insist

insolación (een-soa-lah-*th^yoan*) f sunstroke

insolencia (een-soa-*layn*-th^yah) f insolence

insolente (een-soa-*layn*-tay) adj insolent

insólito (een-*soa*-lee-toa) adj uncommon, unusual

insomnio (een-*soam*-n^yoa) m insomnia

insonorizado (een-soa-noa-ree-*thah*-dhoa) adj soundproof

insoportable (een-soa-poar-*tah*-bhlay) adj intolerable

inspección (eens-payk-*th^yoan*) f inspection; ~ **de pasaportes** passport control

inspeccionar (eens-payk-th^yoa-*nahr*) v inspect

inspector (eens-payk-*toar*) m inspector

inspirar (een-spee-*rahr*) v inspire

instalación (eens-tah-lah-*th^yoan*) f installation; plant

instalar (eens-tah-*lahr*) v install; furnish

instantánea (eens-tahn-*tah*-nay-ah) f snapshot

instantáneamente (eens-tahn-tah-nay-ah-*mayn*-tay) adv instantly

instante (eens-*tahn*-tay) m instant; second; **al ~** instantly

instinto (een-*steen*-toa) m instinct

institución (eens-tee-too-*th^yoan*) f institution, institute

*****instituir** (eens-tee-*twee r*) v institute

instituto (eens-tee-*too*-toa) m institution, institute

institutor (eens-tee-too-*toar*) m teacher

instrucción (eens-trook-*th^yoan*) f instruction; direction

instructivo (eens-trook-*tee*-bhoa) adj instructive

instructor (eens-trook-*toar*) m instructor

*****instruir** (eens-*trwee r*) v instruct

instrumento (eens-troo-*mayn*-toa) m instrument; ~ **músico** musical instrument

insuficiente (een-soo-fee-*th^yayn*-tay) adj insufficient

insufrible (een-soo-*free*-bhlay) adj unbearable

insultante (een-sool-*tahn*-tay) adj offensive

insultar (een-sool-*tahr*) v insult; scold, call names

insulto (een-*sool*-toa) m insult

intacto (een-*tahk*-toa) adj intact; unbroken, whole

integral (een-tay-*grahl*) adj integral

integrar (een-tay-*grahr*) v integrate

intelecto (een-tay-*layk*-toa) m intellect

intelectual (een-tay-layk-*twahl*) adj intellectual

inteligencia (een-tay-lee-*khayn*-th^yah) f intelligence, brain

inteligente (een-tay-lee-*khayn*-tay) adj intelligent; clever, smart

intención (een-tayn-*th^yoan*) f intention, purpose; *****tener la ~ de** intend

intencionado (een-tayn-th^yoa-*nah*-dhoa) adj on purpose

intencional (een-tayn-th^yoa-*nahl*) adj intentional

intensidad (een-tayn-see-*dhahdh*) f intensity

intenso (een-*tayn*-soa) adj intense

intentar (een-tayn-*tahr*) v attempt, try; intend

intercambiar (een-tayr-kahm-*b^yahr*) v exchange

interés (een-tay-*rayss*) m interest

interesado (een-tay-ray-*sah*-dhoa) adj interested; concerned; m candidate

interesante (een-tay-ray-*sahn*-tay) adj

interesting
interesar (een-tay-ray-*sahr*) v interest
interferencia (een-tayr-fay-*rayn*-th^yah) f interference
interferir (een-tayr-fay-*reer*) v interfere
ínterin (*een*-tay-reen) m interim
interior (een-tay-r^yoar) adj inside, inner; domestic; m interior, inside
intermediario (een-tayr-may-*dh^yah*-r^yoa) m intermediary
intermedio (een-tayr-*may*-dh^yoa) m interlude
internacional (een-tayr-nah-th^yoa-*nahl*) adj international
internado (een-tayr-*nah*-dhoa) m boarding-school
interno (een-*tayr*-noa) adj internal; resident
interpretar (een-tayr-pray-*tahr*) v interpret
intérprete (een-*tayr*-pray-tay) m interpreter
interrogar (een-tay-rroa-*gahr*) v interrogate
interrogativo (een-tay-rroa-gah-*tee*-bhoa) adj interrogative
interrogatorio (een-tay-rroa-gah-*toa*-r^yoa) m interrogation, examination
interrumpir (een-tay-rroom-*peer*) v interrupt
interrupción (een-tay-rroop-*th^yoan*) f interruption
interruptor (een-tay-rroop-*toar*) m switch
intersección (een-tayr-sayk-*th^yoan*) f intersection
intervalo (een-tayr-*bhah*-loa) m interval
intervención (een-tayr-bhayn-*th^yoan*) f intervention
*intervenir (een-tayr-bhay-*neer*) v intervene
intestino (een-tayss-*tee*-noa) m intestine, gut; ~ **recto** rectum; **intesti-**

nos intestines pl, bowels pl
intimidad (een-tee-mee-*dhahdh*) f privacy
íntimo (*een*-tee-moa) adj intimate; cosy
intoxicación alimentaria (een-toak-see-kah-*th^yoan* ah-lee-mayn-*tah*-r^yah) food poisoning
intransitable (een-trahn-see-*tah*-bhlay) adj impassable
intriga (een-*tree*-gah) f intrigue
introducción (een-troa-dhook-*th^yoan*) f introduction
*introducir (een-troa-dhoo-*theer*) v introduce; *bring up
intruso (een-*troo*-soa) m trespasser
inundación (ee-noon-dah-*th^yoan*) f flood
inusitado (ee-noo-see-*tah*-dhoa) adj unusual
inútil (ee-*noo*-teel) adj useless
inútilmente (ee-noo-teel-*mayn*-tay) adv in vain
invadir (eem-bah-*dheer*) v invade
inválido (eem-*bah*-lee-dhoa) adj invalid, disabled; m invalid
invasión (eem-bah-*s^yoan*) f invasion
invención (eem-bayn-*th^yoan*) f invention
inventar (eem-bayn-*tahr*) v invent
inventario (eem-bayn-*tah*-r^yoa) m inventory
inventivo (eem-bayn-*tee*-bhoa) adj inventive
inventor (eem-bayn-*toar*) m inventor
invernáculo (eem-bayr-*nah*-koo-loa) m greenhouse
invernadero (eem-bayr-nah-*dhay*-roa) m greenhouse
inversión (eem-bayr-*s^yoan*) f investment
inversionista (eem-bayr-s^yoa-*neess*-tah) m investor
inverso (eem-*bayr*-soa) adj reverse

* invertir (eem-bayr-*teer*) *v* invert; invest

investigación (eem-bayss-tee-gah-*thᵞoan*) *f* research; investigation, enquiry

investigador (eem-bhayss-tee-gah-*dhoar*) *m* research worker

investigar (eem-bayss-tee-*gahr*) *v* investigate, enquire

invierno (eem-*bᵞayr*-noa) *m* winter; **deportes de ~** winter sports

invisible (eem-bee-*see*-bhlay) *adj* invisible

invitación (eem-bee-tah-*thᵞoan*) *f* invitation

invitado (eem-bee-*tah*-dhoa) *m* guest

invitar (eem-bee-*tahr*) *v* invite; ask

inyección (een-ᵞayk-*thᵞoan*) *f* shot, injection

inyectar (een-ᵞayk-*tahr*) *v* inject

* ir (eer) *v* *go; **~ por** fetch; *** irse** *v* *go away

Irak (ee-*rahk*) *m* Iraq

Irán (ee-*rahn*) *m* Iran

iraní (ee-rah-*nee*) *adj* Iranian; *m* Iranian

iraquí (ee-rah-*kee*) *adj* Iraqi; *m* Iraqi

irascible (ee-rahss-*thee*-bhlay) *adj* irascible, quick-tempered

Irlanda (eer-*lahn*-dah) *f* Ireland

irlandés (eer-lahn-*dayss*) *adj* Irish; *m* Irishman

ironía (ee-roa-*nee*-ah) *f* irony

irónico (ee-*roa*-nee-koa) *adj* ironical

irrazonable (ee-rrah-thoa-*nah*-bhlay) *adj* unreasonable

irreal (ee-rray-*ahl*) *adj* unreal

irreflexivo (ee-rray-flayk-*see*-bhoa) *adj* rash

irregular (ee-rray-goo-*lahr*) *adj* irregular; uneven

irrelevante (ee-rray-lay-*bhahn*-tay) *adj* insignificant

irreparable (ee-rray-pah-*rah*-bhlay) *adj*

irreparable

irrevocable (ee-rray-bhoa-*kah*-bhlay) *adj* irrevocable

irritable (ee-rree-*tah*-bhlay) *adj* irritable

irritante (ee-rree-*tahn*-tay) *adj* annoying

irritar (ee-rree-*tahr*) *v* annoy, irritate

irrompible (ee-rroam-*pee*-bhlay) *adj* unbreakable

irrupción (ee-rroop-*thᵞoan*) *f* invasion, raid

isla (*eez*-lah) *f* island

islandés (eez-lahn-*dayss*) *adj* Icelandic; *m* Icelander

Islandia (eez-*lahn*-dᵞah) *f* Iceland

Israel (eess-rah-*ayl*) *m* Israel

israelí (eess-rah-ay-*lee*) *adj* Israeli; *m* Israeli

istmo (*eest*-moa) *m* isthmus

Italia (ee-*tah*-lᵞah) *f* Italy

italiano (ee-tah-*lᵞah*-noa) *adj* Italian; *m* Italian

ítem (*ee*-taym) *m* item

itinerario (ee-tee-nay-*rah*-rᵞoa) *m* itinerary

izar (ee-*thahr*) *v* hoist

izquierdo (eeth-*kᵞayr*-dhoa) *adj* left; left-hand

J

jabón (khah-*bhoan*) *m* soap; **~ de afeitar** shaving-soap; **~ en polvo** soap powder, washing-powder

jade (*khah*-dhay) *m* jade

jadear (khah-dhay-*ahr*) *v* pant

jalar (khah-*lahr*) *vMe* *draw

jalea (khah-*lay*-ah) *f* jelly

jamás (khah-*mahss*) *adv* ever

jamón (khah-*moan*) *m* ham

Japón (khah-*poan*) *m* Japan

japonés (khah-poa-*nayss*) *adj* Japanese; *m* Japanese

¡jaque! (*khah*-kay) check!

jarabe (khah-*rah*-bhay) *m* syrup

jardín (khahr-*dheen*) *m* garden; ~ **de infancia** kindergarten; ~ **público** public garden; ~ **zoológico** zoological gardens, zoo

jardinero (khahr-dhee-*nay*-roa) *m* gardener

jarra (*khah*-rrah) *f* jar

jaula (*khou*-lah) *f* cage

jefe (*khay*-fay) *m* chief, manager, boss; leader; chieftain; ~ **de cocina** chef; ~ **de estación** stationmaster; ~ **de Estado** head of state; ~ **de gobierno** premier

jengibre (khayng-*khee*-bhray) *m* ginger

jerarquía (khay-rahr-*kee*-ah) *f* hierarchy

jeringa (khay-*reeng*-gah) *f* syringe

jersey (khayr-*say*) *m* jersey; jumper

jinete (khee-*nay*-tay) *m* horseman, rider

jitomate (khee-toa-*mah*-tay) *mMe* tomato

Jordania (khoar-*dhah*-nʸah) *f* Jordan

jordano (khoar-*dhah*-noa) *adj* Jordanian; *m* Jordanian

jornada (khoar-*nah*-dhah) *f* day trip

joven (*khoa*-bhayn) *adj* young; *m* lad

jovencito (khoa-bhayn-*thee*-toa) *m* teenager

jovial (khoa-*bhʸahl*) *adj* jolly

joya (*khoa*-ʸah) *f* jewel, gem

joyería (khoa-ʸay-*ree*-ah) *f* jewellery

joyero (khoa-ʸay-roa) *m* jeweller

jubilado (khoo-bhee-*lah*-dhoa) *adj* retired

judía (khoo-*dhee*-ah) *f* bean

judío (khoo-*dhee*-oa) *adj* Jewish; *m* Jew

juego (*khway*-goa) *m* game, play; set; ***hacer** ~ **con** match; ~ **de bolos** bowling; ~ **de damas** draughts; ~ **de té** tea-set

jueves (*khway*-bhayss) *m* Thursday

juez (khwayth) *m* judge

jugada (khoo-*gah*-dhah) *f* move

jugador (khoo-gah-*dhoar*) *m* player

***jugar** (khoo-*gahr*) *v* play

juguete (khoo-*gay*-tay) *m* toy

juguetería (khoo-gay-tay-*ree*-ah) *f* toyshop

juicio (*khwee*-thʸoa) *m* sense; judgment

julio (*khoo*-lʸoa) July

junco (*khoong*-koa) *m* rush

jungla (*khoong*-glah) *f* jungle

junio (*khoo*-nʸoa) June

junquillo (khoong-*kee*-lʸoa) *m* reed

junta (*khoon*-tah) *f* meeting

juntamente (khoon-tah-*mayn*-tay) *adv* jointly

juntar (khoon-*tahr*) *v* attach; collect; join; **juntarse** *v* gather

junto a (*khoon*-toa ah) beside; next to

juntos (*khoon*-toass) *adv* together

jurado (khoo-*rah*-dhoa) *m* jury

juramento (khoo-rah-*mayn*-toa) *m* vow, oath; **prestar** ~ vow

jurar (khoo-*rahr*) *v* *swear

jurídico (khoo-*ree*-dhee-koa) *adj* legal

jurista (khoo-*reess*-tah) *m* lawyer

justamente (khooss-tah-*mayn*-tay) *adv* rightly; just

justicia (khooss-*tee*-thʸah) *f* justice

justificar (khooss-tee-fee-*kahr*) *v* justify

justo (*khooss*-toa) *adj* fair, just, righteous, right; correct, appropriate, proper

juvenil (khoo-bhay-*neel*) *adj* juvenile

juventud (khoo-bhayn-*toodh*) *f* youth

juzgar (khoodh-*gahr*) *v* judge

K

Kenya (*kay*-n^yah) *m* Kenya
kilogramo (kee-loa-*grah*-moa) *m* kilogram
kilometraje (kee-loa-may-*trah*-khay) *m* distance in kilometres
kilómetro (kee-*loa*-may-troa) *m* kilometre

L

la (lah) *pron* her
laberinto (lah-bhay-*reen*-toa) *m* maze, labyrinth
labio (*lah*-bh^yoa) *m* lip
labor (lah-*bhoar*) *f* labour
laboratorio (lah-bhoa-rah-*toa*-r^yoa) *m* laboratory; ~ **de lenguas** language laboratory
laca (*lah*-kah) *f* lacquer; ~ **para el cabello** hair-spray
ladera (lah-*dhay*-rah) *f* hillside
lado (*lah*-dhoa) *m* side; way; **al** ~ next-door; **al otro** ~ across; **al otro** ~ **de** across
ladrar (lah-*dhrahr*) *v* bay, bark
ladrillo (lah-*dhroe*l^yoa) *m* brick
ladrón (lah-*dhroan*) *m* thief, robber; burglar
lago (*lah*-goa) *m* lake
lágrima (*lah*-gree-mah) *f* tear
laguna (lah-*goo*-nah) *f* lagoon
lamentable (lah-mayn-*tah*-bhlay) *adj* lamentable
lamentar (lah-mayn-*tahr*) *v* lament; grieve
lamer (lah-*mayr*) *v* lick
lámpara (*lahm*-pah-rah) *f* lamp; ~ **para lectura** reading-lamp; ~ **sorda**

hurricane lamp
lana (*lah*-nah) *f* wool; **de** ~ woollen
landa (*lahn*-dhah) *f* heath
langosta (lahng-*goass*-tah) *f* lobster
lanza (*lahn*-thah) *f* spear
lanzamiento (lahn-thah-*m^yayn*-toa) *m* throw
lanzar (lahn-*thahr*) *v* *cast; launch
lápida (*lah*-pee-dhah) *f* gravestone, tombstone
lápiz (*lah*-peeth) *m* pencil; ~ **labial** lipstick; ~ **para las cejas** eye-pencil
largo (*lahr*-goa) *adj* long; **a lo** ~ **de** along, past; **pasar de** ~ pass by
laringitis (lah-reeng-*khee*-teess) *f* laryngitis
¡qué lástima! (kay *lahss*-tee-mah) what a pity!
lata (*lah*-tah) *f* tin, canister, can
lateralmente (lah-tay-rahl-*mayn*-tay) *adv* sideways
latín (lah-*teen*) *m* Latin
latinoamericano (lah-tee-noa-ah-may-ree-*kah*-noa) *adj* Latin-American
latitud (lah-tee-*toodh*) *f* latitude
latón (lah-*toan*) *m* brass
lavable (lah-*bhah*-bhlay) *adj* washable; fast-dyed
lavabo (lah-*bhah*-bhoa) *m* wash-stand
lavabos (lah-*bhah*-bhoass) *mpl* bathroom; ~ **para caballeros** men's room; ~ **para señoras** ladies' room
lavado (lah-*bhah*-dhoa) *m* washing
lavandería (lah-bhahn-day-*ree*-ah) *f* laundry; **de autoservicio** launderette
lavar (lah-*bhahr*) *v* wash
laxante (lahk-*sahn*-tay) *m* laxative
le (lay) *pron* him; her
leal (lay-*ahl*) *adj* true, loyal
lección (layk-*th^yoan*) *f* lesson
lectura (layk-*too*-rah) *f* reading
leche (*lay*-chay) *f* milk; **batido de** ~ milk-shake

lechería (lay-chay-*ree*-ah) *f* dairy

lechero (lay-*chay*-roa) *m* milkman

lechigada (lay-chee-*gah*-dhah) *f* litter

lechoso (lay-*choa*-soa) *adj* milky

lechuga (lay-*choo*-gah) *f* lettuce

***leer** (lay-*ayr*) *v* *read

legación (lay-gah-*th*Yoan) *f* legation

legal (lay-*gahl*) *adj* legal

legalización (lay-gah-lee-thah-*th*Yoan) *f* legalization

legible (lay-*khee*-bhlay) *adj* legible

legítimo (lay-*khee*-tee-moa) *adj* legitimate, legal

legumbre (lay-*goom*-bray) *f* vegetable

lejano (lay-*khah*-noa) *adj* remote, far, distant

lejos (*lay*-khoass) *adv* far

lema (*lay*-mah) *f* motto, slogan

lengua (*layng*-gwah) *f* tongue; language; ~ **materna** native language, mother tongue

lenguado (layng-*gwah*-dhoa) *m* sole

lenguaje (layng-*gwah*-khay) *m* speech

lente (*layn*-tay) *m/f* lens; ~ **de aumento** magnifying glass; **lentillas** *fpl* contact lenses

lento (*layn*-toa) *adj* slow; slack

león (lay-*oan*) *m* lion

lepra (*lay*-prah) *f* leprosy

lerdo (*layr*-dhoa) *adj* slow

les (layss) *pron* them

lesión (lay-s*Y*oan) *f* injury

letra (*lay*-trah) *f* letter

levadura (lay-bhah-*dhoo*-rah) *f* yeast

levantamiento (lay-bhahn-tah-*m*Yayn-toa) *m* rise; rising

levantar (lay-bhahn-*tahr*) *v* lift; *bring up; **levantarse** *v* *rise, *get up

leve (*lay*-bhay) *adj* slight

ley (lay) *f* law

leyenda (lay-Yayn-dah) *f* legend

liar (l*Y*ahr) *v* bundle

libanés (lee-bhah-*nayss*) *adj* Lebanese; *m* Lebanese

Líbano (*lee*-bhah-noa) *m* Lebanon

liberación (lee-bhay-rah-*th*Yoan) *f* liberation; delivery

liberal (lee-bhay-*rahl*) *adj* liberal

liberalismo (lee-bhay-rah-*leez*-moa) *m* liberalism

Liberia (lee-*bhay*-rYah) *f* Liberia

liberiano (lee-bhay-rYah-noa) *adj* Liberian; *m* Liberian

libertad (lee-bhayr-*tahdh*) *f* liberty, freedom

libra (*lee*-bhrah) *f* pound

libranza (lee-*bhrahn*-thah) *f* money order

librar (lee-*bhrahr*) *v* deliver

libre (*lee*-bhray) *adj* free

librería (lee-bhray-*ree*-ah) *f* bookstore

librero (lee-*bhray*-roa) *m* bookseller

libro (*lee*-bhroa) *m* book; ~ **de bolsillo** paperback; ~ **de cocina** cookery-book; ~ **de reclamaciones** complaints book; ~ **de texto** textbook

licencia (lee-*thayn*-thYah) *f* permission, licence; leave

lícito (*lee*-thee-toa) *adj* lawful

licor (lee-*koar*) *m* liqueur

líder (*lee*-dhayr) *m* leader

liebre (l*Y*ay-bhray) *f* hare

liga (*lee*-gah) *f* union, league

ligero (lee-*khay*-roa) *adj* light; slight

lima (*lee*-mah) *f* file; lime; ~ **para las uñas** nail-file

limitar (lee-mee-*tahr*) *v* limit

límite (*lee*-mee-tay) *m* boundary, limit; ~ **de velocidad** speed limit

limón (lee-*moan*) *m* lemon

limonada (lee-moa-*nah*-dhah) *f* lemonade

limpiaparabrisas (leem-p*Y*ah-pah-rah-*bhree*-sahss) *m* windscreen wiper

limpiapipas (leem-p*Y*ah-*pee*-pahss) *m* pipe cleaner

limpiar (leem-*p*Yahr) *v* clean; ~ **en se-**

co dry-clean
limpieza (leem-*p*ʸ*ay*-thah) *f* cleaning
limpio (*leem*-pʸoa) *adj* clean
lindo (*leen*-doa) *adj* sweet
línea (*lee*-nay-ah) *f* line; ~ **de navegación** shipping line; ~ **de pesca** fishing line; ~ **principal** main line
lino (*lee*-noa) *m* linen
linterna (leen-*tayr*-nah) *f* lantern; torch, flash-light
liquidación (lee-kee-dhah-*th*ʸ*oan*) *f* clearance sale
líquido (*lee*-kee-dhoa) *adj* liquid
liso (*lee*-soa) *adj* smooth
lista (*leess*-tah) *f* list; ~ **de correos** poste restante; ~ **de espera** waiting-list; ~ **de precios** price-list
listín telefónico (leess-*teen* tay-lay-*foa*-nee-koa) telephone directory; telephone book *Am*
listo (*leess*-toa) *adj* bright; clever, smart; ready
litera (lee-*tay*-rah) *f* berth
literario (lee-tay-rah-rʸoa) *adj* literary
literatura (lee-tay-rah-*too*-rah) *f* literature
litoral (lee-toa *rahl*) *m* sea-coast
litro (*lee*-troa) *m* litre
lo (loa) *pron* it; ~ **que** what
lobo (*loa*-bhoa) *m* wolf
local (loa-*kahl*) *adj* local
localidad (loa-kah-lee *dhahdh*) *f* locality; seat
localizar (loa-kah-lee-*thahr*) *v* locate
loción (loa-*th*ʸ*oan*) *f* lotion
loco (*loa*-koa) *adj* crazy; mad
locomotora (loa-koa-moa-*toa*-rah) *f* engine, locomotive
locuaz (loa-*kwahth*) *adj* talkative
locura (loa-*koo*-rah) *f* madness, lunacy
lodo (*loa*-dhoa) *m* mud
lodoso (loa-*dhoa*-soa) *adj* muddy
lógica (*loa*-khee-kah) *f* logic
lógico (*loa*-khee-koa) *adj* logical

lograr (loa-*grahr*) *v* achieve; secure
lona (*loa*-nah) *f* canvas; ~ **impermeable** tarpaulin
longitud (loang-khee-*toodh*) *f* length; longitude; - **do onda** wave length
longitudinalmente (loang-khee-too-dhee-nahl-*mayn*-tay) *adv* lengthways
loro (*loa*-roa) *m* parrot
lotería (loa-tay-*ree*-ah) *f* lottery
loza (*loa*-thah) *f* earthenware; pottery, faience, crockery
lubricación (loo-bhree-kah-*th*ʸ*oan*) *f* lubrication
lubricar (loo-bhree-*kahr*) *v* lubricate
lubrificar (loo-bhree-fee-*kahr*) *v* lubricate
lucio (*loo*-thʸoa) *m* pike
*****lucir** (loo-*theer*) *v* *shine
lucha (*loo*-chah) *f* combat, fight; contest, strife; struggle
luchar (loo-*chahr*) *v* struggle, *fight
luego (*lway*-goa) *adv* later; ¡**hasta luego!** so long!
lugar (loo-*gahr*) *m* place; spot; **en ~ de** instead of; ~ **de camping** camping site; ~ **de descanso** holiday resort; ~ **de nacimiento** place of birth; ~ **de reunión** meeting-place; *****tener ~** *take place
lúgubre (*loo*-goo-bhray) *adj* creepy
lujo (*loo*-khoa) *m* luxury
lujoso (loo-*khoa*-soa) *adj* luxurious
lumbago (loom-*bah*-goa) *m* lumbago
luminoso (loo-mee-*noa*-soa) *adj* luminous
luna (*loo*-nah) *f* moon; ~ **de miel** honeymoon
lunático (loo-*nah*-tee-koa) *adj* insane, lunatic
lunes (*loo*-nayss) *m* Monday
lúpulo (*loo*-poo-loa) *m* hop
lustroso (looss-*troa*-soa) *adj* glossy
luto (*loo*-toa) *m* mourning
luz (looth) *f* light; **luces de freno**

brake lights; ~ **de estacionamiento** parking light; ~ **de la luna** moonlight; ~ **del día** daylight; ~ **del sol** sunlight; ~ **lateral** sidelight; ~ **trasera** rear-light

LL

llaga (*lʸah*-gah) *f* sore

llama (*lʸah*-mah) *f* flame

llamada (lʸah-*mah*-dhah) *f* call; ~ **local** local call; ~ **telefónica** telephone call

llamar (lʸah-*mahr*) *v* cry, call; **así llamado** so-called; ~ **por teléfono** phone; **llamarse** *v* *be called

llano (*lʸah*-noa) *adj* flat; level, even, smooth; *m* plain

llanta (*lʸahn*-tah) *f* rim; *fMe* tire

llave (*lʸah*-bhay) *f* key; **ama de llaves** housekeeper; **guardar con ~** lock up; ~ **de la casa** latchkey; ~ **inglesa** spanner

llegada (lʸay-*gah*-dhah) *f* arrival; coming

llegar (lʸay-*gahr*) *v* arrive; ~ **a** attain

llenar (lʸay-*nahr*) *v* fill; fill in; fill out *Am*; fill up

lleno (*lʸay*-noa) *adj* full

llevar (lʸay-*bhahr*) *v* *take; *bear, carry; *wear; **llevarse** *v* *take away

llorar (lʸoa-*rahr*) *v* cry, *weep

*llover (lʸoa-*bhayr*) *v* rain

llovizna (lʸoa-*bheeth*-nah) *f* drizzle

lluvia (*lʸoo*-bhʸah) *f* rain

lluvioso (lʸoo-*bhʸoa*-soa) *adj* rainy

M

macizo (mah-*thee*-thoa) *adj* solid, massive

machacar (mah-chah-*kahr*) *v* mash

macho (*mah*-choa) *adj* male

madera (mah-*dhay*-rah) *f* wood; **de ~** wooden; ~ **de construcción** timber

madero (mah-*dhay*-roa) *m* log

madrastra (mah-*dhrahss*-trah) *f* stepmother

madre (*mah*-dhray) *f* mother

madriguera (mah-dhree-*gay*-rah) *f* den

madrugada (mah-dhroo-*gah*-dhah) *f* daybreak

madrugar (mah-dhroo-*gahr*) *v* *rise early

madurez (mah-dhoo-*rayth*) *f* maturity

maduro (mah-*dhoo*-roa) *adj* mature, ripe

maestro (mah-*ayss*-troa) *m* master; schoolteacher, schoolmaster, teacher; ~ **particular** tutor

magia (*mah*-khʸah) *f* magic

mágico (*mah*-khee-koa) *adj* magic

magistrado (mah-kheess-*trah*-dhoa) *m* magistrate

magnético (mahg-*nay*-tee-koa) *adj* magnetic

magneto (mahg-*nay*-toa) *m* magneto

magnetófono (mahg-nay-*toa*-foa-noa) *m* tape-recorder

magnífico (mahg-*nee*-fee-koa) *adj* splendid, gorgeous, magnificent, swell

magro (*mah*-groa) *adj* lean

magulladura (mah-goo-lʸah-*dhoo*-rah) *f* bruise

magullar (mah-goo-*lʸahr*) *v* bruise

maíz (mah-*eeth*) *m* maize; ~ **en la mazorca** corn on the cob

majestad (mah-khayss-*tahdh*) *f* majesty

mal (mahl) *m* harm, evil; wrong; mischief

malaria (mah-*lah*-rʸah) *f* malaria

Malasia (mah-*lah*-sʸah) *f* Malaysia

malayo (mah-*lah*-ʸoa) *adj* Malaysian; *m* Malay

*maldecir** (mahl-day-*theer*) *v* curse

maldición (mahl-dee-th*ʸoan*) *f* curse

maleta (mah-*lay*-tah) *f* suitcase, bag

maletín (mah-lay-*teen*) *m* grip *nAm*

malévolo (mah-*lay*-bhoa-loa) *adj* spiteful

malicia (mah-lee-th*ʸah*) *f* mischief

malicioso (mah-lee-th*ʸoa*-soa) *adj* malicious

maligno (mah-*leeg*-noa) *adj* malignant; ill

malo (*mah*-loa) *adj* bad; evil, ill

malva (*mahl*-bhah) *adj* mauve

malvado (mahl-*bhah*-dhoa) *adj* wicked, evil

malla (*mah*-lʸah) *f* mesh

mamífero (mah-*mee*-fay-roa) *m* mammal

mampara (mahm-*pah*-rah) *f* screen

mampostear (mahm-poass-tay-*ahr*) *v* *lay bricks

mamut (mah-*moot*) *m* mammoth

manada (mah-*nah*-dhah) *f* herd

manantial (mah-nahn-t*ʸahl*) *m* spring

mancuernillas (mahn-kwayr-*nee*-lʸahss) *fplMe* cuff-links *pl*

mancha (*mahn*-chah) *f* stain, spot, speck; blot

manchado (mahn-*chah*-dhoa) *adj* soiled

manchar (mahn-*chahr*) *v* stain

mandar (mahn-*dahr*) *v* command; *send; ~ **a buscar** *send for

mandarina (mahn-dah-*ree*-nah) *f* mandarin, tangerine

mandato (mahn-*dah*-toa) *m* mandate; order

mandíbula (mahn-*dee*-bhoo-lah) *f* jaw

mando (*mahn*-doa) *m* command

manejable (mah-nay-*khah*-bhlay) *adj* handy; manageable

manejar (mah-nay-*khahr*) *v* handle

manejo (mah-*nay*-khoa) *m* management

manera (mah-*nay*-rah) *f* way, manner; **de otra ~** otherwise

manga (*mahng*-gah) *f* sleeve

mango (*mahng*-goa) *m* handle

manía (mah-*nee*-ah) *f* craze

manicura (mah-nee-*koo*-rah) *f* manicure; *hacer la ~** manicure

manifestación (mah-nee-fayss-tah-th*ʸoan*) *f* demonstration; *hacer una ~** demonstrate

*manifestar** (mah-nee-fayss-*tahr*) *v* reveal

maniquí (mah-nee-*kee*) *m* model, mannequin

mano (*mah*-noa) *f* hand; **de segunda ~** second-hand; **hecho a ~** handmade

mansión (mahn-s*ʸoan*) *f* mansion

manso (*mahn*-soa) *adj* tame

manta (*mahn*-tah) *f* blanket

mantel (mahn-*tayl*) *m* table-cloth

*mantener** (mahn-tay-*nayr*) *v* maintain

mantenimiento (mahn-tay-nee-m*ʸayn*-toa) *m* maintenance

mantequilla (mahn-tay-kee-*lʸah*) *f* butter

manual (mah-*nwahl*) *adj* manual; *m* handbook; **~ de conversación** phrase-book

manuscrito (mah-nooss-*kree*-toa) *m* manuscript

manutención (mah-noo-tayn-th*ʸoan*) *f* upkeep

manzana (mahn-*thah*-nah) *f* apple; **~ de casas** house block *Am*

mañana (mah-*ñah*-nah) *f* morning;

adv tomorrow; **esta** ~ this morning

mapa (_mah_-pah) _m_ map; ~ **de carreteras** road map

maquillaje (mah-kee-_lʸah_-khay) _m_ make-up

máquina (_mah_-kee-nah) _f_ engine, machine; ~ **de afeitar** razor; ~ **de billetes** ticket machine; ~ **de coser** sewing-machine; ~ **de escribir** typewriter; ~ **de lavar** washing-machine; ~ **tragamonedas** slot-machine

maquinaria (mah-kee-_nah_-rʸah) _f_ machinery

mar (mahr) _m_ sea; **orilla del** ~ seaside, seashore

maravilla (mah-rah-_bhee_-lʸah) _f_ marvel

maravillarse (mah-rah-bhee-_lʸahr_-say) _v_ marvel

maravilloso (mah-rah-bhee-_lʸoa_-soa) _adj_ wonderful, marvellous, fine

marca (_mahr_-kah) _f_ brand; mark; ~ **de fábrica** trademark

marcar (mahr-_kahr_) _v_ mark; score

marco (_mahr_-koa) _m_ frame

marcha (_mahr_-chah) _f_ march; *dar ~ **atrás** reverse; ~ **atrás** reverse

marchar (mahr-_chahr_) _v_ march

marea (mah-_ray_-ah) _f_ tide

mareado (mah-ray-_ah_-dhoa) _adj_ dizzy, giddy; seasick

mareo (mah-_ray_-oa) _m_ giddiness; seasickness

marfil (mahr-_feel_) _m_ ivory

margarina (mahr-gah-_ree_-nah) _f_ margarine

margen (_mahr_-khayn) _m_ margin

marido (mah-_ree_-dhoa) _m_ husband

marina (mah-_ree_-nah) _f_ navy; seascape

marinero (mah-ree-_nay_-roa) _m_ sailor

marino (mah-_ree_-noa) _m_ seaman

mariposa (mah-ree-_poa_-sah) _f_ butterfly

marisco (mah-_reess_-koa) _m_ shellfish

marisma (mah-_reez_-mah) _f_ swamp

marítimo (mah-_ree_-tee-moa) _adj_ maritime

mármol (_mahr_-moal) _m_ marble

marqués (mahr-_kayss_) _m_ marquis

marroquí (mah-rroa-_kee_) _adj_ Moroccan; _m_ Moroccan

Marruecos (mah-_rrway_-koass) _m_ Morocco

martes (_mahr_-tayss) _m_ Tuesday

martillo (mahr-_tee_-lʸoa) _m_ hammer

mártir (_mahr_-teer) _m_ martyr

marzo (_mahr_-thoa) March

mas (mahss) _conj_ but

más (mahss) _adv_ more; plus; **algo** ~ some more; **el** ~ most; ~ **de** over

masa (_mah_-sah) _f_ mass; crowd, lot; dough, batter

masaje (mah-_sah_-khay) _m_ massage; *dar ~ massage; ~ **facial** face massage

masajista (mah-sah-_kheess_-tah) _m_ masseur

máscara (_mahss_-kah-rah) _f_ mask; ~ **facial** face-pack

masculino (mahss-koo-_lee_-noa) _adj_ masculine

masticar (mahss-tee-_kahr_) _v_ chew

mástil (_mahss_-teel) _m_ mast

matar (mah-_tahr_) _v_ kill

mate (_mah_-tay) _adj_ mat, dim, dull

matemáticas (mah-tay-_mah_-tee-kahss) _fpl_ mathematics

matemático (mah-tay-_mah_-tee-koa) _adj_ mathematical

materia (mah-_tay_-rʸah) _f_ matter; ~ **prima** raw material

material (mah-tay-_rʸahl_) _adj_ material, substantial; _m_ material

matiz (mah-_teeth_) _m_ nuance

matorral (mah-toa-_rrahl_) _m_ scrub, bush

matrícula (mah-*tree*-koo-lah) f registration number

matrimonial (mah-tree-moa-n^y*ahl*) adj matrimonial

matrimonio (mah-tree-*moa*-n^yoa) m wedding, marriage; matrimony

matriz (mah-*treeth*) f womb

mausoleo (mou-soa-*lay*-oa) m mausoleum

máximo (*mahk*-see-moa) m maximum

mayo (*mah*-^yoa) May

mayor (mah-*y*oar) adj superior, major; main, eldest; m major

mayoría (mah-^yoa-*ree*-ah) f majority; bulk

mayorista (mah-^yoa-*reess*-tah) m wholesale dealer

mayúscula (mah-^y*ooss*-koo-lah) f capital letter

mazo (*mah*-thoa) m mallet

me (may) pron me; myself

mecánico (may-*kah*-nee-koa) adj mechanical; m mechanic

mecanismo (may-kah-*neez*-moa) m mechanism, machinery

mecanografiar (may-kah-noa-grah-f^y*ahr*) v type

mecer (may-*thayr*) v rock

mecha (*may*-chah) f fuse

medalla (may-*dhah*-l^yah) f medal

media (*may*-dh^yah) f stocking; ~ pantalón panty-hose; medias elásticas support hose

mediador (may-dh^yah-*dhoar*) m mediator

medianamente (may-dh^yah-nah-*mayn*-tay) adv fairly

mediano (may-*dh^yah*-noa) adj medium

medianoche (may-dh^yah-*noa*-chay) f midnight

mediante (may-*dh^yahn*-tay) adv by means of

mediar (may-*dh^yahr*) v mediate

medicamento (may-dhee-kah-*mayn*-toa) m medicine, drug

medicina (may-dhee-*thee*-nah) f medicine

médico (*may*-dhee-koa) adj medical; m doctor, physician; ~ de cabecera general practitioner

medida (may-*dhee*-dhah) f measure; hecho a la ~ made to order, tailor-made

medidor (may-dhee-*dhoar*) m gauge

medieval (may-dh^yay-*bhahl*) adj mediaeval

medio (*may*-dh^yoa) adj half; medium; middle; m midst, middle; means; en ~ de amid; ~ ambiente milieu, environment

mediocre (may-dh^yoa-kray) adj moderate, poor

mediodía (may-dh^yoa-*dhee*-ah) m midday, noon

* **medir** (may-*dheer*) v measure

meditación (may-dhee-tah-*th^yoan*) f meditation

meditar (may-dhee-*tahr*) v meditate

Mediterráneo (may-dhee-tay-*rrah*-nay-oa) Mediterranean

médula (*may*-dhoo-lah) f marrow

medusa (may-*dhoo*-sah) f jelly-fish

mejicano (may-khee-*kah*-noa) adj Mexican; m Mexican

Méjico (*may*-khee-koa) m Mexico

mejilla (may-*khee*-l^yah) f cheek

mejillón (may-khee-*l^yoan*) m mussel

mejor (may-*khoar*) adj better; superior

mejora (may-*khoa*-rah) f improvement

mejorar (may-khoa-*rahr*) v improve

melancolía (may-lahng-koa-*lee*-ah) f melancholy

melancólico (may-lahng-*koa*-lee-koa) adj sad

melocotón (may-loa-koa-*toan*) m peach

melodía (may-loa-*dhee*-ah) f melody
melodioso (may-loa-*dhᵞoa*-soa) adj tuneful
melodrama (may-loa-*dhrah*-mah) m melodrama
melón (may-*loan*) m melon
membrana (maym-*brah*-nah) f diaphragm
memorable (may-moa-*rah*-bhlay) adj memorable
memoria (may-*moa*-rᵞah) f memory; **de ~** by heart
menaje (may-*nah*-khay) m household
mención (mayn-*thᵞoan*) f mention
mencionar (mayn-thᵞoa-*nahr*) v mention
mendigar (mayn-dee-*gahr*) v beg
mendigo (mayn-*dee*-goa) m beggar
menor (may-*noar*) adj minor; junior
menos (may-noass) adv less; minus; but; **a ~ que** unless; **por lo ~** at least
menosprecio (may-noass-*pray*-thᵞoa) m contempt
mensaje (mayn-*sah*-khay) m message
mensajero (mayn-sah-*khay*-roa) m messenger
menstruación (mayns-trwah-*thᵞoan*) f menstruation
mensual (mayn-*swahl*) adj monthly
menta (*mayn*-tah) f mint; peppermint
mental (mayn-*tahl*) adj mental
mente (*mayn*-tay) f mind
*****mentir** (mayn-*teer*) v lie
mentira (mayn-*tee*-rah) f lie
menú (may-*noo*) m menu
menudo (may-*noo*-dhoa) adj minute, small, tiny; **a ~** often
mercado (mayr-*kah*-dhoa) m market; **~ negro** black market
mercancía (mayr-kahn-*thee*-ah) f merchandise
mercería (mayr-thay-*ree*-ah) f haberdashery

mercurio (mayr-*koo*-rᵞoa) m mercury
*****merecer** (may-ray-*thayr*) v merit, deserve
meridional (may-ree-dhᵞoa-*nahl*) adj southern, southerly
merienda (may-*rᵞayn*-dah) f tea
mérito (*may*-ree-toa) m merit
merluza (mayr-*loo*-thah) f whiting
mermelada (mayr-may-*lah*-dhah) f jam
mes (mayss) m month
mesa (*may*-sah) f table
mesera (may-*say*-rah) fMe waitress
mesero (may-*say*-roa) mMe waiter
meseta (may-*say*-tah) f plateau
meta (*may*-tah) f goal; finish
metal (may-*tahl*) m metal
metálico (may-*tah*-lee-koa) adj metal
meter (may-*tayr*) v *put
meticuloso (may-tee-koo-*loa*-soa) adj precise
metódico (may-*toa*-dhee-koa) adj methodical
método (*may*-toa-dhoa) m method
métrico (*may*-tree-koa) adj metric
metro (*may*-troa) m metre; underground; subway nAm
mezcla (*mayth*-klah) f mixture
mezclar (mayth-*klahr*) v mix; **mezclarse en** interfere with
mezquino (mayth-*kee*-noa) adj narrow-minded, stingy; mean
mezquita (mayth-*kee*-tah) f mosque
mi (mee) adj my
micrófono (mee-*kroa*-foa-noa) m microphone
microscopio (mee-kroass-*koa*-pᵞoa) m microscope
microsurco (mee-kroa-*soor*-koa) m long-playing record
miedo (*mᵞay*-dhoa) m fear, fright; *****tener ~** *be afraid
miel (mᵞayl) f honey
miembro (*mᵞaym*-broa) m limb; member

mientras (*m^yayn*-trahss) *conj* whilst, while

miércoles (*m^yayr*-koa-layss) *m* Wednesday

migaja (mee-*gah*-khah) *f* crumb

migraña (mee-*grah*-ñah) *f* migraine

mil (meel) *num* thousand

milagro (mee-lah-*groa*) *m* wonder, miracle

milagroso (mee-lah-*groa*-soa) *adj* miraculous

militar (mee-lee-*tahr*) *adj* military; *m* soldier

milla (*mee*-l^yah) *f* mile

millaje (mee-*l^yah*-khay) *m* mileage

millón (mee-*l^yoan*) *m* million

millonario (mee-l^yoa-nah-r^yoa) *m* millionaire

mimar (mee-*mahr*) *v* *spoil

mina (*mee*-nah) *f* mine; pit; ~ **de oro** goldmine

mineral (mee-nay-*rahl*) *m* mineral; ore

minería (mee-nay-*ree*-ah) *f* mining

minero (mee-nay-roa) *m* miner

miniatura (mee-n^yah-*too*-rah) *f* miniature

mínimo (*mee*-nee-moa) *adj* least

mínimum (*mee*-nee-moom) *m* minimum

ministerio (mee-neess-*tay*-r^yoa) *m* ministry

ministro (mee-*neess*-troa) *m* minister

minoría (mee-noa-*ree*-ah) *f* minority

minorista (mee-noa-*reess*-tah) *m* retailer

minucioso (mee-noo-*th^yoa*-soa) *adj* thorough

minusválido (mee-nooz-*bhah*-lee-*dhoa*) *adj* disabled

minuto (mee-*noo*-toa) *m* minute

mío (*mee*-oa) *pron* mine

miope (*m^yoa*-pay) *adj* short-sighted

mirada (mee-*rah*-dhah) *f* look

mirar (mee-*rahr*) *v* look; watch, view, look at; stare, gaze

mirlo (*meer*-loa) *m* blackbird

misa (*mee*-sah) *f* Mass

misceláneo (mee-thay-*lah*-nay-oa) *adj* miscellaneous

miserable (mee-say-*rah*-bhlay) *adj* miserable

miseria (mee-*say*-r^yah) *f* misery

misericordia (mee-say-ree-*koar*-d^yah) *f* mercy

misericordioso (mee-say-ree-koar-*d^yoa*-soa) *adj* merciful

misión (mee-*s^yoan*) *f* mission

mismo (*meez*-moa) *adj* same

misterio (meess-*tay*-r^yoa) *m* mystery

misterioso (meess-tay-*r^yoa*-soa) *adj* mysterious; obscure

mitad (mee-*tahdh*) *f* half; **partir por la** ~ halve

mito (*mee*-toa) *m* myth

moción (moa-*th^yoan*) *f* motion

mochila (moa-*chee*-lah) *f* rucksack, knapsack

moda (*moa*-dhah) *f* fashion; **a la** ~ fashionable

modales (moa-*dhah*-layss) *mpl* manners *pl*

modelar (moa-dhay-*lahr*) *v* model

modelo (moa-*dhay*-loa) *m* model

moderado (moa-dhay-*rah*-dhoa) *adj* moderate

moderno (moa-*dhayr*-noa) *adj* modern

modestia (moa-dhayss-*t^yah*) *f* modesty

modesto (moa-*dhayss*-toa) *adj* modest

modificación (moa-dhee-fee-kah-*th^yoan*) *f* change

modificar (moa-dhee-fee-*kahr*) *v* change, modify

modismo (moa-*dheez*-moa) *m* idiom

modista (moa-*dheess*-tah) *f* dressmaker

modo (*moa*-dhoa) *m* fashion, manner; **de cualquier** ~ anyhow; **de ningún** ~ by no means; **de todos modos**

any way; at any rate; **en ~ alguno** at all; **~ de empleo** directions for use

mohair (moa-*ayr*) *m* mohair

moho (*moa*-oa) *m* mildew

mojado (moa-*khah*-dhoa) *adj* wet; moist, damp

mojigato (moa-khee-*gah*-toa) *adj* hypocritical

mojón (moa-*khoan*) *m* landmark

*moler (moa-*layr*) *v* *grind

molestar (moa-layss-*tahr*) *v* disturb, trouble, bother

molestia (moa-*layss*-tʸah) *f* trouble, nuisance, bother

molesto (moa-*layss*-toa) *adj* troublesome, inconvenient

molinero (moa-lee-*nay*-roa) *m* miller

molino (moa-*lee*-noa) *m* mill; **~ de viento** windmill

momentáneo (moa-mayn-*tah*-nay-oa) *adj* momentary

momento (moa-*mayn*-toa) *m* moment

monarca (moa-*nahr*-kah) *m* monarch, ruler

monarquía (moa-nahr-*kee*-ah) *f* monarchy

monasterio (moa-nahss-*tay*-rʸoa) *m* monastery

moneda (moa-*nay*-dhah) *f* currency; coin; change; **~ extranjera** foreign currency

monedero (moa-nay-*dhay*-roa) *m* purse

monetario (moa-nay-tah-rʸoa) *adj* monetary; **unidad monetaria** monetary unit

monja (*moang*-khah) *f* nun

monje (*moang*-khay) *m* monk

mono (*moa*-noa) *m* monkey; overalls *pl*

monólogo (moa-*noa*-loa-goa) *m* monologue

monopolio (moa-noa-*poa*-lʸoa) *m* monopoly

monótono (moa-*noa*-toa-noa) *adj* monotonous

monstruo (*moans*-trwoa) *m* monster

montaña (moan-*tah*-ñah) *f* mountain

montañismo (moan-tah-*ñeez*-moa) *m* mountaineering

montañoso (moan-tah-*ño*a-soa) *adj* mountainous

montar (moan-*tahr*) *v* mount, *get on; assemble; *ride

monte (*moan*-tay) *m* mount

montículo (moan-*tee*-koo-loa) *m* mound

montón (moan-*toan*) *m* heap, stack, pile

montuoso (moan-*twoa*-soa) *adj* hilly

monumento (moa-noo-*mayn*-toa) *m* monument; memorial

mora (*moa*-rah) *f* mulberry; blackberry

morado (moa-*rah*-dhoa) *adj* violet

moral (moa-*rahl*) *adj* moral; *f* moral; spirits

moralidad (moa-rah-lee-*dhahdh*) *f* morality

mordaza (moar-*dhah*-thah) *f* clamp

mordedura (moar-dhay-*dhoo*-rah) *f* bite

*morder (moar-*dhayr*) *v* *bite

morena (moa-*ray*-nah) *f* brunette

moreno (moa-*ray*-noa) *adj* brown

moretón (moa-ray-*toan*) *m* bruise

morfina (moar-*fee*-nah) *f* morphine, morphia

*morir (moa-*reer*) *v* die

moro (*moa*-roa) *m* Moor

morral (moa-*rrahl*) *m* haversack

morro (*moa*-rroa) *m* pussy-cat

mortal (moar-*tahl*) *adj* mortal; fatal

mosaico (moa-*sigh*-koa) *m* mosaic

mosca (*moass*-kah) *f* fly

mosquitero (moass-kee-*tay*-roa) *m* mosquito-net

mosquito (moass-*kee*-toa) *m* mosquito
mostaza (moass-*tah*-thah) *f* mustard
mostrador (moass-trah-*dhoar*) *m* counter
***mostrar** (moass-*trahr*) *v* display, *show
mote (*moa*-tay) *m* nickname
moteado (moa-tay-*ah*-dhoa) *adj* spotted
motel (moa-*tayl*) *m* motel
motín (moa-*teen*) *m* riot
motivo (moa-*tee*-bhoa) *m* motive; cause, occasion
motocicleta (moa-toa-thee-*klay*-tah) *f* motor-cycle; motorbike *nAm*
motoneta (moa-toa-*nay*-tah) *f* scooter
motor (moa-*toar*) *m* motor, engine; ~ **de arranque** starter motor
***mover** (moa-*bhayr*) *v* move; stir
movible (moa-*bhee*-bhlay) *adj* movable
móvil (*moa*-bheel) *adj* mobile
movimiento (moa-bhee-*mʸayn*-toa) *m* movement, motion
mozo (*moa*-thoa) *m* boy; porter
muchacha (moo-*chah*-chah) *f* girl; maid
muchacho (moo-*chah*-choa) *m* boy; lad
muchedumbre (moo-chay-*dhoom*-bray) *f* crowd
mucho (*moo* choa) *adv* much; far, very; *adj* much; **con ~** by far; **muchos** *adj* many
mudanza (moo-*dhahn*-thah) *f* move
mudarse (moo-*dhahr*-say) *v* move; change
mudo (*moo*-dhoa) *adj* mute, dumb
muebles (*mway*-bhlayss) *mpl* furniture
muela (*mway*-lah) *f* molar; **dolor de muelas** toothache
muelle (*mway*-lʸay) *m* dock, wharf, quay; pier, jetty; spring
muerte (*mwayr*-tay) *f* death

muerto (*mwayr*-toa) *adj* dead
muestra (*mwayss*-trah) *f* sample
mugir (moo-*kheer*) *v* roar
mujer (moo-*khayr*) *f* woman; wife
mújol (*moo*-khoal) *m* mullet
muleta (moo-*lay*-tah) *f* crutch
mulo (*moo*-loa) *m* mule
multa (*mool*-tah) *f* fine; ticket
multiplicación (mool-tee-plee-kah-*thʸoan*) *f* multiplication
multiplicar (mool-tee-plee-*kahr*) *v* multiply
multitud (mool-tee-*toodh*) *f* crowd
mundial (moon-*dʸahl*) *adj* world-wide, global
mundo (*moon*-doa) *m* world; **todo el ~** everyone
municipal (moo-nee-thee-*pahl*) *adj* municipal
municipalidad (moo-nee-thee-pah-lee-*dhahdh*) *f* municipality
muñeca (moo-*ñay*-kah) *f* doll; wrist
muralla (moo-*rah*-lʸah) *f* wall
muro (*moo*-roa) *m* wall
músculo (*mooss*-koo-loa) *m* muscle
musculoso (mooss-koo-*loa*-soa) *adj* muscular
muselina (moo-say-*lee*-nah) *f* muslin
museo (moo-*say*-oa) *m* museum; ~ **de figuras de cera** waxworks *pl*
musgo (*mooz*-goa) *m* moss
música (*moo*-see-kah) *f* music
musical (moo-see-*kahl*) *adj* musical; **comedia ~** musical comedy
músico (*moo*-see-koa) *m* musician
muslo (*mooz*-loa) *m* thigh
musulmán (moo-sool-*mahn*) *m* Muslim
mutuo (*moo*-twoa) *adj* mutual
muy (moo*ee*) *adv* very, quite

N

nácar (*nah*-kahr) *m* mother-of-pearl

*nacer (nah-*thayr*) *v* *be born

nacido (nah-*thee*-dhoa) *adj* born

nacimiento (nah-thee-*m*ᵞ*ayn*-toa) *m* birth; rise

nación (nah-*th*ᵞ*oan*) *f* nation

nacional (nah-th*ᵞ*oa-*nahl*) *adj* national

nacionalidad (nah-th*ᵞ*oa-nah-lee-*dhahdh*) *f* nationality

nacionalizar (nah-th*ᵞ*oa-nah-lee-*thahr*) *v* nationalize

nada (*nah*-dhah) nothing; nil

nadador (nah-dhah-*dhoar*) *m* swimmer

nadar (nah-*dhahr*) *v* *swim

nadie (*nah*-dh*ᵞ*ay) *pron* nobody, no one

naipe (*nigh*-pay) *m* playing-card

nalga (*nahl*-gah) *m* buttock

naranja (nah-*rahng*-khah) *f* orange

narciso (nahr-*thee*-soa) *m* daffodil

narcosis (nahr-*koa*-seess) *f* narcosis

narcótico (nahr-*koa*-tee-koa) *m* narcotic

nariz (nah-*reeth*) *f* nose

narración (nah-rrah-*th*ᵞ*oan*) *f* account

nata (*nah*-tah) *f* cream

natación (nah-tah-*th*ᵞ*oan*) *f* swimming

nativo (nah-*tee*-bhoa) *adj* native

natural (nah-too-*rahl*) *adj* natural; *m* nature

naturaleza (nah-too-rah-*lay*-thah) *f* nature

naturalmente (nah-too-rahl-*mayn*-tay) *adv* naturally

náusea (*nou*-say-ah) *f* nausea, sickness

navaja (nah-*bhah*-khah) *f* pocket-knife

naval (nah-*bhahl*) *adj* naval

navegable (nah-bhay-*gah*-bhlay) *adj* navigable

navegación (nah-bhay-gah-*th*ᵞ*oan*) *f* navigation

navegar (nah-bhay-*gahr*) *v* sail; navigate

Navidad (nah-bhee-*dhahdh*) *f* Xmas, Christmas

nebuloso (nay-bhoo-*loa*-soa) *adj* misty

necesario (nay-thay-*sah*-r*ᵞ*oa) *adj* necessary; requisite

neceser (nay-thay-*sayr*) *m* toilet case

necesidad (nay-thay-see-*dhahdh*) *f* need, necessity; want; misery

necesitar (nay-thay-see-*tahr*) *v* need

necio (*nay*-th*ᵞ*oa) *adj* foolish, silly

*negar (nay-*gahr*) *v* deny

negativa (nay-gah-*tee*-bhah) *f* refusal

negativo (nay-gah-*tee*-bhoa) *adj* negative; *m* negative

negligencia (nay-glee-*khayn*-th*ᵞ*ah) *f* neglect

negligente (nay-glee-*khayn*-tay) *adj* neglectful, careless

negociación (nay-goa-th*ᵞ*ah-*th*ᵞ*oan*) *f* negotiation

negociante (nay-goa-th*ᵞ*ahn-tay) *m* dealer

negociar (nay-goa-th*ᵞ*ahr) *v* negotiate

negocio (nay-*goa*-th*ᵞ*oa) *m* business; ***hacer negocios con** *deal with; **hombre de negocios** businessman; **~ fotográfico** camera shop; **viaje de negocios** business trip

negro (*nay*-groa) *adj* black; *m* Negro

neón (nay-*oan*) *m* neon

nervio (*nayr*-bh*ᵞ*oa) *m* nerve

nervioso (nayr-*bh*ᵞ*oa*-soa) *adj* nervous

neto (*nay*-toa) *adj* net

neumático (nay°°-*mah*-tee-koa) *adj* pneumatic; *m* tyre, tire; **~ de repuesto** spare tyre; **~ desinflado** flat tyre

neumonía (nay°°-moa-*nee*-ah) *f* pneumonia

neuralgia (nay°°-*rahl*-kh*ᵞ*ah) *f* neu-

ralgia
neurosis (nay⁰⁰-*roa*-seess) *f* neurosis
neutral (nay⁰⁰-*trahl*) *adj* neutral
neutro (*nay⁰⁰*-troa) *adj* neuter
*****nevar** (nay *bhahr*) *v* snow
nevasca (nay-*bhahss*-kah) *f* snowstorm
nevoso (nay-*bhoa*-soa) *adj* snowy
ni ... ni (nee) neither ... nor
nicotina (nee-koa-*tee*-nah) *f* nicotine
nido (*nee*-dhoa) *m* nest
niebla (*nⁱay*-hhlah) *f* mist, fog; haze;
  faro de ~ foglamp
nieta (*nⁱay*-tah) *f* granddaughter
nieto (*nⁱay*-toa) *m* grandson
nieve (*nⁱay*-bhay) *f* snow
Nigeria (nee-*khay*-rⁱah) *f* Nigeria
nigeriano (nee-khay-rⁱah-noa) *adj* Nigerian; *m* Nigerian
ninguno (neeng-*goo*-noa) *adj* no;
  pron none; **~ de los dos** neither
niñera (nee-*ñay*-rah) *f* nurse
niño (*nee*-ñoa) *m* child; kid
níquel (*nee*-kayl) *m* nickel
nitrógeno (nee-*troa*-khay-noa) *m* nitrogen
nivel (nee-*bhayl*) *m* level; **~ de vida**
  standard of living; **paso a ~** level
  crossing
nivelar (nee-bhay-*lahr*) *v* level
no (noa) not; no; **si ~** otherwise, else
noble (*noa*-bhlay) *adj* noble
nobleza (noa-*bhlay*-thah) *f* nobility
noción (noa-*thⁱoan*) *f* notion; idea
nocturno (noak-*toor*-noa) *adj* nightly
noche (*noa*-chay) *f* night; **de ~** overnight, by night; **esta ~** tonight
nogal (noa-*gahl*) *m* walnut
nombramiento (noam-brah-*mⁱayn*-toa)
  m appointment, nomination
nombrar (noam-*brahr*) *v* name, mention; appoint, nominate
nombre (*noam*-bray) *m* noun; name;
  denomination; **en ~ de** on behalf
  of, in the name of; **~ de pila** Chris-

tian name, first name
nominación (noa-mee-nah-*thⁱoan*) *f*
  nomination
nominal (noa-mee-*nahl*) *adj* nominal
nordeste (noar-*dhayss*-tay) *m* north-
  east
norma (*noar*-mah) *f* standard
normal (noar-*mahl*) *adj* normal; regular, standard
noroeste (noa-roa-*ayss*-tay) *m* north-
  west
norte (*noar*-tay) *m* north; **del ~**
  northerly; **polo ~** North Pole
norteño (noar-*tay*-ñoa) *adj* northern
Noruega (noa-*rway*-gah) *f* Norway
noruego (noa-*rway*-goa) *adj* Norwegian; *m* Norwegian
nos (noass) *pron* ourselves
nosotros (noa-*soa*-troass) *pron* we; us
nostalgia (noass-*tahl*-khⁱah) *f* homesickness
nota (*noa*-tah) *f* ticket; note; mark
notable (noa-*tah*-bhlay) *adj* considerable; remarkable, striking, noticeable
notar (noa-*tahr*) *v* notice; note
notario (noa-*tah*-rⁱoa) *m* notary
noticia (noa-*tee*-thⁱah) *f* news, notice;
  noticias *fpl* news, tidings *pl*
noticiario (noa-tee-*thⁱah*-rⁱoa) *m*
  news; newsreel
notificar (noa-tee-fee-*kahr*) *v* notify
notorio (noa-*toa*-rⁱoa) *adj* well-known
novedad (noa-bhay-*dhahdh*) *f* novelty
novela (noa-*bhay*-lah) *f* novel; **~ policíaca** detective story; **~ por entregas** serial
novelista (noa-bhay-*leess*-tah) *m* novelist
noveno (noa-*bhay*-noa) *num* ninth
noventa (noa-*bhayn*-tah) *num* ninety
novia (*noa*-bhⁱah) *f* fiancée; bride
noviazgo (noa-*bhⁱahth*-goa) *m* engagement

noviembre (noa-*bh*ᵞ*aym*-bray) November

***hacer novillos** (ah-*thayr* noa-*bhee*-lᵞoass) play truant

novio (*noa*-bhᵞoa) *m* fiancé; bridegroom

nube (*noo*-bhay) *f* cloud

nublado (noo-*bhlah*-dhoa) *adj* cloudy, overcast

nuca (*noo*-kah) *f* nape of the neck

nuclear (noo-klay-*ahr*) *adj* nuclear

núcleo (*noo*-klay-oa) *m* nucleus; heart, essence, core

nudillo (noo-*dhee*-lᵞoa) *m* knuckle

nudo (*noo*-dhoa) *m* knot; lump; ~ **corredizo** loop

nuestro (*nwayss*-troa) *adj* our

Nueva Zelanda (*nway*-bhah thay-*lahn*-dah) New Zealand

nueve (*nway*-bhay) *num* nine

nuevo (*nway*-bhoa) *adj* new; **de ~** again

nuez (nwayth) *f* nut; ~ **moscada** nutmeg

nulo (*noo*-loa) *adj* invalid, void

numeral (noo-may-*rahl*) *m* numeral

número (*noo*-may-roa) *m* number; digit; quantity; size; act

numeroso (noo-may-*roa*-soa) *adj* numerous

nunca (*noong*-kah) *adv* never

nutritivo (noo-tree-*tee*-bhoa) *adj* nutritious, nourishing

nylon (*nigh*-loan) *m* nylon

O

o (oa) *conj* or; **o … o** either … or

oasis (oa-*ah*-seess) *f* oasis

***obedecer** (oa-bhay-dhay-*thayr*) *v* obey

obediencia (oa-bhay-*dh*ᵞ*ayn*-th*ᵞ*ah) *f* obedience

obediente (oa-bhay-*dh*ᵞ*ayn*-tay) *adj* obedient

obertura (oa-bhayr-*too*-rah) *f* overture

obesidad (oa-bhay-see-*dhahdh*) *f* fatness

obeso (oa-*bhay*-soa) *adj* corpulent

obispo (oa-*bheess*-poa) *m* bishop

objeción (oabh-khay-th*ᵞ*oan) *f* objection; ***hacer ~ a** mind

objetar (oabh-khay-*tahr*) *v* object

objetivo (oabh-khay-*tee*-bhoa) *adj* objective; *m* design, objective, target

objeto (oabh-*khay*-toa) *m* object; **objetos de valor** valuables *pl*; **objetos perdidos** lost and found

oblea (oa-*bhlay*-ah) *f* wafer

oblicuo (oa-*bhlee*-kwoa) *adj* slanting

obligar (oa-bhlee-*gahr*) *v* oblige; force

obligatorio (oa-bhlee-gah-*toa*-rᵞoa) *adj* compulsory, obligatory

oblongo (oa-*bhloang*-goa) *adj* oblong

obra (*oa*-bhrah) *f* work; ~ **de arte** work of art; ~ **de teatro** play; ~ **hecha a mano** handwork; ~ **maestra** masterpiece

obrar (oa-*bhrahr*) *v* work; perform

obrero (oa-*bhray*-roa) *m* workman, worker, labourer; ~ **portuario** docker

obsceno (oabh-*thay*-noa) *adj* obscene

obscuridad (oabhs-koo-ree-*dhahdh*) *f* gloom

obscuro (oabhs-*koo*-roa) *adj* dark, obscure

observación (oabh-sayr-bhah-th*ᵞ*oan) *f* observation; remark; ***hacer una ~** remark

observar (oabh-sayr-*bhahr*) *v* watch, observe, notice, note

observatorio (oabh-sayr-bhah-*toa*-rᵞoa) *m* observatory

obsesión (oabh-say-s*ᵞ*oan) *f* obsession

obstáculo (oabhs-*tah*-koo-loa) *m* obstacle

no obstante (noa oabhs-*tahn*-tay) nevertheless

obstinado (oabhs-tee-*nah*-dhoa) *adj* dogged, obstinate

***obstruir** (oabhs-*trweer*) *v* block

***obtener** (oabh-tay-*nayr*) *v* obtain

obtenible (oabh-tay-*nee*-bhlay) *adj* available

obtuso (oabh-*too*-soa) *adj* blunt

obvio (*oabh*-bhᵛoa) *adj* apparent, obvious

oca (*oa*-kah) *f* goose

ocasión (oa-kah-sᵛoan) *f* occasion; chance

ocasionalmente (oa-kah-sᵛoa-nahl-*mayn*-tay) *adv* occasionally

ocaso (oa-*kah*-soa) *m* sunset

occidental (oak-thee-dhayn-*tahl*) *adj* westerly; western

occidente (oak-thee-*dhayn*-tay) *m* west

océano (oa-*thay*-ah-noa) *m* ocean; **Océano Pacífico** Pacific Ocean

ocio (*oa*-thᵛoa) *m* leisure

ocioso (oa-*thᵛoa*-soa) *adj* idle

octavo (oak-*tah*-bhoa) *num* eighth

octubre (oak-*too*-bhray) October

oculista (oa-koo-*leess*-tah) *m* oculist

ocultar (oa-kool-*tahr*) *v* *hide

ocupación (oa-koo-pah-*thᵛoan*) *f* occupation; business

ocupante (oa-koo-*pahn*-tay) *m* occupant

ocupar (oa-koo-*pahr*) *v* occupy; *take up; **ocupado** *adj* engaged, busy; occupied; **ocuparse de** look after

ocurrencia (oa-koo-*rrayn*-thᵛah) *f* idea

ocurrir (oa-koo-*rreer*) *v* occur

ochenta (oa-*chayn*-tah) *num* eighty

ocho (*oa*-choa) *num* eight

odiar (oa-*dhᵛahr*) *v* hate

odio (*oa*-dhᵛoa) *m* hatred, hate

oeste (oa-*ayss*-tay) *m* west

ofender (oa-fayn-*dayr*) *v* wound, *hurt, offend, injure

ofensa (oa-*fayn*-sah) *f* offence

ofensivo (oa-fayn-*see*-bhoa) *adj* offensive; *m* offensive

oferta (oa-*fayr*-tah) *f* offer, supply

oficial (oa-fee-*thᵛahl*) *adj* official; *m* officer; ~ **de aduanas** Customs officer

oficina (oa-fee-*thee*-nah) *f* office; ~ **de cambio** exchange office; ~ **de colocación** employment exchange; ~ **de informaciones** information bureau; ~ **de objetos perdidos** lost property office

oficinista (oa-fee-thee-*neess*-tah) *m* clerk

oficio (oa-*fee*-thᵛoa) *m* trade

***ofrecer** (oa-fray-*thayr*) *v* offer

oído (oa-*ee*-dhoa) *m* hearing; **dolor de oídos** earache

***oír** (oa-*eer*) *v* *hear

ojal (oa-*khahl*) *m* buttonhole

ojeada (oa-khay-*ah*-dhah) *f* glimpse, glance; look

ojear (oa-khay-*ahr*) *v* glance

ojo (*oa*-khoa) *m* eye

ola (*oa*-lah) *f* wave

***oler** (oa-*layr*) *v* *smell

olmo (*oal*-moa) *m* elm

olor (oa-*loar*) *m* smell, odour

olvidadizo (oal-bhee-dhah-*dhee*-thoa) *adj* forgetful

olvidar (oal-bhee-*dhahr*) *v* *forget

olla (*oa*-lᵛah) *f* pot; kettle; ~ **a presión** pressure-cooker

ombligo (oam-*blee*-goa) *m* navel

omitir (oa-mee-*teer*) *v* *leave out, omit; fail

omnipotente (oam-nee-poa-*tayn*-tay) *adj* omnipotent

once (*oan*-thay) *num* eleven

onceno (oan-*thay*-noa) *num* eleventh

onda (*oan*-dah) *f* wave

ondulación (oan-doo-lah-*thᵛoan*) *f*

wave; ~ **permanente** permanent wave

ondulado (oan-doo-*lah*-dhoa) *adj* wavy

ondulante (oan-doo-*lahn*-tay) *adj* undulating

ónix (*oa*-neeks) *m* onyx

ópalo (*oa*-pah-loa) *m* opal

opcional (oap-thᵞoa-*nahl*) *adj* optional

ópera (*oa*-pay-rah) *f* opera

operación (oa-pay-rah-*thᵞoan*) *f* operation, surgery

operar (oa-pay-*rahr*) *v* operate

opereta (oa-pay-*ray*-tah) *f* operetta

opinar (oa-pee-*nahr*) *v* consider

opinión (oa-pee-*nᵞoan*) *f* view, opinion

*oponerse (oa-poa-*nayr*-say) *v* oppose; ~ **a** object to

oportunidad (oa-poar-too-nee-*dhahdh*) *f* chance, opportunity

oportuno (oa-poar-*too*-noa) *adj* convenient

oposición (oa-poa-see-*thᵞoan*) *f* opposition

oprimir (oa-pree-*meer*) *v* oppress

óptico (*oap*-tee-koa) *m* optician

optimismo (oap-tee-*meez*-moa) *m* optimism

optimista (oap-tee-*meess*-tah) *adj* optimistic; *m* optimist

óptimo (*oap*-tee-moa) *adj* best

opuesto (oa-*pwayss*-toa) *adj* opposite; averse

oración (oa-rah-*thᵞoan*) *f* prayer

oral (oa-*rahl*) *adj* oral

orar (oa-*rahr*) *v* pray

orden (*oar*-dhayn) *f* command; order; *m* method; **de primer** ~ first-rate; ~ **del día** agenda

ordenar (oar-dhay-*nahr*) *v* arrange; order

ordinario (oar-dhee-*nah*-rᵞoa) *adj* simple, ordinary; common, vulgar

oreja (oa-*ray*-khah) *f* ear

orfebre (oar-*fay*-bhray) *m* goldsmith

orgánico (oar-*gah*-nee-koa) *adj* organic

organillo (oar-gah-*nee*-lᵞoa) *m* street-organ

organismo (oar-gah-*neez*-moa) *m* organism

organización (oar-gah-nee-thah-*thᵞoan*) *f* organization

organizar (oar-gah-nee-*thahr*) *v* organize; arrange

órgano (*oar*-gah-noa) *m* organ

orgullo (oar-*goo*-lᵞoa) *m* pride

orgulloso (oar-goo-*lᵞoa*-soa) *adj* proud

orientación (oa-rᵞayn-tah-*thᵞoan*) *f* orientation

oriental (oa-rᵞayn-*tahl*) *adj* eastern, easterly; oriental

orientarse (oa-rᵞayn-*tahr*-say) *v* orientate

oriente (oa-rᵞayn-tay) *m* Orient

origen (oa-*ree*-khayn) *m* origin

original (oa-ree-khee-*nahl*) *adj* original

originalmente (oa-ree-khee-nahl-*mayn*-tay) *adv* originally

originar (oa-ree-khee-*nahr*) *v* originate

orilla (oa-*ree*-lᵞah) *f* bank; shore

orina (oa-*ree*-nah) *f* urine

orlón (oar-*loan*) *m* orlon

ornamental (oar-nah-mayn-*tahl*) *adj* ornamental

oro (*oa*-roa) *m* gold

orquesta (oar-*kayss*-tah) *f* orchestra; band

ortodoxo (oar-toa-*dhoak*-soa) *adj* orthodox

os (oass) *pron* you

osar (oa-*sahr*) *v* dare

oscilar (oa-thee-*lahr*) *v* *swing

oscuridad (oass-koo-ree-*dhahdh*) *f* dark

oscuro (oass-*koo*-roa) *adj* dark, dim, obscure

oso (*oa*-soa) *m* bear

ostentación (oass-tayn-tah-thⁱoan) *f* fuss

ostra (*oass*-trah) *f* oyster

otoño (oa-*toa*-ñoa) *m* autumn; fall *nAm*

otro (*oa*-troa) *adj* other, different; another; ~ **más** another

ovalado (oa-bhah-*lah*-dhoa) *adj* oval

oveja (oa-*bhay*-khah) *f* sheep

overol (oa-bhay-*roal*) *mMe* overalls *pl*

oxidado (oak-see-*dhah*-dhoa) *adj* rusty

oxígeno (oak-*see*-khay-noa) *m* oxygen

oyente (oa-ⁱyayn-tay) *m* auditor, listener

P

pabellón (pah-bhay-*lⁱoan*) *m* pavilion

***pacer** (pah-*thayr*) *v* graze

paciencia (pah-*thⁱayn*-thⁱah) *f* patience

paciente (pah-*thⁱayn*-tay) *adj* patient; *m* patient

pacifismo (pah-thee-*feez*-moa) *m* pacifism

pacifista (pah-thee-*feess*-tah) *adj* pacifist; *m* pacifist

***padecer** (pah-dhay-*thayr*) *v* suffer

padrastro (pah-*dhrahss*-troa) *m* stepfather

padre (*pah*-dhray) *m* father

padres (*pah*-dhrayss) *mpl* parents *pl*; **adoptivos** foster parents *pl*; **políticos** parents-in-law *pl*

padrino (pah-*dhree*-noa) *m* godfather

paga (*pah*-gah) *f* wages *pl*

pagano (pah-*gah*-noa) *adj* heathen, pagan; *m* heathen, pagan

pagar (pah-*gahr*) *v* *pay; **pagado por adelantado** prepaid; ~ **a plazos** *pay on account

página (*pah*-khee-nah) *f* page

pago (*pah*-goa) *m* payment; **primer** ~ down payment

painel (pigh-*nayl*) *m* panel

país (pah-*eess*) *m* country, land; ~ **natal** native country

paisaje (pigh-*sah*-khay) *m* scenery, landscape

paisano (pigh-*sah*-noa) *m* civilian

Países Bajos (pah-*ee*-sayss -*bah*-khoass) *mpl* the Netherlands

paja (*pah*-khah) *f* straw

pájaro (*pah*-khah-roa) *m* bird

paje (*pah*-khay) *m* page-boy

pala (*pah*-lah) *f* spade, shovel

palabra (pah-*lah*-bhrah) *f* word

palacio (pah-*lah*-thⁱoa) *m* palace

palanca (pah-*lahng*-kah) *f* lever; ~ **de cambios** gear lever

palangana (pah-lahng-*gah*-nah) *f* basin; wash-basin

pálido (*pah*-lee-dhoa) *adj* pale; dull; light

palillo (pah-*lee*-lⁱoa) *m* toothpick

palma (*pahl*-mah) *f* palm

palo (*pah*-loa) *m* stick; ~ **de golf** golf-club

paloma (pah-*loa*-mah) *f* pigeon

palpable (pahl-*pah*-bhlay) *adj* palpable

palpar (pahl-*pahr*) *v* *feel

palpitación (pahl-pee-tah-*thⁱoan*) *f* palpitation

pan (pahn) *m* bread, loaf; ~ **integral** wholemeal bread; ~ **tostado** toast

pana (*pah*-nah) *f* corduroy, velveteen

panadería (pah-nah-dhay-*ree*-ah) *f* bakery

panadero (pah-nah-*dhay*-roa) *m* baker

panecillo (pah-nay-*thee*-lⁱoa) *m* roll

pánico (*pah*-nee-koa) *m* panic

pantalones (pahn-tah-*loa*-nayss) *mpl* trousers *pl*; slacks *pl*; pants *plAm*; ~ **cortos** shorts *pl*; ~ **de esquí** ski pants; ~ **de gimnasia** trunks *pl*

pantalla (pahn-*tah*-lⁱah) *f* lampshade;

screen

pantano (pahn-*tah*-noa) *m* marsh, bog

pantanoso (pahn-tah-*noa*-soa) *adj* marshy

pantorrilla (pahn-toa-*rree*-lʸah) *f* calf

pañal (pah-*ñahl*) *m* nappy; diaper *nAm*

pañería (pah-ñay-*ree*-ah) *f* drapery

pañero (pah-*ñay*-roa) *m* draper

paño (*pah*-ñoa) *m* cloth; ~ **higiénico** sanitary towel

pañuelo (pah-*ñway*-loa) *m* handkerchief; ~ **de papel** tissue, Kleenex®

Papa (*pah*-pah) *m* pope

papa (*pah*-pah) *fMe* potato

papá (pah-*pah*) *m* dad

papaíto (pah-pah-*ee*-toa) *m* daddy

papel (pah-*payl*) *m* paper; **de ~** paper; ~ **carbón** carbon paper; ~ **de envolver** wrapping paper; ~ **de escribir** writing-paper; ~ **de estaño** tinfoil; ~ **de lija** sandpaper; ~ **higiénico** toilet-paper; ~ **para cartas** notepaper; ~ **para mecanografiar** typing paper; ~ **pintado** wallpaper; ~ **secante** blotting paper

papelería (pah-pay-lay-*ree*-ah) *f* stationery; stationer's

paperas (pah-*pay*-rahss) *fpl* mumps

paquete (pah-*kay*-tay) *m* packet, package, parcel; bundle

Paquistán (pah-keess-*tahn*) *m* Pakistan

paquistaní (pah-keess-tah-*nee*) *adj* Pakistani; *m* Pakistani

par (pahr) *adj* even; *m* pair

para (*pah*-rah) *prep* to, for; to, in order to; ~ **con** towards; ~ **que** what for

parabrisas (pah-rah-*bhree*-sahss) *m* windscreen; windshield *nAm*

parachoques (pah-rah-*choa*-kayss) *m* fender, bumper

parada (pah-*rah*-dhah) *f* parade; stop;

~ **de taxis** taxi rank; taxi stand *Am*

parado (pah-*rah*-dhoa) *adjMe* erect

parador (pah-rah-*dhoar*) *m* roadhouse

parafina (pah-rah-*fee*-nah) *f* paraffin

paraguas (pah-*rah*-gwahss) *m* umbrella

paraíso (pah-rah-*ee*-soa) *m* paradise

paralelo (pah-rah-*lay*-loa) *adj* parallel; *m* parallel

paralítico (pah-rah-*lee*-tee-koa) *adj* lame

paralizar (pah-rah-lee-*thahr*) *v* paralise

pararse (pah-*rahr*-say) *v* halt; pull up

parcela (pahr-*thay*-lah) *f* plot

parcial (pahr-*thʸahl*) *adj* partial

parecer (pah-ray-*thayr*) *m* view, opinion

** **parecer** (pah-ray-*thayr*) *v* appear, seem, look

parecido (pah-ray-*thee*-dhoa) *adj* alike; **bien ~** good-looking

pared (pah-*raydh*) *f* wall

pareja (pah-*ray*-khah) *f* couple; partner

pariente (pah-*rʸayn*-tay) *m* relative, relation

parlamentario (pahr-lah-mayn-*tah*-rʸoa) *adj* parliamentary

parlamento (pahr-lah-*mayn*-toa) *m* parliament

párpado (*pahr*-pah-dhoa) *m* eyelid

parque (*pahr*-kay) *m* park; ~ **de estacionamiento** car park; ~ **de reserva zoológica** game reserve; ~ **nacional** national park

parquímetro (pahr-*kee*-may-troa) *m* parking meter

párrafo (*pahr*-rrah-foa) *m* paragraph

parrilla (pah-*rree*-lʸah) *f* grill; grill-room; **asar en ~** grill

parroquia (pah-*rroa*-kʸah) *f* parish

parsimonioso (pahr-see-moa-*nʸoa*-soa) *adj* economical

parte (*pahr*-tay) *f* part; share; **en al-**

guna ~ somewhere; **en ninguna** ~ nowhere; **en** ~ partly; **otra** ~ elsewhere; ~ **posterior** rear; ~ **superior** top, top side; **por otra** ~ besides; **por todas partes** everywhere, throughout

participante (pahr-tee-thee-*pahn*-tay) *m* participant

participar (pahr-tee-thee-*pahr*) *v* participate

particular (pahr-tee-koo-*lahr*) *adj* private; particular; **en** ~ specially, in particular

particularidad (pahr-tee-koo-lah-ree-*dhahdh*) *f* detail; peculiarity

partida (pahr-*tee*-dhah) *f* departure

partido (pahr-*tee*-dhoa) *m* side, party; match; ~ **de fútbol** football match

partir (pahr-*teer*) *v* *leave, depart, pull out, *set out; **a** ~ **de** as from; from

parto (*pahr*-toa) *m* childbirth, delivery

párvulo (*pahr*-bhoo-loa) *m* toddler; **escuela de párvulos** kindergarten

pasa (*pah*-sah) *f* raisin; ~ **de Corinto** currant

pasado (pah-*sah*-dhoa) *adj* past; *m* past

pasaje (pah-*san*-khay) *m* passage

pasajero (pah-sah-*khay*-roa) *m* passenger

pasaporte (pah-sah-*poar*-tay) *m* passport

pasar (pah-*sahr*) *v* happen; *go through; pass; *spend; ~ **por alto** overlook; **pasarse sin** spare

pasarela (pah-sah-*ray*-lah) *f* gangway

Pascua (*pahss*-kwah) Easter

paseante (pah-say-*ahn*-tay) *m* walker

pasear (pah-say-*ahr*) *v* walk, stroll

paseo (pah-*say*-oa) *m* stroll; ride; promenade

pasillo (pah-*see*-l^yoa) *m* corridor; aisle

pasión (pah-s^yoan) *f* passion

pasivo (pah-*see*-bhoa) *adj* passive

paso (*pah*-soa) *m* step, pace; move, gait; crossing; mountain pass; **de** ~ casual; ~ **a nivel** crossing; **prioridad de** ~ right of way; **prohibido el** ~ no entry

pasta (*pahss*-tah) *f* paste; ~ **dentífrica** toothpaste

pastel (pahss-*tayl*) *m* cake

pastelería (pahss-tay-lay-*ree*-ah) *f* pastry, cake; pastry shop

pastilla (pahss-*tee*-l^yah) *f* tablet

pastor (pahss-*toar*) *m* shepherd; clergyman, parson, rector

pata (*pah*-tah) *f* paw; leg

patada (pah-*tah*-dhah) *f* kick

patata (pah-*tah*-tah) *f* potato; **patatas fritas** chips

patear (pah-tay-*ahr*) *v* kick; stamp

patente (pah-*tayn*-tay) *f* patent

patillas (pah-*tee*-l^yahss) *fpl* whiskers *pl*, sideburns *pl*

patín (pah-*teen*) *m* skate; scooter

patinaje (pah-tee-*nah*-khay) *m* skating

patinar (pah-tee-*nahr*) *v* skate; skid

pato (*pah*-toa) *m* duck

patria (*pah*-tr^yah) *f* native country, fatherland

patriota (pah-tr^yoa-tah) *m* patriot

patrón (pah-*troan*) *m* boss, master; employer; landlord

patrona (pah-*troa*-nah) *f* landlady

patrulla (pah-*troo*-l^yah) *f* patrol

patrullar (pah-troo-l^y*ahr*) *v* patrol

paulatinamente (pou-lah-tee-nah-*mayn*-tay) *adv* gradually

pausa (*pou*-sah) *f* pause; ˙**hacer una** ~ pause

pavimentar (pah-bhee-mayn-*tahr*) *v* pave

pavimento (pah-bhee-*mayn*-toa) *m* pavement

pavo (*pah*-bhoa) *m* peacock; turkey

payaso (pah-^y*ah*-soa) *m* clown

paz (pahth) f peace; quiet

peaje (pay-ah-khay) m toll

peatón (pay-ah-toan) m pedestrian; **prohibido para los peatones** no pedestrians

pecado (pay-kah-dhoa) m sin

pecio (pay-thʸoa) m wreck

peculiar (pay-koo-lʸahr) adj peculiar

pecho (pay-choa) m chest; bosom

pedal (pay-dhahl) m pedal

pedazo (pay-dhah-thoa) m piece; scrap

pedernal (pay-dhayr-nahl) m flint

pedicuro (pay-dhee-koo-roa) m chiropodist, pedicure

pedido (pay-dhee-dhoa) m order

*****pedir** (pay-dheer) v beg; order; charge

pegajoso (pay-gah-khoa-soa) adj sticky

pegar (pay-gahr) v smack, slap, *hit; *stick, paste; **pegarse** v *burn

peinado (pay-nah-dhoa) m hair-do

peinar (pay-nahr) v comb

peine (pay-nay) m comb; ~ **de bolsillo** pocket-comb

pelar (pay-lahr) v peel

peldaño (payl-dah-ñoa) m step

pelea (pay-lay-ah) f battle

peletero (pay-lay-tay-roa) m furrier

pelícano (pay-lee-kah-noa) m pelican

película (pay-lee-koo-lah) f film; ~ **en colores** colour film

peligro (pay-lee-groa) m danger; peril, risk; distress

peligroso (pay-lee-groa-soa) adj dangerous; perilous

pelmazo (payl-mah-thoa) m bore

pelota (pay-loa-tah) f ball

peluca (pay-loo-kah) f wig

peluquero (pay-loo-kay-roa) m hairdresser

pelvis (payl-bheess) m pelvis

pellizcar (pay-lʸeeth-kahr) v pinch

pena (pay-nah) f sorrow; pains; penalty; ~ **de muerte** death penalty

pendiente (payn-dʸayn-tay) adj slanting; m earring, pendant; f gradient, slope

penetrar (pay-nay-trahr) v penetrate

penicilina (pay-nee-thee-lee-nah) f penicillin

península (pay-neen-soo-lah) f peninsula

pensador (payn-sah-dhoar) m thinker

pensamiento (payn-sah-mʸayn-toa) m idea, thought

*****pensar** (payn-sahr) v *think; ~ **en** *think of

pensativo (payn-sah-tee-bhoa) adj thoughtful

pensión (payn-sʸoan) f guest-house, pension, boarding-house; board; ~ **alimenticia** alimony; ~ **completa** full board, board and lodging

Pentecostés (payn-tay-koass-tayss) m Whitsun

peña (pay-ñah) f boulder

peón (pay-oan) m pawn

peor (pay-oar) adj worse; adv worse

pepino (pay-pee-noa) m cucumber

pepita (pay-pee-tah) f pip

pequeño (pay-kay-ñoa) adj small, little; petty, minor

pera (pay-rah) f pear

perca (payr-kah) f perch, bass

percepción (payr-thayp-thʸoan) f perception

perceptible (payr-thayp-tee-bhlay) adj perceptible, noticeable

percibir (payr-thee-bheer) v perceive

percha (payr-chah) f hanger, coat-hanger, peg; hat rack

*****perder** (payr-dhayr) v *lose; miss; waste

pérdida (payr-dhee-dhah) f loss

perdiz (payr-dheeth) f partridge

perdón (payr-dhoan) m pardon;

grace; ¡perdón! sorry!

perdonar (payr-dhoa-*nahr*) *v* *forgive

perecedero (pay-ray-thay-*dhay*-roa) *adj* perishable

***perecer** (pay-rav-*thavr*) *v* perish

peregrinación (pay-ray-gree-nah-*th*ᵞ*oan*) *f* pilgrimage

peregrino (pay-ray-*gree*-noa) *m* pilgrim

perejil (pay-ray-*kheel*) *m* parsley

perezoso (pay-ray-*thoa*-soa) *adj* lazy

perfección (payr-fayk-*th*ᵞ*oan*) *f* perfection

perfecto (payr-*fayk*-toa) *adj* perfect; faultless

perfil (payr-*feel*) *m* profile

perfume (payr-*foo*-may) *m* perfume; scent

periódico (pay-*r*ᵞ*oa*-dhee-koa) *adj* periodical; *m* periodical, paper; **vendedor de periódicos** newsagent

periodismo (pay-*r*ᵞ*oa*-*deez*-moa) *m* journalism

periodista (pay-*r*ᵞ*oa*-*dheess*-tah) *m* journalist

período (pay-*ree*-oa-dhoa) *m* period, term

perito (pay-*ree*-toa) *m* expert, connoisseur

perjudicar (payr-khoo-dhee-*kahr*) *v* harm

perjudicial (payr-khoo-dhee-*th*ᵞ*ahl*) *adj* harmful, hurtful

perjuicio (payr-*khwee*-th*ᵞ*oa) *m* harm, damage

perjurio (payr-*khoo*-r*ᵞ*oa) *m* perjury

perla (*payr*-lah) *f* pearl

***permanecer** (payr-mah-nay-*thayr*) *v* remain

permanente (payr-mah-*nayn*-tay) *adj* permanent; **planchado** ~ permanent press

permiso (payr-*mee*-soa) *m* permission, authorization; permit, licence; ~ **de**

conducir driving licence; ~ **de pesca** fishing licence; ~ **de residencia** residence permit; ~ **de trabajo** work permit; labor permit *Am*

permitir (payr-mee-*teer*) *v* permit, allow; enable; **permitirse** *v* afford

perno (*payr*-noa) *m* bolt

pero (*pay*-roa) *conj* yet, only, but

peróxido (pay-*roak*-see-dhoa) *m* peroxide

perpendicular (payr-payn-dee-koo-*lahr*) *adj* perpendicular

perpetuo (payr-*pay*-twoa) *adj* perpetual

perra (*pay*-rrah) *f* bitch

perrera (pay-*rray*-rah) *f* kennel

perro (*pay*-rroa) *m* dog; ~ **lazarillo** guide-dog

persa (*payr*-sah) *adj* Persian; *m* Persian

***perseguir** (payr-say-*geer*) *v* pursue

perseverar (payr-say-bhay-*rahr*) *v* *keep up

Persia (*payr*-sᵞah) *f* Persia

persiana (payr-sᵞah-nah) *f* shutter, blind

persistir (payr-seess-*teer*) *v* insist

persona (payr-*soa*-nah) *f* person; **por** ~ per person

personal (payr-soa-*nahl*) *adj* personal, private; *m* personnel, staff

personalidad (payr-soa-nah-lee-*dhahdh*) *f* personality

perspectiva (payrs-payk-*tee*-bhah) *f* perspective; prospect

persuadir (payr-swah-dheer) *v* persuade

***pertenecer** (payr-tay-nay-*thayr*) *v* belong

pertenencias (payr-tay-*nayn*-thᵞahss) *fpl* belongings *pl*

pertinaz (pay-tee-*nahth*) *adj* obstinate

pesado (pay-*sah*-dhoa) *adj* heavy

pesadumbre (pay-sah-*dhoom*-bray) *f*

grief

pesar (pay-*sahr*) *v* weigh; **a ~ de** despite, in spite of

pesca (*payss*-kah) *f* fishing; fishing industry

pescadería (payss-kah-dhay-*ree*-ah) *f* fish shop

pescador (payss-kah-*dhoar*) *m* fisherman

pescar (payss-*kahr*) *v* fish; **~ con caña** angle

pesebre (pay-*say*-bhray) *m* manger

pesimismo (pay-see-*meez*-moa) *m* pessimism

pesimista (pay-see-*meess*-tah) *adj* pessimistic; *m* pessimist

pésimo (*pay*-see-moa) *adj* worst; terrible

peso (*pay*-soa) *m* weight; burden

pestaña (payss-*tah*-ñah) *f* eyelash

petaca (pay-*tah*-kah) *f* pouch; tobacco pouch

pétalo (*pay*-tah-loa) *m* petal

petición (pay-tee-*th*ʸ*oan*) *f* petition

petirrojo (pay-tee-*rroa*-khoa) *m* robin

petróleo (pay-*troa*-lay-oa) *m* petroleum, oil; **~ lampante** kerosene; **pozo de ~** oil-well; **refinería de ~** oil-refinery

pez (payth) *m* fish

piadoso (pʸah-*dhoa*-soa) *adj* pious

pianista (pʸah-*neess*-tah) *m* pianist

piano (*p*ʸ*ah*-noa) *m* piano; **~ de cola** grand piano

picadero (pee-kah-*dhay*-roa) *m* riding-school

picadura (pee-kah-*dhoo*-rah) *f* sting, bite; cigarette tobacco

picante (pee-*kahn*-tay) *adj* spicy, savoury

picar (pee-*kahr*) *v* itch; mince; *sting

pícaro (*pee*-kah-roa) *m* rascal

picazón (pee-kah-*thoan*) *f* itch

pico (*pee*-koa) *m* beak; peak; pick-

axe

pie (pʸay) *m* foot; **a ~** on foot; walking; **de ~** upright; *estar de ~ *stand; **~ de cabra** crowbar

piedad (pʸay-*dhahdh*) *f* pity; *tener ~ de* pity

piedra (*p*ʸ*ay*-dhrah) *f* stone; **de ~** stone; **~ miliar** milestone; **~ pómez** pumice stone; **~ preciosa** stone

piel (pʸayl) *f* skin; fur, hide; peel; **de ~** leather; **~ de cerdo** pigskin

pierna (*p*ʸ*ayr*-nah) *f* leg

pieza (*p*ʸ*ay*-thah) *f* part; **de dos piezas** two-piece; **~ de repuesto** spare part; **~ en un acto** one-act play

pijama (pee-*khah*-mah) *m* pyjamas *pl*

pilar (pee-*lahr*) *m* pillar

píldora (*peel*-doa-rah) *f* pill

pileta (pee-*lay*-tah) *f* sink

piloto (pee-*loa*-toa) *m* pilot

pillo (*pee*-lʸoa) *m* rascal

pimienta (pee-*m*ʸ*ayn*-tah) *f* pepper

pincel (peen-*thayl*) *m* paint-brush

pinchado (peen-*chah*-dhoa) *adj* punctured

pinchar (peen-*chahr*) *v* prick

pinchazo (peen-*chah*-thoa) *m* puncture

pingüino (peeng-*gwee*-noa) *m* penguin

pino (*pee*-noa) *m* fir-tree

pintar (peen-*tahr*) *v* paint

pintor (peen-*toar*) *m* painter

pintoresco (peen-toa-*rayss*-koa) *adj* picturesque, scenic

pintura (peen-*too*-rah) *f* paint; painting; **~ al óleo** oil-painting

pinzas (*peen*-thahss) *fpl* tweezers *pl*

pinzón (peen-*thoan*) *m* finch

piña (*pee*-ñah) *f* pineapple

pío (*pee*-oa) *adj* pious

piojo (*p*ʸ*oa*-khoa) *m* louse

pionero (pʸoa-*nay*-roa) *m* pioneer

pipa (*pee*-pah) *f* pipe

pirata (pee-*rah*-tah) *m* pirate

pisar (pee-*sahr*) *v* step

piscina (pee-*thee*-nah) *f* swimming pool

piso (*pee*-soa) *m* storey, floor; flat; apartment *nAm*; ~ **bajo** ground floor

pista (*peess*-tah) *f* ring; track; lane; ~ **de aterrizaje** runway; ~ **de patinaje** skating-rink; ~ **para carreras** race-course

pistola (peess-*toa*-lah) *f* pistol

pistón (peess-*toan*) *m* piston

pitillera (pee-tee-*l^yay*-rah) *f* cigarette-case

pizarra (pee-*thah*-rrah) *f* slate; blackboard

placa (*plah*-kah) *f* registration plate

placer (plah-*thayr*) *m* pleasure

*****placer** (plah-*thayr*) *v* please

plaga (*plah*-gah) *f* plague

plan (plahn) *m* plan, project

plancha (*plahn*-chah) *f* iron; **no precisa** ~ wash and wear, drip-dry

planchar (plahn-*chahr*) *v* iron; press

planeador (plah-nay-ah-*dhoar*) *m* glider

planear (plah-nay-*ahr*) *v* plan

planeta (plah-*nay*-tah) *m* planet

planetario (plah-nay-*tah*-r^yoa) *m* planetarium

plano (*plah*-noa) *adj* level, even, plane; *m* plan, map; **primer** ~ foreground

planta (*plahn*-tah) *f* plant

plantación (plahn-tah-*th^yoan*) *f* plantation

plantar (plahn-*tahr*) *v* plant

plantear (plahn-tay-*ahr*) *v* *put

plástico (*plahss*-tee-koa) *m* plastic; **de** ~ plastic

plata (*plah*-tah) *f* silver; **de** ~ silver; ~ **labrada** silverware

plátano (*plah*-tah-noa) *m* banana

platero (plah-*tay*-roa) *m* silversmith

platija (plah-*tee*-khah) *f* plaice

platillo (plah-*tee*-l^yoa) *m* saucer

platino (plah-*tee*-noa) *m* platinum

plato (*plah*-toa) *m* dish, plate; course; ~ **para sopa** soup-plate

playa (*plah*-^yah) *f* beach; ~ **de veraneo** seaside resort; ~ **para nudistas** nudist beach

plaza (*plah*-thah) *f* square; ~ **de mercado** market-place; ~ **de toros** bullring; ~ **fuerte** stronghold

plazo (*plah*-thoa) *m* term; instalment; **compra a plazos** hire-purchase

pleamar (play-ah-*mahr*) *f* high tide

*****plegar** (play-*gahr*) *v* crease

pliegue (*pl^yay*-gay) *m* crease, fold

plomero (ploa-*may*-roa) *m* plumber

plomo (*ploa*-moa) *m* lead

pluma (*ploo*-mah) *f* feather; pen

plural (ploo-*rahl*) *m* plural

población (poa-bhlah-*th^yoan*) *f* population

pobre (*poa*-bhray) *adj* poor

pobreza (poa-*bhray*-thah) *f* poverty

poco (*poa*-koa) *adj* little; *m* bit; **dentro de** ~ presently; **pocos** *adj* few; **un** ~ some

poder (poa-*dhayr*) *m* power; authority

*****poder** (poa-*dhayr*) *v* *be able to, *can; *might, *may

poderoso (poa-dhay-*roa*-soa) *adj* powerful

podrido (poa-*dhree*-dhoa) *adj* rotten

poema (poa-*ay*-mah) *m* poem; ~ **épico** epic

poesía (poa-ay-*see*-ah) *f* poetry

poeta (poa-*ay*-tah) *m* poet

poético (poa-*ay*-tee-koa) *adj* poetic

polaco (poa-*lah*-koa) *adj* Polish; *m* Pole

polea (poa-*lay*-ah) *f* pulley

policía (poa-lee-*thee*-ah) *f* police *pl*

polifacético (poa-lee-fah-*thay*-tee-koa) *adj* all-round

polilla (poa-*lee*-l∀ah) *f* moth

polio (*poa*-l∀oa) *f* polio

poliomielitis (poa-l∀oa-m∀ay-*lee*-teess) *f* polio

política (poa-*lee*-tee-kah) *f* policy; politics

político (poa-*lee*-tee-koa) *adj* political; *m* politician

póliza (*poa*-lee-thah) *f* policy

Polonia (poa-*loa*-n∀ah) *f* Poland

polución (poa-loo-th∀oan) *f* pollution

polvera (poal-*bhay*-rah) *f* powder compact

polvo (*poal*-bhoa) *m* dust; powder; grit; ~ **facial** face-powder; ~ **para los dientes** toothpowder; ~ **para los pies** foot powder

pólvora (*poal*-bhoa-rah) *f* gunpowder

polvoriento (poal-bhoa-r∀ayn-toa) *adj* dusty

pollero (poa-*l∀ay*-roa) *m* poulterer

pollo (*poa*-l∀oa) *m* chicken

pomelo (poa-*may*-loa) *m* grapefruit

pómulo (*poa*-moo-loa) *m* cheek-bone

ponderado (poan-day-*rah*-dhoa) *adj* sober

*__poner__ (poa-*nayr*) *v* place, *lay, *put, *set; *__ponerse__ *v* *put on

pony (*poa*-nee) *m* pony

popelín (poa-pay-*leen*) *m* poplin

popular (poa-poo-*lahr*) *adj* popular; vulgar; **canción** ~ folk song; **danza** ~ folk-dance

populoso (poa-poo-*loa*-soa) *adj* populous

por (poar) *prep* by; for; via; times

porcelana (poar-thay-*lah*-nah) *f* china, porcelain

porcentaje (poar-thayn-*tah*-khay) *m* percentage

porción (poar-*th∀oan*) *f* portion, helping

porque (*poar*-kay) *conj* because, for, as; **por qué** why

porra (*poa*-rrah) *f* club

portabagajes (poar-tah-bah-*khah*-gayss) *m* luggage rack

portador (poar-tah-*dhoar*) *m* bearer

portaequipajes (poar-tah-ay-kee-*pah*-khayss) *m* boot; trunk *nAm*

portafolio (poar-tah-*foa*-l∀oa) *m* attaché case, briefcase

portaligas (poar-tah-*lee*-gahss) *m* suspender belt

portátil (poar-*tah*-teel) *adj* portable

portero (poar-*tay*-roa) *m* doorman, door-keeper, porter; goalkeeper

pórtico (*poar*-tee-koa) *m* arcade

portilla (poar-tee-l∀ah) *f* porthole

portón (poar-*toan*) *m* gate

Portugal (poar-too-*gahl*) *m* Portugal

portugués (poar-too-*gayss*) *adj* Portuguese; *m* Portuguese

porvenir (poar-bhay-*neer*) *m* future

posada (poa-*sah*-dhah) *f* inn

posadero (poa-sah-*dhay*-roa) *m* innkeeper

*__poseer__ (poa-say-*ayr*) *v* own, possess

posesión (poa-say-s∀oan) *f* possession

posibilidad (poa-see-bhee-lee-*dhahdh*) *f* possibility

posible (poa-*see*-bhlay) *adj* possible

posición (poa-see-th∀oan) *f* position

positiva (poa-see-*tee*-bhah) *f* positive, print

positivo (poa-see-*tee*-bhoa) *adj* positive

postal ilustrada (poass-*tahl* ee-loos-*trah*-dhah) picture postcard

poste (*poass*-tay) *m* post, pole; ~ **de farol** lamp-post; ~ **de indicador** signpost

posterior (poass-tay-r∀oar) *adj* subsequent

postizo (poass-*tee*-thoa) *m* hair piece

postre (*poass*-tray) *m* dessert

potable (poa-*tah*-bhlay) *adj* for drinking

potencia (poa-*tayn*-th^Yah) *f* capacity; power

pozo (*poa*-thoa) *m* well; ~ **de petróleo** oil-well

práctica (*prahk*-tee-kah) *f* practice

prácticamente (*prahk*-tee-kah-mayn-tay) *adv* practically

practicar (prahk-tee-*kahr*) *v* practise

práctico (*prahk*-tee-koa) *adj* practical; business-like; *m* pilot

prado (*prah*-dhoa) *m* meadow, pasture

precario (pray-*kah*-r^Yoa) *adj* critical, precarious

precaución (pray-kou-*th*^Yoan) *f* precaution

precaverse (pray-kah-*bhayr*-say) *v* beware

precedente (pray-thay-*dhayn*-tay) *adj* previous, preceding, last

preceder (pray-thay-*dhayr*) *v* precede

precio (*pray*-th^Yoa) *m* price; charge, cost, rate; ~ **de compra** purchase price; ~ **del billete** fare

precioso (pray-*th*^Yoa-soa) *adj* precious; lovely

precipicio (pray-thee-*pee*-th^Yoa) *m* precipice

precipitación (pray-thee-pee-tah-*th*^Yoan) *f* precipitation

precipitarse (pray-thee-pee-*tahr*-say) *v* rush; crash; **precipitado** *adj* rash

preciso (pray-*thee*-soa) *adj* precise; very

predecesor (pray-dhay-thay-*soar*) *m* predecessor

*****predecir** (pray-dhay-*theer*) *v* predict

predicar (pray-dhee-*kahr*) *v* preach

preferencia (pray-fay-*rayn*-th^Yah) *f* preference

preferible (pray-fay-*ree*-bhlay) *adj* preferable

*****preferir** (pray-fay-*reer*) *v* prefer; **preferido** *adj* favourite

prefijo (pray-*fee*-khoa) *m* prefix

pregunta (pray-*goon*-tah) *f* question; query, inquiry

preguntar (pray goon *tahr*) *v* ask; enquire; **preguntarse** *v* wonder

prejuicio (pray-*khwee*-th^Yoa) *m* prejudice

preliminar (pray-lee-mee-*nahr*) *adj* preliminary

prematuro (pray-mah-*too*-roa) *adj* premature

premio (*pray*-m^Yoa) *m* award, prize; ~ **de consolación** consolation prize

prender (prayn-*dayr*) *v* attach

prensa (*prayn*-sah) *f* press; **conferencia de** ~ press conference

preocupación (pray-oa-koo-pah-*th*^Yoan) *f* concern, anxiety, worry; trouble

preocupado (pray-oa-koo-pah-dhoa) *adj* concerned, anxious

preocuparse de (pray-oa-koo-*pahr*-say) care about

preparación (pray-pah-rah-*th*^Yoan) *f* preparation

preparado (pray-pah-*rah*-dhoa) *adj* prepared, ready

preparar (pray-pah-*rahr*) *v* prepare; cook

preposición (pray-poa-see-*th*^Yoan) *f* preposition

presa (*pray*-sah) *f* dam

prescindir (pray-theen-*deer*) *v* omit; disregard; **prescindiendo de** apart from

prescribir (prayss-kree-*bheer*) *v* prescribe

prescripción (prayss-kreep-*th*^Yoan) *f* prescription

presencia (pray-*sayn*-th^Yah) *f* presence

presenciar (pray-sayn-*th*^Y*ahr*) *v* witness

presentación (pray-sayn-tah-*th*^Yoan) *f* introduction

presentar (pray-sayn-*tahr*) *v* introduce,

present; offer; **presentarse** v report
presente (pray-*sayn*-tay) adj present; m present
preservar (pray-sayr-*bhahr*) v preserve
presidente (pray-see-*dhayn*-tay) m president, chairman
presidir (pray-see-*dheer*) v preside at
presión (pray-sᵞoan) f pressure; ~ **atmosférica** atmospheric pressure; ~ **del aceite** oil pressure; ~ **del neumático** tyre pressure
preso (*pray*-soa) m prisoner; **coger** ~ capture
prestamista (prayss-tah-*meess*-tah) m pawnbroker
préstamo (*prayss*-tah-moa) m loan
prestar (prayss-*tahr*) v *lend; ~ **atención a** attend to, *pay attention to; **tomar prestado** borrow
prestidigitador (prayss-tee-dhee-khee-tah-*dhoar*) m magician
prestigio (prayss-*tee*-khᵞoa) m prestige
presumible (pray-soo-*mee*-bhlay) adj presumable
presumido (pray-soo-*mee*-dhoa) adj presumptuous
presumir (pray-soo-*meer*) v assume; boast
presuntuoso (pray-soon-*twoa*-soa) adj conceited; presumptuous
presupuesto (pray-soo-*pwayss*-toa) m budget
pretender (pray-tayn-*dayr*) v claim
pretensión (pray-tayn-sᵞoan) f claim
pretexto (pray-*tayks*-toa) m pretext, pretence
*prevenir** (pray-bhay-*neer*) v anticipate, prevent
preventivo (pray-bhayn-*tee*-bhoa) adj preventive
*prever** (pray-*bhayr*) v anticipate
previo (*pray*-bhᵞoa) adj previous
previsión (pray-bhee-sᵞoan) f outlook,

forecast
prima (*pree*-mah) f cousin; premium
primario (pree-*mah*-rᵞoa) adj primary
primavera (pree-mah-*bhay*-rah) f springtime, spring
primero (pree-*may*-roa) num first; adj foremost; primary
primitivo (pree-mee-*tee*-bhoa) adj primitive
primo (*pree*-moa) m cousin
primordial (pree-moar-*dhᵞahl*) adj primary
princesa (preen-*thay*-sah) f princess
principal (preen-thee-*pahl*) adj principal; chief, main, cardinal; m principal
principalmente (preen-thee-pahl-*mayn*-tay) adv mainly
príncipe (*preen*-thee-pay) m prince
principiante (preen-thee-*pᵞahn*-tay) m beginner, learner
principio (preen-*thee*-pᵞoa) m principle; **al** ~ at first
prioridad (prᵞoa-ree-*dhahdh*) f priority
prisa (*pree*-sah) f haste, speed, hurry; *dar** ~ *speed; *darse** ~ hurry; **de** ~ in a hurry
prisión (pree-sᵞoan) f prison
prisionero (pree-sᵞoa-*nay*-roa) m prisoner; ~ **de guerra** prisoner of war
prismáticos (preez-*mah*-tee-koass) mpl binoculars pl
privado (pree-*bhah*-dhoa) adj private
privar de (pree-*bhahr*) deprive of
privilegio (pree-bhee-*lay*-khᵞoa) m privilege
probable (proa-*bhah*-bhlay) adj probable; likely
probablemente (proa-bhah-bhlay-*mayn*-tay) adv probably
probador (proa-bhah-*dhoar*) m fitting room
*probar** (proa-*bhahr*) v attempt; test; taste; *probarse** v try on

problema (proa-*bhlay*-mah) *m* problem, question

procedencia (proa-thay-*dhayn*-thᵞah) *f* origin

proceder (proa-thay-*dhayr*) *v* proceed

procedimiento (proa-thay-dhee-*mᵞayn*-toa) *m* procedure; process

procesión (proa-thay-*sᵞoan*) *f* procession

proceso (proa-*thay*-soa) *m* process, trial, lawsuit

proclamar (proa-klah-*mahr*) *v* proclaim

procurador (proa-koo-rah-*dhoar*) *m* solicitor

procurar (proa-koo-*rahr*) *v* furnish

pródigo (*proa*-dhee-goa) *adj* lavish

producción (proa-dhook-*thᵞoan*) *f* production, output; ~ **en serie** mass production

*****producir** (proa-dhoo-*theer*) *v* produce

producto (proa-*dhook*-toa) *m* product, produce

productor (proa-dhook-*toar*) *m* producer

profano (proa-*fah*-noa) *m* layman

profesar (proa-fay-*sahr*) *v* confess

profesión (proa-fay-*sᵞoan*) *f* profession

profesional (proa-fay-sᵞoa-*nahl*) *adj* professional

profesor (proa-fay-*soar*) *m* master, teacher; professor

profesora (proa-fay-*soa*-rah) *f* teacher

profeta (proa-*fay*-tah) *m* prophet

profundidad (proa-foon-dee-*dhahdh*) *f* depth

profundo (proa-*foon*-doa) *adj* low, profound

programa (proa-*grah*-mah) *m* programme

progresista (proa-gray-*seess*-tah) *adj* progressive

progresivo (proa-gray-*see*-bhoa) *adj* progressive

progreso (proa-*gray*-soa) *m* progress

prohibición (proa-ee-bhee-*thᵞoan*) *f* prohibition

prohibido (proa-ee-*bhee*-dhoa) *adj* prohibited

prohibir (proa-ee-*bheer*) *v* prohibit, *forbid

prolongación (proa-loang-gah-*thᵞoan*) *f* prolongation

prolongar (proa-loang-*gahr*) *v* extend

promedio (proa-*may*-dhᵞoa) *adj* average; *m* average, mean; **en ~** on the average

promesa (proa-*may*-sah) *f* promise

prometer (proa-may-*tayr*) *v* promise

prometido (proa-may-*tee*-dhoa) *adj* engaged

promoción (proa-moa-*thᵞoan*) *f* promotion

promontorio (proa-moan-*toa*-rᵞoa) *m* headland

*****promover** (proa-moa-*bhayr*) *v* promote

pronombre (proa-*noam*-bray) *m* pronoun

pronosticar (proa-noass-tee-*kahr*) *v* forecast

pronto (*proan*-toa) *adj* prompt; *adv* soon, shortly; **tan ~ como** as soon as

pronunciación (proa-noon-thᵞah-*thᵞoan*) *f* pronunciation

pronunciar (proa-noon-*thᵞahr*) *v* pronounce

propaganda (proa-pah-*gahn*-dah) *f* propaganda

propicio (proa-*pee*-thᵞoa) *adj* favourable; well-disposed

propiedad (proa-pᵞay-*dhahdh*) *f* property; estate

propietario (proa-pᵞay-*tah*-rᵞoa) *m* owner, proprietor; landlord

propina (proa-*pee*-nah) *f* gratuity, tip

propio (*proa*-pᵞoa) *adj* own

* proponer (proa-poa-*nayr*) *v* propose

proporción (proa-poar-*th*ʸ*oan*) *f* proportion

proporcional (proa-poar-th*ʸ*oa-*nahl*) *adj* proportional

proporcionar (proa-poar-th*ʸ*oa-*nahr*) *v* adjust; procure

propósito (proa-*poa*-see-toa) *m* purpose; **a ~** by the way

propuesta (proa-*pwayss*-tah) *f* proposition, proposal

prórroga (*proa*-rroa-gah) *f* extension

prosa (*proa*-sah) *f* prose

* proseguir (proa-say-*geer*) *v* proceed, continue, carry on

prospecto (proass-*payk*-toa) *m* prospectus

prosperidad (proass-pay-ree-*dhahdh*) *f* prosperity

próspero (*proass*-pay-roa) *adj* prosperous

prostituta (proass-tee-*too*-tah) *f* prostitute

protección (proa-tayk-*th*ʸ*oan*) *f* protection

proteger (proa-tay-*khayr*) *v* protect

proteína (proa-tay-ee-nah) *f* protein

protesta (proa-*tayss*-tah) *f* protest

protestante (proa-tayss-*tahn*-tay) *adj* Protestant

protestar (proa-tayss-*tahr*) *v* protest

provechoso (proa-bhay-*choa*-soa) *adj* profitable

* proveer (proa-bhay-*ayr*) *v* provide; **~ de** furnish with

proverbio (proa-*bhayr*-bh*ʸ*oa) *m* proverb

provincia (proa-*bheen*-th*ʸ*ah) *f* province

provincial (proa-bheen-*th*ʸ*ahl*) *adj* provincial

provisional (proa-bhee-s*ʸ*oa-*nahl*) *adj* provisional, temporary

provisiones (proa-bhee-s*ʸ*oa-nayss) *fpl* provisions *pl*

provocar (proa-bhoa-*kahr*) *v* cause

próximamente (*proak*-see-mah-mayn-tay) *adv* shortly

próximo (*proak*-see-moa) *adj* next

proyectar (proa-*ʸ*ayk-*tahr*) *v* project

proyecto (proa-*ʸ*ayk-toa) *m* project, scheme

proyector (proa-*ʸ*ayk-*toar*) *m* spotlight

prudente (proo-*dhayn*-tay) *adj* cautious, wary, gentle

prueba (*prway*-bhah) *f* experiment, trial, test; proof, token, evidence; **a ~** on approval

prurito (proo-*ree*-toa) *m* itch

psicoanalista (see-koa-ah-nah-*leess*-tah) *m* analyst, psychoanalyst

psicología (see-koa-loa-*khee*-ah) *f* psychology

psicológico (see-koa-*loa*-khee-koa) *adj* psychological

psicólogo (see-*koa*-loa-goa) *m* psychologist

psiquiatra (see-k*ʸ*ah-trah) *m* psychiatrist

psíquico (*see*-kee-koa) *adj* psychic

publicación (poo-bhlee-kah-*th*ʸ*oan*) *f* publication

publicar (poo-bhlee-*kahr*) *v* publish

publicidad (poo-bhlee-thee-*dhahdh*) *f* advertising, publicity

público (*poo*-bhlee-koa) *adj* public; *m* public

pueblo (*pway*-bhloa) *m* nation, people; village

puente (*pwayn*-tay) *m* bridge; **~ colgante** suspension bridge; **~ levadizo** drawbridge; **~ superior** main deck

puerta (*pwayr*-tah) *f* door; **~ corrediza** sliding door; **~ giratoria** revolving door

puerto (*pwayr*-toa) *m* harbour, port; **~ de mar** seaport

pues (pwayss) *conj* since

puesta (*pwayss*-tah) *f* bet

puesto (loo-*gahr*) *m* spot; job, post, position; stand, stall, booth; ~ **de gasolina** service station; gas station *Am*; ~ **de libros** bookstand

puesto que (*pwayss*-toa kay) because, since

pulcro (*pool*-kroa) *adj* neat

pulgar (pool-*gahr*) *m* thumb

pulir (poo-*leer*) *v* polish

pulmón (pool-*moan*) *m* lung

pulóver (poo-*loa*-bhayr) *m* pullover

púlpito (*pool*-pee-toa) *m* pulpit

pulpo (*pool*-poa) *m* octopus

pulsera (pool-*say*-rah) *f* bracelet, bangle

pulso (*pool*-soa) *m* pulse

pulverizador (pool-bhay-ree-thah-*dhoar*) *m* atomizer

punta (*poon*-tah) *f* tip, point

puntiagudo (poon-tᵛah-*goo*-dhoa) *adj* pointed

puntilla (poon-*tee*-lᵛah) *f* lace

punto (*poon*-toa) *m* point; item, issue; period, full stop; stitch; **géneros de** ~ hosiery; *hacer* ~ *knit; ~ **de congelación** freezing-point; ~ **de partida** starting-point; ~ **de vista** point of view; ~ **y coma** semicolon

puntual (poon-*twahl*) *adj* punctual

punzada (poon-*thah*-dhah) *f* stitch

punzar (poon-*thahr*) *v* pierce

puñado (poo-*ñah*-dhoa) *m* handful

puñetazo (poo ñay tah thoa) *m* punch; *dar puñetazos* punch

puño (*poo*-ñoa) *m* fist; cuff

pupitre (poo-*pee*-tray) *m* desk

purasangre (poo-rah-*sahng*-gray) *adj* thoroughbred

puro (*poo*-roa) *adj* pure; clean, neat, sheer; *m* cigar

purpúreo (poor-*poo*-ray-oa) *adj* purple

pus (pooss) *f* pus

Q

que (kay) *pron* who, which, that; *conj* that; as, than

qué (kay) *pron* what; *adv* how

quebradizo (kay-bhrah-*dhee*-thoa) *adj* crisp

quebrantar (kay-bhrahn-*tahr*) *v* *break

*quebrar** (kay-*bhrahr*) *v* crack, *break, *burst

quedar (kay-*dhahr*) *v* remain; **quedarse** *v* remain, stay

queja (*kay*-khah) *f* complaint

quejarse (kay-*khahr*-say) *v* complain

quemadura (kay-mah-*dhoo*-rah) *f* burn; ~ **del sol** sunburn

quemar (kay-*mahr*) *v* *burn

*querer** (kay-*rayr*) *v* *will, want; like, *be fond of

querida (kay-*ree*-dhah) *f* sweetheart; mistress

querido (kay-*ree*-dhoa) *adj* beloved, dear; precious; *m* darling

queso (*kay*-soa) *m* cheese

quien (kᵛayn) *pron* who; **a** ~ whom

quienquiera (kᵛayng-*kᵛay*-rah) *pron* whoever

quieto (kᵛay-toa) *adj* still, quiet; *estarse** ~ *keep quiet

quilate (kee-*lah*-tay) *m* carat

quilla (*kee*-lᵛah) *f* keel

química (*kee*-mee-kah) *f* chemistry

químico (*kee*-mee-koa) *adj* chemical

quincalla (keeng-*kah*-lᵛah) *f* hardware

quince (*keen*-thay) *num* fifteen

quincena (keen-*thay*-nah) *f* fortnight

quinceno (keen-*thay*-noa) *num* fifteenth

quinina (kee-*nee*-nah) *f* quinine

quinta (*keen*-tah) *f* country house

quinto¹ (*keen*-toa) *num* fifth

quinto² (*keen*-toa) *m* conscript

quiosco (*kʸoass*-koa) *m* kiosk; **~ de periódicos** newsstand

quitamanchas (kee-tah-*mahn*-chahss) *m* cleaning fluid, stain remover

quitar (kee-*tahr*) *v* *take away

quitasol (kee-tah-*soal*) *m* sunshade

quizás (kee-*thahss*) *adv* maybe, perhaps

R

rábano (*rah*-bhah-noa) *m* radish; **~ picante** horseradish

rabia (*rah*-bhʸah) *f* rage; rabies

rabiar (rah-*bhʸahr*) *v* rage

rabioso (rah-*bhʸoa*-soa) *adj* mad

racial (rah-*thʸahl*) *adj* racial

ración (rah-*thʸoan*) *f* ration

radiador (rah-dhʸah-*dhoar*) *m* radiator

radical (rah-dhee-*kahl*) *adj* radical

radio (*rah*-dhʸoa) *m* radius; spoke; *f* wireless, radio

radiografía (rah-dhʸoa-grah-*fee*-ah) *f* X-ray

radiografiar (rah-dhʸoa-grah-*fʸahr*) *v* X-ray

raedura (rah-ay-*dhoo*-rah) *f* scratch; ***hacer raeduras** scratch

ráfaga (*rah*-fah-gah) *f* gust, blow

raíz (rah-*eeth*) *f* root

rallar (rah-*lʸahr*) *v* grate

rama (*rah*-mah) *f* branch, bough

ramita (rah-*mee*-tah) *f* twig

ramo (*rah*-moa) *m* bouquet, bunch

rampa (*rahm*-pah) *f* ramp

rana (*rah*-nah) *f* frog

rancio (*rahn*-thʸoa) *adj* rancid

rancho (*rahn*-choa) *mMe* farmhouse

rango (*rahng*-goa) *m* rank

ranura (rah-*noo*-rah) *f* slot

rápidamente (*rah*-pee-dah-mayn-tay) *adv* soon

rapidez (*rah*-pee-dhayth) *f* speed

rápido (*rah*-pee-dhoa) *adj* fast, rapid, quick; **rápidos de río** rapids *pl*

raqueta (rah-*kay*-tah) *f* racquet

raro (*rah*-roa) *adj* uncommon, rare; strange, odd; **raras veces** rarely

rascacielos (rahss-kah-*thʸay*-loass) *m* skyscraper

rascar (rahss-*kahr*) *v* scratch

rasgar (rahz-*gahr*) *v* rip

rasgo (*rahz*-goa) *m* trait; feature; **~ característico** characteristic

rasgón (rahz-*goan*) *m* tear

rasguño (rahz-*goo*-ñoa) *m* scratch

raso (*rah*-soa) *adj* bare; *m* satin

raspar (rahss-*pahr*) *v* scrape

rastrear (rahss-tray-*ahr*) *v* trace

rastrillo (rahss-*tree*-lʸoa) *m* rake

rastro (*rahss*-troa) *m* trail

rasurarse (rah-soo-*rahr*-say) *v* shave

rata (*rah*-tah) *f* rat

rato (*rah*-toa) *m* while

ratón (rah-*toan*) *m* mouse

raya (*rah*-ʸah) *f* line, stripe; crease; parting

rayado (rah-*ʸah*-dhoa) *adj* striped

rayador (rah-ʸah-*dhoar*) *m* grater

rayo (*rah*-ʸoa) *m* beam, ray

rayón (rah-*ʸoan*) *m* rayon

raza (*rah*-thah) *f* race; breed

razón (rah-*thoan*) *f* wits *pl*, sense, reason; **no *tener ~** *be wrong; ***tener ~** * be right

razonable (rah-thoa-*nah*-bhlay) *adj* reasonable

razonar (rah-thoa-*nahr*) *v* reason

reacción (ray-ahk-*thʸoan*) *f* reaction

reaccionar (ray-ahk-thʸoa-*nahr*) *v* react

real (ray-*ahl*) *adj* factual, true, substantial; royal

realidad (ray-ah-lee-*dhahdh*) *f* reality;

en ~ actually, as a matter of fact, really, in effect

realizable (ray-ah-lee-*thah*-bhlay) *adj* feasible, realizable

realización (ray-ah-lee-thah-*th ͮoan*) *f* achievement

realizar (ray-ah-lee-*thahr*) *v* realize; carry out

rebaja (ray-*bhah*-khah) *f* reduction, rebate; **rebajas** *fpl* sales

rebajar (ray-bhah-*khahr*) *v* lower, reduce

rebaño (ray-*bhah*-ñoa) *m* flock

rebelde (ray-*bhayl*-day) *m* rebel

rebelión (ray-bhay-*l ͮoan*) *f* revolt, rebellion

recado (ray-*kah*-dhoa) *m* errand

recambio (ray-*kahm*-b ͮoa) *m* spare part

recaudar (ray-kou-*dhahr*) *v* raise

recepción (ray-thayp-*th ͮoan*) *f* reception

recepcionista (ray-thayp-th ͮoa-*neess*-tah) *f* receptionist

receptáculo (ray-thayp-*tah*-koo-loa) *m* container

receptor (ray-thayp-*toar*) *m* receiver

receta (ray-*thay*-tah) *f* recipe

recibir (ray-thee-*bheer*) *v* receive

recibo (ray-*thee*-bhoa) *m* voucher, receipt; **oficina de** ~ reception office

recién (ray-*th ͮayn*) *adv* recently

reciente (ray-*th ͮayn*-tay) *adj* recent

recientemente (ray-th ͮayn-tay-*mayn*-tay) *adv* lately, recently

recio (ray-*th ͮoa*) *adj* strong

recíproco (ray-*thee*-proa-koa) *adj* mutual

recital (ray-thee-*tahl*) *m* recital

reclamar (ray-klah-*mahr*) *v* claim

recluta (ray-*kloo*-tah) *m* recruit

recoger (ray-koa-*khayr*) *v* pick up, pick; collect, gather; *overtake

recogida (ray-koa-*khee*-dhah) *f* collec-

tion

recomendación (ray-koa-mayn-dah-*th ͮoan*) *f* recommendation

* **recomendar** (ray-koa-mayn-*dahr*) *v* recommend

* **recomenzar** (ray-koa-mayn-*thahr*) *v* recommence

recompensa (ray-koam-*payn*-sah) *f* prize, reward

recompensar (ray-koam-payn-*sahr*) *v* reward

reconciliación (ray-koan-thee-l ͮah-*th ͮoan*) *f* reconciliation

* **reconocer** (ray-koa-noa-*thayr*) *v* recognize; admit, confess, acknowledge; realize

reconocimiento (ray-koa-noa-thee-*m ͮayn*-toa) *m* recognition; check-up

récord (*ray*-koardh) *m* record

* **recordar** (ray-koar-*dhahr*) *v* remind; *think of

recorrer (ray-koa-*rrayr*) *v* cross

recortar (ray-koar-*tahr*) *v* trim

recreación (ray-kray-ah-*th ͮoan*) *f* recreation

recreo (ray-*kray*-oa) *m* recreation; **patio de** ~ playground

recriar (ray-kr ͮahr) *v* *breed

rectangular (rayk-tahng-goo-*lahr*) *adj* rectangular

rectángulo (rayk-*tahng*-goo-loa) *m* oblong, rectangle

rectificación (rayk-tee-fee-kah-*th ͮoan*) *f* correction

recto (*rayk*-toa) *adj* erect

rector (rayk-*toar*) *m* rector

rectoría (rayk-toa-*ree*-ah) *f* rectory

recuerdo (ray-*kwayr*-dhoa) *m* remembrance, memory; souvenir

recuperación (ray-koo-pay-rah-*th ͮoan*) *f* revival

recuperar (ray-koo-pay-*rahr*) *v* recover

rechazar (ray-chah-*thahr*) *v* reject, turn down

red (raydh) f net; network; ~ **de ca-rreteras** road system; ~ **de pescar** fishing net

redacción (ray-dhahk-*th*ʸoan) f wording; editorial staff

redactar (ray-dhahk-*tahr*) v *make up; *draw up

redactor (ray-dhahk-*toar*) m editor

redecilla (ray-dhay-*thee*-lʸah) f hairnet

redimir (ray-dhee-*meer*) v redeem

rédito (*ray*-dhee-toa) m interest

redondeado (ray-dhoan-day-*ah*-dhoa) adj rounded

redondo (ray-dhoan-doa) adj round

reducción (ray-dhook-*th*ʸoan) f reduction, rebate

*** reducir** (ray-dhoo-*theer*) v *cut, decrease, reduce

reembolsar (ray-aym-boal-*sahr*) v reimburse

reemplazar (ray-aym-plah-*thahr*) v replace

reemprender (ray-aym-prayn-*dayr*) v resume

reexpedir (ray-ayks-pay-*dheer*) v forward

referencia (ray-fay-*rayn*-thʸah) f reference; **punto de** ~ landmark

*** referir** (ray-fay-*reer*) v refer; narrate

refinería (ray-fee-nay-*ree*-ah) f refinery

reflector (ray-flayk-*toar*) m reflector; searchlight

reflejar (ray-flay-*khahr*) v reflect

reflejo (ray-*flay*-khoa) m reflection

reflexionar (ray-flayk-sʸoa-*nahr*) v *think

Reforma (ray-*foar*-mah) f reformation

refractario (ray-frahk-*tah*-rʸoa) adj fireproof

refrenar (ray-fray-*nahr*) v curb

refrescar (ray-frayss-*kahr*) v refresh

refresco (ray-*frayss*-koa) m refreshment

refrigerador (ray-free-khay-rah-*dhoar*) m fridge, refrigerator

refugio (ray-*foo*-khʸoa) m cover, shelter

refunfuñar (ray-foon-foo-*ñahr*) v grumble

regalar (ray-gah-*lahr*) v present

regaliz (ray-gah-*leeth*) m liquorice

regalo (ray-*gah*-loa) m present, gift

regata (ray-*gah*-tah) f regatta

regatear (ray-gah-tay-*ahr*) v bargain

régimen (*ray*-khee-mayn) m (pl regímenes) régime; government, rule; diet

regimiento (ray-khee-*m*ʸayn-toa) m regiment

región (ray-*kh*ʸoan) f region; zone, country, area

regional (ray-khʸoa-*nahl*) adj regional

*** regir** (ray-*kheer*) v govern, rule

registrar (ray-kheess-*trahr*) v book, record

registro (ray-*kheess*-troa) m record

regla (*ray*-glah) f rule; regulation; ruler; **en** ~ in order; **por** ~ **general** as a rule

reglamento (ray-glah-*mayn*-toa) m regulation

regocijo (ray-goa-*thee*-khoa) m joy

regordete (ray-goar-*dhay*-tay) adj plump

regresar (ray-gray-*sahr*) v *go back, *get back

regreso (ray-*gray*-soa) m return; **viaje de** ~ return journey; **vuelo de** ~ return flight

regulación (ray-goo-lah-*th*ʸoan) f regulation

regular (ray-goo-*lahr*) v regulate; adj regular

rehabilitación (ray-ah-bhee-lee-tah-*th*ʸoan) f rehabilitation

rehén (ray-*ayn*) m hostage

rehusar (rayᵒᵒ-*sahr*) v refuse; reject

reina (*ray*-nah) *f* queen
reinado (ray-*nah*-dhoa) *m* reign
reino (*ray*-noa) *m* kingdom
reintegrar (rayn-tay-*grahr*) *v* *repay, refund
reintegro (rayn-*tay*-groa) *m* repayment, refund
*reír** (ray-*eer*) *v* laugh
reivindicación (ray-bheen-dee-kah-*th^yoan*) *f* claim
reivindicar (ray-bheen-dee-*kahr*) *v* claim
reja (*ray*-khah) *f* grate; fence, gate
rejilla (ray-*khee*-l^yah) *f* luggage rack
relación (ray-lah-*th^yoan*) *f* connection, relation; reference; report
relacionar (ray-lah-th^yoa-*nahr*) *v* relate
relajación (ray-lah-khah-*th^yoan*) *f* relaxation
relajado (ray-lah-*khah*-dhoa) *adj* easygoing
relámpago (ray-*lahm*-pah-goa) *m* lightning; flash
relatar (ray-lah-*tahr*) *v* report
relativo (ray-lah-*tee*-bhoa) *adj* comparative, relative; ~ **a** regarding
relato (ray-*lah*-toa) *m* talc
relevar (ray-lay-*bhahr*) *v* relieve
relieve (ray-*l^yay*-bhay) *m* relief
religión (ray-lee-*kh^yoan*) *f* religion
religioso (ray-lee-*kh^yoa*-soa) *adj* religious
reliquia (ray-*lee*-k^yah) *f* relic
reloj (ray-*loakh*) *m* clock; watch; ~ **de bolsillo** pocket-watch; ~ **de pulsera** wrist-watch
relojero (ray-loa-*khay*-roa) *m* watchmaker
reluciente (ray-loo-*th^yayn*-tay) *adj* bright
*relucir** (ray-loo-*theer*) *v* *shine
rellenado (ray-l^yay-*nah*-doa) *adj* stuffed

relleno (ray-*l^yay*-noa) *m* stuffing; filling
remanente (ray-mah-*nayn*-tay) *m* remnant
remar (ray-*mahr*) *v* row
remedio (ray-*may*-dh^yoa) *m* remedy
*remendar** (ray-mayn-*dahr*) *v* mend; patch
remesa (ray-*may*-sah) *f* remittance
remitir (ray-mee-*teer*) *v* remit; ~ **a** refer to
remo (*ray*-moa) *m* paddle, oar
remoción (ray-moa-*th^yoan*) *f* removal
remojar (ray-moa-*khahr*) *v* soak
remolacha (ray-moa-*lah*-chah) *f* beetroot, beet
remolcador (ray-moal-kah-*dhoar*) *m* tug
remolcar (ray-moal-*kahr*) *v* tug, tow
remolque (ray-*moal*-kay) *m* trailer
remoto (ray-*moa*-toa) *adj* remote, faraway, far-off
*remover** (ray-moa-*bhayr*) *v* remove
remuneración (ray-moo-nay-rah-*th^yoan*) *f* remuneration
remunerar (ray-moo-nay-*rahr*) *v* remunerate
Renacimiento (ray-nah-thee-*m^yayn*-toa) *m* Renaissance
rendición (rayn-dee-*th^yoan*) *f* surrender
*rendir** (rayn-*deer*) *v* *pay; ~ **homenaje** honour; *rendirse** *v* surrender
renglón (rayng-*gloan*) *m* line
reno (*ray*-noa) *m* reindeer
renombre (ray-*noam*-bray) *m* reputation
*renovar** (ray-noa-*bhahr*) *v* renew
renta (*rayn*-tah) *f* revenue
rentable (rayn-*tah*-bhlay) *adj* paying
renunciar (ray-noon-*th^yahr*) *v* *give up
*reñir** (ray-*ñeer*) *v* dispute, quarrel
reparación (ray-pah-rah-*th^yoan*) *f* reparation; repair

reparar (ray-pah-*rahr*) v repair, mend
repartir (ray-pahr-*teer*) v divide, *deal
reparto (ray-*pahr*-toa) m delivery; **camioneta de ~** pick-up van
repelente (ray-pay-*layn*-tay) adj repellent, revolting
repentinamente (ray-payn-tee-nah-*mayn*-tay) adv suddenly
repertorio (ray-payr-*toa*-rʸoa) m repertory
repetición (ray-pay-tee-*thʸoan*) f repetition
repetidamente (ray-pay-tee-dhah-*mayn*-tay) adv again and again
*repetir (ray-pay-*teer*) v repeat
repleto (ray-*play*-toa) adj chock-full, crowded
reportero (ray-poar-*tay*-roa) m reporter
reposado (ray-poa-*sah*-dhoa) adj restful
reposo (ray-*poa*-soa) m rest
reprender (ray-prayn-*dayr*) v reprimand, scold
representación (ray-pray-sayn-tah-*thʸoan*) f representation; show, performance
representante (ray-pray-sayn-*tahn*-tay) m agent
representar (ray-pray-sayn-*tahr*) v represent
representativo (ray-pray-sayn-tah-*tee*-bhoa) adj representative
reprimir (ray-pree-*meer*) v suppress
*reprobar (ray-proa-*bhahr*) v reject
reprochar (ray-proa-*chahr*) v reproach
reproche (ray-*proa*-chay) m reproach, blame
reproducción (ray-proa-dhook-*thʸoan*) f reproduction
*reproducir (ray-proa-dhoo-*theer*) v reproduce
reptil (rayp-*teel*) m reptile
república (ray-*poo*-bhlee-kah) f republic

republicano (ray-poo-bhlee-*kah*-noa) adj republican
repuesto (ray-*pwayss*-toa) m store; refill
repugnancia (ray-poog-*nahn*-thʸah) f dislike
repugnante (ray-poog-*nahn*-tay) adj repellent, disgusting, revolting
repulsivo (ray-pool-*see*-bhoa) adj repulsive
reputación (ray-poo-tah-*thʸoan*) f reputation, fame
requerimiento (ray-kay-ree-*mʸayn*-toa) m requirement
*requerir (ray-kay-*reer*) v require, demand
resaca (ray-*sah*-kah) f undercurrent; hangover
resbaladizo (rayz-bhah-lah-*dhee*-thoa) adj slippery
resbalar (rayz-bhah-*lahr*) v slip, glide
rescatar (rayss-kah-*tahr*) v rescue
rescate (rayss-*kah*-tay) m rescue; ransom
*resentirse por (ray-sayn-*teer*-say) resent
reseña (ray-*say*-ñah) f review
reserva (ray-*sayr*-bhah) f qualification; reserve; booking; **de ~** spare
reservación (ray-sayr-bhah-*thʸoan*) f reservation, booking
reservar (ray-sayr-*bhahr*) v engage; reserve, book
resfriado (rayss-*frʸah*-dhoa) m cold
resfriarse (rayss-*frʸahr*-say) v catch a cold
residencia (ray-see-*dhayn*-thʸah) f residence
residente (ray-see-*dhayn*-tay) adj resident; m resident
residir (ray-see-*dheer*) v reside
residuo (ray-*see*-dhwoa) m remnant
resignación (ray-seeg-nah-*thʸoan*) f resignation

resignar (ray-seeg-*nahr*) *v* resign

resina (ray-*see*-nah) *f* resin

resistencia (ray-seess-*tayn*-th^yah) *f* resistance

resistir (ray-seess-*teer*) *v* resist

resolución (ray-soa-loo-*th^yoan*) *f* resolution

*__resolver__ (ray-soal-*bhayr*) *v* solve

*__resonar__ (ray-soa-*nahr*) *v* sound

respectivo (rayss-payk-*tee*-bhoa) *adj* respective

respecto a (rayss-*payk*-toa ah) about, regarding

respetable (rayss-pay-*tah*-bhlay) *adj* respectable

respetar (rayss-pay-*tahr*) *v* respect

respeto (rayss-*pay*-toa) *m* respect, esteem, regard

respetuoso (rayss-pay-*twoa*-soa) *adj* respectful

respiración (rayss-pee-rah-*th^yoan*) *f* respiration, breathing

respirar (rayss-pee-*rahr*) *v* breathe

*__resplandecer__ (rayss-plahn-day-*thayr*) *v* *shine

resplandor (rayss-plahn-*doar*) *m* glare

responder (rayss-poan-*dayr*) *v* reply, answer

responsabilidad (rayss-poan-sah-bhee-lee-*dhahdh*) *f* responsibility; liability

responsable (rayss-poan-*sah*-bhlay) *adj* responsible; liable

respuesta (rayss-*pwayss*-tah) *f* reply, answer

*__restablecerse__ (rayss-tah-bhlay-*thayr*-say) *v* recover

restablecimiento (rayss-tah-bhlay-thee-*m^yayn*-toa) *m* recovery

restante (rayss-*tahn*-tay) *adj* remaining

restar (rayss-*tahr*) *v* subtract

restaurante (rayss-tou-*rahn*-tay) *m* restaurant; ~ **de autoservicio** self-service restaurant

resto (*rayss*-toa) *m* rest; remnant, remainder

restricción (rayss-treek-*th^yoan*) *f* restriction; qualification

resuelto (ray-*swayl*-toa) *adj* resolute, determined

resultado (ray-sool-*tah*-dhoa) *m* result; issue, outcome, effect

resultar (ray-sool-*tahr*) *v* result; prove

resumen (ray-*soo*-mayn) *m* résumé, survey, summary

retardar (ray-tahr-*dhahr*) *v* delay

*__retener__ (ray-tay-*nayr*) *v* *hold

retina (ray-*tee*-nah) *f* retina

retirar (ray-tee-*rahr*) *v* *withdraw

reto (*ray*-toa) *m* challenge

retrasado (ray-trah-*sah*-dhoa) *adj* late

retraso (ray-*trah*-soa) *m* delay

retrato (ray-*trah*-toa) *m* portrait

retrete (ray-*tray*-tay) *m* toilet

retroceso (ray-troa-*thay*-soa) *m* recession

retumbo (ray-*toom*-boa) *m* roar

reumatismo (ray^{oo}-mah-*teez*-moa) *m* rheumatism

reunión (ray^{oo}-*n^yoan*) *f* meeting, assembly, rally

reunir (ray^{oo}-*neer*) *v* join, assemble; reunite

revelación (ray-bhay-lah-*th^yoan*) *f* revelation

revelar (ray-hhay-*lahr*) *v* reveal; *give away; develop

*__reventar__ (ray-bhayn-*tahr*) *v* crack, *burst

reventón (ray-bhayn-*toan*) *m* blow-out

reverencia (ray-bhay-*rayn*-th^yah) *f* respect

reverso (ray-*bhayr*-soa) *m* reverse

revés (ray-*bhayss*) *m* reverse; **al** ~ the other way round; upside-down; inside out

revisar (ray-bhee-*sahr*) v revise, overhaul

revisión (ray-bhee-s*Υ*oan) f revision

revisor (ray-bhee-*soar*) m ticket collector

revista (ray-*bheess*-tah) f journal; review, magazine; revue; ~ **mensual** monthly magazine

revocar (ray-bhoa-*kahr*) v recall

revolución (ray-bhoa-loo-th*Υ*oan) f revolution

revolucionar (ray-bhoa-loo-th*Υ*oa-*nahr*) v rebel

revolucionario (ray-bhoa-loo-th*Υ*oa-nah-r*Υ*oa) adj revolutionary

*****revolver** (ray-bhoal-*bhayr*) v stir

revólver (ray-*bhoal*-bhayr) m revolver, gun

revuelta (ray-*bhwayl*-tah) f revolt

rey (ray) m king

rezar (ray-*thahr*) v pray

riada (r*Υ*ah-dhah) f flood

ribera (ree-*bhay*-rah) f riverside, river bank, shore

rico (ree-koa) adj rich; wealthy; nice, enjoyable, tasty

ridiculizar (ree-dhee-koo-lee-*thahr*) v ridicule

ridículo (ree-*dhee*-koo-loa) adj ridiculous, ludicrous

riesgo (r*Υ*ayz-goa) m hazard, chance, risk

rigoroso (ree-goa-*roa*-soa) adj severe

riguroso (ree-goo-*roa*-soa) adj bleak

rima (*ree*-mah) f rhyme

rímel (*ree*-mayl) m mascara

rincón (reeng-*koan*) m angle

rinoceronte (ree-noa-thay-*roan*-tay) m rhinoceros

riña (*ree*-ñah) f dispute

riñón (ree-*ñoan*) m kidney

río (*ree*-oa) m river; ~ **abajo** downstream; ~ **arriba** upstream

riqueza (ree-*kay*-thah) f riches pl,

wealth

risa (*ree*-sah) f laughter, laugh

ritmo (*reet*-moa) m rhythm; pace

rival (ree-*bhahl*) m rival

rivalidad (ree-bhah-lee-*dhahdh*) f rivalry

rivalizar (ree-bhah-lee-*thahr*) v rival

rizador (ree-thah-*dhoar*) m curling-tongs pl; **rizadores** mpl hair rollers

rizar (ree-*thahr*) v curl

rizo (*ree*-thoa) m curl

robar (roa-*bhahr*) v rob; burgle

roble (*roa*-bhlay) m oak

robo (*roa*-bhoa) m robbery, theft

robusto (roa-*bhooss*-toa) adj solid, robust

roca (*roa*-kah) f rock

rocío (roa-*thee*-oa) m dew

rocoso (roa-*koa*-soa) adj rocky

rodaballo (roa-dhah-*bhah*-l*Υ*oa) m brill

*****rodar** (roa-*dhahr*) v roll

rodear (roa-dhay-*ahr*) v circle, surround; by-pass

rodilla (roa-*dhee*-l*Υ*ah) f knee

*****rogar** (roa-*gahr*) v ask

rojo (*roa*-khoa) adj red

rollo (*roa*-l*Υ*oa) m roll

romano (roa-*mah*-noa) adj Roman

Romanticismo (roa-mahn-tee-*theez*-moa) m Romanticism

romántico (roa-*mahn*-tee-koa) adj romantic

rompecabezas (roam-pay-kah-*bhay*-thahss) m puzzle; jigsaw puzzle

romper (roam-*payr*) v *break

roncar (roang-*kahr*) v snore

ronco (*roang*-koa) adj hoarse

ropa (*roa*-pah) f clothes pl; ~ **blanca** linen; ~ **de cama** bedding; ~ **interior** underwear; ~ **interior de mujer** lingerie; ~ **sucia** washing, laundry

rosa (*roa*-sah) f rose; adj rose

rosado (roa-*sah*-dhoa) adj pink

rosario (roa-*sah*-r^yoa) *m* beads *pl*, rosary
rostro (*roas*-troa) *m* face
rota (*roa*-tah) *f* rattan
roto (*roa*-toa) *adj* broken
rótula (*roa*-too-lah) *f* kneecap
rotular (roa-too-*lahr*) *v* label
rótulo (*roa*-too-loa) *m* label
rozadura (roa-thah-*dhoo*-rah) *f* graze
rubí (roo-*bhee*) *m* ruby
rubia (*roo*-bh^yah) *f* blonde
rubio (*roo*-bh^yoa) *adj* fair
ruborizarse (roo-bhoa-ree-*thahr*-say) blush
rubricar (roo-bhree-*kahr*) *v* initial
rueda (*rway*-dhah) *f* wheel; **patinaje de ruedas** roller-skating; ~ **de repuesto** spare wheel
ruego (*rway*-goa) *m* request
rugido (roo-*khee*-dhoa) *m* roar
rugir (roo-*kheer*) *v* roar
ruibarbo (rwee-*bhahr*-bhoa) *m* rhubarb
ruido (*rwee*-dhoa) *m* noise
ruidoso (rwee-*dhoa*-soa) *adj* noisy
ruina (*rwee*-nah) *f* ruins; ruin, destruction
ruinoso (rwee-*noa*-soa) *adj* dilapidated
ruiseñor (rwee-say-*ñoar*) *m* nightingale
ruleta (roo-*lay*-tah) *f* roulette
rulo (*roo*-loa) *m* curler
Rumania (roo-*mah*-n^yah) *f* Rumania
rumano (roo-*mah*-noa) *adj* Rumanian; *m* Rumanian
rumbo (*room*-boa) *m* course
rumor (roo-*moar*) *m* rumour
rural (roo-*rahl*) *adj* rural
Rusia (*roo*-s^yah) *f* Russia
ruso (*roo*-soa) *adj* Russian; *m* Russian
rústico (*rooss*-tee-koa) *adj* rustic
ruta (*roo*-tah) *f* route; ~ **principal** thoroughfare

rutina (roo-*tee*-nah) *f* routine

S

sábado (*sah*-bhah-dhoa) *m* Saturday
sábana (*sah*-bhah-nah) *f* sheet
sabañón (sah-bhah-*ñoan*) *m* chilblain
* **saber** (sah-*bhayr*) *v* *know; *be able to; **a** ~ namely; ~ **a** taste
sabiduría (sah-bhee-dhoo-*ree*-ah) *f* wisdom
sabio (*sah*-bh^yoa) *adj* wise
sabor (sah-*bhoar*) *m* flavour
sabroso (sah-*bhroa*-soa) *adj* savoury, tasty
sacacorchos (sah-kah-*koar*-choass) *mpl* corkscrew
sacapuntas (sah-kah-*poon*-tahss) *m* pencil-sharpener
sacar (sah-*kahr*) *v* *take out; *draw; ~ **brillo** brush
sacarina (sah-kah-*ree*-nah) *f* saccharin
sacerdote (sah-thayr-*dhoa*-tay) *m* priest
saco (*sah*-koa) *m* sack; *mMe* jacket; ~ **de compras** shopping bag; ~ **de dormir** sleeping-bag
sacrificar (sah-kree-fee-*kahr*) *v* sacrifice
sacrificio (sah-kree-*fee*-th^yoa) *m* sacrifice
sacrilegio (sah-kree-*lay*-kh^yoa) *m* sacrilege
sacristán (sah-kreess-*tahn*) *m* sexton
sacudir (sah-koo-*dheer*) *v* *shake
sagrado (sah-*grah*-dhoa) *adj* sacred
sainete (sigh-*nay*-tay) *m* farce
sal (sahl) *f* salt; **sales de baño** bath salts
sala (*sah*-lah) *f* hall; ~ **de conciertos** concert hall; ~ **de espera** waiting-room; ~ **de estar** sitting-room, liv-

ing-room; ~ **de lectura** reading-room; ~ **para fumar** smoking-room

salado (sah-*lah*-dhoa) *adj* salty

salario (sah-*lah*-rʸoa) *m* pay

salchicha (sahl-*chee*-chah) *f* sausage

saldo (*sahl*-doa) *m* balance

salero (sah-*lay*-roa) *m* salt-cellar

salida (sah-*lee*-dhah) *f* issue, exit, way out; ~ **de emergencia** emergency exit

***salir** (sah-*leer*) *v* *go out; appear

saliva (sah-*lee*-bhah) *f* spit

salmón (sahl-*moan*) *m* salmon

salón (sah-*loan*) *m* salon, lounge, drawing-room; ~ **de baile** ball-room; ~ **de belleza** beauty parlour; ~ **de demostraciones** showroom; ~ **de té** tea-shop

salpicadera (sahl-pee-kah-*dhay*-rah) *fMe* mud-guard

salpicar (sahl-pee-*kahr*) *v* splash

salsa (*sahl*-sah) *f* sauce; gravy

saltamontes (sahl-tah-*moan*-tayss) *m* grasshopper

saltar (sahl-*tahr*) *v* jump, *leap; skip

salto (*sahl*-toa) *m* jump, leap, hop

salud (sah-*loodh*) *f* health

saludable (sah-loo-*dhah*-bhlay) *adj* wholesome

saludar (sah-loo-*dhahr*) *v* greet; salute

saludo (sah-*loo*-dhoa) *m* greeting

salvador (sahl-bhah-*dhoar*) *m* saviour

salvaje (sahl-*bhah*-khay) *adj* wild, savage; fierce, desert

salvar (sahl-*bhahr*) *v* save

sanatorio (sah-nah-*toa*-rʸoa) *m* sanatorium

sandalia (sahn-*dah*-lʸah) *f* sandal; **sandalias de gimnasia** gym shoes

sandía (sahn-*dee*-ah) *f* watermelon

sangrar (sahng-*grahr*) *v* *bleed

sangre (*sahng*-gray) *f* blood

sangriento (sahng-grʸ*ayn*-toa) *adj* bloody

sanitario (sah-nee-*tah*-rʸoa) *adj* sanitary

sano (*sah*-noa) *adj* healthy, well

santo (*sahn*-toa) *adj* holy; *m* saint; ~ **y seña** password

santuario (sahn-*twah*-rʸoa) *m* shrine

sapo (*sah*-poa) *m* toad

sarampión (sah-rahm-pʸ*oan*) *m* measles

sardina (sahr-*dhee*-nah) *f* sardine

sartén (sahr-*tayn*) *f* pan; frying-pan

sastre (*sahss*-tray) *m* tailor

satélite (sah-*tay*-lee-tay) *m* satellite

satisfacción (sah-teess-fahk-*thʸoan*) *f* satisfaction

***satisfacer** (sah-teess-fah-*thayr*) *v* satisfy; **satisfecho** satisfied

saudí (sou-*dhee*) *adj* Saudi Arabian

sauna (*sou*-nah) *f* sauna

sazonar (sah-thoa-*nahr*) *v* flavour

se (say) *pron* himself; herself; yourselves; themselves

secadora (say-kah-*dhoa*-rah) *f* dryer

secar (say-*kahr*) *v* dry

sección (sayk-*thʸoan*) *f* section; agency

seco (*say*-koa) *adj* dry

secretaria (say-kray-*tah*-rʸah) *f* secretary

secretario (say-kray-*tah*-rʸoa) *m* secretary; clerk

secreto (say-*kray*-toa) *adj* secret; *m* secret

sector (sayk-*toar*) *m* sector

secuencia (say-*kwayn*-thʸah) *f* shot

secuestrador (say-kwayss-trah-*dhoar*) *m* hijacker

secundario (say-koon-*dah*-rʸoa) *adj* secondary; minor

sed (saydh) *f* thirst

seda (*say*-dhah) *f* silk

sede (*say*-dhay) *f* seat

sediento (say-*dhʸ*ayn-toa) *adj* thirsty

sedoso (say-*dhoa*-soa) *adj* silken

*seducir (say-dhoo-*theer*) v seduce

en seguida (ayn say-*gee*-dhah) straight away, at once, presently

*seguir (say-*geer*) v follow; ~ el paso *keep up with; todo seguido straight on, straight ahead

según (say-*goon*) prep according to

segundo (say-*goon*-doa) num second; m second

seguramente (say-goo-rah-*mayn*-tay) adv surely

seguridad (say-goo-ree-*dhahdh*) f security, safety; cinturón de ~ safety-belt

seguro (say-*goo*-roa) adj safe; sure; m insurance; póliza de ~ insurance policy; ~ de viaje travel insurance; ~ de vida life insurance

seis (sayss) num six

selección (say-layk-th*Y*oan) f selection; choice

seleccionado (say-layk-th*Y*oa-*nah*-dhoa) adj select

seleccionar (say-layk-th*Y*oa-*nahr*) v select

selecto (say-*layk*-toa) adj select

selva (*sayl*-bhah) f jungle, forest

selvoso (sayl-*bhoa*-soa) adj wooded

sellar (say-*lY*ahr) v stamp

sello (say-*lY*oa) m stamp; seal

semáforo (say-*mah*-foa-roa) m traffic light

semana (say-*mah*-nah) f week; fin de ~ weekend

semanal (say-mah-*nahl*) adj weekly

*sembrar (saym-*brahr*) v *sow

semejante (say-may-*khahn*-tay) adj like

semejanza (say-may-*khahn*-thah) f resemblance, similarity

semi- (say-mee) semi-

semicírculo (say-mee-*theer*-koo-loa) m semicircle

semilla (say-mee-*lY*ah) f seed

senado (say-*nah*-dhoa) m senate

senador (say-nah-*dhoar*) m senator

sencillo (sayn-*thee*-lY*oa) adj plain

senda (*sayn*-dah) f footpath

sendero (sayn-*day*-roa) m trail

senil (say-*neel*) adj senile

seno (*say*-noa) m bosom; breast

sensación (sayn-sah-*th*Y*oan) f sensation; feeling

sensacional (sayn-sah-th*Y*oa-*nahl*) adj sensational

sensato (sayn-*sah*-toa) adj sensible; down-to-earth

sensibilidad (sayn-see-bhee-lee-*dhahdh*) f sensibility

sensible (sayn-*see*-bhlay) adj sensitive; perceptible

sensitivo (sayn-see-*tee*-bhoa) adj sensitive

*sentarse (sayn-*tahr*-say) v *sit down; *estar sentado *sit; *sentar bien *become

sentencia (sayn-*tayn*-th*Y*ah) f sentence, verdict

sentenciar (sayn-tayn-th*Y*ahr) v sentence

sentido (sayn-*tee*-dhoa) m sense; reason; ~ del honor sense of honour; sin ~ meaningless

sentimental (sayn-tee-mayn-*tahl*) adj sentimental

sentimiento (sayn-tee-m*Y*ayn-toa) m sentiment

*sentir (sayn-*teer*) v *feel, sense; regret

seña (*say*-ñah) f sign; señas personales description

señal (say-*ñahl*) f signal, sign, indication; m token, tick; *hacer señales signal; wave; ~ de alarma distress signal

señalar (say-ñah-*lahr*) v tick off, indicate

señor (say-*ñoar*) m mister; sir

señora (say-*ñoa*-rah) *f* lady; mistress; madam

señorita (say-ñoa-*ree*-tah) *f* miss

separación (say-pah-rah-*th*ᵞ*oan*) *f* division

separadamente (say-pah-rah-dhah-*mayn*-tay) *adv* apart

separado (say-pah-*rah*-dhoa) *adj* separate; **por ~** apart, separately

separar (say-pah-*rahr*) *v* separate, part; divide; detach

septentrional (sayp-tayn-tr*ᵞ*oa-*nahl*) *adj* north

septicemia (sayp-tee-*thay*-mᵞah) *f* blood-poisoning

séptico (*sayp*-tee-koa) *adj* septic

septiembre (sayp-t*ᵞaym*-bray) September

séptimo (*sayp*-tee-moa) *num* seventh

sepulcro (say-*pool*-kroa) *m* sepulchre

sepultura (say-pool-*too*-rah) *f* grave

sequía (say-*kee*-ah) *f* drought

ser (sayr) *m* being, creature; **~ humano** human being

* **ser** (sayr) *v* *be

sereno (say-*ray*-noa) *adj* serene

serie (*say*-rᵞay) *f* series; sequence

seriedad (say-rᵞay-*dhahdh*) *f* seriousness, gravity

serio (*say*-rᵞoa) *adj* serious

sermón (sayr-*moan*) *m* sermon

serpentear (sayr-payn-tay-*ahr*) *v* *wind

serrín (say-*rreen*) *m* sawdust

servicial (sayr-bhee-*th*ᵞ*ahl*) *adj* helpful

servicio (sayr-*bhee*-thᵞoa) *m* service; service charge; **~ de habitación** room service; **~ de mesa** dinnerservice; **~ postal** postal service

servilleta (sayr-bhee-*l*ᵞ*ay*-tah) *f* napkin, serviette; **~ de papel** paper napkin

* **servir** (sayr-*bheer*) *v* serve; attend on, wait on; *be of use

sesenta (say-*sayn*-tah) *num* sixty

sesión (say-s*ᵞoan*) *f* session

seta (*say*-tah) *f* mushroom

setenta (say-*tayn*-tah) *num* seventy

seto (*say*-toa) *m* hedge

severo (say-*bhay*-roa) *adj* harsh, strict, severe

sexo (*sayk*-soa) *m* sex

sexto (*sayks*-toa) *num* sixth

sexual (sayk-*swahl*) *adj* sexual

sexualidad (sayk-swah-lee-*dhahdh*) *f* sexuality; sex

si (see) *conj* if; in case; whether; **si ... o** whether ... or; **~ bien** though

sí (see) yes

Siam (sᵞahm) *m* Siam

siamés (sᵞah-*mayss*) *adj* Siamese; *m* Siamese

siempre (s*ᵞaym*-pray) *adv* ever, always

sien (sᵞayn) *f* temple

sierra (s*ᵞay*-rrah) *f* saw

siesta (s*ᵞayss*-tah) *f* nap

siete (s*ᵞay*-tay) *num* seven

sifón (see-*foan*) *m* siphon, syphon

siglo (*see*-gloa) *m* century

significado (seeg-nee-fee-*kah*-dhoa) *m* meaning

significar (seeg-nee-fee-*kahr*) *v* *mean

significativo (seeg-nee-fee-kah-*tee*-bhoa) *adj* significant

signo (*seeg*-noa) *m* sign; **~ de interrogación** question mark

siguiente (see-g*ᵞayn*-tay) *adj* following

sílaba (*see*-lah-bhah) *f* syllable

silbar (seel-*bhahr*) *v* whistle

silbato (seel-*bhah*-toa) *m* whistle

silenciador (see-layn-th*ᵞah*-*dhoar*) *m* silencer

silencio (see-*layn*-thᵞoa) *m* stillness, quiet, silence

silencioso (see-layn-th*ᵞoa*-soa) *adj* silent

silla (*see*-lᵞah) *f* chair; saddle; **~ de ruedas** wheelchair; **~ de tijera**

deck chair

sillón (see-*lᵞoan*) *m* armchair

simbólico (seem-*boa*-lee-koa) *adj* symbolic

símbolo (*seem*-boa-loa) *m* symbol

similar (see-mee-*lahr*) *adj* similar

simpatía (seem-pah-*tee*-ah) *f* sympathy

simpático (seem-*pah*-tee-koa) *adj* nice, pleasant; obliging

simple (*seem*-play) *adj* simple

simular (see-moo-*lahr*) *v* simulate

simultáneo (see-mool-*tah*-nay-oa) *adj* simultaneous

sin (seen) *prep* without

sinagoga (see-nah-*goa*-gah) *f* synagogue

sincero (seen-*thay*-roa) *adj* sincere; open, honest

sindicato (seen-dee-*kah*-toa) *m* trade-union

sinfonía (seen-foa *nee* ah) *f* symphony

singular (seeng-goo-*lahr*) *adj* singular, queer; *m* singular

siniestro (see-*nᵞayss*-troa) *adj* ominous, sinister

sino (*see*-noa) *conj* but

sinónimo (see-*noa*-nee-moa) *m* synonym

sintético (seen-*tay*-tee-koa) *adj* synthetic

síntoma (*seen*-toa-mah) *m* symptom

sintonizar (seen-toa-nee-*thahr*) *v* tune in

siquiera (see-*kᵞay*-rah) *adv* at least; *conj* even though

sirena (coo *ray* nah) *f* siren; mermaid

Siria (*see*-rᵞah) *f* Syria

sirio (*see*-rᵞoa) *adj* Syrian; *m* Syrian

sirviente (seer-*bhᵞayn*-tay) *m* domestic; boy

sistema (seess-*tay*-mah) *m* system; ~ **decimal** decimal system; ~ **de lubricación** lubrication system; ~ **de**

refrigeración cooling system

sistemático (seess-tay-*mah*-tee-koa) *adj* systematic

sitio (*see*-tᵞoa) *m* site; seat, room; siege

situación (see-twah-*thᵞoan*) *f* situation

situado (see-*twah*-dhoa) *adj* situated

situar (see-*twahr*) *v* locate

slogan (*sloa*-gahn) *m* slogan

smoking (*smoa*-keeng) *m* dinner-jacket; tuxedo *nAm*

soberano (soa-bhay-*rah*-noa) *m* sovereign

soberbio (soa-*bhayr*-bhᵞoa) *adj* superb

sobornar (soa-bhoar-*nahr*) *v* bribe

soborno (soa-*bhoar*-noa) *m* bribery

sobra (*soa*-bhrah) *f* surplus

sobrar (soa-*bhrahr*) *v* *be left over; *be in plenty

sobre (*soa*-bhray) *prep* on, upon; *m* envelope

sobrecubierta (soa-bhray-koo-*bhᵞayr*-tah) *f* jacket

sobreexcitado (soa-bhray-ayk-thee-*tah*-dhoa) *adj* overstrung

sobrepeso (soa-bhray-*pay*-soa) *m* overweight

sobretasa (soa-bhray-*tah*-sah) *f* surcharge

sobretodo (soa-bhray-*toa*-dhoa) *m* coat, topcoat

sobrevivir (soa-bhray-bhee-*bhoor*) *v* survive

sobrina (soa-*bhree*-nah) *f* niece

sobrino (soa-*bhree*-noa) *m* nephew

sobrio (*soa* bhrᵞoa) *adj* sober

social (soa-*thᵞahl*) *adj* social

socialismo (soa-thᵞah-*leez*-moa) *m* socialism

socialista (soa-thᵞah-*leess*-tah) *adj* socialist; *m* socialist

sociedad (soa-thᵞay-*dhahdh*) *f* community, society; company

socio (*soa*-thᵞoa) *m* associate; partner

socorro (soa-*koa*-rroa) *m* aid; **puesto de ~** first-aid post

soda (*soa*-dhah) *f* soda-water

sofá (sa-*fah*) *m* sofa

sofocante (so-foa-*kahn*-tay) *adj* stuffy

sofocarse (so-foa-*kahr*-say) *v* choke

soga (*soa*-gah) *f* rope

sol (soal) *m* sun; **tomar el ~** sunbathe

solamente (soa-lah-*mayn*-tay) *adv* merely, only

solapa (soa-*lah*-pah) *f* lapel

soldado (soal-*dah*-dhoa) *m* soldier

soldador (soal-dah-*dhoar*) *m* soldering-iron

soldadura (soal-dah-*dhoo*-rah) *f* joint

*soldar** (soal-*dahr*) *v* solder; weld

soleado (soa-lay-*ah*-dhoa) *adj* sunny

soledad (soa-lay-*dhahdh*) *f* solitude

solemne (soa-*laym*-nay) *adj* solemn

*soler** (soa-*layr*) *v* would

solicitar (soa-lee-thee-*tahr*) *v* request; **~ un puesto** apply

solicitud (soa-lee-thee-*toodh*) *f* application

sólido (*soa*-lee-dhoa) *adj* solid, firm; *m* solid

solitario (soa-lee-*tah*-rʸoa) *adj* lonely

solo (*soa*-loa) *adj* only, single

sólo (*soa*-loa) *adv* alone; only

*soltar** (soal-*tahr*) *v* loosen

soltero (soal-*tay*-roa) *adj* single; *m* bachelor

solterona (soal-tay-*roa*-nah) *f* spinster

soluble (soa-*loo*-bhlay) *adj* soluble

solución (soa-loo-*thʸoan*) *f* solution

sombra (*soam*-brah) *f* shade; shadow; **~ para los ojos** eye-shadow

sombreado (soam-bray-*ah*-dhoa) *adj* shady

sombrerera (soam-bray-*ray*-rah) *f* milliner

sombrero (soam-*bray*-roa) *m* hat

sombrío (soam-*bree*-oa) *adj* sombre, gloomy

someter (soa-may-*tayr*) *v* subject; **someterse** *v* submit

somnífero (soam-*nee*-fay-roa) *m* sleeping-pill

*sonar** (soa-*nahr*) *v* sound; *ring

sonido (soa-*nee*-dhoa) *m* sound

sonreír (soan-ray-*eer*) *v* smile

sonrisa (soan-*ree*-sah) *f* smile

*soñar** (soa-*ñahr*) *v* *dream

soñoliento (soa-ñoa-lʸayn-toa) *adj* sleepy

sopa (*soa*-pah) *f* soup

soplar (soa-*plahr*) *v* *blow

soportar (soa-poar-*tahr*) *v* *bear, endure, sustain; support

sóquet (*soa*-kayt) *mMe* socket

sorbo (*soar*-bhoa) *m* sip

sórdido (*soar*-dhee-dhoa) *adj* filthy

sordo (*soar*-dhoa) *adj* deaf

sorprender (soar-prayn-*dayr*) *v* surprise; *catch

sorpresa (soar-*pray*-sah) *f* surprise; astonishment

sorteo (soar-*tay*-oa) *m* draw

sosegado (soa-say-*gah*-dhoa) *adj* sedate

sospecha (soass-*pay*-chah) *f* suspicion

sospechar (soass-pay-*chahr*) *v* suspect

sospechoso (soass-pay-*choa*-soa) *adj* suspicious; **persona sospechosa** suspect

sostén (soass-*tayn*) *m* brassiere, bra

*sostener** (soass-tay-*nayr*) *v* support, *hold up

sota (*soa*-tah) *f* knave

sótano (*soa*-tah-noa) *m* basement; cellar

soto (*soa*-toa) *m* grove

soviético (soa-bhʸay-tee-koa) *adj* Soviet

starter (*stahr*-tayr) *m* choke

su (soo) *adj* his; her; their

suahili (swah-*ee*-lee) *m* Swahili

suave (*swah*-bhay) *adj* mild, mellow; gentle

subacuático (soo-bhah-*kwah*-tee-koa) *adj* underwater

subalterno (soo-bhahl-*tayr*-noa) *adj* subordinate

subasta (soo-*bhahss*-tah) *f* auction

súbdito (*soobh*-dhee-toa) *m* subject

subestimar (soo-bhayss-tee-*mahr*) *v* underestimate

subida (soo-*bhee*-dhah) *f* climb, rise, ascent

subir (soo-*bheer*) *v* *rise, ascend; *get on

súbito (*soo*-bhee-toa) *adj* sudden

sublevación (soo-bhlay-bhah-*th^yoan*) *f* rebellion

sublevarse (soo-bhlay-*bhahr*-say) *v* revolt

subordinado (soo-bhoar-dhee-*nah*-dhoa) *adj* subordinate

subrayar (soobh-rah-*^yahr*) *v* underline

subsidio (soobh-*see*-dh^yoa) *m* subsidy

substancia (soobhs-*tahn*-th^yah) *f* substance

substantivo (soobh-stahn-*tee*-bhoa) *m* noun

*substituir** (soobhs-tee-*tweer*) *v* replace

subterráneo (soobh-tay-*rrah*-nay-oa) *adj* underground

subtítulo (soobh-*tee*-too-loa) *m* subtitle

suburbano (soo-bhoor-*bhah*-noa) *adj* suburban; *m* commuter

suburbio (soo-*bhoor*-bh^yoa) *m* suburb

subvención (soobh-hhayn-*th^yoan*) *f* grant

subyugar (soobh-^yoo-*gahr*) *v* overwhelm

suceder (soo-thay-*dhayr*) *v* happen, occur; succeed

sucesión (soo-thay-*s^yoan*) *f* sequence

suceso (soo-*thay*-soa) *m* event

suciedad (soo-th^yay-*dhahdh*) *f* dirt; muck

sucio (*soo*-th^yoa) *adj* dirty; unclean, foul

sucumbir (soo-koom-*beer*) *v* succumb

sucursal (soo-koor-*sahl*) *f* branch

sudar (soo-*dhahr*) *v* perspire, sweat

sudeste (soo-*dhayss*-tay) *m* south-east

sudoeste (soo-dhoa-*ayss*-tay) *m* south-west

sudor (soo-*dhoar*) *m* perspiration, sweat

Suecia (*sway*-th^yah) *f* Sweden

sueco (*sway*-koa) *adj* Swedish; *m* Swede

suegra (*sway*-grah) *f* mother-in-law

suegro (*sway*-groa) *m* father-in-law

suela (*sway*-lah) *f* sole

sueldo (*swayl*-doa) *m* salary, pay; **aumento de** ~ rise; raise *nAm*

suelo (*sway*-loa) *m* soil, earth; floor

suelto (*swayl*-toa) *adj* loose

sueño (*sway*-ñoa) *m* sleep; dream

suero (*sway*-roa) *m* serum

suerte (*swayr*-tay) *f* luck; fortune, lot; chance; **mala** ~ bad luck

suéter (*sway*-tayr) *m* sweater

suficiente (soo-fee-*th^yayn*-tay) *adj* enough, sufficient; *ser ~ *do

sufragio (soo-*frah*-kh^yoa) *m* suffrage

sufrimiento (soo-free-*m^yayn*-toa) *m* affliction, sorrow, suffering

sufrir (soo-*freer*) *v* suffer

*sugerir** (soo-khay-*reer*) *v* suggest

sugestión (soo-khayss-*t^yoan*) *f* suggestión

suicidio (swee-*thee*-dh^yoa) *m* suicide

Suiza (*swee*-thah) *f* Switzerland

suizo (*swee*-thoa) *adj* Swiss; *m* Swiss

sujetador (soo-khay-tah-*dhoar*) *m* brassiere, bra

sujeto (soo-*khay*-toa) *m* subject; theme

sujeto a (soo-*khay*-toa ah) liable to,

subject to

suma (*soo*-mah) f amount, sum

sumar (soo-*mahr*) v add; amount to

sumario (soo-*mah*-rʸoa) m summary

suministrar (soo-mee-neess-*trahr*) v furnish, supply

suministro (soo-mee-*neess*-troa) m supply

a lo sumo (*soo*-moa) at most

superar (soo-pay-*rahr*) v exceed, *outdo

superficial (soo-payr-fee-*th*ʸ*ahl*) adj superficial

superficie (soo-payr-*fee*-thʸay) f surface; area

superfluo (soo-*payr*-flwoa) adj superfluous, redundant

superior (soo-pay-*r*ʸ*oar*) adj superior, upper; top

superlativo (soo-payr-lah-*tee*-bhoa) adj superlative; m superlative

supermercado (soo-payr-mayr-*kah*-dhoa) m supermarket

superstición (soo-payrs-tee-*th*ʸ*oan*) f superstition

supervisar (soo-payr-bhee-*sahr*) v supervise

supervisión (soo-payr-bhee-*s*ʸ*oan*) f supervision

supervisor (soo-payr-bhee-*soar*) m supervisor

supervivencia (soo-payr-bhee-*bhayn*-thʸah) f survival

suplemento (soo-play-*mayn*-toa) m supplement

suplicar (soo-plee-*kahr*) v beg

***suponer** (soo-poa-*nayr*) v assume, suppose

supositorio (soo-poa-see-*toa*-rʸoa) m suppository

supremo (soo-*pray*-moa) adj supreme

suprimir (soo-pree-*meer*) v discontinue

por supuesto (poar soo-*pwayss*-toa)

naturally, of course

sur (soor) m south; **polo** ~ South Pole

surco (*soor*-koa) m groove

surgir (soor-*kheer*) v *arise

surtido (soor-*tee*-dhoa) m assortment

suscribir (sooss-kree-*bheer*) v sign

suscripción (sooss-kreep-*th*ʸ*oan*) f subscription

suscrito (sooss-*kree*-toa) m undersigned

suspender (sooss-payn-*dayr*) v suspend; *ser suspendido** fail

suspensión (sooss-payn-*s*ʸ*oan*) f suspension

suspicacia (sooss-pee-*kah*-thʸah) f suspicion

suspicaz (sooss-pee-*kahth*) adj suspicious

sustancia (sooss-*tahn*-thʸah) f substance

sustancial (sooss-tahn-*th*ʸ*ahl*) adj substantial

sustento (sooss-*tayn*-toa) m livelihood

***sustituir** (sooss-tee-*tweer*) v substitute

sustituto (sooss-tee-*too*-toa) m deputy, substitute

susto (*sooss*-toa) m scare

susurrar (soo-soo-*rrahr*) v whisper

susurro (soo-*soo*-rroa) m whisper

sutil (soo-*teel*) adj subtle

sutura (soo-*too*-rah) f stitch; *hacer una** ~ sew up

suyo (*soo*-ʸoa) pron his

T

tabaco (tah-*bhah*-koa) m tobacco; ~ **de pipa** pipe tobacco

taberna (tah-*bhayr*-nah) f public house, pub; tavern; **moza de** ~

barmaid

tabique (tah-*bhee*-kay) *m* partition

tabla (*tah*-bhlah) *f* board; chart, table; ~ **de conversión** conversion chart; ~ **para surf** surf-board

tablero (tah-*bhlay*-roa) *m* board; ~ **de ajedrez** checkerboard *nAm*; ~ **de damas** draught-board; ~ **de instrumentos** dashboard

tablón (tah-*bhloan*) *m* plank

tabú (tah-*bhoo*) *m* taboo

tacón (tah-*koan*) *m* heel

táctica (*tahk*-tee-kah) *f* tactics *pl*

tacto (*tahk*-toa) *m* touch

tailandés (tigh-lahn-*dayss*) *adj* Thai; *m* Thai

Tailandia (tigh-*lahn*-dᵞah) *f* Thailand

tajada (tah-*khah*-dhah) *f* slice

tajar (tah-*khahr*) *v* chop

tal (tahl) *adj* such; **con ~ que** provided that; ~ **como** such as

taladrar (tah-lah-*dhrahr*) drill, bore

taladro (tah-*lah*-dhroa) *m* drill

talco (*tahl*-koa) *m* talc powder

talento (tah-*layn*-toa) *m* gift, talent

talentoso (tah-layn-*toa*-soa) *adj* gifted

talismán (tah-leez-*mahn*) *m* lucky charm

talón (tah-*loan*) *m* heel; counterfoil, stub

talonario (tah-loa-*nah*-rᵞoa) *m* chequebook; check-book *nAm*

talla (*tah*-lᵞah) *f* wood-carving, carving

tallar (tah-*lᵞahr*) *v* carve

taller (tah-*lᵞayr*) *m* workshop

tallo (*tah*-lᵞoa) *m* stem

tamaño (tah-*mah*-ño a) *m* size; ~ **extraordinario** outsize

también (tahm-*bᵞayn*) *adv* too, also, as well; **así ~** likewise

tambor (tahm-*boar*) *m* drum; ~ **del freno** brake drum

tamiz (tah-*meeth*) *m* sieve

tamizar (tah-mee-*thahr*) *v* sift, sieve

tampoco (tahm-*poa*-koa) *adv* not ... either

tan (tahn) *adv* so, such

tangible (tahng-*khee*-bhlay) *adj* tangible

tanque (*tahng*-kay) *m* tank

tanteo (tahn-*tay*-oa) *m* score

tanto (*tahn*-toa) *adv* as much; as; **por lo ~** therefore; **por ~** so; **tanto ... como** both ... and

tapa (*tah*-pah) *f* lid, top, cover; appetizer

tapiz (tah-*peeth*) *m* tapestry

tapizar (tah-pee-*thahr*) *v* upholster

tapón (tah-*poan*) *m* stopper, cork; tampon

taquigrafía (tah-kee-grah-*fee*-ah) *f* shorthand

taquígrafo (tah-*kee*-grah-foa) *m* stenographer

taquilla (tah-kee-*lᵞah*) *f* box-office

tararear (tah-rah-ray-*ahr*) *v* hum

tardanza (tahr-*dhahn*-thah) *f* delay

tarde (*tahr*-dhay) *f* afternoon; evening

tardío (tahr-*dhee*-oa) *adj* late

tarea (tah-*ray*-ah) *f* duty, task; job

tarifa (tah-*ree*-fah) *f* rate; ~ **nocturna** night rate

tarjeta (tahr-*khay*-tah) *f* card; ~ **de crédito** credit card; charge plate *Am*; ~ **de temporada** season-ticket; ~ **de visita** visiting-card; ~ **postal** postcard, card; ~ **postal ilustrada** picture postcard; ~ **verde** green card

tarta (*tahr*-tah) *f* cake

taxi (*tahk*-see) *m* cab, taxi

taxímetro (tahk-*see*-may-troa) *m* taximeter

taxista (tahk-*seess*-tah) *m* cab-driver, taxi-driver

taza (*tah*-thah) *f* cup; mug; ~ **de té** teacup

tazón (tah-*thoan*) *m* bowl, basin

te (tay) *pron* yourself

té (tay) *m* tea

teatro (tay-*ah*-troa) *m* drama; theatre; ~ **de la ópera** opera house; ~ **de variedades** music-hall, variety theatre; ~ **guiñol** puppet-show

tebeo (tay-*bhay*-oa) *m* comics *pl*

técnica (*tayk*-nee-kah) *f* technique

técnico (*tayk*-nee-koa) *adj* technical; *m* technician

tecnología (tayk-noa-loa-*khee*-ah) *f* technology

techo (*tay*-choa) *m* roof; ~ **de paja** thatched roof

teja (*tay*-khah) *f* tile

tejedor (tay-khay-*dhoar*) *m* weaver

tejer (tay-*khayr*) *v* *weave

tejido (tay-*khee*-dhoa) *m* fabric, tissue, material

tela (*tay*-lah) *f* cloth; ~ **para toallas** towelling

telaraña (tay-lah-*rah*-ñah) *f* spider's web

telefonear (tay-lay-foa-nay-*ahr*) *v* phone; call up *Am*

telefonista (tay-lay-foa-*neess*-tah) *f* telephonist, telephone operator

teléfono (tay-*lay*-foa-noa) *m* phone, telephone; **llamar por** ~ ring up

telegrafiar (tay-lay-grah-*fYahr*) *v* telegraph

telegrama (tay-lay-*grah*-mah) *m* telegram

telémetro (tay-*lay*-may-troa) *m* range-finder

teleobjetivo (tay-lay-oabh-khay-*tee*-bhoa) *m* telephoto lens

telepatía (tay-lay-pah-*tee*-ah) *f* telepathy

telesilla (tay-lay-*see*-lYah) *m* ski-lift

televisión (tay-lay-bhee-*sYoan*) *f* television

televisor (tay-lay-bhee-*soar*) *m* television set

télex (*tay*-layks) *m* telex

telón (tay-*loan*) *m* curtain

tema (*tay*-mah) *m* theme

temblar (taym-*bhlahr*) *v* tremble, shiver

temer (tay-*mayr*) *v* fear, dread

temor (tay-*moar*) *m* fear, dread

temperamento (taym-pay-rah-*mayn*-toa) *m* temperament

temperatura (taym-pay-rah-*too*-rah) *f* temperature; ~ **ambiente** room temperature

tempestad (taym-payss-*tahdh*) *f* tempest

tempestuoso (taym-payss-*twoa*-soa) *adj* stormy

templo (*taym*-ploa) *m* temple

temporada (taym-poa-*rah*-dhah) *f* season; **apogeo de la** ~ high season; ~ **baja** low season

temporal (taym-poa-*rahl*) *adj* temporary

temprano (taym-*prah*-noa) *adj* early

tenazas (tay-*nah*-thahss) *f* tongs *pl*, pincers *pl*

tendencia (tayn-*dayn*-thYah) *f* tendency

tender a (tayn-*dayr*) tend; *tenderse* *v* *lie down

tendero (tayn-*day*-roa) *m* shopkeeper; tradesman

tendón (tayn-*doan*) *m* sinew, tendon

tenedor (tay-nay-*dhoar*) *m* fork

tener (tay-*nayr*) *v* *have; *keep, *hold; ~ **que** *must; *ought to, *should; *shall; *be obliged to; **tenga usted** here you are

teniente (tay-nYayn-tay) *m* lieutenant

tenis (*tay*-neess) *m* tennis; ~ **de mesa** ping-pong, table tennis

tensión (tayn-*sYoan*) *f* strain, pressure, tension; ~ **arterial** blood pressure

tenso (*tayn*-soa) *adj* tense

tentación (tayn-tah-*th*ʸoan) *f* temptation

*__tentar__ (tayn-*tahr*) *v* tempt

tentativa (tayn-tah-*tee*-bhah) *f* attempt, try

tentempié (tayn-taym-*p*ʸay) *m* snack

*__teñir__ (tay-*ñeer*) *v* dye

teología (tay-oa-loa-*khee*-ah) *f* theology

teoría (tay-oa-*ree*-ah) *f* theory

teórico (tay-*oa*-ree-koa) *adj* theoretical

terapia (tay-*rah*-p*ʸ*ah) *f* therapy

tercero (tayr-*thay*-roa) *num* third

terciopelo (tayr-th*ʸ*oa-*pay*-loa) *m* velvet

terilene (tay-ree-*lay*-nay) *m* terylene

terminación (tayr mee-nah-*th*ʸoan) *f* finish

terminar (tayr-mee-*nahr*) *v* end, finish; accomplish; **terminarse** *v* expire, end

término (*tayr*-mee-noa) *m* term; issue

termo (*tayr*-moa) *m* vacuum flask, thermos flask

termómetro (tayr-*moa*-may-troa) *m* thermometer

termostato (tayr-moass-*tah* toa) *m* thermostat

ternero (tayr-*nay*-roa) *m* calf

ternura (tayr-*noo*-rah) *f* tenderness

terraplén (tay-rrah-*playn*) *m* embankment

terraza (tay-*rrah*-thah) *f* terrace

terremoto (tay-rray-*moa*-toa) *m* earthquake

terreno (tay-*rray*-noa) *m* terrain; field, grounds

terrible (tay-*rree*-bhlay) *adj* frightful; awful, horrible, terrible, dreadful

territorio (tay-rree-*toa*-r*ʸ*oa) *m* territory

terrón (tay-*rroan*) *m* lump

terror (tay-*rroar*) *m* terror; terrorism

terrorismo (tay-rroa-*reez*-moa) *m* terrorism

terrorista (tay-rroa-*reess*-tah) *m* terrorist

tesis (*tay*-seess) *f* thesis

Tesorería (tay-soa-ray-*ree*-ah) *f* treasury

tesorero (tay-soa-*ray*-roa) *m* treasurer

tesoro (tay-*soa*-roa) *m* treasure

testamento (tayss-tah-*mayn*-toa) *m* will

testarudo (tayss-tah-*roo*-dhoa) *adj* pigheaded, stubborn

testigo (tayss-*tee*-goa) *m* witness; ~ **de vista** eye-witness

testimoniar (tayss-tee-moa-n*ʸ*ahr) *v* testify

testimonio (tayss-tee-*moa*-n*ʸ*oa) *m* testimony

tetera (tay-*tay*-rah) *f* teapot

textil (tayks-*teel*) *m* textile

texto (*tayks*-toa) *m* text

textura (tayks-*too*-rah) *f* texture

tez (tayth) *f* complexion

ti (tee) *pron* you

tía (*tee*-ah) *f* aunt

tibio (*tee*-bh*ʸ*oa) *adj* tepid, lukewarm

tiburón (tee-bhoo-*roan*) *m* shark

tiempo (t*ʸ*aym-poa) *m* time; weather; **a** ~ in time; ~ **libre** spare time

tienda (t*ʸ*ayn-dah) *f* shop; tent

tierno (t*ʸ*ayr-noa) *adj* gentle, tender

tierra (t*ʸ*ay-rrah) *f* earth; ground, soil; land; **en** ~ ashore; ~ **baja** lowlands *pl*; ~ **firme** mainland

tieso (t*ʸ*ay-soa) *adj* stiff

tifus (*tee*-fooss) *m* typhoid

tigre (*tee*-gray) *m* tiger

tijeras (tee-*khay*-rahss) *fpl* scissors *pl*; ~ **para las uñas** nail-scissors *pl*

tilo (*tee*-loa) *m* limetree, lime

timbre (*teem*-bray) *m* tone; bell; doorbell; *mMe* postage stamp

timidez (tee-mee-*dhayth*) *f* timidity, shyness

tímido (*tee*-mee-dhoa) *adj* timid, embarrassed, shy

timón (tee-*moan*) *m* helm, rudder

timonel (tee-moa-*nayl*) *m* steersman

timonero (tee-moa-*nay*-roa) *m* helmsman

tímpano (*teem*-pah-noa) *m* ear-drum

tinta (*teen*-tah) *f* ink

tintorería (teen-toa-ray-*ree*-ah) *f* dry-cleaner's

tintura (teen-*too*-rah) *f* dye

tío (*tee*-oa) *m* uncle

típico (*tee*-pee-koa) *adj* typical, characteristic

tipo (*tee*-poa) *m* type; fellow, guy

tirada (tee-*rah*-dhah) *f* issue

tirano (tee-*rah*-noa) *m* tyrant

tirantes (tee-*rahn*-tayss) *mpl* braces *pl*; suspenders *plAm*

tirar (tee-*rahr*) *v* pull; *throw; *shoot

tiritar (tee-ree-*tahr*) *v* shiver

tiro (*tee*-roa) *m* shot

tirón (tee-*roan*) *m* wrench

titular (tee-too-*lahr*) *m* headline

título (*tee*-too-loa) *m* heading, title; degree

toalla (toa-*ah*-lⱽah) *f* towel; ~ **de baño** bath towel

tobera (toa-*bhay*-rah) *f* nozzle

tobillo (toa-*bhee*-lⱽoa) *m* ankle

tobogán (toa-bhoa-*gahn*) *m* slide

tocadiscos (toa-kah-*deess*-koass) *m* record-player

tocador (toa-kah-*dhoar*) *m* dressing-table; powder-room; **artículos de** ~ toiletry

tocante a (toa-*kahn*-tay ah) regarding

tocar (toa-*kahr*) *v* touch, *hit; play; **no** ~ *keep off

tocino (toa-*thee*-noa) *m* bacon

todavía (toa-dhah-*bhee*-ah) *adv* still, however

todo (*toa*-dhoa) *adj* all; entire; *pron* everything; **sobre** ~ most of all, essentially, especially; **todos** *pron* everybody

toldo (*toal*-doa) *m* awning

tolerable (toa-lay-*rah*-bhlay) *adj* tolerable

tomar (toa-*mahr*) *v* *catch; *take; ~ **el pelo** tease

tomate (toa-*mah*-tay) *m* tomato

tomillo (toa-*mee*-lⱽoa) *m* thyme

tomo (*toa*-moa) *m* volume

tonada (toa-*nah*-dhah) *f* tune

tonel (toa-*nayl*) *m* barrel, cask

tonelada (toa-nay-*lah*-dhah) *f* ton

tónico (*toa*-nee-koa) *m* tonic; ~ **para el cabello** hair tonic

tono (*toa*-noa) *m* tone; note; shade

tontería (toan-tay-*ree*-ah) *f* nonsense, rubbish; *decir tonterías talk rubbish

tonto (*toan*-toa) *adj* foolish; *m* fool

topetar (toa-pay-*tahr*) *v* bump

topetón (toa-pay-*toan*) *m* bump

toque (*toa*-kay) *m* touch

torcedura (toar-thay-*dhoo*-rah) *f* sprain

*torcer (toar-*thayr*) *v* twist; *torcerse *v* sprain

tordo (*toar*-dhoa) *m* thrush

tormenta (toar-*mayn*-tah) *f* storm

tormento (toar-*mayn*-toa) *m* torment

tormentoso (toar-mayn-*toa*-soa) *adj* thundery

tornar (toar-*nahr*) *v* return

torneo (toar-*nay*-oa) *m* tournament

tornillo (toar-*nee*-lⱽoa) *m* screw

en torno (ayn *toar*-noa) about, around

en torno de (ayn *toar*-noa day) round, around

toro (*toa*-roa) *m* bull

toronja (toa-*roan*-khah) *fMe* grapefruit

torpe (*toar*-pay) *adj* clumsy, awkward

torre (*toa*-rray) *f* tower

torsión (toar-sⱽoan*) *f* twist

tortilla (toar-*tee*-lⱽah) *f* omelette

tortuga (toar-*too*-gah) *f* turtle

tortuoso (toar-*twoa*-soa) *adj* winding

tortura (toar-*too*-rah) *f* torture

torturar (toar-too *rahr*) *v* torture

tos (toass) *f* cough

toser (toa-*sayr*) *v* cough

tostado (toass-*tah*-dhoa) *adj* tanned

total (toa-*tahl*) *adj* total; overall, utter; *m* total; whole; **en** ~ altogether

totalitario (toa-tah-lee-*tah*-rʸoa) *adj* totalitarian

totalizador (toa-tah-lee-thah-*dhoar*) *m* totalizator

totalmente (toa-tahl-*mayn*-tay) *adv* completely, altogether, wholly

tóxico (*toak*-see-koa) *adj* toxic

trabajar (trah-bhah-*khahr*) *v* work

trabajo (trah-*bhah*-khoa) *m* work, labour; difficulty; ~ **manual** handicraft

tractor (trahk-*toar*) *m* tractor

tradición (trah-dhee-*thʸoan*) *f* tradition

tradicional (trah-dhee-thʸoa-*nahl*) *adj* traditional

traducción (trah-dhook-*thʸoan*) *f* translation

*****traducir** (trah-dhoo-*theer*) *v* translate

traductor (trah-dhook-*toar*) *m* translator

*****traer** (trah-*ayr*) *v* *****bring

tragar (trah-*gahr*) *v* swallow

tragedia (trah-*khay*-dhʸah) *f* drama, tragedy

trágico (*trah*-khee-koa) *adj* tragic

traición (trigh-*thʸoan*) *f* treason

traicionar (trigh-thʸoa-*nahr*) *v* betray

traidor (trigh-*dhoar*) *m* traitor

traílla (trah-ee-*lʸ*ah) *f* lead

traje (*trah*-khay) *m* suit; gown; robe; ~ **de baño** bathing-suit; ~ **de etiqueta** evening dress; ~ **del país** national dress; ~ **de malla** tights *pl*; ~ **pantalón** pant-suit

trama (*trah*-mah) *f* plot

trampa (*trahm*-pah) *f* trap; hatch

tranquilidad (trahng-kee-lee-*dhahdh*) *f* tranquillity

tranquilizar (trahng-kee-lee-*thahr*) *v* reassure

tranquilo (trahng-*kee*-loa) *adj* tranquil, quiet, calm; peaceful

transacción (trahn-sahk-*thʸoan*) *f* transaction, deal; **volumen de transacciones** turnover

transatlántico (trahn-saht-*lahn*-tee-koa) *adj* transatlantic

transbordador (trahnz-bhoar-dhah-*dhoar*) *m* ferry-boat; ~ **de trenes** train ferry

transcurrir (trahns-koo-*rrer*) *v* pass

transeúnte (trahn-say-*oon*-tay) *m* passer-by

*****transferir** (trahns-fay-*reer*) *v* transfer

transformador (trahns-foar-mah-*dhoar*) *m* transformer

transformar (trahns-foar-*mahr*) *v* transform

transgredir (trahnz-gray-*deer*) *v* offend

transición (trahn-see-*thʸoan*) *f* transition

tránsito (*trahn*-see-toa) *m* traffic

transmisión (trahnz-mee-*sʸoan*) *f* transmission, broadcast

transmitir (trahnz-mee-*teer*) *v* transmit

transparente (trahns pah *rayn* tay) *adj* transparent

transpiración (trahns-pee-rah-*thʸoan*) *f* perspiration

transpirar (trahns-pee-*rahr*) *v* perspire

transportar (trahns-poar-*tahr*) *v* transport; ship

transporte (trahns-*poar*-tay) *m* transportation, transport

tranvía (trahm-*bee*-ah) *m* tram; street-car *nAm*

trapo (*trah*-poa) *m* rag; ~ **de cocina** tea-cloth

tras (trahss) *prep* behind
*hacer trasbordo (ah-*thayr* trahz-*bhoar*-dhoa) *v* change
trasero (trah-*say*-roa) *m* bottom
trasladar (trahz-lah-*dhahr*) *v* move
traslúcido (trahz-*loo*-thee-dhoa) *adj* sheer
trastornado (trahss-toar-*nah*-dhoa) *adj* upset
trastornar (trahss-toar-*nahr*) *v* upset
trastos (*trahss*-toass) *mpl* litter
tratado (trah-*tah*-dhoa) *m* essay; treaty
tratamiento (trah-tah-*m*ᵛ*ayn*-toa) *m* treatment; ~ **de belleza** beauty treatment
tratar (trah-*tahr*) *v* handle, treat; ~ **con** *deal with
trato (*trah*-toa) *m* intercourse
a través de (ah trah-*bhayss day*) across, through
travesía (trah-bhay-*see*-ah) *f* crossing, passage
travieso (trah-*bh*ᵛ*ay*-soa) *adj* naughty, bad; mischievous
trazar (trah-*thahr*) *v* sketch
trébol (*tray*-bhoal) *m* clover, shamrock
trece (*tray*-thay) *num* thirteen
treceno (tray-*thay*-noa) *num* thirteenth
trecho (*tray*-choa) *m* stretch
treinta (*trayn*-tah) *num* thirty
treintavo (trayn-*tah*-bhoa) *num* thirtieth
tremendo (tray-*mayn*-doa) *adj* awful, terrible; tremendous, terrific
trementina (tray-mayn-*tee*-nah) *f* turpentine
tren (trayn) *m* train; ~ **de cercanías** stopping train; ~ **de mercancías** goods train; ~ **de pasajeros** passenger train; ~ **directo** through train; ~ **expreso** express train; ~ **nocturno** night train; ~ **ómnibus** local train

trenza (*trayn*-thah) *f* twine
trepar (tray-*pahr*) *v* climb
tres (trayss) *num* three
triangular (trᵛahng-goo-*lahr*) *adj* triangular
triángulo (*trᵛ*ahng-goo-loa) *m* triangle
tribu (*tree*-bhoo) *m* tribe
tribuna (tree-*bhoo*-nah) *f* stand
tribunal (tree-bhoo-*nahl*) *m* court, law court
trigal (tree-*gahl*) *m* cornfield
trigo (*tree*-goa) *m* grain, corn; wheat
trimestral (tree-mayss-*trahl*) *adj* quarterly
trimestre (tree-*mayss*-tray) *m* quarter
trinchar (treen-*chahr*) *v* carve
trineo (tree-*nay*-oa) *m* sleigh, sledge
triste (*treess*-tay) *adj* sad
tristeza (treess-*tay*-thah) *f* sorrow, sadness
triturar (tree-too-*rahr*) *v* *grind
triunfante (trᵛoon-*fahn*-tay) *adj* triumphant
triunfar (trᵛoon-*fahr*) *v* triumph
triunfo (trᵛoon-foa) *m* triumph
*trocar (troa-*kahr*) *v* swap
trolebús (troa-lay-*bhooss*) *m* trolleybus
trompeta (troam-*pay*-tah) *f* trumpet
tronada (troa-*nah*-dhah) *f* thunderstorm
*tronar (troa-*nahr*) *v* thunder
tronco (*troang*-koa) *m* trunk
trono (*troanoa*) *m* throne
tropas (*troa*-pahss) *fpl* troops *pl*
*tropezarse (troa-pay-*thahr*-say) *v* stumble
tropical (troa-pee-*kahl*) *adj* tropical
trópicos (*troa*-pee-koass) *mpl* tropics *pl*
trozo (*troa*-thoa) *m* chunk, morsel, bit; fragment, passage
truco (*troo*-koa) *m* trick
trucha (*troo*-chah) *f* trout

trueno (*trway*-noa) *m* thunder
tu (too) *adj* your
tú (too) *pron* you
tuberculosis (too-bhayr-koo-*loa*-seess)
  f tuberculosis
tubo (*too*-bhoa) *m* tube
tuerca (*twayr*-kah) *f* nut
tulipán (too-lee-*pahn*) *m* tulip
tumba (*toom*-bah) *f* tomb
tumor (*too-moar*) *m* growth, tumour
tunecino (too-nay-*thee*-noa) *adj* Tunisian; *m* Tunisian
túnel (*too*-nayl) *m* tunnel
Túnez (*too*-nayth) *m* Tunisia
túnica (*too*-nee-kah) *f* tunic
turbar (toor-*bhahr*) *v* embarrass
turbera (toor-*bhay*-rah) *f* moor
turbina (toor-*bhee*-nah) *f* turbine
turco (*toor*-koa) *adj* Turkish; *m* Turk
turismo (too-*reez*-moa) *m* tourism
turista (too-*reess*-tah) *m* tourist; **oficina para turistas** tourist office
turno (*toor*-noa) *m* turn; shift
Turquía (toor-*kee*-ah) *f* Turkey
turrón (too-*rroan*) *m* nougat
tutela (too-*tay*-lah) *f* custody
tutor (too-*toar*) *m* tutor; guardian
tuyos (*too*-Yoass) *adj* your

U

ubicación (oo-bhee-kah-*th*Yoan) *f* situation, location
ujier (oo kh*Y*ayr) *m* bailiff
úlcera (*ool*-thay-rah) *f* ulcer, sore; ~ **gástrica** gastric ulcer
ulterior (ool-tay-r*Y*oar) *adj* further
últimamente (*ool*-tee-mah-mayn-tay) *adv* lately
último (*ool*-tee-moa) *adj* ultimate; last
ultraje (ool-*trah*-khay) *m* outrage
ultramar (ool-trah-*mahr*) *adv* overseas

ultravioleta (ool-trah-bh*Y*oa-*lay*-tah)
  adj ultraviolet
umbral (oom-*brahl*) *m* threshold
un (oon) *art* a *art*
unánime (oo-*nah*-nee-may) *adj* likeminded, unanimous
ungüento (oong-*gwayn*-toa) *m* ointment, salve
únicamente (*oo*-nee-kah-mayn-tay)
  adv exclusively
único (*oo*-nee-koa) *adj* unique, sole
unidad (oo-nee-*dhahdh*) *f* unity; unit
unido (oo-*nee*-dhoa) *adj* joint
uniforme (oo-nee-*foar*-may) *adj* uniform; *m* uniform
unilateral (oo-nee-lah-tay-*rahl*) *adj* one-sided
unión (oo-n*Y*oan) *f* union
Unión Soviética (oo-n*Y*oan soa-bh*Y*aytee-kah) Soviet Union
unir (oo-*neer*) *v* unite; combine; **unirse a** join
universal (oo-nee-bhayr-*sahl*) *adj* universal
universidad (oo-nee-bhayr-see-*dhahdh*) *f* university
universo (oo-nee-*bhayr*-soa) *m* universe
uno (*oo*-noa) *num* one; *pron* one; **unos** *adj* some; *pron* some
uña (*oo*-nah) *f* nail
urbano (oor-*bhah*-noa) *adj* urban
urgencia (oor-*khayn*-th*Y*ah) *f* urgency; emergency; **botiquín de** ~ first-aid kit
urgente (oor-*khayn*-tay) *adj* pressing, urgent
urraca (oo-*rrah*-kah) *f* magpie
Uruguay (oo-roo-*gwigh*) *m* Uruguay
uruguayo (oo-roo-*gwah*-Yoa) *adj* Uruguayan; *m* Uruguayan
usar (oo-*sahr*) *v* use
uso (*oo*-soa) *m* use, usage
usted (ooss-*taydh*) *pron* you; **a** ~

you; **de** ~ your

usual (oo-*swahl*) *adj* common, customary, usual

usuario (oo-swah-r‿oa) *m* user

utensilio (oo-tayn-*see*-l‿oa) *m* utensil

útil (*oo*-teel) *adj* useful

utilidad (oo-tee-lee-*dhahdh*) *f* utility, use

utilizable (oo-tee-lee-*thah*-bhlay) *adj* usable

utilizar (oo-tee-lee-*thahr*) *v* utilize

uvas (*oo*-bhahss) *fpl* grapes *pl*

V

vaca (*bah*-kah) *f* cow

vacaciones (bah-kah-*th‿oa*-nayss) *fpl* holiday, vacation; **de** ~ on holiday

vacante (bah-*kahn*-tay) *adj* vacant; *f* vacancy

vaciar (bah-*th‿ahr*) *v* empty; vacate

vacilante (bah-thee-lahn-tay) *adj* unsteady, shaky

vacilar (bah-thee-*lahr*) *v* hesitate; falter

vacío (bah-*thee*-oa) *adj* empty; *m* vacuum

vacunación (bah-koo-nah-*th‿oan*) *f* vaccination

vacunar (bah-koo-*nahr*) *v* vaccinate, inoculate

vadear (bah-dhay-*ahr*) *v* wade

vado (*bah*-dhoa) *m* ford

vagabundear (bah-gah-bhoon-day-*ahr*) *v* tramp, roam

vagabundo (bah-gah-*bhoon*-doa) *m* tramp

vagancia (bah-*gahn*-th‿ah) *f* vagrancy

vagar (bah-*gahr*) *v* wander

vago (*bah*-goa) *adj* vague; faint, dim; idle

vagón (bah-*goan*) *m* waggon, carriage; coach

vainilla (bigh-*nee*-l‿ah) *f* vanilla

vale (*bah*-lay) *m* banknote

***valer** (bah-*layr*) *v* *be worth; ~ **la pena** *be worth-while

valiente (bah-*l‿ayn*-tay) *adj* courageous, plucky, brave

valija (bah-*lee*-khah) *f* case

valioso (bah-*l‿oa*-soa) *adj* valuable

valor (bah-*loar*) *m* worth, value; courage; **bolsa de valores** stock exchange; **sin** ~ worthless

vals (bahls) *m* waltz

valuar (bah-*lwahr*) *v* value; appreciate

válvula (*bahl*-bhoo-lah) *f* valve

valle (*bah*-l‿ay) *m* valley

vanidoso (bah-nee-*dhoa*-soa) *adj* vain

vano (*bah*-noa) *adj* idle, vain; **en** ~ in vain

vapor (bah-*poar*) *m* steam, vapour; steamer; ~ **de línea** liner

vaporizador (bah-poa-ree-thah-*dhoar*) *m* atomizer

vaqueros (bah-*kay*-roass) *mpl* jeans *pl*

variable (bah-r‿*ah*-bhlay) *adj* variable

variación (bah-r‿ah-*th‿oan*) *f* variation

variado (bah-r‿*ah*-dhoa) *adj* varied

variar (bah-r‿*ahr*) *v* vary

varice (*bah*-ree-thay) *f* varicose vein

varicela (bah-ree-*thay*-lah) *f* chickenpox

variedad (bah-r‿ay-*dhahdh*) *f* variety; **espectáculo de variedades** variety show

varios (*bah*-r‿oass) *adj* various, several

vaselina (bah-say-*lee*-nah) *f* vaseline

vasija (bah-*see*-khah) *f* vessel

vaso (*bah*-soa) *m* glass; mug, tumbler; vase; ~ **sanguíneo** bloodvessel

vasto (*bahss*-toa) *adj* wide, vast; extensive

vatio (*bah*-t‿oa) *m* watt

vecindad (bay-theen-*dahdh*) *f* neighbourhood, vicinity

vecindario (bay-theen-dah-r^yoa) *m* community

vecino (bay-*thee*-noa) *adj* neighbouring; *m* neighbour

vegetación (bay-khay-tah-th^yoan) *f* vegetation

vegetariano (bay-khay-tah-r^yah-noa) *m* vegetarian

vehículo (bay-*ee*-koo-loa) *m* vehicle

veinte (*bayn*-tay) *num* twenty

vejez (bay-*khayth*) *f* old age

vejiga (bay-*khee*-gah) *f* bladder

vela (*bay*-lah) *f* sail; **deporte de ~** yachting

velo (*bay*-loa) *m* veil

velocidad (bay-loa-thee-*dhahdh*) *f* speed; rate; gear; **límite de ~** speed limit; **~ de cruce** cruising speed

velocímetro (bay-loa-*thee*-may-troa) *m* speedometer

veloz (bay-*loath*) *adj* swift

vena (*bay*-nah) *f* vein

vencedor (bayn-thay-*dhoar*) *m* winner

vencer (bayn-*thayr*) *v* *overcome, conquer; *win

vencimiento (bayn-thee-m^yayn-toa) *m* expiry

vendaje (bayn-*dah*-khay) *m* bandage

vendar (bayn-*dahr*) *v* dress

vendedor (bayn-day-*dhoar*) *m* salesman

vendedora (bayn-day-*dhoa*-rah) *f* salesgirl

vender (bayn-*dayr*) *v* *sell; **~ al detalle** retail

vendible (bayn-*dee*-bhlay) *adj* saleable

vendimia (bayn-*dee*-m^yah) *f* vintage

veneno (bay-*nay*-noa) *m* poison

venenoso (bay-nay-*noa*-soa) *adj* poisonous

venerable (bay-nay-*rah*-bhlay) *adj* venerable

venerar (bay-nay-*rahr*) *v* worship

venezolano (bay-nay-thoa-*lah*-noa) *adj* Venezuelan; *m* Venezuelan

Venezuela (bay-nay-*thway*-lah) *f* Venezuela

venganza (bayng-*gahn*-thah) *f* revenge

venidero (bay-nee-*dhay*-roa) *adj* oncoming

venir (bay-*neer*) *v* *come

venta (*bayn*-tah) *f* sale; **de ~** for sale; **~ al por mayor** wholesale

ventaja (bayn-*tah*-khah) *f* benefit, advantage; profit; lead

ventajoso (bayn-tah-*khoa*-soa) *adj* advantageous

ventana (bayn-*tah*-nah) *f* window; **~ de la nariz** nostril

ventarrón (bayn-tah-*rroan*) *m* gale

ventilación (bayn-tee-lah-th^yoan) *f* ventilation

ventilador (bayn-tee-lah-*dhoar*) *m* fan, ventilator

ventilar (bayn-tee-*lahr*) *v* ventilate

ventisca (bhayn-*teess*-kah) *f* blizzard

ventoso (bayn-*toa*-soa) *adj* windy

ver (bayr) *v* *see, notice

veranda (bay-*rahn*-dah) *f* veranda

verano (bay-*rah*-noa) *m* summer; **pleno ~** midsummer

verbal (bayr-*bhahl*) *adj* verbal

verbo (*bavr*-bhoa) *m* verb

verdad (bayr-*dhahdh*) *f* truth

verdaderamente (bayr-dhah-dhay-rah-*mayn*-tay) *adv* really

verdadero (bayr-dhah-*dhay*-roa) *adj* true, real, very; actual

verde (*bayr*-dhay) *adj* green

verdulero (bayr-dhoo-*lay*-roa) *m* greengrocer

veredicto (bay-ray-*dheek*-toa) *m* verdict

vergel (*bayr*-gayl) *m* orchard

vergüenza (bayr-*gwayn*-thah) *f* shame;

¡qué vergüenza! shame!

verídico (bay-*ree*-dhee-koa) *adj* truthful

verificar (bay-ree-fee-*kahr*) *v* check, verify

verosímil (bay-roa-*see*-meel) *adj* credible

versión (bayr-s^y*oan*) *f* version

verso (*bayr*-soa) *m* verse

*__verter__ (bayr-*tayr*) *v* pour; *spill

vertical (bayr-tee-*kahl*) *adj* vertical

vértigo (*bayr*-tee-goa) *m* dizziness, vertigo

vestíbulo (bayss-*tee*-bhoo-loa) *m* hall, lobby; foyer

vestido (bayss-*tee*-dhoa) *m* frock, dress; **vestidos** *mpl* clothes *pl*

*__vestir__ (bayss-*teer*) *v* dress; *vestirse* *v* dress

vestuario (bayss-*twah*-r^yoa) *m* wardrobe; dressing-room

veterinario (bay-tay-ree-*nah*-r^yoa) *m* veterinary surgeon

vez (bayth) *f* time; **alguna** ~ some time; **a veces** sometimes; **de** ~ **en cuando** occasionally, now and then; **otra** ~ again, once more; **pocas veces** seldom; **una** ~ once

vía (*bee*-ah) *f* track; ~ **del tren** railroad *nAm*; ~ **navegable** waterway

viaducto (b^yah-*dhook*-toa) *m* viaduct

viajar (b^yah-*khahr*) *v* travel

viaje (b^y*ah*-khay) *m* journey; trip, voyage

viajero (b^yah-*khay*-roa) *m* traveller

vibración (bee-bhrah-*th*^y*oan*) *f* vibration

vibrar (bee-*bhrahr*) *v* tremble, vibrate

vicario (bee-kah-r^yoa) *m* vicar

vicepresidente (bee-thay-pray-see-*dhayn*-tay) *m* vice-president

vicioso (bee-*th*^y*oa*-soa) *adj* vicious

víctima (*beek*-tee-mah) *f* casualty, victim

victoria (beek-*toa*-r^yah) *f* victory

vid (beedh) *f* vine

vida (*bee*-dhah) *f* life; lifetime; **en** ~ alive; ~ **privada** privacy

vidrio (*bee*-dhr^yoa) *m* glass; **de** ~ glass; ~ **de color** stained glass

viejo (b^y*ay*-khoa) *adj* old; ancient, aged; stale

viento (b^y*ayn*-toa) *m* wind

vientre (b^y*ayn*-tray) *m* belly

viernes (b^y*ayr*-nayss) *m* Friday

viga (*bee*-gah) *f* beam

vigente (bee-*khayn*-tay) *adj* valid

vigésimo (bee-*khay*-see-moa) *num* twentieth

vigilar (bee-khee-*lahr*) *v* watch, patrol

vigor (bee-*goar*) *m* strength; stamina

vil (beel) *adj* foul

villa (*bee*-l^yah) *f* villa

villano (bee-l^y*ah*-noa) *m* villain

vinagre (bee-*nah*-gray) *m* vinegar

vinatero (bee-nah-*tay*-roa) *m* wine-merchant

vino (*bee*-noa) *m* wine

viña (*bee*-ñah) *f* vineyard

violación (b^yoa-lah-*th*^y*oan*) *f* violation

violar (b^yoa-*lahr*) *v* assault, rape

violencia (b^yoa-*layn*-th^yah) *f* violence

violento (b^yoa-*layn*-toa) *adj* violent; fierce, severe

violeta (b^yoa-*lay*-tah) *f* violet

violín (b^yoa-*leen*) *m* violin

virgen (*beer*-khayn) *f* virgin

virtud (beer-*toodh*) *f* virtue

viruelas (bee-*rr*way-lahss) *fpl* smallpox

visado (bee-*sah*-dhoa) *m* visa

visar (bee-*sahr*) *v* endorse

visibilidad (bee-see-bhee-lee-*dhahdh*) *f* visibility

visible (bee-*see*-bhlay) *adj* visible

visión (bee-s^y*oan*) *f* vision

visita (bee-*see*-tah) *f* visit, call

visitante (bee-see-*tahn*-tay) *m* visitor

visitar (bee-see-*tahr*) *v* visit, call on

vislumbrar (beez-loom-*brahr*) v glimpse

vislumbre (beez-*loom*-bray) m glimpse

visón (bee-*soan*) m mink

visor (bee-*soar*) m view-finder

vista (*beess*-tah) f sight; view; **punto de** ~ outlook

vistoso (beess-*toa*-soa) adj striking

vital (bee-*tahl*) adj vital

vitamina (bee-tah-*mee*-nah) f vitamin

vitrina (bee-*tree*-nah) f show-case

viuda (bᵞoo-dhah) f widow

viudo (bᵞoo-dhoa) m widower

vivaz (bee-*bhahth*) adj active

vivero (bee-*bhay*-roa) m nursery

vivienda (bee-bhᵞ*ayn*-dah) f house

vivir (bee-*bheer*) v live; experience

vivo (*bee*-bhoa) adj alive, live; brisk, vivid, lively

vocabulario (boa-kah-bhoo-*lah*-rᵞoa) m vocabulary

vocación (boa-kah-*th*ᵞoan) f vocation

vocal (boa-*kahl*) f vowel; adj vocal

vocalista (boa-kah-*leess*-tah) m vocalist

volante (boa-*lahn*-tay) m steering-wheel

*****volar** (boa-*lahr*) v *fly

volatería (boa-lah-tay-*ree*-ah) f fowl

volcán (boal-*kahn*) m volcano

voltaje (boal-*tah*-khay) m voltage

voltio (*boal*-tᵞoa) m volt

volumen (boa-*loo*-mayn) m volume

voluminoso (boa-loo-mee-*noa*-soa) adj bulky; big

voluntad (boa-loon-*tahdh*) f will; **buena** ~ goodwill

voluntario (boa-loon-*tah*-rᵞoa) adj voluntary; m volunteer

*****volver** (boal-*bhayr*) v return, turn back; turn over, turn, turn round; ~ **a casa** *go home; *volverse* v turn round

vomitar (boa-mee-*tahr*) v vomit

vosotros (boa-*soa*-troass) pron you

votación (boa-tah-*th*ᵞoan) f vote

votar (boa-*tahr*) v vote

voto (*boa*-toa) m vote; vow

voz (boath) f voice; cry; **en** ~ **alta** aloud

vuelo (*bway*-loa) m flight; ~ **fletado** charter flight; ~ **nocturno** night flight

vuelta (*bwayl*-tah) f return journey, way back; tour; turning, turn; round; **ida y** ~ round trip *Am*

vuestro (*bwayss*-troa) adj your

vulgar (bool-*gahr*) adj vulgar

vulnerable (bool-nay-*rah*-bhlay) adj vulnerable

Y

y (ee) conj and

ya (ᵞah) adv already; ~ **no** no longer; ~ **que** as

*****yacer** (ᵞah-*thayr*) v *lie

yacimiento (ᵞah-thee-mᵞ*ayn*-toa) m deposit

yate (ᵞah-tay) m yacht

yegua (ᵞay-gwah) f mare

yema (ᵞay-mah) f yolk

yerno (ᵞayr-noa) m son-in-law

yeso (ᵞay-soa) m plaster

yo (ᵞoa) pron I

yodo (ᵞoa-dhoa) m iodine

yugo (ᵞoo-goa) m yoke

Yugoslavia (ᵞoo-goaz-*lah*-bhᵞah) f Yugoslavia, Jugoslavia

yugoslavo (ᵞoo-goaz-*lah*-bhoa) adj Jugoslav; m Yugoslav, Jugoslav

Z

zafiro (thah-*fee*-roa) *m* sapphire
zanahoria (thah-nah-*oa*-rʸah) *f* carrot
zanja (*thahng*-khah) *f* ditch
zapatería (thah-pah-tay-*ree*-ah) *f* shoe-shop
zapatero (thah-pah-*tay*-roa) *m* shoemaker
zapatilla (thah-pah-*tee*-lʸah) *f* slipper
zapato (thah-*pah*-toa) *m* shoe; **zapatos de gimnasia** plimsolls *pl*; sneakers *plAm*; **zapatos de tenis** tennis shoes

zatara (thah-*tah*-rah) *f* raft
zodíaco (thoa-*dhee*-ah-koa) *m* zodiac
zona (*thoa*-nah) *f* zone; area; **~ industrial** industrial area
zoología (thoa-oa-loa-*khee*-ah) *f* zoology
zorro (*thoa*-rroa) *m* fox
zueco (*thway*-koa) *m* wooden shoe
zumo (*thoo*-moa) *m* juice; squash
zumoso (thoo-*moa*-soa) *adj* juicy
zurcir (thoor-*theer*) *v* darn
zurdo (*thoor*-dhoa) *adj* left-handed
zurra (*thoo*-rrah) *f* spanking

Menu Reader

Food

a caballo steak topped with two eggs
acedera sorrel
aceite oil
aceituna olive
achicoria endive (US chicory)
(al) adobo marinated
aguacate avocado (pear)
ahumado smoked
ajiaceite garlic mayonnaise
ajiaco bogotano chicken soup with potatoes
(al) ajillo cooked in garlic and oil
ajo garlic
al, a la in the style of, with
albahaca basil
albaricoque apricot
albóndiga spiced meat- or fishball
alcachofa artichoke
alcaparra caper
aliñado seasoned
alioli garlic mayonnaise
almeja clam, cockle
almejas a la marinera cooked in hot, pimento sauce
almendra almond
  ∼ **garrapiñada** sugared almond
almíbar syrup
almuerzo lunch
alubia bean

anchoa anchovy
anguila eel
angula baby eel
anticucho beef heart grilled on a skewer with green peppers
apio celery
a punto medium (done)
arenque herring
  ∼ **en escabeche** marinated, pickled herring
arepa flapjack made of maize (corn)
arroz rice
  ∼ **blanco** boiled, steamed
  ∼ **escarlata** with tomatoes and prawns
  ∼ **a la española** with chicken liver, pork, tomatoes, fish stock
  ∼ **con leche** rice pudding
  ∼ **primavera** with spring vegetables
  ∼ **a la valenciana** with vegetables, chicken, shellfish (and sometimes eel)
asado roast
  ∼ **antiguo a la venezolana mechado** roast beef stuffed with capers
asturias a strong, fermented cheese with a sharp flavour

atún tunny (US tuna)
avellana hazelnut
azafrán saffron
azúcar sugar
bacalao cod
   ~ **a la vizcaína** with green peppers, potatoes, tomato sauce
barbo barbel (fish)
batata sweet potato, yam
becada woodcock
berberecho cockle
berenjena aubergine (US eggplant)
berraza parsnip
berro cress
berza cabbage
besugo sea bream
bien hecho well-done
biftec, bistec beef steak
bizcocho sponge cake, sponge finger (US ladyfinger)
   ~ **borracho** cake steeped in rum (or wine) and syrup
bizcotela glazed biscuit (US cookie)
blando soft
bocadillo 1) sandwich 2) sweet (Colombia)
bollito, bollo roll, bun
bonito a kind of tunny (US tuna)
boquerón 1) anchovy 2) whitebait
(en) brocheta (on a) skewer
budín blancmange, custard
buey ox
buñuelo 1) doughnut 2) fritter with ham, mussels and prawns (sometimes flavoured with brandy)
burgos a popular soft, creamy cheese named after the Spanish province of its origin
butifarra spiced sausage
caballa fish of the mackerel family
cabeza de ternera calf's head

cabra goat
cabrales blue-veined goat's-milk cheese
cabrito kid
cacahuete peanut
cachelos diced potatoes boiled with cabbage, paprika, garlic, bacon, *chorizo* sausage
calabacín vegetable marrow, courgette (US zucchini)
calabaza pumpkin
calamar squid
calamares a la romana squids fried in batter
caldereta de cabrito kid stew (often cooked in red wine)
caldillo de congrio conger-eel soup with tomatoes and potatoes
caldo consommé
   ~ **gallego** meat and vegetable broth
callos tripe (often served in pimento sauce)
   ~ **a la madrileña** in piquant sauce with *chorizo* sausage and tomatoes
camarón shrimp
canela cinnamon
cangrejo de mar crab
cangrejo de río crayfish
cantarela chanterelle mushroom
caracol snail
carbonada criolla baked pumpkin stuffed with diced beef
carne meat
   ~ **asada al horno** roast meat
   ~ **molida** minced beef
   ~ **a la parrilla** charcoal-grilled steak
   ~ **picada** minced beef
carnero mutton
carpa carp
casero home made

castaña chestnut
castañola sea perch
(a la) catalana with onions, parsley, tomatoes and herbs
caza game
(a la) cazadora with mushrooms, spring onions, herbs in wine
cazuela de cordero lamb stew with vegetables
cebolla onion
cebolleta chive
cebrero blue-veined cheese of creamy texture with a pale, yellow rind; sharp taste
cena dinner, supper
centolla spider-crab, served cold
cerdo pork
cereza cherry
ceviche fish marinated in lemon and lime juice
cigala Dublin Bay prawn
cincho a hard cheese made from sheep's milk
ciruela plum
 ~ **pasa** prune
cocido 1) cooked, boiled 2) stew of beef with ham, fowl, chick peas, potatoes and vegetables (the broth is eaten first)
cochifrito de cordero highly seasoned stew of lamb or kid
codorniz quail
col cabbage
 ~ **de Bruselas** brussels sprout
coliflor cauliflower
comida meal
compota stewed fruit
conejo rabbit
confitura jam
congrio conger eel
consomé al jerez chicken broth with sherry
copa nuria egg-yolk and egg-white, whipped and served with

jam
corazón de alcachofa artichoke heart
corazonada heart stewed in sauce
cordero lamb
 ~ **recental** spring lamb
cortadillo small pancake with lemon
corzo deer
costilla chop
crema 1) cream or mousse
 ~ **batida** whipped cream
 ~ **española** dessert of milk, eggs, fruit jelly
 ~ **nieve** frothy egg-yolk, sugar, rum (or wine)
crema 2) soup
criadillas (de toro) glands (of bull)
(a la) criolla with green peppers, spices and tomatoes
croqueta croquette, fish or meat dumpling
crudo raw
cubierto cover charge
cuenta bill (US check)
curanto dish consisting of seafood, vegetables and suck(l)ing pig, all cooked in an earthen well, lined with charcoal
chabacano apricot
chalote shallot
champiñón mushroom
chancho adobado pork braised with sweet potatoes, orange and lemon juice
chanfaina goat's liver and kidney stew, served in a thick sauce
chanquete whitebait
chile chili pepper
chiles en nogada green peppers stuffed with whipped cream and nut sauce
chimichurri hot parsley sauce
chipirón small squid

chopa a kind of sea bream

chorizo pork sausage, highly seasoned with garlic and paprika

chuleta cutlet

chupe de mariscos scallops served with a creamy sauce and gratinéed with cheese

churro sugared tubular fritter

damasco variety of apricot

dátil date

desayuno breakfast

dorada gilt-head

dulce sweet

  ~ **de naranja** marmalade

durazno peach

embuchado stuffed with meat

embutido spicy sausage

empanada pie or tart with meat or fish filling

  ~ **de horno** dough filled with minced meat, similar to ravioli

empanadilla small patty stuffed with seasoned meat or fish

empanado breaded

emperador swordfish

encurtido pickle

enchilada a maizeflour (US cornmeal) pancake *(tortilla)* stuffed and usually served with vegetable garnish and sauce

  ~ **roja** sausage-filled maizeflour pancake dipped into a red sweet-pepper sauce

  ~ **verde** maizeflour pancake stuffed with meat or fowl and braised in a green-tomato sauce

endibia chicory (US endive)

eneldo dill

ensalada salad

  ~ **común** green

  ~ **de frutas** fruit salad

  ~ **(a la) primavera** spring

  ~ **valenciana** with green peppers, lettuce and oranges

ensaladilla rusa diced cold vegetables with mayonnaise

entremés appetizer, hors-d'oeuvre

erizo de mar sea urchin

(en) escabeche marinated, pickled

  ~ **de gallina** chicken marinated in vinegar

escarcho red gurnard (fish)

escarola endive (US chicory)

espalda shoulder

(a la) española with tomatoes

espárrago asparagus

especia spice

especialidad de la casa chef's speciality

espinaca spinach

esqueixada mixed fish salad

(al) estilo de in the style of

estofado stew(ed)

estragón tarragon

fabada (asturiana) stew of pork, beans, bacon and sausage

faisán pheasant

fiambres cold meat (US cold cuts)

fideo thin noodle

filete steak

  ~ **de lomo** fillet steak (US tenderloin)

  ~ **de res** beef steak

  ~ **de lenguado empanado** breaded fillet of sole

(a la) flamenca with onions, peas, green peppers, tomatoes and spiced sausage

flan caramel mould, custard

frambuesa raspberry

(a la) francesa sautéed in butter

fresa strawberry

  ~ **de bosque** wild

fresco fresh, chilled

fresón large strawberry

fricandó veal bird, thin slice of meat rolled in bacon and braised

frijol bean

frijoles refritos fried mashed beans

frío cold

frito 1) fried 2) fry
~ **de patata** deep-fried potato croquette

fritura fry
~ **mixta** meat, fish or vegetables deep-fried in batter

fruta fruit
~ **escarchada** crystallized (US candied) fruit

galleta salted or sweet biscuit (US cracker or cookie)
~ **de nata** cream biscuit (US sandwich cookie)

gallina hen
~ **de Guinea** guinea fowl

gallo cockerel

gamba shrimp
~ **grande** prawn

gambas con mayonesa shrimp cocktail

ganso goose

garbanzo chick pea

gazpacho seasoned broth made of raw onions, garlic, tomatoes, cucumber and green pepper; served chilled

(a la) gitanilla with garlic

gordo fatty, rich (of food)

granada pomegranate

grande large

(al) gratín gratinéed

gratinado gratinéed

grelo turnip greens

grosella currant
~ **espinosa** gooseberry
~ **negra** blackcurrant
~ **roja** redcurrant

guacamole a purée of avocado and spices used as a dip, in a salad, for a *tortilla* filling or as a garnish

guarnición garnish, trimming

guayaba guava (fruit)

guinda sour cherry

guindilla chili pepper

guisado stew(ed)

guisante green pea

haba broad bean

habichuela verde French bean (US green bean)

hamburguesa hamburger

hayaca central maizeflour (US cornmeal) pancake, usually with a minced-meat filling

helado ice-cream, ice

hervido 1) boiled 2) stew of beef and vegetables (Latin America)

hielo ice

hierba herb

hierbas finas finely chopped mixture of herbs

hígado liver

higo fig

hinojo fennel

hongo mushroom

(al) horno baked

hortaliza greens

hueso bone

huevo egg
~ **cocido** boiled
~ **duro** hard-boiled
~ **escalfado** poached
~ **a la española** stuffed with tomatoes and served with cheese sauce
~ **a la flamenca** baked with asparagus, peas, peppers, onions, tomatoes and sausage
~ **frito** fried
~ **al nido** egg-yolk placed into small, soft roll, fried, then covered with egg-white
~ **pasado por agua** soft-boiled
~ **revuelto** scrambled

~ **con tocino** bacon and egg

humita boiled maize (US corn) with tomatoes, green peppers, onions and cheese

(a la) inglesa 1) underdone (of meat) 2) boiled 3) served with boiled vegetables

jabalí wild boar

jalea jelly

jamón ham

~ **cocido** boiled (often referred to as *jamón de York*)

~ **en dulce** boiled and served cold

~ **gallego** smoked and cut thinly

~ **serrano** cured and cut thinly

(a la) jardinera with carrots, peas and other vegetables

jengibre ginger

(al) jerez braised in sherry

judía bean

~ **verde** French bean (US green bean)

jugo gravy, meat juice

en su ~ in its own juice

juliana with shredded vegetables

jurel variety of mackerel

lacón shoulder of pork

~ **curado** salted pork

lamprea lamprey

langosta spiny lobster

langostino Norway lobster, Dublin Bay prawn

laurel bay leaf

lechón suck(l)ing pig

lechuga lettuce

legumbre vegetable

lengua tongue

lenguado sole, flounder

~ **frito** fried fillet of sole on bed of vegetables

lenteja lentil

liebre hare

~ **estofada** jugged hare

lima 1) lime 2) sweet lime (Latin America)

limón lemon

lista de platos menu

lista de vinos wine list

lobarro a variety of bass

lombarda red cabbage

lomo loin

longaniza long, highly seasoned sausage

lonja slice of meat

lubina bass

macarrones macaroni

(a la) madrileña with *chorizo* sausage, tomatoes and paprika

magras al estilo de Aragón cured ham in tomato sauce

maíz maize (US corn)

(a la) mallorquina usually refers to highly seasoned fish and shellfish

manchego hard cheese from La Mancha, made from sheep's milk, white or golden-yellow in colour

maní peanut

mantecado 1) small butter cake 2) custard ice-cream

mantequilla butter

manzana apple

~ **en dulce** in honey

(a la) marinera usually with mussels, onions, tomatoes, herbs and wine

marisco seafood

matambre rolled beef stuffed with vegetables

mayonesa mayonnaise

mazapán marzipan, almond paste

mejillón mussel

mejorana marjoram

melaza treacle, molasses

melocotón peach

membrillo quince
menestra boiled green vegetable soup
  ~ **de pollo** chicken and vegetable soup
menta mint
menú menu
  ~ **del día** set menu
  ~ **turístico** tourist menu
menudillos giblets
merengue meringue
merienda snack
merluza hake
mermelada jam
mezclado mixed
miel honey
(a la) milanesa with cheese, generally baked
minuta menu
mixto mixed
mole poblano chicken served with a sauce of chili peppers, spices and chocolate
molusco mollusc (snail, mussel, clam)
molleja sweetbread
mora mulberry
morcilla black pudding (US blood sausage)
morilla morel mushroom
moros y cristianos rice and black beans with diced ham, garlic, green peppers and herbs
mostaza mustard
mújol mullet
nabo turnip
naranja orange
nata cream
  ~ **batida** whipped cream
natillas custard
  ~ **al limón** lemon cream
níspola medlar (fruit)
nopalito young cactus leaf served with salad dressing

nuez nut
  ~ **moscada** nutmeg
olla stew
  ~ **gitana** vegetable stew
  ~ **podrida** stew made of vegetables, meat, fowl and ham
ostra oyster
oveja ewe
pabellón criollo beef in tomato sauce garnished with beans, rice and bananas
paella consists basically of saffron rice with assorted seafood and sometimes meat
  ~ **alicantina** with green peppers, onions, tomatoes, artichokes and fish
  ~ **catalana** with sausages, pork, squid, tomatoes, red sweet peppers and peas
  ~ **marinera** with fish, shellfish and meat
  ~ **(a la) valenciana** with chicken, shrimps, peas, tomatoes, mussels and garlic
palmito palm heart
palta avocado (pear)
pan bread
panecillo roll
papa potato
papas a la huancaína with cheese and green peppers
(a la) parrilla grilled
parrillada mixta mixed grill
pasado done, cooked
  bien ~ well-done
  poco ~ underdone (US rare)
pastas noodles, macaroni, spaghetti
pastel cake, pie
  ~ **de choclo** maize with minced beef, chicken, raisins and olives
pastelillo small tart
pata trotter (US foot)

patatas potatoes
  ~ **fritas** fried; usually chips (US french fries)
  ~ **(a la) leonesa** with onions
  ~ **nuevas** new
pato duck, duckling
pavo turkey
pechuga breast (of fowl)
pepinillo gherkin (US pickle)
pepino cucumber
(en) pepitoria stewed with onions, green peppers and tomatoes
pera pear
perca perch
percebe barnacle (shellfish)
perdiz partridge
  ~ **en escabeche** cooked in oil with vinegar, onions, parsley, carrots and green pepper; served cold
  ~ **estofada** stewed and served with a white-wine sauce
perejil parsley
perifollo chervil
perilla a firm, bland cheese
pescadilla whiting
pescado fish
pez espada swordfish
picadillo minced meat, hash
picado minced
picante sharp, spicy, highly seasoned
picatoste deep-fried slice of bread
pichoncillo young pigeon (US squab)
pierna leg
pimentón chili pepper
pimienta pepper
pimiento sweet pepper
  ~ **morrón** red (sweet) pepper
pincho moruno grilled meat (often kidneys) on a skewer, sometimes served with spicy sauces
pintada guinea fowl

piña pineapple
pisto diced and sautéed vegetables: mainly aubergines, green peppers and tomatoes; served cold
(a la) plancha grilled on a girdle
plátano banana
plato plate, dish, portion
  ~ **típico de la región** regional speciality
pollito spring chicken
pollo chicken
  ~ **pibil** simmered in fruit juice and spices
polvorón hazelnut biscuit (US cookie)
pomelo grapefruit
porción portion
porotos granados shelled beans served with pumpkin and maize (US corn)
postre dessert, sweet
potaje vegetable soup
puchero stew
puerro leek
pulpo octopus
punta de espárrago asparagus tip
punto de nieve dessert of whipped cream with beaten egg-whites
puré de patatas mashed potatoes
queso cheese
quisquilla shrimp
rábano radish
  ~ **picante** horse-radish
raja slice or portion
rallado grated
rape angler fish
ravioles ravioli
raya skate, ray
rebanada slice
rebozado breaded or fried in batter
recargo extra charge
rehogada sautéed

relleno stuffed
remolacha beetroot
repollo cabbage
requesón a fresh-curd cheese
riñón kidney
róbalo haddock
rodaballo turbot, flounder
(a la) romana dipped in batter and
    fried
romero rosemary
roncal cheese made from sheep's
    milk; close grained and hard in
    texture with a few small holes;
    piquant flavour
ropa vieja cooked, left-over meat
    and vegetables, covered with to-
    matoes and green peppers
rosbif roast beef
rosquilla doughnut
rubio red mullet
ruibarbo rhubarb
sal salt
salado salted, salty
salchicha small pork sausage for
    frying
salchichón salami
salmón salmon
salmonete red mullet
salsa sauce
    ~ **blanca** white
    ~ **española** brown sauce with
    herbs, spices and wine
    ~ **mayordoma** butter and pars-
    ley
    ~ **picante** hot pepper
    ~ **romana** bacon or ham egg,
    cream (sometimes flavoured
    with nutmeg)
    ~ **tártara** tartar
    ~ **verde** parsley
salsifi salsify
salteado sauté(ed)
salvia sage
san simón a firm, bland cheese

resembling *perilla*; shiny yellow
    rind
sandía watermelon
sardina sardine, pilchard
sémola semolina
sencillo plain
sepia cuttlefish
servicio service
    ~ **(no) incluido** (not) included
sesos brains
seta mushroom
sobrasada salami
solomillo fillet steak (US tender-
    loin)
sopa soup
    ~ **(de) cola de buey** oxtail
    ~ **sevillana** a highly spiced fish
    soup
suave soft
suflé soufflé
suizo bun
surtido assorted
taco wheat or maizeflour (US
    cornmeal) pancake usually with
    a meat filling and garnished
    with a spicy sauce
tajada slice
tallarín noodle
tamal a pastry dough of coarsely
    ground maizeflour with meat or
    fruit filling, steamed in maize-
    husks (US corn husks)
tapa appetizer, snack
tarta cake, tart
    ~ **helada** ice-cream tart
ternera veal
tocino bacon
    ~ **de cielo** 1) caramel mould 2)
    custard-filled cake
tomate tomato
tomillo thyme
tordo thrush
toronja variety of grapefruit
tortilla 1) omelet 2) a type of

pancake made with maizeflour (US cornmeal)

~ **de chorizo** with pieces of a spicy sausage

~ **a la española** with onions, potatoes and seasoning

~ **a la francesa** plain

~ **gallega** potatoes with ham, red sweet peppers and peas

~ **a la jardinera** with mixed, diced vegetables

~ **al ron** rum

tortita waffle

tortuga turtle

tostada toast

tripas tripe

trucha trout

~ **frita a la asturiana** floured and fried in butter, garnished with lemon

trufa truffle

turrón nougat

ulloa a soft cheese from Galicia, rather like a mature camembert

uva grape

~ **pasa** raisin

vaca salada corned beef

vainilla vanilla

(a la) valenciana with rice, toma-toes and garlic

variado varied, assorted

varios sundries

venado venison

venera scallop, coquille St. Jacques

verdura greens

vieira scallop

villalón a cheese from sheep's milk

vinagre vinegar

vinagreta a piquant vinegar dressing (vinaigrette) to accompany salads

(a la) ~ marinated in oil and vinegar or lemon juice with mixed herbs

(a la) vizcaína with green peppers, tomatoes, garlic and paprika

yema egg-yolk

yemas a dessert of whipped egg-yolks and sugar

zanahoria carrot

zarzamora blackberry

zarzuela savoury stew of assorted fish and shellfish

~ **de mariscos** seafood stew

~ **de pescado** selection of fish served with a highly seasoned sauce

~ **de verduras** vegetable stew

Drinks

abocado sherry made from a blend of sweet and dry wines

agua water

aguardiente spirits

Alicante this region to the south of Valencia produces a large quantity of red table wine and some good rosé, particularly from Yecla

Amontillado medium-dry sherry,

light amber in colour, with a
nutty flavour

Andalucía a drink of dry sherry
and orange juice

Angélica a Basque herb liqueur
similar to yellow Chartreuse

anís aniseed liqueur

Anís del Mono a Calatonian aniseed liqueur

anís seco aniseed brandy

anisado an aniseed-based soft
drink which may be slightly
alcoholic

batido milk shake

bebida drink

Bobadilla Gran Reserva a wine-
distilled brandy

botella bottle

  media ~ half bottle

café coffee

  ~ **cortado** small cup of strong
  coffee with a dash of milk or
  cream

  ~ **descafeinado** coffeine-free

  ~ **exprés** espresso

  ~ **granizado** iced (white)

  ~ **con leche** white

  ~ **negro/solo** black

Calisay a quinine-flavoured liqueur

Carlos I a wine-distilled brandy

Cataluña Catalonia; this region
southwest of Barcelona is
known for its *xampañ*, bearing
little resemblance to the famed
French sparkling wine

Cazalla an aniseed liqueur

cerveza beer

  ~ **de barril** draught (US draft)

  ~ **dorada** light

  ~ **negra** dark

cola de mono a blend of coffee,
milk, rum and *pisco*

coñac 1) French Cognac 2) term

applied to any Spanish wine-
distilled brandy

Cordoníu a brand-name of Catalonian sparkling wine locally referred to as *xampañ* (champagne)

cosecha harvest; indicates the
vintage of wine

crema de cacao cocoa liqueur,
crème de cacao

Cuarenta y Tres an egg liqueur

Cuba libre rum and Coke

champán, champaña 1) French
Champagne 2) term applied to
any Spanish sparkling wine

chicha de manzana apple brandy

Chinchón an aniseed liqueur

chocolate chocolate drink

  ~ **con leche** hot chocolate with
  milk

Dulce dessert wine

Fino dry sherry wine, very pale
and straw-coloured

Fundador a wine-distilled brandy

Galicia this Atlantic coastal region
has good table wines

gaseosa fizzy (US carbonated)
water

ginebra gin

gran vino term found on Chilean
wine labels to indicate a wine of
exceptional quality

granadina pomegranate syrup
mixed with wine or brandy

horchata de almendra (or **de chu-
fa)** drink made from ground al-
monds (or Jerusalem artichoke)

Jerez 1) sherry 2) the Spanish
region near the Portuguese border, internationally renowned
for its *Jerez*

jugo fruit juice

leche milk

limonada lemonade, lemon

squash

Málaga 1) dessert wine 2) the region in the south of Spain, is particularly noted for its dessert wine

Manzanilla dry sherry, very pale and straw-coloured

margarita *tequila* with lime juice

Montilla a dessert wine from near Cordoba, often drunk as an aperitif

Moscatel fruity dessert wine

naranjada orangeade

Oloroso sweet, dark sherry, drunk as dessert wine, resembles brown cream sherry

Oporto port (wine)

pisco grape brandy

ponche crema egg-nog liquor

Priorato the region south of Barcelona produces good quality red and white wine but also a dessert wine, usually called *Priorato* but renamed *Tarragona* when it is exported

refresco a soft drink

reservado term found on Chilean wine labels to indicate a wine of exceptional quality

Rioja the northern region near the French border is considered to produce Spain's best wines—especially red; some of the finest Rioja wines resemble good Bordeaux wines

ron rum

sangría a mixture of red wine, ice, orange, lemon, brandy and sugar

sangrita *tequila* with tomato, orange and lime juices

sidra cider

sol y sombra a blend of wine-distilled brandy and aniseed liqueur

sorbete (iced) fruit drink

té tea

tequila brandy made from agave (US aloe)

tinto 1) red wine 2) black coffee with sugar (Colombia)

Tío Pepe a brand-name sherry

Triple Seco an orange liqueur

Valdepeñas the region south of Madrid is an important wine-producing area

vermú vermouth

Veterano Osborne a wine-distilled brandy

vino wine

~ **blanco** white

~ **clarete** rosé

~ **común** table wine

~ **dulce** dessert

~ **espumoso** sparkling

~ **de mesa** table wine

~ **del país** local wine

~ **rosado** rosé

~ **seco** dry

~ **suave** sweet

~ **tinto** red

xampañ Catalonian sparkling wine

Yerba mate South American holly tea

zumo juice

Spanish Verbs

Below are some examples of Spanish verbs in the three regular conjugations, grouped by families according to their infinitive endings, *-ar, -er* and *-ir*. Verbs which do not follow the conjugations below are considered irregular (see irregular verb list). Note that there are some verbs which follow the regular conjugation of the category they belong to, but present some minor changes in spelling. Examples: *tocar, toque; cargar, cargue.* The personal pronoun is not generally expressed, since the verb endings clearly indicate the person.

		1st conj. am ar *(to love)*	2nd conj. tem er *(to fear)*	3rd conj. viv ir *(to live)*
Infinitive				
Present	(yo)	am o	tem o	viv o
	(tú)	am as	tem es	viv es
	(él)	am a	tem e	viv e
	(nosotros)	am amos	tem emos	viv imos
	(vosotros)	am áis	tem éis	viv ís
	(ellos)	am an	tem en	viv en
Imperfect	(yo)	am aba	tem ía	viv ía
	(tú)	am abas	tem ías	viv ías
	(él)	am aba	tem ía	viv ía
	(nosotros)	am ábamos	tem íamos	viv íamos
	(vosotros)	am abais	tem íais	viv íais
	(ellos)	am aban	tem ían	viv ían
Past. def.	(yo)	am é	tem í	viv í
	(tú)	am aste	tem iste	viv iste
	(él)	am ó	tem ió	viv ió
	(nosotros)	am amos	tem imos	viv imos
	(vosotros)	am asteis	tem isteis	viv isteis
	(ellos)	am aron	tem ieron	viv ieron
Future	(yo)	am aré	tem eré	viv iré
	(tú)	am arás	tem erás	viv irás
	(él)	am ará	tem erá	viv irá
	(nosotros)	am aremos	tem eremos	viv iremos
	(vosotros)	am aréis	tem eréis	viv iréis
	(ellos)	am arán	tem erán	viv irán
Conditional	(yo)	am aría	tem ería	viv iría
	(tú)	am arías	tem erías	viv irías
	(él)	am aría	tem ería	viv iría
	(nosotros)	am aríamos	tem eríamos	viv iríamos
	(vosotros)	am aríais	tem eríais	viv iríais
	(ellos)	am arían	tem erían	viv irían
Subj. Pres.	(yo)	am e	tem a	viv a
	(tú)	am es	tem as	viv as
	(él)	am e	tem a	viv a
	(nosotros)	am emos	tem amos	viv amos
	(vosotros)	am éis	tem áis	viv áis
	(ellos)	am en	tem an	viv an

| Pres. Part./Gerund | am **ando** | tem **iendo** | viv **iendo** |
| Past. Part. | am **ado** | tem **ido** | viv **ido** |

Auxiliary verbs

The verb **to have** is translated either by *haber* or by *tener*. *Haber* is the auxiliary (e.g. he has gone) and *tener* (see list of irregular verbs) is a transitive verb, which conveys the idea of possession (e.g. she has a house).

The verb **to be** is translated either by *ser* or *estar*. *Ser* is used as an auxiliary verb to form the passive (e.g. they are understood) and to express an intrinsic quality of a fundamental characteristic (e.g. man is mortal). *Estar* (see list of irregular verbs) expresses a state or an attitude, whether lasting or not, of a thing or a person (e.g. she is hungry).

	haber *(to have)*		**ser** *(to be)*	
	Present	*Imperfect*	*Present*	*Imperfect*
(yo)	he	había	soy	era
(tú)	has	habías	eres	eras
(él)	ha	había	es	era
(nosotros)	hemos	habíamos	somos	éramos
(vosotros)	habéis	habíais	sois	erais
(ellos)	han	habían	son	eran
	Future	*Conditional*	*Future*	*Conditional*
(yo)	habré	habría	seré	sería
(tú)	habrás	habrías	serás	serías
(él)	habrá	habría	será	sería
(nosotros)	habremos	habríamos	seremos	seríamos
(vosotros)	habréis	habríais	seréis	seríais
(ellos)	habrán	habrían	serán	serían
	Present subjunctive	*Present perfect*	*Present subjunctive*	*Present perfect*
(yo)	haya	he habido	sea	he sido
(tú)	hayas	has habido	seas	has sido
(él)	haya	ha habido	sea	ha sido
(nosotros)	hayamos	hemos habido	seamos	hemos sido
(vosotros)	hayáis	habéis habido	seáis	habéis sido
(ellos)	hayan	han habido	sean	han sido
	Present participle	*Past participle*	*Present participle*	*Past participle*
	habiendo	habido	siendo	sido

Irregular verbs

Below is a list of the verbs and tenses commonly used in spoken Spanish. In the listing, a) stands for the present tense, b) for the imperfect, c) for the past def., d) for the future, e) for the present participle and f) for the past participle. The only forms given below are the irregular ones commonly used. There can be other irregular forms, but they are considered rare. In tenses other than present, all persons can be regularly formed from the first person. Unless otherwise indicated, verbs with prefixes (ad-, ante-, com-, con-, de-, des-, dis-, en-, ex-, im-, pos-, pre-, pro-, re-, sobre-, sub-, tras-, etc.) are conjugated like the stem verb.

abstenerse
refrain
→tener

acertar
guess
→cerrar

acontecer
happen
→agradecer

acordar
agree ; decide
→contar

acostarse
lie down
→contar

acrecentar
increase ; advance
→cerrar

adormecer
put to sleep
→agradecer

adquirir
acquire
a) adquiero, adquieres, adquiere, adquirimos, adquirís, adquieren; b) adquiría; c) adquirí; d) adquiriré; e) adquiriendo; f) adquirido

advertir
notice
→sentir

agradecer
thank
a) agradezco, agradeces, agradece, agradecemos, agradecéis, agradecen; b) agradecía; c) agradecí; d) agradeceré; e) agradeciendo; f) agradecido

alentar
encourage
→cerrar

almorzar
have lunch
→contar

amanecer
dawn
→agradecer

andar
walk
a) ando, andas, anda, andamos, andáis, andan; b) andaba; c) anduve; d) andaré; e) andando; f) andado

anochecer
begin to get dark
→agradecer

apetecer
want
→agradecer

apostar
bet
→contar

apretar
tighten, squeeze
→cerrar

arrendar →cerrar
let, lease, rent

arrepentirse →sentir
repent, regret

ascender →perder
climb, reach

atenerse →tener
obey; rely on

atravesar →cerrar
cross, pierce

atribuir →instruir
attribute

aventar →cerrar
fan, air

avergonzar →contar
put to shame,
embarrass

bendecir →decir
bless

caber a) quepo, cabes, cabe, cabemos, cabéis, caben;
contain; fit b) cabía; c) cupe; d) cabré; e) cabiendo; f) cabido

caer a) caigo, caes, cae, caemos, caéis, caen; b) caía;
fall c) caí; d) caeré; e) cayendo; f) caído

calentar →cerrar
heat

carecer →agradecer
lack

cegar →cerrar
blind

cerrar a) cierro, cierras, cierra, cerramos, cerráis, cierran;
close b) cerraba; c) cerré; d) cerraré; e) cerrando; f) cerrado

cocer a) cuezo, cueces, cuece, cocemos, cocéis, cuecen;
boil b) cocía; c) cocí; d) coceré; e) cociendo; f) cocido

colar →contar
strain; filter

colgar →contar
hang

comenzar →cerrar
begin

competir →pedir
compete

concebir →pedir
conceive

concernir →sentir
concern

concluir →instruir
conclude, finish

concordar →contar
agree, reconcile

conducir →traducir
drive

conferir →sentir
confer

confesar →cerrar
confess

conocer a) conozco, conoces, conoce, conocemos, conocéis,
know conocen; b) conocía; c) conocí; d) conoceré;
e) conociendo; f) conocido

consolar →contar
console, comfort

constituir →instruir
constitute, be

construir →instruir
build, erect

contar a) cuento, cuentas, cuenta, contamos, contáis, cuentan;
count, bear in mind b) contaba; c) conté; d) contaré; e) contando;
f) contado

contribuir →instruir
contribute

convertir →sentir
convert

corregir →pedir
correct

costar →contar
cost

crecer →agradecer
grow, rise

dar a) doy, das, da, damos, dais, dan; b) daba; c) di;
give d) daré; e) dando; f) dado

decir a) digo, dices, dice, decimos, decis, dicen; b) decía;
say c) dije; d) diré e) diciendo; f) dicho

deducir →traducir
deduce

defender →perder
defend

derretir →pedir
melt

descender *descend, let down*	→perder
descollar *be outstanding*	→contar
desconcertar *damage; upset*	→cerrar
despertar *awaken, revive*	→cerrar
desterrar *banish*	→cerrar
destituir *deprive, dismiss*	→instruir
destruir *destroy*	→instruir
desvanecer *make disappear,* *take out*	→agradecer
diferir *defer*	→sentir
digerir *digest*	→sentir
diluir *dilute*	→instruir
discernir *discern*	→sentir
disminuir *diminish*	→instruir
disolver *dissolve*	→morder
distribuir *distribute*	→instruir
divertir *entertain, distract*	→sentir
doler *hurt*	→morder
dormir *sleep*	a) duermo, duermes, duerme, dormimos, dormís duermen; b) dormía; c) dormí; d) dormiré; e) durmiendo; f) dormido
elegir *elect, choose*	→pedir
embestir *assault*	→pedir
empezar *begin, start*	→cerrar

enaltecer	→agradecer
exalt, praise	
enardecer	→agradecer
excite; inflame	
encender	→perder
light, ignite	
encomendar	→cerrar
entrust	
encontrar	→contar
find	
engrandecer	→agradecer
enlarge, exaggerate	
enloquecer	→agradecer
madden	
enmendar	→cerrar
emend, correct	
enmudecer	→agradecer
silence	
enorgullecer	→agradecer
fill with pride	
enriquecer	→agradecer
enrich	
ensangrentar	→cerrar
stain with blood	
ensoberbecer	→agradecer
make proud	
ensordecer	→agradecer
deafen	
enternecer	→agradecer
soften; affect	
enterrar	→cerrar
bury	
entristecer	→agradecer
sadden	
envejecer	→agradecer
age	
errar	→cerrar
miss; wander	
escarmentar	→cerrar
chastise, punish	
escarnecer	→agradecer
scoff	
establecer	→agradecer
establish	

| **estar** | a) estoy, estás, está, estamos, estáis, están; b) estaba; |
| *be* | c) estuve; d) estaré; e) estando; f) estado |

estremecer →agradecer
shake

excluir →instruir
exclude

fallecer →agradecer
die

favorecer →agradecer
favour

florecer →agradecer
blossom

fluir →instruir
flow

fortalecer →agradecer
strengthen

forzar →contar
compel, force

fregar →cerrar
wash up; scrub

freír →reír
fry

gemir →pedir
groan

gobernar →cerrar
govern

| **gruñir** | a) gruño, gruñes, gruñe, gruñimos, gruñís, gruñen; |
| *grunt* | b) gruñía;c) gruñí; d) gruñiré; e) gruñiendo; f) gruñido |

| **haber** | a) he, has, ha, hemos, habéis, han; b) había; c) hube; |
| *have* | d) habré; e) habiendo; f) habido |

| **hacer** | a) hago, haces, hace, hacemos, hacéis, hacen; b) hacía; |
| *make* | c) hice; d) haré; e) haciendo; f) hecho |

heder →perder
stink

helar →cerrar
freeze

hender →perder
crack

herir →sentir
injure

hervir →sentir
boil

huir →instruir
escape

humedecer *humidify*	→agradecer
incluir *include*	→instruir
inducir *induce*	→traducir
ingerir *swallow; consume*	→sentir
instituir *institute*	→instruir
instruir *instruct*	a) instruyo, instruyes, instruye, instruimos, instruis, instruyen; b) instruía; c) instruí; d) instruiré; e) instruyendo; f) instruido
introducir *introduce*	→traducir
invertir *invest*	→sentir
ir *go*	a) voy, vas, va, vamos, vais, van; b) iba; c) fui; d) iré; e) yendo; f) ido
jugar *play*	a) juego, juegas, juega, jugamos, jugáis, juegan; b) jugaba; c) jugué; d) jugaré; e) jugando; f) jugado
lucir *shine*	a) luzco, luces, luce, lucimos, lucís, lucen; b) lucía; c) lucí; d) luciré; e) luciendo; f) lucido
llover *rain*	a) llueve; b) llovía; c) llovió; d) lloverá; e) lloviendo; f) llovido
manifestar *manifest*	→cerrar
mantener *maintain*	→tener
medir *measure*	→pedir
mentir *tell a lie*	→sentir
merecer *deserve*	→agradecer
merendar *have tea, snack*	→cerrar
moler *grind*	→morder
morder *bite*	a) muerdo, muerdes, muerde, mordemos, mordéis, muerden; b) mordía; c) mordí; d) morderé; e) mordiendo; f) mordido
morir *die*	→dormir

mostrar *show*	→contar
mover *move*	→morder
nacer *be born*	a) nazco, naces, nace, nacemos, nacéis, nacen; b) nacía; c) nací; d) naceré; e) naciendo; f) nacido
negar *deny*	→cerrar
nevar *snow*	a) nieva; b) nevaba; c) nevó; d) nevará; e) nevando; f) nevado
obedecer *obey*	→agradecer
obscurecer *darken*	→agradecer
obstruir *obstruct*	→instruir
obtener *obtain*	→tener
ofrecer, *offer*	→agradecer
oír *hear, listen*	a) oigo, oyes, oye, oímos, oís, oyen; b) oía; c) oí; d) oiré; e) oyendo; f) oído
oler *smell*	→morder
pacer *graze*	→nacer
padecer *suffer*	→agradecer
parecer *seem*	→agradecer
pedir *ask for, request*	a) pido, pides, pide, pedimos, pedís, piden; b) pedía; c) pedí; d) pediré; e) pidiendo; f) pedido
pensar *think*	→cerrar
perder *lose*	a) pierdo, pierdes, pierde, perdemos, perdéis, pierden; b) perdía; c) perdí; d) perderé; e) perdiendo; f) perdido
perecer *perish*	→agradecer
permanecer *stay*	→agradecer
pertenecer *belong to*	→agradecer
pervertir *pervert*	→sentir

placer *please*	a) plazco, places, place, placemos, placéis, placen; b) placía; c) plací; d) placeré; e) placiendo; f) placido
plegar *fold*	→cerrar
poblar *populate*	→contar
poder *can, be able*	a) puedo, puedes, puede, podemos, podéis, pueden; b) podía; c) pude; d) podré; e) pudiendo; f) podido
poner *put*	a) pongo, pones, pone, ponemos, ponéis, ponen; b) ponía; c) puse; d) pondré; e) poniendo; f) puesto
preferir *prefer*	→sentir
probar *try*	→contar
producir *produce*	→traducir
proferir *utter*	→sentir
quebrar *break*	→cerrar
querer *want, wish*	a) quiero, quieres, quiere, queremos, queréis, quieren; b) quería; c) quise; d) querré; e) queriendo; f) querido
recomendar *recommend*	→cerrar
recordar *remember*	→contar
reducir *reduce*	→traducir
referir *refer, relate*	→sentir
regar *water*	→cerrar
regir *govern*	→pedir
reír *laugh*	a) río, ríes, ríe, reímos, reís, ríen; b) reía; c) reí; d) reiré; e) riendo, f) reído
remendar *mend*	→cerrar
rendir *produce; overcome*	→pedir
renovar *renew*	→contar
reñir *scold; quarrel*	→teñir

repetir →pedir
repeat

requerir →sentir
request

resolver →morder
resolve

resplandecer →agradecer
shine

restituir →instruir
restore, return

retribuir →instruir
pay ; reward

reventar →cerrar
burst

robustecer →agradecer
strengthen

rodar →contar
drive ; roll

rogar →contar
beg, plead

saber a) sé, sabes, sabe, sabemos, sabéis, saben;)b sabía;
know c) supe; d) sabré; e) sabiendo; f) sabido

salir a) salgo, sales, sale, salimos, salís, salen; b) salía;
go out c) salí; d) saldré; e) saliendo; f) salido

satisfacer →hacer
satisfy

seducir →traducir
seduce

seguir →pedir
follow

sembrar →cerrar
sow

sentar →cerrar
sit, seat

sentir a) siento, sientes, siente, sentimos, sentís, sienten;
feel b) sentía; c) sentí; d) sentiré; e) sintiendo; f) sentido

ser a) soy, eres, es, somos, sois, son; b) era c) fui; d) seré;
be e) siendo; f) sido

servir →pedir
serve

soldar →contar
solder ; join

soler a) suelo, sueles, suele, solemos, soléis, suelen; b) solía;
be used to c) solí; e) soliendo; f) solido

soltar	→contar
release ; loosen	
sonar	→contar
ring, sound	
soñar	→contar
dream	
sugerir	→sentir
suggest	
sustituir	→instruir
substitute	
temblar	→cerrar
tremble	
tender	→perder
stretch, extend	
tener	a) tengo, tienes, tiene, tenemos, tenéis, tienen; b) tenía;
have (got)	c) tuve; d) tendré; e) teniendo; f) tenido
tentar	→cerrar
touch ; try	
teñir	a) tiño, tiñes, tiñe, teñimos, teñís, tiñen; b) teñía;
dye	c) teñí; d) teñiré; e) tiñiendo; f) teñido
torcer	→cocer
twist	
tostar	→contar
roast	
traducir	a) traduzco, traduces, traduce, traducimos, traducís,
translate	traducen; b) traducía; c) traduje; d) traduciré;
	e) traduciendo; f) traducido
traer	a) traigo, traes, trae, traemos, traéis, traen; b) traía;
bring	c) traje; d) traeré; e) trayendo; f) traido
transferir	→sentir
transfer	
trocar	→contar
(ex)change	
tronar	a) trueno, truenas, truena, tronamos, tronáis, truenan;
thunder	b) tronaba; c) troné; d) tronaré; e) tronando; f) tronado
tropezar	→cerrar
stumble	
valer	a) valgo, vales, vale, valemos, valéis, valen; b) valía;
protect ; be worth	c) valí; d) valdré; e) valiendo; f) valido
venir	a) vengo, vienes, viene, venimos, venís, vienen; b) venía;
come	c) vine; d) vendré; e) viniendo; f) venido
ver	a) veo, ves, ve, vemos, veis, ven; b) veía; c) vi; d) veré;
see	e) viendo; f) visto

verter →perder
pour ; spill

vestir →pedir
dress

volar →contar
fly

volcar →contar
tip over

volver →morder
(re)turn

yacer →nacer
lie, rest

zambullir a) zambullo, zambulles, zambulle, zambullimos,
plunge zambullís, zambullen; b) zambullía; c) zambullí;
d) zambulliré; e) zambullendo; f) zambullido

Spanish Abbreviations

a.C.	*antes de Cristo*	B.C.
A.C.	*año de Cristo*	A.D.
admón.	*administración*	administration
A.L.A.L.C.	*Asociación Latino-Americana de Libre Comercio*	Latin American Free Trade Association
apdo.	*apartado de correos*	P.O. Box
Av./Avda.	*Avenida*	avenue
Barna.	*Barcelona*	Barcelona
C/	*Calle*	street, road
c/c.	*cuenta corriente*	current account
Cía.	*Compañía*	company
ct(s).	*céntimo(s)*	1/100 of a peseta
cta.	*cuenta*	account; bill
cte.	*corriente*	inst., of this month
CV.	*caballos de vapor*	horsepower
D.	*Don*	courtesy title for gentlemen, only used together with the Christian name
D.ª	*Doña*	courtesy title for ladies, only used together with the Christian name
dcha.	*derecha*	right (direction)
D.N.I.	*Documento Nacional de Identidad*	identity card
d.v.	*días de visita*	open days
EE.UU.	*Estados Unidos*	USA
Exc.ª	*Excelencia*	Your Excellency
f.c.	*ferrocarril*	railway
G.C.	*Guardia Civil*	Spanish police force
gral.	*general*	general
h.	*hora*	hour
hab.	*habitantes*	inhabitants, population
hnos.	*hermanos*	brothers (in firms)
íd.	*ídem*	ditto
igla.	*iglesia*	church
izq./izqda.	*izquierda*	left (direction)
lic.	*licenciado*	licentiate; lawyer
M.I.T.	*Ministerio de Información y Turismo*	Spanish Ministry of Information and Tourism
Mons.	*Monseñor*	Roman Catholic title (approx. Your Grace)

N.ª S.ª	*Nuestra Señora*	Our Lady, Virgin Mary
n.º/núm.	*número*	number
O.E.A.	*Organización de Estados Americanos*	Organization of American States
P.	*Padre*	Father (ecclesiastical title)
pág.	*página*	page
P.D.	*posdata*	P.S.
p. ej.	*por ejemplo*	e.g.
P.P.	*porte pagado*	postage paid
pta(s).	*peseta(s)*	peseta(s)
P.V.P.	*precio de venta al público*	retail price
R.A.C.E.	*Real Automóvil Club de España*	Royal Automobile Association of Spain
R.A.E.	*Real Academia Española*	Royal Academy of the Spanish Language
R.C.	*Real Club…*	Royal… Association
RENFE	*Red Nacional de los Ferrocarriles Españoles*	Spanish National Railways
R.M.	*Reverenda Madre*	Mother Superior, abbess
R.P.	*Reverendo Padre*	Reverend Father (title for Catholic priests and abbots)
Rte.	*Remite, Remitente*	sender (of a letter)
RTVE	*Radio Televisión Española*	Spanish Radio and Television Corporation
S./Sto./ Sta.	*San/Santo/Santa*	saint
S.A.	*Sociedad Anónima*	Ltd., Inc.
S.A.R.	*Su Alteza Real*	His/Her Royal Highness
s.a.s.s.	*su atento y seguro servidor*	approx. Yours faithfully
S.E.	*Su Excelencia*	His Excellency
sgte.	*siguiente*	following
S.M.	*Su Majestad*	His/Her Majesty
Sr.	*Señor*	Mr.
Sra.	*Señora*	Mrs.
S.R.C.	*se ruega contestación*	please reply
Sres./Srs.	*Señores*	Sirs, Gentlemen
Srta.	*Señorita*	Miss
S.S.	*Su Santidad*	His Holiness
Ud./Vd.	*Usted*	you (singular)
Uds./Vds.	*Ustedes*	you (plural)
Vda.	*viuda*	widow
v.g./v.gr.	*verbigracia*	e.g.

Numerals

Cardinal numbers		Ordinal numbers	
0	cero	1.°	primero
1	uno	2.°	segundo
2	dos	3.°	tercero
3	tres	4.°	cuarto
4	cuatro	5.°	quinto
5	cinco	6.°	sexto
6	seis	7.°	séptimo
7	siete	8.°	octavo
8	ocho	9.°	noveno (nono)
9	nueve	10.°	décimo
10	diez	11.°	undécimo
11	once	12.°	duodécimo
12	doce	13.°	decimotercero
13	trece	14.°	decimocuarto
14	catorce	15.°	decimoquinto
15	quince	16.°	decimosexto
16	dieciséis	17.°	decimoséptimo
17	diecisiete	18.°	decimoctavo
18	dieciocho	19.°	decimonoveno
19	diecinueve	20.°	vigésimo
20	veinte	21.°	vigésimo primero
21	veintiuno	22.°	vigésimo segundo
30	treinta	30.°	trigésimo
31	treinta y uno	40.°	cuadragésimo
40	cuarenta	50.°	quincuagésimo
50	cincuenta	60.°	sexagésimo
60	sesenta	70.°	septuagésimo
70	setenta	80.°	octogésimo
80	ochenta	90.°	nonagésimo
90	noventa	100.°	centésimo
100	ciento (cien)	230.°	ducentésimo trigésimo
101	ciento uno	300.°	tricentésimo
230	doscientos treinta	400.°	cuadringentésimo
500	quinientos	500.°	quingentésimo
700	setecientos	600.°	sexcentésimo
900	novecientos	700.°	septingentésimo
1.000	mil	800.°	octingentésimo
100.000	cien mil	900.°	noningentésimo
1.000.000	un millón	1.000.°	milésimo

Time

Although official time in Spain is based on the 24-hour clock, the 12-hour system is used in conversation.

la una

la una y cinco

la una y diez

la una y cuarto

la una y veinte

la una y veinticinco

la una y media

las dos menos veinticinco

las dos menos veinte

las dos menos cuarto

las dos menos diez

las dos menos cinco

In some Latin American countries you can specify *a.m.* or *p.m.* as in English, but it is far more common to add *de la mañana, de la tarde* or *de la noche* as in Spain.

Thus:

las ocho de la mañana	8 a.m.
la una de la tarde	1 p.m.
las ocho de la noche	8 p.m.

Days of the Week

domingo	Sunday	*jueves*	Thursday
lunes	Monday	*viernes*	Friday
martes	Tuesday	*sábado*	Saturday
miércoles	Wednesday		

176

C°	F°
100	212
40	105
36,9	98,6
35	
30	90
25	80
20	70
15	60
10	50
5	40
0	32
	30
−5	20
−10	
	10
−15	0
−20	

Conversion tables/
Tablas de conversión

Metres and feet
The figure in the middle stands for both metres and feet, e.g. 1 metre = 3.281 ft. and 1 foot = 0.30 m.

Metros y pies
La columna del centro corresponde a metros y pies, por ejemplo 1 metro = 3,281 pies y 1 pie = 0,30 metros.

Metres/Metros		Feet/Pies
0.30	1	3.281
0.61	2	6.563
0.91	3	9.843
1.22	4	13.124
1.52	5	16.403
1.83	6	19.686
2.13	7	22.967
2.44	8	26.248
2.74	9	29.529
3.05	10	32.810
3.66	12	39.372
4.27	14	45.934
6.10	20	65.620
7.62	25	82.023
15.24	50	164.046
22.86	75	246.069
30.48	100	328.092

Temperature
To convert Centigrade to Fahrenheit, multiply by 1.8 and add 32.
To convert Fahrenheit to Centigrade, subtract 32 from Fahrenheit and divide by 1.8.

Temperatura
Para convertir grados centígrados en Fahrenheit multiplique los centígrados por 1,8 y sume 32 al resultado.
Para convertir grados Fahrenheit en centígrados reste 32 de los Fahrenheit y divida el resultado entre 1,8.

Some Basic Phrases

Algunas expresiones útiles

Please.	Por favor.
Thank you very much.	Muchas gracias.
Don't mention it.	No hay de qué.
Good morning.	Buenos días.
Good afternoon.	Buenas tardes.
Good evening.	Buenas noches.
Good night.	Buenas noches (despedida).
Good-bye.	Adiós.
See you later.	Hasta luego.
Where is/Where are…?	¿Dónde está/Dónde están…?
What do you call this?	¿Cómo se llama esto?
What does that mean?	¿Qué quiere decir eso?
Do you speak English?	¿Habla usted inglés?
Do you speak German?	¿Habla usted alemán?
Do you speak French?	¿Habla usted francés?
Do you speak Spanish?	¿Habla usted español?
Do you speak Italian?	¿Habla usted italiano?
Could you speak more slowly, please?	¿Puede usted hablar más despacio, por favor?
I don't understand.	No comprendo.
Can I have…?	¿Puede darme…?
Can you show me…?	¿Puede usted enseñarme…?
Can you tell me…?	¿Puede usted decirme…?
Can you help me, please?	¿Puede usted ayudarme, por favor?
I'd like…	Quisiera…
We'd like…	Quisiéramos…
Please give me…	Por favor, déme…
Please bring me…	Por favor, tráigame…
I'm hungry.	Tengo hambre.
I'm thirsty.	Tengo sed.
I'm lost.	Me he perdido.
Hurry up!	¡Dése prisa!

| There is/There are... | Hay... |
| There isn't/There aren't... | No hay... |

Arrival / Llegada

Your passport, please.	Su pasaporte, por favor.
Have you anything to declare?	¿Tiene usted algo que declarar?
No, nothing at all.	No, nada en absoluto.
Can you help me with my luggage, please?	¿Puede usted ayudarme con mi equipaje, por favor?
Where's the bus to the centre of town, please?	¿Dónde está el autobús que va al centro, por favor?
This way, please.	Por aquí, por favor.
Where can I get a taxi?	¿Dónde puedo coger un taxi?
What's the fare to...?	¿Cuánto es la tarifa a...?
Take me to this address, please.	Lléveme a esta dirección, por favor.
I'm in a hurry.	Tengo mucha prisa.

Hotel / Hotel

My name is...	Me llamo...
Have you a reservation?	¿Ha hecho usted una reserva?
I'd like a room with a bath.	Quisiera una habitación con baño.
What's the price per night?	¿Cuánto cuesta por noche?
May I see the room?	¿Puedo ver la habitación?
What's my room number, please?	¿Cuál es el número de mi habitación, por favor?
There's no hot water.	No hay agua caliente.
May I see the manager, please?	¿Puedo ver al director, por favor?
Did anyone telephone me?	¿Me ha llamado alguien?
Is there any mail for me?	¿Hay correo para mí?
May I have my bill (check), please?	¿Puede darme mi cuenta, por favor?

Eating out	**Restaurante**
Do you have a fixed-price menu?	¿Tiene usted un menú de precio fijo?
May I see the menu?	¿Puedo ver la carta?
May we have an ashtray, please?	¿Nos puede traer un cenicero, por favor?
Where's the toilet, please?	¿Dónde están los servicios, por favor?
I'd like an hors d'œuvre (starter).	Quisiera un entremés.
Have you any soup?	¿Tiene usted sopa?
I'd like some fish.	Quisiera pescado.
What kind of fish do you have?	¿Qué clases de pescado tiene usted?
I'd like a steak.	Quisiera un bistec.
What vegetables have you got?	¿Qué verduras tiene usted?
Nothing more, thanks.	Nada más, gracias.
What would you like to drink?	¿Qué le gustaría beber?
I'll have a beer, please.	Tomaré una cerveza, por favor.
I'd like a bottle of wine.	Quisiera una botella de vino.
May I have the bill (check), please?	¿Podría darme la cuenta, por favor?
Is service included?	¿Está incluido el servicio?
Thank you, that was a very good meal.	Gracias. Ha sido una comida muy buena.

Travelling	**Viajes**
Where's the railway station, please?	¿Dónde está la estación de ferrocarril, por favor?
Where's the ticket office, please?	¿Dónde está la taquilla, por favor?
I'd like a ticket to...	Quisiera un billete para...
First or second class?	¿Primera o segunda clase?
First class, please.	Primera clase, por favor.
Single or return (one way or roundtrip)?	¿Ida, o ida y vuelta?

Do I have to change trains?	¿Tengo que transbordar?
What platform does the train for... leave from?	¿De qué andén sale el tren para...?
Where's the nearest underground (subway) station?	¿Dónde está la próxima estación de Metro?
Where's the bus station, please?	¿Dónde está la estación de autobuses, por favor?
When's the first bus to...?	¿Cuándo sale el primer autobús para...?
Please let me off at the next stop.	Por favor, deténgase en la próxima parada.

Relaxing | Diversiones

What's on at the cinema (movies)?	¿Qué dan en el cine?
What time does the film begin?	¿A qué hora empieza la película?
Are there any tickets for tonight?	¿Quedan entradas para esta noche?
Where can we go dancing?	¿Dónde se puede ir a bailar?

Meeting people | Presentaciones – Citas

How do you do.	Buenos días Señora/ Señorita/Señor.
How are you?	¿Cómo está usted?
Very well, thank you. And you?	Muy bien, gracias. ¿Y usted?
May I introduce...?	¿Me permite presentarle a...?
My name is...	Me llamo...
I'm very pleased to meet you.	Tanto gusto (en conocerle).
How long have you been here?	¿Cuánto tiempo lleva usted aquí?
It was nice meeting you.	Ha sido un placer conocerle.
Do you mind if I smoke?	¿Le molesta si fumo?
Do you have a light, please?	¿Tiene usted fuego, por favor?
May I get you a drink?	¿Me permite invitarle a una bebida (una copa)?
May I invite you for dinner tonight?	¿Me permite invitarle a cenar esta noche?
Where shall we meet?	¿Dónde quedamos citados?

Shops, stores and services

Where's the nearest bank, please?	Dónde está el banco más cercano, por favor?
Where can I cash some travellers' cheques?	¿Dónde puedo cambiar unos cheques de viaje?
Can you give me some small change, please?	¿Puede usted darme algún dinero suelto, por favor?
Where's the nearest chemist's (pharmacy)?	¿Dónde está la farmacia más cercana?
How do I get there?	¿Cómo podría ir hasta allí?
Is it within walking distance?	¿Se puede ir andando?
Can you help me, please?	¿Puede usted atenderme, por favor?
How much is this? And that?	¿Cuánto cuesta éste? ¿Y ése?
It's not quite what I want.	No es exactamente lo que quiero.
I like it.	Me gusta.
Can you recommend something for sunburn?	¿Podría recomendarme algo para las quemaduras del sol?
I'd like a haircut, please.	Quisiera cortarme el pelo, por favor.
I'd like a manicure, please.	Quisiera una manicura, por favor.

Comercios y servicios

Street directions

Can you show me on the map where I am?	¿Puede enseñarme en el mapa dónde estoy?
You are on the wrong road.	Está usted equivocado de camino.
Go/Walk straight ahead.	Siga todo derecho.
It's on the left/on the right.	Está a la izquierda/a la derecha.

Direcciones

Emergencies

Call a doctor quickly.	Llame a un médico rápidamente.
Call an ambulance.	Llame a una ambulancia.
Please call the police.	Llame a la policía, por favor.

Urgencias

inglés-español
---
english-spanish

Abreviaturas

adj	adjetivo	*n*	nombre
adv	adverbio		(sustantivo)
Am	inglés americano	*nAm*	nombre
art	artículo		(inglés americano)
conj	conjunción	*num*	numeral
f	femenino	*p*	tiempo pasado
fMe	femenino (mexicano)	*pl*	plural
fpl	femenino plural	*plAm*	plural (inglés americano)
fplMe	femenino plural	*pp*	participio pasado
	(mexicano)	*pr*	tiempo presente
m	masculino	*pref*	prefijo
Me	mexicano	*prep*	preposición
mMe	masculino (mexicano)	*pron*	pronombre
mpl	masculino plural	*v*	verbo
mplMe	masculino plural	*vAm*	verbo (inglés americano)
	(mexicano)	*vMe*	verbo (mexicano)

3

Introducción

Este diccionario ha sido concebido para resolver de la mejor manera posible sus problemas prácticos de lenguaje. Se han suprimido las informaciones lingüísticas innecesarias. Los vocablos se suceden en un estricto orden alfabético, sin tener en cuenta si la palabra es simple o compuesta, o si se trata de una expresión formada por dos o más términos separados. Como única excepción, algunas expresiones idiomáticas están colocadas en orden alfabético, considerando para ello la palabra más característica. Cuando un término principal va seguido de otras palabras, expresiones o locuciones, éstas se hallan anotadas también en orden alfabético.

Cada palabra va seguida de una transcripción fonética (véase la guía de pronunciación). Después de la transcripción fonética se encuentra una indicación de la parte de la oración a la que pertenece el vocablo. Cuando una palabra puede desempeñar distintos oficios en la oración, las diferentes traducciones se dan una a continuación de la otra, precedidas de la indicación correspondiente.

Se indica el plural de los nombres cuando son irregulares y en algunos otros casos dudosos.

Cuando haya que repetir una palabra para formar el plural irregular o en las series de palabras se usa la tilde (~) para representar el vocablo principal.

En los plurales irregulares de las palabras compuestas sólo se escribe la parte que cambia, mientras que la parte invariable se representa por un guión (-).

Un asterisco (*) colocado antes de un verbo indica que dicho verbo es irregular. Para más detalles puede consultar la lista de los verbos irregulares.

Las palabras de este diccionario están escritas en su forma inglesa. La forma y significado americanos están señalados como tales (véase la lista de abreviaturas empleadas en el texto).

Guía de pronunciación

Cada vocablo principal de esta parte del diccionario va acompañado de una transcripción fonética destinada a indicar la pronunciación. Esta representación fonética debe leerse como si se tratara del idioma español hablado en Castilla. A continuación figuran tan solo las letras y los símbolos ambiguos o particularmente difíciles de comprender.

Cada sílaba está separada por un guión y la que lleva el acento está impresa en letra *bastardilla*.

Por supuesto, los sonidos de dos lenguas rara vez coinciden exactamente, pero siguiendo con atención nuestras explicaciones, el lector de habla española llegará a pronunciar las palabras extranjeras de manera que pueda ser comprendido. A fin de facilitar su tarea, algunas veces nuestras transcripciones simplifican ligeramente el sistema fonético del idioma, sin dejar por ello de reflejar·las diferencias de sonido esenciales.

Consonantes

b	como en bueno
d	como en día
ð	como d en ruido
dʒ	como la ll argentina, precedida por una d
gh	como g en gato
h	sonido que es una espiración suave
ng	como n en blanco
r	ponga la lengua en la misma posición que para pronunciar ʒ (véase más abajo), luego abra ligeramente la boca y baje la lengua
s	sonido siempre suave y sonoro como en mismo
ʃ	como ch en mucho, pero sin la t inicial que compone el sonido
v	más o menos como en lava; sonido que se obtiene colocando los dientes incisivos superiores sobre el labio inferior y expulsando suavemente el aire
ʒ	como la ll argentina

Vocales y diptongos

æ sonido que combina el de la **a** en caso con el de la **e** en saber

ê como **e** en saber

o como **o** en por

ö vocal neutra; sonido parecido al de la **a** española, pero con los labios extendidos

1) Las vocales largas están impresas a doble.

2) Las letras situadas más arriba que las otras (por ej.: **ᵘi, uö**) deben pronunciarse con menor intensidad y rápidamente.

3) Algunas palabras inglesas toman del francés las vocales nasales, que están indicadas con un símbolo de vocal mas **ng** (por ej.: **ang**). Este signo **ng** *no* se debe pronunciar y sólo sirve para indicar la nasalidad de la vocal precedente. Las vocales nasales se pronuncian con la boca y la nariz simultáneamente.

Pronunciación americana

Nuestra transcripción representa la pronunciación de Gran Bretaña. Aunque existen notables variaciones regionales en la lengua americana, ésta presenta en general algunas diferencias importantes respecto al inglés de Gran Bretaña.

He aquí algunos ejemplos:

1) La **r**, delante de una consonante o al final de una palabra, siempre se pronuncia, lo cual es contrario a la costumbre inglesa.

2) En muchas palabras (por ej.: *ask, castle, laugh,* etc.) la **aa** se transforma en **ææ**.

3) El sonido inglés **o** se pronuncia **a** o también **oo**.

4) En palabras como *duty, tune, new,* etc., el sonido **y** se omite a menudo antes de **uu**.

5) Por último, el acento tónico de algunas palabras puede variar considerablemente.

A

a (ei,ö) *art* (an) un *art*
abbey (*æ*-bi) *n* abadía *f*
abbreviation (ö-brii-vi-*ei*-∫ön) *n* abreviatura *f*
aberration (æ-bö-*rei*-∫ön) *n* anomalía *f*
ability (ö-*bi*-lö-ti) *n* habilidad *f*
able (*ei*-böl) *adj* capaz; hábil; *be ~ to* *ser capaz de; *saber, *poder
abnormal (æb-*noo*-möl) *adj* anormal
aboard (ö-*bood*) *adv* a bordo
abolish (ö-*bo*-li∫) *v* abolir
abortion (ö-*boo*-∫ön) *n* aborto *m*
about (ö-*baut*) *prep* acerca de; respecto a; alrededor de; *adv* hacia, aproximadamente; en torno
above (ö-*bav*) *prep* encima de; *adv* encima
abroad (ö-*brood*) *adv* en el extranjero
abscess (æb-ssèss) *n* absceso *m*
absence (æb-ssönss) *n* ausencia *f*
absent (æb-ssönt) *adj* ausente
absolutely (æh-ssö-luut-li) *adv* absolutamente
abstain from (öb-*sstein*) *abstenerse de
abstract (æb-sstrækt) *adj* abstracto
absurd (öb-*ssööd*) *adj* absurdo
abundance (ö-*ban*-dönss) *n* abundancia *f*
abundant (ö-*ban*-dönt) *adj* abundante
abuse (ö-*byuuss*) *n* abuso *m*
abyss (ö-*biss*) *n* abismo *m*
academy (ö-*kæ*-dö-mi) *n* academia *f*
accelerate (ök-*ssê*-lo-reit) *v* acelerar
accelerator (ök-*ssê*-lö-rei-tö) *n* acelerador *m*
accent (æk-ssönt) *n* acento *m*
accept (ök-*ssêpt*) *v* aceptar
access (æk-ssèss) *n* acceso *m*
accessary (ök-*ssê*-ssö-ri) *n* cómplice *m*
accessible (ök-*ssê*-ssö-böl) *adj* accesible
accessories (ök-*ssê*-ssö-ris) *pl* accesorios *mpl*
accident (æk-ssi-dönt) *n* accidente *m*
accidental (æk-ssi-*dên*-töl) *adj* accidental
accommodate (ö-*ko*-mö-deit) *v* acomodar
accommodation (ö-ko-mö-*dei*-∫ön) *n* acomodación *f*, alojamiento *m*
accompany (ö-*kam*-pö-ni) *v* acompañar
accomplish (ö-*kam*-pli∫) *v* terminar; cumplir
in accordance with (in ö-*koo*-dönss ⁱð) con arreglo a
according to (ö-*koo*-ding tuu) según; conforme a
account (ö-*kaunt*) *n* cuenta *f*; narra-

ción *f*; ~ **for** explicar; **on** ~ **of** a causa de
accountable (ö-*kaun*-tö-böl) *adj* explicable
accurate (*æ*-kyu-röt) *adj* exacto
accuse (ö-*kyuus*) *v* acusar
accused (ö-*kyuusd*) *n* acusado *m*
accustom (ö-*ka*-sstöm) *v* acostumbrar; **accustomed** acostumbrado
ache (eik) *v* *doler; *n* dolor *m*
achieve (ö-*chiiv*) *v* alcanzar; lograr
achievement (ö-*chiiv*-mönt) *n* realización *f*
acid (*æ*-ssid) *n* ácido *m*
acknowledge (ök-*no*-lidʒ) *v* *reconocer; admitir; confirmar
acne (*æk*-ni) *n* acné *m*
acorn (*ei*-koon) *n* bellota *f*
acquaintance (ö-*k*ᵘ*ein*-tönss) *n* conocido *m*
acquire (ö-*k*ᵘ*ai*ᵒ) *v* *adquirir
acquisition (*æ*-kᵘi-*si*-ʃön) *n* adquisición *f*
acquittal (ö-*k*ᵘ*i*-töl) *n* absolución *f*
across (ö-*kross*) *prep* a través de; al otro lado de; *adv* al otro lado
act (*æk*t) *n* acto *m*; número *m*; *v* actuar, *hacer; comportarse
action (*æk*-ʃön) *n* acción *f*
active (*æk*-tiv) *adj* activo; vivaz
activity (*æk*-*ti*-vö-ti) *n* actividad *f*
actor (*æk*-tö) *n* actor *m*
actress (*æk*-triss) *n* actriz *f*
actual (*æk*-chu-öl) *adj* verdadero
actually (*æk*-chu-ö-li) *adv* en realidad
acute (ö-*kyuut*) *adj* agudo
adapt (ö-*dæpt*) *v* adaptar
add (*æd*) *v* sumar, adicionar; añadir
adding-machine (*æ*-ding-mö-ʃiin) *n* calculadora *f*
addition (ö-*di*-ʃön) *n* adición *f*
additional (ö-*di*-ʃö-nöl) *adj* adicional; accesorio
address (ö-*drêss*) *n* dirección *f*; *v*

destinar; dirigirse a
addressee (*æ*-drê-*ssii*) *n* destinatario *m*
adequate (*æ*-di-kᵘöt) *adj* adecuado; conveniente
adjective (*æ*-dʒik-tiv) *n* adjetivo *m*
adjourn (ö-*dʒöön*) *v* aplazar
adjust (ö-*dʒasst*) *v* ajustar
administer (öd-*mi*-ni-sstö) *v* administrar
administration (öd-mi-ni-*sstrei*-ʃön) *n* administración *f*; gestión *f*
administrative (öd-*mi*-ni-sströ-tiv) *adj* gerencial; administrativo; ~ **law** derecho administrativo
admiral (*æd*-mö-röl) *n* almirante *m*
admiration (*æd*-mö-*rei*-ʃön) *n* admiración *f*
admire (öd-*mai*ᵒ) *v* admirar
admission (öd-*mi*-ʃön) *n* entrada *f*; admisión *f*
admit (öd-*mit*) *v* admitir; *reconocer
admittance (öd-*mi*-tönss) *n* admisión *f*; **no** ~ prohibida la entrada
adopt (ö-*dopt*) *v* adoptar
adorable (ö-*doo*-rö-böl) *adj* adorable
adult (*æ*-dalt) *n* adulto *m*; *adj* adulto
advance (öd-*vaanss*) *n* adelanto *m*; anticipo *m*; *v* avanzar; anticipar; **in** ~ por adelantado
advanced (öd-*vaansst*) *adj* avanzado
advantage (öd-*vaan*-tidʒ) *n* ventaja *f*
advantageous (*æd*-vön-*tei*-dʒöss) *adj* ventajoso
adventure (öd-*vên*-chö) *n* aventura *f*
adverb (*æd*-vööb) *n* adverbio *m*
advertisement (öd-*vöö*-tiss-mönt) *n* anuncio *m*
advertising (*æd*-vö-tai-sing) *n* publicidad *f*
advice (öd-*vaiss*) *n* consejo *m*
advise (öd-*vais*) *v* aconsejar
advocate (*æd*-vö-köt) *n* abogado *m*
aerial (*ê*ᵒ-ri-öl) *n* antena *f*

aeroplane (*ê⁰*-rö-plein) *n* avión *m*
affair (ö-*fê⁰*) *n* asunto *m*; amorío *m*
affect (ö-*fêkt*) *v* afectar
affected (ö-*fêk*-tid) *adj* afectado
affection (ö-*fêk*-ʃön) *n* afección *f*; cariño *m*
affectionate (ö-*fêk*-ʃö-nit) *adj* cariñoso
affiliated (ö-*fi*-li-ei-tid) *adj* afiliado
affirmative (ö-*föö*-mö-tiv) *adj* afirmativo
affliction (ü-*flik*-ʃön) *n* sufrimiento *m*
afford (ö-*food*) *v* permitirse
afraid (ö-*freid*) *adj* angustioso, asustado; *be ~ *tener miedo
Africa (*æ*-fri-kö) África *f*
African (*æ*-fri-kön) *adj* africano
after (*aaf*-tö) *prep* después de; detrás de; *conj* después de que
afternoon (aaf-tö-*nuun*) *n* tarde *f*
afterwards (*aaf*-tö-ᵘöds) *adv* después
again (ö-*ghên*) *adv* otra vez; de nuevo; *~ and again* repetidamente
against (ö-*ghênsst*) *prep* contra
age (eidʒ) *n* edad *f*; vejez *f*; *of ~* mayor de edad; *under ~* menor de edad
aged (*ei*-dʒid) *adj* viejo; anciano
agency (*ei*-dʒön-ssi) *n* agencia *f*; sección *f*
agenda (ö *dʒên*-dö) *n* orden del día
agent (*ei*-dʒönt) *n* agente *m*, representante *m*
aggressive (ö-*ghrê*-ssiv) *adj* agresivo
ago (ö-*ghou*) *adv* hace
agrarian (ö-*ghrêᵘ*-ri-on) *adj* agrario, agrícola
agree (ö-*ghrii*) *v* *convenir, *concordar; *consentir; *acordar
agreeable (ö-*ghrii*-ö-böl) *adj* agradable
agreement (ö-*ghrii*-mönt) *n* contrato *m*; acuerdo *m*; conformidad *f*
agriculture (*æ*-ghri-kal-chö) *n* agricul-

tura *f*
ahead (ö-*hêd*) *adv* adelante; *~ of* delante de; *go --* continuar; *straight ~* todo seguido
aid (eid) *n* socorro *m*; *v* asistir, ayudar
ailment (*eil*-mönt) *n* enfermedad *f*
aim (eim) *n* fin *m*; *~ at* apuntar; aspirar a
air (ê⁰) *n* aire *m*; *v* airear
air-conditioning (*ê⁰*-kön-di-ʃö-ning) *n* aire acondicionado; **air-conditioned** *adj* climatizado
aircraft (*ê⁰*-kraaft) *n* (pl ~) avión *m*
airfield (*ê⁰*-fiild) *n* campo de aviación
air-filter (*ê⁰*-fil-tö) *n* filtro de aire
airline (*ê⁰*-lain) *n* aerolínea *f*
airmail (*ê⁰*-meil) *n* correo aéreo
airplane (*ê⁰*-plein) *nAm* avión *m*
airport (*ê⁰*-poot) *n* aeropuerto *m*
air-sickness (*ê⁰*-ssik-nöss) *n* mal de las alturas
airtight (*ê⁰*-tait) *adj* hermético
airy (*ê⁰*-ri) *adj* airoso
aisle (ail) *n* nave lateral; pasillo *m*
alarm (ö-*laam*) *n* alarma *f*; *v* alarmar
alarm-clock (ö-*laam*-klok) *n* despertador *m*
album (*æl*-böm) *n* álbum *m*
alcohol (*æl*-kö-hol) *n* alcohol *m*
alcoholic (æl-kö-*ho*-lik) *adj* alcohólico
ale (eil) *n* cerveza *f*
algebra (*æl*-dʒi-brö) *n* álgebra *f*
Algeria (æl-*dʒiᵒ*-ri-ö) Argelia *f*
Algerian (æl-*dʒiᵒ*-ri-ön) *adj* argelino
alien (*ei*-li-ön) *n* extranjero *m*; *adj* extranjero
alike (ö-*laik*) *adj* igual, parecido; *adv* igualmente
alimony (*æ*-li-mö-ni) *n* pensión alimenticia
alive (ö-*laiv*) *adj* en vida, vivo
all (ool) *adj* todo; *~ in* todo incluido; *~ right!* ¡bien!; *at ~* en modo algu-

no

allergy (æ-lö-dʒi) *n* alergia *f*
alley (æ-li) *n* callejón *m*
alliance (ö-*lai*-önss) *n* alianza *f*
Allies (æ-lais) *pl* Aliados *mpl*
allot (ö-*lot*) *v* asignar
allow (ö-*lau*) *v* permitir, autorizar; ~ to autorizar a; *be allowed *estar autorizado
allowance (ö-*lau*-önss) *n* asignación *f*
all-round (ool-*raund*) *adj* polifacético
almanac (*ool*-mö-næk) *n* almanaque *m*
almond (*aa*-mönd) *n* almendra *f*
almost (*ool*-mousst) *adv* casi; cerca de
alone (ö-*loun*) *adv* sólo
along (ö-*long*) *prep* a lo largo de
aloud (ö-*laud*) *adv* en voz alta
alphabet (æl-fö-bêt) *n* abecedario *m*
already (ool-*rê*-di) *adv* ya
also (*ool*-ssou) *adv* también; asimismo
altar (*ool*-tö) *n* altar *m*
alter (*ool*-tö) *v* cambiar, alterar
alteration (ool-tö-*rei*-fön) *n* cambio *m*, alteración *f*
alternate (ool-*töö*-nöt) *adj* alternativo
alternative (ool-*töö*-nö-tiv) *n* alternativa *f*
although (ool-*ðou*) *conj* aunque
altitude (æl-ti-tyuud) *n* altitud *f*
alto (æl-tou) *n* (pl ~s) contralto *m*
altogether (ool-tö-*ghê*-ðö) *adv* totalmente; en total
always (*ool*-ᵘeis) *adv* siempre
am (æm) *v* (pr be)
amaze (ö-*meis*) *v* extrañar, asombrar
amazement (ö-*meis*-mönt) *n* asombro *m*
ambassador (æm-*bæ*-ssö-dö) *n* embajador *m*
amber (*æm*-bö) *n* ámbar *m*
ambiguous (æm-*bi*-ghyu-öss) *adj* ambiguo; equívoco

ambitious (æm-*bi*-föss) *adj* ambicioso
ambulance (*æm*-byu-lönss) *n* ambulancia *f*
ambush (*æm*-buʃ) *n* emboscada *f*
America (ö-*mê*-ri-kö) América *f*
American (ö-*mê*-ri-kön) *adj* americano
amethyst (æ-mi-zisst) *n* amatista *f*
amid (ö-*mid*) *prep* entre; en medio de
ammonia (ö-*mou*-ni-ö) *n* amoníaco *m*
amnesty (*æm*-ni-ssti) *n* amnistía *f*
among (ö-*mang*) *prep* entre; ~ **other things** entre otras cosas
amount (ö-*maunt*) *n* cantidad *f*; suma *f*; ~ **to** sumar
amuse (ö-*myuus*) *v* *divertir, *entretener
amusement (ö-*myuus*-mönt) *n* distracción *f*, entretenimiento *m*
amusing (ö-*myuu*-sing) *adj* divertido
anaemia (ö-*nii*-mi-ö) *n* anemia *f*
anaesthesia (æ-niss-*zii*-si-ö) *n* anestesia *f*
anaesthetic (æ-niss-*zê*-tik) *n* anestésico *m*
analyse (æ-nö-lais) *v* analizar
analysis (ö-*næ*-lö-ssiss) *n* (pl -ses) análisis *m*
analyst (æ-nö-lisst) *n* analista *m*; psicoanalista *m*
anarchy (æ-nö-ki) *n* anarquía *f*
anatomy (ö-*næ*-tö-mi) *n* anatomía *f*
ancestor (æn-ssê-sstö) *n* antepasado *m*
anchor (*æng*-kö) *n* ancla *f*
anchovy (æn-chö-vi) *n* anchoa *f*
ancient (ein-fönt) *adj* viejo, antiguo; anticuado
and (ænd, önd) *conj* y
angel (ein-dʒöl) *n* ángel *m*
anger (æng-ghö) *n* cólera *f*, enojo *m*; furor *m*
angle (æng-ghöl) *v* pescar con caña; *n* ángulo *m*

angry (æng-ghri) *adj* enfadado, enojado

animal (æ-ni-möl) *n* animal *m*

ankle (æng-köl) *n* tobillo *m*

annex¹ (æ-nêkss) *n* anexo *m*

annex² (ö-nêkss) *v* anexar

anniversary (æ-ni-vöö-ssö-ri) *n* aniversario *m*

announce (ö-naunss) *v* anunciar

announcement (ö-naunss-mönt) *n* anuncio *m*

annoy (ö-noi) *v* irritar, fastidiar; aburrir

annoyance (ö-noi-önss) *n* aburrimiento *m*

annoying (ö-noi-ing) *adj* irritante, importuno

annual (æ-nyu-öl) *adj* anual; *n* anuario *m*

per annum (pör æ-nöm) al año

anonymous (ö-no-ni-möss) *adj* anónimo

another (ö-na-ðö) *adj* otro más; otro

answer (aan-ssö) *v* responder a; *n* respuesta *f*

ant (ænt) *n* hormiga *f*

anthology (æn-zo-lö-dʒi) *n* antología *f*

antibiotic (æn-ti-bai-o-tik) *n* antibiótico *m*

anticipate (æn-ti-ssi peit) *v* *prever; *prevenir

antifreeze (æn-ti-friis) *n* anticongelante *m*

antipathy (æn-ti-pö-zi) *n* antipatía *f*

antique (æn-tiik) *adj* antiguo; *n* antigualla *f*; ~ **dealer** anticuario *m*

antiquity (æn-ti-kʰö-ti) *n* Antigüedad *f*; **antiquities** *pl* antigüedades *fpl*

antiseptic (æn-ti-ssêp-tik) *n* antiséptico *m*

antlers (ænt-lös) *pl* cornamenta *f*

anxiety (æng-sai-ö-ti) *n* preocupación *f*

anxious (ængk-ʃöss) *adj* ansioso; preocupado

any (ê-ni) *adj* alguno

anybody (ê-ni-bo-di) *pron* cualquiera

anyhow (ê-ni-hau) *adv* de cualquier modo

anyone (ê-ni-ᵘan) *pron* cualquiera

anything (ê-ni-zing) *pron* cualquier cosa

anyway (ê-ni-ᵘei) *adv* en todo caso

anywhere (ê-ni-ᵘêᵒ) *adv* en donde sea; dondequiera

apart (ö-paat) *adv* por separado, separadamente; ~ **from** prescindiendo de

apartment (ö-paat-mönt) *nAm* apartamento *m*; piso *m*; ~ **house** *Am* casa de pisos

aperitif (ö-pê-rö-tiv) *n* aperitivo *m*

apologize (ö-po-lö-dʒais) *v* disculparse

apology (ö-po-lö-dʒi) *n* excusa *f*, disculpa *f*

apparatus (æ-pö-rei-töss) *n* aparato *m*

apparent (ö-pæ-rönt) *adj* aparente; obvio

apparently (o-pæ-rönt-li) *adv* por lo visto; evidentemente

apparition (æ-pö-ri-ʃön) *n* aparición *f*

appeal (ö-piil) *n* apelación *f*

appear (ö-piᵒ) *v* *parecer; *salir; *aparecer

appearance (ö-piᵒ-rönss) *n* apariencia *f*; aspecto *m*; entrada *f*

appendicitis (ö-pên-di-ssai-tiss) *n* apendicitis *f*

appendix (ö-pên-dikss) *n* (pl -dices, -dixes) apéndice *m*

appetite (æ-pö-tait) *n* apetito *m*

appetizer (æ-pö-tai-sö) *n* tapa *f*

appetizing (æ-pö-tai-sing) *adj* apetitoso

applause (ö-ploos) *n* aplauso *m*

apple (æ-pöl) *n* manzana *f*

appliance (ö-*plai*-önss) n aparato m

application (æ-pli-*kei*-ʃön) n aplicación f; demanda f; solicitud f

apply (ö-*plai*) v aplicar; solicitar un puesto; aplicarse a

appoint (ö-*point*) v designar, nombrar

appointment (ö-*point*-mönt) n cita f; nombramiento m

appreciate (ö-*prii*-ʃi-eit) v valuar; apreciar

appreciation (ö-prii-ʃi-*ei*-ʃön) n aprecio m

approach (ö-*prouch*) v acercarse; n enfoque m; acceso m

appropriate (ö-*prou*-pri-öt) adj justo, apropiado, adecuado

approval (ö-*pruu*-völ) n aprobación f; consentimiento m, acuerdo m; on ~ a prueba

approve (ö-*pruuv*) v *aprobar; ~ of *estar de acuerdo con

approximate (ö-*prok*-ssi-möt) adj aproximado

approximately (ö-*prok*-ssi-möt-li) adv aproximadamente

apricot (*ei*-pri-kot) n albaricoque m; chabacano mMe

April (*ei*-pröl) abril

apron (*ei*-prön) n delantal m

Arab (æ-röb) adj árabe

arbitrary (*aa*-bi-trö-ri) adj arbitrario

arcade (aa-*keid*) n pórtico m, arcada f

arch (aach) n arco m; bóveda f

archaeologist (aa-ki-o-lö-dʒisst) n arqueólogo m

archaeology (aa-ki-o-lö-dʒi) n arqueología f

archbishop (aach-*bi*-ʃöp) n arzobispo m

arched (aacht) adj arqueado

architect (*aa*-ki-têkt) n arquitecto m

architecture (*aa*-ki-têk-chö) n arquitectura f

archives (*aa*-kaivs) pl archivo m

are (aa) v (pr be)

area (*ê*ᵒ-ri-ö) n región f; zona f; superficie f; ~ code indicativo m

Argentina (aa-dʒön-*tii*-nö) Argentina f

Argentinian (aa-dʒön-*ti*-ni-ön) adj argentino

argue (*aa*-ghyuu) v argumentar, discutir; disputar

argument (*aa*-ghyu-mönt) n argumento m; discusión f; disputa f

arid (æ-rid) adj árido

*arise (ö-*rais*) v surgir

arithmetic (ö-*riz*-mö-tik) n aritmética f

arm (aam) n brazo m; arma f; v armar

armchair (*aam*-chêᵒ) n butaca f, sillón m

armed (aamd) adj armado; ~ forces fuerzas armadas

armour (*aa*-mö) n armadura f

army (*aa*-mi) n ejército m

aroma (ö-*rou*-mö) n aroma m

around (ö-*raund*) prep alrededor de, en torno de; adv en torno

arrange (ö-*reindʒ*) v clasificar, ordenar; organizar

arrangement (ö-*reindʒ*-mönt) n arreglo m

arrest (ö-*rêsst*) v arrestar; n arresto m

arrival (ö-*rai*-völ) n llegada f

arrive (ö-*raiv*) v llegar

arrow (æ-rou) n flecha f

art (aat) n arte m/f; habilidad f; ~ collection colección de arte; ~ exhibition exposición de arte; ~ gallery galería de arte; ~ history historia del arte; arts and crafts artes industriales; ~ school academia de bellas artes

artery (*aa*-tö-ri) n arteria f

artichoke (*aa*-ti-chouk) n alcachofa f

article (*aa*-ti-köl) n artículo m

artifice (aa-ti-fiss) n artificio m
artificial (aa-ti-fi-föl) adj artificial
artist (aa-tisst) n artista m/f
artistic (aa-ti-sstik) adj artístico
as (æs) conj como; tanto; que; ya
  que, porque; ~ from a partir de; ~
  if como si
asbestos (æs-bé-sstoss) n asbesto m
ascend (ö-ssénd) v subir; escalar
ascent (ö-ssént) n subida f
ascertain (æ-ssö-tein) v *comprobar;
  asegurarse de
ash (æf) n ceniza f
ashamed (ö-feimd) adj avergonzado;
  *be ~ *avergonzarse
ashore (ö-foo) adv en tierra
ashtray (æf-trei) n cenicero m
Asia (ei-fö) Asia f
Asian (ei-fön) adj asiático
aside (ö-ssaid) adv aparte
ask (aassk) v preguntar; *rogar; invitar
asleep (ö-ssliip) adj dormido
asparagus (ö-sspæ-rö-ghöss) n espárrago m
aspect (æ-sspêkt) n aspecto m
asphalt (æss-fælt) n asfalto m
aspire (ö-sspai⁰) v aspirar
aspirin (æ-sspö-rin) n aspirina f
ass (œss) n burro m
assassination (ö-ssæ-ssi-nei-fön) n
  asesinato m
assault (ö-ssoolt) v atacar; violar
assemble (ö-ssêm-böl) v reunir; montar
assembly (ö-ssêm-blı) n reunión f,
  asamblea f
assignment (ö-ssain-mönt) n encargo
  m
assign to (ö-ssain) asignar a; *atribuir a
assist (ö-ssisst) v asistir
assistance (ö-ssi-sstönss) n auxilio
  m; apoyo m, asistencia f

assistant (ö-ssi-sstönt) n asistente m
associate¹ (ö-ssou-fi-öt) n compañero
  m, asociado m; aliado m; socio m
associate² (ö-ssou-fi-eit) v asociar; ~
  with frecuentar
association (ö-ssou-ssi-ei-fön) n asociación f
assort (ö-ssoot) v clasificar
assortment (ö-ssoot-mönt) n surtido
  m
assume (ö-ssyuum) v *suponer, presumir
assure (ö-fu⁰) v asegurar
asthma (æss-mö) n asma f
astonish (ö-ssto-nif) v asombrar
astonishing (ö-ssto-ni-fing) adj asombroso
astonishment (ö-ssto-nif-mönt) n sorpresa f
astronomy (ö-sstro-nö-mi) n astronomía f
asylum (ö-ssai-löm) n asilo m
at (æt) prep en, a; hacia
ate (êt) v (p eat)
atheist (ei-zi-isst) n ateo m
athlete (æz-liit) n atleta m
athletics (æz-lê-tikss) pl atletismo m
Atlantic (öt-læn-tik) Atlántico m
atmosphere (æt-möss-fi⁰) n atmósfera f; esfera f, ambiente m
atom (æ-töm) n átomo m
atomic (ö-to-mik) adj atómico
atomizer (æ-tö-mai-sö) n vaporizador
  m; aerosol m, pulverizador m
attach (ö-tæch) v prender; fijar; juntar; attached to encariñado con
attack (o-tæk) v atacar; n ataque m
attain (ö-tein) v llegar a
attainable (ö-tei-nö-böl) adj factible;
  alcanzable
attempt (ö-têmpt) v intentar; *probar; n tentativa f
attend (ö-tênd) v asistir a; ~ on *servir; ~ to cuidar de, *atender a;

prestar atención a
attendance (ö-*tên*-dönss) *n* asistencia *f*
attendant (ö-*tên*-dönt) *n* guardián *m*
attention (ö-*tên*-ʃön) *n* atención *f*; ***pay ~** prestar atención
attentive (ö-*tên*-tiv) *adj* atento
attic (*æ*-tik) *n* buhardilla *f*
attitude (*æ*-ti-tyuud) *n* actitud *f*
attorney (ö-*töö*-ni) *n* abogado *m*
attract (ö-*trækt*) *v* *atraer
attraction (ö-*træk*-ʃön) *n* atracción *f*
attractive (ö-*træk*-tiv) *adj* atractivo
auburn (*oo*-bön) *adj* castaño
auction (*ook*-ʃön) *n* subasta *f*
audible (*oo*-di-böl) *adj* audible
audience (*oo*-di-önss) *n* auditorio *m*
auditor (*oo*-di-tö) *n* oyente *m*
auditorium (oo-di-*too*-ri-öm) *n* aula *f*
August (*oo*-ghösst) agosto
aunt (aant) *n* tía *f*
Australia (o-*sstrei*-li-ö) Australia *f*
Australian (o-*sstrei*-li-ön) *adj* australiano
Austria (*o*-sstri-ö) Austria *f*
Austrian (*o*-sstri-ön) *adj* austriaco
authentic (oo-*zên*-tik) *adj* auténtico
author (*oo*-zö) *n* autor *m*
authoritarian (oo-zo-ri-*tê*ö-ri-ön) *adj* autoritario
authority (oo-*zo*-rö-ti) *n* autoridad *f*; poder *m*
authorization (oo-zö-rai-*sei*-ʃön) *n* autorización *f*; permiso *m*
automatic (oo-tö-*mæ*-tik) *adj* automático
automation (oo-tö-*mei*-ʃön) *n* automatización *f*
automobile (*oo*-tö-mö-biil) *n* automóvil *m*; **~ club** automóvil club
autonomous (oo-*to*-nö-möss) *adj* autónomo
autopsy (*oo*-to-pssi) *n* autopsia *f*
autumn (*oo*-töm) *n* otoño *m*

available (ö-*vei*-lö-böl) *adj* adquirible, obtenible, disponible
avalanche (*æ*-vö-laanʃ) *n* avalancha *f*
avaricious (æ-vö-*ri*-ʃöss) *adj* avaro
avenue (*æ*-vö-nyuu) *n* avenida *f*
average (*æ*-vö-ridʒ) *adj* promedio; *n* promedio *m*; **on the ~** en promedio
averse (ö-*vööss*) *adj* opuesto
aversion (ö-*vöö*-ʃön) *n* aversión *f*
avert (ö-*vööt*) *v* desviar
avoid (ö-*void*) *v* evitar
await (ö-*ᵘeit*) *v* esperar
awake (ö-*ᵘeik*) *adj* despierto
*awake (ö-*ᵘeik*) *v* *despertar
award (ö-*ᵘood*) *n* premio *m*; *v* conceder
aware (ö-*ᵘê*ö) *adj* consciente
away (ö-*ᵘei*) *adv* fuera; ***go ~** *irse
awful (*oo*-föl) *adj* terrible, tremendo
awkward (*oo*-kᵘöd) *adj* embarazoso; torpe
awning (*oo*-ning) *n* toldo *m*
axe (ækss) *n* hacha *f*
axle (*æk*-ssöl) *n* eje *m*

B

baby (*bei*-bi) *n* bebé *m*; **~ carriage** *Am* cochecillo *m*
babysitter (*bei*-bi-ssi-tö) *n* babysitter *m*
bachelor (*bæ*-chö-lö) *n* soltero *m*
back (bæk) *n* espalda *f*; *adv* atrás; ***go ~** regresar
backache (*bæ*-keik) *n* dolor de espalda
backbone (*bæk*-boun) *n* espina dorsal
background (*bæk*-ghraund) *n* fondo *m*; antecedentes *mpl*
backwards (*bæk*-ᵘöds) *adv* hacia atrás

bacon (*bei*-kön) *n* tocino *m*

bacterium (bæk-*tii*-ri-öm) *n* (pl -ria) bacteria *f*

bad (bæd) *adj* malo; grave; travieso

bag (bægh) *n* bolsa *f*; bolso *m*, carte-ra *f*; maleta *f*

baggage (*bæ*-ghidʒ) *n* equipaje *m*; **hand** ~ *Am* equipaje de mano

bail (beil) *n* fianza *f*

bailiff (*bei*-lif) *n* ujier *m*

bait (beit) *n* cebo *m*

bake (beik) *v* hornear

baker (*bei*-kö) *n* panadero *m*

bakery (*bei*-kö-ri) *n* panadería *f*

balance (*bæ*-lönss) *n* equilibrio *m*; balance *m*; saldo *m*

balcony (*bæl*-kö-ni) *n* balcón *m*

bald (boold) *adj* calvo

ball (bool) *n* pelota *f*; baile *m*

ballet (*bæ*-lei) *n* ballet *m*

balloon (bö-*luun*) *n* globo *m*

ballpoint-pen (*bool*-point-pên) *n* bolígrafo *m*

ballroom (*bool* ruum) *n* salón de baile

bamboo (bæm-*buu*) *n* (pl ~s) bambú *m*

banana (bö-*naa*-nö) *n* plátano *m*

band (bænd) *n* orquesta *f*; banda *f*

bandage (*bæn*-didʒ) *n* vendaje *m*

bandit (*bæn*-dit) *n* bandido *m*

bangle (*bæng* ghöl) *n* pulsera *f*

banisters (*bæ*-ni-sstöss) *pl* baranda *f*

bank (bængk) *n* orilla *f*; banco *m*; *v* depositar; ~ **account** cuenta de banco

banknote (*bængk*-nout) *n* valé *m*, billete de banco

bank-rate (*bængk*-reit) *n* descuento bancario

bankrupt (*bængk*-rapt) *adj* en quiebra

banner (*bæ*-nö) *n* bandera *f*

banquet (*bæng*-kᵘit) *n* banquete *m*

banqueting-hall (*bæng*-kᵘi-ting-hool) *n* comedor de gala

baptism (*bæp*-ti-söm) *n* bautismo *m*, bautizo *m*

baptize (bæp-*tais*) *v* bautizar

bar (baa) *n* bar *m*; barra *f*; barrote *m*

barber (*baa*-bö) *n* barbero *m*

bare (bêᵒ) *adj* desnudo; raso

barely (*bêᵒ*-li) *adv* apenas

bargain (*baa*-ghin) *n* ganga *f*; *v* regatear

baritone (*bæ*-ri-toun) *n* barítono *m*

bark (baak) *n* corteza *f*; *v* ladrar

barley (*baa*-li) *n* cebada *f*

barmaid (*baa*-meid) *n* moza de taberna

barman (*baa*-mön) *n* (pl -men) barman *m*

barn (baan) *n* granero *m*

barometer (bö-*ro*-mi-tö) *n* barómetro *m*

baroque (bö-*rok*) *adj* barroco

barracks (*bæ*-rökss) *pl* cuartel *m*

barrel (*bæ* röl) *n* tonel *m*, barril *m*

barrier (*bæ*-ri-ö) *n* barrera *f*

barrister (*bæ*-ri-sstö) *n* abogado *m*

bartender (*baa*-tên-dö) *n* barman *m*

base (beiss) *n* base *f*; fundamento *m*; *v* basar

baseball (*beiss*-bool) *n* béisbol *m*

basement (*beiss*-mönt) *n* sótano *m*

basic (*bei*-ssik) *adj* fundamental

basilica (bö-*si*-li-kö) *n* basílica *f*

basin (*bei*-ssön) *n* tazón *m*, palangana *f*

basis (*bei*-ssiss) *n* (pl bases) fundamento *m*, base *f*

basket (*baa*-sskit) *n* cesta *f*

bass¹ (beiss) *n* bajo *m*

bass² (bæss) *n* (pl ~) perca *f*

bastard (*baa*-sstöd) *n* bastardo *m*; descarado *m*

batch (bæch) *n* carga *f*

bath (baaz) *n* baño *m*; ~ **salts** sales de baño; ~ **towel** toalla de baño

bathe (beið) *v* bañarse
bathing-cap (*bei*-ðing-kæp) *n* gorro de baño
bathing-suit (*bei*-ðing-ssuut) *n* traje de baño
bathing-trunks (*bei*-ðing-trangkss) *n* bañador *m*
bathrobe (*baaz*-roub) *n* bata de baño
bathroom (*baaz*-ruum) *n* cuarto de baño; lavabos *mpl*; baño *mMe*
batter (*bæ*-tö) *n* masa *f*
battery (*bæ*-tö-ri) *n* batería *f*; acumulador *m*
battle (*bæ*-töl) *n* batalla *f*; pelea *f*, combate *m*; *v* combatir
bay (bei) *n* bahía *f*; *v* ladrar
***be** (bii) *v* *estar, *ser
beach (biich) *n* playa *f*; **nudist** ~ playa para nudistas
bead (biid) *n* cuenta *f*; **beads** *pl* collar *m*; rosario *m*
beak (biik) *n* pico *m*
beam (biim) *n* rayo *m*; viga *f*
bean (biin) *n* judía *f*; ejote *mMe*
bear (bëⁿ) *n* oso *m*
***bear** (bëⁿ) *v* llevar; aguantar; soportar
beard (biⁿd) *n* barba *f*
bearer (*bëⁿ*-rö) *n* portador *m*
beast (biisst) *n* animal *m*; ~ **of prey** animal de presa
***beat** (biit) *v* batir, golpear
beautiful (*byuu*-ti-föl) *adj* hermoso
beauty (*byuu*-ti) *n* belleza *f*; ~ **parlour** salón de belleza; ~ **salon** salón de belleza; ~ **treatment** tratamiento de belleza
beaver (*bii*-vö) *n* castor *m*
because (bi-*kos*) *conj* porque; puesto que; ~ **of** a causa de
***become** (bi-*kam*) *v* *hacerse; *sentar bien
bed (bëd) *n* cama *f*; ~ **and board** pensión completa; ~ **and breakfast**

cama y desayuno
bedding (*bê*-ding) *n* ropa de cama
bedroom (*bêd*-ruum) *n* dormitorio *m*
bee (bii) *n* abeja *f*
beech (bii-ch) *n* haya *f*
beef (biif) *n* carne de vaca
beehive (*bii*-haiv) *n* colmena *f*
been (biin) *v* (pp be)
beer (biⁿ) *n* cerveza *f*
beet (biit) *n* remolacha *f*
beetle (*bii*-töl) *n* escarabajo *m*
beetroot (*biit*-ruut) *n* remolacha *f*
before (bi-*foo*) *prep* antes de; delante de; *conj* antes de que; *adv* antes
beg (bêgh) *v* mendigar; suplicar; *pedir
beggar (*bê*-ghö) *n* mendigo *m*
***begin** (bi-*ghin*) *v* *empezar; *comenzar
beginner (bi-*ghi*-nö) *n* principiante *m*
beginning (bi-*ghi*-ning) *n* comienzo *m*
on behalf of (on bi-*haaf* ov) en nombre de; a favor de
behave (bi-*heiv*) *v* comportarse
behaviour (bi-*hei*-vyö) *n* conducta *f*
behind (bi-*haind*) *prep* detrás de; *adv* detrás
beige (beiȝ) *adj* beige
being (*bii*-ing) *n* ser *m*
Belgian (*bêl*-dȝön) *adj* belga
Belgium (*bêl*-dȝöm) Bélgica *f*
belief (bi-*liif*) *n* creencia *f*
believe (bi-*liiv*) *v* *creer
bell (bêl) *n* campana *f*; timbre *m*
bellboy (*bêl*-boi) *n* botones *mpl*
belly (*bê*-li) *n* vientre *m*
belong (bi-*long*) *v* *pertenecer
belongings (bi-*long*-ings) *pl* pertenencias *fpl*
beloved (bi-*lavd*) *adj* querido
below (bi-*lou*) *prep* debajo de; bajo; *adv* debajo
belt (bêlt) *n* cinturón *m*
bench (bênch) *n* banco *m*

bend (bênd) *n* comba *f*, curva *f*

* **bend** (bênd) *v* doblar; ~ **down** bajarse

beneath (bi-*niiz*) *prep* debajo de; *adv* debajo

benefit (*bê*-ni-fit) *n* beneficio *m*; ventaja *f*; *v* aprovechar

bent (bênt) *adj* (pp bend) curvo

beret (*bê*-rei) *n* boina *f*

berry (*bê*-ri) *n* baya *f*

berth (bööz) *n* litera *f*

beside (bi-*ssaid*) *prep* junto a

besides (bi-*ssaids*) *adv* además; por otra parte; *prep* además de

best (bêsst) *adj* óptimo

bet (bêt) *n* apuesta *f*; puesta *f*

* **bet** (bêt) *v* *apostar

betray (bi-*trei*) *v* traicionar

better (*bê*-tö) *adj* mejor

between (bi-*tᵘiin*) *prep* entre

beverage (*bê*-vö-ridʒ) *n* bebida *f*

beware (bi-*ᵘę̂ᵒ*) *v* precaverse, guardarse

bewitch (bi-*ᵘich*) *v* hechizar, encantar

beyond (bi-*yond*) *prep* más allá de; además de; *adv* más allá

bible (*bai*-böl) *n* biblia *f*

bicycle (*bai*-ssi-köl) *n* bicicleta *f*; biciclo *m*

big (bigh) *adj* grande; voluminoso; gordo; importante

bile (bail) *n* bilis *f*

bilingual (bai-*ling*-ghᵘöl) *adj* bilingüe

bill (bil) *n* cuenta *f*; *v* facturar

billiards (*bil*-yöds) *pl* billar *m*

* **bind** (baind) *v* atar

binding (*bain*-ding) *n* atadura *f*

binoculars (bi-*no*-kyö-lös) *pl* prismáticos *mpl*; gemelos *mpl*

biology (bai-*o*-lö-dʒi) *n* biología *f*

birch (bööch) *n* abedul *m*

bird (bööd) *n* pájaro *m*

Biro (*bai*-rou) *n* bolígrafo *m*

birth (bööz) *n* nacimiento *m*

birthday (*bööz*-dei) *n* cumpleaños *m*

biscuit (*biss*-kit) *n* galleta *f*

bishop (*bi*-ʃöp) *n* obispo *m*

bit (bit) *n* trozo *m*; poco *m*

bitch (bich) *n* perra *f*

bite (bait) *n* bocado *m*; mordedura *f*; picadura *f*

* **bite** (bait) *v* *morder

bitter (*bi*-tö) *adj* amargo

black (blæk) *adj* negro; ~ **market** mercado negro

blackberry (*blæk*-bö-ri) *n* mora *f*

blackbird (*blæk*-bööd) *n* mirlo *m*

blackboard (*blæk*-bood) *n* pizarra *f*

black-currant (blæk-*ka*-rönt) *n* grosella negra

blackmail (*blæk*-meil) *n* chantaje *m*; *v* *hacer chantaje

blacksmith (*blæk*-ssmiz) *n* herrero *m*

bladder (*blæ*-dö) *n* vejiga *f*

blade (bleid) *n* hoja *f*; ~ **of grass** brizna de hierba

blame (bleim) *n* culpa *f*; reproche *m*; *v* echar la culpa, culpar

blank (blængk) *adj* blanco

blanket (*blæng*-kit) *n* manta *f*

blast (blaasst) *n* explosión *f*

blazer (*blei*-sö) *n* chaqueta de sport, chaqueta ligera

bleach (bliich) *v* blanquear

bleak (bliik) *adj* riguroso

* **bleed** (bliid) *v* sangrar; chupar la sangre

bless (blêss) *v* *bendecir

blessing (*blê*-ssing) *n* bendición *f*

blind (blaind) *n* persiana *f*; *adj* ciego; *v* *cegar

blister (*bli*-sstö) *n* ampolla *f*

blizzard (*bli*-söd) *n* ventisca *f*

block (blok) *v* *obstruir, bloquear; *n* bloque *m*; ~ **of flats** casa de pisos

blonde (blond) *n* rubia *f*

blood (blad) *n* sangre *f*; ~ **pressure** tensión arterial

blood-poisoning (*blad*-poi-sö-ning) *n* septicemia *f*

blood-vessel (*blad*-vê-ssöl) *n* vaso sanguíneo

blot (blot) *n* borrón *m*; mancha *f*; **blotting paper** papel secante

blouse (blaus) *n* blusa *f*

blow (blou) *n* golpe *m*; ráfaga *f*

blow (blou) *v* soplar

blow-out (*blou*-aut) *n* reventón *m*

blue (bluu) *adj* azul; deprimido

blunt (blant) *adj* desafilado; obtuso

blush (blaʃ) *v* ruborizarse

board (bood) *n* tabla *f*; tablero *m*; pensión *f*; consejo *m*; ~ **and lodging** pensión completa

boarder (*boo*-dö) *n* huésped *m*

boarding-house (*boo*-ding-hauss) *n* pensión *f*

boarding-school (*boo*-ding-sskuul) *n* internado *m*

boast (bousst) *v* presumir

boat (bout) *n* barco *m*, barca *f*

body (*bo*-di) *n* cuerpo *m*

bodyguard (*bo*-di-ghaad) *n* guardia personal

bog (bogh) *n* pantano *m*

boil (boil) *v* *hervir; *n* forúnculo *m*

bold (bould) *adj* audaz; impertinente, descarado

Bolivia (bö-*li*-vi-ö) Bolivia *f*

Bolivian (bö-*li*-vi-ön) *adj* boliviano

bolt (boult) *n* cerrojo *m*; perno *m*

bomb (bom) *n* bomba *f*; *v* bombardear

bond (bond) *n* obligación *f*

bone (boun) *n* hueso *m*; espina *f*; *v* deshuesar

bonnet (*bo*-nit) *n* capó *m*

book (buk) *n* libro *m*; *v* reservar; inscribir, registrar

booking (*bu*-king) *n* reservación *f*, reserva *f*

bookmaker (*buk*-mei-kö) *n* corredor *m*

bookseller (*buk*-ssê-lö) *n* librero *m*

bookstand (*buk*-sstænd) *n* puesto de libros

bookstore (*buk*-sstoo) *n* librería *f*

boot (buut) *n* bota *f*; portaequipajes *m*

booth (buuð) *n* puesto *m*; cabina *f*

border (*boo*-dö) *n* frontera *f*; borde *m*

bore[1] (boo) *v* aburrir; taladrar; *n* pelmazo *m*

bore[2] (boo) *v* (p bear)

boring (*boo*-ring) *adj* aburrido

born (boon) *adj* nacido

borrow (*bo*-rou) *v* tomar prestado; tomar

bosom (*bu*-söm) *n* pecho *m*; seno *m*

boss (boss) *n* jefe *m*, patrón *m*

botany (*bo*-tö-ni) *n* botánica *f*

both (bouz) *adj* ambos; **both ... and** tanto ... como

bother (*bo*-ðö) *v* fastidiar, molestar; *esforzarse; *n* molestia *f*

bottle (*bo*-töl) *n* botella *f*; ~ **opener** destapador de botellas; **hot-water** ~ calorífero *m*

bottleneck (*bo*-töl-nêk) *n* cuello de botella

bottom (*bo*-töm) *n* fondo *m*; trasero *m*; *adj* inferior

bough (bau) *n* rama *f*

bought (boot) *v* (p, pp buy)

boulder (*boul*-dö) *n* peña *f*

bound (baund) *n* frontera *f*; *be ~ **to** deber de; ~ **for** camino de

boundary (*baun*-dö-ri) *n* límite *m*; frontera *f*

bouquet (bu-*kei*) *n* ramo *m*

bourgeois (*buᵊ*-ᴣ^uaa) *adj* burgués

boutique (bu-*tiik*) *n* boutique *f*

bow[1] (bau) *v* inclinar

bow[2] (bou) *n* arco *m*; ~ **tie** corbata de lazo, corbatín *m*

bowels (bau⁶ls) *pl* intestinos *mpl*

bowl (boul) *n* tazón *m*

bowling (*bou*-ling) *n* bowling *m*, juego de bolos; ~ **alley** bolera *f*

box¹ (bokss) *v* boxear; **boxing match** combate de boxeo

box² (bokss) *n* caja *f*

box-office (*bokss*-o-fiss) *n* taquilla *f*

boy (boi) *n* muchacho *m*; chico *m*, mozo *m*; sirviente *m*; ~ **scout** explorador *m*

bra (braa) *n* sujetador *m*, sostén *m*

bracelet (*breiss*-lit) *n* pulsera *f*

braces (*brei*-ssis) *pl* tirantes *mpl*

brain (brein) *n* cerebro *m*; inteligencia *f*

brain-wave (*brein*-ᵘeiv) *n* ocurrencia *f*

brake (breik) *n* freno *m*; ~ **drum** tambor del freno; ~ **lights** luces de freno

branch (braanch) *n* rama *f*; sucursal *f*

brand (brænd) *n* marca *f*

brand-new (brænd-*nyuu*) *adj* flamante

brass (braass) *n* latón *m*; cobre *m*, cobre amarillo; ~ **band** *n* charanga *f*

brassiere (bræ-si⁶) *n* sujetador *m*, sostén *m*

brassware (*braass*-ᵘê⁶) *n* cobres *mpl*

brave (breiv) *adj* valiente

Brazil (brö-*sil*) Brasil *m*

Brazilian (brö-*sil*-yön) *adj* brasileño

breach (briich) *n* brecha *f*

bread (brêd) *n* pan *m*; **wholemeal** ~ pan integral

breadth (brêdz) *n* ancho *m*

break (breik) *n* fractura *f*; descanso *m*

*break (breik) *v* *quebrar, quebrantar; ~ **down** averiarse; analizar

breakdown (*breik*-daun) *n* avería *f*; descompostura *fMe*

breakfast (*brêk*-fösst) *n* desayuno *m*

bream (briim) *n* (pl ~) brema *f*

breast (brêsst) *n* seno *m*

breaststroke (*brêsst*-sstrouk) *n* braza *f*

breath (brêz) *n* aliento *m*; aire *m*

breathe (briið) *v* respirar

breathing (*brii*-ðing) *n* respiración *f*

breed (briid) *n* raza *f*; especie *f*

*breed (briid) *v* recriar

breeze (briis) *n* brisa *f*

brew (bruu) *v* fabricar cerveza

brewery (*bruu*-ö-ri) *n* cervecería *f*

bribe (braib) *v* sobornar

bribery (*brai*-bö-ri) *n* soborno *m*

brick (brik) *n* ladrillo *m*

bricklayer (*brik*-lei⁶) *n* albañil *m*

bride (braid) *n* novia *f*

bridegroom (*braid*-ghruum) *n* novio *m*

bridge (bridȝ) *n* puente *m*; bridge *m*

brief (briif) *adj* breve

briefcase (*briif*-keiss) *n* portafolio *m*

briefs (briifss) *pl* braga *f*, calzoncillos *mpl*

bright (brait) *adj* claro; reluciente; listo

brill (bril) *n* rodaballo *m*

brilliant (*bril*-yönt) *adj* brillante

brim (brim) *n* borde *m*

*bring (bring) *v* *traer; ~ **back** *devolver; ~ **up** educar; *introducir, levantar

brisk (brissk) *adj* vivo

Britain (*bri*-tön) Inglaterra *f*

British (*bri*-tiʃ) *adj* británico

Briton (*bri*-tön) *n* británico *m*; inglés *m*

broad (brood) *adj* ancho; amplio; general

broadcast (*brood*-kaasst) *n* transmisión *f*

*broadcast (*brood*-kaasst) *v* emitir

brochure (*brou*-ʃu⁶) *n* folleto *m*

broke¹ (brouk) *v* (p break)

broke² (brouk) *adj* arruinado

broken (*brou*-kön) *adj* (pp break) estropeado, roto

broker (brou-kŏ) n corredor m
bronchitis (brong-*kai*-tiss) n bronquitis f
bronze (brons) n bronce m; adj de bronce
brooch (brouch) n broche m
brook (bruk) n arroyo m
broom (bruum) n escoba f
brothel (bro-zŏl) n burdel m
brother (bra-ðŏ) n hermano m
brother-in-law (bra-ðŏ-rin-loo) n (pl brothers-) cuñado m
brought (broot) v (p, pp bring)
brown (braun) adj moreno
bruise (bruus) n moretón m, magulladura f; v magullar
brunette (bruu-*nêt*) n morena f
brush (braʃ) n cepillo m; brocha f; v sacar brillo, cepillar
brutal (*bruu*-tŏl) adj brutal
bubble (ba-bŏl) n burbuja f
bucket (ba-kit) n balde m
buckle (ba-kŏl) n hebilla f
bud (bad) n capullo m
budget (ba-dȝit) n presupuesto m
buffet (bu-fei) n buffet m
bug (bagh) n chinche f; escarabajo m; nAm insecto m
build (bild) v *construir
building (bil-ding) n edificio m
bulb (balb) n bulbo m; **light ~** bombilla f; foco mMe
Bulgaria (bal-*ghê*ᵒ-ri-ö) Bulgaria f
Bulgarian (bal-*ghê*ᵒ-ri-ön) adj búlgaro
bulk (balk) n bulto m; mayoría f
bulky (*bal*-ki) adj voluminoso
bull (bul) n toro m
bullet (bu-lit) n bala f
bullfight (*bul*-fait) n corrida de toros
bullring (*bul*-ring) n plaza de toros
bump (bamp) v topetar; chocar; *dar golpes; n golpe m, topetón m
bumper (bam-pŏ) n parachoques m
bumpy (bam-pi) adj lleno de baches

bun (ban) n bollo m
bunch (banch) n ramo m; grupo m
bundle (ban-dŏl) n paquete m; v atar, liar
bunk (bangk) n camastro m
buoy (boi) n boya f
burden (böö-dön) n peso m
bureau (byuᵒ-rou) n (pl ~x, ~s) escritorio m; nAm cómoda f
bureaucracy (byuᵒ-*ro*-krö-ssi) n burocracia f
burglar (böö-ghlö) n ladrón m
burgle (böö-ghöl) v robar
burial (bê-ri-öl) n entierro m
burn (böön) n quemadura f
burn (böön) v quemar; pegarse
burst (böösst) v *reventar; *quebrar
bury (bê-ri) v *enterrar
bus (bass) n autobús m
bush (buʃ) n matorral m
business (bis-nöss) n negocios mpl, comercio m; empresa f, negocio m; ocupación f; asunto m; ~ **hours** horas hábiles, horas de oficina; ~ **trip** viaje de negocios; **on ~** por asuntos de negocio
business-like (bis-niss-laik) adj práctico
businessman (bis-nöss-mön) n (pl -men) hombre de negocios
bust (basst) n busto m
bustle (ba-ssöl) n agitación f
busy (bi-si) adj ocupado; concurrido, atareado
but (bat) conj mas; pero; prep menos
butcher (bu-chö) n carnicero m
butter (ba-tö) n mantequilla f
butterfly (ba-tö-flai) n mariposa f; ~ **stroke** braza de mariposa
buttock (ba-tök) n nalga m
button (ba-tön) n botón m; v abrochar
buttonhole (ba-tön-houl) n ojal m
buy (bai) v comprar; *adquirir

buyer (*bai*-ö) *n* comprador *m*
by (bai) *prep* por; con; cerca de
by-pass (*bai*-paass) *n* cinturón *m*; *v* rodear

C

cab (kæb) *n* taxi *m*
cabaret (*kæ*-bö-rei) *n* cabaret *m*
cabbage (*kæ*-bidʒ) *n* col *m*
cab-driver (*kæb*-drai-vö) *n* taxista *m*
cabin (*kæ*-bin) *n* cabina *f*; cabaña *f*
cabinet (*kæ*-bi-nöt) *n* gabinete *m*
cable (*kei*-böl) *n* cable *m*; cablegrama *m*; *v* cablegrafiar
cadre (*kaa*-dö) *n* cuadro *m*
café (*kæ*-fei) *n* bar *m*
cafeteria (kæ-fö-*ti⁰*-ri-ö) *n* cafetería *f*
caffeine (*kæ*-fiin) *n* cafeína *f*
cage (keidʒ) *n* jaula *f*
cake (keik) *n* pastel *m*; pastelería *f*, tarta *f*, dulces
calamity (kö-*læ*-mö-ti) *n* desastre *m*, catástrofe *f*
calcium (*kæl*-ssi-öm) *n* calcio *m*
calculate (*kæl*-kyu-leit) *v* calcular
calculation (kæl-kyu-*lei*-ʃön) *n* cálculo *m*
calendar (*kæ*-lön-dö) *n* calendario *m*
calf (kaaf) *n* (pl calves) ternero *m*; pantorrilla *f*; ~ skin becerro *m*
call (kool) *v* llamar; *n* llamada *f*; visita *f*; *be called llamarse; ~ names insultar; ~ on visitar; ~ up *Am* telefonear
callus (*kæ*-löss) *n* callo *m*
calm (kaam) *adj* tranquilo; ~ down calmar
calorie (*kæ*-lö-ri) *n* caloría *f*
Calvinism (*kæl*-vi-ni-söm) *n* calvinismo *m*
came (keim) *v* (p come)

camel (*kæ*-möl) *n* camello *m*
cameo (*kæ*-mi-ou) *n* (pl ~s) camafeo *m*
camera (*kæ*-mö-rö) *n* cámara fotográfica; cámara *f*; ~ shop negocio fotográfico
camp (kæmp) *n* campamento *m*; *v* acampar
campaign (kæm-*pein*) *n* campaña *f*
camp-bed (kæmp-*bêd*) *n* catre de campaña, cama de tijera
camper (*kæm*-pö) *n* acampador *m*
camping (*kæm*-ping) *n* camping *m*; ~ site camping *m*, lugar de camping
camshaft (*kæm*-ʃaaft) *n* árbol de levas
can (kæn) *n* lata *f*; ~ opener abrelatas *m*
* can (kæn) *v* *poder
Canada (*kæ*-nö-dö) Canadá *m*
Canadian (kö-*nei*-di-ön) *adj* canadiense
canal (kö-*næl*) *n* canal *m*
canary (ko-*në⁰*-ri) *n* canario *m*
cancel (*kæn*-ssöl) *v* cancelar; anular
cancellation (kæn-ssö-*lei*-ʃön) *n* cancelación *f*
cancer (*kæn*-ssö) *n* cáncer *m*
candelabrum (kæn-dö-*laa*-bröm) *n* (pl -bra) candelabro *m*
candidate (*kæn*-di-döt) *n* candidato *m*, interesado *m*
candle (*kæn*-döl) *n* candela *f*
candy (*kæn*-di) *nAm* bombón *m*; dulces, golosinas
cane (kcin) *n* caña *f*; bastón *m*
canister (*kæ*-ni-ssto) *n* caja metálica, lata *f*
canoe (kö-*nuu*) *n* canoa *f*
canteen (kæn-*tiin*) *n* cantina *f*
canvas (*kæn*-vöss) *n* lona *f*
cap (kæp) *n* gorra *f*, gorro *m*
capable (*kei*-pö-böl) *adj* capaz
capacity (kö-*pæ*-ssö-ti) *n* capacidad

f; potencia *f*; competencia *f*

cape (keip) *n* capa *f*; cabo *m*

capital (*kæ*-pi-töl) *n* capital *f*; capital *m*; *adj* importante, capital; ~ **letter** mayúscula *f*

capitalism (*kæ*-pi-tö-li-söm) *n* capitalismo *m*

capitulation (kö-pi-tyu-*lei*-fön) *n* capitulación *f*

capsule (*kæp*-ssyuul) *n* cápsula *f*

captain (*kæp*-tin) *n* capitán *m*; comandante *m*

capture (*kæp*-chö) *v* coger preso, capturar; conquistar; *n* captura *f*; conquista *f*

car (kaa) *n* coche *m*; carro *mMe*; ~ **hire** alquiler de coches; ~ **park** parque de estacionamiento

carafe (kö-*ræf*) *n* garrafa *f*

caramel (*kæ*-rö-möl) *n* caramelo *m*

carat (*kæ*-röt) *n* quilate *m*

caravan (*kæ*-rö-væn) *n* caravana *f*; carro de gitanos

carburettor (kaa-byu-*rê*-tö) *n* carburador *m*

card (kaad) *n* tarjeta *f*; tarjeta postal

cardboard (*kaad*-bood) *n* cartón *m*; *adj* de cartón

cardigan (*kaa*-di-ghön) *n* chaqueta *f*

cardinal (*kaa*-di-nöl) *n* cardenal *m*; *adj* cardinal, principal

care (kê⁰) *n* cuidado *m*; ~ **about** preocuparse de; ~ **for** gustar; *take ~ of* cuidar de

career (kö-*ri*⁰) *n* carrera *f*

carefree (*kê*⁰-frii) *adj* despreocupado

careful (*kê*⁰-föl) *adj* cuidadoso; escrupuloso

careless (*kê*⁰-löss) *adj* indiferente, negligente

caretaker (*kê*⁰-tei-kö) *n* guardián *m*

cargo (*kaa*-ghou) *n* (pl ~es) carga *f*

carnival (*kaa*-ni-völ) *n* carnaval *m*

carp (kaap) *n* (pl ~) carpa *f*

carpenter (*kaa*-pin-tö) *n* carpintero *m*

carpet (*kaa*-pit) *n* alfombra *f*

carriage (*kæ*-ridʒ) *n* vagón *m*; coche *m*, carruaje *m*

carriageway (*kæ*-ridʒ-ᵘei) *n* calzada *f*

carrot (*kæ*-röt) *n* zanahoria *f*

carry (*kæ*-ri) *v* llevar; *conducir; ~ **on** continuar; *proseguir; ~ **out** realizar

carry-cot (*kæ*-ri-kot) *n* cuna de viaje

cart (kaat) *n* carro *m*

cartilage (*kaa*-ti-lidʒ) *n* cartílago *m*

carton (*kaa*-tön) *n* caja de cartón; cartón *m*

cartoon (kaa-*tuun*) *n* dibujos animados

cartridge (*kaa*-tridʒ) *n* cartucho *m*

carve (kaav) *v* trinchar; entallar, tallar

carving (*kaa*-ving) *n* talla *f*

case (keiss) *n* caso *m*; causa *f*; valija *f*; estuche *m*; **attaché ~** portafolio *m*; **in ~** si; **in ~ of** en caso de

cash (kæʃ) *n* dinero contante, efectivo *m*; *v* cobrar, *hacer efectivo

cashier (kæ-*fi*⁰) *n* cajero *m*; cajera *f*

cashmere (*kæf*-mi⁰) *n* casimir *m*

casino (kö-*ssii*-nou) *n* (pl ~s) casino *m*

cask (kaassk) *n* barril *m*, tonel *m*

cast (kaasst) *n* echada *f*

*cast (kaasst) *v* lanzar; **cast iron** hierro fundido

castle (*kaa*-ssöl) *n* castillo *m*

casual (*kæ*-ʒu-öl) *adj* informal; de paso, por casualidad

casualty (*kæ*-ʒu-öl-ti) *n* víctima *f*

cat (kæt) *n* gato *m*

catacomb (*kæ*-tö-koum) *n* catacumba *f*

catalogue (*kæ*-tö-logh) *n* catálogo *m*

catarrh (kö-*taa*) *n* catarro *m*

catastrophe (kö-*tæ*-sströ-fi) *n* catástrofe *f*

*catch (kæch) *v* coger; sorprender

category (*kæ*-ti-ghö-ri) *n* categoría *f*

cathedral (kö-*zii*-dröl) *n* catedral *f*

catholic (*kæ*-zö-lik) *adj* católico

cattle (*kæ*-töl) *pl* ganado *m*

caught (koot) *v* (p, pp catch)

cauliflower (*ko*-li-flau⁰) *n* coliflor *f*

cause (koos) *v* causar; provocar; *n* causa *f*; motivo *m*; **~ to** *hacer

causeway (*koos*-ᵁei) *n* calzada *f*

caution (*koo*-ʃön) *n* cautela *f*; *v* *advertir

cautious (*koo*-ʃöss) *adj* prudente

cave (keiv) *n* cueva *f*; grieta *f*

cavern (*kæ*-vön) *n* cueva *f*

caviar (*kæ*-vi-aa) *n* caviar *m*

cavity (*kæ*-vö-ti) *n* cavidad *f*

cease (ssiiss) *v* cesar

ceiling (*ssii*-ling) *n* cielo raso

celebrate (*ssé*-li-breit) *v* celebrar

celebration (ssè-li-*brei*-ʃön) *n* celebración *f*

celebrity (ssi-*lé*-brö-ti) *n* celebridad *f*

celery (*ssé*-lö-ri) *n* apio *m*

celibacy (*ssé*-li-bö-ssi) *n* celibato *m*

cell (ssél) *n* celda *f*

cellar (*ssé*-lö) *n* sótano *m*

cellophane (*ssé*-lö-fein) *n* celofán *m*

cement (ssi-*mént*) *n* cemento *m*

cemetery (*ssé*-mi-tri) *n* cementerio *m*

censorship (*ssén*-sso-ʃip) *n* censura *f*

centigrade (*ssén*-ti-ghreid) *adj* centigrado

centimetre (*ssén*-ti-mii-tö) *n* centímetro *m*

central (*ssön* tröl) *adj* central; **~ heating** calefacción central; **~ station** estación central

centralize (*ssén*-trö-lais) *v* centralizar

centre (*ssén*-tö) *n* centro *m*

century (*ssén*-chö-ri) *n* siglo *m*

ceramics (ssi-*ræ*-mikss) *pl* cerámica *f*

ceremony (*ssé*-rö-mö-ni) *n* ceremonia *f*

certain (*ssöö*-tön) *adj* cierto

certificate (ssö-*ti*-fi-köt) *n* certificado *m*; certificación *f*, acta *f*, diploma *m*

chain (chein) *n* cadena *f*

chair (chê⁰) *n* silla *f*

chairman (*chê*⁰-mön) *n* (pl -men) presidente *m*

chalet (*fæ*-lei) *n* chalet *m*

chalk (chook) *n* creta *f*

challenge (*chæ*-löndʒ) *v* desafiar; *n* reto *m*

chamber (*cheim*-bö) *n* cuarto *m*

chambermaid (*cheim*-bö-meid) *n* doncella *f*

champagne (fæm-*pein*) *n* champán *m*

champion (*chæm*-pyön) *n* campeón *m*; defensor *m*

chance (chaanss) *n* azar *m*; oportunidad *f*, ocasión *f*; riesgo *m*; suerte *f*; **by ~** por casualidad

change (cheindʒ) *v* modificar, cambiar; mudarse; *hacer trasbordo; *n* modificación *f*, cambio *m*; moneda *f*

channel (*chæ*-nöl) *n* canal *m*; **English Channel** Canal de la Mancha

chaos (*kei*-oss) *n* caos *m*

chaotic (kei-*o*-tik) *adj* caótico

chap (chæp) *n* hombre *m*

chapel (*chæ*-pöl) *n* iglesia *f*, capilla *f*

chaplain (*chæ* plin) *n* capellán *m*

character (*kæ* rök-tö) *n* carácter *m*

characteristic (kæ-rök-tö-*ri*-sstik) *adj* típico, característico; *n* característica *f*; rasgo característico

characterize (*kæ*-rök-tö-rais) *v* caracterizar

charcoal (*chaa*-koul) *n* carbón de leña

charge (chaadʒ) *v* *pedir; cargar; acusar; *n* precio *m*; carga *f*; acusación *f*; **~ plate** *Am* tarjeta de crédito; **free of ~** gratuito; **in ~ of** encargado de; ***take ~ of** encargarse

de
charity (*chæ*-rö-ti) *n* caridad *f*
charm (chaam) *n* encanto *m*; amuleto *m*
charming (*chaa*-ming) *adj* encantador
chart (chaat) *n* tabla *f*; gráfico *m*; carta marina; **conversion** ~ tabla de conversión
chase (cheiss) *v* cazar; expulsar, ahuyentar; *n* caza *f*
chasm (*kæ*-söm) *n* grieta *f*
chassis (*fæ*-ssi) *n* (pl ~) chasis *m*
chaste (cheisst) *adj* casto
chat (chæt) *v* charlar; *n* charla *f*
chatterbox (*chæ*-tö-bokss) *n* charlatán *m*
chauffeur (*fou*-fö) *n* chófer *m*
cheap (chiip) *adj* barato; económico
cheat (chiit) *v* engañar; estafar
check (chêk) *v* controlar, verificar; *n* escaque *m*; *nAm* cuenta *f*; cheque *m*; **check!** ¡jaque!; ~ **in** inscribirse; ~ **out** *despedirse
check-book (*chêk*-buk) *nAm* talonario *m*
checkerboard (*chê*-kö-bood) *nAm* tablero de ajedrez
checkroom (*chêk*-ruum) *nAm* guardarropa *m*
check-up (*chê*-kap) *n* reconocimiento *m*
cheek (chiik) *n* mejilla *f*
cheek-bone (*chiik*-boun) *n* pómulo *m*
cheer (chi⁰) *v* aclamar; ~ **up** alegrar
cheerful (*chi⁰*-föl) *adj* alegre
cheese (chiis) *n* queso *m*
chef (jêf) *n* jefe de cocina
chemical (*kê*-mi-köl) *adj* químico
chemist (*kê*-misst) *n* farmacéutico *m*; **chemist's** farmacia *f*; droguería *f*
chemistry (*kê*-mi-sstri) *n* química *f*
cheque (chêk) *n* cheque *m*
cheque-book (*chêk*-buk) *n* talonario *m*

chequered (*chê*-köd) *adj* a cuadros, cuadriculado
cherry (*chê*-ri) *n* cereza *f*
chess (chêss) *n* ajedrez *m*
chest (chêsst) *n* pecho *m*; arca *f*; ~ **of drawers** cómoda *f*
chestnut (*chêss*-nat) *n* castaña *f*
chew (chuu) *v* masticar
chewing-gum (*chuu*-ing-gham) *n* goma de mascar, chicle *m*
chicken (*chi*-kin) *n* pollo *m*
chickenpox (*chi*-kin-pokss) *n* varicela *f*
chief (chiif) *n* jefe *m*; *adj* principal
chieftain (*chiif*-tön) *n* jefe *m*
chilblain (*chil*-blein) *n* sabañón *m*
child (chaild) *n* (pl children) niño *m*
childbirth (*chaild*-bööz) *n* parto *m*
childhood (*chaild*-hud) *n* infancia *f*
Chile (*chi*-li) Chile *m*
Chilean (*chi*-li-ön) *adj* chileno
chill (chil) *n* escalofrío *m*
chilly (*chi*-li) *adj* fresco
chimes (chaims) *pl* carillón *m*
chimney (*chim*-ni) *n* chimenea *f*
chin (chin) *n* barbilla *f*
China (*chai*-nö) China *f*
china (*chai*-nö) *n* porcelana *f*
Chinese (chai-*niis*) *adj* chino
chink (chingk) *n* hendidura *f*
chip (chip) *n* astilla *f*; ficha *f*; *v* cortar, astillar; **chips** patatas fritas
chiropodist (ki-*ro*-pö-disst) *n* pedicuro *m*
chisel (*chi*-söl) *n* cincel *m*
chives (chaivs) *pl* cebollino *m*
chlorine (*kloo*-riin) *n* cloro *m*
chock-full (chok-*ful*) *adj* de bote en bote, repleto
chocolate (*cho*-klöt) *n* chocolate *m*; bombón *m*
choice (choiss) *n* elección *f*; selección *f*
choir (k⁰ai⁰) *n* coro *m*

choke (chouk) v sofocarse; estrangular; n starter m

*choose (chuus) v escoger

chop (chop) n chuleta f; v tajar

Christ (kraisst) Cristo

christen (kri-ssön) v bautizar

christening (kri-ssö-ning) n bautizo m

Christian (kriss-chön) adj cristiano; ~ name nombre de pila

Christmas (kriss-möss) Navidad f

chromium (krou-mi-öm) n cromo m

chronic (kro-nik) adj crónico

chronological (kro-nö-lo-dʒi-köl) adj cronológico

chuckle (cha-köl) v *reírse entre dientes

chunk (changk) n trozo m

church (chööch) n iglesia f

churchyard (chööch-yaad) n cementerio m

cigar (ssi-ghaa) n puro m; ~ shop estanco m

cigarette (ssi-ghö-rêt) n cigarrillo m; ~ tobacco picadura f

cigarette-case (ssi-ghö-rêt-keiss) n pitillera f

cigarette-holder (ssi-ghö-rêt-houl-dö) n boquilla f

cigarette-lighter (ssi-ghö-rêt-lai-tö) n encendedor m

cinema (ssi-nö-mö) n cinematógrafo m

cinnamon (ssi-nö-mön) n canela f

circle (ssöö-köl) n círculo m; balcón m; v rodear, circundar

circulation (ssoo-kyu-lei-ʃön) n circulación f; circulación de la sangre

circumstance (ssöö-köm-sstænss) n circunstancia f

circus (ssöö-köss) n circo m

citizen (ssi-ti-sön) n ciudadano m

citizenship (ssi-ti-sön-ʃip) n ciudadanía f

city (ssi-ti) n ciudad f

civic (ssi-vik) adj cívico

civil (ssi-völ) adj civil; cortés; ~ law derecho civil; ~ servant funcionario m

civilian (ssi-vil-yön) adj civil; n paisano m

civilization (ssi-vö-lai-sei-ʃön) n civilización f

civilized (ssi-vö-laisd) adj civilizado

claim (kleim) v reivindicar, reclamar; afirmar; n reivindicación f, pretensión f

clamp (klæmp) n mordaza f; grapa f

clap (klæp) v aplaudir

clarify (klæ-ri-fai) v aclarar, clarificar

class (klaass) n clase f

classical (klæ-ssi-köl) adj clásico

classify (klæ-ssi-fai) v clasificar

class-mate (klaass-meit) n compañero de clase

classroom (klaass-ruum) n clase f

clause (kloos) n cláusula f

claw (kloo) n garra f

clay (klei) n arcilla f

clean (kliin) adj puro, limpio; v limpiar

cleaning (klii-ning) n limpieza f; ~ fluid quitamanchas m

clear (kliö) adj claro; v limpiar

clearing (kliö-ring) n claro m

cleft (klêft) n grieta f

clergyman (klöö-dʒi-mön) n (pl men) pastor m; clérigo m

clerk (klaak) n empleado de oficina, oficinista m; escribano m; secretario m

clever (klê-vö) adj inteligente; astuto, listo

client (klai-önt) n cliente m

cliff (klif) n acantilado m, farallón m

climate (klai-mit) n clima m

climb (klaim) v trepar; n subida f

clinic (kli-nik) n clínica f

cloak (klouk) n capa f

cloakroom (*klouk*-ruum) *n* guardarropa *m*
clock (klok) *n* reloj *m*; **at ... o'clock** a las ...
cloister (*kloi*-sstö) *n* convento *m*
close¹ (klous) *v* *cerrar
close² (klouss) *adj* cercano
closet (*klo*-sit) *n* armario *m*
cloth (kloz) *n* tela *f*; paño *m*
clothes (klouðs) *pl* ropa *f*, vestidos *mpl*
clothes-brush (*klouðs*-braʃ) *n* cepillo de la ropa
clothing (*klou*-ðing) *n* vestido *m*
cloud (klaud) *n* nube *f*
cloud-burst (*klaud*-böösst) *n* chaparrón *m*
cloudy (*klau*-di) *adj* cubierto, nublado
clover (*klou*-vö) *n* trébol *m*
clown (klaun) *n* payaso *m*
club (klab) *n* club *m*; círculo *m*, asociación *f*; porra *f*, garrote *m*
clumsy (*klam*-si) *adj* torpe
clutch (klach) *n* embrague *m*; apretón *m*
coach (kouch) *n* autobús *m*; vagón *m*; carroza *f*; entrenador *m*
coachwork (*kouch*-ᵘöök) *n* carrocería *f*
coagulate (kou-æ-ghyu-leit) *v* coagularse
coal (koul) *n* carbón *m*
coarse (kooss) *adj* burdo; grosero
coast (kousst) *n* costa *f*
coat (kout) *n* sobretodo *m*, abrigo *m*
coat-hanger (*kout*-hæng-ö) *n* percha *f*
cobweb (*kob*-ᵁêb) *n* tela de araña *f*
cocaine (kou-*kein*) *n* cocaína *f*
cock (kok) *n* gallo *m*
cocktail (*kok*-teil) *n* cóctel *m*
coconut (*kou*-kö-nat) *n* coco *m*
cod (kod) *n* (pl ~) bacalao *m*
code (koud) *n* código *m*
coffee (*ko*-fi) *n* café *m*

cognac (*ko*-nyæk) *n* coñac *m*
coherence (kou-*hi*ᵒ-rönss) *n* coherencia *f*
coin (koin) *n* moneda *f*
coincide (kou-in-*ssaid*) *v* coincidir
cold (kould) *adj* frío; *n* frío *m*; resfriado *m*; **catch a** ~ resfriarse
collapse (kö-*læpss*) *v* desplomarse, derrumbarse
collar (*ko*-lö) *n* collar *m*; cuello *m*; ~ **stud** botón del cuello
collarbone (*ko*-lö-boun) *n* clavícula *f*
colleague (*ko*-liigh) *n* colega *m*
collect (kö-*lêkt*) *v* juntar; recoger; *hacer una colecta
collection (kö-*lêk*-ʃön) *n* colección *f*; recogida *f*
collective (kö-*lêk*-tiv) *adj* colectivo
collector (kö-*lêk*-tö) *n* coleccionista *m*; colector *m*
college (*ko*-lidʒ) *n* colegio *m*
collide (kö-*laid*) *v* chocar
collision (kö-*li*-ʒön) *n* colisión *f*
Colombia (kö-*lom*-bi-ö) Colombia *f*
Colombian (kö-*lom*-bi-ön) *adj* colombiano
colonel (*köö*-nöl) *n* coronel *m*
colony (*ko*-lö-ni) *n* colonia *f*
colour (*ka*-lö) *n* color *m*; *v* colorear; ~ **film** película en colores
colourant (*ka*-lö-rönt) *n* colorante *m*
colour-blind (*ka*-lö-blaind) *adj* daltoniano
coloured (*ka*-löd) *adj* de color
colourful (*ka*-lö-föl) *adj* colorado, lleno de color
column (*ko*-löm) *n* columna *f*
coma (*kou*-mö) *n* coma *m*
comb (koum) *v* peinar; *n* peine *m*
combat (*kom*-bæt) *n* lucha *f*, combate *m*; *v* combatir
combination (kom-bi-*nei*-ʃön) *n* combinación *f*
combine (köm-*bain*) *v* combinar; unir

*come (kam) v *venir; ~ across *encontrar; hallar

comedian (kö-*mii*-di-ön) n comediante m; cómico m

comedy (*ko*-mö-di) n comedia f; musical - comedia musical

comfort (*kam*-föt) n comodidad f, confort m; consuelo m; v *consolar

comfortable (*kam*-fö-tö-böl) adj confortable

comic (*ko*-mik) adj cómico

comics (*ko*-mikss) pl tcbeo m

coming (*ka*-ming) n llegada f

comma (*ko*-mö) n coma f

command (kö-*maand*) v mandar; n orden f

commander (kö-*maan*-dö) n comandante m

commemoration (kö-mê-mö-*rei*-fön) n conmemoración f

commence (kö-*mênss*) v *comenzar

comment (*ko*-mênt) n comentario m; v comentar

commerce (*ko*-mööss) n comercio m

commercial (kö-*möö*-föl) adj comercial; n anuncio publicitario; ~ law derecho comercial

commission (kö-*mi*-fön) n comisión f

commit (kö-*mit*) v confiar, entregar; cometer

committee (kö-*mi*-ti) n comisión f, comité m

common (*ko*-mön) adj común; usual; ordinario

commune (*ko*-myuun) n comuna f

communicate (kö-*myuu*-ni-keit) v comunicar

communication (kö-myuu-ni-*kei*-fön) n comunicación f

communiqué (kö-*myuu*-ni-kei) n comunicado m

communism (*ko*-myu-ni-söm) n comunismo m

communist (*ko*-myu-nisst) n comunista m

community (kö-*myuu*-nö-ti) n sociedad f, vecindario m

commuter (kö-*myuu*-tö) n suburbano m

compact (*kom*-pækt) adj compacto

companion (köm-*pæ*-nyön) n compañero m

company (*kam*-pö-ni) n compañía f; sociedad f

comparative (köm-*pæ*-rö-tiv) adj relativo

compare (köm-*pê^ö*) v comparar

comparison (köm-*pæ*-ri-ssön) n comparación f

compartment (köm-*paat*-mönt) n compartimento m

compass (*kam*-pöss) n brújula f

compel (köm-*pêl*) v compeler

compensate (*kom*-pön-sseit) v compensar

compensation (kom-pön-*ssei*-fön) n compensación f; indemnización f

compete (köm-*piit*) v *competir

competition (kom-pö-*ti*-fön) n concurso m; competencia f

competitor (köm-*pê*-ti-tör) n competidor m

compile (köm-*pail*) v compilar

complain (köm-*plein*) v quejarse

complaint (köm-*pleint*) n queja f; complaints book libro de reclamaciones

complete (köm-*pliit*) adj completo; v completar

completely (köm-*pliit*-li) adv enteramente, totalmente, completamente

complex (*kom*-plêkss) n complejo m; adj complejo

complexion (köm-*plêk*-fön) n tez f

complicated (*kom*-pli-kei-tid) adj complicado

compliment (*kom*-pli-mönt) n cumpli-

miento *m*; *v* cumplimentar
compose (köm-*pous*) *v* *componer
composer (köm-*pou*-sö) *n* compositor *m*
composition (kom-pö-*si*-ſön) *n* composición *f*
comprehensive (kom-pri-*hên*-ssiv) *adj* extenso
comprise (köm-*prais*) *v* comprender
compromise (*kom*-prö-mais) *n* compromiso *m*
compulsory (köm-*pal*-ssö-ri) *adj* obligatorio
comrade (*kom*-reid) *n* camarada *m*
conceal (kön-*ssiil*) *v* disimular
conceited (kön-*ssii*-tid) *adj* presuntuoso
conceive (kön-*ssiiv*) *v* *concebir, *entender; imaginar
concentrate (*kon*-ssön-treit) *v* concentrarse
concentration (kon-ssön-*trei*-ſön) *n* concentración *f*
conception (kön-*ssêp*-ſön) *n* entendimiento *m*; concepción *f*
concern (kön-*ssöön*) *v* *concernir, atañer; *n* preocupación *f*; asunto *m*; empresa *f*, consorcio *m*
concerned (kön-*ssöönd*) *adj* preocupado; interesado
concerning (kön-*ssöö*-ning) *prep* en lo que se refiere a, concerniente a
concert (*kon*-ssöt) *n* concierto *m*; ~ **hall** sala de conciertos
concession (kön-*ssê*-ſön) *n* concesión *f*
concierge (kong-ssi-*ê^ôʒ*) *n* conserje *m*
concise (kön-*ssaiss*) *adj* conciso
conclusion (köng-*kluu*-ʒön) *n* conclusión *f*
concrete (*kong*-kriit) *adj* concreto; *n* hormigón *m*
concurrence (köng-*ka*-rönss) *n* coincidencia *f*

concussion (köng-*ka*-ſön) *n* conmoción cerebral
condition (kön-*di*-ſön) *n* condición *f*; estado *m*; circunstancia *f*
conditional (kön-*di*-ſö-nöl) *adj* condicional
conduct[1] (*kon*-dakt) *n* conducta *f*
conduct[2] (kön-*dakt*) *v* *conducir; acompañar
conductor (kön-*dak*-tö) *n* cobrador *m*; director *m*; conductor *mMe*
confectioner (kön-*fêk*-ſö-nö) *n* confitero *m*
conference (*kon*-fö-rönss) *n* conferencia *f*
confess (kön-*fêss*) *v* *reconocer; *confesarse; profesar
confession (kön-*fê*-ſön) *n* confesión *f*
confidence (*kon*-fi-dönss) *n* confianza *f*
confident (*kon*-fi-dönt) *adj* lleno de confianza
confidential (kon-fi-*dên*-ſöl) *adj* confidencial
confirm (kön-*fööm*) *v* confirmar
confirmation (kon-fö-*mei*-ſön) *n* confirmación *f*
confiscate (*kon*-fi-sskeit) *v* embargar, confiscar
conflict (*kon*-flikt) *n* conflicto *m*
confuse (kön-*fyuus*) *v* confundir; **confused** *adj* confuso
confusion (kön-*fyuu*-ʒön) *n* confusión *f*
congratulate (köng-*ghræ*-chu-leit) *v* felicitar
congratulation (köng-ghræ-chu-*lei*-ſön) *n* felicitación *f*
congregation (kong-ghri-*ghei*-ſön) *n* comunidad *f*, congregación *f*
congress (*kong*-ghrêss) *n* congreso *m*
connect (kö-*nêkt*) *v* conectar
connection (kö-*nêk*-ſön) *n* relación *f*; conexión *f*; enlace *m*

connoisseur (ko-nö-*ssöö*) *n* perito *m*

connotation (ko-nö-*tei*-∫ön) *n* connotación *f*

conquer (*kong*-kö) *v* conquistar; vencer

conqueror (*kong*-ko-rö) *n* conquistador *m*

conquest (*kong*-kᵘêsst) *n* conquista *f*

conscience (*kon*-∫önss) *n* conciencia *f*

conscious (*kon*-∫öss) *adj* consciente

consciousness (*kon*-∫öss-nöss) *n* conciencia *f*

conscript (*kon*-sskript) *n* quinto *m*

consent (kön-*ssênt*) *v* *consentir; *n* consentimiento *m*

consequence (*kon*-ssi-kᵘönss) *n* consecuencia *f*

consequently (*kon*-ssi-kᵘönt-li) *adv* por consiguiente

conservative (kön-*ssöö*-vö-tiv) *adj* conservador

consider (kön-*ssi*-dö) *v* considerar; opinar

considerable (kön-*ssi*-dö-rö-böl) *adj* considerable; importante, notable

considerate (kön-*ssi*-dö-röt) *adj* considerado

consideration (kön-ssi-dö-*rei*-∫ön) *n* consideración *f*; atención *f*

considering (kön-*ssi*-dö-ring) *prep* considerando

consignment (kön-*ssain*-mönt) *n* envío *m*

consist of (kön-*ssisst*) constar de

conspire (kön-*sspai*ö) *v* conspirar

constant (*kon*-sstönt) *adj* constante

constipated (*kon*-ooti-pei-tid) *adj* estreñido

constipation (kon-ssti-*pei*-∫ön) *n* estreñimiento *m*

constituency (kön-*ssti*-chu-ön-ssi) *n* distrito electoral

constitution (kon-ssti-*tyuu*-∫ön) *n* constitución *f*

construct (kön-*sstrakt*) *v* *construir; edificar

construction (kön-*sstrak*-∫ön) *n* construcción *f*; edificio *m*

consul (*kon*-ssöl) *n* cónsul *m*

consulate (*kon*-ssyu-löt) *n* consulado *m*

consult (kön-*ssalt*) *v* consultar

consultation (kon-ssöl-*tei*-∫ön) *n* consulta *f*; ~ **hours** *n* horas de consulta

consumer (kön-*ssyuu*-mö) *n* consumidor *m*

contact (*kon*-tækt) *n* contacto *m*; *v* *ponerse en contacto con; ~ **lenses** lentillas *fpl*

contagious (kön-*tei*-dʒöss) *adj* contagioso

contain (kön-*tein*) *v* *contener; comprender

container (kön-*tei*-nö) *n* receptáculo *m*; contenedor *m*

contemporary (kön-*têm*-pö-rö-ri) *adj* contemporáneo; de entonces; *n* contemporáneo *m*

contempt (kön-*têmpt*) *n* desprecio *m*, menosprecio *m*

content (kön-*tênt*) *adj* contento

contents (*kon*-têntss) *pl* contenido *m*

contest (*kon*-tèsst) *n* lucha *f*; concurso *m*

continent (*kon* ti nönt) *n* continente *m*

continental (kon-ti-*nên*-töl) *adj* continental

continual (kön-*ti*-nyu-öl) *adj* continuo

continue (kön-*ti*-nyuu) *v* continuar; *proseguir, durar

continuous (kön-*ti*-nyu-öss) *adj* continuo, ininterrumpido

contour (*kon*-tuö) *n* contorno *m*

contraceptive (kon-trö-*ssêp*-tiv) *n* anticonceptivo *m*

contract[1] (*kon*-trækt) *n* contrato *m*

contract² (kön-*trækt*) v atrapar

contractor (kön-*træk*-tö) n contratista m

contradict (kon-trö-*dikt*) v *contradecir

contradictory (kon-trö-*dik*-tö-ri) adj contradictorio

contrary (*kon*-trö-ri) n contrario m; adj contrario; **on the ~** al contrario

contrast (*kon*-traasst) n contraste m; diferencia f

contribution (kon-tri-*byuu*-[ö]n) n contribución f

control (kön-*troul*) n control m; v controlar

controversial (kon-trö-*vöö*-[ö]l) adj controvertido, controvertible

convenience (kön-*vii*-nyönss) n comodidad f

convenient (kön-*vii*-nyönt) adj cómodo; adecuado, conveniente

convent (*kon*-vönt) n convento m

conversation (kon-vö-*ssei*-[ö]n) n conversación f

convert (kön-*vööt*) v *convertir

convict¹ (kön-*vikt*) v convencer

convict² (*kon*-vikt) n condenado m

conviction (kön-*vik*-[ö]n) n convencimiento m; condena f

convince (kön-*vinss*) v convencer

convulsion (kön-*val*-[ö]n) n convulsión f

cook (kuk) n cocinero m; v cocinar; guisar, preparar

cooker (*ku*-kö) n cocina f; **gas ~** cocina de gas

cookery-book (*ku*-kö-ri-buk) n libro de cocina

cookie (*ku*-ki) nAm bizcocho m

cool (kuul) adj fresco; **cooling system** sistema de refrigeración

co-operation (kou-o-pö-*rei*-[ö]n) n cooperación f; colaboración f

co-operative (kou-o-pö-rö-tiv) adj

cooperativo; cooperador; n cooperativa f

co-ordinate (kou-*oo*-di-neit) v coordinar

co-ordination (kou-oo-di-*nei*-[ö]n) n coordinación f

copper (*ko*-pö) n cobre m

copy (*ko*-pi) n copia f; ejemplar m; v copiar; imitar; **carbon ~** copia f

coral (*ko*-röl) n coral m

cord (kood) n cuerda f; cordón m

cordial (*koo*-di-öl) adj cordial

corduroy (*koo*-dö-roi) n pana f

core (koo) n núcleo m; corazón m

cork (kook) n corcho m; tapón m

corkscrew (*kook*-sskruu) n sacacorchos mpl

corn (koon) n grano m; cereales mpl, trigo m; callo m; **~ on the cob** maíz en la mazorca

corner (*koo*-nö) n esquina f

cornfield (*koon*-fiild) n trigal m

corpse (koopss) n cadáver m

corpulent (*koo*-pyu-lönt) adj corpulento; grueso, obeso

correct (kö-*rêkt*) adj correcto, justo; v *corregir

correction (kö-*rêk*-[ö]n) n corrección f; rectificación f

correctness (kö-*rêkt*-nöss) n exactitud f

correspond (ko-ri-*sspond*) v corresponderse; corresponder

correspondence (ko-ri-*sspon*-dönss) n correspondencia f

correspondent (ko-ri-*sspon*-dönt) n corresponsal m

corridor (*ko*-ri-doo) n pasillo m

corrupt (kö-*rapt*) adj corrupto; v corromper

corruption (kö-*rap*-[ö]n) n corrupción f

corset (*koo*-ssit) n corsé m

cosmetics (kos-*mê*-tikss) pl productos

cosméticos, cosméticos *mpl*
cost (kosst) *n* coste *m*; precio *m*
** **cost** (kosst) *v* *costar*
cosy (kou-si) *adj* íntimo, confortable
cot (kot) *nAm* cama de tijera
cottage (ko-tidʒ) *n* casa de campo
cotton (ko-tön) *n* algodón *m*; de algodón
cotton-wool (ko-tön-ᵘul) *n* algodón *m*
couch (kauch) *n* diván *m*
cough (kof) *n* tos *f*; *v* toser
could (kud) *v* (p can)
council (kaun-ssöl) *n* consejo *m*
councillor (kaun-ssö-lö) *n* consejero *m*
counsel (kaun-ssöl) *n* consejo *m*
counsellor (kaun-ssö-lö) *n* consejero *m*
count (kaunt) *v* *contar; adicionar; *incluir; considerar; *n* conde *m*
counter (kaun-tö) *n* mostrador *m*; barra *f*
counterfeit (kaun-tö-flit) *v* falsificar
counterfoil (kaun-to-toil) *n* talón *m*
counterpane (kaun-tö-pein) *n* colcha *f*
countess (kaun-tiss) *n* condesa *f*
country (kan-tri) *n* país *m*; campo *m*; región *f*; ~ **house** quinta *f*
countryman (kan-tri-mön) *n* (pl -men) compatriota *m*
countryside (kan-tri-ssaid) *n* campo *m*
county (kaun-ti) *n* condado *m*
couple (ka-pöl) *n* pareja *f*
coupon (kuu-pon) *n* cupón *m*
courage (ka-ridʒ) *n* valor *m*
courageous (kö-rei-dʒöss) *adj* valiente
course (kooss) *n* rumbo *m*; plato *m*; curso *m*; **intensive** ~ curso intensivo; **of** ~ por supuesto
court (koot) *n* tribunal *m*; corte *f*
courteous (köö-ti-öss) *adj* cortés
cousin (ka-sön) *n* prima *f*, primo *m*
cover (ka-vö) *v* cubrir; *n* refugio *m*;

tapa *f*; cubierta *f*; ~ **charge** precio del cubierto
cow (kau) *n* vaca *f*
coward (kau-öd) *n* cobarde *m*
cowardly (kau-öd-li) *adj* cobarde
cow-hide (kau-haid) *n* cuero vacuno
crab (kræb) *n* cangrejo *m*
crack (kræk) *n* crujido *m*; hendidura *f*; *v* crujir; *quebrar, *reventar
cradle (krei-döl) *n* cuna *f*
cramp (kræmp) *n* calambre *m*
crane (krein) *n* grúa *f*
crankcase (krængk-keiss) *n* cárter *m*
crankshaft (krængk-ʃaaft) *n* cigüeñal *m*
crash (kræʃ) *n* choque *m*; *v* chocar; precipitarse; ~ **barrier** barrera de protección
crate (kreit) *n* caja *f*
crater (krei-tö) *n* cráter *m*
crawl (krool) *v* arrastrarse; *n* crawl *m*
craze (kreis) *n* manía *f*
crazy (krei-si) *adj* loco
creak (kriik) *v* crujir
cream (kriim) *n* crema *f*; nata *f*; *adj* de color crema
creamy (krii-mi) *adj* cremoso
crease (kriiss) *v* *plegar; *n* raya *f*; pliegue *m*
create (kri-eit) *v* crear
creature (krii-chö) *n* criatura *f*; ser *m*
credible (krê-di-böl) *adj* verosímil
credit (krê-dit) *n* crédito *m*; *v* acreditar; ~ **card** tarjeta de crédito
creditor (krê-di-tö) *n* acreedor *m*
credulous (krê-dyu-löss) *adj* crédulo
creek (kriik) *n* ensenada *f*
** **creep** (kriip) *v* gatear*
creepy (krii-pi) *adj* lúgubre, espeluznante
cremate (kri-meit) *v* incinerar
cremation (kri-mei-ʃön) *n* incineración *f*
crew (kruu) *n* equipo *m*

cricket (*kri*-kit) *n* cricquet *m* ; grillo *m*

crime (kraim) *n* crimen *m*

criminal (*kri*-mi-nöl) *n* delincuente *m*, criminal *m* ; *adj* criminal ; ~ law derecho penal

criminality (kri-mi-*næ*-lö-ti) *n* criminalidad *f*

crimson (*krim*-sön) *adj* carmesí

crippled (*kri*-pöld) *adj* estropeado

crisis (*krai*-ssiss) *n* (pl crises) crisis *f*

crisp (krissp) *adj* crujiente, quebradizo

critic (*kri*-tik) *n* crítico *m*

critical (*kri*-ti-köl) *adj* crítico ; precario

criticism (*kri*-ti-ssi-söm) *n* crítica *f*

criticize (*kri*-ti-ssais) *v* criticar

crochet (krou-ʃei) *v* *hacer croché

crockery (*kro*-kö-ri) *n* cerámica *f*, loza *f*

crocodile (*kro*-kö-dail) *n* cocodrilo *m*

crooked (*kru*-kid) *adj* torcido, curvo ; deshonesto

crop (krop) *n* cosecha *f*

cross (kross) *v* *atravesar ; *adj* enojado, enfadado ; *n* cruz *f*

cross-eyed (*kross*-aid) *adj* bizco

crossing (*kro*-ssing) *n* travesía *f* ; encrucijada *f* ; paso *m* ; paso a nivel

crossroads (*kross*-rouds) *n* cruce *m*

crosswalk (*kross*-ᵘook) *nAm* cruce para peatones

crow (krou) *n* corneja *f*

crowbar (*krou*-baa) *n* pie de cabra

crowd (kraud) *n* masa *f*, muchedumbre *f*

crowded (*krau*-did) *adj* animado ; repleto

crown (kraun) *n* corona *f* ; *v* coronar

crucifix (*kruu*-ssi-fikss) *n* crucifijo *m*

crucifixion (kruu-ssi-*fik*-ʃön) *n* crucifixión *f*

crucify (*kruu*-ssi-fai) *v* crucificar

cruel (kruᵒl) *adj* cruel

cruise (kruus) *n* crucero *m*

crumb (kram) *n* migaja *f*

crusade (kruu-*sseid*) *n* cruzada *f*

crust (krasst) *n* corteza *f*

crutch (krach) *n* muleta *f*

cry (krai) *v* llorar ; gritar ; llamar ; *n* grito *m* ; voz *f*

crystal (*kri*-sstöl) *n* cristal *m* ; *adj* de cristal

Cuba (*kyuu*-bö) Cuba *f*

Cuban (*kyuu*-bön) *adj* cubano

cube (kyuub) *n* cubo *m*

cuckoo (*ku*-kuu) *n* cuclillo *m*

cucumber (*kyuu*-köm-bö) *n* pepino *m*

cuddle (*ka*-döl) *v* acariciar

cudgel (*ka*-dʒöl) *n* garrote *m*

cuff (kaf) *n* puño *m*

cuff-links (*kaf*-lingkss) *pl* gemelos *mpl* ; mancuernillas *fplMe*

cul-de-sac (*kal*-dö-ssæk) *n* callejon sin salida

cultivate (*kal*-ti-veit) *v* cultivar

culture (*kal*-chö) *n* cultura *f*

cultured (*kal*-chöd) *adj* culto

cunning (*ka*-ning) *adj* astuto

cup (kap) *n* taza *f* ; copa *f*

cupboard (*ka*-böd) *n* armario *m*

curb (kööb) *n* bordillo *m* ; *v* refrenar

cure (kyuᵒ) *v* curar ; *n* cura *f* ; curación *f*

curio (*kyu*ᵒ-ri-ou) *n* (pl ~s) curiosidad *f*

curiosity (kyuᵒ-ri-*o*-ssö-ti) *n* curiosidad *f*

curious (*kyu*ᵒ-ri-öss) *adj* curioso

curl (kööl) *v* rizar ; *n* rizo *m*

curler (*köö*-lö) *n* rulo *m*

curling-tongs (*köö*-ling-tongs) *pl* rizador *m*

curly (*köö*-li) *adj* crespo ; chino *adjMe*

currant (*ka*-rönt) *n* pasa de Corinto ; grosella *f*

currency (*ka*-rön-ssi) *n* moneda *f* ; foreign ~ moneda extranjera

current (ka-rönt) n corriente f; adj corriente; **alternating** ~ corriente alterna; **direct** ~ corriente continua

curry (ka-ri) n cari m

curse (kööss) v *maldecir; n maldición f

curtain (köö tön) n cortina f; telón m

curve (kööv) n curva f

curved (köövd) adj curvado, encorvado

cushion (ku-∫ön) n almohadón m

custodian (ka-sstou-di-ön) n guarda m

custody (ka-sstö-di) n detención f; custodia f; tutela f

custom (ka-sstöm) n costumbre f

customary (ka-sstö-mö-ri) adj usual, corriente, acostumbrado

customer (ka-sstö-mö) n cliente m

Customs (ka-sstöms) pl aduana f; ~ **duty** impuesto m; ~ **officer** oficial de aduanas

cut (kat) n incisión f; cortadura f

***cut** (kat) v cortar; *reducir; ~ **off** cortar

cutlery (kat-lö-ri) n cubiertos mpl

cutlet (kat-löt) n chuleta f

cycle (ssai-köl) n biciclo m; bicicleta f; ciclo m

cyclist (ssai-klisst) n ciclista m

cylinder (ssi-lin-dö) n cilindro m; ~ **head** culata del cilindro

cystitis (ssi-sstai-tiss) n cistitis f

Czech (chök) adj checo

Czechoslovakia (chê-kö-sslo-vaa-ki-ö) Checoslovaquia f

D

dad (dæd) n papá m

daddy (dæ-di) n papaíto m

daffodil (dæ-fö-dil) n narciso m

daily (dei-li) adj diario; n diario m

dairy (dê ö-ri) n lechería f

dam (dæm) n presa f; dique m

damage (dæ mid3) n perjuicio m; v dañar

damp (dæmp) adj húmedo; mojado; n humedad f; v *humedecer

dance (daanss) v bailar; n baile m

dandelion (dæn-di-lai-ön) n diente de león

dandruff (dæn-dröf) n caspa f

Dane (dein) n danés m

danger (dein-d3ö) n peligro m

dangerous (dein-d3ö-röss) adj peligroso

Danish (dei-ni∫) adj danés

dare (dê ö) v atreverse, osar; desafiar

daring (dê ö-ring) adj atrevido

dark (daak) adj oscuro, obscuro; n oscuridad f

darling (daa-ling) n amor m, querido m

darn (daan) v zurcir

dash (dæ∫) v correr; n guión m

dashboard (dæ∫-bood) n tablero de instrumentos

data (dei-tö) pl dato m

date¹ (deit) n fecha f; cita f; v datar; **out of** ~ anticuado

date² (deit) n dátil m

daughter (doo-tö) n hija f

dawn (doon) n alba f; aurora f

day (dei) n día m; **hy** ~ de día; ~ **trip** jornada f; **per** ~ a diario; **the** ~ **before yesterday** anteayer

daybreak (dei-breik) n amanecer m

daylight (dei-lait) n luz del día

dead (dêd) adj muerto; difunto

deaf (dêf) adj sordo

deal (diil) n transacción f

***deal** (diil) v repartir; ~ **with** v tratar con; *hacer negocios con

dealer (dii-lö) n negociante m, comerciante m

dear (di ö) adj querido; caro; amado

death (dêz) *n* muerte *f*; ~ **penalty** pena de muerte
debate (di-*beit*) *n* debate *m*
debit (*dê*-bit) *n* debe *m*
debt (dêt) *n* deuda *f*
decaffeinated (dii-*kæ*-fi-nei-tid) *adj* descafeinado
deceit (di-*ssiit*) *n* engaño *m*
deceive (di-*ssiiv*) *v* engañar
December (di-*ssêm*-bö) diciembre
decency (*dii*-ssön-ssi) *n* decencia *f*
decent (*dii*-ssönt) *adj* decente
decide (di-*ssaid*) *v* decidir
decision (di-*ssi*-3ön) *n* decisión *f*
deck (dêk) *n* cubierta *f*; ~ **cabin** camarote en cubierta; ~ **chair** silla de tijera
declaration (dê-klö-*rei*-∫ön) *n* declaración *f*
declare (di-*klêö*) *v* declarar; indicar
decoration (dê-kö-*rei*-∫ön) *n* decoración *f*
decrease (dii-*kriiss*) *v* *reducir; *disminuir; *n* disminución *f*
dedicate (*dê*-di-keit) *v* dedicar
deduce (di-*dyuuss*) *v* *deducir
deduct (di-*dakt*) *v* *deducir
deed (diid) *n* acción *f*, acto *m*
deep (diip) *adj* hondo
deep-freeze (diip-*friis*) *n* congelador *m*
deer (di⁶) *n* (pl ~) ciervo *m*
defeat (di-*fiit*) *v* derrotar; *n* derrota *f*
defective (di-*fêk*-tiv) *adj* defectuoso
defence (di-*fênss*) *n* defensa *f*
defend (di-*fênd*) *v* *defender
deficiency (di-*fi*-∫ön-ssi) *n* deficiencia *f*
deficit (*dê*-fi-ssit) *n* déficit *m*
define (di-*fain*) *v* definir, determinar
definite (*dê*-fi-nit) *adj* determinado; definido
definition (dê-fi-*ni*-∫ön) *n* definición *f*
deformed (di-*foomd*) *adj* contrahecho,

deforme
degree (di-*ghrii*) *n* grado *m*; título *m*
delay (di-*lei*) *v* retardar; *diferir; *n* retraso *m*, tardanza *f*; dilación *f*
delegate (*dê*-li-ghöt) *n* delegado *m*
delegation (dê-li-*ghei*-∫ön) *n* delegación *f*
deliberate¹ (di-*li*-bö-reit) *v* discutir, deliberar
deliberate² (di-*li*-bö-röt) *adj* deliberado
deliberation (di-li-bö-*rei*-∫ön) *n* deliberación *f*
delicacy (*dê*-li-kö-ssi) *n* golosina *f*
delicate (*dê*-li-köt) *adj* delicado; fino
delicatessen (dê-li-kö-*tê*-ssön) *n* gollerías *fpl*; tienda de comestibles finos
delicious (di-*li*-∫öss) *adj* exquisito, delicioso
delight (di-*lait*) *n* delicia *f*, deleite *m*; *v* encantar
delightful (di-*lait*-föl) *adj* delicioso, deleitoso
deliver (di-*li*-vö) *v* entregar; librar
delivery (di-*li*-vö-ri) *n* entrega *f*, reparto *m*; parto *m*; liberación *f*; ~ **van** furgoneta *f*
demand (di-*maand*) *v* *requerir, exigir; *n* exigencia *f*; demanda *f*
democracy (di-*mo*-krö-ssi) *n* democracia *f*
democratic (dê-mö-*kræ*-tik) *adj* democrático
demolish (di-*mo*-li∫) *v* *demoler
demolition (dê-mö-*li*-∫ön) *n* demolición *f*
demonstrate (*dê*-mön-sstreit) *v* *demostrar; *hacer una manifestación
demonstration (dê-mön-*sstrei*-∫ön) *n* manifestación *f*; demostración *f*
den (dên) *n* madriguera *f*
Denmark (*dên*-maak) Dinamarca *f*
denomination (di-no-mi-*nei*-∫ön) *n* denominación *f*

dense (dênss) *adj* denso

dent (dênt) *n* abolladura *f*

dentist (*dén*-tisst) *n* dentista *m*

denture (*dén*-chö) *n* dentadura posti-za

deny (di-*nai*) *v* *negar; *denegar

deodorant (dii-*ou*-dö-rönt) *n* desodo-rante *m*

depart (di-*paat*) *v* partir; *fallecer

department (di-*paat*-mönt) *n* departa-mento *m*; ~ **store** grandes almace-nes

departure (di-*paa*-chö) *n* despedida *f*, partida *f*

dependant (di-*pên*-dönt) *adj* depen-diente

depend on (di-*pênd*) depender de

deposit (di-*po*-sit) *n* depósito *m*; fian-za *f*; capa *f*, yacimiento *m*; *v* ingre-sar

depository (di-*po*-si-tö-ri) *n* almacén *m*

depot (*dê*-pou) *n* almacén *m*; *nAm* estación *f*

depress (di-*prêss*) *v* deprimir

depression (di-*prê*-jön) *n* desánimo *m*; depresión *f*

deprive of (di-*praiv*) privar de

depth (dêpz) *n* profundidad *f*

deputy (*dê*-pyu-ti) *n* diputado *m*; sus-tituto *m*

descend (di-*ssênd*) *v* *descender

descendant (di-*ssên*-dönt) *n* descen-diente *m*

descent (di-*ssênt*) *n* bajada *f*

describe (di-*sskraib*) *v* describir

description (di-*sskrip* jön) *n* descrip-ción *f*; señas personales

desert[1] (*dê*-söt) *n* desierto *m*; *adj* salvaje, desierto

desert[2] (di-*söt*) *v* desertar; dejar

deserve (di-*sööv*) *v* *merecer

design (di-*sain*) *v* diseñar; *n* diseño *m*; objetivo *m*

designate (*dê*-sigh-neit) *v* designar

desirable (di-*sai*[6]-rö-böl) *adj* deseable

desire (di-*sai*[6]) *n* deseo *m*; ganas *fpl*; *v* anhelar, desear

desk (dêssk) *n* escritorio *m*; pupitre *m*

despair (di-*sspê*[ö]) *n* desesperación *f*; *v* *estar desesperado

despatch (di-*sspæch*) *v* despachar

desperate (*dê*-sspö-röt) *adj* desespera-do

despise (di-*sspais*) *v* despreciar

despite (di-*sspait*) *prep* a pesar de

dessert (di-*söt*) *n* postre *m*

destination (dê-ssti-*nei*-jön) *n* destino *m*

destine (*dê*-sstin) *v* destinar

destiny (*dê*-ssti-ni) *n* destino *m*

destroy (di-*sstroi*) *v* *destruir

destruction (di-*sstrak*-jön) *n* destruc-ción *f*; ruina *f*

detach (di-*tæch*) *v* separar

detail (*dii*-teil) *n* particularidad *f*, de-talle *m*

detailed (*dii*-teild) *adj* detallado

detect (di-*têkt*) *v* descubrir

detective (di-*têk*-tiv) *n* detective *m*; ~ **story** novela policíaca

detergent (di-*töö*-dʒönt) *n* detergente *m*

determine (di-*töö*-min) *v* determinar

determined (di-*töö*-mind) *adj* resuelto

detour (*dii*-tu[6]) *n* desvío *m*

devaluation (dii-væl-yu-*ei*-jön) *n* des-valorización *f*

devalue (dii-*væl*-yuu) *v* desvalorizar

develop (di-*vê*-löp) *v* desarrollar; re-velar

development (di-*vê*-löp-mönt) *n* desa-rrollo *m*

deviate (*dii*-vi-eit) *v* desviarse

devil (*dê*-völ) *n* diablo *m*

devise (di-*vais*) *v* idear

devote (di-*vout*) *v* dedicar

dew (dyuu) *n* rocío *m*
diabetes (dai-ö-*bii*-tiis) *n* diabetes *f*
diabetic (dai-ö-*bé*-tik) *n* diabético *m*
diagnose (dai-ögh-*nous*) *v* diagnosticar; *comprobar
diagnosis (dai-ögh-*nou*-ssiss) *n* (pl -ses) diagnosis *m*
diagonal (dai-æ-ghö-nöl) *n* diagonal *f*; *adj* diagonal
diagram (*dai*-ö-ghræm) *n* esquema *m*; gráfico *m*
dialect (*dai*-ö-lêkt) *n* dialecto *m*
diamond (*dai*-ö-mönd) *n* diamante *m*
diaper (*dai*-ö-pö) *nAm* pañal *m*
diaphragm (*dai*-ö-fræm) *n* membrana *f*
diarrhoea (dai-ö-*ri*-ö) *n* diarrea *f*
diary (*dai*-ö-ri) *n* agenda *f*; diario *m*
dictaphone (*dik*-tö-foun) *n* dictáfono *m*
dictate (dik-*teit*) *v* dictar
dictation (dik-*tei*-jön) *n* dictado *m*
dictator (dik-*tei*-tö) *n* dictador *m*
dictionary (*dik*-jö-nö-ri) *n* diccionario *m*
did (did) *v* (p do)
die (dai) *v* *morir
diesel (*dii*-söl) *n* diesel *m*
diet (*dai*-öt) *n* régimen *m*
differ (*di*-fö) *v* *diferir
difference (*di*-fö-rönss) *n* diferencia *f*; distinción *f*
different (*di*-fö-rönt) *adj* diferente; otro
difficult (*di*-fi-költ) *adj* difícil; fastidioso
difficulty (*di*-fi-köl-ti) *n* dificultad *f*; trabajo *m*
*dig (digh) *v* cavar
digest (di-*dʒêsst*) *v* *digerir
digestible (di-*dʒê*-sstö-böl) *adj* digerible
digestion (di-*dʒêss*-chön) *n* digestión *f*

digit (*di*-dʒit) *n* número *m*
dignified (*digh*-ni-faid) *adj* distinguido
dike (daik) *n* dique *m*
dilapidated (di-*læ*-pi-dei-tid) *adj* ruinoso
diligence (*di*-li-dʒönss) *n* celo *m*, diligencia *f*
diligent (*di*-li-dʒönt) *adj* celoso, cuidadoso
dilute (dai-*lyuut*) *v* *diluir
dim (dim) *adj* deslucido, mate; oscuro, vago, difuso
dine (dain) *v* cenar
dinghy (*ding*-ghi) *n* chinchorro *m*
dining-car (*dai*-ning-kaa) *n* coche comedor
dining-room (*dai*-ning-ruum) *n* comedor *m*
dinner (*di*-nö) *n* comida principal; cena *f*
dinner-jacket (*di*-nö-dʒæ-kit) *n* smoking *m*
dinner-service (*di*-nö-ssöö-viss) *n* servicio de mesa
diphtheria (dif-*ziö*-ri-ö) *n* difteria *f*
diploma (di-*plou*-mö) *n* diploma *m*
diplomat (*di*-plö-mæt) *n* diplomático *m*
direct (di-*rêkt*) *adj* directo; *v* dirigir; administrar
direction (di-*rêk*-jön) *n* dirección *f*; instrucción *f*; dirección de escena; administración *f*; **directions for use** modo de empleo
directive (di-*rêk*-tiv) *n* directriz *f*
director (di-*rêk*-tö) *n* director *m*; director de escena
dirt (dööt) *n* suciedad *f*
dirty (*döö*-ti) *adj* sucio
disabled (di-*ssei*-böld) *adj* minusválido, inválido
disadvantage (di-ssöd-*vaan*-tidʒ) *n* desventaja *f*
disagree (di-ssö-*ghrii*) *v* no *estar de

acuerdo, *disentir

disagreeable (di-ssö-*ghrii*-ö-böl) *adj* desagradable

disappear (di-ssö-*piö*) *v* *desaparecer

disappoint (di-ssö-*point*) *v* decepcionar

disappointment (di-ssö-*point*-mönt) *n* desengaño *m*

disapprove (di-ssö-*pruuv*) *v* *desaprobar

disaster (di-*saa*-sstö) *n* desastre *m*; catástrofe *f*, calamidad *f*

disastrous (di-*saa*-sströss) *adj* desastroso

disc (dissk) *n* disco *m*; **slipped ~** hernia intervertebral

discard (di-*sskaad*) *v* desechar

discharge (diss-*chaadʒ*) *v* descargar; **~ of** dispensar de

discipline (*di*-ssi-plin) *n* disciplina *f*

discolour (di-*sska*-lö) *v* *desteñirse*; **discoloured** descolorido

disconnect (di-sskö-*nêkt*) *v* desconectar

discontented (di-sskön-*tên*-tid) *adj* descontento

discontinue (di-sskön-*ti*-nyuu) *v* suprimir, cesar

discount (*di*-sskaunt) *n* descuento *m*

discover (di-*sska*-vö) *v* descubrir

discovery (di-*sska*-vö-ri) *n* descubrimiento *m*

discuss (di-*sskass*) *v* discutir; debatir

discussion (di-*sska*-jön) *n* discusión *f*; conversación *f*, debate *m*

disease (di *siis*) *n* enfermedad *f*

disembark (ui-ssim-*baak*) *v* desembarcar

disgrace (diss-*ghreiss*) *n* deshonor *m*

disguise (diss-*ghais*) *v* disfrazarse; *n* disfraz *m*

disgusting (diss-*gha*-ssting) *adj* repugnante, asqueroso

dish (diʃ) *n* plato *m*; fuente *f*; guiso *m*

dishonest (di-*sso*-nisst) *adj* improbo

disinfect (di-ssin-*fêkt*) *v* desinfectar

disinfectant (di-ssin-*fêk*-tönt) *n* desinfectante *m*

dislike (di-*sslaik*) *v* detestar, no gustar; *n* repugnancia *f*, aversión *f*, antipatía *f*

dislocated (*di*-sslö-kei-tid) *adj* dislocado

dismiss (diss-*miss*) *v* *despedir

disorder (di-*ssoo*-dö) *n* desorden *m*

dispatch (di-*sspæch*) *v* enviar, despachar

display (di-*ssplei*) *v* exhibir; *mostrar; *n* exposición *f*

displease (di-*sspliis*) *v* disgustar, desagradar

disposable (di-*sspou*-sö-böl) *adj* desechable

disposal (di-*sspou*-söl) *n* disposición *f*

dispose of (di-*sspous*) *disponer de

dispute (di-*sspyuut*) *n* disputa *f*; riña *f*, contienda *f*; *v* *reñir, disputar

dissatisfied (di-*ssæ*-tiss-faid) *adj* insatisfecho

dissolve (di *solv*) *v* *disolver

dissuade from (di-*ssᵘeid*) disuadir

distance (*di*-sstönss) *n* distancia *f*; **~ in kilometres** kilometraje *m*

distant (*di*-sstönt) *adj* lejano

distinct (di-*sstingkt*) *adj* claro; distinto

distinction (di-*sstingk*-jön) *n* distinción *f*, diferencia *f*

distinguish (di-*ssting*-ghᵘj) *v* distinguir

distinguished (di-*ssting*-ghᵘiʃt) *adj* distinguido

distress (di-*sstrêss*) *n* peligro *m*; **~ signal** señal de alarma

distribute (di-*sstri*-byuut) *v* *distribuir

distributor (di-*sstri*-byu-tö) *n* distribuidor *m*

district (*di*-sstrikt) *n* distrito *m*; comarca *f*; barrio *m*

disturb (di-*sstööb*) *v* estorbar, molestar

disturbance (di-*sstöö*-bönss) *n* disturbio *m*; confusión *f*

ditch (dich) *n* zanja *f*, cuneta *f*

dive (daiv) *v* bucear

diversion (dai-*vöö*-Jön) *n* desvío *m*; diversión *f*

divide (di-*vaid*) *v* dividir; repartir; separar

divine (di-*vain*) *adj* divino

division (di-*vi*-Zön) *n* división *f*; separación *f*; departamento *m*

divorce (di-*vooss*) *n* divorcio *m*; *v* divorciar

dizziness (*di*-si-nöss) *n* vértigo *m*

dizzy (*di*-si) *adj* mareado

*do (duu) *v* *hacer; *ser suficiente

dock (dok) *n* dock *m*; muelle *m*; *v* atracar

docker (*do*-kö) *n* obrero portuario

doctor (*dok*-tö) *n* médico *m*; doctor *m*

document (*do*-kyu-mönt) *n* documento *m*

dog (dogh) *n* perro *m*

dogged (*do*-ghid) *adj* obstinado

doll (dol) *n* muñeca *f*

dome (doum) *n* cúpula *f*

domestic (dö-*mé*-sstik) *adj* doméstico; interior; *n* sirviente *m*

domicile (*do*-mi-ssail) *n* domicilio *m*

domination (do-mi-*nei*-Jön) *n* dominación *f*

dominion (dö-*mi*-nyön) *n* dominio *m*

donate (dou-*neit*) *v* donar

donation (dou-*nei*-Jön) *n* donación *f*

done (dan) *v* (pp do)

donkey (*dong*-ki) *n* burro *m*

donor (*dou*-nö) *n* donante *m*

door (doo) *n* puerta *f*; **revolving** ~ puerta giratoria; **sliding** ~ puerta

corrediza

doorbell (*doo*-bêl) *n* timbre *m*

door-keeper (*doo*-kii-pö) *n* portero *m*

doorman (*doo*-mön) *n* (pl -men) portero *m*

dormitory (*doo*-mi-tri) *n* dormitorio *m*

dose (douss) *n* dosis *f*

dot (dot) *n* punto *m*

double (*da*-böl) *adj* doble

doubt (daut) *v* dudar; *n* duda *f*; **without** ~ sin duda

doubtful (*daut*-föl) *adj* dudoso; inseguro

dough (dou) *n* masa *f*

down¹ (daun) *adv* abajo; hacia abajo; *adj* abatido; *prep* a lo largo de, debajo de; ~ **payment** primer pago

down² (daun) *n* flojel *m*

downpour (*daun*-poo) *n* aguacero *m*

downstairs (daun-*sstê°*s) *adv* abajo

downstream (daun-*sstriim*) *adv* río abajo

down-to-earth (daun-tu-*ööz*) *adj* sensato

downwards (*daun*-ᵘöds) *adv* hacia abajo

dozen (*da*-sön) *n* (pl ~, ~s) docena *f*

draft (draaft) *n* giro *m*

drag (drægh) *v* arrastrar

dragon (*dræ*-ghön) *n* dragón *m*

drain (drein) *v* desecar; drenar; *n* desagüe *m*

drama (*draa*-mö) *n* drama *m*; tragedia *f*; teatro *m*

dramatic (drö-*mæ*-tik) *adj* dramático

dramatist (*dræ*-mö-tisst) *n* dramaturgo *m*

drank (drængk) *v* (p drink)

draper (*drei*-pö) *n* pañero *m*

drapery (*drei*-pö-ri) *n* pañería *f*

draught (draaft) *n* corriente de aire; **draughts** juego de damas

draught-board (*draaft*-bood) *n* tablero

de damas
draw (droo) *n* sorteo *m*
*****draw** (droo) *v* dibujar; arrastrar; sacar; jalar *vMe*; ~ **up** redactar
drawbridge (*droo*-bridȝ) *n* puente levadizo
drawer (*droo*-o) *n* cajón *m*; **drawers** calzoncillos *mpl*
drawing (*droo*-ing) *n* dibujo *m*
drawing-pin (*droo*-ing-pin) *n* chinche *f*
drawing-room (*droo*-ing-ruum) *n* salón *m*
dread (drêd) *v* temer; *n* temor *m*
dreadful (*drêd*-föl) *adj* terrible, espantoso
dream (driim) *n* sueño *m*
*****dream** (driim) *v* *soñar
dress (drêss) *v* *vestir; *vestirse; vendar; *n* vestido *m*
dressing-gown (*drê*-ssing-ghaun) *n* bata *f*
dressing-room (*drê*-ssing-ruum) *n* vestuario *m*
dressing-table (*drê*-ssing-tei-böl) *n* tocador *m*
dressmaker (*drêss*-mei-kö) *n* modista *f*
drill (dril) *v* taladrar; entrenar; *n* taladro *m*
drink (dringk) *n* aperitivo *m*, bebida *f*
*****drink** (dringk) *v* beber
drinking-water (*dring*-king-ᵘoo-tö) *n* agua potable
drip-dry (drip-*drai*) *adj* no precisa plancha
drive (draiv) *n* calzada *f*; paseo en coche
*****drive** (draiv) *v* *conducir
driver (*drai*-vö) *n* conductor *m*
drizzle (*dri*-söl) *n* llovizna *f*
drop (drop) *v* dejar caer; *n* gota *f*
drought (draut) *n* sequía *f*
drown (draun) *v* ahogar; *be

drowned ahogarse
drug (dragh) *n* estupefaciente *m*; medicamento *m*
drugstore (*dragh*-sstoo) *nAm* droguería *f*, farmacia *f*; almacén *m*
drum (dram) *n* tambor *m*
drunk (drangk) *adj* (pp drink) borracho
dry (drai) *adj* seco; *v* secar
dry-clean (drai-*kliin*) *v* limpiar en seco
dry-cleaner's (drai-*klii*-nös) *n* tintorería *f*
dryer (*drai*-ö) *n* secadora *f*
duchess (da-chiss) *n* duquesa *f*
duck (dak) *n* pato *m*
due (dyuu) *adj* aguardado; adeudado; debido
dues (dyuus) *pl* derechos *mpl*
dug (dagh) *v* (p, pp dig)
duke (dyuuk) *n* duque *m*
dull (dal) *adj* aburrido; pálido, mate; embotado
dumb (dam) *adj* mudo; atontado, estúpido
dune (dyuun) *n* duna *f*
dung (dang) *n* abono *m*
dunghill (*dang*-hil) *n* estercolero *m*
duration (dyu-*rei*-ʃön) *n* duración *f*
during (*dyu*ᵒ-ring) *prep* durante
dusk (dassk) *n* crepúsculo *m*
dust (dasst) *n* polvo *m*
dustbin (*dasst*-bin) *n* cubo de la basura
dusty (*da*-ssti) *adj* polvoriento
Dutch (dach) *adj* holandés
Dutchman (*dach*-mön) *n* (pl -men) holandés *m*
dutiable (*dyuu*-ti-ö-böl) *adj* imponible
duty (*dyuu*-ti) *n* deber *m*; tarea *f*; arancel *m*; **Customs** ~ impuesto de aduana
duty-free (dyuu-ti-*frii*) *adj* exento de impuestos
dwarf (dᵘoof) *n* enano *m*

dye (dai) *v* *teñir; *n* tintura *f*

dynamo (*dai*-nö-mou) *n* (pl ~s) dínamo *f*

dysentery (*di*-ssön-tri) *n* disentería *f*

E

each (iich) *adj* cada; ~ **other** el uno al otro

eager (*ii*-ghö) *adj* ansioso, impaciente

eagle (*ii*-ghöl) *n* águila *m*

ear (i°) *n* oreja *f*

earache (*i°*-reik) *n* dolor de oídos

ear-drum (*i°*-dram) *n* tímpano *m*

earl (ööl) *n* conde *m*

early (*öö*-li) *adj* temprano

earn (öön) *v* ganar

earnest (*öö*-nisst) *n* seriedad *f*

earnings (*öö*-nings) *pl* ingresos *mpl*, ganancias *fpl*

earring (*i°*-ring) *n* pendiente *m*

earth (ööz) *n* tierra *f*; suelo *m*

earthenware (*öö*-zön-ᵘè°) *n* loza *f*

earthquake (*ööz*-kᵘeik) *n* terremoto *m*

ease (iis) *n* desenvoltura *f*, facilidad *f*; bienestar *m*

east (iisst) *n* este *m*

Easter (*ii*-sstö) Pascua

easterly (*ii*-sstö-li) *adj* oriental

eastern (*ii*-sstön) *adj* oriental

easy (*ii*-si) *adj* fácil; cómodo; ~ **chair** butaca *f*

easy-going (*ii*-si-ghou-ing) *adj* relajado

* **eat** (iit) *v* comer; cenar

eavesdrop (*iivs*-drop) *v* escuchar

ebony (*é*-bö-ni) *n* ébano *m*

eccentric (ik-*ssên*-trik) *adj* excéntrico

echo (*é*-kou) *n* (pl ~es) eco *m*

eclipse (i-*klipss*) *n* eclipse *m*

economic (ii-kö-*no*-mik) *adj* económico

economical (ii-kö-*no*-mi-köl) *adj* parsimonioso, económico

economist (i-*ko*-nö-misst) *n* economista *m*

economize (i-*ko*-nö-mais) *v* economizar

economy (i-*ko*-nö-mi) *n* economía *f*

ecstasy (*êk*-sstö-si) *n* éxtasis *m*

Ecuador (*ê*-kᵘö-doo) Ecuador *m*

Ecuadorian (ê-kᵘö-*doo*-ri-ön) *n* ecuatoriano *m*

eczema (*êk*-ssi-mö) *n* eczema *m*

edge (êdʒ) *n* borde *m*

edible (*é*-di-böl) *adj* comestible

edition (i-*di*-ʃön) *n* edición *f*; **morning** ~ edición de mañana

editor (*ê*-di-tö) *n* redactor *m*

educate (*ê*-dʒu-keit) *v* formar, educar

education (ê-dʒu-*kei*-ʃön) *n* educación *f*

eel (iil) *n* anguila *f*

effect (i-*fêkt*) *n* resultado *m*, efecto *m*; *v* efectuar; **in ~** en realidad

effective (i-*fêk*-tiv) *adj* eficaz

efficient (i-*fi*-ʃönt) *adj* eficiente

effort (*ê*-föt) *n* esfuerzo *m*

egg (êgh) *n* huevo *m*

egg-cup (*êgh*-kap) *n* huevera *f*

eggplant (*êgh*-plaant) *n* berenjena *f*

egg-yolk (*êgh*-youk) *n* yema de huevo

egoistic (ê-ghou-*i*-sstik) *adj* egoísta

Egypt (*ii*-dʒipt) Egipto *m*

Egyptian (i-*dʒip*-ʃön) *adj* egipcio

eiderdown (*ai*-dö-daun) *n* edredón *m*

eight (eit) *num* ocho

eighteen (ei-*tiin*) *num* dieciocho

eighteenth (ei-*tiinz*) *num* decimoctavo

eighth (eitz) *num* octavo

eighty (*ei*-ti) *num* ochenta

either (*ai*-öö) *pron* cualquiera de los dos; **either ... or** o ... o, bien ... bien

elaborate (i-*læ*-bö-reit) v elaborar

elastic (i-*læ*-sstik) adj elástico; flexible; ~ **band** cinta de goma

elasticity (ê-læ-*ssti*-ssö-ti) n elasticidad f

elbow (*êl*-bou) n codo m

elder (*êl*-dö) adj mayor

elderly (*êl*-dö-li) adj anciano

eldest (*êl*-disst) adj mayor

elect (i-*lêkt*) v *elegir

election (i-*lêk*-fön) n elección f

electric (i-*lêk*-trik) adj eléctrico; ~ **razor** afeitadora eléctrica

electrician (i-lêk-*tri*-fön) n electricista m

electricity (ı-lêk-*tri*-ssö-ti) n electricidad f

electronic (i-lêk-*tro*-nik) adj electrónico

elegance (ê-li-ghönss) n elegancia f

elegant (ê-li-ghönt) adj elegante

element (ê-li-mönt) n elemento m

elephant (ê-li-fönt) n elefante m

elevator (ê-li-vei tö) nAm ascensor m; elevador mMc

eleven (i-*lê*-vön) num once

eleventh (i-*lê*-vönz) num onceno

elf (êlf) n (pl elves) duende m

eliminate (i-*li*-mi-neit) v eliminar

elm (êlm) n olmo m

else (êlss) adv si no

elsewhere (êl-ss^{u}ê^ö) adv otra parte

elucidate (i-*luu*-ssi-deit) v elucidar

emancipation (i-mæn-ssi-*pei*-fön) n emancipación f

embankment (im-*bæng*k-mont) n terraplén m

embargo (êm-*baa*-ghou) n (pl ~es) embargo m

embark (im-*baak*) v embarcar

embarkation (êm-baa-*kei*-fön) n embarcación f

embarrass (im-*bæ*-röss) v turbar; *desconcertar; estorbar; **embar-**

rassed tímido

embassy (*êm*-bö-ssi) n embajada f

emblem (*êm*-blöm) n emblema m

embrace (im-*breiss*) v abrazar; n abrazo m

embroider (im-*broi*-dö) v bordar

embroidery (im-*broi*-dö-ri) n bordado m

emerald (ê-mö-röld) n esmeralda f

emergency (i-*möö*-dʒön-ssi) n caso de urgencia, urgencia f; emergencia f; ~ **exit** salida de emergencia

emigrant (ê-mi-ghrönt) n emigrante m

emigrate (ê-mi-ghreit) v emigrar

emigration (ê-mi-*ghrei*-fön) n emigración f

emotion (i-*mou*-fön) n emoción f

emperor (êm-pö-rö) n emperador m

emphasize (êm-fö-ssais) v enfatizar, acentuar

empire (êm-pai^ö) n imperio m

employ (im-*ploi*) v emplear

employee (êm-ploi-*ii*) n empleado m

employer (im-*ploi*-ö) n patrón m

employment (im-*ploi*-mönt) n empleo m; ~ **exchange** oficina de colocación

empress (êm-priss) n emperatriz f

empty (êmp-ti) adj vacío; v vaciar

enable (i-*nei*-bol) v permitir

enamel (i-*næ*-möl) n esmalte m

enamelled (i-*næ*-möld) adj esmaltado

enchanting (in-*chaan*-ting) adj espléndido, encantador

encircle (in *ssöö*-köl) v *circuir, cercar, *encerrar

enclose (ing-*klous*) v *incluir

enclosure (ing-*klou*-ʒö) n anexo m

encounter (ing-*kaun*-tö) v *encontrarse con; n encuentro m

encourage (ing-*ka*-ridʒ) v *alentar

encyclopaedia (ên-ssai-klö-*pii*-di-ö) n enciclopedia f

end (ênd) *n* fin *m*, extremo *m*; final *m*; *v* terminar, acabar; terminarse

ending (ên-ding) *n* conclusión *f*

endless (ênd-löss) *adj* infinito

endorse (in-*dooss*) *v* visar, endosar

endure (in-*dyu*ó) *v* soportar

enemy (ê-nö-mi) *n* enemigo *m*

energetic (ê-nö-*dʒê*-tik) *adj* enérgico

energy (ê-nö-dʒi) *n* energía *f*; fuerza *f*

engage (ing-*gheidʒ*) *v* emplear; reservar; comprometerse; **engaged** prometido; ocupado

engagement (ing-*gheidʒ*-mönt) *n* noviazgo *m*; compromiso *m*; ~ **ring** anillo de esponsales

engine (ên-dʒin) *n* máquina *f*, motor *m*; locomotora *f*

engineer (ên-dʒi-*ni*ó) *n* ingeniero *m*

England (*ing*-ghlönd) Inglaterra *f*

English (*ing*-ghliʃ) *adj* inglés

Englishman (*ing*-ghliʃ-mön) *n* (pl - men) inglés *m*

engrave (ing-*ghreiv*) *v* grabar

engraver (ing-*ghrei*-vö) *n* grabador *m*

engraving (ing-*ghrei*-ving) *n* estampa *f*; grabado *m*

enigma (i-*nigh*-mö) *n* enigma *m*

enjoy (in-*dʒoi*) *v* disfrutar, gozar

enjoyable (in-*dʒoi*-ö-böl) *adj* agradable, grato, deleitable; rico

enjoyment (in-*dʒoi*-mönt) *n* goce *m*

enlarge (in-*laadʒ*) *v* ampliar

enlargement (in-*laadʒ*-mönt) *n* ampliación *f*

enormous (i-*noo*-möss) *adj* gigantesco, enorme

enough (i-*naf*) *adv* bastante; *adj* suficiente

enquire (ing-*k*ᵘ*ai*ó) *v* preguntar; investigar

enquiry (ing-*k*ᵘ*ai*ó-ri) *n* información *f*; investigación *f*; encuesta *f*

enter (*ên*-tö) *v* entrar; inscribir

enterprise (*ên*-tö-prais) *n* empresa *f*

entertain (ên-tö-*tein*) *v* *divertir, *entretener; hospedar

entertainer (ên-tö-*tei*-nö) *n* cómico *m*

entertaining (ên-tö-*tei*-ning) *adj* divertido, entretenido

entertainment (ên-tö-*tein*-mönt) *n* diversión *f*, entretenimiento *m*

enthusiasm (in-*zyuu*-si-æ-söm) *n* entusiasmo *m*

enthusiastic (in-zyuu-si-æ-sstik) *adj* entusiasta

entire (in-*tai*ó) *adj* todo, entero

entirely (in-*tai*ó-li) *adv* enteramente

entrance (*ên*-trönss) *n* entrada *f*; acceso *m*

entrance-fee (*ên*-trönss-fii) *n* entrada *f*

entry (*ên*-tri) *n* entrada *f*, ingreso *m*; anotación *f*; **no** ~ prohibido el paso

envelope (*ên*-vö-loup) *n* sobre *m*

envious (*ên*-vi-öss) *adj* envidioso, celoso

environment (in-*vai*ó-rön-mönt) *n* medio ambiente; alrededores *mpl*

envoy (*ên*-voi) *n* enviado *m*

envy (*ên*-vi) *n* envidia *f*; *v* envidiar

epic (ê-pik) *n* poema épico; *adj* épico

epidemic (ê-pi-*dê*-mik) *n* epidemia *f*

epilepsy (*ê*-pi-lêp-ssi) *n* epilepsia *f*

epilogue (*ê*-pi-logh) *n* epílogo *m*

episode (*ê*-pi-ssoud) *n* episodio *m*

equal (*ii*-kᵘöl) *adj* igual; *v* igualar

equality (i-*k*ᵘ*o*-lö-ti) *n* igualdad *f*

equalize (*ii*-kᵘö-lais) *v* igualar

equally (*ii*-kᵘö-li) *adv* igualmente

equator (i-*k*ᵘ*ei*-tö) *n* ecuador *m*

equip (i-*k*ᵘ*ip*) *v* equipar

equipment (i-*k*ᵘ*ip*-mönt) *n* equipo *m*

equivalent (i-*k*ᵘ*i*-vö-lönt) *adj* equivalente

eraser (i-*rei*-sö) *n* goma de borrar

erect (i-*rêkt*) *v* erigir; *adj* erguido, recto; parado *adjMe*

err (öö) v *errar

errand (ê-rönd) n recado m

error (ê-rö) n falta f, error m

escalator (ê-sskö-lei-tö) n escalera móvil

escape (i-sskeip) v escaparse; *huir, escapar; n evasión f

escort[1] (ê-sskoot) n escolta f

escort[2] (i-sskoot) v escoltar

especially (i-sspê-ʃö-li) adv sobre todo, especialmente

esplanade (ê-ssplö-neid) n explanada f

essay (ê-ssei) n ensayo m; tratado m, composición f

essence (ê-ssönss) n esencia f; núcleo m

essential (i-ssên-ʃöl) adj indispensable; esencial

essentially (i-ssên-ʃö-li) adv sobre todo

establish (i-sstæ-bliʃ) v *establecer; *comprobar

estate (i-ssteit) n propiedad f

esteem (i-sstiim) n respeto m, estima f; v estimar

estimate[1] (ê-ssti-meit) v evaluar, estimar

estimate[2] (ê-ssti-möt) n estimación f

estuary (êss-chu-ö-ri) n estuario m

etcetera (êt-ssê-tö-rö) etcétera

etching (ê-ching) n aguafuerte f

eternal (ı-töö-nöl) adj eterno

eternity (i-töö-nö-ti) n eternidad f

ether (ii-zö) n éter m

Ethiopia (i-zi-ou-pi-ö) Etiopía f

Ethiopian (i-zi-ou-pi-ön) adj etíope

Europe (yuᵉ-röp) Europa f

European (yuᵉ-rö-pii-ön) adj europeo

evacuate (i-væ-kyu-eit) v evacuar

evaluate (i-væl-yu-eit) v evaluar

evaporate (i-væ-pö-reit) v evaporar

even (ii-vön) adj llano, plano, igual; constante; par; adv aun

evening (iiv-ning) n tarde f; ~ dress traje de etiqueta

event (i-vênt) n acontecimiento m; caso m

eventual (i-vên-chu-öl) adj eventual; final

ever (ê-vö) adv jamás; siempre

every (êv-ri) adj cada

everybody (êv-ri-bo-di) pron todos

everyday (êv-ri-dei) adj cotidiano

everyone (êv-ri-ᵘan) pron cada uno, todo el mundo

everything (êv-ri-zing) pron todo

everywhere (êv-ri-ᵘêᵒ) adv por todas partes

evidence (ê-vi-dönss) n prueba f

evident (ê-vi-dönt) adj evidente

evil (ii-völ) n mal m; adj malo, malvado

evolution (ii-vö-luu-ʃön) n evolución f

exact (igh-sækt) adj exacto

exactly (igh-sækt-lı) adv exactamente

exaggerate (igh-sæ-dʒö-reit) v exagerar

examination (igh-sæ-mi-nei-ʃön) n examen m; interrogatorio m

examine (igh-sæ-min) v examinar

example (igh-saam-pöl) n ejemplo m; for ~ por ejemplo

excavation (êkss-kö-vei-ʃön) n excavación f

exceed (ik-ssiid) v exceder; superar

excel (ik-ssêl) v distinguirse

excellent (êk-ssö-lönt) adj excelente

except (ik-ssêpt) prep excepto

exception (ik-ssêp-ʃön) n excepción f

exceptional (ık-ssêp-ʃö-nöl) adj extraordinario, excepcional

excerpt (êk-ssööpt) n extracto m

excess (ik-ssêss) n exceso m

excessive (ik-ssê-ssiv) adj excesivo

exchange (ikss-cheindʒ) v intercambiar, cambiar; n cambio m; bolsa f; ~ **office** oficina de cambio; ~

rate cambio *m*

excite (ik-*ssait*) *v* excitar

excitement (ik-*ssait*-mönt) *n* agitación *f*, excitación *f*

exciting (ik-*ssai*-ting) *adj* excitante

exclaim (ik-*sskleim*) *v* exclamar

exclamation (êk-ssklö-*mei*-∫ön) *n* exclamación *f*

exclude (ik-*sskluud*) *v* *excluir

exclusive (ik-*sskluu*-ssiv) *adj* exclusivo

exclusively (ik-*sskluu*-ssiv-li) *adv* exclusivamente, únicamente

excursion (ik-*ssköö*-∫ön) *n* excursión *f*

excuse[1] (ik-*sskyuuss*) *n* excusa *f*

excuse[2] (ik-*sskyuus*) *v* excusar, disculpar

execute (*êk*-ssi-kyuut) *v* ejecutar

execution (êk-ssi-*kyuu*-∫ön) *n* ejecución *f*

executioner (êk-ssi-*kyuu*-∫ö-nö) *n* verdugo *m*

executive (igh-*sê*-kyu-tiv) *adj* ejecutivo; *n* poder ejecutivo; ejecutivo *m*

exempt (igh-*∫êmpt*) *v* dispensar, eximir; *adj* exento

exemption (igh-*sêmp*-∫ön) *n* exención *f*

exercise (*êk*-ssö-ssais) *n* ejercicio *m*; *v* ejercitar; ejercer

exhale (êkss-*heil*) *v* exhalar

exhaust (igh-*soosst*) *n* tubo de escape, escape *m*; *v* extenuar; ~ **gases** gases de escape

exhibit (igh-*si*-bit) *v* *exponer; exhibir

exhibition (êk-ssi-*bi*-∫ön) *n* exposición *f*

exile (*êk*-ssail) *n* exilio *m*; exiliado *m*

exist (igh-*sisst*) *v* existir

existence (igh-*si*-sstönss) *n* existencia *f*

exit (*êk*-ssit) *n* salida *f*

exotic (igh-*so*-tik) *adj* exótico

expand (ik-*sspænd*) *v* *extender;

*desplegar

expect (ik-*sspêkt*) *v* aguardar, esperar

expectation (êk-sspêk-*tei*-∫ön) *n* esperanza *f*

expedition (êk-sspö-*di*-∫ön) *n* envío *m*; expedición *f*

expel (ik-*sspêl*) *v* expulsar

expenditure (ik-*sspên*-di-chö) *n* gasto *m*

expense (ik-*sspênss*) *n* gasto *m*

expensive (ik-*sspên*-ssiv) *adj* caro; costoso

experience (ik-*sspi*[ö]-ri-önss) *n* experiencia *f*; *v* experimentar, vivir; **experienced** experimentado

experiment (ik-*sspê*-ri-mönt) *n* prueba *f*, experimento *m*; *v* experimentar

expert (*êk*-sspööt) *n* perito *m*, experto *m*; *adj* competente

expire (ik-*sspai*[ö]) *v* expirar, terminarse; espirar; **expired** caducado

expiry (ik-*sspai*[ö]-ri) *n* vencimiento *m*

explain (ik-*ssplein*) *v* explicar

explanation (êk-ssplö-*nei*-∫ön) *n* aclaración *f*, explicación *f*

explicit (ik-*sspli*-ssit) *adj* expreso, explícito

explode (ik-*ssploud*) *v* estallar

exploit (ik-*ssploit*) *v* abusar de, explotar

explore (ik-*ssploo*) *v* explorar

explosion (ik-*ssplou*-zön) *n* explosión *f*

explosive (ik-*ssplou*-ssiv) *adj* explosivo; *n* explosivo *m*

export[1] (ik-*sspoot*) *v* exportar

export[2] (*êk*-sspoot) *n* exportación *f*

exportation (êk-sspoo-*tei*-∫ön) *n* exportación *f*

exports (*êk*-sspootss) *pl* exportación *f*

exposition (êk-sspö-*si*-∫ön) *n* exposición *f*

exposure (ik-*sspou*-zö) *n* exposición *f*; ~ **meter** exposímetro *m*

express (ik-*sspréss*) v expresar; *adj* expreso; explícito; ~ **train** tren expreso

expression (ik-*ssprê*-ʃön) n expresión f

exquisite (ik-*sskᵘi*-sit) *adj* exquisito

extend (ik-*ssténd*) v prolongar; ampliar; conceder

extension (ik-*sstên*-ʃön) n prórroga f; ampliación f; extensión f; ~ **cord** cordón de extensión

extensive (ik-*sstên*-ssiv) *adj* extenso; vasto

extent (ik-*sstênt*) n dimensión f

exterior (êk-*ssti*ᵒ-ri-ö) *adj* exterior; n exterior m

external (êk-*sstöö*-nöl) *adj* exterior

extinguish (ik-*ssting*-ghᵘiʃ) v extinguir, apagar

extort (ik-*sstoot*) v extorsionar

extortion (ik-*sstoo*-ʃön) n extorsión f

extra (êk-sströ) *adj* extra

extract[1] (ik-*ssträkt*) v *extraer

extract[2] (êk-ssträkt) n fragmento m

extradite (êk-sströ-dait) v entregar

extraordinary (ik-*sstroo*-dön-ri) *adj* extraordinario

extravagant (ik-*ssträ*-vö-ghönt) *adj* exagerado, extravagante

extreme (ik-*sstriim*) *adj* extremo; n extremo m

exuberant (igh-*syuu*-bö-rönt) *adj* exuberante

eye (ai) n ojo m

eyebrow (*ai*-brau) n ceja f

eyelash (*ai*-læʃ) n pestaña f

eyelid (*al*-lld) n párpado m

eye-pencil (*ai*-pên-ssöl) n lápiz para las cejas

eye-shadow (*ai*-ʃæ-dou) n sombra para los ojos

eye-witness (*ai*-ᵘit-nöss) n testigo de vista

F

fable (*fei*-böl) n fábula f

fabric (*fæ*-brik) n tejido m; estructura f

façade (fö-*ssaad*) n fachada f

face (feiss) n cara f; v enfrentarse con; ~ **massage** masaje facial; **facing** enfrente de

face-cream (*feiss*-kriim) n crema facial

face-pack (*feiss*-pæk) n máscara facial

face-powder (*feiss*-pau-dö) n polvo facial

facility (fö-*ssi*-lö-ti) n facilidad f

fact (tækt) n hecho m; **in** ~ efectivamente

factor (*fæk*-tö) n factor m

factory (*fæk*-tö-ri) n fábrica f

factual (*fæk*-chu-öl) *adj* real

faculty (*fæ*-köl-tı) n facultad f; don m, aptitud f

fad (fæd) n antojo m

fade (feid) v *desteñirse

faience (fai-*angss*) n loza f

fail (feil) v fallar; faltar; omitir; *ser suspendido; **without** ~ sin falta

failure (*feil*-yö) n fracaso m; fiasco m

faint (feint) v desmayarse; *adj* débil, vago

fair (fê*ᵒ*) n feria f; *adj* justo; rubio; bonito

fairly (*fê*ᵒ-li) *adv* bastante, medianamente

fairy (*fê*ᵒ-ri) n hada f

fairytale (*fê*ᵒ-ri-teil) n cuento de hadas

faith (feiz) n fe f; confianza f

faithful (*feiz*-ful) *adj* fiel

fake (feik) n falsificación f

fall (fool) n caída f; nAm otoño m; *fall** (fool) v *caer

false (foolss) *adj* falso; inexacto; ~

teeth dentadura postiza
falter (*fool*-tö) *v* vacilar; balbucear
fame (feim) *n* fama *f*; reputación *f*
familiar (fö-*mil*-yö) *adj* familiar
family (*fæ*-mö-li) *n* familia *f*; ~ **name** apellido *m*
famous (*fei*-möss) *adj* famoso
fan (fæn) *n* ventilador *m*; abanico *m*; admirador *m*; ~ **belt** correa del ventilador
fanatical (fö-*næ*-ti-köl) *adj* fanático
fancy (*fæn*-ssi) *v* gustar, antojarse; imaginarse; *n* capricho *m*; imaginación *f*
fantastic (fæn-*tæ*-sstik) *adj* fantástico
fantasy (*fæn*-tö-si) *n* fantasía *f*
far (faa) *adj* lejano; *adv* mucho; **by** ~ con mucho; **so** ~ hasta ahora
far-away (*faa*-rö-ᵁei) *adj* remoto
farce (faass) *n* sainete *m*, farsa *f*
fare (fê⁶) *n* gastos de viaje, precio del billete; alimento *m*
farm (faam) *n* granja *f*
farmer (*faa*-mö) *n* granjero *m*; **farmer's wife** granjera *f*
farmhouse (*faam*-hauss) *n* cortijo *m*; rancho *mMe*
far-off (*faa*-rof) *adj* remoto
fascinate (*fæ*-ssi-neit) *v* cautivar
fascism (*fæ*-ʃi-söm) *n* fascismo *m*
fascist (*fæ*-ʃisst) *adj* fascista
fashion (*fæ*-ʃön) *n* moda *f*; modo *m*
fashionable (*fæ*-ʃö-nö-böl) *adj* a la moda
fast (faasst) *adj* rápido; firme
fast-dyed (faasst-*daid*) *adj* lavable, no destiñe
fasten (*faa*-ssön) *v* atar; *cerrar
fastener (*faa*-ssö-nö) *n* cierre *m*
fat (fæt) *adj* graso, gordo; *n* grasa *f*
fatal (*fei*-töl) *adj* fatal, mortal
fate (feit) *n* destino *m*
father (*faa*-ðö) *n* padre *m*
father-in-law (*faa*-ðö-rin-loo) *n* (pl fa-

thers-) suegro *m*
fatherland (*faa*-ðö-lönd) *n* patria *f*
fatness (*fæt*-nöss) *n* obesidad *f*
fatty (*fæ*-ti) *adj* grasiento
faucet (*foo*-ssit) *nAm* grifo *m*
fault (foolt) *n* culpa *f*; imperfección *f*, defecto *m*
faultless (*foolt*-löss) *adj* impecable; perfecto
faulty (*fool*-ti) *adj* defectuoso
favour (*fei*-vö) *n* favor *m*; *v* *favorecer
favourable (*fei*-vö-rö-böl) *adj* favorable
favourite (*fei*-vö-rit) *n* favorito *m*; *adj* preferido
fawn (foon) *adj* marrón claro; *n* cervato *m*, corcino *m*
fear (fi⁶) *n* temor *m*, miedo *m*; *v* temer
feasible (*fii*-sö-böl) *adj* realizable
feast (fiisst) *n* fiesta *f*
feat (fiit) *n* gran trabajo
feather (*fê*-ðö) *n* pluma *f*
feature (*fii*-chö) *n* característica *f*; rasgo *m*
February (*fê*-bru-ö-ri) febrero
federal (*fê*-dö-röl) *adj* federal
federation (fê-dö-*rei*-ʃön) *n* federación *f*
fee (fii) *n* honorarios *mpl*
feeble (*fii*-böl) *adj* débil
***feed** (fiid) *v* alimentar; **fed up with** harto de
***feel** (fiil) *v* *sentir; palpar; ~ **like** antojarse
feeling (*fii*-ling) *n* sensación *f*
fell (fêl) *v* (p fall)
fellow (*fê*-lou) *n* tipo *m*
felt¹ (fêlt) *n* fieltro *m*
felt² (fêlt) *v* (p, pp feel)
female (*fii*-meil) *adj* femenino
feminine (*fê*-mi-nin) *adj* femenino
fence (fênss) *n* cerca *f*; reja *f*; *v* es-

grimir

fender (fên-dö) *n* parachoques *m*; defensa *f*Me

ferment (föö-mênt) *v* fermentar

ferry-boat (fê-ri-bout) *n* transbordador *m*

fertile (föö-tail) *adj* fértil

festival (fê-ssti-völ) *n* festival *m*

festive (fê-sstiv) *adj* festivo

fetch (fêch) *v* *ir por; *ir a buscar

feudal (fyuu-döl) *adj* feudal

fever (fii-vö) *n* fiebre *f*

feverish (fii-vö-riʃ) *adj* febril

few (fyuu) *adj* pocos

fiancé (fi-ang-ssei) *n* novio *m*

fiancée (fi-ang-ssei) *n* novia *f*

fibre (fai-bö) *n* fibra *f*

fiction (fik-ʃön) *n* ficción *f*

field (fiild) *n* campo *m*; terreno *m*; ~ **glasses** gemelos de campaña

fierce (fiöss) *adj* fiero; salvaje, violento

fifteen (fif-tiin) *num* quince

fifteenth (fif-tiinz) *num* quinceno

fifth (fifz) *num* quinto

fifty (fif-ti) *num* cincuenta

fig (figh) *n* higo *m*

fight (fait) *n* combate *m*, lucha *f*

*****fight** (fait) *v* combatir, luchar

figure (fi-ghö) *n* estatura *f*, figura *f*; cifra *f*

file (fail) *n* lima *f*; expediente *m*; cola *f*

Filipino (fi-li-pii-nou) *n* filipino *m*

fill (fil) *v* llenar; ~ **in** completar, llenar; **filling station** estación de servicio; - **out** *Am* completar, llenar; ~ **up** llenar

filling (fi-ling) *n* empaste *m*; relleno *m*

film (film) *n* película *f*; *v* filmar

filter (fil-tö) *n* filtro *m*

filthy (fil-zi) *adj* sórdido, inmundo

final (fai-nöl) *adj* final

finance (fai-nænss) *v* financiar

finances (fai-næn-ssis) *pl* finanzas *fpl*

financial (fai-næn-ʃöl) *adj* financiero

finch (finch) *n* pinzón *m*

*****find** (faind) *v* *encontrar

fine (fain) *n* multa *f*; *adj* fino; bello; excelente, maravilloso; ~ **arts** bellas artes

finger (fing-ghö) *n* dedo *m*; **little** ~ dedo auricular

fingerprint (fing-ghö-print) *n* impresión digital

finish (fi-niʃ) *v* terminar; *n* terminación *f*; meta *f*; **finished** acabado

Finland (fin-lönd) Finlandia *f*

Finn (fin) *n* finlandés *m*

Finnish (fi-niʃ) *adj* finlandés

fire (faiö) *n* fuego *m*; incendio *m*; *v* disparar; *despedir

fire-alarm (faiö-rö-laam) *n* alarma de incendio

fire-brigade (faiö-bri-gheid) *n* bomberos *mpl*

fire-escape (faiö-ri-sskeip) *n* escala de incendios

fire-extinguisher (faiö-rik-ssting-ghᵘi-ʃö) *n* extintor *m*

fireplace (faiö-pleiss) *n* chimenea *f*

fireproof (faiö-pruuf) *adj* incombustible; refractario

firm (fööm) *adj* firme; sólido; *n* firma *f*

first (föösst) *num* primero; **at** ~ antes; al principio; ~ **name** nombre de pila

first-aid (föösst-eid) *n* primeros auxilios; ~ **kit** botiquín de urgencia; ~ **post** puesto de socorro

first-class (föösst-klaass) *adj* de primera calidad

first-rate (föösst-reit) *adj* de primer orden, de primera clase

fir-tree (föö-trii) *n* pino *m*

fish[1] (fiʃ) *n* (pl ~, ~es) pez *m*; ~

shop pescadería f
fish² (fiʃ) v pescar; **fishing gear** avíos
de pesca; **fishing fly** mosca artificial; **fishing hook** anzuelo m; **fishing licence** permiso de pesca;
fishing line línea de pesca; **fishing
net** red de pescar; **fishing rod** caña
de pescar; **fishing tackle** aparejo de
pesca
fishbone (fiʃ-boun) n espina f
fisherman (fi-ʃö-mön) n (pl -men)
pescador m
fist (fisst) n puño m
fit (fit) adj apropiado; n ataque m; v
*convenir; **fitting room** probador
m
five (faiv) num cinco
fix (fikss) v arreglar
fixed (fiksst) adj fijo
fizz (fis) n efervescencia f
fjord (fyood) n fiordo m
flag (flægh) n bandera f
flame (fleim) n llama f
flamingo (flö-ming-ghou) n (pl ~s,
~es) flamenco m
flannel (flæ-nöl) n franela f
flash (flæʃ) n relámpago m
flash-bulb (flæʃ-balb) n bombilla de
flash
flash-light (flæʃ-lait) n linterna f
flask (flaassk) n frasco m; **thermos** ~
termo m
flat (flæt) adj llano; n piso m; ~ **tyre**
neumático desinflado
flavour (flei-vö) n sabor m; v sazonar
fleet (fliit) n flota f
flesh (fleʃ) n carne f
flew (fluu) v (p fly)
flex (flèkss) n cordón flexible
flexible (flèk-ssi-böl) adj flexible
flight (flait) n vuelo m; **charter** ~
vuelo fletado
flint (flint) n pedernal m
float (flout) v flotar; n flotador m

flock (flok) n rebaño m
flood (flad) n inundación f; riada f
floor (floo) n suelo m; piso m; ~
show espectáculo de variedades
florist (flo-risst) n florista m
flour (flauº) n harina f
flow (flou) v correr, *fluir
flower (flauº) n flor f
flowerbed (flauº-bêd) n arriate m
flower-shop (flauº-ʃop) n floristería f
flown (floun) v (pp fly)
flu (fluu) n gripe f
fluent (fluu-önt) adj con soltura
fluid (fluu-id) adj fluido; n fluido m
flute (fluut) n flauta f
fly (flai) n mosca f; bragueta f
*fly (flai) v *volar
foam (foum) n espuma f; v espumar
foam-rubber (foum-ra-bö) n goma espumada
focus (fou-köss) n foco m
fog (fogh) n niebla f
foggy (fo-ghi) adj brumoso
foglamp (fogh-læmp) n faro de niebla
fold (fould) v doblar; n pliegue m
folk (fouk) n gente f; ~ **song** canción
popular
folk-dance (fouk-daanss) n danza popular
folklore (fouk-loo) n folklore m
follow (fo-lou) v *seguir; **following**
adj siguiente
*be fond of (bii fond ov) *querer
food (fuud) n comida f; alimento m;
~ **poisoning** intoxicación alimentaria
foodstuffs (fuud-sstafss) pl artículos
alimenticios
fool (fuul) n idiota m, tonto m; v engañar
foolish (fuu-liʃ) adj necio, tonto; absurdo
foot (fut) n (pl feet) pie m; ~ **powder**
polvo para los pies; **on** ~ a pie

football (*fut*-bool) *n* fútbol *m* ; ~
   match partido de fútbol
foot-brake (*fut*-breik) *n* freno de pie
footpath (*fut*-paaz) *n* senda *f*
footwear (*fut*-ᵘêᵒ) *n* calzado *m*
for (too, to) *prep* para ; durante ; a
   causa de, por ; *conj* porque
*****forbid** (fö-*bid*) *v* prohibir
force (fooss) *v* obligar, *forzar ; *n*
   fuerza *f* ; **by** ~ forzosamente ;
   driving ~ fuerza motriz
ford (food) *n* vado *m*
forecast (*foo*-kaasst) *n* previsión *f* ; *v*
   pronosticar
foreground (*foo*-ghraund) *n* primer
   plano
forehead (*fo*-rêd) *n* frente *f*
foreign (*fo*-rin) *adj* extranjero ; extraño
foreigner (*fo*-ri-nö) *n* extranjero *m* ;
   forastero *m*
foreman (*foo*-mön) *n* (pl -men) capataz *m*
foremost (*foo*-mousst) *adj* primero
foresail (*foo*-sseil) *n* foque *m*
forest (*fo*-risst) *n* selva *f*, bosque *m*
forester (*fo*-ri-sstö) *n* guardabosques
   m
forge (food3) *v* falsificar
*****forget** (fö-*ghêt*) *v* olvidar
forgetful (fö-*ghêt*-föl) *adj* olvidadizo
*****forgive** (fö-*ghiv*) *v* perdonar
fork (fook) *n* tenedor *m* ; bifurcación
   f ; *v* bifurcarse
form (foom) *n* forma *f* ; formulario
   m, clase *f* ; *v* formar
formal (*foo* möl) *adj* formal
formality (foo-*mæ*-lö-ti) *n* formalidad
   f
former (*foo*-mö) *adj* antiguo ; anterior ; **formerly** antes
formula (*foo*-myu-lö) *n* (pl ~e, ~s)
   fórmula *f*
fort (foot) *n* fortaleza *f*

fortnight (*foot*-nait) *n* quincena *f*
fortress (*foo*-triss) *n* fortaleza *f*
fortunate (*foo*-chö-nöt) *adj* afortunado
fortune (*foo*-chuun) *n* fortuna *f* ; suerte *f*
forty (*foo*-ti) *num* cuarenta
forward (*foo*-ᵘöd) *adv* hacia adelante,
   adelante ; *v* reexpedir
foster-parents (fo-sstö-pêᵒ-röntss) *pl*
   padres adoptivos
fought (foot) *v* (p, pp fight)
foul (faul) *adj* sucio ; vil
found¹ (faund) *v* (p, pp find)
found² (faund) *v* fundar
foundation (faun-*dei*-jön) *n* fundación
   f ; ~ **cream** crema de base
fountain (*faun*-tin) *n* fuente *f*
fountain-pen (*faun*-tin-pên) *n* estilográfica *f*
four (foo) *num* cuatro
fourteen (foo-*tiin*) *num* catorce
fourteenth (foo-*tiinz*) *num* catorceno
fourth (fooz) *num* cuarto
fowl (faul) *n* (pl ~s, ~) volatería *f*
fox (fokss) *n* zorro *m*
foyer (*foi*-ei) *n* vestíbulo *m*
fraction (*fræk*-jon) *n* fracción *f*
fracture (*fræk*-chö) *v* fracturar ; *n*
   fractura *f*
fragile (*fræ*-dʒail) *adj* frágil
fragment (*frægh*-mönt) *n* fragmento
   m ; trozo *m*
frame (freim) *n* marco *m* ; armadura *f*
France (fraanss) Francia *f*
franchise (*træn*-chais) *n* derecho electoral
fraternity (frö-*töö*-nö-ti) *n* fraternidad
   f
fraud (frood) *n* fraude *m*
fray (frei) *v* deshilacharse
free (frii) *adj* libre ; gratuito ; ~ **of**
   charge gratis ; ~ **ticket** billete gratuito

freedom (*frii*-döm) *n* libertad *f*

***freeze** (friis) *v* *helar; congelar

freezing (*frii*-sing) *adj* helado

freezing-point (*frii*-sing-point) *n* punto de congelación

freight (freit) *n* carga *f*, cargo *m*

French (frênch) *adj* francés

Frenchman (*frênch*-mön) *n* (pl -men) francés *m*

frequency (*frii*-kᵘön-ssi) *n* frecuencia *f*

frequent (*frii*-kᵘönt) *adj* frecuente

fresh (frêʃ) *adj* fresco; ~ **water** agua dulce

friction (*frik*-ʃön) *n* fricción *f*

Friday (*frai*-di) viernes *m*

fridge (fridʒ) *n* frigorífico *m*, refrigerador *m*

friend (frênd) *n* amigo *m*; amiga *f*

friendly (*frênd*-li) *adj* amable; amistoso

friendship (*frênd*-ʃip) *n* amistad *f*

fright (frait) *n* miedo *m*, espanto *m*

frighten (*frai*-tön) *v* espantar

frightened (*frai*-tönd) *adj* espantado; ***be** ~ asustarse

frightful (*frait*-föl) *adj* terrible

fringe (frindʒ) *n* franja *f*

frock (frok) *n* vestido *m*

frog (frogh) *n* rana *f*

from (from) *prep* desde; de; a partir de

front (frant) *n* frente *m*; **in** ~ **of** delante de

frontier (*fran*-tiᵒ) *n* frontera *f*

frost (frosst) *n* escarcha *f*

froth (froz) *n* espuma *f*

frozen (*frou*-sön) *adj* congelado; ~ **food** alimento congelado

fruit (fruut) *n* fruta *f*; fruto *m*

fry (frai) *v* *freír

frying-pan (*frai*-ing-pæn) *n* sartén *f*

fuel (*fyuu*-öl) *n* combustible *m*; ~ **pump** *Am* bomba de gasolina

full (ful) *adj* lleno; ~ **board** pensión completa; ~ **stop** punto *m*; ~ **up** completo

fun (fan) *n* diversión *f*

function (*fangk*-ʃön) *n* función *f*

fund (fand) *n* fondos *mpl*

fundamental (fan-dö-*mên*-töl) *adj* fundamental

funeral (*fyuu*-nö-röl) *n* funerales *mpl*

funnel (*fa*-nöl) *n* embudo *m*

funny (*fa*-ni) *adj* gracioso, cómico; extraño

fur (föö) *n* piel *f*; ~ **coat** abrigo de pieles; **furs** piel *f*

furious (*fyuᵒ*-ri-öss) *adj* furioso

furnace (*föö*-niss) *n* horno *m*

furnish (*föö*-niʃ) *v* suministrar, procurar; instalar, amueblar; ~ **with** *proveer de

furniture (*föö*-ni-chö) *n* muebles *mpl*

furrier (*fa*-ri-ö) *n* peletero *m*

further (*föö*-ðö) *adj* más lejos; ulterior

furthermore (*föö*-ðö-moo) *adv* además

furthest (*föö*-ðisst) *adj* el más alejado

fuse (fyuus) *n* fusible *m*; mecha *f*

fuss (fass) *n* bulla *f*; ostentación *f*, alharaca *f*

future (*fyuu*-chö) *n* porvenir *m*; *adj* futuro

G

gable (*ghei*-böl) *n* faldón *m*

gadget (*ghæ*-dʒit) *n* accesorio *m*

gaiety (*ghei*-ö-ti) *n* alegría *f*

gain (ghein) *v* ganar; *n* ganancia *f*

gait (gheit) *n* paso *m*

gale (gheil) *n* ventarrón *m*

gall (ghool) *n* bilis *f*; ~ **bladder** vesícula biliar

gallery (*ghæ*-lö-ri) *n* galería *f*
gallop (*ghæ*-löp) *n* galope *m*
gallows (*ghæ*-lous) *pl* horca *f*
gallstone (*ghool*-sstoun) *n* cálculo biliar
game (gheim) *n* juego *m*; caza *f*; ~ reserve parque de reserva zoológica
gang (ghæng) *n* banda *f*; equipo *m*
gangway (*ghæng*-ᵁei) *n* pasarela *f*
gaol (dʒeil) *n* cárcel *f*
gap (ghæp) *n* hueco *m*
garage (*ghæ*-raaʒ) *n* garaje *m*; *v* dejar en garaje
garbage (*ghaa*-bidʒ) *n* basura *f*
garden (*ghaa*-dön) *n* jardín *m*; public ~ jardín público; zoological gardens jardín zoológico
gardener (*ghaa*-dö-nö) *n* jardinero *m*
gargle (*ghaa*-ghöl) *v* *hacer gárgaras
garlic (*ghaa*-lik) *n* ajo *m*
gas (ghæss) *n* gas *m*; *nAm* gasolina *f*; ~ cooker cocina de gas; ~ station *Am* puesto de gasolina; ~ stove estufa de gas
gasoline (*ghæ*-ssö-liin) *nAm* gasolina *f*
gastric (*ghæ*-sstrik) *adj* gástrico; ~ ulcer úlcera gástrica
gasworks (*ghæss*-ᵁöökss) *n* fábrica de gas
gate (gheit) *n* portón *m*; reja *f*
gather (*ghæ*-ðö) *v* coleccionar; juntarse; recoger
gauge (gheidʒ) *n* medidor *m*
gauze (ghoos) *n* gasa *f*
gave (gheiv) *v* (p give)
gay (ghei) *adj* alegre; gaitero
gaze (gheis) *v* mirar
gazetteer (ghæ-sö-*tiᵒ*) *n* diccionario geográfico
gear (ghiᵒ) *n* velocidad *f*; aparejo *m*; change ~ cambiar de marcha; ~ lever palanca de cambios
gear-box (*ghiᵒ*-bokss) *n* caja de veloci-

dades
gem (dʒêm) *n* joya *f*, gema *f*; alhaja *f*
gender (*dʒên*-dö) *n* género *m*
general (*dʒê*-nö-röl) *adj* general; *n* general *m*; ~ practitioner médico de cabecera; in ~ en general
generate (*dʒê*-nö-reit) *v* generar
generation (dʒê-nö-*rei*-ſön) *n* generación *f*
generator (*dʒê*-nö-rei-tör) *n* generador *m*
generosity (dʒê-nö-*ro*-ssö-ti) *n* generosidad *f*
generous (*dʒê*-nö-röss) *adj* generoso
genital (*dʒê*-ni-töl) *adj* genital
genius (*dʒii*-ni-öss) *n* genio *m*
gentle (*dʒên*-töl) *adj* gentil; tierno, suave; prudente
gentleman (*dʒên*-töl-mön) *n* (pl -men) caballero *m*
genuine (*dʒê*-nyu-in) *adj* genuino
geography (dʒi-*o*-ghrö-fi) *n* geografía *f*
geology (dʒi-*o*-lö-dʒi) *n* geología *f*
geometry (dʒi-*o*-mo-tri) *n* geometría *f*
germ (dʒööm) *n* germen *m*
German (*dʒöö*-mön) *adj* alemán
Germany (*dʒöö*-mö-ni) Alemania *f*
gesticulate (dʒi-*ssti*-kyu-leit) *v* gesticular
*get (ghêt) *v* *conseguir; *ir a buscar; *hacerse; ~ back regresar; ~ off apearse; ~ on subir, montar; adelantar; ~ up levantarse
ghost (ghousst) *n* fantasma *m*; espíritu *m*
giant (*dʒai*-önt) *n* gigante *m*
giddiness (*ghi*-di-nöss) *n* mareo *m*
giddy (*ghi*-di) *adj* mareado
gift (ghift) *n* regalo *m*; talento *m*
gifted (*ghif*-tid) *adj* talentoso
gigantic (dʒai-*ghæn*-tik) *adj* gigantesco
giggle (*ghi*-ghöl) *v* *soltar risitas

gill (ghil) n branquia f

gilt (ghilt) adj dorado

ginger (dʒin-dʒö) n jengibre m

gipsy (dʒip-ssi) n gitano m

girdle (ghöö-döl) n faja f

girl (ghööl) n muchacha f; ~ **guide** exploradora f

*****give** (ghiv) v *dar; entregar; ~ **away** revelar; ~ **in** ceder; ~ **up** renunciar

glacier (ghlæ-ssi-ö) n glaciar m

glad (ghlæd) adj alegre, contento; **gladly** con mucho gusto, gustosamente

gladness (ghlæd-nöss) n alegría f

glamorous (ghlæ-mö-röss) adj encantador

glamour (ghlæ-mö) n encanto m

glance (ghlaanss) n ojeada f; v ojear

gland (ghlænd) n glándula f

glare (ghlêö) n destello m; resplandor m

glaring (ghlêö-ring) adj deslumbrador

glass (ghlaass) n vaso m; vidrio m; de vidrio; **glasses** anteojos mpl; **magnifying** ~ lente de aumento

glaze (ghleis) v esmaltar

glen (ghlên) n cañada f

glide (ghlaid) v resbalar

glider (ghlai-dö) n planeador m

glimpse (ghlimpss) n vislumbre m; ojeada f; v vislumbrar

global (ghlou-böl) adj mundial

globe (ghloub) n globo m

gloom (ghluum) n obscuridad f

gloomy (ghluu-mi) adj sombrío

glorious (ghloo-ri-öss) adj espléndido

glory (ghloo-ri) n gloria f; honor m, elogio m

gloss (ghloss) n brillo m

glossy (ghlo-ssi) adj lustroso

glove (ghlav) n guante m

glow (ghlou) v brillar; n brillo m

glue (ghluu) n cola f

*****go** (ghou) v *ir; caminar; *hacerse; ~ **ahead** continuar; ~ **away** *irse; ~ **back** regresar; ~ **home** *volver a casa; ~ **in** entrar; ~ **on** continuar; ~ **out** *salir; ~ **through** pasar

goal (ghoul) n meta f; gol m

goalkeeper (ghoul-kii-pö) n portero m

goat (ghout) n cabrón m, cabra f

god (ghod) n dios m

goddess (gho-diss) n diosa f

godfather (ghod-faa-ðö) n padrino m

goggles (gho-ghöls) pl gafas fpl

gold (ghould) n oro m; ~ **leaf** hojas de oro

golden (ghoul-dön) adj dorado

goldmine (ghould-main) n mina de oro

goldsmith (ghould-ssmiz) n orfebre m

golf (gholf) n golf m

golf-club (gholf-klab) n palo de golf

golf-course (gholf-kooss) n campo de golf

golf-links (gholf-lingkss) n campo de golf

gondola (ghon-dö-lö) n góndola f

gone (ghon) adv (pp go) ido

good (ghud) adj bueno

good-bye! (ghud-bai) ¡adiós!

good-humoured (ghud-hyuu-möd) adj de buen humor

good-looking (ghud-lu-king) adj bien parecido

good-natured (ghud-nei-chöd) adj bondadoso

goods (ghuds) pl mercancías fpl, bienes mpl; ~ **train** tren de mercancías

good-tempered (ghud-têm-pöd) adj de buen humor

goodwill (ghud-ᵘil) n buena voluntad f

goose (ghuuss) n (pl geese) oca f

gooseberry (ghus-bö-ri) n grosella espinosa

goose-flesh (ghuuss-flêʃ) n carne de

gallina

gorge (ghoodȝ) n cañón m

gorgeous (*ghoo*-dȝöss) adj magnífico

gospel (*gho*-sspöl) n evangelio m

gossip (*gho*-ssip) n chisme m; v *contar chismes

got (ghot) v (p, pp get)

gourmet (*ghu*ó-mei) n gastrónomo m

gout (ghaut) n gota f

govern (*gha*-vön) v *regir

governess (*gha*-vö-niss) n aya f

government (*gha*-vön-mönt) n régimen m, gobierno m

governor (*gha*-vö-nö) n gobernador m

gown (ghaun) n traje m

grace (ghreiss) n gracia f; perdón m

graceful (*ghreiss*-föl) adj gracioso

grade (ghreid) n grado m; v graduar

gradient (*ghrei*-di-önt) n pendiente f

gradual (*ghræ*-dȝu-öl) adj gradual; **gradually** adv paulatinamente

graduate (*ghræ*-dȝu-eit) v graduarse

grain (ghrein) n grano m, trigo m

gram (ghræm) n gramo m

grammar (*ghræ*-mö) n gramática f

grammatical (ghrö-*mæ*-ti-köl) adj gramatical

gramophone (*ghræ*-mö-foun) n gramófono m

grand (ghrænd) adj imponente

granddad (*ghræn*-dæd) n abuelo m

granddaughter (*ghræn*-dôo-to) n nieta f

grandfather (*ghræn*-faa-ðö) n abuelo m

grandmother (*ghræn*-ma-ðö) n abuela f

grandparents (*ghræn*-pêó-röntss) pl abuelos mpl

grandson (*ghræn*-ssan) n nieto m

granite (*ghræ*-nit) n granito m

grant (ghraant) v conceder; n subvención f, beca f

grapefruit (*ghreip*-fruut) n pomelo m; toronja fMe

grapes (ghreipss) pl uvas fpl

graph (ghræf) n gráfico m

graphic (*ghræ*-fik) adj gráfico

grasp (ghraassp) v agarrar; n agarre m

grass (ghraass) n césped m

grasshopper (*ghraass*-ho-pö) n saltamontes m

grate (ghreit) n reja f; v rallar

grateful (*ghreit*-föl) adj agradecido

grater (*ghrei*-tö) n rayador m

gratis (*ghræ*-tiss) adj gratuito

gratitude (*ghræ*-ti-tyuud) n gratitud f

gratuity (ghrö-*tyuu*-ö-ti) n propina f

grave (ghreiv) n sepultura f; adj grave

gravel (*ghræ*-völ) n grava f

gravestone (*ghreiv*-sstoun) n lápida f

graveyard (*ghreiv*-yaad) n cementerio m

gravity (*ghræ*-vö-ti) n gravedad f; seriedad f

gravy (*ghrei*-vi) n salsa f

graze (ghreis) v *pacer; n rozadura f

grease (ghriiss) n grasa f; v engrasar

greasy (*ghrii*-ssi) adj grasiento, graso-so

great (ghreit) adj grande; **Great Britain** Gran Bretaña

Greece (ghriiss) Grecia f

greed (ghriid) n codicia f

greedy (*ghrii*-di) adj codicioso; glotón

Greek (ghriik) adj griego

green (ghriin) adj verde; ~ **card** tarjeta verde

greengrocer (*ghriin*-ghrou-ssö) n verdulero m

greenhouse (*ghriin*-hauss) n invernadero m, invernáculo m

greens (ghriins) pl legumbres fpl

greet (ghriit) v saludar

greeting (*ghrii*-ting) n saludo m

grey (ghrei) *adj* gris
greyhound (*ghrei*-haund) *n* galgo *m*
grief (ghriif) *n* pesadumbre *f*; aflicción *f*, dolor *m*
grieve (ghriiv) *v* *estar afligido
grill (ghril) *n* parrilla *f*; *v* asar en parrilla
grill-room (*ghril*-ruum) *n* parrilla *f*
grin (ghrin) *v* *sonreír; *n* sonrisa sardónica
*grind** (ghraind) *v* *moler; triturar
grip (ghrip) *v* *asir; *n* agarradero *m*, agarre *m*; *nAm* maletín *m*
grit (ghrit) *n* polvo *m*
groan (ghroun) *v* *gemir
grocer (*ghrou*-ssö) *n* abacero *m*; abarrotero *mMe*; **grocer's** abacería *f*; abarrotería *fMe*
groceries (*ghrou*-ssö-ris) *pl* comestibles *mpl*
groin (ghroin) *n* ingle *f*
groove (ghruuv) *n* surco *m*
gross¹ (ghrouss) *n* (pl ~) gruesa *f*
gross² (ghrouss) *adj* grosero; bruto
grotto (*ghro*-tou) *n* (pl ~es, ~s) gruta *f*
ground¹ (ghraund) *n* fondo *m*, tierra *f*; ~ **floor** piso bajo; **grounds** terreno *m*
ground² (ghraund) *v* (p, pp grind)
group (ghruup) *n* grupo *m*
grouse (ghrauss) *n* (pl ~) gallo de bosque
grove (ghrouv) *n* soto *m*
*grow** (ghrou) *v* *crecer; cultivar; *hacerse
growl (ghraul) *v* *gruñir
grown-up (*ghroun*-ap) *adj* adulto; *n* adulto *m*
growth (ghrouz) *n* crecimiento *m*; tumor *m*
grudge (ghradჳ) *v* envidiar
grumble (*ghram*-böl) *v* refunfuñar
guarantee (ghæ-rön-*tii*) *n* garantía *f*;

v garantizar
guarantor (ghæ-rön-*too*) *n* garante *m*
guard (ghaad) *n* guardia *f*; *v* guardar
guardian (*ghaa*-di-ön) *n* tutor *m*
guess (ghêss) *v* adivinar; *creer, conjeturar; *n* conjetura *f*
guest (ghêsst) *n* huésped *m*, invitado *m*
guest-house (*ghêsst*-hauss) *n* pensión *f*
guest-room (*ghêsst*-ruum) *n* habitación para huéspedes
guide (ghaid) *n* guía *m*; *v* guiar
guidebook (*ghaid*-buk) *n* guía *f*
guide-dog (*ghaid*-dogh) *n* perro lazarillo
guilt (ghilt) *n* culpa *f*
guilty (*ghil*-ti) *adj* culpable
guinea-pig (*ghi*-ni-pigh) *n* conejillo de Indias
guitar (ghi-*taa*) *n* guitarra *f*
gulf (ghalf) *n* golfo *m*
gull (ghal) *n* gaviota *f*
gum (gham) *n* encía *f*; goma *f*; cola *f*
gun (ghan) *n* fusil *m*, revólver *m*; cañón *m*
gunpowder (*ghan*-pau-dö) *n* pólvora *f*
gust (ghasst) *n* ráfaga *f*
gusty (*gha*-ssti) *adj* borrascoso
gut (ghat) *n* intestino *m*; **guts** coraje *m*
gutter (*gha*-tö) *n* cuneta *f*
guy (ghai) *n* tipo *m*
gymnasium (dჳim-*nei*-si-öm) *n* (pl ~s, -sia) gimnasio *m*
gymnast (*dჳim*-næsst) *n* gimnasta *m*
gymnastics (dჳim-*næ*-sstikss) *pl* gimnasia *f*
gynaecologist (ghai-nö-*ko*-lö-dჳisst) *n* ginecólogo *m*

H

haberdashery (hæ-bö-dæ-ſö-ri) *n* mercería *f*

habit (hæ-bit) *n* hábito *m*

habitable (hæ-bi-tö-böl) *adj* habitable

habitual (hö-*bi*-chu-öl) *adj* habitual

had (hæd) *v* (p, pp have)

haddock (hæ-dök) *n* (pl ~) bacalao *m*

haemorrhage (hê-mö ridʒ) *n* hemorragia *f*

haemorrhoids (hê-mö-roids) *pl* hemorroides *fpl*

hail (heil) *n* granizo *m*

hair (hêᵒ) *n* cabello *m*; ~ **cream** brillantina *f*; ~ **piece** postizo *m*; ~ **rollers** rizadores *mpl*; ~ **tonic** tónico para el cabello

hairbrush (hêᵈ-braſ) *n* cepillo para el cabello

haircut (hêᵒ-kat) *n* corte de pelo

hair-do (hêᵒ-duu) *n* peinado *m*

hairdresser (hêᵒ-drê-ssö) *n* peluquero *m*

hair-dryer (hêᵒ-drai-ö) *n* secador para el pelo

hair-grip (hêᵒ-ghrip) *n* horquilla *f*

hair-net (hêᵒ-nêt) *n* redecilla *f*

hair-oil (hêᵒ-roil) *n* aceite para el pelo

hairpin (hêᵒ-pin) *n* horquilla *f*

hair-spray (hêᵈ-ssprei) *n* laca para el cabello

hairy (hêᵒ-ri) *adj* cabelludo

half¹ (haaf) *adj* medio

half² (haat) *n* (pl halves) mitad *f*

half-time (haaf-*taim*) *n* descanso *m*

halfway (haaf-ᵘei) *adv* a mitad de camino

halibut (hæ-li-böt) *n* (pl ~) halibut *m*

hall (hool) *n* vestíbulo *m*; sala *f*

halt (hoolt) *v* pararse

halve (haav) *v* partir por la mitad

ham (hæm) *n* jamón *m*

hamlet (hæm-löt) *n* aldea *f*

hammer (hæ mö) *n* martillo *m*

hammock (hæ-mök) *n* hamaca *f*

hamper (hæm-pö) *n* cesto *m*

hand (hænd) *n* mano *f*; *v* alargar; ~ **cream** crema para las manos

handbag (hænd-bægh) *n* bolso *m*

handbook (hænd-buk) *n* manual *m*

hand-brake (hænd-breik) *n* freno de mano

handcuffs (hænd-kafss) *pl* esposas *fpl*

handful (hænd-ful) *n* puñado *m*

handicraft (hæn-di-kraaft) *n* trabajo manual; artesanía *f*

handkerchief (hæng-kö-chif) *n* pañuelo *m*

handle (hæn-döl) *n* mango *m*; *v* manejar; tratar

hand-made (hænd-*meid*) *adj* hecho a mano

handshake (hænd-ſeik) *n* apretón de manos

handsome (hæn-ssöm) *adj* guapo

handwork (hænd-ᵘöök) *n* obra hecha a mano

handwriting (hænd-rai-ting) *n* escritura *f*

handy (hæn-di) *adj* manejable

*****hang** (hæng) *v* *colgar

hanger (hæng-ö) *n* percha *f*

hangover (hæng-ou-vö) *n* resaca *f*

happen (hæ-pön) *v* suceder, pasar

happening (hæ-pö-ning) *n* acontecimiento *m*

happiness (hæ-pi nöss) *n* felicidad *f*

happy (hæ-pi) *adj* contento, feliz

harbour (haa-bö) *n* puerto *m*

hard (haad) *adj* duro; difícil; **hardly** apenas

hardware (haad-ᵘêᵒ) *n* quincalla *f*; ~ **store** ferretería *f*

hare (hêᵒ) *n* liebre *f*

harm (haam) *n* perjuicio *m*; mal *m*,

daño *m*; *v* perjudicar

harmful (*haam*-fŏl) *adj* perjudicial, dañoso

harmless (*haam*-löss) *adj* inocuo

harmony (*haa*-mö-ni) *n* armonía *f*

harp (haap) *n* arpa *f*

harpsichord (*haap*-ssi-kood) *n* clavicémbalo *m*

harsh (haaʃ) *adj* áspero; severo; cruel

harvest (*haa*-visst) *n* cosecha *f*

has (hæs) *v* (pr have)

haste (heisst) *n* prisa *f*

hasten (*hei*-ssön) *v* apresurarse

hasty (*hei*-ssti) *adj* apresurado

hat (hæt) *n* sombrero *m*; ~ **rack** percha *f*

hatch (hæch) *n* trampa *f*

hate (heit) *v* detestar; odiar; *n* odio *m*

hatred (*hei*-trid) *n* odio *m*

haughty (*hoo*-ti) *adj* altivo

haul (hool) *v* arrastrar

* **have** (hæv) *v* *haber, *tener; *hacer; ~ **to** deber

haversack (*hæ*-vö-ssæk) *n* morral *m*

hawk (hook) *n* azor *m*; halcón *m*

hay (hei) *n* heno *m*; ~ **fever** fiebre del heno

hazard (*hæ*-söd) *n* riesgo *m*

haze (heis) *n* calina *f*; niebla *f*

hazelnut (*hei*-söl-nat) *n* avellana *f*

hazy (*hei*-si) *adj* calinoso; brumoso

he (hii) *pron* él

head (hĕd) *n* cabeza *f*; *v* dirigir; ~ **of state** jefe de Estado; ~ **teacher** director de escuela

headache (*hĕ*-deik) *n* dolor de cabeza

heading (*hĕ*-ding) *n* título *m*

headlamp (*hĕd*-læmp) *n* fanal *m*

headland (*hĕd*-lönd) *n* promontorio *m*

headlight (*hĕd*-lait) *n* faro *m*

headline (*hĕd*-lain) *n* titular *m*

headmaster (hĕd-*maa*-sstö) *n* director

de escuela

headquarters (hĕd-*kᵘoo*-tös) *pl* cuartel general

head-strong (*hĕd*-sstrong) *adj* cabezudo

head-waiter (hĕd-ᵘ*ei*-tö) *n* jefe de camareros

heal (hiil) *v* curar

health (hĕlz) *n* salud *f*; ~ **centre** dispensario *m*; ~ **certificate** certificado de salud

healthy (*hĕl*-zi) *adj* sano

heap (hiip) *n* montón *m*

* **hear** (hiʰ) *v* *oír

hearing (*hiʰ*-ring) *n* oído *m*

heart (haat) *n* corazón *m*; núcleo *m*; **by** ~ de memoria; ~ **attack** ataque cardíaco

heartburn (*haat*-böön) *n* acidez *f*

hearth (haaz) *n* hogar *m*

heartless (*haat*-löss) *adj* insensible

hearty (*haa*-ti) *adj* cordial

heat (hiit) *n* calor *m*; *v* *calentar; **heating pad** almohada eléctrica

heater (*hii*-tö) *n* calefactor *m*; **immersion** ~ calentador de inmersión

heath (hiiz) *n* landa *f*

heathen (*hii*-ðön) *n* pagano *m*

heather (*hĕ*-ðö) *n* brezo *m*

heating (*hii*-ting) *n* calefacción *f*

heaven (*hĕ*-vön) *n* cielo *m*

heavy (*hĕ*-vi) *adj* pesado

Hebrew (*hii*-bruu) *n* hebreo *m*

hedge (hĕdʒ) *n* seto *m*

hedgehog (*hĕdʒ*-hogh) *n* erizo *m*

heel (hiil) *n* talón *m*; tacón *m*

height (hait) *n* altura *f*; colmo *m*, apogeo *m*

hell (hĕl) *n* infierno *m*

hello! (hĕ-*lou*) ¡hola!; ¡buenos días!

helm (hĕlm) *n* timón *m*

helmet (*hĕl*-mit) *n* casco *m*

helmsman (*hĕlms*-mön) *n* timonero *m*

help (hĕlp) *v* ayudar; *n* ayuda *f*

helper (*hêl*-pö) *n* ayudante *m*
helpful (*hêlp*-föl) *adj* servicial
helping (*hêl*-ping) *n* porción *f*
hem (hêm) *n* dobladillo *m*
hemp (hêmp) *n* cáñamo *m*
hen (hên) *n* gallina *f*
henceforth (hênss-*fooz*) *adv* de ahora en adelante
her (höö) *pron* la, le; *adj* su
herb (hööb) *n* hierba *f*
herd (hööd) *n* manada *f*
here (hi^ö) *adv* acá; ~ you are tenga usted
hereditary (hi-*rê*-di-tö-ri) *adj* hereditario
hernia (*höö*-ni-ö) *n* hernia *f*
hero (*hi^ö*-rou) *n* (pl ~-es) héroe *m*
heron (*hê*-rön) *n* garza *f*
herring (*hê*-ring) *n* (pl ~, ~s) arenque *m*
herself (höö-*ssêlf*) *pron* se; ella misma
hesitate (*hê*-si-teit) *v* vacilar
heterosexual (hê-tö-rö-*ssêk*-ʃu-öl) *adj* heterosexual
hiccup (*hi*-kap) *n* hipo *m*
hide (haid) *n* piel *f*
*hide (haid) *v* esconder
hideous (*hi*-di-öss) *adj* horrible
hierarchy (*hai^ö*-raa-ki) *n* jerarquía *f*
high (hai) *adj* alto
highway (*hai*-^uei) *n* carretera *f*; *nAm* autopista *t*
hijack (*hai*-dʒæk) *v* apresar
hijacker (*hai*-dʒæ-kö) *n* secuestrador *m*
hike (haik) *v* caminar
hill (hil) *n* colina *f*
hillside (*hil*-ssaid) *n* ladera *f*
hilltop (*hil*-top) *n* cima *f*
hilly (*hi*-li) *adj* montuoso
him (him) *pron* le
himself (him-*ssêlf*) *pron* se; él mismo
hinder (*hin*-dö) *v* *impedir

hinge (hindʒ) *n* bisagra *f*
hip (hip) *n* cadera *f*
hire (hai^ö) *v* alquilar; for ~ de alquiler
hire-purchase (hai^ö-*pöö*-chöss) *n* compra a plazos
his (his) *adj* su
historian (hi-*sstoo*-ri-ön) *n* historiador *m*
historic (hi-*ssto*-rik) *adj* histórico
historical (hi-*ssto*-ri-köl) *adj* histórico
history (*hi*-sstö-ri) *n* historia *f*
hit (hit) *n* éxito *m*
*hit (hit) *v* pegar; tocar, *acertar
hitchhike (*hich*-haik) *v* *hacer autostop
hitchhiker (*hich*-hai-kö) *n* autoestopista *m*
hoarse (hooss) *adj* ronco
hobby (*ho*-bi) *n* afición *f*
hobby-horse (*ho*-bi-hooss) *n* comidilla *f*
hockey (*ho*-ki) *n* hockey *m*
hoist (hoisst) *v* izar
hold (hould) *n* bodega *f*
*hold (hould) *v* *tener; *retener; ~ on agarrarse; ~ up *sostener
hold-up (*houl*-dap) *n* atraco *m*
hole (houl) *n* bache *m*, agujero *m*
holiday (*ho*-lö-di) *n* vacaciones *fpl*; fiesta *f*; ~ camp colonia veraniega; ~ resort lugar de descanso; on ~ de vacaciones
Holland (*ho*-lönd) Holanda *f*
hollow (*ho*-lou) *adj* hueco
holy (*hou*-li) *adj* santo
homage (*ho*-midʒ) *n* homenaje *m*
home (houm) *n* casa *f*; hospicio *m*; *adv* en casa, a casa; at ~ en casa
home-made (houm-*meid*) *adj* casero
homesickness (*houm*-ssik-nöss) *n* nostalgia *f*
homosexual (hou-mö-*ssêk*-ʃu-öl) *adj* homosexual

honest (*o*-nisst) *adj* honesto; sincero
honesty (*o*-ni-ssti) *n* honradez *f*
honey (*ha*-ni) *n* miel *f*
honeymoon (*ha*-ni-muun) *n* luna de miel
honour (*o*-nö) *n* honor *m*; *v* honrar, *rendir homenaje
honourable (*o*-nö-rö-böl) *adj* honorable; honesto
hood (hud) *n* capucha *f*; *nAm* capó *m*
hoof (huuf) *n* casco *m*
hook (huk) *n* gancho *m*
hoot (huut) *v* tocar la bocina
hooter (*huu*-tö) *n* bocina *f*
hoover (*huu*-vö) *v* pasar el aspirador
hop¹ (hop) *v* brincar; *n* salto *m*
hop² (hop) *n* lúpulo *m*
hope (houp) *n* esperanza *f*; *v* esperar
hopeful (*houp*-föl) *adj* esperanzado
hopeless (*houp*-löss) *adj* desesperado
horizon (hö-*rai*-sön) *n* horizonte *m*
horizontal (ho-ri-*son*-töl) *adj* horizontal
horn (hoon) *n* cuerno *m*; bocina *f*
horrible (*ho*-ri-böl) *adj* horrible; terrible, atroz
horror (*ho*-rö) *n* espanto *m*, horror *m*
hors-d'œuvre (oo-*döövr*) *n* entremeses *mpl*
horse (hooss) *n* caballo *m*
horseman (*hooss*-mön) *n* (pl -men) jinete *m*
horsepower (*hooss*-pauᵒ) *n* caballo de vapor
horserace (*hooss*-reiss) *n* carrera de caballos
horseradish (*hooss*-ræ-diʃ) *n* rábano picante
horseshoe (*hooss*-ʃuu) *n* herradura *f*
horticulture (*hoo*-ti-kal-chö) *n* horticultura *f*
hosiery (*hou*-ʒö-ri) *n* géneros de punto

hospitable (*ho*-sspi-tö-böl) *adj* hospitalario
hospital (*ho*-sspi-töl) *n* hospital *m*
hospitality (ho-sspi-*tæ*-lö-ti) *n* hospitalidad *f*
host (housst) *n* anfitrión *m*
hostage (*ho*-sstidʒ) *n* rehén *m*
hostel (*ho*-sstöl) *n* hospedería *f*
hostess (*hou*-sstiss) *n* azafata *f*
hostile (*ho*-sstail) *adj* hostil
hot (hot) *adj* caliente
hotel (hou-*têl*) *n* hotel *m*
hot-tempered (hot-*têm*-pöd) *adj* colérico
hour (auᵒ) *n* hora *f*
hourly (*auᵒ*-li) *adj* a cada hora
house (hauss) *n* casa *f*; vivienda *f*; inmueble *m*; ~ agent corredor de casas; ~ block *Am* manzana de casas; public ~ café *m*
houseboat (*hauss*-bout) *n* casa flotante
household (*hauss*-hould) *n* menaje *m*
housekeeper (*hauss*-kii-pö) *n* ama de llaves
housekeeping (*hauss*-kii-ping) *n* gobierno de la casa
housemaid (*hauss*-meid) *n* criada *f*
housewife (*hauss*-ᵘaif) *n* ama de casa
housework (*hauss*-ᵘöök) *n* faenas domésticas
how (hau) *adv* cómo; qué; ~ many cuánto; ~ much cuánto
however (hau-ê-vö) *conj* todavía, sin embargo
hug (hagh) *v* abrazar; *n* abrazo *m*
huge (hyuudʒ) *adj* formidable, enorme
hum (ham) *v* tararear
human (*hyuu*-mön) *adj* humano; ~ being ser humano
humanity (hyu-*mæ*-nö-ti) *n* humanidad *f*
humble (*ham*-böl) *adj* humilde

humid (*hyuu*-mid) *adj* húmedo

humidity (hyu-*mi*-dö-ti) *n* humedad *f*

humorous (*hyuu*-mö-röss) *adj* chistoso, gracioso, humorístico

humour (*hyuu*-mö) *n* humor *m*

hundred (*han*-dröd) *n* ciento

Hungarian (hang-*ghê*ǒ-ri-ön) *adj* húngaro

Hungary (*hang*-ghö-ri) Hungría *m*

hunger (*hang*-ghö) *n* hambre *f*

hungry (*hang*-ghri) *adj* hambriento

hunt (hant) *v* cazar; *n* caza *f*; ~ for buscar

hunter (*han*-tö) *n* cazador *m*

hurricane (*ha*-ri-kön) *n* huracán *m*; ~ lamp lámpara sorda

hurry (*ha* ri) *v* *darse prisa, apresurarse; *n* prisa *f*; in a ~ de prisa

*hurt (hööt) *v* *hacer daño, dañar; ofender

hurtful (*hööt*-föl) *adj* perjudicial

husband (*has*-bönd) *n* esposo *m*, marido *m*

hut (hat) *n* cabaña *f*

hydrogen (*hai*-drö-dʒön) *n* hidrógeno *m*

hygiene (*hai*-dʒiin) *n* higiene *f*

hygienic (hai-*dʒii*-nik) *adj* higiénico

hymn (him) *n* himno *m*

hyphen (*hai*-fön) *n* guión *m*

hypocrisy (hi-*po*-krö-ssi) *n* hipocresía *f*

hypocrite (*hi*-pö-krit) *n* hipócrita *m*

hypocritical (hi-pö-*kri*-ti-köl) *adj* hipócrita, mojigato

hysterical (hi-*ssté*-ri-köl) *adj* histérico

I

I (ai) *pron* yo

ice (aiss) *n* hielo *m*

ice-bag (*aiss*-bægh) *n* bolsa de hielo

ice-cream (*aiss*-kriim) *n* helado *m*

Iceland (*aiss*-lönd) Islandia *f*

Icelander (*aiss*-lön-dö) *n* islandés *m*

Icelandic (aiss-*læn*-dik) *adj* islandés

icon (*ai*-kon) *n* icono *m*

idea (ai-*di*ǒ) *n* idea *f*; pensamiento *m*; noción *f*, concepto *m*

ideal (ai-*di*ǒl) *adj* ideal; *n* ideal *m*

identical (ai-*dên*-ti-köl) *adj* idéntico

identification (ai-dên-ti-fi-*kei*-ʃön) *n* identificación *f*

identify (ai-*dên*-ti-fai) *v* identificar

identity (ai-*dên*-tö-ti) *n* identidad *f*; ~ card carnet de identidad

idiom (*i*-di-öm) *n* modismo *m*

idiomatic (i-di-ö-*mæ*-tik) *adj* idiomático

idiot (*i*-di-öt) *n* idiota *m*

idiotic (i-di-*o*-tik) *adj* idiota

idle (*ai*-döl) *adj* ocioso, vago; vano

idol (*ai*-döl) *n* ídolo *m*

if (if) *conj* si

ignition (igh-*ni*-ʃön) *n* encendido *m*; ~ coil bobina del encendido

ignorant (*igh*-nö-rönt) *adj* ignorante

ignore (igh-*noo*) *v* ignorar

ill (il) *adj* enfermo; malo; maligno

illegal (i-*lii*-ghöl) *adj* ilegal

illegible (i-*lê*-dʒö-böl) *adj* ilegible

illiterate (i-*li*-tö-röt) *n* analfabeto *m*

illness (*il*-nöss) *n* enfermedad *f*

illuminate (i-*luu*-mi-neit) *v* iluminar

illumination (i-luu mi-*nei*-ʃön) *n* iluminación *f*

illusion (i-*luu*-ʒön) *n* ilusión *f*

illustrate (*i*-lö-sstreit) *v* ilustrar

illustration (i-lö-*sstrei*-ʃön) *n* ilustración *f*

image (*i*-midʒ) *n* imagen *f*

imaginary (i-*mæ*-dʒi-nö-ri) *adj* imaginario

imagination (i-mæ-dʒi-*nei*-ʃön) *n* imaginación *f*

imagine (i-*mæ*-dʒin) *v* imaginarse; fi-

gurarse
imitate (*i*-mi-teit) *v* imitar
imitation (i-mi-*tei*-şön) *n* imitación *f*
immediate (i-*mii*-dyöt) *adj* inmediato
immediately (i-*mii*-dyöt-li) *adv* inmediatamente, de inmediato
immense (i-*mênss*) *adj* inmenso, enorme
immigrant (*i*-mi-ghrönt) *n* inmigrante *m*
immigrate (*i*-mi-ghreit) *v* inmigrar
immigration (i-mi-*ghrei*-şön) *n* inmigración *f*
immodest (i-*mo*-disst) *adj* inmodesto
immunity (i-*myuu*-nö-ti) *n* inmunidad *f*
immunize (*i*-myu-nais) *v* inmunizar
impartial (im-*paa*-şöl) *adj* imparcial
impassable (im-*paa*-ssö-böl) *adj* intransitable
impatient (im-*pei*-şönt) *adj* impaciente
impede (im-*piid*) *v* *impedir
impediment (im-*pê*-di-mönt) *n* impedimento *m*
imperfect (im-*pöö*-fikt) *adj* imperfecto
imperial (im-*pi*^ö-ri-öl) *adj* imperial
impersonal (im-*pöö*-ssö-nöl) *adj* impersonal
impertinence (im-*pöö*-ti-nönss) *n* impertinencia *f*
impertinent (im-*pöö*-ti-nönt) *adj* grosero, descarado, impertinente
implement[1] (*im*-pli-mönt) *n* herramienta *f*
implement[2] (*im*-pli-mênt) *v* efectuar
imply (im-*plai*) *v* implicar
impolite (im-pö-*lait*) *adj* descortés
import[1] (im-*poot*) *v* importar
import[2] (*im*-poot) *n* importación *f*; ~ **duty** impuestos de importación
importance (im-*poo*-tönss) *n* importancia *f*
important (im-*poo*-tönt) *adj* impor-

tante
importer (im-*poo*-tö) *n* importador *m*
imposing (im-*pou*-sing) *adj* imponente
impossible (im-*po*-ssö-böl) *adj* imposible
impotence (*im*-pö-tönss) *n* impotencia *f*
impotent (*im*-pö-tönt) *adj* impotente
impound (im-*paund*) *v* confiscar
impress (im-*prêss*) *v* impresionar
impression (im-*prê*-şön) *n* impresión *f*
impressive (im-*prê*-ssiv) *adj* impresionante
imprison (im-*pri*-sön) *v* encarcelar
imprisonment (im-*pri*-sön-mönt) *n* encarcelamiento *m*
improbable (im-*pro*-bö-böl) *adj* improbable
improper (im-*pro*-pö) *adj* impropio
improve (im-*pruuv*) *v* mejorar
improvement (im-*pruuv*-mönt) *n* mejora *f*
improvise (*im*-prö-vais) *v* improvisar
impudent (*im*-pyu-dönt) *adj* impudente
impulse (*im*-palss) *n* impulso *m*; estímulo *m*
impulsive (im-*pal*-ssiv) *adj* impulsivo
in (in) *prep* en; dentro de; *adv* adentro
inaccessible (i-næk-*ssê*-ssö-böl) *adj* inaccesible
inaccurate (i-*næ*-kyu-röt) *adj* inexacto
inadequate (i-*næ*-di-k^uöt) *adj* inadecuado
incapable (ing-*kei*-pö-böl) *adj* incapaz
incense (*in*-ssênss) *n* incienso *m*
incident (*in*-ssi-dönt) *n* incidente *m*
incidental (in-ssi-*dên*-töl) *adj* imprevisto
incite (in-*ssait*) *v* incitar
inclination (ing-kli-*nei*-şön) *n* inclinación *f*
incline (ing-*klain*) *n* inclinación *f*

inclined (ing-*klaind*) *adj* dispuesto, inclinado; *be ~ to *v* inclinarse

include (ing-*kluud*) *v* *incluir

inclusive (ing-*kluu*-ssiv) *adj* incluso

income (*ing*-köm) *n* ingresos *mpl*

income-tax (*ing*-köm-tækss) *n* impuesto sobre los ingresos

incompetent (ing-*kom*-pö-tönt) *adj* incompetente

incomplete (in-köm-*pliit*) *adj* incompleto

inconceivable (ing-kön-*ssii*-vo-böl) *adj* inconcebible

inconspicuous (ing-kön-*sspi*-kyu-öss) *adj* discreto

inconvenience (ing-kön-*vii*-nyönss) *n* incomodidad *f*, inconveniencia *f*

inconvenient (ing-kön-*vii*-nyönt) *adj* inoportuno; molesto

incorrect (ing-kö-*rêkt*) *adj* inexacto, incorrecto

increase[1] (ing-*kriiss*) *v* aumentar; incrementar, *acrecentarse

increase[2] (*ing*-kriiss) *n* aumento *m*

incredible (ing-*krê*-dö-böl) *adj* increíble

incurable (ing-*kyu⁰*-rö-böl) *adj* incurable

indecent (in-*dii*-ssönt) *adj* indecente

indeed (in-*diid*) *adv* por cierto

indefinite (in-*dê*-fi-nit) *adj* indefinido

indemnity (in-*dêm*-nö-ti) *n* indemnización *f*

independence (in-di-*pên*-dönss) *n* independencia *f*

independent (in-di-*pên*-dönt) *adj* independiente; autónomo

index (*in*-dêkss) *n* índice *m*; ~ finger índice *m*

India (*in*-di-ö) India *f*

Indian (*in*-di-ön) *adj* indio; *n* indio *m*

indicate (*in*-di-keit) *v* señalar, indicar

indication (in-di-*kei*-ſön) *n* señal *f*, indicación *f*

indicator (*in*-di-kei-tö) *n* indicador *m*

indifferent (in-*di*-fö-rönt) *adj* indiferente

indigestion (in-di-*dʒêss*-chön) *n* indigestión *f*

indignation (in-digh-*nei*-ſön) *n* indignación *f*

indirect (in-di-*rêkt*) *adj* indirecto

individual (in-di-*vi*-dʒu-öl) *adj* aparte, individual; *n* individuo *m*

Indonesia (in-dö-*nii*-si-ö) Indonesia *f*

Indonesian (in-dö-*nii*-si-ön) *adj* indonesio

indoor (*in*-doo) *adj* en casa

indoors (in-*doos*) *adv* en casa

indulge (in-*daldʒ*) *v* ceder

industrial (in-*da*-sstri-ol) *adj* industrial; ~ area zona industrial

industrious (in-*da*-sstri-öss) *adj* diligente

industry (*in*-dö-sstri) *n* industria *f*

inedible (i-*nê*-di-böl) *adj* incomible

inefficient (i-ni-*fi*-ſönt) *adj* ineficiente

inevitable (i-*nê*-vi-tö-böl) *adj* inevitable

inexpensive (i-nik-*sspên*-ssiv) *adj* barato

inexperienced (i-nik-*sspi⁰*-ri-önsst) *adj* inexperto

infant (*in*-fönt) *n* criatura *f*

infantry (*in*-fon-trı) *n* infantería *f*

infect (in-*fêkt*) *v* infectar

infection (in-*fêk*-ſön) *n* infección *f*

infectious (in-*fêk*-ſöss) *adj* contagioso

infer (in-*föö*) *v* *deducir

inferior (in-*fi⁰* ri-ö) *adj* inferior

infinite (*in*-fi-nöt) *adj* infinito

infinitive (in-*fi*-ni-tiv) *n* infinitivo *m*

infirmary (in-*föö*-mö-ri) *n* enfermería *f*

inflammable (in-*flæ*-mö-böl) *adj* inflamable

inflammation (in-flö-*mei*-ſön) *n* inflamación *f*

inflatable (in-*flei*-tö-böl) *adj* inflable
inflate (in-*fleit*) *v* hinchar
inflation (in-*flei*-[ö]n) *n* inflación *f*
influence (*in*-flu-önss) *n* influencia *f*; *v* *influir
influential (in-flu-*ên*-[ö]l) *adj* influyente
influenza (in-flu-*ên*-sö) *n* gripe *f*
inform (in-*foom*) *v* informar; comunicar
informal (in-*foo*-möl) *adj* informal
information (in-fö-*mei*-[ö]n) *n* información *f*; informes *mpl*, comunicado *m*; ~ **bureau** oficina de informaciones
infra-red (in-frö-*rêd*) *adj* infrarrojo
infrequent (in-*frii*-k[u]önt) *adj* infrecuente
ingredient (ing-*ghrii*-di-önt) *n* ingrediente *m*
inhabit (in-*hæ*-bit) *v* habitar
inhabitable (in-*hæ*-bi-tö-böl) *adj* habitable
inhabitant (in-*hæ*-bi-tönt) *n* habitante *m*
inhale (in-*heil*) *v* inhalar
inherit (in-*hê*-rit) *v* heredar
inheritance (in-*hê*-ri-tönss) *n* herencia *f*
initial (i-*ni*-[ö]l) *adj* inicial; *n* inicial *f*; *v* rubricar
initiative (i-*ni*-[ö]-tiv) *n* iniciativa *f*
inject (in-*dʒêkt*) *v* inyectar
injection (in-*dʒêk*-[ö]n) *n* inyección *f*
injure (in-dʒö) *v* *herir; ofender
injury (in-dʒö-ri) *n* herida *f*; lesión *f*
injustice (in-*dʒa*-sstiss) *n* injusticia *f*
ink (ingk) *n* tinta *f*
inlet (*in*-lêt) *n* ensenada *f*
inn (in) *n* posada *f*
inner (*i*-nö) *adj* interior; ~ **tube** cámara de aire
inn-keeper (*in*-kii-pö) *n* posadero *m*
innocence (*i*-nö-ssönss) *n* inocencia *f*

innocent (*i*-nö-ssönt) *adj* inocente
inoculate (i-*no*-kyu-leit) *v* vacunar
inoculation (i-no-kyu-*lei*-[ö]n) *n* inoculación *f*
inquire (ing-k[u]*ai[ö]*) *v* informarse, *pedir informes
inquiry (ing-k[u]*ai[ö]*-ri) *n* pregunta *f*, indagación *f*; encuesta *f*; ~ **office** oficina de informaciones
inquisitive (ing-k[u]*i*-sö-tiv) *adj* curioso
insane (in-*ssein*) *adj* lunático
inscription (in-*sskrip*-[ö]n) *n* inscripción *f*
insect (*in*-ssêkt) *n* insecto *m*; ~ **repellent** insectífugo *m*
insecticide (in-*ssêk*-ti-ssaid) *n* insecticida *m*
insensitive (in-*ssên*-ssö-tiv) *adj* insensible
insert (in-*ssööt*) *v* insertar
inside (in-*ssaid*) *n* interior *m*; *adj* interior; *adv* adentro; dentro; *prep* en, dentro de; ~ **out** al revés; **insides** entrañas *fpl*
insight (*in*-ssait) *n* entendimiento *m*
insignificant (in-ssigh-*ni*-fi-könt) *adj* insignificante; irrelevante; baladí
insist (in-*ssisst*) *v* insistir; persistir
insolence (*in*-ssö-lönss) *n* insolencia *f*
insolent (*in*-ssö-lönt) *adj* insolente
insomnia (in-*ssom*-ni-ö) *n* insomnio *m*
inspect (in-*sspêkt*) *v* inspeccionar
inspection (in-*sspêk*-[ö]n) *n* inspección *f*; control *m*
inspector (in-*sspêk*-tö) *n* inspector *m*
inspire (in-*sspai[ö]*) *v* inspirar
install (in-*sstool*) *v* instalar
installation (in-sstö-*lei*-[ö]n) *n* instalación *f*
instalment (in-*sstool*-mönt) *n* plazo *m*
instance (*in*-sstönss) *n* ejemplo *m*; caso *m*; **for** ~ por ejemplo
instant (*in*-sstönt) *n* instante *m*

instantly (*in*-sstönt-li) *adv* instantáneamente, inmediatamente, al instante

instead of (in-*sstéd* ov) en lugar de

instinct (*in*-sstingkt) *n* instinto *m*

institute (*in*-ssti-tyuut) *n* instituto *m*; institución *f*; *v* *instituir

institution (in-ssti-*tyuut*-fön) *n* instituto *m*, institución *f*

instruct (in-*sstrakt*) *v* *instruir

instruction (in-*sstrak*-fön) *n* instrucción *f*

instructive (in-*sstrak*-tiv) *adj* instructivo

instructor (in-*sstrak*-tö) *n* instructor *m*

instrument (*in*-sstru-mönt) *n* instrumento *m*; **musical** ~ instrumento músico

insufficient (in-ssö-*fi*-fönt) *adj* insuficiente

insulate (*in*-ssyu-leit) *v* aislar

insulation (in-ssyu-*lei*-fön) *n* aislamiento *m*

insulator (*in*-ssyu-lei-tö) *n* aislador *m*

insult[1] (in-*ssalt*) *v* insultar

insult[2] (*in*-ssalt) *n* insulto *m*

insurance (in-*fu^o*-rönss) *n* seguro *m*; ~ **policy** póliza de seguro

insure (in-*fu^o*) *v* asegurar

intact (in-*tækt*) *adj* intacto

intellect (*in*-tö-lêkt) *n* intelecto *m*

intellectual (in-tö-*lêk*-chu-öl) *adj* intelectual

intelligence (in-*tê*-li-dзönss) *n* inteligencia *t*

intelligent (in-*tê*-li-dзönt) *adj* inteligente

intend (in-*tênd*) *v* intentar, *tener la intención de

intense (in-*tênss*) *adj* intenso

intention (in-*tên*-fön) *n* intención *f*

intentional (in-*tên*-fö-nöl) *adj* intencional

intercourse (*in*-tö-kooss) *n* trato *m*

interest (*in*-tröst) *n* interés *m*; rédito *m*; *v* interesar

interesting (*in*-trö-ssting) *adj* interesante

interfere (in-tö-*fi^ö*) *v* interferir; ~ **with** mezclarse en

interference (in-tö-*fi^ö*-rönss) *n* interferencia *f*

interim (*in*-tö-rim) *n* interin *m*

interior (in-*ti^ö*-ri-ö) *n* interior *m*

interlude (*in*-tö-luud) *n* intermedio *m*

intermediary (in-tö-*mii*-dyö-ri) *n* intermediario *m*

intermission (in-tö-*mi*-fön) *n* entreacto *m*

internal (in-*töö*-nöl) *adj* interno

international (in-tö-*næ*-fö-nöl) *adj* internacional

interpret (in-*töö*-prit) *v* interpretar

interpreter (in-*töö*-pri-tö) *n* intérprete *m*

interrogate (in-*tê*-rö-gheit) *v* interrogar

interrogation (in-tê-rö-*ghei*-fön) *n* interrogatorio *m*

interrogative (in-tö-*ro*-ghö-tiv) *adj* interrogativo

interrupt (in-tö-*rapt*) *v* interrumpir

interruption (in-tö-*rap*-fön) *n* interrupción *f*

intersection (in-tö-*ssêk*-fön) *n* intersección *f*

interval (*in*-tö-völ) *n* intervalo *m*

intervene (in-tö-*viin*) *v* *intervenir

interview (*in*-tö-vyuu) *n* entrevista *f*

intestine (in-*tê*-sstin) *n* intestino *m*

intimate (*in*-ti-möt) *adj* íntimo

into (*in*-tu) *prep* dentro de

intolerable (in-*to*-lö-rö-böl) *adj* insoportable

intoxicated (in-*tok*-ssi-kei-tid) *adj* embriagado

intrigue (in-*triigh*) *n* intriga *f*

introduce (in-trö-*dyuuss*) *v* presentar; *introducir

introduction (in-trö-*dak*-ʃön) *n* presentación *f*; introducción *f*

invade (in-*veid*) *v* invadir

invalid¹ (*in*-vö-liid) *n* inválido *m*; *adj* inválido

invalid² (in-*væ*-lid) *adj* nulo

invasion (in-*vei*-ʒön) *n* irrupción *f*, invasión *f*

invent (in-*vênt*) *v* inventar

invention (in-*vên*-ʃön) *n* invención *f*

inventive (in-*vên*-tiv) *adj* inventivo

inventor (in-*vên*-tö) *n* inventor *m*

inventory (*in*-vön-tri) *n* inventario *m*

invert (in-*vööt*) *v* *invertir

invest (in-*vêsst*) *v* *invertir

investigate (in-*vê*-ssti-gheit) *v* investigar

investigation (in-vê-ssti-*ghei*-ʃön) *n* investigación *f*

investment (in-*vêsst*-mönt) *n* inversión *f*

investor (in-*vê*-sstö) *n* inversionista *m*

invisible (in-*vi*-sö-böl) *adj* invisible

invitation (in-vi-*tei*-ʃön) *n* invitación *f*

invite (in-*vait*) *v* invitar, convidar

invoice (*in*-voiss) *n* factura *f*

involve (in-*volv*) *v* *envolver; **involved** implicado

inwards (*in*-ᵘöds) *adv* hacia adentro

iodine (*ai*-ö-diin) *n* yodo *m*

Iran (i-*raan*) Irán *m*

Iranian (i-*rei*-ni-ön) *adj* iraní

Iraq (i-*raak*) Irak *m*

Iraqi (i-*raa*-ki) *adj* iraquí

irascible (i-*ræ*-ssi-böl) *adj* irascible

Ireland (*aiᵒ*-lönd) Irlanda *f*

Irish (*aiᵒ*-riʃ) *adj* irlandés

Irishman (*aiᵒ*-riʃ-mön) *n* (pl -men) irlandés *m*

iron (*ai*-ön) *n* hierro *m*; plancha *f*; de hierro; *v* planchar

ironical (ai-*ro*-ni-köl) *adj* irónico

ironworks (*ai*-ön-ᵘöökss) *n* herrería *f*

irony (*aiᵒ*-rö-ni) *n* ironía *f*

irregular (i-*rê*-ghyu-lö) *adj* irregular

irreparable (i-*rê*-pö-rö-böl) *adj* irreparable

irrevocable (i-*rê*-vö-kö-böl) *adj* irrevocable

irritable (*i*-ri-tö-böl) *adj* irritable

irritate (*i*-ri-teit) *v* irritar

is (is) *v* (pr be)

island (*ai*-lönd) *n* isla *f*

isolate (*ai*-ssö-leit) *v* aislar

isolation (ai-ssö-*lei*-ʃön) *n* aislamiento *m*

Israel (*is*-reil) Israel *m*

Israeli (is-*rei*-li) *adj* israelí

issue (*i*-ʃuu) *v* *distribuir; *n* emisión *f*, tirada *f*, edición *f*; cuestión *f*, punto *m*; consecuencia *f*, resultado *m*, conclusión *f*, término *m*; salida *f*

isthmus (*iss*-möss) *n* istmo *m*

it (it) *pron* lo

Italian (i-*tæl*-yön) *adj* italiano

italics (i-*tæ*-likss) *pl* cursiva *f*

Italy (*i*-tö-li) Italia *f*

itch (ich) *n* picazón *f*; prurito *m*; *v* picar

item (*ai*-töm) *n* ítem *m*; punto *m*

itinerant (ai-*ti*-nö-rönt) *adj* ambulante

itinerary (ai-*ti*-nö-rö-ri) *n* itinerario *m*

ivory (*ai*-vö-ri) *n* marfil *m*

ivy (*ai*-vi) *n* hiedra *f*

J

jack (dʒæk) *n* gato *m*

jacket (*dʒæ*-kit) *n* americana *f*, chaqueta *f*; sobrecubierta *f*; saco *mMe*

jade (dʒeid) *n* jade *m*

jail (dʒeil) *n* cárcel *f*

jailer (*dʒei*-lö) *n* carcelero *m*

jam (dʒæm) *n* mermelada *f*; congestión *f*

janitor (*dʒæ*-ni-tö) *n* conserje *m*

January (*dʒæ*-nyu-ö-ri) enero

Japan (dʒö-*pæn*) Japón *m*

Japanese (dʒæ-pö-*niis*) *adj* japonés

jar (dʒaa) *n* jarra *f*

jaundice (*dʒoon*-diss) *n* ictericia *f*

jaw (dʒoo) *n* mandíbula *f*

jealous (*dʒê*-löss) *adj* celoso

jealousy (*dʒê*-lö-ssi) *n* celos

jeans (dʒiins) *pl* vaqueros *mpl*

jelly (*dʒê*-li) *n* jalea *f*

jelly-fish (*dʒê*-li-fiʃ) *n* medusa *f*

jersey (*dʒöö*-si) *n* jersey *m*

jet (dʒêt) *n* chorro *m*; avión a reacción

jetty (*dʒê*-ti) *n* muelle *m*

Jew (dʒuu) *n* judío *m*

jewel (*dʒuu*-öl) *n* joya *f*

jeweller (*dʒuu*-ö-lö) *n* joyero *m*

jewellery (*dʒuu*-öl-ri) *n* joyería *f*

Jewish (*dʒuu*-iʃ) *adj* judío

job (dʒob) *n* tarea *f*; puesto *m*, empleo *m*

jockey (*dʒo*-ki) *n* jockey *m*

join (dʒoin) *v* juntar; unirse a, asociarse a; ensamblar, reunir

joint (dʒoint) *n* articulación *f*; soldadura *f*; *adj* unido, en común

jointly (*dʒoint*-li) *adv* juntamente

joke (dʒouk) *n* broma *f*

jolly (*dʒo*-li) *adj* jovial

Jordan (*dʒoo*-dön) Jordania *f*

Jordanian (dʒoo-*dei*-ni-ön) *adj* jordano

journal (*dʒöö*-nöl) *n* revista *f*

journalism (*dʒöö*-nö-li-söm) *n* periodismo *m*

journalist (*dʒöö*-nö-lisst) *n* periodista *m*

journey (*dʒöö*-ni) *n* viaje *m*

joy (dʒoi) *n* delicia *f*, regocijo *m*

joyful (*dʒoi*-föl) *adj* contento, alegre

jubilee (*dʒuu*-bi-lii) *n* aniversario *m*

judge (dʒadʒ) *n* juez *m*; *v* juzgar

judgment (*dʒadʒ*-mönt) *n* juicio *m*

jug (dʒagh) *n* cántaro *m*

Jugoslav (yuu-ghö-*sslaav*) *adj* yugoslavo

Jugoslavia (yuu-ghö-*sslaa*-vi-ö) Yugoslavia *f*

juice (dʒuuss) *n* zumo *m*

juicy (*dʒuu*-ssi) *adj* zumoso

July (dʒu-*lai*) julio

jump (dʒamp) *v* saltar; *n* salto *m*

jumper (*dʒam*-pö) *n* jersey *m*

junction (*dʒangk*-ʃön) *n* encrucijada *f*; empalme *m*

June (dʒuun) junio

jungle (*dʒang*-ghöl) *n* selva *f*, jungla *f*

junior (*dʒuu*-nyö) *adj* menor

junk (dʒangk) *n* cachivache *m*

jury (*dʒuᵒ*-ri) *n* jurado *m*

just (dʒasst) *adj* justo; *adv* apenas; justamente

justice (*dʒa*-sstiss) *n* derecho *m*; justicia *f*

juvenile (*dʒuu*-vö-nail) *adj* juvenil

K

kangaroo (kæng-ghö-*ruu*) *n* canguro *m*

keel (kiil) *n* quilla *f*

keen (kiin) *adj* entusiasta; agudo

*keep (kiip) *v* *tener; guardar; continuar; ~ away from *mantenerse alejado de; ~ off no tocar; ~ on continuar; ~ quiet *estarse quieto; ~ up perseverar; ~ up with *seguir el paso

keg (kêgh) *n* barrilete *m*

kennel (*kê*-nöl) *n* perrera *f*; perrera *m*

Kenya (*kê*-nyö) Kenya *m*

kerosene (*kê*-rö-ssiin) *n* petróleo lampante

kettle (*kê*-töl) *n* olla *f*

key (kii) *n* llave *f*

keyhole (*kii*-houl) *n* ojo de la cerradura

khaki (*kaa*-ki) *n* caqui *m*

kick (kik) *v* patear; *n* patada *f*

kick-off (ki-*kof*) *n* saque inicial

kid (kid) *n* niño *m*, chico *m*; cabritilla *f*; *v* embromar

kidney (*kid*-ni) *n* riñón *m*

kill (kil) *v* matar

kilogram (*ki*-lö-ghræm) *n* kilogramo *m*

kilometre (*ki*-lö-mii-tö) *n* kilómetro *m*

kind (kaind) *adj* amable, bondadoso; bueno; *n* género *m*

kindergarten (*kin*-dö-ghaa-tön) *n* escuela de párvulos, jardín de infancia

king (king) *n* rey *m*

kingdom (*king*-döm) *n* reino *m*

kiosk (*kii*-ossk) *n* quiosco *m*

kiss (kiss) *n* beso *m*; *v* besar

kit (kit) *n* avíos *mpl*

kitchen (*ki*-chin) *n* cocina *f*; ~ **garden** huerto *m*

Kleenex® (*klii*-nêkss) *n* pañuelo de papel

knapsack (*næp*-ssæk) *n* mochila *f*

knave (neiv) *n* sota *f*

knee (nii) *n* rodilla *f*

kneecap (*nii*-kæp) *n* rótula *f*

***kneel** (niil) *v* arrodillarse

knew (nyuu) *v* (p know)

knickers (*ni*-kös) *pl* braga *f*

knife (naif) *n* (pl knives) cuchillo *m*

knight (nait) *n* caballero *m*

***knit** (nit) *v* *hacer punto

knob (nob) *n* botón *m*

knock (nok) *v* golpear; *n* golpe *m*; ~ **against** chocar contra; ~ **down** derribar

knot (not) *n* nudo *m*; *v* anudar

***know** (nou) *v* *saber, *conocer

knowledge (*no*-lidȝ) *n* conocimiento *m*

knuckle (*na*-köl) *n* nudillo *m*

L

label (*lei*-böl) *n* rótulo *m*; *v* rotular

laboratory (lö-*bo*-rö-tö-ri) *n* laboratorio *m*

labour (*lei*-bö) *n* trabajo *m*, labor *f*; dolores *mpl*; *v* ajetrearse, bregar; **labor permit** *Am* permiso de trabajo

labourer (*lei*-bö-rö) *n* obrero *m*

labour-saving (*lei*-bö-ssei-ving) *adj* economizador de trabajo

labyrinth (*læ*-bö-rinz) *n* laberinto *m*

lace (leiss) *n* puntilla *f*; cordón *m*

lack (læk) *n* falta *f*; *v* *carecer

lacquer (*læ*-kö) *n* laca *f*

lad (læd) *n* joven *m*, muchacho *m*

ladder (*læ*-dö) *n* escalera de mano

lady (*lei*-di) *n* señora *f*; **ladies' room** lavabos para señoras

lagoon (lö-*ghuun*) *n* laguna *f*

lake (leik) *n* lago *m*

lamb (læm) *n* cordero *m*

lame (leim) *adj* paralítico, cojo

lamentable (*læ*-mön-tö-böl) *adj* lamentable

lamp (læmp) *n* lámpara *f*

lamp-post (*læmp*-pousst) *n* poste de farol

lampshade (*læmp*-ʃeid) *n* pantalla *f*

land (lænd) *n* país *m*, tierra *f*; *v* aterrizar; desembarcar

landlady (*lænd*-lei-di) *n* patrona *f*

landlord (*lænd*-lood) *n* propietario *m*, dueño *m*; patrón *m*

landmark (*lænd*-maak) *n* punto de re-

ferencia; mojón m
landscape (lænd-sskeip) n paisaje m
lane (lein) n callejón m; pista f
language (læng-gh^uidʒ) n lengua f; ~
    laboratory laboratorio de lenguas
lantern (læn-tön) n linterna f
lapel (lö-pêl) n solapa f
larder (laa-dö) n despensa f
large (laadʒ) adj grande; espacioso
lark (laak) n alondra f
laryngitis (læ-rin-dʒai-tiss) n laringitis
    f
last (laasst) adj último; precedente; v
    durar; at ~ al fin; al final
lasting (laa-ssting) adj duradero
latchkey (læch-kii) n llave de la casa
late (leit) adj tardío; retrasado
lately (leit-li) adv últimamente, re-
    cientemente
lather (laa-ðö) n espuma f
Latin America (læ-tin ö-mê-ri-kö)
    América Latina
Latin-American (læ-tin-ö-mê-ri-kön)
    adj latinoamericano
latitude (læ-ti-tyuud) n latitud f
laugh (laaf) v *reír; n risa f
laughter (laaf-tö) n risa f
launch (loonch) v lanzar; n buque a
    motor
launching (loon-ching) n botadura f
launderette (loon-dö-rêt) n lavandería
    de autoservicio
laundry (loon dri) n lavandería f; ro-
    pa sucia
lavatory (læ-vö-tö-ri) n cuarto de aseo
lavish (læ-viʃ) adj pródigo
law (loo) n ley f; derecho m; ~
    court tribunal m
lawful (loo-föl) adj lícito
lawn (loon) n césped m
lawsuit (loo-ssuut) n proceso m, cau-
    sa f
lawyer (loo-yö) n abogado m; jurista
    m

laxative (læk-ssö-tiv) n laxante m
*lay (lei) v colocar, *poner; ~ bricks
    mampostear
layer (lei^ö) n capa f
layman (lei-mön) n profano m
lazy (lei-si) adj perezoso
lead¹ (liid) n ventaja f; dirección f;
    traílla f
lead² (lêd) n plomo m
*lead (liid) v *conducir
leader (lii-dö) n jefe m, líder m
leadership (lii-dö-ʃip) n dirección f
leading (lii-ding) adj dominante, prin-
    cipal
leaf (liif) n (pl leaves) hoja f
league (liigh) n liga f
leak (liik) v gotear; n goteo m
leaky (lii-ki) adj que tiene escapes
lean (liin) adj magro
*lean (liin) v apoyarse
leap (liip) n salto m
*leap (liip) v saltar
leap-year (liip-yi^ö) n año bisiesto
*learn (löön) v aprender
learner (löö-no) n principiante m
lease (liiss) n contrato de arrenda-
    miento; arrendamiento m; v
    *arrendar, alquilar
leash (liiʃ) n correa f
least (liisst) adj mínimo, menos; at ~
    por lo menos
leather (lê-ðö) n cuero m; de piel
leave (liiv) n licencia f
*leave (liiv) v partir, dejar; ~ out
    omitir
Lebanese (lê-bö niis) adj libanés
Lebanon (lê-bö-nön) Líbano m
lecture (lêk-chö) n curso m, conferen-
    cia f
left¹ (lêft) adj izquierdo
left² (lêft) v (p, pp leave)
left-hand (lêft-hænd) adj izquierdo, de
    izquierda
left-handed (lêft-hæn-did) adj zurdo

leg (lêgh) *n* pata *f*, pierna *f*
legacy (*lê*-ghö-ssi) *n* herencia *f*
legal (*lii*-ghöl) *adj* legítimo, legal; jurídico
legalization (lii-ghö-lai-*sei*-[ʃ]ön) *n* legalización *f*
legation (li-*ghei*-[ʃ]ön) *n* legación *f*
legible (*lê*-dʒi-böl) *adj* legible
legitimate (li-*dʒi*-ti-möt) *adj* legítimo
leisure (*lê*-ʒö) *n* ocio *m*; comodidad *f*
lemon (*lê*-mön) *n* limón *m*
lemonade (lê-mö-*neid*) *n* limonada *f*
***lend** (lênd) *v* prestar
length (lêngz) *n* longitud *f*
lengthen (*lêng*-zön) *v* alargar
lengthways (*lêngz*-ᵘeis) *adv* longitudinalmente
lens (lêns) *n* lente *m/f*; **telephoto** ~ teleobjetivo *m*; **zoom** ~ lente de foco regulable
leprosy (*lê*-prö-ssi) *n* lepra *f*
less (lêss) *adv* menos
lessen (*lê*-ssön) *v* *disminuir
lesson (*lê*-ssön) *n* lección *f*
***let** (lêt) *v* dejar; alquilar; ~ **down** decepcionar
letter (*lê*-tö) *n* carta *f*; letra *f*; ~ **of credit** carta de crédito; ~ **of recommendation** carta de recomendación
letter-box (*lê*-tö-bokss) *n* buzón *m*
lettuce (*lê*-tiss) *n* lechuga *f*
level (*lê*-völ) *adj* igual; plano, llano; *n* nivel *m*; *v* igualar, nivelar; ~ **crossing** paso a nivel
lever (*lii*-vö) *n* palanca *f*
Levis (*lii*-vais) *pl* jeans *mpl*
liability (lai-ö-*bi*-lö-ti) *n* responsabilidad *f*
liable (*lai*-ö-böl) *adj* responsable; ~ **to** sujeto a
liberal (*li*-bö-röl) *adj* liberal; generoso, dadivoso

liberation (li-bö-*rei*-[ʃ]ön) *n* liberación *f*
Liberia (lai-*bi*ᵒ-ri-ö) Liberia *f*
Liberian (lai-*bi*ᵒ-ri-ön) *adj* liberiano
liberty (*li*-bö-ti) *n* libertad *f*
library (*lai*-brö-ri) *n* biblioteca *f*
licence (*lai*-ssönss) *n* licencia *f*; permiso *m*; **driving** ~ permiso de conducir
license (*lai*-ssönss) *v* autorizar
lick (lik) *v* lamer
lid (lid) *n* tapa *f*
lie (lai) *v* *mentir; *n* mentira *f*
***lie** (lai) *v* *yacer; ~ **down** *tenderse
life (laif) *n* (pl lives) vida *f*; ~ **insurance** seguro de vida
lifebelt (*laif*-bêlt) *n* chaleco salvavidas
lifetime (*laif*-taim) *n* vida *f*
lift (lift) *v* levantar; *n* ascensor *m*; elevador *mMe*
light (lait) *n* luz *f*; *adj* ligero; pálido; ~ **bulb** bulbo *m*
***light** (lait) *v* *encender
lighter (*lai*-tö) *n* encendedor *m*
lighthouse (*lait*-hauss) *n* faro *m*
lighting (*lai*-ting) *n* alumbrado *m*
lightning (*lait*-ning) *n* relámpago *m*
like (laik) *v* *querer; gustar; *adj* semejante; *conj* como
likely (*lai*-kli) *adj* probable
like-minded (laik-*main*-did) *adj* unánime
likewise (*laik*-ᵘais) *adv* así también, asimismo
lily (*li*-li) *n* azucena *f*
limb (lim) *n* miembro *m*
lime (laim) *n* cal *f*; tilo *m*; lima *f*
limetree (*laim*-trii) *n* tilo *m*
limit (*li*-mit) *n* límite *m*; *v* limitar
limp (limp) *v* cojear; *adj* inerte
line (lain) *n* renglón *m*; raya *f*; cordón *m*; línea *f*; cola *f*
linen (*li*-nin) *n* lino *m*; ropa blanca
liner (*lai*-nö) *n* vapor de línea
lingerie (*long*-ʒö-rii) *n* ropa interior de

mujer

lining (*lai*-ning) *n* forro *m*

link (lingk) *v* enlazar; *n* enlace *m*; eslabón *m*

lion (*lai*-ön) *n* león *m*

lip (lip) *n* labio *m*

lipsalve (*lip*-ssaav) *n* manteca de cacao

lipstick (*lip*-sstik) *n* lápiz labial

liqueur (li-*kyu^o*) *n* licor *m*

liquid (*li*-k^uid) *adj* líquido; *n* líquido *m*

liquor (*li*-kö) *n* bebidas alcohólicas

liquorice (*li*-kö-riss) *n* regaliz *m*

list (lisst) *n* lista *f*; *v* inscribir

listen (*li*-ssön) *v* escuchar

listener (*liss*-nö) *n* oyente *m*

literary (*li*-trö-ri) *adj* literario

literature (*li*-trö-chö) *n* literatura *f*

litre (*lii*-tö) *n* litro *m*

litter (*li*-tö) *n* desperdicio *m*; trastos *mpl*; lechigada *f*

little (*li*-töl) *adj* pequeño; poco

live[1] (liv) *v* vivir

live[2] (laiv) *adj* vivo

livelihood (*laiv*-li-hud) *n* sustento *m*

lively (*laiv*-li) *adj* vivo

liver (*li*-vö) *n* hígado *m*

living-room (*li*-ving-ruum) *n* sala de estar, living *m*

load (loud) *n* carga *f*; fardo *m*; *v* cargar

loaf (louf) *n* (pl loaves) pan *m*

loan (loun) *n* préstamo *m*

lobby (*lo*-bi) *n* vestíbulo *m*

lobster (*lob*-sstö) *n* langosta *f*

local (*lou*-köl) *adj* local; ~ **call** llamada local; ~ **train** tren ómnibus

locality (lou-*kæ*-lö-ti) *n* localidad *f*

locate (lou-*keit*) *v* localizar

location (lou-*kei*-fön) *n* ubicación *f*

lock (lok) *v* *cerrar con llave; *n* cerradura *f*; esclusa *f*; ~ **up** guardar con llave

locomotive (lou-kö-*mou*-tiv) *n* locomotora *f*

lodge (lodʒ) *v* alojar; *n* apeadero de caza

lodger (*lo*-dʒö) *n* huésped *m*

lodgings (*lo*-dʒings) *pl* alojamiento *m*

log (logh) *n* madero *m*

logic (*lo*-dʒik) *n* lógica *f*

logical (*lo*-dʒi-köl) *adj* lógico

lonely (*loun*-li) *adj* solitario

long (long) *adj* largo; ~ **for** anhelar; **no longer** ya no

longing (*long*-ing) *n* anhelo *m*

longitude (*lon*-dʒi-tyuud) *n* longitud *f*

look (luk) *v* mirar; *parecer, *tener aires de; *n* ojeada *f*, mirada *f*; aspecto *m*; ~ **after** ocuparse de, cuidar de; ~ **at** mirar; ~ **for** buscar; ~ **out** prestar atención, *tener cuidado; ~ **up** buscar

looking-glass (*lu*-king-ghlaass) *n* espejo *m*

loop (luup) *n* nudo corredizo

loose (luuss) *adj* suelto

loosen (*luu*-ssön) *v* *soltar

lord (lood) *n* lord *m*

lorry (*lo*-ri) *n* camión *m*

***lose** (luus) *v* *perder

loss (loss) *n* pérdida *f*

lost (losst) *adj* perdido; desaparecido; ~ **and found** objetos perdidos; ~ **property office** oficina de objetos perdidos

lot (lot) *n* suerte *f*, destino *m*; masa *f*, cantidad *f*

lotion (lou*fön) *n* loción *f*, **aftershave** ~ loción para después de afeitarse

lottery (*lo*-tö-ri) *n* lotería *f*

loud (laud) *adj* fuerte

loud-speaker (laud-*sspii*-kö) *n* altavoz *m*

lounge (laundʒ) *n* salón *m*

louse (lauss) *n* (pl lice) piojo *m*

love (lav) v amar; n amor m; **in ~ enamorado**

lovely (*lav*-li) adj delicioso, precioso, bonito

lover (*la*-vö) n amante m

love-story (*lav*-sstoo-ri) n historia de amor

low (lou) adj bajo; profundo; deprimido; **~ tide** bajamar f

lower (*lou*-ö) v bajar; rebajar; arriar; adj inferior

lowlands (*lou*-lönds) pl tierra baja

loyal (*loi*-öl) adj leal

lubricate (*luu*-bri-keit) v lubrificar, lubricar

lubrication (luu-bri-*kei*-∫ön) n lubricación f; **~ oil** aceite lubricante; **~ system** sistema de lubricación

luck (lak) n éxito m, suerte f; azar m

lucky (*la*-ki) adj afortunado; **~ charm** talismán m

ludicrous (*luu*-di-kröss) adj ridículo, grotesco

luggage (*la*-ghidʒ) n equipaje m; **hand ~** equipaje de mano; **left ~ office** consigna f; **~ rack** portabagajes m, rejilla f; **~ van** furgón de equipajes

lukewarm (*luuk*-ᵘoom) adj tibio

lumbago (lam-*bei*-ghou) n lumbago m

luminous (*luu*-mi-nöss) adj luminoso

lump (lamp) n nudo m, grumo m, terrón m; chichón m; **~ of sugar** terrón de azúcar; **~ sum** suma global

lumpy (*lam*-pi) adj apelmazado

lunacy (*luu*-nö-ssi) n locura f

lunatic (*luu*-nö-tik) adj lunático; n alienado m

lunch (lanch) n almuerzo m

luncheon (*lan*-chön) n almuerzo m

lung (lang) n pulmón m

lust (lasst) n concupiscencia f

luxurious (lagh-ʒuᵒ-ri-öss) adj lujoso

luxury (*lak*-∫ö-ri) n lujo m

M

machine (mö-*∫iin*) n aparato m, máquina f

machinery (mö-*∫ii*-nö-ri) n maquinaria f; mecanismo m

mackerel (*mæ*-kröl) n (pl ~) escombro m

mackintosh (*mæ*-kin-to∫) n impermeable m

mad (mæd) adj loco; rabioso

madam (*mæ*-döm) n señora f

madness (*mæd*-nöss) n locura f

magazine (mæ-ghö-*siin*) n revista f

magic (*mæ*-dʒik) n magia f; adj mágico

magician (mö-*dʒi*-∫ön) n prestidigitador m

magistrate (*mæ*-dʒi-sstreit) n magistrado m

magnetic (mægh-*nê*-tik) adj magnético

magneto (mægh-*nii*-tou) n (pl ~s) magneto m

magnificent (mægh-*ni*-fi-ssönt) adj magnífico; grandioso, espléndido

magpie (*mægh*-pai) n urraca f

maid (meid) n muchacha f

maiden name (*mei*-dön neim) apellido de soltera

mail (meil) n correo m; v enviar por correo

mailbox (*meil*-bokss) nAm buzón m

main (mein) adj principal; mayor; **~ deck** puente superior; **~ line** línea principal; **~ road** camino principal; **~ street** calle mayor

mainland (*mein*-lönd) n tierra firme

mainly (*mein*-li) adv principalmente

mains (meins) pl conducción principal

maintain (mein-*tein*) *v* *mantener

maintenance (*mein*-tö-nönss) *n* mantenimiento *m*

maize (meis) *n* maíz *m*

major (*mei*-dʒö) *adj* grande; mayor; *n* mayor *m*

majority (mo-*dʒo*-rö-ti) *n* mayoría *f*

*make (meik) *v* *hacer; ganar; *conseguir; ~ do with arreglarse con; ~ good compensar; ~ up redactar

make-up (*mei*-kap) *n* maquillaje *m*

malaria (mö-*lê*ᵃ-ri-ö) *n* malaria *f*

Malay (mö-*lei*) *n* malayo *m*

Malaysia (mö-*lei*-si-ö) Malasia *f*

Malaysian (mö-*lei*-si-ön) *adj* malayo

male (meil) *adj* macho

malicious (mö-*li*-ʃöss) *adj* malicioso

malignant (mö-*ligh*-nönt) *adj* maligno

mallet (*mæ*-lit) *n* mazo *m*

malnutrition (mæl-nyu-*tri*-ʃön) *n* desnutrición *f*

mammal (*mæ*-möl) *n* mamífero *m*

mammoth (*mæ*-möz) *n* mamut *m*

man (mæn) *n* (pl men) hombre *m*; men's room lavabos para caballeros

manage (*mæ*-nidʒ) *v* administrar; *tener éxito

manageable (*mæ*-ni-dʒö-böl) *adj* manejable

management (*mæ*-nidʒ-mönt) *n* manejo *m*; gestión *f*

manager (*mæ*-ni-dʒö) *n* jefe *m*, director *m*

mandarin (*mæn*-dö-rin) *n* mandarina *f*

mandate (*mæn*-deit) *n* mandato *m*

manger (*mein*-dʒö) *n* pesebre *m*

manicure (*mæ*-ni-kyuᵃ) *n* manicura *f*; *v* *hacer la manicura

mankind (mæn-*kaind*) *n* humanidad *f*

mannequin (*mæ*-nö-kin) *n* maniquí *m*

manner (*mæ*-nö) *n* modo *m*, manera *f*; manners *pl* modales *mpl*

man-of-war (mæ-növ-ᵘoo) *n* buque de guerra

manor-house (*mæ*-no-hauss) *n* casa señorial

mansion (*mæn*-ʃön) *n* mansión *f*

manual (*mæ*-nyu-öl) *adj* manual

manufacture (mæ-nyu-*fæk*-chö) *v* fabricar

manufacturer (mæ-nyu-*fæk*-chö-rö) *n* fabricante *m*

manure (mö-*nyu*ᵃ) *n* abono *m*

manuscript (*mæ*-nyu-sskript) *n* manuscrito *m*

many (*mê*-ni) *adj* muchos

map (mæp) *n* carta *f*; mapa *m*; plano *m*

maple (*mei*-pöl) *n* arce *m*

marble (*maa*-böl) *n* mármol *m*; canica *f*

March (maach) marzo

march (maach) *v* marchar; *n* marcha *f*

mare (mê ᵃ) *n* yegua *f*

margarine (maa-dʒö-*riin*) *n* margarina *f*

margin (*maa*-dʒin) *n* margen *m*

maritime (*mæ*-ri-taim) *adj* marítimo

mark (maak) *v* marcar; caracterizar; *n* marca *f*; nota *f*; blanco *m*

market (*maa*-kit) *n* mercado *m*

market-place (*maa*-kit-pleiss) *n* plaza de mercado

marmalade (*maa*-mö-leid) *n* confitura *f*

marriage (*mæ*-ridʒ) *n* matrimonio *m*

marrow (*mæ*-rou) *n* médula *f*

marry (*mæ*-ri) *v* casarse; married couple cónyuges *mpl*

marsh (maaʃ) *n* pantano *m*

marshy (*maa*-ʃi) *adj* pantanoso

martyr (*maa*-tö) *n* mártir *m*

marvel (*maa*-völ) *n* maravilla *f*; *v* maravillarse

marvellous (*maa*-vö-löss) *adj* maravilloso

mascara (mæ-*sskaa*-rö) *n* rímel *m*

masculine (*mæ*-sskyu-lin) *adj* masculino

mash (mæʃ) *v* machacar

mask (maassk) *n* máscara *f*

Mass (mæss) *n* misa *f*

mass (mæss) *n* masa *f*; ~ **production** producción en serie

massage (*mæ*-ssaaʒ) *n* masaje *m*; *v* *dar masaje

masseur (mæ-*ssöö*) *n* masajista *m*

massive (*mæ*-ssiv) *adj* macizo

mast (maasst) *n* mástil *m*

master (*maa*-sstö) *n* maestro *m*; patrón *m*; profesor *m*; *v* dominar

masterpiece (*maa*-sstö-piiss) *n* obra maestra

mat (mæt) *n* estera *f*; *adj* mate, apagado

match (mæch) *n* cerilla *f*; partido *m*; cerillo *mMe*; *v* *hacer juego con

match-box (*mæch*-bokss) *n* caja de cerillas

material (mö-*tiⁱ*-ri-öl) *n* material *m*; tejido *m*; *adj* material

mathematical (mæ-zö-*mæ*-ti-köl) *adj* matemático

mathematics (mæ-zö-*mæ*-tikss) *n* matemáticas *fpl*

matrimonial (mæ-tri-*mou*-ni-öl) *adj* matrimonial

matrimony (*mæ*-tri-mö-ni) *n* matrimonio *m*

matter (*mæ*-tö) *n* materia *f*; asunto *m*, cuestión *f*; *v* *tener importancia; **as a ~ of fact** efectivamente, en realidad

matter-of-fact (mæ-tö-röv-*fækt*) *adj* desapasionado

mattress (*mæ*-tröss) *n* colchón *m*

mature (mö-*tyuⁱ*) *adj* maduro

maturity (mö-*tyuⁱ*-rö-ti) *n* madurez *f*

mausoleum (moo-ssö-*lii*-öm) *n* mau-

soleo *m*

mauve (mouv) *adj* malva

May (mei) mayo

*** may** (mei) *v* *poder

maybe (*mei*-bii) *adv* quizás

mayor (mê⁰) *n* alcalde *m*

maze (meis) *n* laberinto *m*

me (mii) *pron* me

meadow (*mê*-dou) *n* prado *m*

meal (miil) *n* comida *f*

mean (miin) *adj* mezquino; *n* promedio *m*

*** mean** (miin) *v* significar; *querer decir

meaning (*mii*-ning) *n* significado *m*

meaningless (*mii*-ning-löss) *adj* sin sentido

means (miins) *n* medio *m*; **by no ~** en ningún caso, de ningún modo

in the meantime (in ðö *miin*-taim) entretanto

meanwhile (*miin*-ᵘail) *adv* entretanto

measles (*mii*-söls) *n* sarampión *m*

measure (*mê*-ʒö) *v* *medir; *n* medida *f*

meat (miit) *n* carne *f*

mechanic (mi-*kæ*-nik) *n* mecánico *m*

mechanical (mi-*kæ*-ni-köl) *adj* mecánico

mechanism (*mê*-kö-ni-söm) *n* mecanismo *m*

medal (*mê*-döl) *n* medalla *f*

mediaeval (mê-di-*ii*-völ) *adj* medieval

mediate (*mii*-di-eit) *v* mediar

mediator (*mii*-di-ei-tö) *n* mediador *m*

medical (*mê*-di-köl) *adj* médico

medicine (*mêd*-ssin) *n* medicamento *m*; medicina *f*

meditate (*mê*-di-teit) *v* meditar

Mediterranean (mê-di-tö-*rei*-ni-ön) Mediterráneo

medium (*mii*-di-öm) *adj* mediano, medio

*** meet** (miit) *v* *encontrarse con

meeting (*mii*-ting) *n* asamblea *f*, reunión *f*; encuentro *m*

meeting-place (*mii*-ting-pleiss) *n* lugar de reunión

melancholy (*mê*-löng-kö-li) *n* melancolía *f*

mellow (*mê*-lou) *adj* suave

melodrama (*mê*-lö-draa-mö) *n* melodrama *m*

melody (*mê*-lö-di) *n* melodía *f*

melon (*mê*-lön) *n* melón *m*

melt (mêlt) *v* fundir

member (*mêm*-bö) *n* miembro *m*; **Member of Parliament** diputado *m*

membership (*mêm*-bö-ſip) *n* afiliación *f*

memo (*mê*-mou) *n* (pl ~s) apunte *m*

memorable (*mê*-mö-rö-böl) *adj* memorable

memorial (mö-*moo*-ri-öl) *n* monumento *m*

memorize (*mê*-mö-rais) *v* aprenderse de memoria

memory (*mê*-mö-ri) *n* memoria *f*; recuerdo *m*

mend (mênd) *v* reparar, *remendar

menstruation (mên-sstru-*ei*-ſön) *n* menstruación *f*

mental (*mên*-töl) *adj* mental

mention (*mên*-ſön) *v* nombrar, mencionar; *n* mención *f*

menu (*mê*-nyu) *n* menú *m*

merchandise (*möö*-chön-dais) *n* mercancía *f*

merchant (*möö*-chönt) *n* comerciante *m*

merciful (*möö*-ssi-föl) *adj* misericordioso

mercury (*möö*-kyu-ri) *n* mercurio *m*

mercy (*möö*-ssi) *n* misericordia *f*, clemencia *f*

mere (mi⁸) *adj* puro

merely (*mi⁸*-li) *adv* solamente

merger (*möö*-dʒö) *n* fusión *f*

merit (*mê*-rit) *v* *merecer; *n* mérito *m*

mermaid (*möö*-meid) *n* sirena *f*

merry (*mê*-ri) *adj* alegre

merry-go-round (*mê*-ri-ghou-raund) *n* caballitos *mpl*

mesh (mêſ) *n* malla *f*

mess (mêss) *n* desorden *m*; ~ **up** estropear

message (*mê*-ssidʒ) *n* mensaje *m*

messenger (*mê*-ssin-dʒö) *n* mensajero *m*

metal (*mê*-töl) *n* metal *m*; metálico

meter (*mii*-tö) *n* contador *m*

method (*mê*-zöd) *n* método *m*; orden *m*

methodical (mö-*zo*-di-köl) *adj* metódico

methylated spirits (*mê*-zö-lei-tid *sspi*-ritss) alcohol de quemar

metre (*mii*-tö) *n* metro *m*

metric (*mê*-trik) *adj* métrico

Mexican (*mêk*-ssi-kön) *adj* mejicano; *n* mejicano *m*

Mexico (*mêk*-ssi-kou) Méjico *m*

mezzanine (*mê*-sö-niin) *n* entresuelo *m*

microphone (*mai*-krö-foun) *n* micrófono *m*

midday (*mid*-dei) *n* mediodía *m*

middle (*mi*-döl) *n* medio *m*; *adj* medio; **Middle Ages** Edad Media; ~ **class** clase media; **middle-class** *adj* burgués

midnight (*mid*-nait) *n* medianoche *f*

midst (midsst) *n* medio *m*

midsummer (*mid*-ssa-mö) *n* pleno verano

midwife (*mid*-ᵘaif) *n* (pl -wives) comadrona *f*

might (mait) *n* fuerza *f*

***might** (mait) *v* *poder

mighty (*mai*-ti) *adj* fuerte

migraine (*mi*-ghrein) *n* migraña *f*
mild (maild) *adj* suave
mildew (*mil*-dyu) *n* moho *m*
mile (mail) *n* milla *f*
mileage (*mai*-lidӡ) *n* millaje *m*
milepost (*mail*-pousst) *n* cipo *m*
milestone (*mail*-sstoun) *n* piedra miliar
milieu (*mii*-lyöö) *n* medio ambiente
military (*mi*-li-tö-ri) *adj* militar; ~ **force** fuerzas armadas
milk (milk) *n* leche *f*
milkman (*milk*-mön) *n* (pl -men) lechero *m*
milk-shake (*milk*-ʃeik) *n* batido de leche
milky (*mil*-ki) *adj* lechoso
mill (mil) *n* molino *m*; fábrica *f*
miller (*mi*-lö) *n* molinero *m*
milliner (*mi*-li-nö) *n* sombrerera *f*
million (*mil*-yön) *n* millón *m*
millionaire (mil-yö-*nêᵒ*) *n* millonario *m*
mince (minss) *v* picar
mind (maind) *n* mente *f*; *v* *hacer objeción a; fijarse en, *tener cuidado con
mine (main) *n* mina *f*
miner (*mai*-nö) *n* minero *m*
mineral (*mi*-nö-röl) *n* mineral *m*; ~ **water** agua mineral
miniature (*min*-yö-chö) *n* miniatura *f*
minimum (*mi*-ni-möm) *n* mínimum *m*
mining (*mai*-ning) *n* minería *f*
minister (*mi*-ni-sstö) *n* ministro *m*; clérigo *m*; **Prime Minister** Presidente de Consejo de ministros
ministry (*mi*-ni-sstri) *n* ministerio *m*
mink (mingk) *n* visón *m*
minor (*mai*-nö) *adj* pequeño, escaso, menor; secundario; *n* menor de edad
minority (mai-*no*-rö-ti) *n* minoría *f*
mint (mint) *n* menta *f*

minus (*mai*-nöss) *prep* menos
minute[1] (*mi*-nit) *n* minuto *m*; **minutes** actas
minute[2] (mai-*nyuut*) *adj* menudo
miracle (*mi*-rö-köl) *n* milagro *m*
miraculous (mi-*ræ*-kyu-löss) *adj* milagroso
mirror (*mi*-rö) *n* espejo *m*
misbehave (miss-bi-*heiv*) *v* portarse mal
miscarriage (miss-*kæ*-ridӡ) *n* aborto *m*
miscellaneous (mi-ssö-*lei*-ni-öss) *adj* misceláneo
mischief (*miss*-chif) *n* diabluras *fpl*; mal *m*, daño *m*, malicia *f*
mischievous (*miss*-chi-vöss) *adj* travieso
miserable (*mi*-sö-rö-böl) *adj* miserable
misery (*mi*-sö-ri) *n* miseria *f*; necesidad *f*
misfortune (miss-*foo*-chên) *n* contratiempo *m*, infortunio *m*
*****mislay** (miss-*lei*) *v* extraviar
misplaced (miss-*pleisst*) *adj* inoportuno; fuera de lugar
mispronounce (miss-prö-*naunss*) *v* pronunciar mal
miss[1] (miss) señorita *f*
miss[2] (miss) *v* *perder
missing (*mi*-ssing) *adj* que falta; ~ **person** desaparecido *m*
mist (misst) *n* niebla *f*
mistake (mi-*ssteik*) *n* error *m*, equivocación *f*
*****mistake** (mi-*ssteik*) *v* confundir
mistaken (mi-*sstei*-kön) *adj* equivocado; *be ~ equivocarse
mister (*mi*-sstö) señor *m*
mistress (*mi*-sströss) *n* señora *f*; dueña *f*; querida *f*
mistrust (miss-*trasst*) *v* desconfiar de
misty (*mi*-ssti) *adj* nebuloso
*****misunderstand** (mi-ssan-dö-*sstænd*)

v comprender mal

misunderstanding (mi-ssan-dö-*sstæn*-ding) *n* equivocación *f*

misuse (miss-*yuuss*) *n* abuso *m*

mittens (*mi*-töns) *pl* guantes *mpl*

mix (mikss) *v* mezclar ; ~ **with** alternar con

mixed (miksst) *adj* mezclado

mixer (*mik*-ssö) *n* batidora *f*

mixture (*mikss*-chö) *n* mezcla *f*

moan (moun) *v* *gemir

moat (mout) *n* foso *m*

mobile (*mou*-bail) *adj* móvil

mock (mok) *v* burlarse de

mockery (*mo*-kö-ri) *n* burla *f*

model (*mo*-döl) *n* modelo *m* ; maniquí *m* ; *v* modelar

moderate (*mo*-dö-röt) *adj* moderado ; mediocre

modern (*mo*-dön) *adj* moderno

modest (*mo*-disst) *adj* modesto

modesty (*mo*-di-ssti) *n* modestia *f*

modify (*mo*-di-fai) *v* modificar

mohair (*mou*-hê⁸) *n* mohair *m*

moist (moisst) *adj* mojado, húmedo

moisten (*moi*-ssön) *v* *humedecer

moisture (*moiss*-chö) *n* humedad *f* ; **moisturizing cream** crema hidratante

molar (*mou*-lö) *n* muela *f*

moment (*mou*-mönt) *n* momento *m*

momentary (*mou*-mön-tö-ri) *adj* momentáneo

monarch (*mo*-nök) *n* monarca *m*

monarchy (*mo*-nö-ki) *n* monarquía *f*

monastery (*mö*-nö-sstri) *n* monasterio *m*

Monday (*man*-di) lunes *m*

monetary (*ma*-ni-tö-ri) *adj* monetario ; ~ **unit** unidad monetaria

money (*ma*-ni) *n* dinero *m* ; ~ **exchange** oficina de cambio ; ~ **order** libranza *f*

monk (mangk) *n* monje *m*

monkey (*mang*-ki) *n* mono *m*

monologue (*mo*-no-logh) *n* monólogo *m*

monopoly (mö-*no*-pö-li) *n* monopolio *m*

monotonous (mö-*no*-tö-nöss) *adj* monótono

month (manz) *n* mes *m*

monthly (*manz*-li) *adj* mensual ; ~ **magazine** revista mensual

monument (*mo*-nyu-mönt) *n* monumento *m*

mood (muud) *n* humor *m*

moon (muun) *n* luna *f*

moonlight (*muun*-lait) *n* luz de la luna

moor (mu⁸) *n* brezal *m*, turbera *f*

moose (muuss) *n* (pl ~, ~s) alce *m*

moped (*mou*-pêd) *n* bicimotor *m*

moral (*mo*-röl) *n* moral *f* ; *adj* moral ; **morals** costumbres

morality (mö-*ræ*-lö-ti) *n* moralidad *f*

more (moo) *adj* más ; **once** ~ otra vez

moreover (moo-*rou*-vö) *adv* además

morning (*moo*-ning) *n* mañana *f* ; ~ **paper** diario matutino

Moroccan (mö-*ro*-kön) *adj* marroquí

Morocco (mö-*ro*-kou) Marruecos *m*

morphia (*moo*-fi-ö) *n* morfina *f*

morphine (*moo*-fiin) *n* morfina *f*

morsel (*moo*-ssöl) *n* trozo *m*

mortal (*moo*-töl) *adj* fatal, mortal

mortgage (*moo*-ghidჳ) *n* hipoteca *f*

mosaic (mö-*sei*-ik) *n* mosaico *m*

mosque (mossk) *n* mezquita *f*

mosquito (mö-*sskii*-tou) *n* (pl ~ es) mosquito *m*

mosquito-net (mö-*sskii*-tou-nêt) *n* mosquitero *m*

moss (moss) *n* musgo *m*

most (mousst) *adj* el más ; **at** ~ a lo sumo, como máximo ; ~ **of all** sobre todo

mostly (*mousst*-li) *adv* generalmente

motel (mou-*têl*) *n* motel *m*

moth (moz) *n* polilla *f*

mother (*ma*-ðö) *n* madre *f*; ~ **tongue** lengua materna

mother-in-law (*ma*-ðö-rin-loo) *n* (pl mothers-) suegra *f*

mother-of-pearl (ma-ðö-röv-*pööl*) *n* nácar *m*

motion (*mou*-ʃön) *n* movimiento *m*; moción *f*

motive (*mou*-tiv) *n* motivo *m*

motor (*mou*-tö) *n* motor *m*; *v* *ir en coche; **starter** ~ motor de arranque

motorbike (*mou*-tö-baik) *nAm* motocicleta *f*

motor-boat (*mou*-tö-bout) *n* bote a motor

motor-car (*mou*-tö-kaa) *n* automóvil *m*

motor-cycle (*mou*-tö-ssai-köl) *n* motocicleta *f*

motoring (*mou*-tö-ring) *n* automovilismo *m*

motorist (*mou*-tö-risst) *n* automovilista *m*

motorway (*mou*-tö-ᵘei) *n* autopista *f*

motto (*mo*-tou) *n* (pl ~es, ~s) lema *f*

mouldy (*moul*-di) *adj* enmohecido

mound (maund) *n* montículo *m*

mount (maunt) *v* montar; *n* monte *m*

mountain (*maun*-tin) *n* montaña *f*; ~ **pass** paso *m*; ~ **range** cordillera *f*

mountaineering (maun-ti-*niº*-ring) *n* montañismo *m*

mountainous (*maun*-ti-nöss) *adj* montañoso

mourning (*moo*-ning) *n* luto *m*

mouse (mauss) *n* (pl mice) ratón *m*

moustache (mö-*sstaa*ʃ) *n* bigote *m*

mouth (mauz) *n* boca *f*; hocico *m*; desembocadura *f*

mouthwash (*mauz*-ᵘoʃ) *n* enjuague bucal

movable (*muu*-vö-böl) *adj* movible

move (muuv) *v* *mover; trasladar;

mudarse; *conmover; *n* jugada *f*, paso *m*; mudanza *f*

movement (*muuv*-mönt) *n* movimiento *m*

movie (*muu*-vi) *n* filme *m*

much (mach) *adj* mucho; **as** ~ tanto

muck (mak) *n* suciedad *f*

mud (mad) *n* lodo *m*

muddle (*ma*-döl) *n* dédalo *m*, embrollo *m*; *v* embrollar

muddy (*ma*-di) *adj* lodoso

mud-guard (*mad*-ghaad) *n* guardabarros *m*; salpicadera *fMe*

mug (magh) *n* vaso *m*, taza *f*

mulberry (*mal*-bö-ri) *n* mora *f*

mule (myuul) *n* mulo *m*

mullet (*ma*-lit) *n* mújol *m*

multiplication (mal-ti-pli-*kei*-ʃön) *n* multiplicación *f*

multiply (*mal*-ti-plai) *v* multiplicar

mumps (mampss) *n* paperas *fpl*

municipal (myuu-*ni*-ssi-pöl) *adj* municipal

municipality (myuu-ni-ssi-*pæ*-lö-ti) *n* municipalidad *f*

murder (*möö*-dö) *n* asesinato *m*; *v* asesinar

murderer (*möö*-dö-rö) *n* asesino *m*

muscle (*ma*-ssöl) *n* músculo *m*

muscular (*ma*-sskyu-lö) *adj* musculoso

museum (myuu-*sii*-öm) *n* museo *m*

mushroom (*maʃ*-ruum) *n* seta *f*; hongo *m*

music (*myuu*-sik) *n* música *f*; ~ **academy** conservatorio *m*

musical (*myuu*-si-köl) *adj* musical; *n* comedia musical

music-hall (*myuu*-sik-hool) *n* teatro de variedades

musician (myuu-*si*-ʃön) *n* músico *m*

muslin (*mas*-lin) *n* muselina *f*

mussel (*ma*-ssöl) *n* mejillón *m*

must (masst) *v* *tener que

mustard (*ma*-sstöd) *n* mostaza *f*

mute (myuut) *adj* mudo
mutiny (myuu-ti-ni) *n* amotinamiento *m*
mutton (ma-tön) *n* carnero *m*
mutual (myuu-chu-öl) *adj* mutuo, recíproco
my (mai) *adj* mi
myself (mai-ssêlf) *pron* me; yo mismo
mysterious (mi-ssti⁰-ri-öss) *adj* misterioso
mystery (mi-sstö-ri) *n* enigma *m*, misterio *m*
myth (miz) *n* mito *m*

N

nail (neil) *n* uña *f*; clavo *m*
nailbrush (neil-braʃ) *n* cepillo para las uñas
nail-file (neil-fail) *n* lima para las uñas
nail-polish (neil-po-liʃ) *n* barniz para las uñas
nail-scissors (neil-ssi-sös) *pl* tijeras para las uñas
naïve (naa-iiv) *adj* ingenuo
naked (nei-kid) *adj* desnudo
name (neim) *n* nombre *m*; *v* nombrar; **in the ~ of** en nombre de
namely (neim-li) *adv* a saber
nap (næp) *n* siesta *f*
napkin (næp-kin) *n* servilleta *f*
nappy (næ-pi) *n* pañal *m*
narcosis (naa-kou-ssiss) *n* (pl -ses) narcosis *f*
narcotic (naa-ko-tik) *n* narcótico *m*
narrow (næ-rou) *adj* angosto, estrecho
narrow-minded (næ-rou-main-did) *adj* mezquino
nasty (naa-ssti) *adj* antipático, desagradable
nation (nei-ʃön) *n* nación *f*; pueblo *m*

national (næ-ʃö-nöl) *adj* nacional; del Estado; **~ anthem** himno nacional; **~ dress** traje del país; **~ park** parque nacional
nationality (næ-ʃö-næ-lö-ti) *n* nacionalidad *f*
nationalize (næ-ʃö-nö-lais) *v* nacionalizar
native (nei-tiv) *n* indígena *m*; *adj* nativo; **~ country** patria *f*, país natal; **~ language** lengua materna
natural (næ-chö-röl) *adj* natural; innato
naturally (næ-chö-rö-li) *adv* naturalmente, por supuesto
nature (nei-chö) *n* naturaleza *f*; natural *m*
naughty (noo-ti) *adj* travieso
nausea (noo-ssi-ö) *n* náusea *f*
naval (nei-völ) *adj* naval
navel (nei-völ) *n* ombligo *m*
navigable (næ-vi-ghö-böl) *adj* navegable
navigate (næ-vi-gheit) *v* navegar
navigation (næ-vi-ghei-ʃön) *n* navegación *f*
navy (nei-vi) *n* marina *f*
near (ni⁰) *prep* cerca de; *adj* cercano
nearby (ni⁰-bai) *adj* cercano
nearly (ni⁰-li) *adv* casi
neat (niit) *adj* pulcro; puro
necessary (nê-ssö-ssö-ri) *adj* necesario
necessity (nö-ssê-ssö-ti) *n* necesidad *f*
neck (nêk) *n* cuello *m*; **nape of the ~** nuca *f*
necklace (nêk-loss) *n* collar *m*
necktie (nêk-tai) *n* corbata *f*
need (niid) *v* deber, necesitar; *n* necesidad *f*; **~ to** deber
needle (nii-döl) *n* aguja *f*
needlework (nii-döl-ᵘöök) *n* labor de aguja
negative (nê-ghö-tiv) *adj* negativo; *n*

negativo *m*

neglect (ni-*ghlêkt*) *v* descuidar; *n* negligencia *f*

neglectful (ni-*ghlêkt*-föl) *adj* negligente

negligee (*nê*-ghli-ʒei) *n* bata suelta

negotiate (ni-*ghou-ʃi*-eit) *v* negociar

negotiation (ni-ghou-ʃi-*ei*-ʃön) *n* negociación *f*

Negro (*nii*-ghrou) *n* (pl ~es) negro *m*

neighbour (*nei*-bö) *n* vecino *m*

neighbourhood (*nei*-bö-hud) *n* vecindad *f*

neighbouring (*nei*-bö-ring) *adj* contiguo, vecino

neither (*nai*-ðö) *pron* ninguno de los dos; **neither ... nor** ni ... ni

neon (*nii*-on) *n* neón *m*

nephew (*nê*-fyuu) *n* sobrino *m*

nerve (nööv) *n* nervio *m*; audacia *f*

nervous (*nöö*-vöss) *adj* nervioso

nest (nêsst) *n* nido *m*

net (nêt) *n* red *f*; *adj* neto

the Netherlands (*nê*-ðö-lönds) Países Bajos *mpl*

network (*nêt*-ᵁöök) *n* red *f*

neuralgia (nyu-ö-*ræl*-dʒö) *n* neuralgia *f*

neurosis (nyu-ö-*rou*-ssiss) *n* neurosis *f*

neuter (*nyuu*-tö) *adj* neutro

neutral (*nyuu*-tröl) *adj* neutral

never (*nê*-vö) *adv* nunca

nevertheless (nê-vö-ðö-*lêss*) *adv* no obstante

new (nyuu) *adj* nuevo; **New Year** año nuevo

news (nyuus) *n* noticiario *m*, noticia *f*; noticias *fpl*

newsagent (*nyuu*-sei-dʒönt) *n* vendedor de periódicos

newspaper (*nyuus*-pei-pö) *n* diario *m*

newsreel (*nyuus*-riil) *n* noticiario *m*

newsstand (*nyuus*-sstænd) *n* quiosco de periódicos

New Zealand (nyuu *sii*-lönd) Nueva

Zelanda

next (nêksst) *adj* próximo; ~ **to** junto a

next-door (nêksst-*door*) *adv* al lado

nice (naiss) *adj* agradable, bonito, ameno; rico; simpático

nickel (*ni*-köl) *n* níquel *m*

nickname (*nik*-neim) *n* mote *m*

nicotine (*ni*-kö-tiin) *n* nicotina *f*

niece (niiss) *n* sobrina *f*

Nigeria (nai-*dʒiö*-ri-ö) Nigeria *f*

Nigerian (nai-*dʒiö*-ri-ön) *adj* nigeriano

night (nait) *n* noche *f*; **by** ~ de noche; ~ **flight** vuelo nocturno; ~ **rate** tarifa nocturna; ~ **train** tren nocturno

nightclub (*nait*-klab) *n* cabaret *m*

night-cream (*nait*-kriim) *n* crema de noche

nightdress (*nait*-drêss) *n* camisón *m*

nightingale (*nai*-ting-gheil) *n* ruiseñor *m*

nightly (*nait*-li) *adj* nocturno

nil (nil) nada

nine (nain) *num* nueve

nineteen (nain-*tiin*) *num* diecinueve

nineteenth (nain-*tiinz*) *num* decimonono

ninety (*nain*-ti) *num* noventa

ninth (nainz) *num* noveno

nitrogen (*nai*-trö-dʒön) *n* nitrógeno *m*

no (nou) no; *adj* ninguno; ~ **one** nadie

nobility (nou-*bi*-lö-ti) *n* nobleza *f*

noble (*nou*-böl) *adj* noble

nobody (*nou*-bo-di) *pron* nadie

nod (nod) *n* cabeceo *m*; *v* cabecear

noise (nois) *n* ruido *m*; alboroto *m*

noisy (*noi*-si) *adj* ruidoso

nominal (*no*-mi-nöl) *adj* nominal

nominate (*no*-mi-neit) *v* nombrar

nomination (no-mi-*nei*-ʃön) *n* nominación *f*; nombramiento *m*

none (nan) *pron* ninguno

nonsense (*non*-ssönss) *n* tontería *f*
noon (nuun) *n* mediodía *m*
normal (*noo*-möl) *adj* normal
north (nooz) *n* norte *m*; *adj* septentrional; **North Pole** polo norte
north-east (nooz-*iisst*) *n* nordeste *m*
northerly (*noo*-ðö-li) *adj* del norte
northern (*noo*-ðön) *adj* norteño
north-west (nooz-ᵘ*êsst*) *n* noroeste *m*
Norway (*noo*-ᵘei) Noruega *f*
Norwegian (noo-ᵘ*ii*-dʒön) *adj* noruego
nose (nous) *n* nariz *f*
nosebleed (*nous*-bliid) *n* hemorragia
nasal
nostril (*no*-sstril) *n* ventana de la nariz
not (not) *adv* no
notary (*nou*-tö-ri) *n* notario *m*
note (nout) *n* apunte *m*, esquela *f*;
nota *f*; tono *m*; *v* notar; observar,
*comprobar
notebook (*nout*-buk) *n* libreta de
apuntes
noted (*nou*-tid) *adj* afamado
notepaper (*nout*-pei-pö) *n* papel de
escribir, papel para cartas
nothing (*na*-zing) *n* nada *f*, nada
notice (*nou*-tiss) *v* observar, notar,
*advertir; *ver; *n* aviso *m*, noticia
f; atención *f*
noticeable (*nou*-ti-ssö-böl) *adj* perceptible; notable
notify (*nou*-ti-fai) *v* notificar
notion (*nou*-ʃön) *n* noción *f*
notorious (nou-*too*-ri-öss) *adj* de mala
fama
nougat (*nuu*-ghaa) *n* turrón *m*
nought (noot) *n* cero *m*
noun (naun) *n* nombre *m*, substantivo *m*
nourishing (*na*-ri-ʃing) *adj* nutritivo
novel (*no*-völ) *n* novela *f*
novelist (*no*-vö-lisst) *n* novelista *m*
November (nou-*vêm*-bö) noviembre

now (nau) *adv* ahora; actualmente;
~ **and then** de vez en cuando
nowadays (*nau*-ö-deis) *adv* hoy en día
nowhere (*nou*-ᵘêð) *adv* en ninguna
parte
nozzle (*no*-söl) *n* tobera *f*
nuance (nyuu-*angss*) *n* matiz *m*
nuclear (*nyuu*-kli-ö) *adj* nuclear; ~
energy energía nuclear
nucleus (*nyuu*-kli-öss) *n* núcleo *m*
nude (nyuud) *adj* desnudo; *n* desnudo *m*
nuisance (*nyuu*-ssönss) *n* molestia *f*
numb (nam) *adj* entumecido; aterido
number (*nam*-bö) *n* número *m*; cifra
f; cantidad *f*
numeral (*nyuu*-mö-röl) *n* numeral *m*
numerous (*nyuu*-mö-röss) *adj* numeroso
nun (nan) *n* monja *f*
nunnery (*na*-nö-ri) *n* convento *m*
nurse (nööss) *n* enfermera *f*; niñera
f; *v* *atender a; amamantar
nursery (*nöö*-ssö-ri) *n* cuarto de niños; guardería *f*; vivero *m*
nut (nat) *n* nuez *f*; tuerca *f*
nutcrackers (*nat*-kræ-kös) *pl* cascanueces *m*
nutmeg (*nat*-mêgh) *n* nuez moscada
nutritious (nyuu-*tri*-ʃöss) *adj* nutritivo
nutshell (*nat*-ʃêl) *n* cáscara de nuez
nylon (*nai*-lon) *n* nylon *m*

O

oak (ouk) *n* roble *m*
oar (oo) *n* remo *m*
oasis (ou-*ei*-ssiss) *n* (pl oases) oasis *f*
oath (ouz) *n* juramento *m*
oats (outss) *pl* avena *f*
obedience (ö-*bii*-di-önss) *n* obediencia
f

obedient (ö-*bii*-di-önt) *adj* obediente

obey (ö-*bei*) *v* *obedecer

object[1] (*ob*-dʒikt) *n* objeto *m*

object[2] (öb-*dʒêkt*) *v* objetar; ~ **to** *oponerse a

objection (öb-*dʒêk*-ʃön) *n* objeción *f*

objective (öb-*dʒêk*-tiv) *adj* objetivo; *n* objetivo *m*

obligatory (ö-*bli*-ghö-tö-ri) *adj* obligatorio

oblige (ö-*blaidʒ*) *v* obligar; *be obliged to *estar obligado a; *tener que

obliging (ö-*blai*-dʒing) *adj* simpático

oblong (*ob*-long) *adj* oblongo; *n* rectángulo *m*

obscene (öb-*ssiin*) *adj* obsceno

obscure (öb-*sskyuᵒ*) *adj* obscuro, misterioso, oscuro

observation (ob-sö-*vei*-ʃön) *n* observación *f*

observatory (öb-*söö*-vö-tri) *n* observatorio *m*

observe (öb-*sööv*) *v* observar

obsession (öb-*ssê*-ʃön) *n* obsesión *f*

obstacle (*ob*-sstö-köl) *n* obstáculo *m*

obstinate (*ob*-ssti-nöt) *adj* obstinado; pertinaz

obtain (öb-*tein*) *v* *conseguir, *obtener

obtainable (öb-*tei*-nö-böl) *adj* adquirible

obvious (*ob*-vi-öss) *adj* obvio

occasion (ö-*kei*-ʒön) *n* ocasión *f*; motivo *m*

occasionally (ö-*kei*-ʒö-nö-li) *adv* de vez en cuando, ocasionalmente

occupant (*o*-kyu-pönt) *n* ocupante *m*

occupation (o-kyu-*pei*-ʃön) *n* ocupación *f*

occupy (*o*-kyu-pai) *v* ocupar

occur (ö-*köö*) *v* suceder, ocurrir, *acontecer

occurrence (ö-*ka*-rönss) *n* acontecimiento *m*

ocean (*ou*-ʃön) *n* océano *m*

October (ok-*tou*-bö) octubre

octopus (*ok*-tö-pöss) *n* pulpo *m*

oculist (*o*-kyu-lisst) *n* oculista *m*

odd (od) *adj* raro; impar

odour (*ou*-dö) *n* olor *m*

of (ov, öv) *prep* de

off (of) *adv* fuera; *prep* de

offence (ö-*fênss*) *n* falta *f*; ofensa *f*, escándalo *m*

offend (ö-*fênd*) *v* ofender; transgredir

offensive (ö-*fên*-ssiv) *adj* ofensivo; insultante; *n* ofensivo *m*

offer (*o*-fö) *v* *ofrecer; presentar; oferta *f*

office (*o*-fiss) *n* oficina *f*; cargo *m*; ~ **hours** horas de oficina

officer (*o*-fi-ssö) *n* oficial *m*

official (ö-*fi*-föl) *adj* oficial

off-licence (*of*-lai-ssönss) *n* almacén de licores

often (*o*-fön) *adv* a menudo, frecuentemente

oil (oil) *n* aceite *m*; petróleo *m*; **fuel** ~ combustible líquido; ~ **filter** filtro del aceite; ~ **pressure** presión del aceite

oil-painting (oil-*pein*-ting) *n* pintura al óleo

oil-refinery (*oil*-ri-fai-nö-ri) *n* refinería de petróleo

oil-well (*oil*-ᵘêl) *n* pozo de petróleo

oily (*oi*-li) *adj* aceitoso

ointment (*oint*-mönt) *n* ungüento *m*

okay! (ou-*kei*) ¡de acuerdo!

old (ould) *adj* viejo; ~ **age** vejez *f*

old-fashioned (ould-*fæ*-ʃönd) *adj* anticuado

olive (*o*-liv) *n* aceituna *f*; ~ **oil** aceite de oliva

omelette (*om*-löt) *n* tortilla *f*

ominous (*o*-mi-nöss) *adj* siniestro

omit (ö-*mit*) *v* omitir

omnipotent (om-*ni*-pö-tönt) *adj* omnipotente

on (on) *prep* sobre; a

once (^uanss) *adv* una vez; **at ~** en seguida; **~ more** otra vez

oncoming (*on*-ka-ming) *adj* venidero

one (^uan) *num* uno; *pron* uno

oneself (^uan-*ssêlf*) *pron* uno mismo

onion (a-nyön) *n* cebolla *f*

only (*oun*-li) *adj* solo; *adv* sólo, solamente; *conj* pero

onwards (*on*-^uöds) *adv* adelante

onyx (*o*-nikss) *n* ónix *m*

opal (*ou*-pöl) *n* ópalo *m*

open (*ou*-pön) *v* abrir; *adj* abierto; sincero

opening (*ou*-pö-ning) *n* abertura *f*

opera (*o*-pö-rö) *n* ópera *f*; **~ house** teatro de la ópera

operate (*o*-pö-reit) *v* operar, funcionar

operation (o-pö-*rei*-fön) *n* funcionamiento *m*; operación *f*

operator (*o*-pö-rei-tö) *n* telefonista *f*

operetta (o pö-*rê*-tö) *n* opereta *f*

opinion (ö-*pi*-nyön) *n* parecer *m*, opinión *f*

opponent (ö *pou*-nönt) *n* contrincante *m*

opportunity (o-pö-*tyuu*-nö-ti) *n* oportunidad *f*

oppose (ö-*pous*) *v* *oponerse

opposite (*o*-pö-sit) *prep* enfrente de; *adj* contrario, opuesto

opposition (o-pö-*si*-fön) *n* oposición *f*

oppress (ö pcss) *v* oprimir

optician (op-*ti*-fön) *n* óptico *m*

optimism (*op*-ti-mi-söm) *n* optimismo *m*

optimist (*op*-ti-misst) *n* optimista *m*

optimistic (op-ti-*mi*-sstik) *adj* optimista

optional (*op*-fö-nöl) *adj* opcional

or (oo) *conj* o

oral (*oo*-röl) *adj* oral

orange (*o*-rindჳ) *n* naranja *f*; *adj* de color naranja

orchard (*oo*-chöd) *n* vergel *m*

orchestra (*oo*-ki-sströ) *n* orquesta *f*; **~ seat** *Am* butaca *f*

order (*oo*-dö) *v* ordenar; *pedir; *n* orden *m*; orden *f*, mandato *m*; pedido *m*; **in ~** en regla; **in ~ to** para; **made to ~** hecho a la medida; **out of ~** averiado; **postal ~** giro postal

order-form (*oo*-dö-foom) *n* hoja de pedido

ordinary (*oo*-dön-ri) *adj* común, ordinario

ore (oo) *n* mineral *m*

organ (*oo*-ghön) *n* órgano *m*

organic (oo-*ghæ*-nik) *adj* orgánico

organization (oo-ghö-nai-*sei*-fön) *n* organización *f*

organize (*oo*-ghö-nais) *v* organizar

Orient (*oo*-ri-önt) *n* oriente *m*

oriental (oo-ri-*ên*-töl) *adj* oriental

orientate (*oo*-ri-ön-teit) *v* orientarse

origin (*o*-ri-dჳin) *n* origen *m*; descendencia *f*, procedencia *f*

original (o-*ri*-dჳi-nöl) *adj* auténtico, original

originally (ö-*ri*-dჳi-nö-li) *adv* originalmente

orlon (*oo*-lon) *n* orlón *m*

ornament (*oo*-nö-mönt) *n* adorno *m*

ornamental (oo-nö-*mên*-töl) *adj* ornamental

orphan (*oo*-tön) *n* huérfano *m*

orthodox (*oo*-zö-dokss) *adj* ortodoxo

ostrich (*o*-sstrich) *n* avestruz *m*

other (a-öö) *adj* otro

otherwise (a-öö-^uais) *conj* si no; *adv* de otra manera

*ought to (oot) *tener que

our (au^ö) *adj* nuestro

ourselves (au^ö-*ssêlvs*) *pron* nos; nosotros mismos

out (aut) *adv* fuera; ~ of fuera ðe, de

outbreak (*aut*-breik) *n* explosión *f*

outcome (*aut*-kam) *n* resultado *m*

*overtake (aut-*duu*) *v* superar

outdoors (aut-*doos*) *adv* afuera

outer (*au*-tö) *adj* exterior

outfit (*aut*-fit) *n* equipo *m*

outline (*aut*-lain) *n* contorno *m*; *v* bosquejar

outlook (*aut*-luk) *n* previsión *f*; punto de vista

output (*aut*-put) *n* producción *f*

outrage (*aut*-reidʒ) *n* ultraje *m*

outside (aut-*ssaid*) *adv* afuera; *prep* fuera de; *n* exterior *m*

outsize (*aut*-ssais) *n* tamaño extraordinario

outskirts (*aut*-ssköötss) *pl* afueras *fpl*

outstanding (aut-*sstæn*-ding) *adj* eminente, destacado

outward (*aut*-ᵘöd) *adj* externo

outwards (*aut*-ᵘöds) *adv* hacia afuera

oval (*ou*-völ) *adj* ovalado

oven (*a*-vön) *n* horno *m*

over (*ou*-vö) *prep* encima de; más de; *adv* encima; abajo; *adj* acabado; ~ there allá

overall (*ou*-vö-rool) *adj* total

overalls (*ou*-vö-rools) *pl* mono *m*; overol *mMe*

overcast (*ou*-vö-kaasst) *adj* nublado

overcoat (*ou*-vö-kout) *n* abrigo *m*

*overcome (ou-vö-*kam*) *v* vencer

overdue (ou-vö-*dyuu*) *adj* atrasado

overgrown (ou-vö-*ghroun*) *adj* cubierto de verdor

overhaul (ou-vö-*hool*) *v* revisar

overhead (ou-vö-*hêd*) *adv* en alto

overlook (ou-vö-*luk*) *v* pasar por alto

overnight (ou-vö-*nait*) *adv* de noche

overseas (ou-vö-*ssiis*) *adj* ultramar

oversight (*ou*-vö-ssait) *n* descuido *m*

*oversleep (ou-vö-*ssliip*) *v* quedarse dormido

overstrung (ou-vö-*sstrang*) *adj* sobreexcitado

*overtake (ou-vö-*teik*) *v* recoger; no overtaking prohibido adelantar

over-tired (ou-vö-*taiᵒd*) *adj* exhausto

overture (*ou*-vö-chö) *n* obertura *f*

overweight (*ou*-vö-ᵘeit) *n* sobrepeso *m*

overwhelm (ou-vö-ᵘêlm) *v* *desconcertar, subyugar

overwork (ou-vö-ᵘöök) *v* trabajar demasiado

owe (ou) *v* deber; owing to a causa de, debido a

owl (aul) *n* buho *m*

own (oun) *v* *poseer; *adj* propio

owner (*ou*-nö) *n* propietario *m*

ox (okss) *n* (pl oxen) buey *m*

oxygen (*ok*-ssi-dʒön) *n* oxígeno *m*

oyster (*oi*-sstö) *n* ostra *f*

P

pace (peiss) *n* andares *mpl*; paso *m*; ritmo *m*

Pacific Ocean (pö-*ssi*-fik *ou*-ʃön) Océano Pacífico

pacifism (*pæ*-ssi-fi-söm) *n* pacifismo *m*

pacifist (*pæ*-ssi-fisst) *n* pacifista *m*

pack (pæk) *v* embalar; ~ up empaquetar

package (*pæ*-kidʒ) *n* paquete *m*

packet (*pæ*-kit) *n* paquete *m*

packing (*pæ*-king) *n* embalaje *m*

pad (pæd) *n* almohadilla *f*; bloque *m*

paddle (*pæ*-döl) *n* remo *m*

padlock (*pæd*-lok) *n* candado *m*

pagan (*pei*-ghön) *adj* pagano; *n* pagano *m*

page (peidʒ) *n* página *f*

page-boy (peidȝ-boi) n paje m
pail (peil) n balde m
pain (pein) n dolor m; **pains** pena f
painful (pein-föl) adj dolorido
painless (pein-löss) adj sin dolor
paint (point) n pintura f; v pintar
paint-box (peint-bokss) n caja de colores
paint-brush (peint-braʃ) n pincel m
painter (pein-tö) n pintor m
painting (pein-ting) n pintura f
pair (pêô) n par m
Pakistan (paa-ki-sstaan) Paquistán m
Pakistani (paa-ki-sstaa-ni) adj paquistaní
palace (pæ-löss) n palacio m
pale (peil) adj pálido
palm (paam) n palma f
palpable (pæl-pö-böl) adj palpable
palpitation (pæl-pi-tei-ʃön) n palpitación f
pan (pæn) n sartén f
pane (pein) n cristal m
panel (pæ-nöl) n painel m, cuarterón m
panelling (pæ-nö-ling) n enmaderado m
panic (pæ-nik) n pánico m
pant (pænt) v jadear
panties (pæn-tis) pl braga f
pants (pæntss) pl calzoncillos mpl; plAm pantalones mpl
pant-suit (pænt-ssuut) n traje pantalón
panty-hose (pæn-ti-hous) n media pantalón
paper (pei-pö) n papel m; periódico m; de papel; **carbon** ~ papel carbón; ~ **bag** bolsa de papel; ~ **napkin** servilleta de papel; **typing** ~ papel para mecanografiar; **wrapping** ~ papel de envolver
paperback (pei-pö-bæk) n libro de bolsillo

paper-knife (pei-pö-naif) n abrecartas m
parade (pö-reid) n parada f, desfile m
paraffin (pæ-rö-fin) n parafina f
paragraph (pæ-rö-ghraaf) n párrafo m
parakeet (pæ-rö-kiit) n cotorra f
paralise (pæ-rö-lais) v paralizar
parallel (pæ-rö-lêl) adj paralelo; n paralelo m
parcel (paa-ssöl) n paquete m
pardon (paa-dön) n perdón m; indulto m
parents (pêô-röntss) pl padres mpl
parents-in-law (pêô-röntss-in-loo) pl padres políticos
parish (pæ-riʃ) n parroquia f
park (paak) n parque m; v estacionar
parking (paa-king) n aparcamiento m; **no** ~ prohibido estacionarse; ~ **fee** derechos de estacionamiento; ~ **light** luz de estacionamiento; ~ **lot** Am estacionamiento m; ~ **meter** parquímetro m; ~ **zone** zona de aparcamiento
parliament (paa-lö-mont) n parlamento m
parliamentary (paa-lö-mên-tö-ri) adj parlamentario
parrot (pæ-röt) n loro m
parsley (paa-ssli) n perejil m
parson (paa-ssön) n pastor m
parsonage (paa-ssö-nidȝ) n curato m
part (paat) n parte f; pieza f; v separar; **spare** ~ recambio m
partial (paa-ʃöl) adj parcial
participant (paa-ti-ssi-pönt) n participante m
participate (paa-ti-ssi-peit) v participar
particular (pö-ti-kyu-lö) adj especial, particular; exigente; **in** ~ en particular
parting (paa-ting) n despedida f; raya f

partition (paa-*ti*-∫ön) n tabique m
partly (*paat*-li) adv en parte
partner (*paat*-nö) n pareja f; socio m
partridge (*paa*-trid3) n perdiz f
party (*paa*-ti) n partido m; guateque m, fiesta f; grupo m
pass (paass) v transcurrir, pasar; *aprobar; ~ by pasar de largo; ~ through *atravesar
passage (*pæ*-ssid3) n pasaje m; travesía f; trozo m
passenger (*pæ*-ssön-d3ö) n pasajero m; ~ train tren de pasajeros
passer-by (paa-ssö-*bai*) n transeúnte m
passion (*pæ*-∫ön) n pasión f; cólera f
passionate (*pæ*-∫ö-nöt) adj apasionado
passive (*pæ*-ssiv) adj pasivo
passport (*paass*-poot) n pasaporte m; ~ control inspección de pasaportes; ~ photograph fotografía de pasaporte
password (*paass*-ᵘ ööd) n santo y seña
past (paasst) n pasado m; adj pasado; transcurrido; prep a lo largo de, más allá de
paste (peisst) n pasta f; v pegar
pastry (*pei*-sstri) n pastelería f; ~ shop pastelería f
pasture (*paass*-chö) n prado m
patch (pæch) v *remendar
patent (*pei*-tönt) n patente f
path (paaz) n senda f
patience (*pei*-∫önss) n paciencia f
patient (*pei*-∫önt) adj paciente; n paciente m
patriot (*pei*-tri-öt) n patriota m
patrol (pö-*troul*) n patrulla f; v patrullar; vigilar
pattern (*pæ*-tön) n diseño m
pause (poos) n pausa f; v *hacer una pausa
pave (peiv) v pavimentar

pavement (*peiv*-mönt) n acera f; pavimento m
pavilion (pö-*vil*-yön) n pabellón m
paw (poo) n pata f
pawn (poon) v empeñar; n peón m
pawnbroker (*poon*-brou-kö) n prestamista m
pay (pei) n salario m, sueldo m
*pay (pei) v pagar; *rendir; ~ attention to prestar atención a; paying rentable; ~ off amortizar; ~ on account pagar a plazos
pay-desk (*pei*-dèssk) n caja f
payee (pei-*ii*) n favorecido m
payment (*pei*-mönt) n pago m
pea (pii) n guisante m
peace (piiss) n paz f
peaceful (*piiss*-föl) adj tranquilo
peach (piich) n melocotón m
peacock (*pii*-kok) n pavo m
peak (piik) n pico m; cumbre f; ~ hour hora punta; ~ season apogeo de la temporada
peanut (*pii*-nat) n cacahuete m; cacahuate mMe
pear (pêᵒ) n pera f
pearl (pööl) n perla f
peasant (*pê*-sönt) n campesino m
pebble (*pê*-böl) n guijarro m
peculiar (pi-*kyuul*-yö) adj extraño; especial, peculiar
peculiarity (pi-kyuu-li-æ-rö-ti) n particularidad f
pedal (*pê*-döl) n pedal m
pedestrian (pi-*dê*-sstri-ön) n peatón m; no pedestrians prohibido para los peatones; ~ crossing cruce para peatones
pedicure (*pê*-di-kyuᵒ) n pedicuro m
peel (piil) v pelar; n piel f
peep (piip) v espiar
peg (pêgh) n percha f
pelican (*pê*-li-kön) n pelícano m
pelvis (*pêl*-viss) n pelvis m

pen (pên) *n* pluma *f*

penalty (*pê*-nöl-ti) *n* pena *f*; castigo *m*; ~ **kick** penalty *m*

pencil (*pên*-ssöl) *n* lápiz *m*

pencil-sharpener (*pên*-ssöl-ʃaap-nö) *n* sacapuntas *m*

pendant (*pên*-dönt) *n* pendiente *m*

penetrate (*pê*-ni-treit) *v* penetrar

penguin (*pêng*-ghᵘin) *n* pingüino *m*

penicillin (pê-ni-*ssi*-lin) *n* penicilina *f*

peninsula (pö-*nin*-ssyu-lö) *n* península *f*

penknife (*pên*-naif) *n* (pl -knives) cortaplumas *m*

pension[1] (*pang*-ssi-ong) *n* pensión *f*

pension[2] (*pên*-ʃön) *n* pensión *f*

people (*pii*-pöl) *pl* gente *f*; *n* pueblo *m*

pepper (*pê*-pö) *n* pimienta *f*

peppermint (*pê*-pö-mint) *n* menta *f*

perceive (pö-*ssiiv*) *v* percibir

percent (pö-*ssênt*) *n* por ciento

percentage (pö-*ssên*-tidʒ) *n* porcentaje *m*

perceptible (pö-*ssêp*-ti-böl) *adj* perceptible

perception (pö-*ssêp*-ʃön) *n* percepción *f*

perch (pööch) (pl ~) perca *f*

percolator (*pöö*-kö-lei-tö) *n* cafetera filtradora

perfect (*pöö*-fikt) *adj* perfecto

perfection (pü-*fêk*-ʃön) *n* perfección *f*

perform (pö-*foom*) *v* ejecutar, desempeñar

performance (pö fóo mönss) *n* representación *f*

perfume (*pöö*-fyuum) *n* perfume *m*

perhaps (pö-*hæpss*) *adv* quizás

peril (*pê*-ril) *n* peligro *m*

perilous (*pê*-ri-löss) *adj* peligroso

period (*piᵃ*-ri-öd) *n* época *f*, período *m*; punto *m*

periodical (piᵃ-ri-*o*-di-köl) *n* periódico

m; *adj* periódico

perish (*pê*-riʃ) *v* *perecer

perishable (*pê*-ri ʃö-böl) *adj* perecedero

perjury (*pöö*-dʒö-ri) *n* perjurio *m*

permanent (*pöö*-mö-nönt) *adj* duradero, permanente; estable, fijo; ~ **press** planchado permanente; ~ **wave** ondulación permanente

permission (pö-*mi*-ʃön) *n* permiso *m*, autorización *f*; licencia *f*

permit[1] (po-*mit*) *v* permitir

permit[2] (*pöö*-mit) *n* permiso *m*

peroxide (pö-*rok*-ssaid) *n* peróxido *m*

perpendicular (pöö-pön-*di*-kyu-lö) *adj* perpendicular

Persia (*pöö*-ʃö) Persia *f*

Persian (*pöö*-ʃön) *adj* persa

person (*pöö*-ssön) *n* persona *f*; **per** ~ por persona

personal (*pöö*-ssö-nöl) *adj* personal

personality (pöö-ssö-*næ*-lö-ti) *n* personalidad *f*

personnel (pöö-ssö-*nêl*) *n* personal *m*

perspective (po-*sspêk*-tiv) *n* perspectiva *f*

perspiration (pöö-sspö-*rei*-ʃön) *n* transpiración *f*, sudor *m*

perspire (pö-*sspaiᵒ*) *v* transpirar, sudar

persuade (pö-*ssᵘeid*) *v* persuadir; convencer

persuasion (pö-*ssᵘei*-ʒön) *n* convicción *f*

pessimism (*pê*-ssi-mi-sᵒm) *n* pesimismo *m*

pessimist (*pê*-ssi-misst) *n* pesimista *m*

pessimistic (pê-ssi-*mi*-sstik) *adj* pesimista

pet (pêt) *n* animal doméstico; cariño *m*; favorito

petal (*pê*-töl) *n* pétalo *m*

petition (pi-*ti*-ʃön) *n* petición *f*

petrol (*pê*-tröl) *n* gasolina *f*; ~ **pump**

bomba de gasolina; ~ **station** puesto de gasolina; ~ **tank** depósito de gasolina

petroleum (pi-*trou*-li-öm) *n* petróleo *m*

petty (*pê*-ti) *adj* pequeño, fútil, insignificante; ~ **cash** calderilla *f*

pewit (*pii*-ᵘit) *n* avefría *f*

pewter (*pyuu*-tö) *n* estaño *m*

phantom (*fæn*-töm) *n* fantasma *m*

pharmacology (faa-mö-*ko*-lö-dʒi) *n* farmacología *f*

pharmacy (*faa*-mö-ssi) *n* farmacia *f*; droguería *f*

phase (feis) *n* fase *f*

pheasant (*fê*-sönt) *n* faisán *m*

Philippine (*fi*-li-pain) *adj* filipino

Philippines (*fi*-li-piins) *pl* Filipinas *fpl*

philosopher (fi-*lo*-ssö-fö) *n* filósofo *m*

philosophy (fi-*lo*-ssö-fi) *n* filosofía *f*

phone (foun) *n* teléfono *m*; *v* llamar por teléfono, telefonear

phonetic (fö-*nê*-tik) *adj* fonético

photo (*fou*-tou) *n* (pl ~s) foto *f*

photograph (*fou*-tö-ghraaf) *n* fotografía *f*; *v* fotografiar

photographer (fö-*to*-ghrö-fö) *n* fotógrafo *m*

photography (fö-*to*-ghrö-fi) *n* fotografía *f*

photostat (*fou*-tö-sstæt) *n* fotocopia *f*

phrase (freis) *n* frase *f*

phrase-book (*freis*-buk) *n* manual de conversación

physical (*fi*-si-köl) *adj* físico

physician (fi-*si*-jön) *n* médico *m*

physicist (*fi*-si-ssisst) *n* físico *m*

physics (*fi*-sikss) *n* física *f*

physiology (fi-si-*o*-lö-dʒi) *n* fisiología *f*

pianist (*pii*-ö-nisst) *n* pianista *m*

piano (pi-*æ*-nou) *n* piano *m*; **grand ~** piano de cola

pick (pik) *v* recoger; escoger; *n* elec-

ción *f*; ~ **up** recoger; *ir a buscar; **pick-up van** camioneta de reparto

pick-axe (*pi*-kækss) *n* pico *m*

pickles (*pi*-köls) *pl* encurtidos *mpl*

picnic (*pik*-nik) *n* día de campo; *v* *hacer un día de campo

picture (*pik*-chö) *n* cuadro *m*; ilustración *f*, grabado *m*; imagen *f*; ~ **postcard** tarjeta postal ilustrada, postal ilustrada; **pictures** cine *m*

picturesque (pik-chö-*rêssk*) *adj* pintoresco

piece (piiss) *n* fragmento *m*, pedazo *m*

pier (piᵒ) *n* muelle *m*

pierce (piᵒss) *v* punzar

pig (pigh) *n* cerdo *m*

pigeon (*pi*-dʒön) *n* paloma *f*

pig-headed (pigh-*hê*-did) *adj* testarudo

piglet (*pigh*-löt) *n* cochinillo *m*

pigskin (*pigh*-sskin) *n* piel de cerdo

pike (paik) (pl ~) *n* lucio *m*

pile (pail) *n* montón *m*; *v* amontonar; **piles** *pl* hemorroides *fpl*

pilgrim (*pil*-ghrim) *n* peregrino *m*

pilgrimage (*pil*-ghri-midʒ) *n* peregrinación *f*

pill (pil) *n* píldora *f*

pillar (*pi*-lö) *n* columna *f*, pilar *m*

pillar-box (*pi*-lö-bokss) *n* buzón *m*

pillow (*pi*-lou) *n* almohadón *m*, almohada *f*

pillow-case (*pi*-lou-keiss) *n* funda de almohada

pilot (*pai*-löt) *n* piloto *m*; práctico *m*

pimple (*pim*-pöl) *n* grano *m*

pin (pin) *n* alfiler *m*; *v* clavar; **bobby ~** *Am* horquilla *f*

pincers (*pin*-ssös) *pl* tenazas *fpl*

pinch (pinch) *v* pellizcar

pineapple (*pai*-næ-pöl) *n* piña *f*

ping-pong (*ping*-pong) *n* tenis de mesa

pink (pingk) *adj* rosado

pioneer (pai-ö-*ni⁰*) *n* pionero *m*

pious (*pai*-öss) *adj* pío

pip (pip) *n* pepita *f*

pipe (paip) *n* pipa *f*; conducto *m*; ~ **cleaner** limpiapipas *m*; ~ **tobacco** tabaco de pipa

pirate (*pai⁰*-röt) *n* pirata *m*

pistol (*pi*-sstöl) *n* pistola *f*

piston (*pi*-sstön) *n* pistón *m*; ~ **ring** aro de émbolo

piston-rod (*pi*-sstön-rod) *n* biela *f*

pit (pit) *n* hoyo *m*; mina *f*

pitcher (*pi*-chö) *n* cántaro *m*

pity (*pi*-ti) *n* piedad *f*; *v* *tener piedad de, compadecerse de; **what a pity!** ¡qué lástima!

placard (*plæ*-kaad) *n* cartel *m*

place (pleiss) *n* lugar *m*; *v* *poner, colocar; ~ **of birth** lugar de nacimiento; *take ~ *tener lugar

plague (pleigh) *n* plaga *f*

plaice (pleiss) (pl ~) platija *f*

plain (plein) *adj* claro; corriente, sencillo; *n* llano *m*

plan (plæn) *n* plan *m*; plano *m*; *v* planear

plane (plein) *adj* plano; *n* avión *m*; ~ **crash** accidente aéreo

planet (*plæ*-nit) *n* planeta *m*

planetarium (plæ-ni-*tê⁰* ri-öm) *n* planetario *m*

plank (plængk) *n* tablón *m*

plant (plaant) *n* planta *f*; instalación *f*; *v* plantar

plantation (plæn-*tei*-jön) *n* plantación *f*

plaster (*plaa*-sstö) *n* estuco *m*, yeso *m*; esparadrapo *m*

plastic (*plæ*-sstik) *adj* de plástico; *n* plástico *m*

plate (pleit) *n* plato *m*; chapa *f*

plateau (*plæ*-tou) *n* (pl ~x, ~s) meseta *f*

platform (*plæt*-foom) *n* andén *m*; ~ **ticket** billete de andén

platinum (*plæ*-ti-nöm) *n* platino *m*

play (plei) *v* *jugar; tocar; *n* juego *m*; obra de teatro; **one-act** ~ pieza en un acto; ~ **truant** *hacer novillos

player (plei⁰) *n* jugador *m*

playground (*plei*-ghraund) *n* patio de recreo

playing-card (*plei*-ing-kaad) *n* naipe *m*

playwright (*plei*-rait) *n* dramaturgo *m*

plea (plii) *n* defensa *f*

plead (pliid) *v* informar

pleasant (*plê*-sönt) *adj* agradable, simpático

please (pliis) por favor; *v* *placer; **pleased** contento; **pleasing** agradable

pleasure (*plê*-зö) *n* placer *m*, diversión *f*

plentiful (*plên*-ti-föl) *adj* abundante

plenty (*plên*-ti) *n* abundancia *f*

pliers (plai⁰s) *pl* alicates *mpl*

plimsolls (*plim*-ssöls) *pl* zapatos de gimnasia

plot (plot) *n* conjuración *f*, complot *m*; trama *f*; parcela *f*

plough (plau) *n* arado *m*; *v* arar

plucky (*pla*-kı) *adj* valiente

plug (plagh) *n* enchufe *m*; ~ **in** enchufar

plum (plam) *n* ciruela *f*

plumber (*pla*-mö) *n* plomero *m*

plump (plamp) *adj* regordete

plural (*plu⁰*-röl) *n* plural *m*

plus (plass) *prep* más

pneumatic (nyuu-*mæ*-tik) *adj* neumático

pneumonia (nyuu-*mou*-ni-ö) *n* neumonía *f*

poach (pouch) *v* cazar en vedado

pocket (*po*-kit) *n* bolsillo *m*

pocket-book (*po*-kit-buk) *n* bolsa *f*

pocket-comb (*po*-kit-koum) *n* peine de bolsillo

pocket-knife (*po*-kit-naif) *n* (pl -knives) navaja *f*

pocket-watch (*po*-kit-ᵘoch) *n* reloj de bolsillo

poem (*pou*-im) *n* poema *m*

poet (*pou*-it) *n* poeta *m*

poetry (*pou*-i-tri) *n* poesía *f*

point (point) *n* punto *m*; punta *f*; *v* señalar con el dedo; ~ **of view** punto de vista; ~ **out** apuntar

pointed (*poin*-tid) *adj* puntiagudo

poison (*poi*-sön) *n* veneno *m*; *v* envenenar

poisonous (*poi*-sö-nöss) *adj* venenoso

Poland (*pou*-lönd) Polonia *f*

Pole (poul) *n* polaco *m*

pole (poul) *n* poste *m*

police (pö-*liiss*) *pl* policía *f*

policeman (pö-*liiss*-mön) *n* (pl -men) agente de policía, guardia *m*

police-station (pö-*liiss*-sstei-ʃön) *n* comisaría *f*

policy (*po*-li-ssi) *n* política *f*; póliza *f*

polio (*pou*-li-ou) *n* polio *f*, poliomielitis *f*

Polish (*pou*-liʃ) *adj* polaco

polish (*po*-liʃ) *v* pulir

polite (pö-*lait*) *adj* cortés

political (pö-*li*-ti-köl) *adj* político

politician (po-li-*ti*-ʃön) *n* político *m*

politics (*po*-li-tikss) *n* política *f*

pollution (pö-*luu*-ʃön) *n* contaminación *f*, polución *f*

pond (pond) *n* estanque *m*

pony (*pou*-ni) *n* pony *m*

poor (puᵒ) *adj* pobre; mediocre

pope (poup) *n* Papa *m*

poplin (*po*-plin) *n* popelín *m*

pop music (pop *myuu*-sik) música pop

poppy (*po*-pi) *n* amapola *f*; adormidera *f*

popular (*po*-pyu-lö) *adj* popular

population (po-pyu-*lei*-ʃön) *n* población *f*

populous (*po*-pyu-löss) *adj* populoso

porcelain (*poo*-ssö-lin) *n* porcelana *f*

porcupine (*poo*-kyu-pain) *n* puerco espín

pork (pook) *n* carne de cerdo

port (poot) *n* puerto *m*; babor *m*

portable (*poo*-tö-böl) *adj* portátil

porter (*poo*-tö) *n* mozo *m*; portero *m*

porthole (*poot*-houl) *n* portilla *f*

portion (*poo*-ʃön) *n* porción *f*

portrait (*poo*-trit) *n* retrato *m*

Portugal (*poo*-tyu-ghöl) Portugal *m*

Portuguese (poo-tyu-*ghiis*) *adj* portugués

position (pö-*si*-ʃön) *n* posición *f*; actitud *f*; puesto *m*

positive (*po*-sö-tiv) *adj* positivo; *n* positiva *f*

possess (pö-*sèss*) *v* *poseer; **possessed** *adj* poseído

possession (pö-*sê*-ʃön) *n* posesión *f*; **possessions** bienes *mpl*

possibility (po-ssö-*bi*-lö-ti) *n* posibilidad *f*

possible (*po*-ssö-böl) *adj* posible; eventual

post (pousst) *n* poste *m*; puesto *m*; correo *m*; *v* echar al correo; **post-office** casa de correos

postage (*pou*-sstidʒ) *n* franqueo *m*; ~ **paid** franco; ~ **stamp** sello de correos; timbre *mMe*

postcard (*pousst*-kaad) *n* tarjeta postal; tarjeta postal ilustrada

poster (*pou*-sstö) *n* cartel *m*, poster *m*

poste restante (pousst rê-*sstangt*) lista de correos

postman (*pousst*-mön) *n* (pl -men) cartero *m*

post-paid (pousst-*peid*) *adj* franco

postpone (pö-*sspoun*) *v* aplazar

pot (pot) *n* olla *f*

potato (pö-*tei*-tou) *n* (pl ~es) patata *f*; papa *fMe*

pottery (*po*-tö-ri) *n* cerámica *f*; loza *f*

pouch (pauch) *n* petaca *f*

poulterer (*poul*-tö-rö) *n* pollero *m*

poultry (*poul*-trı) *n* aves de corral

pound (paund) *n* libra *f*

pour (poo) *v* *verter

poverty (*po*-vö-ti) *n* pobreza *f*

powder (*pau*-dö) *n* polvo *m*; ~ **compact** polvera *f*; **talc** ~ talco *m*

powder-puff (*pau*-dö-paf) *n* borla para empolvarse

powder-room (*pau*-dö-ruum) *n* tocador *m*

power (pau⁰) *n* fuerza *f*, energía *f*; poder *m*; potencia *f*

powerful (*pau⁰*-föl) *adj* poderoso; fuerte

powerless (*pau⁰*-löss) *adj* impotente

power-station (*pau⁰*-sstei-ʃön) *n* central eléctrica

practical (*præk*-ti-köl) *adj* práctico

practically (*præk*-ti-kli) *adv* prácticamente

practice (*præk*-tiss) *n* práctica *f*

practise (*præk*-tiss) *v* practicar; ensayarse

praise (preis) *v* alabar; *n* elogio *m*

pram (præm) *n* cochecillo *m*

prawn (proon) *n* gamba *f*

pray (prei) *v* orar

prayer (pre⁰) *n* oración *f*

preach (priich) *v* predicar

precarious (pri-*kê⁰*-ri-öss) *adj* precario

precaution (pri-*koo*-ʃön) *n* precaución *f*

precede (pri-*ssiid*) *v* preceder

preceding (pri-*ssii*-ding) *adj* precedente

precious (*prê*-ʃöss) *adj* precioso; querido

precipice (*prê*-ssi-piss) *n* precipicio *m*

precipitation (pri-ssi-pi-*tei*-ʃön) *n* precipitación *f*

precise (pri *ssaiss*) *adj* preciso, exacto; meticuloso

predecessor (*prii*-di-ssê-ssö) *n* predecesor *m*

predict (pri-*dikt*) *v* *predecir

prefer (pri-*föö*) *v* *preferir

preferable (*prê*-fö-rö-böl) *adj* preferible

preference (*prê*-fö-rönss) *n* preferencia *f*

prefix (*prii*-fikss) *n* prefijo *m*

pregnant (*prêgh*-nönt) *adj* encinta, embarazada

prejudice (*prê*-dʒö-diss) *n* prejuicio *m*

preliminary (pri-*li*-mi-no-rı) *adj* preliminar

premature (*prê*-mö-chu⁰) *adj* prematuro

premier (*prêm*-i⁰) *n* jefe de gobierno

premises (*prê*-mi-ssis) *pl* finca *f*

premium (*prii*-mi-öm) *n* prima *f*

prepaid (prii-*peid*) *adj* pagado por adelantado

preparation (prê-pö-*rei*-ʃön) *n* preparación *f*

prepare (pri-*pê⁰*) *v* preparar

preposition (prê-pö-*si*-ʃön) *n* preposición *f*

prescribe (pri-*sskraib*) *v* prescribir

prescription (pri-*sskrip*-ʃön) *n* prescripción *f*

presence (*prê*-sönss) *n* presencia *f*

present[1] (*prê*-sönt) *n* regalo *m*, presente *m*; *adj* actual; presente

present[2] (pri-*sênt*) *v* presentar

presently (*prê*-sönt-li) *adv* en seguida, dentro de poco

preservation (prê-sö-*vei*-ʃön) *n* conservación *f*

preserve (pri-*sööv*) *v* preservar; conservar

president (*prê*-si-dönt) *n* presidente *m*

press (prèss) *n* prensa *f*; *v* empujar, *apretar; planchar; ~ **conference** conferencia de prensa

pressing (prê-ssing) *adj* urgente

pressure (prê-ʃö) *n* presión *f*; tensión *f*; **atmospheric** ~ presión atmosférica

pressure-cooker (prê-ʃö-ku-kö) *n* olla a presión

prestige (prè-sstiiʒ) *n* prestigio *m*

presumable (pri-syuu-mö-böl) *adj* presumible

presumptuous (pri-samp-ʃöss) *adj* presuntuoso; presumido

pretence (pri-ténss) *n* pretexto *m*

pretend (pri-ténd) *v* fingir

pretext (prii-tèksst) *n* pretexto *m*

pretty (pri-ti) *adj* bonito; *adv* bastante

prevent (pri-vênt) *v* *impedir; *prevenir

preventive (pri-vên-tiv) *adj* preventivo

previous (prii-vi-öss) *adj* precedente, anterior, previo

pre-war (prii-ᵘoo) *adj* de la preguerra

price (praiss) *n* precio *m*; *v* fijar el precio

priceless (praiss-löss) *adj* inapreciable

price-list (praiss-lisst) *n* lista de precios

prick (prik) *v* pinchar

pride (praid) *n* orgullo *m*

priest (priisst) *n* cura *m*

primary (prai-mö-ri) *adj* primario; primero, primordial; elemental

prince (prinss) *n* príncipe *m*

princess (prin-ssèss) *n* princesa *f*

principal (prin-ssö-pöl) *adj* principal; *n* director de escuela, principal *m*

principle (prin-ssö-pöl) *n* principio *m*

print (print) *v* *imprimir; *n* positiva *f*; grabado *m*; **printed matter** impreso *m*

prior (prai⁶) *adj* anterior

priority (prai-o-rö-ti) *n* prioridad *f*

prison (pri-sön) *n* prisión *f*

prisoner (pri-sö-nö) *n* preso *m*, prisionero *m*; ~ **of war** prisionero de guerra

privacy (prai-vö-ssi) *n* intimidad *f*, vida privada

private (prai-vit) *adj* particular, privado; personal

privilege (pri-vi-lidʒ) *n* privilegio *m*

prize (prais) *n* premio *m*; recompensa *f*

probable (pro-bö-böl) *adj* probable

probably (pro-bö-bli) *adv* probablemente

problem (pro-blöm) *n* problema *m*

procedure (prö-ssii-dʒö) *n* procedimiento *m*

proceed (prö-ssiid) *v* *proseguir; proceder

process (prou-ssèss) *n* procedimiento *m*, proceso *m*

procession (prö-ssê-ʃön) *n* procesión *f*, comitiva *f*

proclaim (prö-kleim) *v* proclamar

produce¹ (prö-dyuuss) *v* *producir

produce² (prod-yuuss) *n* producto *m*

producer (prö-dyuu-ssö) *n* productor *m*

product (pro-dakt) *n* producto *m*

production (prö-dak-ʃön) *n* producción *f*

profession (prö-fê-ʃön) *n* profesión *f*

professional (prö-fê-ʃö-nöl) *adj* profesional

professor (prö-fê-ssö) *n* profesor *m*

profit (pro-fit) *n* beneficio *m*, ganancia *f*; ventaja *f*; *v* aprovechar

profitable (pro-fi-tö-böl) *adj* provechoso

profound (prö-faund) *adj* profundo

programme (prou-ghræm) *n* programa *m*

progress¹ (prou-ghrèss) *n* progreso *m*

progress² (prö-*ghrêss*) v progresar

progressive (prö-*ghrê*-ssiv) adj progresista; progresivo

prohibit (prö-*hi*-bit) v prohibir

prohibition (prou-i-*bi*-ʃön) n prohibición f

prohibitive (prö-*hi*-bi-tiv) adj exorbitante

project (*pro*-dʒêkt) n plan m, proyecto m

promenade (pro-mö-*naad*) n paseo m

promise (*pro*-miss) n promesa f; v prometer

promote (prö-*mout*) v *promover

promotion (prö-*mou*-ʃön) n promoción f

prompt (prompt) adj inmediato, pronto

pronoun (*prou*-naun) n pronombre m

pronounce (prö-*naunss*) v pronunciar

pronunciation (prö-nan-ssi-*ei*-ʃön) n pronunciación f

proof (pruuf) n prueba f

propaganda (pro-pö-*ghæn*-dö) n propaganda f

propel (prö-*pêl*) v impeler

propeller (prö-*pê*-lö) n hélice f

proper (*pro*-pö) adj justo; debido, conveniente, apropiado

property (*pro*-pö-ti) n propiedad f; cualidad f

prophet (*pro*-fit) n profeta m

proportion (prö-*poo*-ʃön) n proporción f

proportional (prö-*poo*-ʃö-nöl) adj proporcional

proposal (prö-*pou*-söl) n propuesta f

propose (prö-*pous*) v *proponer

proposition (pro-pö-*si*-ʃön) n propuesta f

proprietor (prö-*prai*-ö-tö) n propietario m

prospect (*pro*-sspêkt) n perspectiva f

prospectus (prö-*sspêk*-töss) n prospecto m

prosperity (pro-*sspê*-rö-ti) n prosperidad f

prosperous (*pro*-sspö-röss) adj próspero

prostitute (*pro*-ssti-tyuut) n prostituta f

protect (prö-*têkt*) v proteger

protection (prö-*têk*-ʃön) n protección f

protein (*prou*-tiin) n proteína f

protest¹ (*prou*-têsst) n protesta f

protest² (prö-*têsst*) v protestar

Protestant (*pro*-ti-sstönt) adj protestante

proud (praud) adj orgulloso

prove (pruuv) v *demostrar, *comprobar; resultar

proverb (*pro*-vööb) n proverbio m

provide (prö-*vaid*) v *proveer; **provided that** con tal que

province (*pro*-vinss) n provincia f

provincial (prö-*vin*-ʃöl) adj provincial

provisional (pro-*vi*-ʒö-nöl) adj provisional

provisions (prö-*vi*-ʒöns) pl provisiones fpl

prune (pruun) n ciruela pasa

psychiatrist (ssai-*kai*-ö-trisst) n psiquiatra m

psychic (*ssai*-kik) adj psíquico

psychoanalyst (ssai-kou-*æ*-nö-lisst) n psicoanalista m

psychological (ssai-ko-*lo*-dʒi-köl) adj psicológico

psychologist (ssai-*ko*-lö-dʒisst) n psicólogo m

psychology (ssai-*ko*-lö-dʒi) n psicología f

pub (pab) n taberna f

public (*pa*-blik) adj público; general; n público m; ~ **garden** jardín público; ~ **house** taberna f

publication (pa-bli-*kei*-ʃön) n publica-

ción f
publicity (pa-*bli*-ssö-ti) n publicidad f
publish (*pa*-blif) v publicar
publisher (*pa*-bli-fö) n editor m
puddle (*pa*-döl) n charco m
pull (pul) v tirar; ~ **out** partir; ~ **up** pararse
pulley (*pu*-li) n (pl ~s) polea f
Pullman (*pul*-mön) n coche Pullman
pullover (*pu*-lou-vö) n pulóver m
pulpit (*pul*-pit) n púlpito m
pulse (palss) n pulso m
pump (pamp) n bomba f; v bombear
punch (panch) v *dar puñetazos; n puñetazo m
punctual (*pangk*-chu-öl) adj puntual
puncture (*pangk*-chö) n pinchazo m
punctured (*pangk*-chöd) adj pinchado
punish (*pa*-nif) v castigar
punishment (*pa*-nif-mönt) n castigo m
pupil (*pyuu*-pöl) n alumno m
puppet-show (*pa*-pit-fou) n teatro guiñol
purchase (*pöö*-chöss) v comprar; n compra f; ~ **price** precio de compra; ~ **tax** impuesto sobre la venta
purchaser (*pöö*-chö-ssö) n comprador m
pure (pyuᵒ) adj casto, puro
purple (*pöö*-pöl) adj purpúreo
purpose (*pöö*-pöss) n propósito m, fin m, intención f; **on ~** intencionado
purse (pööss) n bolsa f, monedero m
pursue (pö-*ssyuu*) v *perseguir
pus (pass) n pus f
push (puf) n empujón m; v empujar
push-button (*puf*-ba-tön) n botón m
*put (put) v colocar, *poner; meter; plantear; ~ **away** guardar; ~ **off** aplazar; ~ **on** *ponerse; ~ **out** apagar
puzzle (*pa*-söl) n rompecabezas m;

enigma m; v confundir; **jigsaw ~** rompecabezas m
puzzling (*pas*-ling) adj embarazoso
pyjamas (pö-*dʒaa*-mös) pl pijama m

Q

quack (kᵘæk) n curandero m, charlatán m
quail (kᵘeil) n (pl ~, ~s) codorniz f
quaint (kᵘeint) adj curioso; anticuado
qualification (kᵘo-li-fi-*kei*-fön) n aptitud f; reserva f, restricción f
qualified (*kᵘo*-li-faid) adj calificado; competente
qualify (*kᵘo*-li-fai) v *ser capaz de, *ser apto para
quality (*kᵘo*-lö-ti) n calidad f; característica f
quantity (*kᵘon*-tö-ti) n cantidad f; número m
quarantine (*kᵘo*-rön-tiin) n cuarentena f
quarrel (*kᵘo*-röl) v disputar, *reñir; n disputa f
quarry (*kᵘo*-ri) n cantera f
quarter (*kᵘoo*-tö) n cuarto m; trimestre m; barrio m; ~ **of an hour** cuarto de hora
quarterly (*kᵘoo*-tö-li) adj trimestral
quay (kii) n muelle m
queen (kᵘiin) n reina f
queer (kᵘiᵒ) adj singular, extraño
query (*kᵘiᵒ*-ri) n pregunta f; v indagar; *poner en duda
question (*kᵘêss*-chön) n pregunta f; cuestión f, problema m; v interrogar; *poner en duda; ~ **mark** signo de interrogación
queue (kyuu) n cola f; v *hacer cola
quick (kᵘik) adj rápido
quick-tempered (kᵘik-*têm*-pöd) adj

irascible

quiet (kʷai-öt) adj quieto, tranquilo; n silencio m, paz f

quilt (kʷilt) n colcha f

quinine (kʷi-niin) n quinina f

quit (kʷit) v cesar

quite (kʷait) adv enteramente, completamente; bastante; muy

quiz (kʷis) n (pl ~zes) concurso m

quota (kʷou-tö) n cuota f

quotation (kʷou-tei-∫ön) n cita f; ~ **marks** comillas fpl

quote (kʷout) v citar

R

rabbit (ræ-bit) n conejo m

rabies (rei-bis) n rabia f

race (reiss) n carrera f; raza f

race-course (reiss-kooss) n pista para carreras, hipódromo m

race-horse (reiss-hooss) n caballo de carrera

race-track (reiss-træk) n pista para carreras

racial (rei-∫öl) adj racial

racket (ræ-kit) n alboroto m

racquet (ræ-kit) n raqueta f

radiator (rei-di-ei-tö) n radiador m

radical (ræ-di-köl) adj radical

radio (rei-di-ou) n radio t

radish (ræ-di∫) n rábano m

radius (rei-di-öss) n (pl radii) radio m

raft (raaft) n zatara f

rag (rægh) n trapo m

rage (reidʒ) n furor m, rabia f; v rabiar

raid (reid) n irrupción f

rail (reil) n barandilla f, barrera f

railing (rei-ling) n barandilla f

railroad (reil-roud) nAm vía del tren, ferrocarril m

railway (reil-ʷei) n ferrocarril m

rain (rein) n lluvia f; v *llover

rainbow (rein-bou) n arco iris

raincoat (rein-kout) n impermeable m

rainproof (rein-pruuf) adj impermeable

rainy (rei-ni) adj lluvioso

raise (reis) v alzar; aumentar; educar, cultivar, criar; recaudar; nAm aumento de sueldo

raisin (rei-sön) n pasa f

rake (reik) n rastrillo m

rally (ræ-li) n reunión f

ramp (ræmp) n rampa f

ramshackle (ræm-∫æ-köl) adj destartalado

rancid (ræn-ssid) adj rancio

rang (ræng) v (p ring)

range (reindʒ) n alcance m

range-finder (reindʒ-fain-dö) n telémetro m

rank (rængk) n rango m; fila f

ransom (ræn-ssöm) n rescate m

rape (reip) v violar

rapid (ræ-pid) adj rápido

rapids (ræ-pids) pl rápidos de río

rare (rêö) adj raro

rarely (rêö-li) adv raras veces

rascal (raa-ssköl) n pícaro m, pillo m

rash (ræ∫) n erupción f; adj precipitado, irreflexivo

raspberry (raas-bö-ri) n frambuesa f

rat (ræt) n rata f

rate (reit) n precio m, tarifa f; velocidad f; **at any** ~ de todos modos, en todo caso; ~ **of exchange** cambio m

rather (raa-öö) adv bastante; más bien

ration (ræ-∫ön) n ración f

rattan (ræ-tæn) n rota f

raven (rei-vön) n cuervo m

raw (roo) adj crudo; ~ **material** materia prima

ray (rei) n rayo m
rayon (rei-on) n rayón m
razor (rei-sö) n máquina de afeitar
razor-blade (rei-sö-bleid) n hoja de
afeitar
reach (riich) v alcanzar; n alcance m
reaction (ri-æk-ʃön) n reacción f
* read (riid) v *leer
reading (rii-ding) n lectura f
reading-lamp (rii-ding-læmp) n lámpara para lectura
reading-room (rii-ding-ruum) n sala de
lectura
ready (rê-di) adj preparado, listo
ready-made (rê-di-meid) adj confeccionado
real (riºl) adj verdadero
reality (ri-æ-lö-ti) n realidad f
realizable (riº-lai-sö-böl) adj realizable
realize (riº-lais) v *reconocer; realizar
really (riº-li) adv verdaderamente, en
realidad; de veras
rear (riº) n parte posterior; v criar
rear-light (riº-lait) n luz trasera
reason (rii-sön) n causa f, razón f;
sentido m; v razonar
reasonable (rii-sö-nö-böl) adj razonable
reassure (rii-ö-ʃuº) v tranquilizar
rebate (rii-beit) n reducción f, rebaja
f
rebellion (ri-bêl-yön) n sublevación f,
rebelión f
recall (ri-kool) v *acordarse; llamar;
revocar
receipt (ri-ssiit) n recibo m
receive (ri-ssiiv) v recibir
receiver (ri-ssii-vö) n receptor m
recent (rii-ssönt) adj reciente
recently (rii-ssönt-li) adv el otro día,
recientemente
reception (ri-ssêp-ʃön) n recepción f;
acogida f; ~ office oficina de reci-

bo
receptionist (ri-ssêp-ʃö-nisst) n recepcionista f
recession (ri-ssê-ʃön) n retroceso m
recipe (rê-ssi-pi) n receta f
recital (ri-ssai-töl) n recital m
reckon (rê-kön) v calcular; considerar; *creer
recognition (rê-kögh-ni-ʃön) n reconocimiento m
recognize (rê-kögh-nais) v *reconocer
recollect (rê-kö-lêkt) v *acordarse
recommence (rii-kö-mênss) v *recomenzar
recommend (rê-kö-mênd) v *recomendar; aconsejar
recommendation (rê-kö-mên-dei-ʃön)
n recomendación f
reconciliation (rê-kön-ssi-li-ei-ʃön) n
reconciliación f
record¹ (rê-kood) n disco m; récord
m; registro m; long-playing ~ microsurco m
record² (ri-kood) v registrar
recorder (ri-koo-dö) n magnetófono
m
recording (ri-koo-ding) n grabación f
record-player (rê-kood-pleiº) n tocadiscos m
recover (ri-ka-vö) v recuperar; *resta-
blecerse, curarse
recovery (ri-ka-vö-ri) n curación f,
restablecimiento m
recreation (rê-kri-ei-ʃön) n recreación
f, recreo m; ~ centre centro de recreo; ~ ground terreno de recreo
público
recruit (ri-kruut) n recluta f
rectangle (rêk-tæng-ghöl) n rectángulo m
rectangular (rêk-tæng-ghyu-lö) adj
rectangular
rector (rêk-tö) n pastor m, rector m
rectory (rêk-tö-ri) n rectoría f

rectum (rêk-töm) *n* intestino recto

red (rêd) *adj* rojo

redeem (ri-*diim*) *v* redimir

reduce (ri-*dyuuss*) *v* *reducir, *disminuir, rebajar

reduotion (ri-*dak*-fön) *n* rebaja *f*, reducción *f*

redundant (ri-*dan*-dönt) *adj* superfluo

reed (riid) *n* junquillo *m*

reef (riif) *n* arrecife *m*

reference (*rêf*-rönss) *n* referencia *f*; relación *f*; **with ~ to** con respecto a

refer to (ri-*föö*) remitir a

refill (*rii*-fil) *n* repuesto *m*

refinery (ri-*fai*-nö-ri) *n* refinería *f*

reflect (ri-*flêkt*) *v* reflejar

reflection (ri-*flêk*-fön) *n* reflejo *m*; imagen reflejada

reflector (ri-*flêk*-tö) *n* reflector *m*

reformation (rê-fö-*mei*-fön) *n* Reforma *f*

refresh (ri-*frêf*) *v* refrescar

refreshment (ri-*frêf*-mönt) *n* refresco *m*

refrigerator (ri-*fri*-dʒö-rei-tö) *n* refrigerador *m*

refund[1] (ri-*fand*) *v* reintegrar

refund[2] (*rii* fand) *n* reintegro *m*

refusal (ri-*fyuu*-söl) *n* negativa *f*

refuse[1] (ri-*fyuus*) *v* rehusar

refuse[2] (*rê*-fyuuss) *n* desecho *m*

regard (ri-*ghaad*) *v* considerar; *n* respeto *m*, **as regards** en cuanto a, por lo que se refiere a

regarding (ri-*ghaa*-ding) *prep* relativo a, tooante a; respecto a

regatta (ri-*ghæ*-tö) *n* regata *f*

régime (rei-*ʒiim*) *n* régimen *m*

region (*rii*-dʒön) *n* región *f*

regional (*rii*-dʒö-nöl) *adj* regional

register (*rê*-dʒi-sstö) *v* inscribirse; certificar; **registered letter** carta certificada

registration (rê-dʒi-*sstrei*-fön) *n* inscripción *f*; **~ form** formulario de matriculación; **~ number** matrícula *f*; **~ plate** placa *f*

regret (ri-*ghrêt*) *v* *sentir; *n* arrepentimiento *m*

regular (*re*-ghyu-lö) *adj* regular; corriente, normal

regulate (*rê*-ghyu-leit) *v* regular

regulation (rê-ghyu-*lei*-fön) *n* reglamento *m*, regulación *f*; regla *f*

rehabilitation (rii-hö-bi-li-*tei*-fön) *n* rehabilitación *f*

rehearsal (ri-*höö*-ssöl) *n* ensayo *m*

rehearse (ri-*hööss*) *v* ensayar

reign (rein) *n* reinado *m*; *v* *gobernar

reimburse (rii-im-*bööss*) *v* reembolsar

reindeer (*rein* diº) *n* (pl ~) reno *m*

reject (ri-*dʒêkt*) *v* rehusar, rechazar; *reprobar

relate (ri-*leit*) *v* *contar

related (ri-*lei*-tid) *adj* emparentado

relation (ri-*lei*-fön) *n* relación *f*; pariente *m*

relative (*rê*-lö-tiv) *n* pariente *m*; *adj* relativo

relax (ri-*lækss*) *v* descansar

relaxation (ri-læk-*ssei*-fön) *n* relajación *f*

reliable (ri-*lai*-ö-böl) *adj* fiable

relic (*rê*-lik) *n* reliquia *f*

relief (ri *liif*) *n* alivio *m*; ayuda *f*; relieve *m*

relieve (ri-*liiv*) *v* relevar

religion (ri-*li*-dʒön) *n* religión *f*

religious (ri-*li*-dʒöss) *adj* religioso

rely on (ri-*lai*) *contar con

remain (ri *mein*) *v* quedarse; quedar

remainder (ri-*mein*-dö) *n* resto *m*

remaining (ri-*mei*-ning) *adj* demás, restante

remark (ri-*maak*) *n* observación *f*; *v* *hacer una observación

remarkable (ri-*maa*-kö-böl) *adj* notable

remedy (*rê*-mö-di) *n* remedio *m*

remember (ri-*mêm*-bö) *v* *acordarse

remembrance (ri-*mêm*-brönss) *n* recuerdo *m*

remind (ri-*maind*) *v* *recordar

remit (ri-*mit*) *v* remitir

remittance (ri-*mi*-tönss) *n* remesa *f*

remnant (*rêm*-nönt) *n* resto *m*, residuo *m*, remanente *m*

remote (ri-*mout*) *adj* remoto, lejano

removal (ri-*muu*-völ) *n* remoción *f*

remove (ri-*muuv*) *v* *remover

remunerate (ri-*myuu*-nö-reit) *v* remunerar

remuneration (ri-myuu-nö-*rei*-ʃön) *n* remuneración *f*

renew (ri-*nyuu*) *v* *renovar; alargar

rent (rênt) *v* alquilar; *n* alquiler *m*

repair (ri-*pêⁿ*) *v* arreglar, reparar; *n* reparación *f*

reparation (rê-pö-*rei*-ʃön) *n* reparación *f*

*repay (ri-*pei*) *v* reintegrar

repayment (ri-*pei*-mönt) *n* reintegro *m*

repeat (ri-*piit*) *v* *repetir

repellent (ri-*pê*-lönt) *adj* repugnante, repelente

repentance (ri-*pên*-tönss) *n* arrepentimiento *m*

repertory (*rê*-pö-tö-ri) *n* repertorio *m*

repetition (rê-pö-*ti*-ʃön) *n* repetición *f*

replace (ri-*pleiss*) *v* reemplazar

reply (ri-*plai*) *v* responder; *n* respuesta *f*; in ~ en contestación

report (ri-*poot*) *v* relatar; informar; presentarse; *n* relación *f*, informe *m*

reporter (ri-*poo*-tö) *n* reportero *m*

represent (rê-pri-*sênt*) *v* representar

representation (rê-pri-sên-*tei*-ʃön) *n* representación *f*

representative (rê-pri-*sên*-tö-tiv) *adj* representativo

reprimand (*rê*-pri-maand) *v* reprender

reproach (ri-*prouch*) *n* reproche *m*; *v* reprochar

reproduce (rii-prö-*dyuuss*) *v* *reproducir

reproduction (rii-prö-*dak*-ʃön) *n* reproducción *f*

reptile (*rêp*-tail) *n* reptil *m*

republic (ri-*pa*-blik) *n* república *f*

republican (ri-*pa*-bli-kön) *adj* republicano

repulsive (ri-*pal*-ssiv) *adj* repulsivo

reputation (rê-pyu-*tei*-ʃön) *n* reputación *f*; renombre *m*

request (ri-*kʷêsst*) *n* ruego *m*; demanda *f*; *v* solicitar

require (ri-*kʷaiⁿ*) *v* *requerir

requirement (ri-*kʷaiⁿ*-mönt) *n* requerimiento *m*

requisite (*rê*-kʷi-sit) *adj* necesario

rescue (*rê*-sskyuu) *v* rescatar; *n* rescate *m*

research (ri-*ssööch*) *n* investigación *f*

resemblance (ri-*sêm*-blönss) *n* semejanza *f*

resemble (ri-*sêm*-böl) *v* asemejarse

resent (ri-*sênt*) *v* *resentirse por

reservation (rê-sö-*vei*-ʃön) *n* reservación *f*

reserve (ri-*sööv*) *v* reservar; *n* reserva *f*

reserved (ri-*söövd*) *adj* reservado

reservoir (*rê*-sö-vʷaa) *n* embalse *m*

reside (ri-*said*) *v* residir

residence (*rê*-si-dönss) *n* residencia *f*; ~ permit permiso de residencia

resident (*rê*-si-dönt) *n* residente *m*; *adj* residente; interno

resign (ri-*sain*) *v* resignar

resignation (rê-sigh-*nei*-ʃön) *n* resignación *f*

resin (*rê*-sin) *n* resina *f*

resist (ri-*sisst*) *v* resistir

resistance (ri-*si*-sstönss) *n* resistencia

f

resolute (*rê-sö-luut*) *adj* resuelto, decidido

respect (ri-*sspêkt*) *n* respeto *m*; estimación *f*, reverencia *f*; *v* respetar

respectable (ri-*sspêk*-tö-böl) *adj* respetable

respectful (ri-*sspêkt*-föl) *adj* respetuoso

respective (ri-*sspêk*-tiv) *adj* respectivo

respiration (rê-sspö-*rei*-ʃön) *n* respiración *f*

respite (*rê*-sspait) *n* dilación *f*

responsibility (ri-sspon-ssö-*bi*-lö-ti) *n* responsabilidad *f*

responsible (ri-*sspon*-ssö-böl) *adj* responsable

rest (rêsst) *n* descanso *m*; resto *m*; *v* *hacer reposo, descansar

restaurant (*rê*-sstö-rong) *n* restaurante *m*

restful (*rêsst*-föl) *adj* reposado

rest-home (*rêsst*-houm) *n* casa de reposo

restless (*rêsst*-löss) *adj* inquieto

restrain (ri-*sstrein*) *v* *contener, *impedir

restriction (ri-*sstrik*-ʃön) *n* restricción *f*

result (ri-*salt*) *n* resultado *m*; consecuencia *f*; *v* resultar

resume (ri-*syuum*) *v* reemprender

résumé (*rê*-syu-mei) *n* resumen *m*

retail (*rii*-teil) *v* vender al detalle; ~ **trade** comercio al por menor

retailer (*rii*-tei-lö) *n* comerciante al por menor, minorista *m*, revendedor *m*

retina (*rê*-ti-nö) *n* retina *f*

retired (ri-*tai*ᵒd) *adj* jubilado

return (ri-*töön*) *v* *volver; *n* regreso *m*; ~ **flight** vuelo de regreso; ~ **journey** vuelta *f*, viaje de regreso

reunite (rii-yuu-*nait*) *v* reunir

reveal (ri-*viil*) *v* *manifestar, revelar

revelation (rê-vö-*lei*-ʃön) *n* revelación *f*

revenge (ri-*vêndʒ*) *n* venganza *f*

revenue (*rê*-vö-nyuu) *n* ingresos *mpl*, renta *f*

reverse (ri-*vööss*) *n* contrario *m*; reverso *m*; marcha atrás; revés *m*; *adj* inverso; *v* *dar marcha atrás

review (ri-*vyuu*) *n* reseña *f*; revista *f*

revise (ri-*vais*) *v* revisar

revision (ri-*vi*-ʒön) *n* revisión *f*

revival (ri-*vai*-völ) *n* recuperación *f*

revolt (ri-*voult*) *v* sublevarse; *n* rebelión *f*, revuelta *f*

revolting (ri-*voul*-ting) *adj* repugnante, chocante, repelente

revolution (rê-vö-*luu*-ʃön) *n* revolución *f*

revolutionary (rê-vö-*luu*-ʃö-nö-ri) *adj* revolucionario

revolver (ri-*vol*-vo) *n* revólver *m*

revue (ri-*vyuu*) *n* revista *f*

reward (ri-ᵘ*ood*) *n* recompensa *f*; *v* recompensar

rheumatism (*ruu*-mö-ti-söm) *n* reumatismo *m*

rhinoceros (rai-*no*-ssö-röss) *n* (pl ~, ~es) rinoceronte *m*

rhubarb (*ruu*-baab) *n* ruibarbo *m*

rhyme (raim) *n* rima *f*

rhythm (*ri*-ðöm) *n* ritmo *m*

rib (rib) *n* costilla *f*

ribbon (*ri*-bön) *n* cinta *f*

rice (raiss) *n* arroz *m*

rich (rich) *adj* rico

riches (*ri*-chis) *pl* riqueza *f*

riddle (*ri*-döl) *n* adivinanza *f*

ride (raid) *n* paseo *m*

*ride** (raid) *v* *ir en coche; montar

rider (*rai*-dö) *n* jinete *m*

ridge (ridʒ) *n* cresta *f*

ridicule (*ri*-di-kyuul) *v* ridiculizar

ridiculous (ri-*di*-kyu-löss) *adj* ridículo

riding (*rai*-ding) *n* equitación *f*
riding-school (*rai*-ding-sskuul) *n* picadero *m*
rifle (*rai*-föl) *v* rifle *m*
right (rait) *n* derecho *m*; *adj* correcto; derecho; justo; **all right!** ¡de acuerdo!; * **be** ~ *tener razón; ~ **of way** prioridad de paso
righteous (*rai*-chöss) *adj* justo
right-hand (*rait*-hænd) *adj* derecho
rightly (*rait*-li) *adv* justamente
rim (rim) *n* llanta *f*; borde *m*
ring (ring) *n* anillo *m*; círculo *m*; pista *f*
* **ring** (ring) *v* *sonar; ~ **up** llamar por teléfono
rinse (rinss) *v* enjuagar; *n* enjuague *m*
riot (*rai*-öt) *n* motín *m*
rip (rip) *v* rasgar
ripe (raip) *adj* maduro
rise (rais) *n* aumento de sueldo, aumento *m*; levantamiento *m*; subida *f*; nacimiento *m*
* **rise** (rais) *v* levantarse; subir
rising (*rai*-sing) *n* levantamiento *m*
risk (rissk) *n* riesgo *m*; peligro *m*; *v* arriesgar
risky (*ri*-sski) *adj* arriesgado
rival (*rai*-völ) *n* rival *m*; competidor *m*; *v* rivalizar
rivalry (*rai*-völ-ri) *n* rivalidad *f*; competencia *f*
river (*ri*-vö) *n* río *m*; ~ **bank** ribera *f*
riverside (*ri*-vö-ssaid) *n* ribera *f*
roach (rouch) *n* (pl ~) escarcho *m*
road (roud) *n* calle *f*, camino *m*; ~ **fork** *n* bifurcación *f*; ~ **map** mapa de carreteras; ~ **system** red de carreteras; ~ **up** camino en obras
roadhouse (*roud*-hauss) *n* parador *m*
roadside (*roud*-ssaid) *n* borde del camino
roam (roum) *v* vagabundear

roar (roo) *v* mugir, rugir; *n* rugido *m*, retumbo *m*
roast (rousst) *v* asar, asar en parrilla
rob (rob) *v* robar
robber (*ro*-bö) *n* ladrón *m*
robbery (*ro*-bö-ri) *n* robo *m*
robe (roub) *n* traje largo
robin (*ro*-bin) *n* petirrojo *m*
robust (rou-*basst*) *adj* robusto
rock (rok) *n* roca *f*; *v* mecer
rocket (*ro*-kit) *n* cohete *m*
rocky (*ro*-ki) *adj* rocoso
rod (rod) *n* barra *f*
roe (rou) *n* huevos de los peces, hueva *f*
roll (roul) *v* *rodar; *n* rollo *m*; panecillo *m*
roller-skating (*rou*-lö-sskei-ting) *n* patinaje de ruedas
Roman Catholic (*rou*-mön *kæ*-zö-lik) católico
romance (rö-*mænss*) *n* amorío *m*
romantic (rö-*mæn*-tik) *adj* romántico
roof (ruuf) *n* techo *m*; **thatched** ~ techo de paja
room (ruum) *n* habitación *f*; espacio *m*, sitio *m*; ~ **and board** pensión completa; ~ **service** servicio de habitación; ~ **temperature** temperatura ambiente
roomy (*ruu*-mi) *adj* espacioso
root (ruut) *n* raíz *f*
rope (roup) *n* soga *f*
rosary (*rou*-sö-ri) *n* rosario *m*
rose (rous) *n* rosa *f*; *adj* rosa
rotten (*ro*-tön) *adj* podrido
rouge (ruuჳ) *n* colorete *m*
rough (raf) *adj* áspero
roulette (ruu-*lêt*) *n* ruleta *f*
round (raund) *adj* redondo; *prep* alrededor de, en torno de; *n* vuelta *f*; ~ **trip** *Am* ida y vuelta
roundabout (*raun*-dö-baut) *n* glorieta *f*

rounded (*raun*-did) *adj* redondeado
route (ruut) *n* ruta *f*
routine (ruu-*tiin*) *n* rutina *f*
row[1] (rou) *n* fila *f*; *v* remar
row[2] (rau) *n* bronca *f*
rowdy (*rau*-di) *adj* alborotador
rowing-boat (*rou*-ing-bout) *n* bote *m*
royal (*roi*-öl) *adj* real
rub (rab) *v* frotar
rubber (*ra*-bö) *n* caucho *m*; goma de borrar; hule *mMe*; ~ **band** elástico *m*
rubbish (*ra*-biʃ) *n* basura *f*; habladuría *f*, tontería *f*; **talk ~** *decir tonterías
rubbish-bin (*ra*-biʃ-bin) *n* cubo de la basura
ruby (*ruu*-bi) *n* rubí *m*
rucksack (*rak*-ssæk) *n* mochila *f*
rudder (*ra*-dö) *n* timón *m*
rude (ruud) *adj* grosero
rug (ragh) *n* alfombrilla *f*
ruin (*ruu*-in) *v* arruinar; *n* ruina *f*
ruination (ruu-i-*nei*-ʃön) *n* hundimiento *m*
rule (ruul) *n* regla *f*; régimen *m*, gobierno *m*, dominio *m*; *v* *gobernar, *regir; **as a ~** generalmente, por regla general
ruler (*ruu*-lö) *n* monarca *m*, gobernante *m*; regla *f*
Rumania (ruu-*mei*-ni-ö) Rumania *f*
Rumanian (ruu-*mei*-ni-ön) *adj* rumano
rumour (*ruu*-mö) *n* rumor *m*
***run** (ran) *v* correr; ~ **into** *encontrarse con
runaway (*ra*-nö-ᵁei) *n* fugitivo *m*
rung (ran) *v* (pp ring)
runway (*ran*-ᵁei) *n* pista de aterrizaje
rural (*ruᵒ*-röl) *adj* rural
ruse (ruus) *n* astucia *f*
rush (raʃ) *v* precipitarse; *n* junco *m*
rush-hour (*raʃ*-auᵒ) *n* hora de afluencia

Russia (*ra*-ʃö) Rusia *f*
Russian (*ra*-ʃön) *adj* ruso
rust (rasst) *n* herrumbre *f*
rustic (*ra*-sstik) *adj* rústico
rusty (*ra*-ssti) *adj* oxidado

S

saccharin (*ssæ*-kö-rin) *n* sacarina *f*
sack (ssæk) *n* saco *m*
sacred (*ssei*-krid) *adj* sagrado
sacrifice (*ssæ*-kri-faiss) *n* sacrificio *m*; *v* sacrificar
sacrilege (*ssæ*-kri-lidʒ) *n* sacrilegio *m*
sad (ssæd) *adj* triste; afligido, melancólico
saddle (*ssæ*-döl) *n* silla *f*
sadness (*ssæd*-nöss) *n* tristeza *f*
safe (sseif) *adj* seguro; *n* caja fuerte, caja de caudales
safety (*sseif*-ti) *n* seguridad *f*
safety-belt (*sseif*-ti-bëlt) *n* cinturón de seguridad
safety-pin (*sseif*-ti-pin) *n* imperdible *m*
safety-razor (*sseif*-ti-rei-so) *n* máquina de afeitar
sail (sseil) *v* navegar; *n* vela *f*
sailing-boat (*ssei*-ling-bout) *n* buque velero
sailor (*ssei*-lö) *n* marinero *m*
saint (sseint) *n* santo *m*
salad (*ssæ*-löd) *n* ensalada *f*
salad-oil (*ssæ*-lod-oil) *n* aceite de mesa
salary (*ssæ*-lö-ri) *n* sueldo *m*
sale (sseil) *n* venta *f*; **clearance ~** liquidación *f*; **for ~** de venta; **sales** rebajas *fpl*
saleable (*ssei*-lö-böl) *adj* vendible
salesgirl (*sseils*-ghööl) *n* vendedora *f*
salesman (*sseils*-mön) *n* (pl -men)

vendedor *m*

salmon (*ssæ*-mön) *n* (pl ~) salmón *m*

salon (*ssæ-long*) *n* salón *m*

saloon (ssö-*luun*) *n* bar *m*; cantina *f Me*

salt (ssoolt) *n* sal *f*

salt-cellar (*ssoolt*-ssê-lö) *n* salero *m*

salty (*ssool*-ti) *adj* salado

salute (ssö-*luut*) *v* saludar

salve (ssaav) *n* ungüento *m*

same (sseim) *adj* mismo

sample (*ssaam*-pöl) *n* muestra *f*

sanatorium (ssæ-nö-*too*-ri-öm) *n* (pl ~s, -ria) sanatorio *m*

sand (ssænd) *n* arena *f*

sandal (*ssæn*-döl) *n* sandalia *f*

sandpaper (*ssænd*-pei-pö) *n* papel de lija

sandwich (*ssæn*-ᵁidჳ) *n* bocadillo *m*; emparedado *m*

sandy (*ssæn*-di) *adj* arenoso

sanitary (*ssæ*-ni-tö-ri) *adj* sanitario; ~ **towel** paño higiénico

sapphire (*ssæ*-faiᵒ) *n* zafiro *m*

sardine (ssaa-*diin*) *n* sardina *f*

satchel (*ssæ*-chöl) *n* cartera *f*

satellite (*ssæ*-tö-lait) *n* satélite *m*

satin (*ssæ*-tin) *n* raso *m*

satisfaction (ssæ-tiss-*fæk*-ʃön) *n* satisfacción *f*

satisfy (*ssæ*-tiss-fai) *v* *satisfacer

Saturday (*ssæ*-tö-di) *n* sábado *m*

sauce (ssooss) *n* salsa *f*

saucepan (*ssooss*-pön) *n* cacerola *f*

saucer (*ssoo*-ssö) *n* platillo *m*

Saudi Arabia (ssau-di-ö-ö-*rei*-bi-ö) Arabia Saudí

Saudi Arabian (ssau-di-ö-ö-*rei*-bi-ön) *adj* saudí

sauna (*ssoo*-nö) *n* sauna *f*

sausage (sso-ssidჳ) *n* salchicha *f*

savage (*ssæ*-vidჳ) *adj* salvaje

save (sseiv) *v* salvar; ahorrar

savings (*ssei*-vings) *pl* ahorros *mpl*;

~ **bank** caja de ahorros

saviour (*ssei*-vyö) *n* salvador *m*

savoury (*ssei*-vö-ri) *adj* sabroso; picante

saw¹ (ssoo) *v* (p see)

saw² (ssoo) *n* sierra *f*

sawdust (*ssoo*-dasst) *n* serrín *m*

saw-mill (*ssoo*-mil) *n* serrería de maderas

*say (ssei) *v* *decir

scaffolding (*sskæ*-föl-ding) *n* andamio *m*

scale (sskeil) *n* escala *f*; escala musical; escama *f*; **scales** *pl* balanza *f*

scandal (*sskæn*-döl) *n* escándalo *m*

Scandinavia (sskæn-di-*nei*-vi-ö) Escandinavia *f*

Scandinavian (sskæn-di-*nei*-vi-ön) *adj* escandinavo

scapegoat (*sskeip*-ghout) *n* cabeza de turco

scar (sskaa) *n* cicatriz *f*

scarce (sskêᵒss) *adj* escaso

scarcely (*sskêᵒ*-ssli) *adv* apenas

scarcity (*sskêᵒ*-ssö-ti) *n* escasez *f*

scare (sskêᵒ) *v* asustar; *n* susto *m*

scarf (sskaaf) *n* (pl ~s, scarves) bufanda *f*

scarlet (*sskaa*-löt) *adj* escarlata

scary (*sskêᵒ*-ri) *adj* alarmante

scatter (*sskæ*-tö) *v* esparcir

scene (ssiin) *n* escena *f*

scenery (*ssii*-nö-ri) *n* paisaje *m*

scenic (*ssii*-nik) *adj* pintoresco

scent (ssênt) *n* perfume *m*

schedule (*ʃê*-dyuul) *n* horario *m*

scheme (sskiim) *n* esquema *m*; proyecto *m*

scholar (*ssko*-lö) *n* erudito *m*; alumno *m*

scholarship (*ssko*-lö-ʃip) *n* beca *f*

school (sskuul) *n* escuela *f*

schoolboy (*sskuul*-boi) *n* alumno *m*

schoolgirl (*sskuul*-ghööl) *n* alumna *f*

schoolmaster (*sskuul*-maa-sstö) *n* maestro *m*

schoolteacher (*sskuul*-tii-chö) *n* maestro *m*

science (*ssai*-önss) *n* ciencia *f*

scientific (ssai-ön-*ti*-fik) *adj* científico

scientist (*ssai*-ön-tisst) *n* científico *m*

scissors (*ssi*-sös) *pl* tijeras *fpl*

scold (sskould) *v* reprender; insultar

scooter (*sskuu*-tö) *n* motoneta *f*; patín *m*

score (sskoo) *n* tanteo *m* ; *v* marcar

scorn (sskoon) *n* escarnio *m*, desprecio *m* ; *v* despreciar

Scot (sskot) *n* escocés *m*

Scotch (sskoch) *adj* escocés; **scotch tape** cinta adhesiva

Scotland (*sskot*-lönd) Escocia *f*

Scottish (*ssko*-tiʃ) *adj* escocés

scout (sskaut) *n* explorador *m*

scrap (sskræp) *n* pedazo *m*

scrap-book (*sskræp*-buk) *n* álbum *m*

scrape (sskreip) *v* raspar

scrap-iron (*sskræ*-paiⁿn) *n* chatarra *f*

scratch (sskræch) *v* *hacer raeduras, rascar ; *n* raedura *f*, rasguño *m*

scream (sskriim) *v* gritar, chillar ; *n* grito *m*, chillido *m*

screen (sskriin) *n* mampara *f*; pantalla *f*

screw (sskruu) *n* tornillo *m* ; *v* atornillar

screw-driver (*sskruu*-drai-vö) *n* destornillador *m*

scrub (sskrab) *v* *fregar ; *n* matorral *m*

sculptor (*sskalp* tö) *n* escultor *m*

sculpture (*sskalp*-chö) *n* escultura *f*

sea (ssii) *n* mar *m*

sea-bird (*ssii*-bööd) *n* ave marina

sea-coast (*ssii*-kousst) *n* litoral *m*

seagull (*ssii*-ghal) *n* gaviota *f*

seal (ssiil) *n* sello *m* ; foca *f*

seam (ssiim) *n* costura *f*

seaman (*ssii*-mön) *n* (pl -men) marino *m*

seamless (*ssiim*-löss) *adj* sin costura

seaport (*ssii*-poot) *n* puerto de mar

search (ssööch) *v* buscar; cachear ; *n* búsqueda *f*

searchlight (*ssööch*-lait) *n* reflector *m*

seascape (*ssii*-sskeip) *n* marina *f*

sea-shell (*ssii*-ʃêl) *n* concha *f*

seashore (*ssii*-ʃoo) *n* orilla del mar

seasick (*ssii*-ssik) *adj* mareado

seasickness (*ssii*-ssik-nöss) *n* mareo *m*

seaside (*ssii*-ssaid) *n* orilla del mar ; ~ **resort** playa de veraneo

season (*ssii*-sön) *n* temporada *f*, estación *f*; **high** ~ apogeo de la temporada; **low** ~ temporada baja; **off** ~ fuera de temporada

season-ticket (*ssii*-sön-ti-kit) *n* tarjeta de temporada

seat (ssiit) *n* asiento *m* ; sitio *m*, localidad *f*; sede *f*

seat-belt (*ssiit*-bêlt) *n* cinturón de seguridad

sea-urchin (*ssii*-öö-chin) *n* erizo de mar

sea-water (*ssii*-ᵘoo-tö) *n* agua de mar

second (*ssê*-könd) *num* segundo; *n* segundo *m* ; instante *m*

secondary (*ssê*-kön-dö-ri) *adj* secundario; ~ **school** escuela secundaria

second-hand (*ssê*-könd-*hænd*) *adj* de segunda mano

secret (*ssii*-kröt) *n* secreto *m* ; *adj* secreto

secretary (*ssê*-krö-tri) *n* secretaria *f*; secretario *m*

section (*ssêk*-ʃön) *n* sección *f*; división *f*, departamento *m*

secure (ssi-*kyuᵒ*) *adj* firme ; *v* lograr

security (ssi-*kyuᵒ*-rö-ti) *n* seguridad *f*; fianza *f*

sedate (ssi-*deit*) *adj* sosegado

sedative (ssé-dö-tiv) n calmante m

seduce (ssi-dyuuss) v *seducir

* see (ssii) v *ver; comprender, *darse cuenta; ~ to *atender a

seed (ssiid) n semilla f

* seek (ssiik) v buscar

seem (ssiim) v *parecer

seen (ssiin) v (pp see)

seesaw (ssii-ssoo) n columpio m

seize (ssiis) v agarrar

seldom (ssél-döm) adv pocas veces

select (ssi-lékt) v seleccionar, *elegir; adj seleccionado, selecto

selection (ssi-lék-ʃön) n elección f, selección f

self-centred (ssélf-ssén-töd) adj egocéntrico

self-employed (ssél-fim-ploid) adj independiente

self-evident (ssél-fé-vi-dönt) adj evidente

self-government (ssélf-gha-vö-mönt) n autonomía f

selfish (ssél-fiʃ) adj egoísta

selfishness (ssél-fiʃ-nöss) n egoísmo m

self-service (ssélf-ssöö-viss) n autoservicio m

* sell (ssél) v vender

semblance (ssém-blönss) n apariencia f

semi- (ssé-mi) semi-

semicircle (ssé-mi-ssöö-köl) n semicírculo m

semi-colon (ssé-mi-kou-lön) n punto y coma

senate (ssé-nöt) n senado m

senator (ssé-nö-tö) n senador m

* send (ssénd) v enviar, mandar; ~ back *devolver; ~ for mandar a buscar; ~ off despachar

senile (ssii-nail) adj senil

sensation (ssén-ssei-ʃön) n sensación f

sensational (ssén-ssei-ʃö-nöl) adj sensacional

sense (ssénss) n sentido m; juicio m, razón f; v *sentir; ~ of honour sentido del honor

senseless (ssénss-löss) adj insensato

sensible (ssén-ssö-böl) adj sensato

sensitive (ssén-ssi-tiv) adj sensitivo

sentence (ssén-tönss) n frase f; sentencia f; v sentenciar

sentimental (ssén-ti-mén-töl) adj sentimental

separate¹ (ssé-pö-reit) v separar

separate² (ssé-pö-röt) adj separado

separately (ssé-pö-röt-li) adv por separado

September (ssép-têm-bö) septiembre

septic (ssép-tik) adj séptico; * become ~ infectarse

sequel (ssii-kʷöl) n continuación f

sequence (ssii-kʷönss) n sucesión f; serie f

serene (ssö-riin) adj sereno; claro

serial (ssiö-ri-öl) n novela por entregas

series (ssiö-riis) n (pl ~) serie f

serious (ssiö-ri-öss) adj serio

seriousness (ssiö-ri-öss-nöss) n seriedad f

sermon (ssöö-mön) n sermón m

serum (ssiö-röm) n suero m

servant (ssöö-vönt) n criado m

serve (ssööv) v *servir

service (ssöö-viss) n servicio m; ~ charge servicio m; ~ station puesto de gasolina

serviette (ssöö-vi-êt) n servilleta f

session (ssé-ʃön) n sesión f

set (ssét) n juego m, grupo m

* set (ssét) v *poner; ~ menu cubierto a precio fijo; ~ out partir

setting (ssé-ting) n escena f; ~ lotion fijador m

settle (ssé-töl) v arreglar; ~ down

arraigarse
settlement (*ssê*-töl-mönt) *n* acuerdo *m*, arreglo *m*, convenio *m*
seven (*ssê*-vön) *num* siete
seventeen (ssê-vön-*tiin*) *num* diecisiete
seventeenth (ssê-vön-*tiinz*) *num* decimoséptimo
seventh (*ssê*-vönz) *num* séptimo
seventy (*ssê*-vön-ti) *num* setenta
several (*ssê*-vö-röl) *adj* varios
severe (ssi-*vi*ᵒ) *adj* violento, rigoroso, severo
sew (ssou) *v* coser; ~ **up** *hacer una sutura
sewer (*ssuu*-ö) *n* desagüe *m*
sewing-machine (*ssou*-ing-mö-ʃiin) *n* máquina de coser
sex (ssêkss) *n* sexo *m*; sexualidad *f*
sexton (*ssêk*-sstön) *n* sacristán *m*
sexual (*ssêk*-ʃu-öl) *adj* sexual
sexuality (ssêk-ʃu-æ-lö-ti) *n* sexualidad *f*
shade (ʃeid) *n* sombra *f*; tono *m*
shadow (*ʃæ*-dou) *n* sombra *f*
shady (*ʃei*-di) *adj* sombreado
*shake** (ʃeik) *v* sacudir
shaky (*ʃei*-ki) *adj* vacilante
*shall** (ʃæl) *v* *tener que
shallow (*ʃæ*-lou) *adj* poco profundo
shame (ʃeim) *n* vergüenza *f*; deshonra *f*; shame! ¡qué vergüenza!
shampoo (ʃæm-*puu*) *n* champú *m*
shamrock (*ʃæm*-rok) *n* trébol *m*
shape (ʃeip) *n* forma *f*; *v* formar
share (ʃêᵃ) *v* compartir, *n* parte *f*, acción *f*
shark (ʃaak) *n* tiburón *m*
sharp (ʃaap) *adj* afilado
sharpen (*ʃaa*-pön) *v* afilar
shave (ʃeiv) *v* rasurarse, afeitarse
shaver (*ʃei*-vö) *n* máquina de afeitar
shaving-brush (*ʃei*-ving-braʃ) *n* brocha de afeitar

shaving-cream (*ʃei*-ving-kriim) *n* crema de afeitar
shaving-soap (*ʃei*-ving-ssoup) *n* jabón de afeitar
shawl (ʃool) *n* chal *m*
she (ʃii) *pron* ella
shed (ʃêd) *n* cobertizo *m*
*shed** (ʃêd) *v* derramar; esparcir
sheep (ʃiip) *n* (pl ~) oveja *f*
sheer (ʃiᵒ) *adj* absoluto, puro; fino, traslúcido
sheet (ʃiit) *n* sábana *f*; hoja *f*; chapa *f*
shelf (ʃêlf) *n* (pl shelves) estante *m*
shell (ʃêl) *n* concha *f*; cáscara *f*
shellfish (*ʃêl*-fiʃ) *n* marisco *m*
shelter (*ʃêl*-tö) *n* refugio *m*; *v* abrigar
shepherd (*ʃê*-pöd) *n* pastor *m*
shift (ʃift) *n* turno *m*
*shine** (ʃain) *v* *relucir; brillar, *resplandecer
ship (ʃip) *n* buque *m*; *v* transportar; **shipping line** línea de navegación
shipowner (*ʃi*-pou-nö) *n* armador *m*
shipyard (*ʃip*-yaad) *n* astillero *m*
shirt (ʃööt) *n* camisa *f*
shiver (*ʃi*-vö) *v* *temblar, tiritar; *n* escalofrío *m*
shivery (*ʃi*-vö-ri) *adj* estremecido
shock (ʃok) *n* choque *m*; *v* chocar; ~ **absorber** amortiguador *m*
shocking (*ʃo*-king) *adj* chocante
shoe (ʃuu) *n* zapato *m*; **gym shoes** sandalias de gimnasia; ~ **polish** betún *m*; grasa *fMe*
shoe-lace (*ʃuu*-leiss) *n* cordón *m*
shoemaker (*ʃuu*-mei-kö) *n* zapatero *m*
shoe-shop (*ʃuu*-ʃop) *n* zapatería *f*
shook (ʃuk) *v* (p shake)
*shoot** (ʃuut) *v* tirar
shop (ʃop) *n* tienda *f*; *v* *ir de compras; ~ **assistant** dependiente *m*; **shopping bag** saco de compras; **shopping centre** centro comercial

shopkeeper (ʃop-kii-pö) n tendero m

shop-window (ʃop-ᵘin-dou) n escaparate m

shore (ʃoo) n ribera f, orilla f

short (ʃoot) adj corto; bajo; ~ **circuit** cortocircuito m

shortage (ʃoo-tidʒ) n carencia f, escasez f

shortcoming (ʃoot-ka-ming) n deficiencia f

shorten (ʃoo-tön) v acortar

shorthand (ʃoot-hænd) n taquigrafía f

shortly (ʃoot-li) adv pronto, próximamente

shorts (ʃootss) pl pantalones cortos; plAm calzoncillos mpl

short-sighted (ʃoot-ssai-tid) adj miope

shot (ʃot) n disparo m; inyección f; secuencia f

***should** (ʃud) v *tener que

shoulder (ʃoul-dö) n hombro m

shout (ʃaut) v gritar; n grito m

shovel (ʃa-völ) n pala f

show (ʃou) n representación f, espectáculo m; exposición f

***show** (ʃou) v *mostrar; enseñar; *demostrar

show-case (ʃou-keiss) n vitrina f

shower (ʃauᵒ) n ducha f; aguacero m

showroom (ʃou-ruum) n salón de demostraciones

shriek (ʃriik) v chillar; n chillido m

shrimp (ʃrimp) n camarón m

shrine (ʃrain) n santuario m

***shrink** (ʃringk) v encogerse

shrinkproof (ʃringk-pruuf) adj no encoge

shrub (ʃrab) n arbusto m

shudder (ʃa-dö) n estremecimiento m

shuffle (ʃa-föl) v barajar

***shut** (ʃat) v *cerrar; ~ **in** *encerrar

shutter (ʃa-tö) n persiana f

shy (ʃai) adj esquivo, tímido

shyness (ʃai-nöss) n timidez f

Siam (ssai-æm) Siam m

Siamese (ssai-ö-miis) adj siamés

sick (ssik) adj enfermo; que tiene náuseas

sickness (ssik-nöss) n enfermedad f; náusea f

side (ssaid) n lado m; partido m; **one-sided** adj unilateral

sideburns (ssaid-bööns) pl patillas fpl

sidelight (ssaid-lait) n luz lateral

side-street (ssaid-sstriit) n calle lateral

sidewalk (ssaid-ᵘook) nAm acera f

sideways (ssaid-ᵘeis) adv lateralmente

siege (ssiidʒ) n sitio m

sieve (ssiv) n tamiz m; v tamizar

sift (ssift) v tamizar

sight (ssait) n vista f; aspecto m; curiosidad f

sign (ssain) n signo m, señal f; gesto m, seña f; v suscribir, firmar

signal (ssigh-nöl) n señal f; v *hacer señales

signature (ssigh-nö-chö) n firma f

significant (ssigh-ni-fi-könt) adj significativo

signpost (ssain-pousst) n poste de indicador

silence (ssai-lönss) n silencio m; v acallar

silencer (ssai-lön-ssö) n silenciador m

silent (ssai-lönt) adj callado; *be ~ callarse

silk (ssilk) n seda f

silken (ssil-kön) adj sedoso

silly (ssi-li) adj necio, bobo

silver (ssil-vö) n plata f; de plata

silversmith (ssil-vö-ssmiz) n platero m

silverware (ssil-vö-ᵘeᵒ) n plata labrada

similar (ssi-mi-lö) adj similar

similarity (ssi-mi-læ-rö-ti) n semejanza f

simple (ssim-pöl) adj ingenuo, sim-

ple; ordinario
simply (*ssim*-pli) *adv* simplemente
simulate (*ssi* myu loit) *v* simular
simultaneous (ssi-möl-*tei*-ni-öss) *adj* simultáneo
sin (ssin) *n* pecado *m*
since (ssinss) *prep* desde; *adv* desde entonces; *conj* desde que; puesto que
sincere (ssin-*ssiö*) *adj* sincero
sinew (*ssi*-nyuu) *n* tendón *m*
*****sing** (ssing) *v* cantar
singer (*ssing*-ö) *n* cantante *m*; cantadora *f*
single (*ssing*-ghöl) *adj* solo; soltero
singular (*ssing*-ghyu-lö) *n* singular *m*; *adj* singular
sinister (*ssi*-ni-sstö) *adj* siniestro
sink (ssingk) *n* pileta *f*
*****sink** (ssingk) *v* hundirse
sip (ssip) *n* sorbo *m*
siphon (*ssai*-fön) *n* sifón *m*
sir (ssöö) señor *m*
siren (*ssaiö*-rön) *n* sirena *f*
sister (*ssi*-sstö) *n* hermana *f*
sister-in-law (*ssi*-sstö-rin-loo) *n* (pl sisters-) cuñada *f*
*****sit** (ssit) *v* *estar sentado; ~ **down** *sentarse
site (ssait) *n* sitio *m*
sitting-room (*ssi*-ting-ruum) *n* sala de estar
situated (*ssi*-chu-ei-tid) *adj* situado
situation (ssi-chu-*ei*-fön) *n* situación *f*; ubicación *f*
six (ssikss) *num* seis
sixteen (ssikss-*tíín*) *num* dieciséis
sixteenth (ssikss-*tiinz*) *num* decimosexto
sixth (ssikssz) *num* sexto
sixty (*ssikss*-ti) *num* sesenta
size (ssais) *n* tamaño *m*, número *m*; dimensión *f*; formato *m*
skate (sskeit) *v* patinar; *n* patín *m*

skating (*sskei*-ting) *n* patinaje *m*
skating-rink (*sskei*-ting-ringk) *n* pista de patinaje
skeleton (*sskê*-li-tön) *n* esqueleto *m*
sketch (sskêch) *n* dibujo *m*, bosquejo *m*; *v* dibujar, bosquejar
sketch-book (*sskêch*-buk) *n* cuaderno de diseño
ski¹ (sskii) *v* esquiar
ski² (sskii) *n* (pl ~, ~s) esquí *m*; ~ **boots** botas de esquí; ~ **pants** pantalones de esquí; ~ **sticks** bastones de esquí
skid (sskid) *v* patinar
skier (*sskii*-ö) *n* esquiador *m*
skiing (*sskii*-ing) *n* esquí *m*
ski-jump (*sskii*-dʒamp) *n* salto de esquí
skilful (*sskil*-föl) *adj* hábil, diestro
ski-lift (*sskii*-lift) *n* telesilla *m*
skill (sskil) *n* habilidad *f*
skilled (sskild) *adj* hábil; especializado
skin (sskin) *n* piel *f*; cáscara *f*; ~ **cream** crema para la piel
skip (sskip) *v* saltar; brincar
skirt (sskööt) *n* falda *f*
skull (sskal) *n* cráneo *m*
sky (sskai) *n* cielo *m*; aire *m*
skyscraper (*sskai*-sskrei-pö) *n* rascacielos *m*
slack (sslæk) *adj* lento
slacks (sslækss) *pl* pantalones *mpl*
slam (sslæm) *v* *dar un portazo
slander (*sslaan*-dö) *n* calumnia *f*
slant (sslaant) *v* inclinarse
slanting (*sslaan*-ting) *adj* oblicuo, pendiente, inclinado
slap (sslæp) *v* pegar; *n* bofetada *f*
slate (ssleit) *n* pizarra *f*
slave (ssleiv) *n* esclavo *m*
sledge (sslêdʒ) *n* trineo *m*
sleep (ssliip) *n* sueño *m*
*****sleep** (ssliip) *v* *dormir

sleeping-bag (*sslii*-ping-bægh) *n* saco de dormir

sleeping-car (*sslii*-ping-kaa) *n* coche cama

sleeping-pill (*sslii*-ping-pil) *n* somnífero *m*

sleepless (*ssliip*-löss) *adj* desvelado

sleepy (*sslii*-pi) *adj* soñoliento

sleeve (ssliiv) *n* manga *f*; funda *f*

sleigh (sslei) *n* trineo *m*

slender (*sslên*-dö) *adj* esbelto

slice (sslaiss) *n* tajada *f*

slide (sslaid) *n* desliz *m*; tobogán *m*; diapositiva *f*

* **slide** (sslaid) *v* deslizarse

slight (sslait) *adj* ligero; leve

slim (sslim) *adj* esbelto; *v* adelgazar

slip (sslip) *v* deslizarse, resbalar; *n* desliz *m*; combinación *f*; fondo *mMe*

slipper (*sslí*-pö) *n* zapatilla *f*

slippery (*sslí*-pö-ri) *adj* resbaladizo

slogan (*sslou*-ghön) *n* lema *m*, slogan *m*

slope (ssloup) *n* pendiente *f*; *v* inclinarse

sloping (*sslou*-ping) *adj* inclinado

sloppy (*sslo*-pi) *adj* chapucero

slot (sslot) *n* ranura *f*

slot-machine (*sslot*-mö-ʃiin) *n* máquina tragamonedas

slovenly (*sla*-vön-li) *adj* descuidado

slow (sslou) *adj* lerdo, lento; ~ **down** desacelerar, *ir más despacio; frenar

sluice (ssluuss) *n* compuerta *f*

slum (sslam) *n* barrio bajo

slump (sslamp) *n* baja *f*

slush (sslaʃ) *n* aguanieve *f*

sly (sslai) *adj* astuto

smack (ssmæk) *v* pegar; *n* bofetada *f*

small (ssmool) *adj* pequeño; menudo

smallpox (*ssmool*-pokss) *n* viruelas *fpl*

smart (ssmaat) *adj* elegante; inteli-

gente, listo

smell (ssmêl) *n* olor *m*

* **smell** (ssmêl) *v* *oler; *heder

smelly (*ssmê*-li) *adj* hediondo

smile (ssmail) *v* sonreír; *n* sonrisa *f*

smith (ssmiz) *n* herrero *m*

smoke (ssmouk) *v* fumar; *n* humo *m*; **no smoking** prohibido fumar

smoker (*ssmou*-kö) *n* fumador *m*; compartimento para fumadores

smoking-compartment (*ssmou*-king-köm-paat-mönt) *n* compartimento para fumadores

smoking-room (*ssmou*-king-ruum) *n* sala para fumar

smooth (ssmuuð) *adj* llano, liso; dulce

smuggle (*ssma*-ghöl) *v* contrabandear

snack (ssnæk) *n* tentempié *m*

snack-bar (*ssnæk*-baa) *n* cafetería *f*

snail (ssneil) *n* caracol *m*

snake (ssneik) *n* culebra *f*

snapshot (*ssnæp*-ʃot) *n* instantánea *f*

sneakers (*ssnii*-kös) *plAm* zapatos de gimnasia

sneeze (ssniis) *v* estornudar

sniper (*ssnai*-pö) *n* francotirador *m*

snooty (*ssnuu*-ti) *adj* arrogante

snore (ssnoo) *v* roncar

snorkel (*ssnoo*-köl) *n* esnórquel *m*

snout (ssnaut) *n* hocico *m*

snow (ssnou) *n* nieve *f*; *v* *nevar

snowstorm (*ssnou*-sstoom) *n* nevasca *f*

snowy (*ssnou*-i) *adj* nevoso

so (ssou) *conj* por tanto; *adv* así; a tal grado, tan; **and** ~ **on** etcétera; ~ **far** hasta ahora; ~ **that** así que, a fin de

soak (ssouk) *v* empapar, remojar

soap (ssoup) *n* jabón *m*; ~ **powder** jabón en polvo

sober (*ssou*-bö) *adj* sobrio; ponderado

so-called (ssou-*koold*) *adj* así llamado

soccer (*sso*-kö) *n* fútbol *m*; ~ **team** equipo *m*

social (*ssou*-fól) *adj* social

socialism (*ssou*-fö-li-söm) *n* socialismo *m*

socialist (*ssou*-fö-lisst) *adj* socialista; *n* socialista *m*

society (ssö-*ssai*-ö-ti) *n* sociedad *f*; asociación *f*; compañía *f*

sock (ssok) *n* calcetín *m*

socket (*sso*-kit) *n* casquillo *m*; sóquet *mMe*

soda-water (*ssou*-dö-*u*oo-tö) *n* agua de soda, soda *f*

sofa (*ssou*-fö) *n* sofá *m*

soft (ssoft) *adj* blando; ~ **drink** bebida no alcohólica

soften (*sso*-fön) *v* ablandar

soil (ssoil) *n* suelo *m*; tierra *f*

soiled (ssoild) *adj* manchado

sold (ssould) *v* (p, pp sell); ~ **out** agotado

solder (*ssol*-dö) *v* *soldar

soldering-iron (*ssol*-dö-ring-ai°n) *n* soldador *m*

soldier (*ssoul*-dʒö) *n* militar *m*, soldado *m*

sole[1] (ssoul) *adj* único

sole[2] (ssoul) *n* suela *f*; lenguado *m*

solely (*ssoul*-li) *adv* exclusivamente

solemn (*sso*-löm) *adj* solemne

solicitor (ssö-*li*-ssi-tö) *n* procurador *m*, abogado *m*

solid (*sso*-lid) *adj* robusto, sólido; macizo; *n* sólido *m*

soluble (*sso*-lyu-böl) *adj* soluble

solution (ssö-*luu*-fön) *n* solución *f*

solve (ssolv) *v* *resolver

sombre (*ssom*-bö) *adj* sombrío

some (ssam) *adj* algunos, unos; *pron* algunos, unos; un poco; ~ **day** uno u otro día; ~ **more** algo más; ~ **time** alguna vez

somebody (*ssam*-bö-di) *pron* alguien

somehow (*ssam*-hau) *adv* de un modo u otro

someone (*ssam*-ʷan) *pron* alguien

something (*ssam*-zing) *pron* algo

sometimes (*ssam*-taims) *adv* a veces

somewhat (*ssam*-ʷot) *adv* algo

somewhere (*ssam*-ʷê°) *adv* en alguna parte

son (ssan) *n* hijo *m*

song (ssong) *n* canción *f*

son-in-law (*ssa*-nin-loo) *n* (pl sons-) yerno *m*

soon (ssuun) *adv* rápidamente, pronto, en breve; **as** ~ **as** tan pronto como

sooner (*ssuu*-nö) *adv* más bien

sore (ssoo) *adj* doloroso; *n* llaga *f*; úlcera *f*; ~ **throat** dolor de garganta

sorrow (*sso*-rou) *n* tristeza *f*, sufrimiento *m*, pena *f*

sorry (*sso*-ri) *adj* apenado; **sorry!** ¡dispense usted!, ¡disculpe!, ¡perdón!

sort (ssoot) *v* clasificar, *disponer; *n* clase *f*; **all sorts of** toda clase de

soul (ssoul) *n* alma *f*

sound (ssaund) *n* sonido *m*; *v* *sonar, *resonar; *adj* bueno

soundproof (*ssaund*-pruuf) *adj* insonorizado

soup (ssuup) *n* sopa *f*

soup-plate (*ssuup*-pleit) *n* plato para sopa

soup spoon (*ssuup*-sspuun) *n* cuchara *f*

sour (ssauʰ) *adj* agrio

source (ssooss) *n* fuente *f*

south (ssauz) *n* sur *m*; **South Pole** polo sur

South Africa (ssauz æ-fri-kö) África del Sur

south-east (ssauz-*iisst*) *n* sudeste *m*

southerly (*ssa*-ŏŏ-li) *adj* meridional
southern (*ssa*-ŏŏn) *adj* meridional
south-west (ssauz-ᵘêsst) *n* sudoeste *m*
souvenir (*ssuu*-vö-niᵒ) *n* recuerdo *m*
sovereign (*ssov*-rin) *n* soberano *m*
Soviet (*ssou*-vi-öt) *adj* soviético
Soviet Union (*ssou*-vi-öt *yuu*-nyön) Unión Soviética
* **sow** (ssou) *v* *sembrar
spa (sspaa) *n* balneario *m*
space (sspeiss) *n* espacio *m*; distancia *f*; *v* espaciar
spacious (*sspei*-föss) *adj* espacioso
spade (sspeid) *n* azada *f*, pala *f*
Spain (sspein) España *f*
Spaniard (*sspæ*-nyöd) *n* español *m*
Spanish (*sspæ*-niʃ) *adj* español
spanking (*sspæng*-king) *n* zurra *f*
spanner (*sspæ*-nö) *n* llave inglesa *f*
spare (sspêᵒ) *adj* de reserva, disponible; *v* pasarse sin; ~ **part** pieza de repuesto; ~ **room** cuarto para huéspedes; ~ **time** tiempo libre; ~ **tyre** neumático de repuesto; ~ **wheel** rueda de repuesto
spark (sspaak) *n* chispa *f*
sparking-plug (*sspaa*-king-plagh) *n* bujía *f*
sparkling (*sspaa*-kling) *adj* centelleante; espumante
sparrow (*sspæ*-rou) *n* gorrión *m*
* **speak** (sspiik) *v* hablar
spear (sspiᵒ) *n* lanza *f*
special (*sspê*-föl) *adj* especial; ~ **delivery** por expreso
specialist (*sspê*-fö-lisst) *n* especialista *m*
speciality (sspê-ʃi-æ-lö-ti) *n* especialidad *f*
specialize (*sspê*-fö-lais) *v* especializarse
specially (*sspê*-fö-li) *adv* en particular
species (*sspii*-ʃiis) *n* (pl ~) especie *f*

specific (sspö-*ssi*-fik) *adj* específico
specimen (*sspê*-ssi-mön) *n* espécimen *m*
speck (sspêk) *n* mancha *f*
spectacle (*sspêk*-tö-köl) *n* espectáculo *m*; **spectacles** anteojos *mpl*
spectator (sspêk-*tei*-tö) *n* espectador *m*
speculate (*sspê*-kyu-leit) *v* especular
speech (sspiich) *n* habla *f*; discurso *m*; lenguaje *m*
speechless (*sspiich*-löss) *adj* atónito
speed (sspiid) *n* velocidad *f*; rapidez *f*, prisa *f*; **cruising** ~ velocidad de cruce; ~ **limit** límite de velocidad
* **speed** (sspiid) *v* *dar prisa; correr demasiado
speeding (*sspii*-ding) *n* exceso de velocidad
speedometer (sspii-*do*-mi-tö) *n* velocímetro *m*
spell (sspêl) *n* encanto *m*
* **spell** (sspêl) *v* deletrear
spelling (*sspê*-ling) *n* deletreo *m*
* **spend** (sspênd) *v* gastar; pasar
sphere (ssfiᵒ) *n* esfera *f*
spice (sspaiss) *n* especia *f*
spiced (sspaisst) *adj* condimentado
spicy (*sspai*-ssi) *adj* picante
spider (*sspai*-dö) *n* araña *f*; **spider's web** telaraña *f*
* **spill** (sspil) *v* *verter
* **spin** (sspin) *v* hilar; *hacer girar
spinach (*sspi*-nidʒ) *n* espinacas *fpl*
spine (sspain) *n* espinazo *m*
spinster (*sspin*-sstö) *n* solterona *f*
spire (sspaiᵒ) *n* aguja *f*
spirit (*sspi*-rit) *n* espíritu *m*; humor *m*; **spirits** bebidas espirituosas; moral *f*; ~ **stove** calentador de alcohol
spiritual (*sspi*-ri-chu-öl) *adj* espiritual
spit (sspit) *n* esputo *m*, saliva *f*; espetón *m*

*spit (sspit) v escupir

in spite of (in sspait ov) a pesar de

spiteful (sspait-föl) adj malévolo

splash (ssplæʃ) v salpicar

splendid (ssplên-did) adj magnífico, espléndido

splendour (ssplên-dö) n esplendor m

splint (ssplint) n tablilla f

splinter (ssplin-tö) n astilla f

*split (ssplit) v *hender

*spoil (sspoil) v echar a perder; mimar

spoke¹ (sspouk) v (p speak)

spoke² (sspouk) n radio m

sponge (sspandȝ) n esponja f

spook (sspuuk) n fantasma m

spool (sspuul) n bobina f

spoon (sspuun) n cuchara f

spoonful (sspuun-ful) n cucharada f

sport (sspoot) n deporte m

sports-car (sspootss-kaa) n coche de carreras

sports-jacket (sspootss-dȝæ-kit) n chaqueta de deporte

sportsman (sspootss-mön) n (pl -men) deportista m

sportswear (sspootss-ᵘệ̂ᵒ) n conjunto de deporte

spot (sspot) n mancha f; lugar m, puesto m

spotless (sspot-löss) adj inmaculado

spotlight (sspot-lait) n proyector m

spotted (sspo-tid) adj moteado

spout (sspaut) n chorro m

sprain (ssprein) v *torcerse; n torcedura f

*spread (sspred) v *extender

spring (sspring) n primavera f; muelle m; manantial m

springtime (sspring-taim) n primavera f

sprouts (ssprautss) pl col de Bruselas

spy (sspai) n espía m

squadron (sskᵘo-drön) n escuadrilla f

square (sskᵘệ̂ᵒ) adj cuadrado; n cuadrado m; plaza f

squash (sskᵘoʃ) n zumo m

squirrel (sskᵘi-röl) n ardilla f

squirt (sskᵘööt) n chisguete m

stable (sstei-böl) adj estable; n establo m

stack (sstæk) n montón m

stadium (sstei-di-öm) n estadio m

staff (sstaaf) n personal m

stage (ssteidȝ) n escenario m; fase f; etapa f

stain (sstein) v manchar; n mancha f; stained glass vidrio de color; ~ remover quitamanchas m

stainless (sstein-löss) adj inmaculado; ~ steel acero inoxidable

staircase (sstê̂ᵒ-keiss) n escalera f

stairs (sstê̂ᵒss) pl escalera f

stale (ssteil) adj viejo

stall (sstool) n puesto m; butaca f

stamina (sstæ-mi-nö) n vigor m

stamp (sstæmp) n sello m; v sellar; patear; n estampilla fMe; ~ machine máquina expendedora de sellos

stand (sstænd) n puesto m; tribuna f

*stand (sstænd) v *estar de pie

standard (sstæn-död) n norma f; normal; ~ of living nivel de vida

stanza (sstæn-sö) n estrofa f

staple (sstei-pöl) n grapa f

star (sstaa) n estrella f

starboard (sstaa-böd) n estribor m

starch (sstaach) n almidón m; v almidonar

stare (sstê̂ᵒ) v mirar

starling (sstaa-ling) n estornino m

start (sstaat) v *empezar; n comienzo m; starter motor arranque m

starting-point (sstaa-ting-point) n punto de partida

state (ssteit) n Estado m; estado m; v declarar; the States Estados Unidos

statement (*sseit*-mönt) *n* declaración
f

statesman (*sseitss*-mön) *n* (pl -men)
estadista *m*

station (*sstei*-ʃön) *n* estación *f*; puesto *m*

stationary (*sstei*-ʃö-nö-ri) *adj* estacionario

stationer's (*sstei*-ʃö-nös) *n* papelería *f*

stationery (*sstei*-ʃö-nö-ri) *n* papelería
f

station-master (*sstei*-ʃön-maa-sstö) *n*
jefe de estación

statistics (sstö-*ti*-sstikss) *pl* estadística
f

statue (*sstæ*-chuu) *n* estatua *f*

stay (sstei) *v* quedarse; hospedarse;
n estancia *f*

steadfast (*sstêd*-faasst) *adj* constante

steady (*sstê*-di) *adj* firme

steak (ssteik) *n* bistec *m*

* **steal** (sstiil) *v* hurtar

steam (sstiim) *n* vapor *m*

steamer (*sstii*-mö) *n* vapor *m*

steel (sstiil) *n* acero *m*

steep (sstiip) *adj* abrupto

steeple (*sstii*-pöl) *n* campanario *m*

steering-column (*sstiᵒ*-ring-ko-löm) *n*
columna del volante

steering-wheel (*sstiᵒ*-ring-ᵁiil) *n* volante *m*

steersman (*sstiᵒs*-mön) *n* (pl -men) timonel *m*

stem (sstêm) *n* tallo *m*

stenographer (sstê-*no*-ghrö-fö) *n* taquígrafo *m*

step (sstêp) *n* paso *m*; peldaño *m*; *v*
pisar

stepchild (*sstêp*-chaild) *n* (pl
-children) hijastro *m*

stepfather (*sstêp*-faa-ðö) *n* padrastro
m

stepmother (*sstêp*-ma-ðö) *n* madras-

tra *f*

sterile (*sstê*-rail) *adj* estéril

sterilize (*sstê*-ri-lais) *v* esterilizar

steward (*sstyuu*-öd) *n* camarero *m*

stewardess (*sstyuu*-ö-dêss) *n* azafata
f

stick (sstik) *n* palo *m*

* **stick** (sstik) *v* pegar

sticky (*ssti*-ki) *adj* pegajoso

stiff (sstif) *adj* tieso

still (sstil) *adv* todavía; sin embargo;
adj quieto

stillness (*sstil*-nöss) *n* silencio *m*

stimulant (*ssti*-myu-lönt) *n* estimulante *m*

stimulate (*ssti*-myu-leit) *v* estimular

sting (ssting) *n* picadura *f*

* **sting** (ssting) *v* picar

stingy (*sstin*-dʒi) *adj* mezquino

* **stink** (sstingk) *v* apestar

stipulate (*ssti*-pyu-leit) *v* estipular

stipulation (ssti-pyu-*lei*-ʃön) *n* estipulación *f*

stir (sstöö) *v* *mover; *revolver

stirrup (*ssti*-röp) *n* estribo *m*

stitch (sstich) *n* punto *m*, punzada *f*;
sutura *f*

stock (sstok) *n* existencias *fpl*; *v* *tener en existencia; ~ **exchange** bol-
sa de valores, bolsa *f*; ~ **market**
bolsa *f*; **stocks and shares** acciones *fpl*

stocking (*ssto*-king) *n* media *f*

stole¹ (sstoul) *v* (p steal)

stole² (sstoul) *n* estola *f*

stomach (*ssta*-mök) *n* estómago *m*

stomach-ache (*ssta*-mö-keik) *n* dolor
de estómago

stone (sstoun) *n* piedra *f*; piedra preciosa; hueso *m*; de piedra; **pumice**
~ piedra pómez

stood (sstud) *v* (p, pp stand)

stop (sstop) *v* cesar; dejar de; *n* parada *f*; **stop!** ¡alto!

stopper (*ssto*-pö) *n* tapón *m*

storage (*sstoo*-ridჳ) *n* almacenaje *m*

store (sstoo) *n* repuesto *m*; almacén *m*; *v* almacenar

store-house (*sstoo*-hauss) *n* almacén *m*

storey (*sstoo*-ri) *n* piso *m*

stork (sstook) *n* cigüeña *f*

storm (sstoom) *n* tormenta *f*

stormy (*sstoo*-mi) *adj* tempestuoso

story (*sstoo*-ri) *n* cuento *m*

stout (sstaut) *adj* gordo, corpulento

stove (sstouv) *n* estufa *f*; cocina *f*

straight (sstreit) *adj* derecho; honesto; *adv* directamente; ~ ahead todo seguido; ~ away directamente, en seguida; ~ on todo seguido

strain (sstrein) *n* esfuerzo *m*; tensión *f*; *v* *forzar; filtrar

strainer (*sstrei*-nö) *n* escurridor *m*

strange (sstreindჳ) *adj* extraño; raro

stranger (*sstrein*-dჳö) *n* extranjero *m*; forastero *m*

strangle (*ssträng*-ghöl) *v* estrangular

strap (ssträp) *n* correa *f*

straw (sstroo) *n* paja *f*

strawberry (*sstroo*-bö-ri) *n* fresa *f*

stream (sstriim) *n* arroyo *m*; corriente *f*; *v* *fluir

street (sstriit) *n* calle *f*

streetcar (*sstriit*-kaa) *nAm* tranvía *m*

street-organ (*sstrii*-too-ghön) *n* organillo *m*

strength (ssträngz) *n* fuerza *f*, vigor *m*

stress (ssträss) *n* esfuerzo *m*; énfasis *m*, *v* acentuar

stretch (ssträch) *v* estirar; *n* trecho *m*

strict (sstrikt) *adj* estricto; severo

strife (sstraif) *n* lucha *f*

strike (sstraik) *n* huelga *f*

*strike (sstraik) *v* golpear; atacar; impresionar; *estar en huelga; arriar

striking (*sstrai*-king) *adj* impresionante, notable, vistoso

string (sstring) *n* cordel *m*; cuerda *f*

strip (sstrip) *n* faja *f*

stripe (sstraip) *n* raya *f*

striped (sstraipt) *adj* rayado

stroke (sstrouk) *n* ataque *m*

stroll (sstroul) *v* pasear; *n* paseo *m*

strong (sstrong) *adj* fuerte

stronghold (*sstrong*-hould) *n* plaza fuerte

structure (*sstrak*-chö) *n* estructura *f*

struggle (*sstra*-ghöl) *n* combate *m*, lucha *f*; *v* luchar

stub (sstab) *n* talón *m*

stubborn (*ssta*-bön) *adj* testarudo

student (*sstyuu*-dönt) *n* estudiante *m*; estudiante *f*

study (*ssta*-di) *v* estudiar; *n* estudio *m*; despacho *m*

stuff (sstaf) *n* substancia *f*; cachivache *m*

stuffed (sstaft) *adj* rellenado

stuffing (*ssta*-fing) *n* relleno *m*

stuffy (*ssta*-ti) *adj* sofocante

stumble (*sstam*-böl) *v* *tropezarse

stung (sstang) *v* (p, pp sting)

stupid (*sstyuu*-pid) *adj* estúpido

style (sstail) *n* estilo *m*

subject¹ (*ssab*-dჳikt) *n* sujeto *m*; súbdito *m*; ~ to sujeto a

subject² (ssöb-*dჳêkt*) *v* someter

submit (ssöb-*mit*) *v* someterse

subordinate (ssö-*boo*-di-nöt) *adj* subalterno; subordinado

subscriber (ssöb-*sskrai*-bö) *n* abonado *m*

subscription (ssöb-*sskrip*-[ön) *n* suscripción *f*

subsequent (*ssab*-ssi-k^uönt) *adj* posterior

subsidy (*ssab*-ssi-di) *n* subsidio *m*

substance (*ssab*-sstönss) *n* sustancia *f*

substantial (ssöb-*sstæn*-[öl) *adj* mate-

rial; real; sustancial
substitute (*ssab*-ssti-tyuut) *v* *sustituir; *n* sustituto *m*
subtitle (*ssab*-tai-töl) *n* subtítulo *m*
subtle (*ssa*-töl) *adj* sutil
subtract (ssöb-*trækt*) *v* restar
suburb (*ssa*-bööb) *n* suburbio *m*
suburban (ssö-*böö*-bön) *adj* suburbano
subway (*ssab*-ᵘei) *nAm* metro *m*
succeed (ssök-*ssiid*) *v* *tener éxito; suceder
success (ssök-*ssêss*) *n* éxito *m*
successful (ssök-*ssêss*-föl) *adj* de éxito
succumb (ssö-*kam*) *v* sucumbir
such (ssach) *adj* tal; *adv* tan; ~ **as** tal como
suck (ssak) *v* chupar
sudden (*ssa*-dön) *adj* súbito
suddenly (*ssa*-dön-li) *adv* repentinamente
suede (ssᵘeid) *n* gamuza *f*
suffer (*ssa*-fö) *v* sufrir
suffering (*ssa*-fö-ring) *n* sufrimiento *m*
suffice (ssö-*faiss*) *v* bastar
sufficient (ssö-*fi*-ʃönt) *adj* suficiente, bastante
suffrage (*ssa*-fridʒ) *n* derecho electoral, sufragio *m*
sugar (*ʃu*-ghö) *n* azúcar *m/f*
suggest (ssö-*dʒêsst*) *v* *sugerir
suggestion (ssö-*dʒêss*-chön) *n* sugestión *f*
suicide (*ssuu*-i-ssaid) *n* suicidio *m*
suit (ssuut) *v* *convenir; adaptar; *ir bien; *n* traje *m*
suitable (*ssuu*-tö-böl) *adj* apropiado, apto
suitcase (*ssuut*-keiss) *n* maleta *f*
suite (ssᵘiit) *n* apartamento *m*
sum (ssam) *n* suma *f*
summary (*ssa*-mö-ri) *n* resumen *m*, sumario *m*

summer (*ssa*-mö) *n* verano *m*; ~ **time** horario de verano
summit (*ssa*-mit) *n* cima *f*
summons (*ssa*-möns) *n* (pl ~es) citación *f*
sun (ssan) *n* sol *m*
sunbathe (*ssan*-beið) *v* tomar el sol
sunburn (*ssan*-böön) *n* quemadura del sol
Sunday (*ssan*-di) domingo *m*
sun-glasses (*ssan*-ghlaa-ssis) *pl* gafas de sol
sunlight (*ssan*-lait) *n* luz del sol
sunny (*ssa*-ni) *adj* soleado
sunrise (*ssan*-rais) *n* amanecer *m*
sunset (*ssan*-ssêt) *n* ocaso *m*
sunshade (*ssan*-ʃeid) *n* quitasol *m*
sunshine (*ssan*-ʃain) *n* sol *m*
sunstroke (*ssan*-sstrouk) *n* insolación *f*
suntan oil (*ssan*-tæn-oil) aceite bronceador
superb (ssu-*pööb*) *adj* grandioso, soberbio
superficial (ssuu-pö-*fi*-ʃöl) *adj* superficial
superfluous (ssu-*pöö*-flu-öss) *adj* superfluo
superior (ssu-*piᵒ*-ri-ö) *adj* mejor, mayor, superior
superlative (ssu-*pöö*-lö-tiv) *adj* superlativo; *n* superlativo *m*
supermarket (*ssuu*-pö-maa-kit) *n* supermercado *m*
superstition (ssuu-pö-*ssti*-ʃön) *n* superstición *f*
supervise (*ssuu*-pö-vais) *v* supervisar
supervision (ssuu-pö-*vi*-ʒön) *n* supervisión *f*
supervisor (*ssuu*-pö-vai-sö) *n* supervisor *m*
supper (*ssa*-pö) *n* cena *f*
supple (*ssa*-pöl) *adj* flexible, ágil
supplement (*ssa*-pli-mönt) *n* suple-

mento *m*

supply (ssö-*plai*) *n* abastecimiento *m*, suministro *m*; existencias *fpl*; oferta *f*; *v* suministrar

support (ssö-*poot*) *v* apoyar, *sostener, soportar; *n* apoyo *m*; ~ **hose** medias elásticas

supporter (ssö-*poo*-tö) *n* aficionado *m*

suppose (ssö-*pous*) *v* *suponer; **supposing that** dado que

suppository (ssö-*po*-si-tö-ri) *n* supositorio *m*

suppress (ssö-*prêss*) *v* reprimir

surcharge (*ssöö*-chaadʒ) *n* sobretasa *f*

sure (ʃuᵒ) *adj* seguro

surely (ʃuᵒ-li) *adv* seguramente

surface (*ssöö*-fiss) *n* superficie *f*

surf-board (*ssööf*-bood) *n* tabla para surf

surgeon (*ssöö*-dʒön) *n* cirujano *m*; **veterinary** ~ veterinario *m*

surgery (*ssöö*-dʒö-ri) *n* operación *f*; consultorio *m*

surname (*ssöö*-neim) *n* apellido *m*

surplus (*ssöö*-plöss) *n* sobra *f*

surprise (ssö-*prais*) *n* sorpresa *f*; *v* sorprender; extrañar

surrender (ssö-*rên*-dö) *v* *rendirse; *n* rendición *f*

surround (ssö-*raund*) *v* rodear, cercar

surrounding (ssö *raun* ding) *adj* circundante

surroundings (ssö-*raun*-dings) *pl* alrededores *mpl*

survey (*ssöö*-vei) *n* resumen *m*

survival (ssö-*vai*-völ) *n* supervivencia *f*

survive (ssö-*vaiv*) *v* sobrevivir

suspect[1] (ssö-*sspêkt*) *v* sospechar

suspect[2] (ssa-sspêkt) *n* persona sospechosa

suspend (ssö-*sspênd*) *v* suspender

suspenders (ssö-*sspên*-dös) *plAm* tirantes *mpl*; **suspender belt** portaligas *m*

suspension (ssö-*sspên*-ʃön) *n* suspensión *f*; ~ **bridge** puente colgante

suspicion (ssö-*sspi*-ʃön) *n* sospecha *f*; suspicacia *f*, desconfianza *f*

suspicious (ssö-*sspi*-ʃöss) *adj* sospechoso; suspicaz, desconfiado

sustain (ssö-*sstein*) *v* soportar

Swahili (ssᵘö-*hii*-li) *n* suahili *m*

swallow (*ssᵘo*-lou) *v* tragar; *n* golondrina *f*

swam (ssᵘæm) *v* (p swim)

swamp (ssᵘomp) *n* marisma *f*

swan (ssᵘon) *n* cisne *m*

swap (ssᵘop) *v* *trocar

***swear** (ssᵘêᵒ) *v* jurar

sweat (ssᵘêt) *n* sudor *m*; *v* sudar

sweater (*ssᵘê*-tö) *n* suéter *m*

Swede (ssᵘiid) *n* sueco *m*

Sweden (*ssᵘii*-dön) Suecia *f*

Swedish (*ssᵘii*-diʃ) *adj* sueco

***sweep** (ssᵘiip) *v* barrer

sweet (ssᵘiit) *adj* dulce; lindo; *n* caramelo *m*; dulce *m*

sweeten (*ssᵘii*-tön) *v* endulzar

sweetheart (*ssᵘiit*-haat) *n* amor *m*, querida *f*

sweetshop (*ssᵘiit*-ʃop) *n* confitería *f*

swell (ssᵘêl) *adj* magnífico

***swell** (ssᵘêl) *v* hincharse

swelling (*ssᵘê*-ling) *n* hinchazón *f*

swift (ssᵘift) *adj* veloz

***swim** (ssᵘim) *v* nadar

swimmer (*ssᵘi*-mö) *n* nadador *m*

swimming (*ssᵘi*-ming) *n* natación *f*; ~ **pool** piscina *f*

swimming-trunks (*ssᵘi*-ming-trangkss) *n* calzón de baño

swim-suit (*ssᵘim*-ssuut) *n* traje de baño

swindle (*ssᵘin*-döl) *v* estafar; *n* estafa *f*

swindler (*ssᵘin*-dlö) *n* estafador *m*

swing (ss^{u}ing) *n* columpio *m*

*swing (ss^{u}ing) *v* oscilar; columpiar-se

Swiss (ss^{u}iss) *adj* suizo

switch (ss^{u}ich) *n* interruptor *m*; *v* cambiar; ~ off apagar; ~ on *encender

switchboard (ss^{u}ich-bood) *n* cuadro de distribución

Switzerland (ss^{u}it-ssö-lönd) Suiza *f*

sword (ssood) *n* espada *f*

swum (ss^{u}am) *v* (pp swim)

syllable (ssi-lö-böl) *n* sílaba *f*

symbol (ssim-böl) *n* símbolo *m*

sympathetic (ssim-pö-zê-tik) *adj* cordial, compasivo

sympathy (ssim-pö-zi) *n* simpatía *f*; compasión *f*

symphony (ssim-fö-ni) *n* sinfonía *f*

symptom (ssim-töm) *n* síntoma *m*

synagogue (ssi-nö-ghogh) *n* sinagoga *f*

synonym (ssi-nö-nim) *n* sinónimo *m*

synthetic (ssin-zê-tik) *adj* sintético

syphon (ssai-fön) *n* sifón *m*

Syria (ssi-ri-ö) Siria *f*

Syrian (ssi-ri-ön) *adj* sirio

syringe (ssi-*rind*ʒ) *n* jeringa *f*

syrup (ssi-röp) *n* jarabe *m*

system (ssi-sstöm) *n* sistema *m*; decimal ~ sistema decimal

systematic (ssi-sstö-*mæ*-tik) *adj* sistemático

T

table (*tei*-böl) *n* mesa *f*; tabla *f*; ~ of contents índice *m*; ~ tennis tenis de mesa

table-cloth (*tei*-böl-kloz) *n* mantel *m*

tablespoon (*tei*-böl-sspuun) *n* cuchara *f*

tablet (*tæ*-blit) *n* pastilla *f*

taboo (tö-*buu*) *n* tabú *m*

tactics (*tæk*-tikss) *pl* táctica *f*

tag (tægh) *n* etiqueta *f*

tail (teil) *n* cola *f*

tail-light (*teil*-lait) *n* farol trasero

tailor (*tei*-lö) *n* sastre *m*

tailor-made (*tei*-lö-meid) *adj* hecho a la medida

*take (teik) *v* coger; tomar; llevar; comprender, *entender; ~ away quitar; llevarse; ~ off despegar; ~ out sacar; ~ over encargarse de; ~ place *tener lugar; ~ up ocupar

take-off (*tei*-kof) *n* despegue *m*

tale (teil) *n* cuento *m*

talent (*tæ*-lönt) *n* talento *m*

talented (*tæ*-lön-tid) *adj* dotado

talk (took) *v* hablar; *n* conversación *f*

talkative (*too*-kö-tiv) *adj* locuaz

tall (tool) *adj* alto

tame (teim) *adj* manso, domesticado; *v* domesticar

tampon (*tæm*-pön) *n* tapón *m*

tangerine (tæn-dʒö-*riin*) *n* mandarina *f*

tangible (*tæn*-dʒi-böl) *adj* tangible

tank (tængk) *n* tanque *m*

tanker (*tæng*-kö) *n* buque cisterna

tanned (tænd) *adj* tostado

tap (tæp) *n* grifo *m*; golpecito *m*; *v* golpear

tape (teip) *n* cinta *f*; adhesive ~ cinta adhesiva; esparadrapo *m*

tape-measure (*teip*-mê-ʒö) *n* centímetro *m*, cinta métrica

tape-recorder (*teip*-ri-koo-dö) *n* magnetófono *m*

tapestry (*tæ*-pi-sstri) *n* tapiz *m*

tar (taa) *n* brea *f*

target (*taa*-ghit) *n* objetivo *m*, blanco *m*

tariff (*tæ*-rif) *n* arancel *m*

tarpaulin (taa-*poo*-lin) *n* lona impermeable

task (taassk) *n* tarea *f*

taste (teisst) *n* gusto *m*; *v* *saber a; *probar

tasteless (teisst-löss) *adj* insípido

tasty (tei-ssti) *adj* rico, sabroso

taught (toot) *v* (p, pp teach)

tavern (tæ-vön) *n* taberna *f*

tax (tækss) *n* impuesto *m*; *v* *imponer contribuciones

taxation (tæk-ssei-fön) *n* impuesto *m*

tax-free (tækss-frii) *adj* libre de impuestos

taxi (tæk-ssi) *n* taxi *m*; ~ **rank** parada de taxis; ~ **stand** *Am* parada de taxis

taxi-driver (tæk-ssi-drai-vö) *n* taxista *m*

taxi-meter (tæk-ssi-mii-tö) *n* taxímetro *m*

tea (tii) *n* té *m*; merienda *f*

***teach** (tiich) *v* enseñar

teacher (tii-chö) *n* profesor *m*, maestro *m*; profesora *f*; institutor *m*

teachings (tii-chings) *pl* enseñanza *f*

tea-cloth (tii-kloz) *n* trapo de cocina

teacup (tii-kap) *n* taza de té

team (tiim) *n* equipo *m*

teapot (tii-pot) *n* tetera *f*

tear¹ (tiö) *n* lágrima *f*

tear² (téö) *n* rasgón *m*; ***tear** *v* desgarrar

tear-jerker (tiö-dʒöö-kö) *n* cuplé lacrimoso

tease (tiis) *v* tomar el pelo

tea-set (tii ssöt) *n* juego de té

tea-shop (tii-fop) *n* salón de té

teaspoon (tii-sspuun) *n* cucharilla *f*

teaspoonful (tii-sspuun-ful) *n* cucharadita *f*

technical (ték-ni-köl) *adj* técnico

technician (tek-ni-fön) *n* técnico *m*

technique (tek-niik) *n* técnica *f*

technology (tek-no-lö-dʒi) *n* tecnolo-

gía *f*

teenager (tii-nei-dʒö) *n* jovencito *m*

teetotaller (tii-tou-tö-lö) *n* abstemio *m*

telegram (té-li-ghræm) *n* telegrama *m*

telegraph (té-li-ghraaf) *v* telegrafiar

telepathy (ti-lé-pö-zi) *n* telepatía *f*

telephone (té-li-foun) *n* teléfono *m*; ~ **book** *Am* listín telefónico, guía telefónica; ~ **booth** cabina telefónica; ~ **call** llamada telefónica; ~ **directory** guía telefónica, listín telefónico; directorio telefónico *Me*; ~ **exchange** central telefónica; ~ **operator** telefonista *f*

telephonist (ti-lé-fö-nisst) *n* telefonista *f*

television (té-li-vi-ʒön) *n* televisión *f*; ~ **set** televisor *m*

telex (té-lêkss) *n* télex *m*

***tell** (têl) *v* *decir; *contar

temper (têm-pö) *n* cólera *f*

temperature (têm-prö-chö) *n* temperatura *f*

tempest (têm-pisst) *n* tempestad *f*

temple (têm-pöl) *n* templo *m*; sien *f*

temporary (têm-pö-rö-ri) *adj* provisional, temporal

tempt (têmpt) *v* *tentar

temptation (têmp-tei-fön) *n* tentación *f*

ten (tên) *num* diez

tenant (tê-nönt) *n* inquilino *m*

tend (tênd) *v* *tender a; cuidar de; ~ **to** *tender a

tendency (tên-dön-ssi) *n* inclinación *f*, tendencia *f*

tender (tên-dö) *adj* tierno, delicado

tendon (tên-dön) *n* tendón *m*

tennis (tê-niss) *n* tenis *m*; ~ **shoes** zapatos de tenis

tennis-court (tê-niss-koot) *n* campo de tenis, cancha *f*

tense (tênss) *adj* tenso

tension (tên-ʃön) *n* tensión *m*
tent (tênt) *n* tienda *f*
tenth (tênz) *num* décimo
tepid (tê-pid) *adj* tibio
term (tööm) *n* término *m*; período *m*, plazo *m*; condición *f*
terminal (töö-mi-nöl) *n* estación terminal
terrace (tê-röss) *n* terraza *f*
terrain (tê-*rein*) *n* terreno *m*
terrible (tê-ri-böl) *adj* tremendo, terrible, pésimo
terrific (tö-*ri*-fik) *adj* tremendo
terrify (tê-ri-fai) *v* aterrorizar; **terrifying** aterrador
territory (tê-ri-tö-ri) *n* territorio *m*
terror (tê-rö) *n* terror *m*
terrorism (tê-rö-ri-söm) *n* terrorismo *m*, terror *m*
terrorist (tê-rö-risst) *n* terrorista *m*
terylene (tê-rö-liin) *n* terilene *m*
test (tèsst) *n* prueba *f*, ensayo *m*; *v* *probar, ensayar
testify (tê-ssti-fai) *v* testimoniar
text (têksst) *n* texto *m*
textbook (têkss-buk) *n* libro de texto
textile (têk-sstail) *n* textil *m*
texture (têkss-chö) *n* textura *f*
Thai (tai) *adj* tailandés
Thailand (tai-lænd) Tailandia *f*
than (ðæn) *conj* que
thank (zæ̃ngk) *v* *agradecer; ~ you gracias
thankful (zæ̃ngk-föl) *adj* agradecido
that (ðæt) *adj* aquel, ese; *pron* aquél, eso; que; *conj* que
thaw (zoo) *v* descongelarse; *n* deshielo *m*
the (ðö, ði) *art* el *art*; **the ... the** cuanto más ... más
theatre (ziö-tö) *n* teatro *m*
theft (zêft) *n* robo *m*
their (ðêö) *adj* su
them (ðêm) *pron* les

theme (ziim) *n* tema *m*, sujeto *m*
themselves (ðöm-*ssêlvs*) *pron* se; ellos mismos
then (ðên) *adv* entonces; después; en tal caso
theology (zi-*o*-lö-dʒi) *n* teología *f*
theoretical (zi*ö*-*rê*-ti-köl) *adj* teórico
theory (zi*ö*-ri) *n* teoría *f*
therapy (zê-rö-pi) *n* terapia *f*
there (ðêö) *adv* allí; hacia allá
therefore (ðêö-foo) *conj* por lo tanto
thermometer (zö-*mo*-mi-tö) *n* termómetro *m*
thermostat (zöö-mö-sstæt) *n* termostato *m*
these (ðiis) *adj* éstos
thesis (zii-ssiss) *n* (pl theses) tesis *f*
they (ðei) *pron* ellos
thick (zik) *adj* espeso; denso
thicken (zi-kön) *v* espesar
thickness (zik-nöss) *n* espesor *m*
thief (ziif) *n* (pl thieves) ladrón *m*
thigh (zai) *n* muslo *m*
thimble (zim-böl) *n* dedal *m*
thin (zin) *adj* delgado; flaco
thing (zing) *n* cosa *f*
think (zingk) *v* *pensar; reflexionar; ~ of *pensar en; *recordar; ~ over considerar
thinker (zing-kö) *n* pensador *m*
third (zööd) *num* tercero
thirst (zöösst) *n* sed *f*
thirsty (zöö-ssti) *adj* sediento
thirteen (zöö-*tiin*) *num* trece
thirteenth (zöö-*tiinz*) *num* treceno
thirtieth (zöö-ti-öz) *num* treintavo
thirty (zöö-ti) *num* treinta
this (ðiss) *adj* este, esto; *pron* éste
thistle (zi-ssöl) *n* cardo *m*
thorn (zoon) *n* espina *f*
thorough (za-rö) *adj* minucioso
thoroughbred (za-rö-brêd) *adj* purasangre
thoroughfare (za-rö-fêö) *n* ruta prin-

cipal, arteria principal

those (ðous) *adj* aquellos; *pron* aquéllos

though (ðou) *conj* si bien, aunque;
adv sin embargo

thought[1] (zoot) *v* (p, pp think)

thought[2] (zoot) *n* pensamiento *m*

thoughtful (zoot-föl) *adj* pensativo;
atento

thousand (zau-sönd) *num* mil

thread (zrêd) *n* hilo *m*; *v* enhebrar

threadbare (zrêd-bêº) *adj* gastado

threat (zrêt) *n* amenaza *f*

threaten (zrê-tön) *v* amenazar;
threatening amenazador

three (zrii) *num* tres

three-quarter (zrii-k"oo-tö) *adj* trcs
cuartos

threshold (zrê-ʃould) *n* umbral *m*

threw (zruu) *v* (p throw)

thrifty (zrif-ti) *adj* económico

throat (zrout) *n* garganta *f*

throne (zroun) *n* trono *m*

through (zruu) *prcp* a través de

throughout (zruu-aut) *adv* por todas
partes

throw (zrou) *n* lanzamiento *m*

*****throw** (zrou) *v* tirar, arrojar

thrush (zraʃ) *n* tordo *m*

thumb (zam) *n* pulgar *m*

thumbtack (zam-tæk) *nAm* chinche *f*

thump (zamp) *v* golpear

thunder (zan-dö) *n* trueno *m*; *v* *tronar

thunderstorm (zan-dö-sstoom) *n* tronada *f*

thundery (zan-dö-ri) *adj* tormentoso

Thursday (zöös-di) jueves *m*

thus (ðass) *adv* así

thyme (taim) *n* tomillo *m*

tick (tik) *n* señal *f*; ~ **off** señalar

ticket (ti-kit) *n* billete *m*; multa *f*;
boleto *mMe*; ~ **collector** revisor
m; ~ **machine** máquina de billetes

tickle (ti-köl) *v* cosquillear

tide (taid) *n* marea *f*; **high** ~ pleamar
f; **low** ~ bajamar *f*

tidings (tai-dings) *pl* noticias *fpl*

tidy (tai-di) *adj* aseado; ~ **up** arreglar

tie (tai) *v* anudar, atar; *n* corbata *f*

tiger (tai-ghö) *n* tigre *m*

tight (tait) *adj* estrecho; angosto,
apretado; *adv* fuertemente

tighten (tai-tön) *v* estrechar, *apretar; estrecharse

tights (taitss) *pl* traje de malla

tile (tail) *n* azulejo *m*; teja *f*

till (til) *prep* hasta; *conj* hasta que

timber (tim-bö) *n* madera de construcción

time (taim) *n* tiempo *m*; vez *f*; **all
the** ~ continuamente; **in** ~ a tiempo; ~ **of arrival** hora de llegada; ~
of departure hora de salida

time-saving (taim-ssei-ving) *adj* que
economiza ticmpo

timetable (taim-tei-böl) *n* horario *m*

timid (ti-mid) *adj* tímido

timidity (ti-mi-dö-ti) *n* timidez *f*

tin (tin) *n* estaño *m*; lata *f*; **tinned
food** conservas *fpl*

tinfoil (tin-foil) *n* papel de estaño

tin-opener (ti-nou-pö-nö) *n* abrelatas
m

tiny (tai-ni) *adj* menudo

tip (tip) *n* punta *f*; propina *f*

tire[1] (taiº) *n* neumático *m*; llanta
fMe

tire[2] (taiº) *v* cansar

tired (taiºd) *adj* cansado; ~ **of** harto
dc

tissue (ti-ʃuu) *n* tejido *m*; pañuelo de
papel

title (tai-töl) *n* título *m*

to (tuu) *prep* hasta; a, para, en, hacia

toad (toud) *n* sapo *m*

toadstool (toud-sstuul) *n* hongo *m*

toast (tousst) *n* pan tostado; brindis

m

tobacco (tö-*bæ*-kou) *n* (pl ~s) tabaco *m*; ~ **pouch** petaca *f*

tobacconist (tö-*bæ*-kö-nisst) *n* estanquero *m*; **tobacconist's** estanco *m*

today (tö-*dei*) *adv* hoy

toddler (*tod*-lö) *n* párvulo *m*

toe (tou) *n* dedo del pie

toffee (*to*-fi) *n* caramelo *m*

together (tö-*ghê*-ðö) *adv* juntos

toilet (*toi*-löt) *n* retrete *m*; ~ **case** neceser *m*

toilet-paper (*toi*-löt-pei-pö) *n* papel higiénico

toiletry (*toi*-lö-tri) *n* artículos de tocador

token (*tou*-kön) *n* señal *f*; prueba *f*; ficha *f*

told (tould) *v* (p, pp tell)

tolerable (*to*-lö-rö-böl) *adj* tolerable

toll (toul) *n* peaje *m*

tomato (tö-*maa*-tou) *n* (pl ~es) tomate *m*; jitomate *mMe*

tomb (tuum) *n* tumba *f*

tombstone (*tuum*-sstoun) *n* lápida *f*

tomorrow (tö-*mo*-rou) *adv* mañana

ton (tan) *n* tonelada *f*

tone (toun) *n* tono *m*; timbre *m*

tongs (tongs) *pl* tenazas *f*

tongue (tang) *n* lengua *f*

tonic (*to*-nik) *n* tónico *m*

tonight (tö-*nait*) *adv* esta noche

tonsilitis (ton-ssö-*lai*-tiss) *n* amigdalitis *f*

tonsils (*ton*-ssöls) *pl* amígdalas *fpl*

too (tuu) *adv* demasiado; también

took (tuk) *v* (p take)

tool (tuul) *n* herramienta *f*; ~ **kit** bolsa de herramientas

tooth (tuuz) *n* (pl teeth) diente *m*

toothache (*tuu*-zeik) *n* dolor de muelas

toothbrush (*tuuz*-braʃ) *n* cepillo de dientes

toothpaste (*tuuz*-peisst) *n* pasta dentífrica

toothpick (*tuuz*-pik) *n* palillo *m*

toothpowder (*tuuz*-pau-dö) *n* polvo para los dientes

top (top) *n* cima *f*; parte superior; tapa *f*; superior; **on** ~ **of** encima de; ~ **side** parte superior

topcoat (*top*-kout) *n* sobretodo *m*

topic (*to*-pik) *n* asunto *m*

topical (*to*-pi-köl) *adj* actual

torch (tooch) *n* antorcha *f*; linterna *f*

torment[1] (too-*mênt*) *v* atormentar

torment[2] (*too*-mênt) *n* tormento *m*

torture (*too*-chö) *n* tortura *f*; *v* torturar

toss (toss) *v* echar

tot (tot) *n* niño pequeño

total (*tou*-töl) *adj* total; completo, absoluto; *n* total *m*

totalitarian (tou-tæ-li-*tê*ᵒ-ri-ön) *adj* totalitario

totalizator (*tou*-tö-lai-sei-tö) *n* totalizador *m*

touch (tach) *v* tocar; *concernir; *n* contacto *m*, toque *m*; tacto *m*

touching (*ta*-ching) *adj* conmovedor

tough (taf) *adj* duro

tour (tuᵒ) *n* vuelta *f*

tourism (*tu*ᵒ-ri-söm) *n* turismo *m*

tourist (*tu*ᵒ-risst) *n* turista *m*; ~ **class** clase turista; ~ **office** oficina para turistas

tournament (*tu*ᵒ-nö-mönt) *n* torneo *m*

tow (tou) *v* remolcar

towards (tö-ᵘ*oods*) *prep* hacia; para con

towel (*tau*ᵒl) *n* toalla *f*

towelling (*tau*ᵒ-ling) *n* tela para toallas

tower (*tau*ᵒ) *n* torre *f*

town (taun) *n* ciudad *f*; ~ **centre** centro de la ciudad; ~ **hall** ayunta-

miento *m*
townspeople (*tauns*-pii-pöl) *pl* ciuda-
danos *mpl*
toxic (*tok*-ssik) *adj* tóxico
toy (toi) *n* juguete *m*
toyshop (*toi*-ʃop) *n* juguetería *f*
trace (treiss) *n* huella *f*; *v* rastrear
track (træk) *n* vía *f*; pista *f*
tractor (*træk*-tö) *n* tractor *m*
trade (treid) *n* comercio *m*; oficio *m*;
v comerciar
trademark (*treid*-maak) *n* marca de fábrica
trader (*trei*-dö) *n* comerciante *m*
tradesman (*treids*-mön) *n* (pl -men)
tendero *m*
trade-union (treid *yuu*-nyön) *n* sindicato *m*
tradition (trö-*di*-ʃön) *n* tradición *f*
traditional (trö-*di*-ʃö-nöl) *adj* tradicional
traffic (*træ*-fik) *n* tránsito *m*; ~ **jam**
embotellamiento *m*; ~ **light** semáforo *m*
trafficator (*træ*-fi-kei-tö) *n* indicador
m
tragedy (*træ*-dʒö-di) *n* tragedia *f*
tragic (*træ*-dʒik) *adj* trágico
trail (treil) *n* rastro *m*, sendero *m*
trailer (*trei*-lö) *n* remolque *m*; *nAm*
caravana *f*
train (trein) *n* tren *m*; *v* amaestrar,
entrenar; **stopping** ~ tren de cercanías; **through** ~ tren directo; ~
ferry transbordador de trenes
training (*trei*-ning) *n* entrenamiento
m
trait (treit) *n* rasgo *m*
traitor (*trei*-tö) *n* traidor *m*
tram (træm) *n* tranvía *m*
tramp (træmp) *n* vagabundo *m*; *v* vagabundear
tranquil (*træng*-kᵘil) *adj* tranquilo
tranquillizer (*træng*-kᵘi-lai-sö) *n* cal-

mante *m*
transaction (træn-*sæk*-ʃön) *n* transacción *f*
transatlantic (træn-söt-*læn*-tik) *adj*
transatlántico
transfer (trænss-*föö*) *v* *transferir
transform (trænss-*foom*) *v* transformar
transformer (trænss-*foo*-mö) *n* transformador *m*
transition (træn-*ssi*-ʃön) *n* transición *f*
translate (trænss-*leit*) *v* *traducir
translation (trænss-*lei*-ʃön) *n* traducción *f*
translator (trænss-*lei*-tö) *n* traductor
m
transmission (træns-*mi*-ʃön) *n* transmisión *f*
transmit (træns-*mit*) *v* transmitir
transmitter (træns-*mi*-tö) *n* emisor *m*
transparent (træn-*sspéᵒ*-rönt) *adj*
transparente
transport[1] (*træn*-sspoot) *n* transporte
m
transport[2] (træn-*sspoot*) *v* transportar
transportation (træn-sspoo-*tei*-ʃön) *n*
transporte *m*
trap (træp) *n* trampa *f*
trash (træʃ) *n* basura *f*
travel (*træ*-völ) *v* viajar; ~ **agency**
agencia de viajes; ~ **agent** agente
de viajes; ~ **insurance** seguro de
viaje; **travelling expenses** gastos
de viaje
traveller (*træ*-vö-lö) *n* viajero *m*;
traveller's cheque cheque de viajero
tray (trei) *n* bandeja *f*; charola *fMe*
treason (*trii*-sön) *n* traición *f*
treasure (trê-ʒö) *n* tesoro *m*
treasurer (trê-ʒö-rö) *n* tesorero *m*
treasury (trê-ʒö-ri) *n* Tesorería *f*
treat (triit) *v* tratar
treatment (*triit*-mönt) *n* tratamiento

m

treaty (*trii*-ti) *n* tratado *m*

tree (trii) *n* árbol *m*

tremble (*trêm*-böl) *v* *temblar; vibrar

tremendous (tri-*mên*-döss) *adj* tremendo

trespass (*trêss*-pöss) *v* infringir

trespasser (*trêss*-pö-ssö) *n* intruso *m*

trial (trai⁶l) *n* proceso *m*; prueba *f*

triangle (*trai*-æng-ghöl) *n* triángulo *m*

triangular (trai-*æng*-ghyu-lö) *adj* triangular

tribe (traib) *n* tribu *m*

tributary (*tri*-byu-tö-ri) *n* afluente *m*

tribute (*tri*-byuut) *n* homenaje *m*

trick (trik) *n* truco *m*

trigger (*tri*-ghö) *n* gatillo *m*

trim (trim) *v* recortar

trip (trip) *n* excursión *f*, viaje *m*

triumph (*trai*-ömf) *n* triunfo *m*; *v* triunfar

triumphant (trai-*am*-fönt) *adj* triunfante

trolley-bus (*tro*-li-bass) *n* trolebús *m*

troops (truupss) *pl* tropas *fpl*

tropical (*tro*-pi-köl) *adj* tropical

tropics (*tro*-pikss) *pl* trópicos *mpl*

trouble (tra-böl) *n* preocupación *f*, molestia *f*; *v* molestar

troublesome (*tra*-böl-ssöm) *adj* molesto

trousers (*trau*-sös) *pl* pantalones *mpl*

trout (traut) *n* (pl ~) trucha *f*

truck (trak) *nAm* camión *m*

true (truu) *adj* verdadero; real, auténtico; leal, fiel

trumpet (*tram*-pit) *n* trompeta *f*

trunk (trangk) *n* baúl *m*; tronco *m*; *nAm* portaequipajes *m*; **trunks** *pl* pantalones de gimnasia

trunk-call (*trangk*-kool) *n* conferencia interurbana

trust (trasst) *v* confiar en; *n* confianza *f*

trustworthy (*trasst*-ᵘöö-ði) *adj* confiable

truth (truuz) *n* verdad *f*

truthful (*truuz*-föl) *adj* verídico

try (trai) *v* intentar; *esforzarse; *n* tentativa *f*; ~ **on** *probarse

tube (tyuub) *n* tubo *m*

tuberculosis (tyuu-böö-kyu-*lou*-ssiss) *n* tuberculosis *f*

Tuesday (*tyuus*-di) martes *m*

tug (tagh) *v* remolcar; *n* remolcador *m*; estirón *m*

tuition (tyuu-*i*-ʃön) *n* enseñanza *f*

tulip (*tyuu*-lip) *n* tulipán *m*

tumbler (*tam*-blö) *n* vaso *m*

tumour (*tyuu*-mö) *n* tumor *m*

tuna (*tyuu*-nö) *n* (pl ~, ~s) atún *m*

tune (tyuun) *n* tonada *f*; ~ **in** sintonizar

tuneful (*tyuun*-föl) *adj* melodioso

tunic (*tyuu*-nik) *n* túnica *f*

Tunisia (tyuu-*ni*-si-ö) Túnez *m*

Tunisian (tyuu-*ni*-si-ön) *adj* tunecino

tunnel (*ta*-nöl) *n* túnel *m*

turbine (*töö*-bain) *n* turbina *f*

turbojet (töö-bou-*dʒêt*) *n* avión turborreactor

Turk (töök) *n* turco *m*

Turkey (*töö*-ki) Turquía *f*

turkey (*töö*-ki) *n* pavo *m*

Turkish (*töö*-kiʃ) *adj* turco; ~ **bath** baño turco

turn (töön) *v* girar; *volver; *n* cambio *m*, vuelta *f*; curva *f*; turno *m*; ~ **back** *volver; ~ **down** rechazar; ~ **into** *convertirse en; ~ **off** *cerrar; ~ **on** *encender; abrir; ~ **over** *volver; ~ **round** *volver; *volverse

turning (*töö*-ning) *n* vuelta *f*

turning-point (*töö*-ning-point) *n* punto decisivo

turnover (*töö*-nou-vö) *n* volumen de transacciones; ~ **tax** impuesto sobre la venta

turnpike (*töön*-paik) *nAm* autopista de peaje

turpentine (*töö*-pön-tain) *n* trementina *f*

turtle (*töö*-töl) *n* tortuga *f*

tutor (*tyuu*-tö) *n* maestro particular; tutor *m*

tuxedo (tak-*ssii*-dou) *nAm* (pl ~s, ~es) smoking *m*

tweed (t^uiid) *n* lana tweed

tweezers (t^u*ii*-sös) *pl* pinzas *fpl*

twelfth (t^uêlfz) *num* duodécimo

twelve (t^uêlv) *num* doce

twentieth (t^u*ên*-ti-öz) *num* vigésimo

twenty (t^u*ên*-ti) *num* veinte

twice (t^uaiss) *adv* dos veces

twig (t^uigh) *n* ramita *f*

twilight (t^u*ai*-lait) *n* crepúsculo *m*

twine (t^uain) *n* trenza *f*

twins (t^uins) *pl* gemelos *mpl*; **twin beds** camas gemelas

twist (t^uisst) *v* *torcer; *n* torsión *f*

two (tuu) *num* dos

two-piece (tuu-*piiss*) *adj* de dos piezas

type (taip) *v* escribir a máquina, mecanografiar; *n* tipo *m*

typewriter (*taip*-rai-tö) *n* máquina de escribir

typewritten (*taip*-ri-tön) mecanografiado

typhoid (*tai*-foid) *n* tifus *m*

typical (*ti*-pi-köl) *adj* característico, típico

typist (*tai*-pisst) *n* dactilógrafa *f*

tyrant (*tai*^ö rönt) *n* tirano *m*

tyre (tai^ö) *n* neumático *m*; ~ **pressure** presión del neumático

U

ugly (*a*-ghli) *adj* feo

ulcer (*al*-ssö) *n* úlcera *f*

ultimate (*al*-ti-möt) *adj* último

ultraviolet (al-trö-*vai*^ö-löt) *adj* ultravioleta

umbrella (am-*brê*-lö) *n* paraguas *m*

umpire (*am*-pai^ö) *n* árbitro *m*

unable (a-*nei*-böl) *adj* incapaz

unacceptable (a-nök-*ssêp*-tö-böl) *adj* inaceptable

unaccountable (a-nö-*kaun*-tö-böl) *adj* inexplicable

unaccustomed (a-nö-*ka*-sstömd) *adj* desacostumbrado

unanimous (yuu-*næ*-ni-möss) *adj* unánime

unanswered (a-*naan*-ssöd) *adj* sin contestación

unauthorized (a-*noo*-zö-raisd) *adj* desautorizado

unavoidable (a-nö-*voi*-dö-böl) *adj* inevitable

unaware (a-nö-^u*ê*^ö) *adj* inconsciente

unbearable (an-*bê*^ö-rö-böl) *adj* insufrible

unbreakable (an-*brei*-kö-böl) *adj* irrompible

unbroken (an-*brou*-kön) *adj* intacto

unbutton (an-*ba*-tön) *v* desabotonar

uncertain (an-*ssöö*-tön) *adj* incierto

uncle (*ang*-köl) *n* tío *m*

unclean (an-*kliin*) *adj* sucio

uncomfortable (an-*kam*-tö-tö-böl) *adj* incómodo

uncommon (an-*ko*-mön) *adj* insólito, raro

unconditional (an-kön-*di*-fö-nöl) *adj* incondicional

unconscious (an-*kon*-föss) *adj* inconsciente

uncork (an-*kook*) v descorchar
uncover (an-*ka*-vö) v destapar
uncultivated (an-*kal*-ti-vei-tid) adj inculto
under (*an*-dö) prep debajo de, bajo
undercurrent (*an*-dö-ka-rönt) n resaca f
underestimate (an-dö-*rê*-ssti-meit) v subestimar
underground (*an*-dö-ghraund) adj subterráneo; n metro m
underline (an-dö-*lain*) v subrayar
underneath (an-dö-*niiz*) adv debajo
undershirt (*an*-dö-ʃööt) n camiseta f
undersigned (*an*-dö-ssaind) n suscrito m
*understand (an-dö-*sstænd*) v comprender
understanding (an-dö-*sstæn*-ding) n comprensión m
*undertake (an-dö-*teik*) v emprender
undertaking (an-dö-*tei*-king) n empresa f
underwater (*an*-dö-ᵘoo-tö) adj subacuático
underwear (*an*-dö-ᵘêô) n ropa interior
undesirable (an-di-*sai*ô-rö-böl) adj indeseable
*undo (an-*duu*) v desatar
undoubtedly (an-*dau*-tid-li) adv sin duda
undress (an-*drêss*) v desnudarse
undulating (*an*-dyu-lei-ting) adj ondulante
unearned (a-*nöönd*) adj inmerecido
uneasy (a-*nii*-si) adj inquieto
uneducated (a-*nê*-dyu-kei-tid) adj inculto
unemployed (a-nim-*ploid*) adj desocupado
unemployment (a-nim-*ploi*-mönt) n desempleo m
unequal (a-*nii*-kᵘöl) adj desigual

uneven (a-*nii*-vön) adj desigual; irregular
unexpected (a-nik-*sspêk*-tid) adj imprevisto, inesperado
unfair (an-*fêô*) adj ímprobo, injusto
unfaithful (an-*feiz*-föl) adj infiel
unfamiliar (an-fö-*mil*-yö) adj desconocido
unfasten (an-*faa*-ssön) v desatar
unfavourable (an-*fei*-vö-rö-böl) adj desfavorable
unfit (an-*fit*) adj inadecuado
unfold (an-*fould*) v *desplegar
unfortunate (an-*foo*-chö-nöt) adj desafortunado
unfortunately (an-*foo*-chö-nöt-li) adv por desgracia, desgraciadamente
unfriendly (an-*frênd*-li) adj poco amistoso
unfurnished (an-*föö*-niʃt) adj desamueblado
ungrateful (an-*ghreit*-föl) adj ingrato
unhappy (an-*hæ*-pi) adj desdichado
unhealthy (an-*hêl*-zi) adj insalubre
unhurt (an-*hööt*) adj ileso
uniform (*yuu*-ni-foom) n uniforme m; adj uniforme
unimportant (a-nim-*poo*-tönt) adj insignificante
uninhabitable (a-nin-*hæ*-bi-tö-böl) adj inhabitable
uninhabited (a-nin-*hæ*-bi-tid) adj inhabitado
unintentional (a-nin-*tên*-ʃö-nöl) adj no intencional
union (*yuu*-nyön) n unión f; liga f, confederación f
unique (yuu-*niik*) adj único
unit (*yuu*-nit) n unidad f
unite (yuu-*nait*) v unir
United States (yuu-*nai*-tid ssteitss) Estados Unidos
unity (*yuu*-nö-ti) n unidad f
universal (yuu-ni-*vöö*-ssöl) adj gene-

ral, universal

universe (yuu-ni-vööss) n universo m

university (yuu-ni-vöö-ssö-ti) n universidad f

unjust (an-dʒasst) adj injusto

unkind (an-kaind) adj desagradable, arisco

unknown (an-noun) adj desconocido

unlawful (an-loo-föl) adj ilegal

unlearn (an-löön) v desacostumbrar

unless (ön-léss) conj a menos que

unlike (an-laik) adj diferente

unlikely (an-lai-kli) adj improbable

unlimited (an-li-mi-tid) adj ilimitado

unload (an-loud) v descargar

unlock (an-lok) v abrir

unlucky (an-la-ki) adj desafortunado

unnecessary (an-nê-ssö-ssö-ri) adj innecesario

unoccupied (a-no-kyu-paid) adj desocupado

unofficial (a-nö-fi-jöl) adj extraoficial

unpack (an-pæk) v desempaquetar

unpleasant (an-plê-sönt) adj desagradable; antipático

unpopular (an-po-pyu-lö) adj impopular

unprotected (an-prö-têk-tid) adj indefenso

unqualified (an-kuo-li-faid) adj incompetente

unreal (an-riöl) adj irreal

unreasonable (an-rii-so-no-bol) adj irrazonable

unreliable (an-ri-lai-ö-böl) adj no confiable

unrest (an-rêsst) n desasosiego m; inquietud f

unsafe (an-sseif) adj inseguro

unsatisfactory (an-ssæ-tiss-fæk-tö-ri) adj poco satisfactorio

unscrew (an-sskruu) v destornillar

unselfish (an-ssêl-fij) adj desinteresado

unskilled (an-sskild) adj no especializado

unsound (an-ssaund) adj enfermizo

unstable (an-sstei-böl) adj inestable

unsteady (an-sstê-di) adj vacilante, inestable

unsuccessful (an-ssök-ssêss-föl) adj fracasado

unsuitable (an-ssuu-tö-böl) adj inadecuado

unsurpassed (an-ssö-paasst) adj sin igual

untidy (an-tai-di) adj desaliñado

untie (an-tai) v desatar

until (ön-til) prep hasta

untrue (an-truu) adj falso

untrustworthy (an-trasst-vöö-ði) adj indigno de confianza

unusual (an-yuu-ʒu-öl) adj inusitado, insólito

unwell (an-uêl) adj indispuesto

unwilling (an-ui-ling) adj desinclinado

unwise (an-uais) adj imprudente

unwrap (an-ræp) v *desenvolver

up (ap) adv hacia arriba, arriba

upholster (ap-houl-sstö) v tapizar

upkeep (ap-kiip) n manutención f

uplands (ap-lönds) pl altiplano m

upon (ö-pon) prep sobre

upper (a-pö) adj superior

upright (ap-rait) adj derecho; adv de pie

upset (ap-ssêt) v trastornar; adj trastornado

upside-down (ap-ssaid-daun) adv al revés

upstairs (ap-sstêös) adv arriba

upstream (ap-sstriim) adv río arriba

upwards (ap-uöds) adv hacia arriba

urban (öö-bön) adj urbano

urge (öödʒ) v estimular; n impulso m

urgency (öö-dʒön-ssi) n urgencia f

urgent (öö-dʒönt) adj urgente

urine (*yuᵒ*-rin) *n* orina *f*

Uruguay (*yuᵒ*-rö-ghᵘai) Uruguay *m*

Uruguayan (yuᵒ-rö-*ghᵘai*-ön) *adj* uruguayo

us (ass) *pron* nosotros

usable (*yuu*-sö-böl) *adj* utilizable

usage (*yuu*-sidʒ) *n* uso *m*

use¹ (yuus) *v* usar; *be used to *estar acostumbrado a; ~ up consumir

use² (yuuss) *n* uso *m*; utilidad *f*; *be of ~ *servir

useful (*yuuss*-föl) *adj* útil

useless (*yuuss*-löss) *adj* inútil

user (*yuu*-sö) *n* usuario *m*

usher (*a*-ʃö) *n* acomodador *m*

usherette (a-ʃö-*rêt*) *n* acomodadora *f*

usual (*yuu*-ʒu-öl) *adj* usual

usually (*yuu*-ʒu-ö-li) *adv* habitualmente

utensil (yuu-*tên*-ssöl) *n* herramienta *f*, utensilio *m*

utility (yuu-*ti*-lö-ti) *n* utilidad *f*

utilize (*yuu*-ti-lais) *v* utilizar

utmost (*at*-mousst) *adj* extremo

utter (*a*-tö) *adj* completo, total; *v* emitir

V

vacancy (*vei*-kön-ssi) *n* vacante *f*

vacant (*vei*-könt) *adj* vacante

vacate (vö-*keit*) *v* vaciar

vacation (vö-*kei*-ʃön) *n* vacaciones *fpl*

vaccinate (*væk*-ssi-neit) *v* vacunar

vaccination (væk-ssi-*nei*-ʃön) *n* vacunación *f*

vacuum (*væ*-kyu-öm) *n* vacío *m*; ~ cleaner aspirador *m*; ~ flask termo *m*

vagrancy (*vei*-ghrön-ssi) *n* vagancia *f*

vague (veigh) *adj* vago

vain (vein) *adj* vanidoso; vano; in ~

inútilmente, en vano

valet (*væ*-lit) *n* ayuda de cámara

valid (*væ*-lid) *adj* vigente

valley (*væ*-li) *n* valle *m*

valuable (*væ*-lyu-böl) *adj* valioso; valuables *pl* objetos de valor

value (*væ*-lyuu) *n* valor *m*; *v* valuar

valve (vælv) *n* válvula *f*

van (væn) *n* camioneta *f*

vanilla (vö-*ni*-lö) *n* vainilla *f*

vanish (*væ*-niʃ) *v* *desaparecer

vapour (*vei*-pö) *n* vapor *m*

variable (*vêᵒ*-ri-ö-böl) *adj* variable

variation (vêᵒ-ri-*ei*-ʃön) *n* variación *f*; cambio *m*

varied (*vêᵒ*-rid) *adj* variado

variety (vö-*rai*-ö-ti) *n* variedad *f*; ~ show espectáculo de variedades; ~ theatre teatro de variedades

various (*vêᵒ*-ri-öss) *adj* varios

varnish (*vaa*-niʃ) *n* barniz *m*; *v* barnizar

vary (*vêᵒ*-ri) *v* variar; cambiar; *diferir

vase (vaas) *n* vaso *m*

vaseline (*væ*-ssö-liin) *n* vaselina *f*

vast (vaasst) *adj* vasto

vault (voolt) *n* bóveda *f*; caja de caudales

veal (viil) *n* carne de ternera

vegetable (*vê*-dʒö-tö-böl) *n* legumbre *f*

vegetarian (vê-dʒi-*têᵒ*-ri-ön) *n* vegetariano *m*

vegetation (vê-dʒi-*tei*-ʃön) *n* vegetación *f*

vehicle (*vii*-ö-köl) *n* vehículo *m*

veil (veil) *n* velo *m*

vein (vein) *n* vena *f*; varicose ~ varice *f*

velvet (*vêl*-vit) *n* terciopelo *m*

velveteen (vêl-vi-*tiin*) *n* pana *f*

venerable (*vê*-nö-rö-böl) *adj* venerable

venereal disease (vi-*ni*ᵒ-ri-öl di-*siis*) enfermedad venérea

Venezuela (vê-ni-sᵘei-lö) Venezuela *f*

Venezuelan (vê-ni-sᵘei-lön) *adj* venezolano

ventilate (*vên*-ti-leit) *v* ventilar; airear

ventilation (vën-ti-*lei*-ʃon) *n* ventilación *f*; aireo *m*

ventilator (*vên*-ti-lei-tö) *n* ventilador *m*

venture (*vên*-chö) *v* arriesgar

veranda (vö-*ræn*-dö) *n* veranda *f*

verb (vööb) *n* vcrbo *m*

verbal (*vöö*-böl) *adj* verbal

verdict (*vöö*-dikt) *n* sentencia *f*, veredicto *m*

verge (vööd₃) *n* borde *m*

verify (*vê*-ri-fai) *v* verificar

verse (vööss) *n* verso *m*

version (*vöö*-ʃon) *n* versión *f*

versus (*vöö*-ssöss) *prep* contra

vertical (*vöö*-ti-köl) *adj* vertical

vertigo (*vöö*-ti-ghou) *n* vértigo *m*

very (*vê*-ri) *adv* mucho, muy; *adj* preciso, verdadero; extremo

vessel (*vê*-ssöl) *n* embarcación *f*, buque *m*; vasija *f*

vest (vêsst) *n* camiseta *f*; *nAm* chaleco *m*

veterinary surgeon (*vê*-tri-nö-ri *ssöö*-d₃ön) veterinario *m*

via (vaiᵒ) *prep* por

viaduct (*vai*ᵒ-dakt) *n* viaducto *m*

vibrate (vai-*breit*) *v* vibrar

vibration (vai-*brei*-ʃön) *n* vibración *f*

vicar (*vi*-kö) *n* vicario *m*

vicarage (*vi*-kö-rid₃) *n* casa del párroco

vice-president (vaiss-*prê*-si-dönt) *n* vicepresidente *m*

vicinity (vi-*ssi*-nö-ti) *n* vecindad *f*

vicious (*vi*-ʃöss) *adj* vicioso

victim (*vik*-tim) *n* víctima *f*

victory (*vik*-tö-ri) *n* victoria *f*

view (vyuu) *n* vista *f*; parecer *m*, opinión *f*; *v* mirar

view-finder (*vyuu*-fain-dö) *n* visor *m*

vigilant (*vi*-d₃i-lönt) *adj* despierto

villa (*vi*-lö) *n* villa *f*

village (*vi*-lid₃) *n* pueblo *m*

villain (*vi*-lön) *n* villano *m*

vine (vain) *n* vid *f*

vinegar (*vi*-ni-ghö) *n* vinagre *m*

vineyard (*vin*-yöd) *n* viña *f*

vintage (*vin*-tid₃) *n* vendimia *f*

violation (vaiᵒ-*lei*-ʃön) *n* violación *f*

violence (*vai*ᵒ lönss) *n* violencia *f*

violent (*vai*ᵒ-lönt) *adj* violento; impetuoso

violet (*vai*ᵒ-löt) *n* violeta *f*; *adj* morado

violin (vaiᵒ-*lin*) *n* violín *m*

virgin (*vöö*-d₃in) *n* virgen *f*

virtue (*vöö*-chuu) *n* virtud *f*

visa (*vii*-sö) *n* visado *m*

visibility (vi-sö-*bi*-lö-ti) *n* visibilidad *f*

visible (*vi*-sö-böl) *adj* visible

vision (*vi*-ʒön) *n* visión *f*

visit (*vi*-sit) *v* visitar; *n* visita *f*; **visiting hours** horas de visita

visiting-card (*vi*-si-ting-kaad) *n* tarjeta de visita

visitor (*vi*-si-tö) *n* visitante *m*

vital (*vai*-töl) *adj* esencial

vitamin (*vi*-tö-min) *n* vitamina *f*

vivid (*vi*-vid) *adj* vivo

vocabulary (vö-*kæ*-byu-lö-ri) *n* vocabulario *m*; glosario *m*

vocal (*vou*-köl) *adj* vocal

vocalist (*vou*-kö-lisst) *n* vocalista *m*

voice (vöiss) *n* voz *f*

void (void) *adj* nulo

volcano (vol-*kei*-nou) *n* (pl ~es, ~s) volcán *m*

volt (voult) *n* voltio *m*

voltage (*voul*-tid₃) *n* voltaje *m*

volume (*vo*-lyum) *n* volumen *m*; tomo *m*

voluntary (*vo*-lön-tö-ri) *adj* voluntario
volunteer (vo-lön-*tiô*) *n* voluntario *m*
vomit (*vo*-mit) *v* vomitar
vote (vout) *v* votar; *n* voto *m*; votación *f*
voucher (*vau*-chö) *n* recibo *m*, comprobante *m*
vow (vau) *n* voto *m*, juramento *m*; *v* prestar juramento
vowel (vau*ô*l) *n* vocal *f*
voyage (*voi*-id3) *n* viaje *m*
vulgar (*val*-ghö) *adj* vulgar; popular, ordinario
vulnerable (*val*-nö-rö-böl) *adj* vulnerable
vulture (*val*-chö) *n* buitre *m*

W

wade (ᵘeid) *v* vadear
wafer (ᵘ*ei*-fö) *n* oblea *f*
waffle (ᵘ*o*-föl) *n* barquillo *m*
wages (ᵘ*ei*-d3is) *pl* paga *f*
waggon (ᵘ*æ*-ghön) *n* vagón *m*
waist (ᵘeisst) *n* cintura *f*
waistcoat (ᵘ*eiss*-kout) *n* chaleco *m*
wait (ᵘeit) *v* esperar; ~ **on** *verbo servir
waiter (ᵘ*ei*-tö) *n* camarero *m*; mesero *mMe*
waiting *n* espera *f*
waiting-list (ᵘ*ei*-ting-lisst) *n* lista de espera
waiting-room (ᵘ*ei*-ting-ruum) *n* sala de espera
waitress (ᵘ*ei*-triss) *n* camarera *f*; mesera *fMe*
*****wake** (ᵘeik) *v* *despertar; ~ **up** *despertarse
walk (ᵘook) *v* *andar; pasear; *n* caminata *f*; andadura *f*; **walking** a pie
walker (ᵘ*oo*-kö) *n* paseante *m*

walking-stick (ᵘ*oo*-king-sstik) *n* bastón *m*
wall (ᵘool) *n* muro *m*; pared *f*
wallet (ᵘ*o*-lit) *n* cartera *f*
wallpaper (ᵘ*ool*-pei-pö) *n* papel pintado
walnut (ᵘ*ool*-nat) *n* nogal *m*
waltz (ᵘoolss) *n* vals *m*
wander (ᵘ*on*-dö) *v* vagar, *errar
want (ᵘont) *v* *querer; desear; *n* necesidad *f*; carencia *f*, falta *f*
war (ᵘoo) *n* guerra *f*
warden (ᵘ*oo*-dön) *n* guardián *m*
wardrobe (ᵘ*oo*-droub) *n* guardarropa *m*, vestuario *m*
warehouse (ᵘ*ê*ᵒ-hauss) *n* almacén *m*
wares (ᵘê*ᵒs) *pl* mercancías *fpl*
warm (ᵘoom) *adj* caliente; *v* *calentar
warmth (ᵘoomz) *n* calor *m*
warn (ᵘoon) *v* *advertir
warning (ᵘ*oo*-ning) *n* advertencia *f*
wary (ᵘ*ê*ᵒ-ri) *adj* prudente
was (ᵘos) *v* (p be)
wash (ᵘoʃ) *v* lavar; ~ **and wear** no precisa plancha; ~ **up** *fregar
washable (ᵘ*o*-ʃö-böl) *adj* lavable
wash-basin (ᵘ*oʃ*-bei-ssön) *n* palangana *f*
washing (ᵘ*o*-ʃing) *n* lavado *m*; ropa sucia
washing-machine (ᵘ*o*-ʃing-mö-ʃiin) *n* máquina de lavar
washing-powder (ᵘ*o*-ʃing-pau-dö) *n* jabón en polvo
washroom (ᵘ*oʃ*-ruum) *nAm* cuarto de aseo
wash-stand (ᵘ*oʃ*-sstænd) *n* lavabo *m*
wasp (ᵘossp) *n* avispa *f*
waste (ᵘeisst) *v* *perder; *n* desperdicio *m*; *adj* baldío
wasteful (ᵘ*eisst*-föl) *adj* derrochador
wastepaper-basket (ᵘeisst-*pei*-pö-baasskit) *n* cesto para papeles

watch (ᵁoch) v mirar, observar; vigilar; n reloj m; ~ **for** acechar; ~ **out** *tener cuidado

watch-maker (ᵁoch-mei-kö) n relojero m

watch-strap (ᵁoch-sstræp) n correa de reloj

water (ᵁoo-tö) n agua f; **iced** ~ agua helada; **running** ~ agua corriente; ~ **pump** bomba de agua; ~ **ski** esquí acuático

water-colour (ᵁoo-tö-ka-lö) n color de aguada; acuarela f

watercress (ᵁoo-tö-krèss) n berro m

waterfall (ᵁoo-tö-fool) n cascada f

watermelon (ᵁoo-tö-mê-lön) n sandía f

waterproof (ᵁoo-tö-pruuf) adj impermeable

water-softener (ᵁoo-tö-ssof-nö) n ablandador m

waterway (ᵁoo-tö-ᵁei) n vía navegable

watt (ᵁot) n vatio m

wave (ᵁeiv) n ondulación f, ola f; v *hacer señales

wave-length (ᵁeiv-lêngz) n longitud de onda

wavy (ᵁei-vi) adj ondulado

wax (ᵁækss) n cera f

waxworks (ᵁækss-ᵁöökss) pl museo de figuras de cera

way (ᵁei) n manera f; camino m; lado m, dirección f; distancia f; **any** ~ de todos modos; **by the** ~ a propósito; **one-way traffic** dirección única; **out of the** ~ apartado; **the other** ~ **round** al revés; ~ **back** vuelta f; ~ **in** entrada f; ~ **out** salida f

wayside (ᵁei-ssaid) n borde del camino

we (ᵁii) pron nosotros

weak (ᵁiik) adj débil; flojo

weakness (ᵁiik-nöss) n debilidad f

wealth (ᵁêlz) n riqueza f

wealthy (ᵁêl-zi) adj rico

weapon (ᵁê-pön) n arma f

***wear** (ᵁêᵒ) v llevar; ~ **out** gastar

weary (ᵁiᵒ-ᵢi) adj cansado

weather (ᵁê-ðö) n tiempo m; ~ **forecast** boletín meteorológico

***weave** (ᵁiiv) v tejer

weaver (ᵁii-vö) n tejedor m

wedding (ᵁê-ding) n matrimonio m, boda f

wedding-ring (ᵁê-ding-ring) n anillo de boda

wedge (ᵁêdʒ) n cuña f

Wednesday (ᵁêns-di) miércoles m

weed (ᵁiid) n mala hierba

week (ᵁiik) n semana f

weekday (ᵁiik-dei) n día laborable

weekend (ᵁii-kênd) n fin de semana

weekly (ᵁii-kli) adj semanal

***weep** (ᵁiip) v llorar

weigh (ᵁei) v pesar

weighing-machine (ᵁei-ing-mö-ʃiin) n báscula f

weight (ᵁeit) n peso m

welcome (ᵁêl-köm) adj bienvenido; n bienvenida f; v *dar la bienvenida

weld (ᵁêld) v *soldar

welfare (ᵁêl-fêᵒ) n bienestar m

well¹ (ᵁêl) adv bien; adj sano; **as** ~ también; **as** ~ **as** así como; **well!** ¡bueno!

well² (ᵁêl) n pozo m

well-founded (ᵁêl-faun-did) adj fundamentado

well-known (ᵁêl-noun) adj notorio

well-to-do (ᵁêl-tö-duu) adj acomodado

went (ᵁênt) v (p go)

were (ᵁöö) v (p be)

west (ᵁêsst) n occidente m, oeste m

westerly (ᵁê-sstö-li) adj occidental

western (ᵁê-sstön) adj occidental

wet (ᵁêt) *adj* mojado; húmedo

whale (ᵁeil) *n* ballena *f*

wharf (ᵁoof) *n* (pl ~s, wharves) muelle *m*

what (ᵁot) *pron* qué; lo que; ~ **for** para que

whatever (ᵁo-tê-vö) *pron* cualquier cosa que

wheat (ᵁiit) *n* trigo *m*

wheel (ᵁiil) *n* rueda *f*

wheelbarrow (ᵁiil-bæ-rou) *n* carretilla *f*

wheelchair (ᵁiil-chêô) *n* silla de ruedas

when (ᵁên) *adv* cuándo; *conj* cuando

whenever (ᵁê-nê-vö) *conj* cuando quiera que

where (ᵁêô) *adv* dónde; *conj* donde

wherever (ᵁêô-rê-vö) *conj* dondequiera que

whether (ᵁê-ðö) *conj* si; **whether ... or** si ... o

which (ᵁich) *pron* cuál; que

whichever (ᵁi-ché-vö) *adj* cualquiera

while (ᵁail) *conj* mientras; *n* rato *m*

whilst (ᵁailsst) *conj* mientras

whim (ᵁim) *n* antojo *m*, capricho *m*

whip (ᵁip) *n* azote *m*; *v* batir

whiskers (ᵁi-sskös) *pl* patillas *fpl*

whisper (ᵁi-sspö) *v* susurrar; *n* susurro *m*

whistle (ᵁi-ssöl) *v* silbar; *n* silbato *m*

white (ᵁait) *adj* blanco

whitebait (ᵁait-beit) *n* boquerón *m*

whiting (ᵁai-ting) *n* (pl ~) merluza *f*

Whitsun (ᵁit-ssön) Pentecostés *m*

who (huu) *pron* quien; que

whoever (huu-ê-vö) *pron* quienquiera

whole (houl) *adj* completo, entero; intacto; *n* total *m*

wholesale (houl-sseil) *n* venta al por mayor; ~ **dealer** mayorista *m*

wholesome (houl-ssöm) *adj* saludable

wholly (houl-li) *adv* totalmente

whom (huum) *pron* a quien

whore (hoo) *n* puta *f*

whose (huus) *pron* cuyo; de quien

why (ᵁai) *adv* por qué

wicked (ᵁi-kid) *adj* malvado

wide (ᵁaid) *adj* vasto, ancho

widen (ᵁai-dön) *v* ensanchar

widow (ᵁi-dou) *n* viuda *f*

widower (ᵁi-dou-ö) *n* viudo *m*

width (ᵁidz) *n* anchura *f*

wife (ᵁaif) *n* (pl wives) esposa *f*, mujer *f*

wig (ᵁigh) *n* peluca *f*

wild (ᵁaild) *adj* salvaje; feroz

will (ᵁil) *n* voluntad *f*; testamento *m*

***will** (ᵁil) *v* *querer

willing (ᵁi-ling) *adj* dispuesto

willingly (ᵁi-ling-li) *adv* gustosamente

will-power (ᵁil-pauô) *n* fuerza de voluntad

***win** (ᵁin) *v* vencer

wind (ᵁind) *n* viento *m*

***wind** (ᵁaind) *v* serpentear; *dar cuerda, enrollar

winding (ᵁain-ding) *adj* tortuoso

windmill (ᵁind-mil) *n* molino de viento

window (ᵁin-dou) *n* ventana *f*

window-sill (ᵁin-dou-ssil) *n* antepecho *m*

windscreen (ᵁind-sskriin) *n* parabrisas *m*; ~ **wiper** limpiaparabrisas *m*

windshield (ᵁind-ʃiild) *nAm* parabrisas *m*

windy (ᵁin-di) *adj* ventoso

wine (ᵁain) *n* vino *m*

wine-cellar (ᵁain-ssê-lö) *n* cueva *f*

wine-list (ᵁain-lisst) *n* carta de vinos

wine-merchant (ᵁain-möö-chönt) *n* vinatero *m*

wine-waiter (ᵁain-ᵁei-tö) *n* camarero *m*

wing (ᵁing) *n* ala *f*

winkle (ᵁing-köl) *n* caracol marino

winner (ᵘi-nö) n vencedor m

winning (ᵘi-ning) adj ganador; winnings pl ganancias fpl

winter (ᵘin-tö) n invierno m; ~ sports deportes de invierno

wipe (ᵘaip) v enjugar

wire (ᵘaiᵊ) n alambre m

wireless (ᵘaiᵊ-löss) n radio f

wisdom (ᵘis-döm) n sabiduría f

wise (ᵘais) adj sabio

wish (ᵘiʃ) v desear; n deseo m

witch (ᵘich) n bruja f

with (ᵘið) prep con; de

*withdraw (ᵘið-droo) v retirar

within (ᵘi-ðin) prep dentro de; adv de dentro

without (ᵘi-ðaut) prep sin

witness (ᵘit-nöss) n testigo m

wits (ᵘitss) pl razón f

witty (ᵘi-ti) adj chistoso

wolf (ᵘulf) n (pl wolves) lobo m

woman (ᵘu-mön) n (pl women) mujer f

womb (ᵘuum) n matriz f

won (ᵘan) v (p, pp win)

wonder (ᵘan-dö) n milagro m; asombro m; v preguntarse

wonderful (ᵘan-dö-föl) adj estupendo, maravilloso; delicioso

wood (ᵘud) n madera f; bosque m

wood-carving (ᵘud-kaa-ving) n talla f

wooded (ᵘu-did) adj selvoso

wooden (ᵘu-dön) adj de madera, ~ shoe zueco m

woodland (ᵘud-lönd) n arbolado m

wool (ᵘul) n lana f; darning hilo de zurcir

woollen (ᵘu-lön) adj de lana

word (ᵘööd) n palabra f

wore (ᵘoo) v (p wear)

work (ᵘöök) n obra f; trabajo m; v trabajar; funcionar; working day día de trabajo; ~ of art obra de arte; ~ permit permiso de trabajo

worker (ᵘöö-kö) n obrero m

working (ᵘöö-king) n funcionamiento m

workman (ᵘöök-mön) n (pl -men) obrero m

works (ᵘöökss) pl fábrica f

workshop (ᵘöök-ʃop) n taller m

world (ᵘööld) n mundo m; ~ war guerra mundial

world-famous (ᵘööld-fei-möss) adj de fama mundial

world-wide (ᵘööld-ᵘaid) adj mundial

worm (ᵘööm) n gusano m

worn (ᵘoon) adj (pp wear) gastado

worn-out (ᵘoon-aut) adj gastado

worried (ᵘa-rid) adj inquieto

worry (ᵘa-ri) v inquietarse; n preocupación f, inquietud f

worse (ᵘööss) adj peor; adv peor

worship (ᵘöö-ʃip) v venerar; n culto m

worst (ᵘöösst) adj pésimo; adv peor

worsted (ᵘu-sstid) n estambre m/f

worth (ᵘööz) n valor m; *be ~ *valer; *be worth-while *valer la pena

worthless (ᵘöö-löss) adj sin valor

worthy of (ᵘöö-ði öv) digno de

would (ᵘud) v (p will) *soler

wound¹ (ᵘuund) n herida f; v ofender, *herir

wound² (ᵘaund) v (p, pp wind)

wrap (ræp) v *envolver

wreck (rēk) n pecio m; v *destruir

wrench (rēnch) n llave f; tirón m; v dislocar

wrinkle (ring-köl) n arruga f

wrist (risst) n muñeca f

wrist-watch (risst-ᵘoch) n reloj de pulsera

*write (rait) v escribir; in writing por escrito; ~ down anotar

writer (rai-tö) n escritor m

writing-pad (rai-ting-pæd) n bloque m; bloc mMe

writing-paper (*rai*-ting-pei-pö) *n* papel de escribir

written (*ri*-tön) *adj* (pp write) por escrito

wrong (rong) *adj* impropio, erróneo; *n* mal *m*; *v* agraviar; *be ~ no *tener razón

wrote (rout) *v* (p write)

X

Xmas (*kriss*-möss) Navidad *f*

X-ray (*ékss*-rei) *n* radiografía *f*; *v* radiografiar

Y

yacht (yot) *n* yate *m*

yacht-club (*yot*-klab) *n* club de yates

yachting (*yo*-ting) *n* deporte de vela

yard (yaad) *n* corral *m*

yarn (yaan) *n* hilo *m*

yawn (yoon) *v* bostezar

year (yi^o) *n* año *m*

yearly (*yi^o*-li) *adj* anual

yeast (yiisst) *n* levadura *f*

yell (yêl) *v* gritar; *n* grito *m*

yellow (*yê*-lou) *adj* amarillo

yes (yêss) sí

yesterday (*yê*-sstö-di) *adv* ayer

yet (yêt) *adv* aun; *conj* pero, sin embargo

yield (yiild) *v* producir; ceder

yoke (youk) *n* yugo *m*

yolk (youk) *n* yema *f*

you (yuu) *pron* tú; a ti; usted; a usted; vosotros; os; ustedes

young (yang) *adj* joven

your (yoo) *adj* de usted; tu; vuestro, tuyos

yourself (yoo-*ssêlf*) *pron* te; tú mismo; usted mismo

yourselves (yoo-*ssêlvs*) *pron* se; vosotros mismos; ustedes mismos

youth (yuuz) *n* juventud *f*; ~ **hostel** albergue para jóvenes

Yugoslav (yuu-ghö-*sslaav*) *n* yugoslavo *m*

Yugoslavia (yuu-ghö-*sslaa*-vi-ö) Yugoslavia *f*

Z

zeal (siil) *n* celo *m*

zealous (*sê*-löss) *adj* celoso

zebra (*sii*-brö) *n* cebra *f*

zenith (*sê*-niz) *n* cenit *m*; apogeo *m*

zero (*si^o*-rou) *n* (pl ~s) cero *m*

zest (sêsst) *n* energía *f*

zinc (singk) *n* cinc *m*

zip (sip) *n* cremallera *f*; ~ **code** *Am* código postal

zipper (*si*-pö) *n* cierre relámpago

zodiac (*sou*-di-æk) *n* zodíaco *m*

zone (soun) *n* zona *f*; región *f*

zoo (suu) *n* (pl ~s) jardín zoológico

zoology (sou-*o*-lö-dʒi) *n* zoología *f*

Léxico gastronómico

Comidas

almond almendra

anchovy anchoa

angel food cake pastel confeccionado con clara de huevo

angels on horseback ostras envueltas en tocino, asadas y servidas en pan tostado

appetizer entremés

apple manzana

  ~ **charlotte** pastel de compota de manzanas y pan rallado

  ~ **dumpling** pastel de manzanas

  ~ **sauce** puré de manzanas

apricot albaricoque

Arbroath smoky róbalo ahumado

artichoke alcachofa

asparagus espárrago

  ~ **tip** punta de espárrago

aspic (en) gelatina

assorted variado

aubergine berenjena

avocado (pear) aguacate

bacon tocino

  ~ **and eggs** huevos con tocino

bagel panecillo en forma de corona

baked al horno

  ~ **Alaska** helado cubierto con merengue, dorado en el horno;

se sirve flameado como postre

  ~ **beans** judías blancas en salsa de tomates

  ~ **potato** patata sin pelar cocida al horno

Bakewell tart pastel de almendras con mermelada de frambuesas

baloney especie de mortadela

banana plátano

  ~ **split** dos mitades de plátano servidas con helado y nueces, rociadas con almíbar o crema de chocolate

barbecue 1) carne picada de ternera en una salsa a base de tomates, servida en un panecillo 2) comida al aire libre

  ~ **sauce** salsa de tomates muy picante

barbecued asado a la parrilla con carbón de leña

basil albahaca

bass lubina (pescado)

bean judía, haba, frijol

beef carne de ternera

  ~ **olive** rollo de carne de ternera

beefburger bistec de carne picada, asado y a veces servido en un panecillo

beet, beetroot remolacha
bilberry arándano
bill cuenta
  ~ **of fare** lista de platos
biscuit 1) galleta (GB) 2) panecillo (US)
black pudding morcilla
blackberry zarzamora
blackcurrant grosella negra
bloater arenque salado, ahumado
blood sausage morcilla
blueberry arándano
boiled hervido
Bologna (sausage) especie de mortadela
bone hueso
boned deshuesado
Boston baked beans judías blancas con tocino y melaza
Boston cream pie torta rellena de nata en capas superpuestas, cubierta de chocolate
brains sesos
braised asado
bramble pudding pudín de zarzamoras (a menudo con manzanas)
braunschweiger salchichón de hígado ahumado
bread pan
breaded empanado
breakfast desayuno
bream brema (pescado)
breast pecho, pechuga
brisket pecho
broad bean haba
broth caldo
brown Betty especie de compota de manzanas, con especias y cubierta de pan rallado
brunch comida que reemplaza el desayuno y el almuerzo
brussels sprout col de Bruselas
bubble and squeak patatas y coles

picadas que se fríen, mezcladas a veces con trozos de carne de ternera (especie de tortilla)
bun 1) panecillo dulce confeccionado con frutas secas 2) especie de panecillo (US)
butter mantequilla
buttered con mantequilla
cabbage col, repollo
Caesar salad ensalada verde con ajo, anchoas, cuscurro y queso rallado
cake pastel, torta
cakes galletas, pastelillos
calf ternera
Canadian bacon lomo de cerdo ahumado que se corta en lonchas finas
cantaloupe melón
caper alcaparra
capercaillie, capercailzie urogallo grande
caramel caramelo
carp carpa
carrot zanahoria
cashew anacardo
casserole cacerola
catfish siluro (pescado)
catsup salsa de tomate
cauliflower coliflor
celery apio
cereal cereal
  hot ~ gachas
chateaubriand solomillo de ternera
check cuenta
Cheddar (cheese) queso de textura firme y de sabor ligeramente ácido
cheese queso
  ~ **board** bandeja de quesos
  ~ **cake** pastel de queso doble crema, ligeramente azucarado
cheeseburger bistec de carne pica-

da, asado con una loncha de queso, servido en un panecillo

chef's salad ensalada de jamón, pollo, huevos cocidos, tomates, lechuga y queso

cherry cereza

chestnut castaña

chicken pollo

chicory 1) endibia (GB) 2) escarola, achicoria (US)

chili pepper chile, ají

chips 1) patatas fritas (GB) 2) chips (US)

chitt(er)lings tripas de cerdo

chive cebolleta

choice elección, surtido

chop costilla

~ **suey** plato hecho con carne picada de cerdo o de pollo, arroz y legumbres

chopped picado

chowder sopa espesa a base de mariscos

Christmas pudding pudín inglés hecho con frutas secas, a veces flameado, muy nutritivo y que se sirve en Navidad

chutney condimento indio muy sazonado, con sabor agridulce

cinnamon canela

clam almeja

club sandwich bocadillo doble con tocino, pollo, tomates, lechuga y mayonesa

cobbler compota de frutas cubierta con una capa de pasta

cock-a-leekie soup sopa de pollo y puerros

coconut coco

cod bacalao

Colchester oyster ostra inglesa muy afamada

cold cuts/meat fiambres

coleslaw ensalada de col

compote compota

condiment condimento

cooked cocido

cookie galleta

corn 1) trigo (GB) 2) maíz (US)

~ **on the cob** mazorca de maíz

cornflakes copos de maíz

corned beef carne de ternera sazonada

cottage cheese requesón

cottage pie carne picada que se cuece con cebollas y se cubre con puré de patatas

course plato

cover charge precio del cubierto

crab cangrejo de mar

cracker galletita salada

cranberry arándano agrio

~ **sauce** mermelada de arándanos agrios

crawfish, crayfish 1) cangrejo de río 2) langosta (GB) 3) langostino (US)

cream 1) nata 2) crema (sopa) 3) crema (postre)

~ **cheese** queso doble crema

~ **puff** pastelillo con nata

creamed potatoes patatas cortadas en forma de dados en salsa blanca

creole plato muy condimentado con tomates, pimientos y cebollas; suele servirse con arroz blanco

cress berro

crisps patatas a la inglesa, chips

croquette croqueta

crumpet especie de panecillo redondo, asado y untado de mantequilla

cucumber pepino

Cumberland ham jamón ahumado, muy conocido

Cumberland sauce jalea de grosellas sazonada de vino, jugo de naranja y especias

cupcake pastelillo, hojaldre

cured salado y ahumado

currant 1) pasa de Corinto 2) grosella

curried con curry

custard 1) crema 2) flan

cutlet 1) chuleta 2) escalope 3) fina lonja de carne

dab lenguado

Danish pastry pastelillos hojaldrados

date dátil

Derby cheese queso blando picante, de color amarillo claro

dessert postre

devilled con aliño muy fuerte

devil's food cake torta de chocolate muy nutritiva

devils on horseback ciruelas pasas cocidas en vino tinto, rellenas de almendras y anchoas, envueltas en tocino, asadas y servidas en una tostada

Devonshire cream crema doble muy espesa

diced cortado en daditos

diet food alimento dietético

dill eneldo

dinner cena

dish plato

donut, doughnut buñuelo en forma de anillo, rosquilla

double cream doble crema, nata

Dover sole lenguado de Dover, muy afamado

dressing 1) salsa para ensalada 2) relleno para aves (US)

Dublin Bay prawn langostino

duck pato

duckling anadón

dumpling albóndiga de pasta

Dutch apple pie tarta de manza

nas, cubierta con una capa de azúcar negra y mantequilla

éclair pastelillo relleno de crema de chocolate o de café

eel anguila

egg huevo
  boiled ~ pasado por agua
  fried ~ frito
  hard-boiled ~ duro
  poached ~ escalfado
  scrambled ~ revuelto
  soft-boiled ~ poco pasado por agua

eggplant berenjena

endive 1) escarola, achicoria (GB) 2) endibia (US)

entrecôte solomo de ternera

entrée 1) entrada (GB) 2) plato principal (US)

fennel hinojo

fig higo

filet mignon solomillo

fillet filete de carne o de pescado

finnan haddock róbalo ahumado

fish pescado
  ~ **and chips** filetes de pescado y patatas fritas
  ~ **cake** albóndigas, galleta de pescado y patatas

flan tarta de frutas

flapjack hojuela espesa

flounder fleso (pescado)

forcemeat relleno, picadillo

fowl ave

frankfurter salchicha de Francfort

French bean judía verde

French bread pan francés

French dressing 1) vinagreta (GB) 2) salsa cremosa de ensalada con salsa de tomates (US)

french fries patatas fritas

French toast rebanada de pan, mojada en huevos batidos, frita en una sartén y servida con

mermelada o azúcar
fresh fresco
fried frito, asado
fritter buñuelo
frogs' legs ancas de rana
frosting capa de azúcar garrapiñado
fruit fruta
fry fritura
galantine trozos de carne y picadillo cocidos en gelatina
game caza
gammon jamón ahumado
garfish anguila de mar
garlic ajo
garnish aderezo
gherkin pepinillo
giblets menudillos de ave
ginger jengibre
goose ganso
 ∼ **berry** grosella espinosa
grape uva
 ∼ **fruit** pomelo, toronja
grated rallado
gravy jugo de carne, salsa
grayling pescado de la familia del salmón
green bean judía verde
green pepper pimiento verde
green salad ensalada verde
greens verduras
grilled asado a la parrilla
grilse salmón joven
grouse urogallo
gumbo 1) legumbre de origen africano 2) plato criollo a base de *okra*, con carne o pescado y tomates
haddock róbalo
haggis panza de cordero rellena de copos de avena
hake merluza
half mitad, semi
ham jamón

 ∼ **and eggs** huevos con jamón
hamburger hamburguesa
hare liebre
haricot bean alubia blanca
hash 1) carne picada 2) picadillo de carne de ternera cubierto con patatas y legumbres
hazelnut avellana
heart corazón
herb hierba aromática
herring arenque
home-made de confección casera
hominy grits crema espesa de harina de maíz, especie de polenta
honey miel
 ∼ **dew melon** tipo de melón cuya carne es de color verde amarillento
hors-d'œuvre entremeses
horse-radish rábano picante
hot 1) caliente 2) con especias
 ∼ **cross bun** bollito con pasas (que se come durante la Cuaresma)
 ∼ **dog** salchicha caliente en un panecillo
huckleberry especie de arándano
hush puppy buñuelo a base de harina de maíz
ice-cream helado
iced helado
icing capa de azúcar garrapiñado
Idaho baked potato patata sin pelar cocida al horno
Irish stew guisado de cordero con cebollas y patatas
Italian dressing vinagreta
jam confitura
jellied en gelatina
Jell-O postre a la gelatina
jelly gelatina o jalea de frutas
Jerusalem artichoke aguaturma
John Dory especie de dorada
jugged hare estofado de liebre

juice jugo, zumo
juniper berry baya de enebro
junket leche cuajada azucarada
kale col rizada
kedgeree migajas de pescado ade-
rezadas con arroz, huevos y
mantequilla
ketchup salsa de tomates
kidney riñón
kipper arenque ahumado
lamb cordero
Lancashire hot pot guisado de
chuletas y riñones de cordero,
con patatas y cebollas
larded mechado
lean magro
leek puerro
leg pierna, muslo, corvejón
lemon limón
~ **sole** especie de platija
lentil lenteja
lettuce lechuga, ensalada verde
lima bean haba grande
lime lima (limón verde)
liver hígado
loaf pan, hogaza
lobster bogavante
loin lomo
Long Island duck pato de Long
Island, muy afamado
low-calorie pobre en calorías
lox salmón ahumado
lunch almuerzo
macaroni macarrones
macaroon macarrón (almendra-
do)
mackerel caballa
maize maíz
mandarin mandarina
maple syrup jarabe de arce
marinade escabeche
marinated en escabeche
marjoram mejorana
marmalade mermelada de naranja

u otros sabores
marrow tuétano
~ **bone** hueso con tuétano
marshmallow dulce de malvavisco
marzipan mazapán
mashed potatoes puré de patatas
mayonnaise mayonesa
meal comida
meat carne
~**ball** albóndiga de carne
~ **loaf** carne picada preparada
en forma de un pan y que se
cuece al horno
medium (done) a punto
melted derretido
Melton Mowbray pie especie de
empanada de carne
menu lista de platos
meringue merengue
milk leche
mince picadillo
~ **pie** tarta de frutas confitadas
cortadas en daditos, con manzanas y especias (con o sin carne)
minced picado
~ **meat** carne picada
mint menta
mixed mezclado, surtido
~ **grill** brocheta de carne
molasses melaza
morel morilla
mousse postre de nata aromatizada
mulberry mora
mullet mújol (pescado)
mulligatawny soup sopa de pollo
muy picante de origen indio
mushroom champiñón
muskmelon tipo de melón
mussel mejillón
mustard mostaza
mutton carnero
noodle tallarín
nut nuez

oatmeal (porridge) gachas de avena

oil aceite

okra fruto del *gumbo* utilizado generalmente para espesar las sopas y guisados

olive aceituna

omelet tortilla

onion cebolla

orange naranja

ox tongue lengua de buey

oxtail cola de buey (sopa)

oyster ostra

pancake hojuela espesa, torta de sartén

paprika pimiento

Parmesan (cheese) queso parmesano

parsley perejil

parsnip chirivía

partridge perdiz

pastry pastel, pastelillo

pasty empanadilla de carne

pea guisante

peach melocotón

peanut cacahuete, maní
  ~ **butter** manteca de cacahuete

pear pera

pearl barley cebada perlada

pepper pimienta

peppermint menta

perch perca

persimmon caqui

pheasant faisán

pickerel lucio pequeño (pescado)

pickle 1) legumbre o fruta en vinagre 2) pepinillo (US)

pickled conservado en salmuera o vinagre

pie torta a menudo cubierta con una capa de pasta, rellena de carne, legumbres, frutas o crema inglesa

pig cerdo

pigeon pichón

pike lucio

pineapple piña

plaice platija, acedía

plain natural

plate plato

plum ciruela, ciruela pasa
  ~ **pudding** pudín inglés hecho con frutas secas, a veces flameado, muy nutritivo y que se sirve en Navidad

poached escalfado

popcorn palomitas de maíz

popover panecillo esponjoso cocido en el horno

pork cerdo

porridge gachas

porterhouse steak lonja espesa de solomillo de res

pot roast carne de ternera asada y legumbres

potato patata, papa
  ~ **chips** 1) patatas fritas (GB) 2) chips (US)
  ~ **in its jacket** patata sin pelar

potted shrimps mantequilla sazonada, derretida y enfriada, servida con camarones

poultry ave de corral

prawn camarón grande

prune ciruela seca

ptarmigan perdiz blanca

pudding pudín blando o consistente hecho con harina, relleno de carne, pescado, legumbres o frutas

pumpernickel pan hecho con harina gruesa de centeno

pumpkin calabaza

quail codorniz

quince membrillo

rabbit conejo

radish rábano

rainbow trout trucha arco iris

raisin pasa
rare poco hecho
raspberry frambuesa
raw crudo
red mullet salmonete
red (sweet) pepper pimiento morrón
redcurrant grosella roja
relish condimento hecho con trocitos de legumbres y vinagre
rhubarb ruibarbo
rib (of beef) costilla (de ternera)
rib-eye steak solomillo
rice arroz
rissole croqueta de pescado o carne
river trout trucha de río
roast(ed) asado
Rock Cornish hen pollo tomatero
roe huevos de pescado
roll panecillo
rollmop herring filete de arenque escabechado con vino blanco, enrollado con un pepinillo en medio
round steak filete de pierna de ternera
Rubens sandwich carne de ternera en pan tostado, con col fermentada, queso suizo y salsa para ensalada; se sirve caliente
rump steak filete de lomo de ternera
rusk rebanadas tostadas de pan de molde
rye bread pan de centeno
saddle cuarto trasero
saffron azafrán
sage salvia
salad ensalada
  ~ **bar** surtido de ensaladas
  ~ **cream** salsa cremosa para ensalada, ligeramente azucarada

  ~ **dressing** salsa para ensalada
salmon salmón
  ~ **trout** trucha asalmonada
salt(ed) sal(ado)
sandwich bocadillo, emparedado
sardine sardina
sauce salsa
sauerkraut col fermentada
sausage salchicha
sauté(ed) salteado
scallop 1) venera 2) escalope de ternera
scampi langostino
scone panecillo tierno hecho con harina de avena o cebada
Scotch broth caldo a base de carne de carnero o de buey y legumbres
Scotch woodcock pan tostado con huevos revueltos y crema de anchoas
sea bass róbalo, lubina
sea kale col marina
seafood mariscos y peces marinos
(in) season (en su) época (estación del año)
seasoning condimento, sazón
service servicio
  ~ **charge** importe que se paga por el servicio
  ~ **(not) included** servicio (no) incluido
set menu menú fijo
shad alosa, sábalo
shallot chalote
shellfish marisco
sherbet sorbete
shoulder espalda
shredded wheat hojuelas de trigo en croquetas (se sirven en el desayuno)
shrimp camarón, gamba
silverside (of beef) codillo (de ternera)

sirloin steak bistec del solomillo

skewer brocheta

slice loncha, rodaja

sliced cortado en lonchas

sloppy Joe carne picada de ternera con una salsa picante de tomates, se sirve en un panecillo

smelt eperlano

smoked ahumado

snack comida ligera

sole lenguado

soup sopa, crema

sour agrio

soused herring arenque conservado en vinagre y especias

spaghetti espaguetis

spare rib costilla de cerdo casi descarnada

spice especia

spinach espinaca

spiny lobster langosta

(on a) spit (en un) espetón

sponge cake bizcocho ligero y esponjoso

sprat arenque pequeño, sardineta

squash calabaza

starter entrada

steak and kidney pie empanada de carne de ternera y riñones

steamed cocido al vapor

stew guisado

Stilton (cheese) queso inglés atamado (blanco o con mohos azules)

strawberry fresa

string bean judía verde

stuffed relleno

stuffing (el) relleno

suck(l)ing pig lechón

sugar azúcar

sugarless sin azúcar

sundae copa de helado con frutas, nueces, nata batida y a veces jarabe

supper comida ligera de la noche, cena

swede naba de Suecia

sweet 1) dulce 2) postre

~ **corn** maíz blanco

~ **potato** patata dulce

sweetbread lechecillas

Swiss cheese queso suizo (Emmenthal)

Swiss roll bizcocho enrollado y relleno de mermelada

Swiss steak lonja de ternera asada con legumbres y especias

T-bone steak bistec y filete de ternera separados por un hueso en forma de T

table d'hôte menú fijo

tangerine especie de mandarina

tarragon estragón

tart tarta de frutas

tenderloin filete de carne

Thousand Island dressing salsa para ensalada, sazonada, hecha de mayonesa y pimientos

thyme tomillo

toad-in-the-hole carne de ternera (o salchicha) cubierta de pasta y cocida al horno

toast pan tostado, tostada

toasted tostado

~ **cheese** pan tostado con queso derretido

tomato tomate

tongue lengua

tournedos bistec espeso del filete (ternera)

treacle melaza

trifle pastel con jerez o aguardiente, hecho con almendras, mermelada y crema batida o natillas y crema de vainilla

tripe tripas, callos

trout trucha

truffle trufa

tuna, tunny atún
turbot rodaballo, rombo
turkey pavo
turnip nabo
turnover pastelillo relleno de compota o mermelada
turtle tortuga
underdone poco hecho
vanilla vainilla
veal ternera
~ bird pulpeta de ternera
vegetable legumbre
~ marrow calabacín
venison caza, corzo
vichyssoise sopa fría preparada con puerros, patatas y crema
vinegar vinagre
Virginia baked ham jamón cocido al horno, adornado con clavos de especia, rebanadas de piña y cerezas; se le baña con el jugo de las frutas
vol-au-vent pastel de hojaldre relleno de salsa con crema, trozos de carne y champiñones
wafer barquillo
waffle especie de barquillo caliente
walnut nuez
water ice sorbete
watercress berro de agua
watermelon sandía
well-done bastante hecho
Welsh rabbit/rarebit queso derretido sobre una tostada
whelk buccino (molusco)
whipped cream nata batida
whitebait boquerón
Wiener schnitzel escalope de ternera empanado
wine list lista de vinos
woodcock becada
Worcestershire sauce condimento líquido picante a base de vinagre, soja y ajo
yoghurt yogur
York ham jamón de York (ahumado)
Yorkshire pudding especie de pasta de hojuelas que se sirve con el rosbif
zucchini calabacín
zwieback rebanadas tostadas de pan de molde

Bebidas

ale cerveza negra, ligeramente azucarada, fermentada a elevada temperatura
bitter ~ negra, amarga y más bien pesada
brown ~ negra de botella, ligeramente azucarada
light ~ dorada de botella
mild ~ negra de barril, bastante fuerte
pale ~ dorada de botella
angostura esencia aromática amarga que se añade a los cócteles
applejack aguardiente de manzanas

Athol Brose bebida escocesa hecha con whisky, miel, agua y a veces copos de avena

Bacardi cocktail cóctel de ron con ginebra, jarabe de granadina y jugo de limón

barley water bebida refrescante a base de cebada y aromatizada con limón

barley wine cerveza negra muy alcoholizada

beer cerveza
   bottled ~ de botella
   draft, draught ~ de barril

bitters aperitivos y digestivos a base de raíces, corteza o hierbas

black velvet champán mezclado con *stout* (acompaña con frecuencia las ostras)

bloody Mary vodka, jugo de tomate y especias

bourbon whisky americano, a base de maíz

brandy 1) denominación genérica de los aguardientes de uvas y otras frutas 2) coñac
   ~ **Alexander** mezcla de aguardiente, crema de cacao y nata

British wines vino fermentado en Gran Bretaña, fabricado a base de uvas o jugo de uvas importados

cherry brandy licor de cerezas

cider sidra
   ~ **cup** mezcla de sidra, especias, azúcar y hielo

claret vino tinto de Burdeos

cobbler *long drink* helado a base de frutas, al que se añade vino o licor

coffee café
   ~ **with cream** con nata
   black ~ solo
   caffeine-free ~ descafeinado

   white ~ con leche, cortado

cordial licor estimulante y digestivo

cream nata

cup bebida refrescante a base de vino helado, sifón, un espirituoso y adornada con una raja de naranja, de limón o de pepino

daiquiri cóctel de ron con jugo de limón y de piña

double doble porción

Drambuie licor a base de whisky y miel

dry martini 1) vermú seco (GB) 2) cóctel de ginebra con algo de vermú seco (US)

egg-nog bebida de ron u otro licor fuerte con yemas de huevos batidas y azúcar

gin ginebra

gin and it mezcla de ginebra y vermú italiano

gin-fizz mezcla de ginebra, jugo de limón, sifón y azúcar

ginger ale bebida sin alcohol, perfumada con extracto de jengibre

ginger beer bebida ligeramente alcohólica, a base de jengibre y azúcar

grasshopper mezcla de crema de menta, crema de cacao y nata

Guinness (stout) cerveza negra, con gusto muy pronunciado y algo dulce, con mucha malta y lúpulo

half pint aproximadamente 3 decilitros

highball whisky o aguardiente diluido con agua, soda o *ginger ale*

iced helado

Irish coffee café con azúcar y whisky irlandés, cubierto con nata batida (Chantilly)

Irish Mist licor irlandés a base de whisky y miel

Irish whiskey whisky irlandés menos áspero que el whisky escocés *(scotch);* además de cebada contiene centeno, avena y trigo

juice jugo, zumo

lager cerveza dorada ligera

lemon squash zumo de limón

lemonade limonada

lime juice zumo de lima (limón verde)

liqueur licor, poscafé

liquor aguardiente

long drink licor diluido en agua o tónica y servido con cubitos de hielo

madeira vino de Madera

Manhattan whisky americano, vermú y *angostura*

milk leche

~ **shake** batido

mineral water agua mineral

mulled wine vino caliente con especias

neat bebida pura, sola, sin hielo y sin agua

old-fashioned whisky, *angostura*, cerezas con marrasquino y azúcar

on the rocks con cubitos de hielo

Ovaltine Ovomaltina

Pimm's cup(s) bebida alcohólica compuesta por alguno de los siguientes licores; se mezcla con zumo de fruta y algunas veces con agua de Seltz

~ **No. 1** a base de ginebra

~ **No. 2** a base de whisky

~ **No. 3** a base de ron

~ **No. 4** a base de aguardiente

pink champagne champán rosado

pink lady mezcla de clara de huevo, Calvados, zumo de limón, jarabe de granadina y ginebra

pint aproximadamente 6 decilitros

port (wine) (vino de) Oporto

porter cerveza negra y amarga

punch ponche

quart 1,14 litro (US 0,95 litro)

root beer bebida edulcorada efervescente, aromatizada con hierbas y raíces

rum ron

rye (whiskey) whisky de centeno, más pesado y más áspero que el *bourbon*

scotch (whisky) whisky escocés, mezcla de whisky de trigo y de whisky de cebada

screwdriver vodka y zumo de naranja

shandy *bitter ale* mezclada con zumo de limón o con una *ginger beer*

sherry jerez

short drink todo licor no diluido, puro

shot dosis de cualquier licor espirituoso

sloe gin-fizz licor de endrina con sifón y zumo de limón

soda water agua gaseosa

soft drink bebida sin alcohol

spirits aguardientes

stinger coñac y crema de menta

stout cerveza negra con mucho lúpulo y alcohol

straight alcohol que se bebe seco, sin mezcla

tea té

toddy ponche hecho de ron, agua, limón y azúcar

Tom Collins ginebra, zumo de limón, sifón y azúcar

tonic (water) (agua) tónica, agua gaseosa, a base de quinina

vermouth vermú
water agua
whisky sour whisky, zumo de
  limón, azúcar y sifón
wine vino
  dessert ~ de postre

dry ~ seco
red ~ tinto
rosé ~ clarete, rosado
sparkling ~ espumoso
sweet ~ dulce (de postre)
white ~ blanco

Verbos irregulares ingleses

En la siguiente lista damos los verbos irregulares ingleses. Los verbos compuestos o los que llevan un prefijo se conjugan como los verbos simples, por ej.: *mistake* y *overdrive* se conjugan como *take* y *drive*.

Infinitivo	Pret. indefinido	Participio pasado	
arise	arose	arisen	*levantarse*
awake	awoke	awoken	*despertarse*
be	was	been	*ser, estar*
bear	bore	borne	*soportar*
beat	beat	beaten	*batir*
become	became	become	*llegar a ser*
begin	began	begun	*comenzar*
bend	bent	bent	*doblar*
bet	bet	bet	*apostar*
bid	bade/bid	bidden/bid	*pedir*
bind	bound	bound	*atar*
bite	bit	bitten	*morder*
bleed	bled	bled	*sangrar*
blow	blew	blown	*soplar*
break	broke	broken	*romper*
breed	bred	bred	*criar*
bring	brought	brought	*traer*
build	built	built	*construir*
burn	burnt/burned	burnt/burned	*quemar*
burst	burst	burst	*reventar*
buy	bought	bought	*comprar*
can*	could	—	*poder*
cast	cast	cast	*arrojar*
catch	caught	caught	*coger*
choose	chose	chosen	*escoger*
cling	clung	clung	*adherirse*
clothe	clothed/clad	clothed/clad	*vestir*
come	came	come	*venir*
cost	cost	cost	*costar*
creep	crept	crept	*arrastrar*
cut	cut	cut	*cortar*
deal	dealt	dealt	*distribuir*
dig	dug	dug	*cavar*
do (he does)	did	done	*hacer*
draw	drew	drawn	*dibujar*
dream	dreamt/dreamed	dreamt/dreamed	*soñar*
drink	drank	drunk	*beber*
drive	drove	driven	*conducir*
dwell	dwelt	dwelt	*habitar*
eat	ate	eaten	*comer*
fall	fell	fallen	*caer*

* presente de indicativo

feed	fed	fed	*alimentar*
feel	felt	felt	*sentir*
fight	fought	fought	*luchar*
find	found	found	*encontrar*
flee	fled	fled	*huir*
fling	flung	flung	*lanzar*
fly	flew	flown	*volar*
forsake	forsook	forsaken	*renunciar*
freeze	froze	frozen	*helar*
get	got	got	*obtener*
give	gave	given	*dar*
go	went	gone	*ir*
grind	ground	ground	*moler*
grow	grew	grown	*crecer*
hang	hung	hung	*colgar*
have	had	had	*tener*
hear	heard	heard	*oír*
hew	hewed	hewed/hewn	*cortar*
hide	hid	hidden	*esconder*
hit	hit	hit	*golpear*
hold	held	held	*sostener*
hurt	hurt	hurt	*herir*
keep	kept	kept	*guardar*
kneel	knelt	knelt	*arrodillarse*
knit	knitted/knit	knitted/knit	*juntar*
know	knew	known	*saber*
lay	laid	laid	*acostar*
lead	led	led	*dirigir*
lean	leant/leaned	leant/leaned	*apoyarse*
leap	leapt/leaped	leapt/leaped	*saltar*
learn	learnt/learned	learnt/learned	*aprender*
leave	left	left	*marcharse*
lend	lent	lent	*prestar*
let	let	let	*permitir*
lie	lay	lain	*acostarse*
light	lit/lighted	lit/lighted	*encender*
lose	lost	lost	*perder*
make	made	made	*hacer*
may*	might	—	*poder*
mean	meant	meant	*significar*
meet	met	met	*encontrar (personas)*
mow	mowed	mowed/mown	*segar*
must*	—	—	*tener que*
ought (to)*	—	—	*deber*
pay	paid	paid	*pagar*
put	put	put	*poner*
read	read	read	*leer*
rid	rid	rid	*desembarazar*
ride	rode	ridden	*cabalgar*

* presente de indicativo

ring	rang	rung	*sonar*
rise	rose	risen	*ascender*
run	ran	run	*correr*
saw	sawed	sawn	*aserrar*
say	said	said	*decir*
see	saw	seen	*ver*
seek	sought	sought	*buscar*
sell	sold	sold	*vender*
send	sent	sent	*enviar*
set	set	set	*poner*
sew	sewed	sewed/sewn	*coser*
shake	shook	shaken	*agitar*
shall*	should	—	*deber*
shed	shed	shed	*desprenderse*
shine	shone	shone	*brillar*
shoot	shot	shot	*tirar*
show	showed	shown	*mostrar*
shrink	shrank	shrunk	*encogerse*
shut	shut	shut	*cerrar*
sing	sang	sung	*cantar*
sink	sank	sunk	*hundir*
sit	sat	sat	*sentarse*
sleep	slept	slept	*dormir*
slide	slid	slid	*resbalar*
sling	slung	slung	*lanzar*
slink	slunk	slunk	*escabullirse*
slit	slit	slit	*rajar*
smell	smelled/smelt	smelled/smelt	*oler*
sow	sowed	sown/sowed	*sembrar*
speak	spoke	spoken	*hablar*
speed	sped/speeded	sped/speeded	*apresurarse*
spell	spelt/spelled	spelt/spelled	*deletrear*
spend	spent	spent	*gastar*
spill	spilt/spilled	spilt/spilled	*derramar*
spin	spun	spun	*girar*
spit	spat	spat	*escupir*
split	split	split	*rajar*
spoil	spoilt/spoiled	spoilt/spoiled	*estropear*
spread	spread	spread	*extender*
spring	sprang	sprung	*saltar*
stand	stood	stood	*estar de pie*
steal	stole	stolen	*robar*
stick	stuck	stuck	*hundir*
sting	stung	stung	*picar*
stink	stank/stunk	stunk	*apestar*
strew	strewed	strewed/strewn	*esparcir*
stride	strode	stridden	*andar a pasos largos*
strike	struck	struck/stricken	*golpear*
string	strung	strung	*atar*

* presente de indicativo

strive	strove	striven	*esforzarse*
swear	swore	sworn	*jurar*
sweep	swept	swept	*barrer*
swell	swelled	swollen	*hinchar*
swim	swam	swum	*nadar*
swing	swung	swung	*balancearse*
take	took	taken	*tomar*
teach	taught	taught	*enseñar*
tear	tore	torn	*desgarrar*
tell	told	told	*decir*
think	thought	thought	*pensar*
throw	threw	thrown	*arrojar*
thrust	thrust	thrust	*impeler*
tread	trod	trodden	*pisotear*
wake	woke/waked	woken/waked	*despertar*
wear	wore	worn	*llevar puesto*
weave	wove	woven	*tejer*
weep	wept	wept	*llorar*
will*	would	—	*querer*
win	won	won	*ganar*
wind	wound	wound	*enrollar*
wring	wrung	wrung	*torcer*
write	wrote	written	*escribir*

---

* presente de indicativo

Abreviaturas inglesas

AA	*Automobile Association*	Asociación Automovilística
AAA	*American Automobile Association*	Asociación Automovilística de los Estados Unidos
ABC	*American Broadcasting Company*	Sociedad Privada de Radiodifusión y Televisión (EE.UU.)
A.D.	*anno Domini*	año de Cristo
Am.	*America; American*	América; americano
a.m.	*ante meridiem (before noon)*	de la mañana (de 00.00 a 12.00 h.)
Amtrak	*American railroad corporation*	Sociedad Privada de Compañías de Ferrocarriles Americanos
AT & T	*American Telephone and Telegraph Company*	Compañía Americana de Teléfonos y Telégrafos
Ave.	*avenue*	avenida
BBC	*British Broadcasting Corporation*	Sociedad Británica de Radiodifusión y Televisión
B.C.	*before Christ*	antes de Cristo
bldg.	*building*	edificio
Blvd.	*boulevard*	bulevar
B.R.	*British Rail*	Ferrocarriles Británicos
Brit.	*Britain; British*	Gran Bretaña; británico
Bros.	*brothers*	hermanos
¢	*cent*	1/100 de dólar
Can.	*Canada; Canadian*	Canadá; canadiense
CBS	*Columbia Broadcasting System*	Sociedad Privada de Radiodifusión y Televisión (EE.UU.)
CID	*Criminal Investigation Department*	Oficina de Investigación Criminal
CNR	*Canadian National Railway*	Ferrocarriles Canadienses
c/o	*(in) care of*	al cuidado de
Co.	*company*	compañía
Corp.	*corporation*	compañía
CPR	*Canadian Pacific Railways*	Compañía Privada de Ferrocarriles Canadienses
D.C.	*District of Columbia*	Distrito de Columbia (Washington, D.C.)
DDS	*Doctor of Dental Science*	Dentista

dept.	department	departamento, división administrativa
EEC	European Economic Community	Comunidad Económica Europea
e.g.	for instance	por ejemplo, verbigracia
Eng.	England; English	Inglaterra; inglés
excl.	excluding; exclusive	no incluido
ft.	foot/feet	pie/pies (medida: 30,5 cm.)
GB	Great Britain	Gran Bretaña
H.E.	His/Her Excellency; His Eminence	Su Excelencia; Su Eminencia
H.H.	His Holiness	Su Santidad
H.M.	His/Her Majesty	Su Majestad
H.M.S.	Her Majesty's ship	navío de guerra británico
hp	horsepower	caballos de vapor
Hwy	highway	carretera principal
i.e.	that is to say	a saber, es decir
in.	inch	pulgada (medida: 2,54 cm.)
Inc.	incorporated	Sociedad Anónima
incl.	including, inclusive	incluido
£	pound sterling	libra esterlina
L.A.	Los Angeles	Los Angeles
Ltd.	limited	Sociedad Anónima
M.D.	Doctor of Medicine	médico
M.P.	Member of Parliament	Miembro del Parlamento
mph	miles per hour	millas por hora
Mr.	Mister	Señor
Mrs.	Missis	Señora
Ms.	Missis/Miss	Señora/Señorita
nat.	national	nacional
NBC	National Broadcasting Company	Sociedad Privada de Radiodifusión y Televisión (EE.UU.)
No.	number	número
N.Y.C.	New York City	Ciudad de Nueva York
O.B.E.	Officer (of the Order) of the British Empire	Caballero de la Orden del Imperio Británico
p.	page; penny/pence	página; 1/100 de libra
p.a.	per annum	por año
Ph.D.	Doctor of Philosophy	Doctor en Filosofía
p.m.	post meridiem (after noon)	de la tarde/noche (de 12.00 a 24.00 h.)
PO	Post Office	Oficina de Correos
POO	post office order	giro postal

pop.	*population*	población
P.T.O.	*please turn over*	vuelva la página, por favor
RAC	*Royal Automobile Club*	Real Club Autómovil (Gran Bretaña)
RCMP	*Royal Canadian Mounted Police*	Policía Montada de Canadá
Rd.	*road*	carretera
ref.	*reference*	referencia
Rev.	*reverend*	Reverendo (pastor de la Iglesia Anglicana)
RFD	*rural free delivery*	distribución del correo en el campo
RR	*railroad*	ferrocarril
RSVP	*please reply*	se ruega contestación
$	*dollar*	dólar
Soc.	*society*	sociedad
St.	*saint; street*	santo(a); calle
STD	*Subscriber Trunk Dialling*	teléfono automático
UN	*United Nations*	Organización de las Naciones Unidas
UPS	*United Parcel Service*	Compañía Privada de Expedición de Paquetes (EE.UU.)
US	*United States*	Estados Unidos de América
USS	*United States Ship*	navío de guerra (EE.UU.)
VAT	*value added tax*	tasa al valor añadido
VIP	*very important person*	persona importante que beneficia de ventajas particulares
Xmas	*Christmas*	Navidad
yd.	*yard*	yarda (medida: 91,44 cm.)
YMCA	*Young Men's Christian Association*	Asociación Cristiana de Muchachos
YWCA	*Young Women's Christian Association*	Asociación Cristiana de Muchachas
ZIP	*ZIP code*	número de distrito postal

Numerales

Cardinales		Ordinales	
0	zero	1st	first
1	one	2nd	second
2	two	3rd	third
3	three	4th	fourth
4	four	5th	fifth
5	five	6th	sixth
6	six	7th	seventh
7	seven	8th	eighth
8	eight	9th	ninth
9	nine	10th	tenth
10	ten	11th	eleventh
11	eleven	12th	twelfth
12	twelve	13th	thirteenth
13	thirteen	14th	fourteenth
14	fourteen	15th	fifteenth
15	fifteen	16th	sixteenth
16	sixteen	17th	seventeenth
17	seventeen	18th	eighteenth
18	eighteen	19th	nineteenth
19	nineteen	20th	twentieth
20	twenty	21st	twenty-first
21	twenty-one	22nd	twenty-second
22	twenty-two	23rd	twenty-third
23	twenty-three	24th	twenty-fourth
24	twenty-four	25th	twenty-fifth
25	twenty-five	26th	twenty-sixth
30	thirty	27th	twenty-seventh
40	forty	28th	twenty-eighth
50	fifty	29th	twenty-ninth
60	sixty	30th	thirtieth
70	seventy	40th	fortieth
80	eighty	50th	fiftieth
90	ninety	60th	sixtieth
100	a/one hundred	70th	seventieth
230	two hundred and thirty	80th	eightieth
		90th	ninetieth
1,000	a/one thousand	100th	hundredth
10,000	ten thousand	230th	two hundred and thirtieth
100,000	a/one hundred thousand		
1,000,000	a/one million	1,000th	thousandth

La hora

Los británicos y los americanos utilizan el sistema de 12 horas. abreviatura *a.m. (ante meridiem)* designa las horas anteriores al mediodía, *p.m. (post meridiem)* las de la tarde o de la noche. Sin embargo, en Gran Bretaña existe la tendencia, cada vez más acentuada, a indicar los horarios como en el continente.

I'll come at seven a.m.	Vendré a las 7 de la mañana.
I'll come at two p.m.	Vendré a las 2 de la tarde.
I'll come at eight p.m.	Vendré a las 8 de la noche.

Los días de la semana

Sunday	domingo	*Thursday*	jueves
Monday	lunes	*Friday*	viernes
Tuesday	martes	*Saturday*	sábado
Wednesday	miércoles		

MANUALES DE CONVERSACION BERLITZ

Estos libros ofrecen, además de abundancia de frases y de un vocabulario muy útil acompañado de pronunciación, interesantes detalles relativos a propinas, datos útiles y sugerencias. Manejables y eficaces, son una ayuda valiosa para darse a entender.

Francés

Inglés
(Edición Británica)

Inglés
(Edición Norteamericana)

CASSETTES BERLITZ

La mayoría de los Manuales de Conversación pueden combinarse con una cassette que le ayudará a mejorar su acento. Cada cassette, grabada en alta fidelidad, va acompañada de un folleto de 32 páginas impresas con el texto completo de la grabación.